MOON HANDBOOKS®

PENNSYLVANIA

THIRD EDITION

JOANNE MILLER

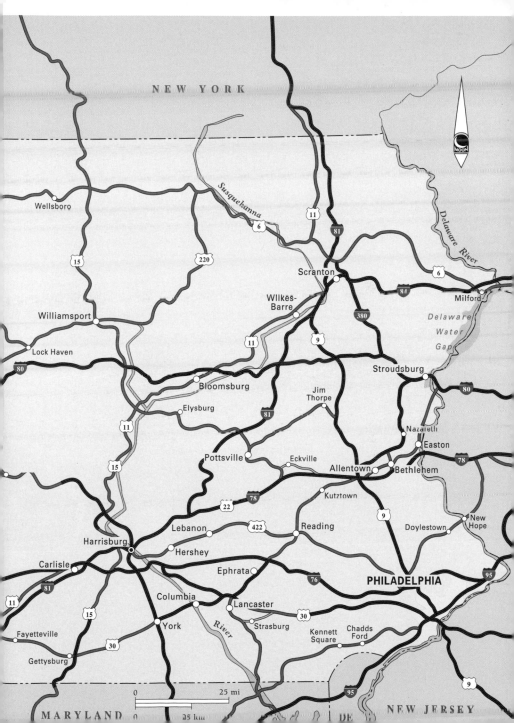

CONTENTS

Discover Pennsylvania

Explore Pennsylvania

Philadelphia 26

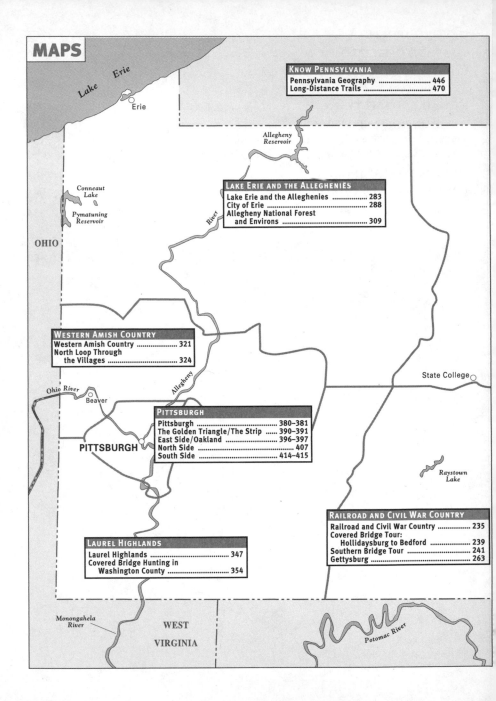

MAPS

Lake Erie

Erie

Allegheny
Reservoir

Conneaut
Lake

Pymatuning
Reservoir

River

OHIO

State College

Ohio River

Allegheny

Beaver

PITTSBURGH

Raystown
Lake

Monongahela
River

WEST

VIRGINIA

Potomac River

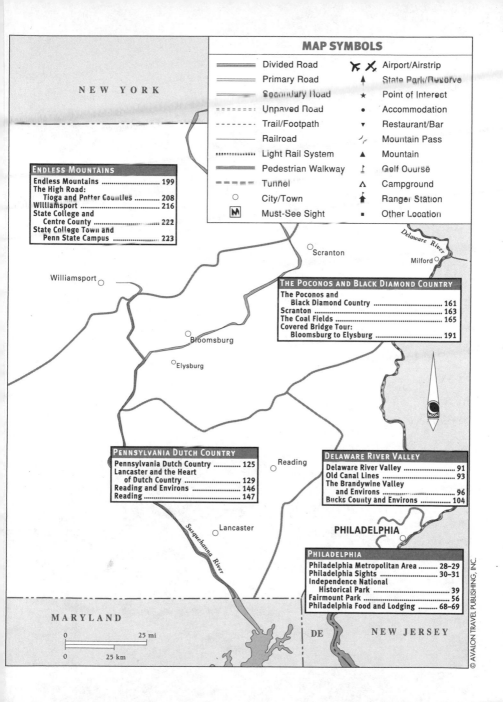

MAP SYMBOLS

Divided Road	✕ ✕ Airport/Airstrip
Primary Road	▲ State Park/Reserve
Secondary Road	★ Point of Interest
Unpaved Road	• Accommodation
Trail/Footpath	▼ Restaurant/Bar
Railroad	⌐ Mountain Pass
Light Rail System	▲ Mountain
Pedestrian Walkway	⅃ Golf Course
Tunnel	∧ Campground
○ City/Town	♦ Ranger Station
Ⓜ Must-See Sight	▪ Other Location

NEW YORK

Scranton

Milford

Delaware River

Williamsport

Bloomsburg

Elysburg

Reading

Susquehanna River

Lancaster

PHILADELPHIA

MARYLAND

0 _____ 25 mi

0 _____ 25 km

DE   NEW JERSEY

Discover Pennsylvania

The beauty of Pennsylvania is almost inexpressible. Perhaps as you read this, it's a misty fall afternoon in the Pocono Mountains; the failing soft gray of the light heightens the jewel tones of the sentinel-like trees that line the road. At every curve in the asphalt, the darkness parts as if by magic, revealing new combinations of ruby, topaz, and emerald. If winter has come, the thin, clean smell of frost accompanies a sunset striped in pink and blue closing quickly over dairy farms in Lancaster County; each is newly spread with pristine white icing, and black-and-white cows, fully aware of their place in the scene, space themselves neatly over the landscape. In spring, the rivers rush past a dizzying array of peridot-green buds, slipping past nodding mountain laurel to freshen the air in the spires of Philadelphia or Pittsburgh. Or, in the aftermath of a summer storm over Lake Erie, light pierces iron-colored clouds and pours like honey onto the pale sand shores of Presque Isle. To some, the state is merely a remnant of America's industrial past; to those who live here, and to those who visit, now-quiet steel mills are being reinvented into shops and gathering places, and black hills of coal-mine tailings sparkle in the June sun, reborn as homes for songbirds and bright wildflowers. Pennsylvania is a populated wilderness; its cities are mighty and prosperous, filled with all the riches that humanity can create, though much of it remains as free of the signposts of modern civilization as when the first European walked ashore and saw infinite possibilities rooted in the forests and flowing around the boulders of the great rivers.

The state—officially a commonwealth—is a year-round feast for the senses, spirit, and intellect. Within its boundaries, two major cities offer rich troves of history, art, and sophisticated urban activities. At the same time, no visitor to Pennsylvania is more than 25 miles from one of 117 state parks. These green treasures, along with the Poconos, Laurel Highlands, and the 516,000-acre Allegheny National Forest, offer recreational activities as diverse as canoeing, fishing, skiing, snowmobiling, and the opportunity to just be.

Pennsylvania is a place of new beginnings. Founded as a haven of religious freedom by renegade aristocrat (and Quaker) William Penn, "Penns Woods" have welcomed successive groups of immigrants who sought a tolerance unknown in the Old World. Today, the state continues to reflect its origins with a thriving diversity of religious beliefs and ethnic cultures. Pennsylvania has been the birthplace of many other firsts, too: the original lending library, zoo, university, newspaper, savings bank, firefighting company, independent hospital, stock exchange, steam locomotive, steamship, oil well, computer, electron microscope, and robotics institute were all developed within its boundaries.

The United States itself was created in Pennsylvania. As one of the original colonies, Pennsylvania attracted firebrands who would become leaders in the American Revolution; Philadelphia, the City of Brotherly Love, midwifed our nation in Independence Hall. That building, along with the Liberty Bell and other significant historical attractions, has drawn visitors from the world over.

Philadelphia, Gettysburg, Erie, Johnstown, Pittsburgh, Bird-in-Hand, Hershey—each name holds a place in our national memory. The first two remind us of painful episodes in American history—the Revolutionary War and the Civil War. Erie evokes memories of tall ships and tragedies on the Great Lakes, Johnstown a cataclysmic flood—an act of God that captured the attention of the world. Pittsburgh, once characterized as "hell with the lid off" once symbolized the worst—and now the highest redemption—of the effluvia of the industrial revolution. Bird-in-Hand brings to mind the simple, unworldly way of life of Old Order Amish. And Hershey remains a synonym for chocolate—in World War II, U.S. soldiers made the name a universal symbol of American generosity all over war-weary Europe.

But Pennsylvania offers much more than instantly recognizable city names. It's a place of scenic back roads and small towns—towns like Jim Thorpe, a thoroughly Victorian settlement named for an Olympian, or Wellsboro, a time-warp holdover from the 1950s on the edge of Pennsylvania's own interpretation of the Grand Canyon.

From Revolutionary War days to the present, the state has often led the nation in industrial production, though agriculture remains Pennsylvania's number-one income-producing industry, due in large part to small farmers, a rural dairy industry, and more than 40 commercial wineries. The Erie region is the largest Concord grape-growing area east of the Mississippi River. Pennsylvania offers travelers opportunities to milk cows on bucolic farms only a few miles from the world's premier collections of fine art.

The state is home to 28 downhill ski areas, hundreds of miles of cross-country and hiking trails, and heart-stopping displays of fall color. Outdoor recreation of all types is popular among Pennsylvanians, who began to explore and enjoy the rural charms of the (then-distant) Pocono Mountains as early as 1815. In fact, tourism may surpass agriculture as the supreme industry in Pennsylvania. Visitors, singly, in pairs, in families and in groups, from within the United States or from around the world, are made welcome everywhere. Traveling to Pennsylvania is traveling to our own fantasy of America—a gentler, less complicated place with strong values and unspoiled wilderness.

WHEN TO GO

I've lived in Pennsylvania year-round, and every season seduces with unique scenic attractions and activities. In most areas, especially those that feature outdoor theme parks, there is a definite "season"—roughly from Memorial Day (end of May) to Labor Day (beginning of September). The largest number of facilities around the state are in operation during that time—and lodging prices are always up a few dollars in the more visited areas.

However, May–June and September–early November are great times to plan a visit if you can. The weather is (usually) mild, prices are down, and many facilities continue to operate on a limited schedule. For those with urban cultural interests, Pittsburgh is uncrowded and offers numerous top quality museums, restaurants, and other amusements every time of year, including the summer. Philadelphia offers an even greater variety of attractions, including unique forays into American history, but is often crowded during the summer months. Early spring, winter, and late fall are great, uncrowded times to visit this historic city.

If spectacular vistas are of interest, the place to be is *anywhere* in the state in spring or autumn. The combination of charming small towns; well-maintained, lightly traveled back roads; manicured farms; and verdant forests and fields is unbeatable. One striking feature of the countryside is that homes, no matter how isolated, are meticulously cared for and often decorated for the season—a definite statement about the people and the place.

Winter is an especially fine time to visit both city and country. Outdoor sports, such as downhill and cross-country skiing, ice fishing, snowmobiling, and snowshoeing are available everywhere, often accompanied by local festivals and celebrations. Some towns, such as Bellefonte, near State College in north-central Pennsylvania, decorate with their Victorian past in mind. Winter is also a wonderful time to visit Amish country, when the trees reveal the landscape and life goes on as usual in the farming communities and markets.

WHAT TO TAKE

Pennsylvania experiences four distinct seasons (see Climate, Know Pennsylvania chapter). Winter brings ice and snow, even to the lowest and most protected elevations, and temperatures occasionally drop below zero, even in the cities. Country roads, especially in the more isolated areas, may not be regularly maintained, so stick to the main roads and ask locals about conditions before venturing off into the unknown. All of the larger towns and cities know snow well, and aren't caught off-guard for more than a few hours by the sneakiest blizzard. Expect underheated exteriors and over-heated interiors—dress in layers.

Spring and fall can be full of surprises, weather-wise. May is often cold, September can be boiling hot—again, layers. Summer is uniformly warm and often muggy—humidity and temperature sometimes race each other to the top of the indicator. Rain is common—that's why it's so green out there. In the cities, dress tends to be more related to age than to formal strictures (though the standing joke is, you can tell an American tourist anywhere in the world: baggy shirt or T-shirt, shorts, sandals or sneakers with socks). Philadelphia is a more formal city, Pittsburgh, less so. Jeans or casual pants are perfect for the country.

If you are traveling by car, by all means have a detailed, recent map on hand. The interstates and large highways have frequent rest stops; however, if you plan to tour the back roads, take water, toilet paper, and snacks. Villages in rural areas may be few and far between, and there's no guarantee that stores will be present, let alone open, even during the day. For back-road touring, a map bought at a local gas station is a must (county and farm roads are often designated by numbers and aren't shown on general maps), and a compass isn't a bad idea, either.

The electrical current in use in Pennsylvania is the same as in the rest of the United States. It functions on 110 volts, 60 cycles of alternating current (AC). Appliances requiring the normal European voltage of 220 will not work. Almost all hotels, B&Bs, and inns provide hairdryers; some provide in-room coffee service, and irons and ironing boards.

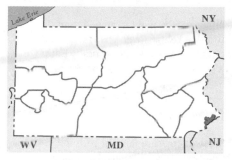

PHILADELPHIA

Philadelphia, one of Pennsylvania's most popular destinations, is the state's oldest and largest city. Colonial-era buildings share narrow streets with modern steel and glass towers; landmarks of American history—the Liberty Bell, Independence Hall—anchor a renovated city center that draws visitors from around the globe.

You'll find world-class museums stuffed with art, history, and science. In addition to a booming gallery scene, and the vast fine- and decorative-art collection at the Philadelphia Museum of Art, the Barnes Foundation art collection of postimpressionist paintings and sculpture has been called the best in the world.

Philadelphia is a cuisine-savvy city—seven of America's top-rated eateries are in town. Comfortable, classic hotels (including the superb duo of the Ritz and Four Seasons) and cozy historic inns abound. A lively nightclub and entertainment scene complete the picture. The Avenue of the Arts (formerly Broad Street), a $300 million project, added new venues for opera; ballet; popular, jazz, and symphonic music; drama; and musical theater. New properties such as the Wilma Theater, Arts Bank, and Orchestra Hall were added to landmarks such as the Academy of Music.

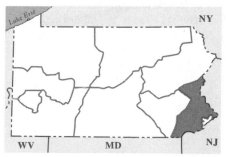

DELAWARE RIVER VALLEY

Counties that nestle along the Delaware River are dotted with upscale suburban and rural towns and villages. The variety of destinations makes for perfect day trips (or longer) from Philadelphia.

To the west of the city, the Brandywine River flows through Brandywine Valley, home to beautiful Longwood Gardens. The Brandywine River Museum displays the works of some of America's most well-loved illustrators and painters. This area is also significant in American history, thanks to Valley Forge and Brandywine Battlefield parks.

Northeast of Philadelphia, in Bucks County, the village of New Hope is a favored getaway for romantic overnights, and Doylestown offers an art museum, two collections of artifacts and craftwork, and good shopping. Pleasant history lessons may be found in William Penn's "country house" and Washington Crossing Historic Park.

Upriver to the north, the Lehigh Valley once set the night aflame; America's largest steel mills pounded out tonnage along the Lehigh River. The Crayola Museum and Bethlehem and Easton historic sites are a worthy draw; pretty Bethlehem has become the "Christmas City," a great place to stay over the holidays.

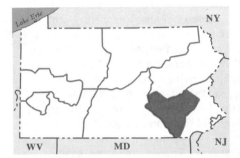

PENNSYLVANIA DUTCH COUNTRY

Most visitors are familiar with the attributes of Dutch Country: horse-drawn buggies, men in wide-brimmed hats, and women in bonnets; the Amish are nearly synonymous with Pennsylvania. The Piedmont region continues to reflect the agrarian interests of its large Amish and Mennonite population, with nearly 5,000 small farms spread throughout the area. Three towns anchor Dutch Country: Lancaster (the county seat), Harrisburg (the state capital), and Reading (a shopper's destination and a great base to visit the surrounding area).

Lancaster County and the Lebanon Valley come complete with unforgettable village names like Blue Ball and Bird-in-Hand, and dozens of activities and amusements celebrating the Amish lifestyle and much more. A chocoholic's mecca, Hershey offers an amusement park and other attractions. In the Reading area, Hopewell Furnace and the Daniel Boone Homestead are outdoor history adventures; and don't miss the nearby Mary Merritt Doll Museum and Merritt Museum of Childhood—two tiny museums filled to the rafters with fascinating dolls, toys, and collectibles.

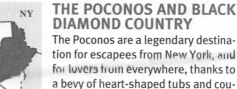

THE POCONOS AND BLACK DIAMOND COUNTRY

The Poconos are a legendary destination for escapees from New York, and for lovers from everywhere, thanks to a bevy of heart-shaped tubs and couples resorts. The gentle, forested mountains are dotted with ski and sports destinations, towns with discount shopping such as Tannersville and Stroudsburg, and pretty rural villages with surprises—a fabulous museum or good restaurant. The Delaware Water Gap (and the entire northern run of the Delaware River) is a scenic area that shines; It's one of the best features of the Poconos year round.

The mountains of northeastern Pennsylvania sit upon a rare geological phenomenon—anthracite coal fields. So valuable it's sometimes referred to as black diamonds, anthracite coal and the mining industry that grew around it shaped the cities and lands of the region. The museums, historic sites, and restaurants of commercial centers Scranton and Wilkes-Barre are a worthy draw; towns like Jim Thorpe have become known for active tourism. Pennsylvania's oldest brewery is here (in Pottersville), still going strong. Take time for the driving tour through black diamond country—a fascinating look at one of the industries that forged America's character.

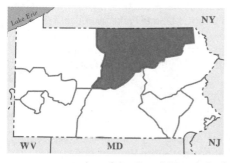

ENDLESS MOUNTAINS

North-central Pennsylvania is the state's largest outdoor recreational area. It's the least-populated part of the commonwealth, carpeted with lush second-growth forests; the region contains more than 30 interconnected state parks and wilderness areas, stretching from Allegheny National Forest in the west to Pennsylvania's own version of the Grand Canyon in the east.

The main access route to this great outdoors is US 6, one of the country's most scenic roads. Starting near Scranton in eastern Pennsylvania, US 6 touches the boundaries of several state parks and passes through small towns, forests of pine and beech, and neat farms, wandering through the Allegheny National Forest before ending a few miles south of Lake Erie.

During the warm months, the area draws bird-watchers, hikers, white-water rafters, canoeists, and anglers. Cold weather brings hunters, cross-country and downhill skiers, snowshoe hikers, and snowmobilers—most parks are laced with trails.

State College, home of Penn State, is one of the two largest towns in the area; the other is Williamsport, with a good history museum. These two, along with villages and small towns that pepper the region, have managed to retain their all-American hometown feel.

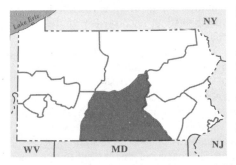

RAILROAD AND CIVIL WAR COUNTRY

A transitional area between the rela-tively flat, fertile farmlands of west Piedmont and the folded mountains and valleys of the Allegheny Plateau, south-central Pennsylvania was set-tled early by German Amish and Scotch-Irish farmers and remains farm-land today, dotted by towns and vil-lages along the early trade routes initially bound by waterways.

Around the time of the Civil War, railroads created access to the Allegheny Ridge and beyond, opening a gateway to the west. The Altoona area, with its railcar repair facilities, museums, and historic sites, has become a steely mecca for rail pilgrims.

Gettysburg, with its moving memorial park on the battlefield, and the sur-rounding Civil War Trail are the area's most popular attractions.

Outdoor recreation, particularly around Blue Knob State Park (favored for ski-ing), Raystown Lake, and Yellow Breeches Creek (boating and fishing), is a big draw for sports enthusiasts. The limestone caves of Huntingdon County provide an opportunity for visitors to explore and enjoy a unique natural feature.

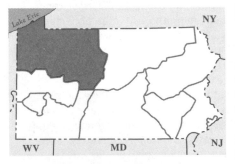

LAKE ERIE AND THE ALLEGHENIES

The undergrowth and dense forests of northwestern Pennsylvania were virtually impassable to 18th-cen-tury homesteaders. This section of the state still retains much of that forested character in the vast Al-legheny National Forest and Cook State Forest, two of many areas that have been preserved.

Erie, third-largest of Pennsylvania's urban areas, is adapting well to its new popularity as a vacation spot offering the best of city and country. The state's scenic "wine country" is centered in the pleasant village of North East. Franklin is a well-preserved Victorian town, and the area boasts interesting museums and a pretty state park—a living shrine to the development of one useful and well-known product: oil (yes, it all started here). Two other towns are worthy of note: Punxsutawney, home of the spring-forecasting groundhog, and Saint Marys, a quiet forest town with a wonderful brewery.

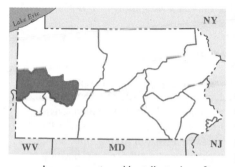

WESTERN AMISH COUNTRY

In colonial times, mountainous western Pennsylvania was the "wild west." The Industrial Revolution turned the area into a series of booming factory towns, but by the mid-20th century, western Pennsylvania shed its industrial trappings to return to rural life and take on a new role as a scenic recreational area. Peaceful farmlands here are watered by tributaries of two of the state's mightiest rivers: the Ohio and the Allegheny.

Hiking and biking trails can be found in parks and on two-lane byways lined with Amish farms. Boating and fishing locations are a short drive in any direction. Small towns such as Beaver, Zelienople, and Harmony (historical site of a 19th-century religious community) retain their individual charm—as well as several good restaurants. The area around New Castle is especially rich in Amish culture, and Volant provides visitors with strolling and shopping opportunities. You might plan a drive out to the Amish farms around Smicksburg, and make a stop in actor Jimmy Stewart's hometown, Indiana, to visit the museum in his honor. It's an unhurried, unadorned place, made for leisurely sightseeing and day trips from Pittsburgh.

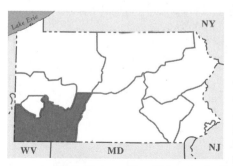

LAUREL HIGHLANDS

The Laurel Highlands has it all—spas, resorts, architectural gems (two Frank Lloyd Wright–designed homes open to the public), elegant getaways, outdoor adventure, peaceful villages— and all a short trip from Pittsburgh. Johnstown offers an excellent historical museum and several other historic attractions. Somerset began life as a market village and is still famous for its maple syrup and living history center. Greensburg is a thriving city with a sophisticated art museum. Ligonier, a small mountain town arranged around a diamond in which band concerts still take place, is filled with pleasant shops, lodgings, and restaurants. It's also home to Fort Ligonier, a worthwhile stop for visitors with an interest in colonial history. Nearby Idlewild Park has been a place of fun and entertainment for families for a century.

Outdoor activities reign supreme here: downhill and cross-country skiers will find paradise among the resorts and parks. Hiking, biking, and fishing opportunities abound, and Ohiopyle State Park is a well-known white-water rafting destination.

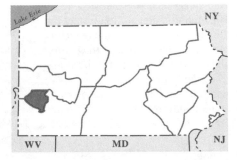

PITTSBURGH

Once one of America's most polluted cities, Pittsburgh led other urban areas in remaking itself into a clean, environmentally aware, people-friendly town. Resurrected from a shambling warehouse past, the Strip has become a trendy shopping area, and first-class universities, museums, parks, and amusements sit firmly in a foundation of family-based neighborhoods. Recently, Pittsburgh was ranked 4th in the United States as an art-related tourist attraction; several richly supported art museums, such as the ultramodern Warhol, the quirky Mattress Factory, and the venerable Carnegie, beckon visitors, and a lively art scene lights up galleries all over town. A unique collection of architecture is part of everyday life. The sciences are well represented, with the Carnegie Science Center, named among the top five museums in the nation; the vast Carnegie Institute collection; the world's largest indoor walk-through aviary; and a charming zoo. Pittsburgh breeds rabid sports fans—PNC Park was ranked "Best Stadium in Major League Baseball" by ESPN. Kennywood Park, one of Pennsylvania's oldest amusement parks, remains cutting edge with new (and old) thrill rides.

Philadelphia is so tightly packed with things to do and see, one week barely affords enough time. In addition to the many sites of historic merit around town including those in Independence National Park, the city offers a number of quirky and unique attractions, such as the nation's first penitentiary, an 18th-century physician's teaching facility, and a Masonic meeting hall that gives new meaning to the term "period architecture." Downtown Philadelphia, site of the majority of the attractions, is continuously undergoing upgrading and is very walkable. Public transportation to Fairmount Park, University City, and Chestnut Hill is easy and accessible. And lest we forget—Philadelphia is recognized as one of the world's greatest food cities. Every block offers eateries that range from four stars down to black holes—let your instincts (and this book) be your guide.

DAY 1:
Start at the Independence National Historical Park visitors center, followed by a tour of Independence Hall and the Liberty Bell (2–3 hours).

Liberty Bell

Round two at Independence National Park: Second Bank of the United States, followed by one of the local heritage museums or Atwater-Kent Museum or Independence Seaport Museum (average 2 hours each). Have dinner at the City Tavern.

DAY 2:
Take a tour of the U.S. Mint (1–2 hours; you've made reservations through your congressional representative, of course) and the Masonic Temple (1–2 hours), followed by lunch in Reading Terminal Market or Chinatown. After, look around the Pennsylvania Academy of Fine Arts (1–2 hours), then take a cab out to Eastern State Penitentiary for the final tour of the day (1–2 hours), and do dinner in the area.

DAY 3:
Time out! Off to Fairmount Park to spend the day in the zoo, walking the trails, checking out Laurel Hill Cemetery, the waterworks, the historic houses. Pack a picnic for lunch, and have dinner at Valley Green.

DAY 4:
Head to either the Franklin Institute Science Museum or Academy of Natural Sciences (2–4 hours). Then, a light lunch—don't want to overindulge

before seeing the displays at the College of Physicians of Philadelphia (2 hours). Wander around Rittenhouse Square, and pick a place for dinner.

DAY 5:

Sensible you! You've booked 30 days ahead and have a reservation at the Barnes Foundation. Marvel at the incredible artwork, and return to town for a late lunch. Enjoy the collections at the Rosenbach Museum and Library (1–2 hours), or go directly to the South Street area and enjoy the Philadelphia Mummers Museum (1–2 hours). Have dinner on South Street or around Headhouse Square.

DAY 6:

Take in the Philadelphia Museum of Art (2–4 hours), in Fairmount Park—and any other sights there you may have missed. Drop down for lunch in University City, and visit the University of Pennsylvania Museum of Archaeology and Anthropology (1–2 hours). Do dinner in the neighborhood.

DAY 7:

Plan to spend the day wandering around Chestnut Hill. As a fond farewell to the city of brotherly love, consider catching the Lights of Liberty show that evening.

Pittsburgh is full of surprises to the uninitiated—a rich variety of world-class fine art venues (the too-cool Warhol Museum, celebrating hometown boy Andy, for one), natural history and science museums, parks, diverse neighborhoods, and—perhaps best of all—Midwestern prices in restaurants, hotels, and amusements. Thanks to the steel magnates of the late 19th century including another hometown boy named Andy (Carnegie), the city offers stunning period architecture; the Pittsburgh millionaires, in their race to outdo one another, created and funded some of western Pennsylvania's finest attractions (Carnegie Institutes, Phipps Conservatory, Frick Park—the list goes on). Today, modern skyscrapers, nationally recognized universities, and cutting-edge medical research facilities are all products of Pittsburgh's ongoing renaissance. From a lofty vantage point you'll see two sparkling rivers, the Allegheny and the Monongahela, flow through the town, and then combine to create the mighty Ohio. Once you get your feet wet, you'll dive in with delight.

DAY 1:

On the morning of the first day, get the big picture—ride one of the inclines up Mt. Washington and take in the gorgeous skyline from the Grandview Overlook—the view ranked second most beautiful in America by *USA Weekend Magazine*. Ride down to the South Side and enjoy the shops and funky atmosphere of East Carson Street. Have dinner in one of the excellent choices on the street or in Station Square.

DAY 2:

Make the Carnegie Institutes (3–4 hours) your destination, followed by lunch on Forbes Avenue; either relax at Phipps Conservatory and Schenley Park in the afternoon (1–2 hours), and/or stop by the University of Pittsburgh's Nationality Classrooms (1–2 hours). Alternatively, the Frick Art Museum/Clayton (1–2 hours) combines a verdant park with historic buildings and a small art museum.

DAY 3:

This is art day—a trip to the Warhol Museum (1–2 hours) on the North Side in the morning, and the Mattress Factory (2 hours) in the afternoon. That evening, if possible, take in the show at the Allegheny Observatory (3 hours, Thursday and Friday only, make sure to book ahead).

DAY 4:

If it's a Saturday, take in the shopping scene at the Strip (1–4 hours), have lunch from one of the many vendors, and stop by the Senator John Heinz Pittsburgh Regional History Center (2 hours) in the afternoon. Don't miss the pickle pins!

DAY 5:

A lovely day to be out and about. Drive up to the Pittsburgh Zoo and Aquarium (2 hours), or stay in town and take in the National Aviary (2–3 hours) in the morning. Have lunch at Penn Brewery and play the afternoon away at the Carnegie Science Center and UPMC SportsWorks (2–4 hours).

DAY 6:

Plan to spend all day at Kennywood and enjoy the free shows and rides or cool off at Sandcastle Water Park.

© JOANNE MILLER

Big Splash at Old Kennywood

DAY 7:

This day—depending on your level of energy and the amount of time you have in the area—could be spent visiting one or more of the other interesting sites and activities listed in this chapter—churches, walking tours, parks—or cheering at a ball game or watching a Broadway show. If you choose to stay downtown, leave the car at home—most destinations of interest (the sole exception being the zoo) are within walking distance or easily accessible public transportation (including taxicabs). If you stay outside the Golden Triangle, a car comes in handy, and parking isn't difficult.

Pennsylvania has always been a place where art and artists have heard a clarion call. Thomas Eakins, Mary Cassatt, the Wyeth family, and dozens of others, from early portraitist Benjamin West to pop-art icon Andy Warhol, have gotten their start or enhanced their careers here. Though Pennsylvania's bucolic vistas have provided plenty of fodder for the brush and camera, its factories were responsible for the pop-art movement: Andy Warhol's "factory" in New York City—where he produced much of his work—relied on consumer design (Campbell's soup cans and Brillo Pad boxes were among his early subjects), repetitive visuals (silkscreen portraits of the not-necessarily-famous-but-definitely-rich), and other influences from his industrial Pittsburgh upbringing.

Pittsburgh is one of two great cities in Pennsylvania in which enormous amounts of wealth have been concentrated; Philadelphia is the other. Thanks to renowned art schools and an appreciative audience in each city, art scenes are flourishing. Both offer spectacular fine art museums and cutting-edge galleries, as well as a multitude of cultural performances including accomplished symphonies, operas, vocal performances, ballet, and other forms of dance.

PHILADELPHIA AND VICINITY

The Barnes Foundation (3–5 hours) stands out as the world's premier private collection of French modern and postimpressionist paintings, featuring artists Henri Matisse, Pablo Picasso, and Claude Monet, among others. The Philadelphia Museum of Art (2–5 hours) is a superb museum that attracts major exhibitions to supplement a mind-boggling collection; the colorful modern mobiles of sculptor Alexander Calder are often on view here, in addition to exhibits covering such diverse styles as Salvador Dali's surrealist paintings and portraits from Renaissance-era Florence. The Pennsylvania Academy of Fine Arts (1–3 hours) spans the history of American painting, featuring classic works by Charles Willson Peale and Thomas Eakins, and contemporary works by the best modern American artists, many of whom have passed through the Academy; the building itself is worth the trip. The Philadelphia Art Alliance (1–4 hours) combines varied exhibits—a recent photography exhibit showcased the work of Alfred Stieglitz—with music and dance performances.

The Institute of Contemporary Art (1–2 hours) in University City goes ultramodern with works by multimedia artists such as Yoshitomo Nara and performer Patti Smith. Woodmere Art Museum (1–2 hours) in Chestnut Hill concentrates on works by Philadelphia area artists, including Daniel Garber, Thomas Pollock Anshutz, Violet Oakley, Benjamin West, and N. C. Wyeth.

Beyond Philadelphia in the Greater Delaware Valley, the Brandywine River Museum (1–2 hours) is home to one of the largest collections of notable works by three generations of the Wyeth family (illustrator N. C. Wyeth and his five children, including Henriette Wyeth Hurd, Carolyn Wyeth, Andrew Wyeth, and their offspring), plus works by other well-known artists and illustrators.

PITTSBURGH AND VICINITY

In Pittsburgh, the Andy Warhol Museum (1–3 hours), an ultramodern facility dedicated to the work of the founder of pop art and his cohorts, is a sleek testament to the playful side of art—with an occasional reference to Warhol's darker side. The Mattress Factory (2–3 hours) is the country's don't-miss premier art collection specializing in large-scale, site-specific installations such as Yayoi Kusama's mirrored room filled with neon dots. The Carnegie Museums (2 hours–2 days) on the East Side, consisting of the Museums of Art and Natural History, display a mind-boggling array of dinosaurs (giant skeletons are always popular with kids), gems, animal specimens, fine art (Edgar Degas and Vincent van Gogh are represented here, not far from modern works by Elizabeth Peyton), sculpture, architectural models (a life-size cast of the Romanesque facade of French Benedictine Abbey St.-Gilles-du-Gard dominates) and more. The Frick Art Museum (1–3 hours), which features revolving art exhibits (a recent one concentrated on Japanese painting), and Clayton, restored Victorian home of industrialist Henry Clay Frick, are within Frick Park, a superbly maintained six-acre preserve.

Beyond Pittsburgh, the Westmoreland Museum of Art (1–3 hours) in the Laurel Highlands features an outstanding collection of works by American artists including Mary Cassatt, John Singer Sargent, and Winslow Homer. Plan to stop by Kentuck Knob (1.5–3 hours) for Lord Palumbo's outstanding (literally—it's all on the grounds surrounding the house) art collection as well as Frank Lloyd Wright's "home for everyman."

In Pittsburgh proper, an interest in architecture could lead beyond the Carnegie Hall of Sculpture and Architecture and Heinz Architectural Center (2–5 hours, both in the Institute of Architecture) to the Triangle History Walk (all day), representing the vast spread of local architecture, such as early wooden buildings on the city's former waterfront, Civil War–era cottages, and mixed marble beaux arts business palaces; and walking tours of Schenley Farms (1–2 hours), an early-20th-century "planned community"; Allegheny Cemetery (1 hour–all day), exemplifying the Victorian obsession with mourning complete with ornate tombs, angels, obelisks, weeping willows, and lush landscaping; and the North Side on Foot (1–2 hours), a combination of post–Mexican War workers' housing and fancy Victorian homes.

The entire Commonwealth of Pennsylvania offers lessons in American history, spanning our colonial beginnings, the Revolution, Civil War, expansion, Industrial Revolution, up to modern America.

For the historian and the curious, each section of Pennsylvania in this book has something to offer. Those with a focus on the Commonwealth's history of religious communes and the Amish will find something of interest in every chapter, particularly Delaware River Valley, Dutch Country, and Western Amish Country. The Poconos and Black Diamond Country lay out the lives of anthracite miners—many of them immigrants in the New World—and their families in Scranton and on the Black Diamond Trail (see Six Days in the Poconos and Black Diamond Country, below). Lake Erie and the Alleghenies touch on the naval battles of the War of 1812, and the founding of America's oil industry; and Pittsburgh and environs provide evidence of industry, from early coal production through big steel.

U.S. history is highly focused in two areas: Philadelphia and environs are notable for colonial preservation and the American Revolution; and Railroad and Civil War Country sings a paean to the railroads that made Western expansion possible and details Pennsylvania's involvement in the War between the States, including Gettysburg's key role.

PHILADELPHIA AND VICINITY

Independence National Historical Park, in toto, would take at five days at a leisurely pace. Add to this additional historic attractions and walks, a matter of individual interest, such as the National Constitution Center (1 hour), a modern building exploring the Constitution and its origins; Elfreth's Alley (.25–1 hour), a collection of colonial buidlings; Arch Street Meeting House (.5 hour), a Quaker hot spot; Pennsylvania Horticultural Society (.25–1 hour)—William Penn wanted plenty of green space in his "City of Brotherly Love"; Edgar Allan Poe National Historic Site (1 hour); and the Betsy Ross House (1 hour). An interest in historic museums might include the Atwater-Kent Museum (1–2 hours), all about the city of Philadelphia, and/or Independence Seaport Museum (2 hours–all day), about ships and their handlers.

If you're in the mood to see additional historic areas on foot, check out Society Hill (1–2 hours), a walk around the brick colonial townhouses that now comprise one of Philadelphia's toniest neighborhoods, and Queens Village/Headhouse Square (1–2 hours), a mixed bag of architectural styles.

You may want to add a tour of City Hall (.5–1 hour); Eastern State Penitentiary (1–2 hours), the Quaker solution to the criminal mind; the Civil War Library and Museum (1 hour); and possibly stop by Gloria Dei Church (.5 hour), established by Philadelphia's original settlers.

Beyond Philadelphia, Valley Forge National Historical Park (2-4 hours) was the site of Washington's headquarters and encampments during the Revolutionary War, and Washington Crossing Historical Park (1–3 hours) features historic buildings and a botanical garden.

RAILROAD AND CIVIL WAR COUNTRY

In this region, especially Altoona, rail fans will enjoy the Conrail Viewing Platform (.5–2 hours) that spans modern railyards and a locomotive repair facility, and nearby Horseshoe Curve

© JOANNE MILLER

Conrail Yard

National Historic Landmark (1 hour), which changed the nature of travel from one end of the state to the other. Visitors ride an incline car up to a viewing platform on the curve and may watch trains rocket around this engineering marvel of the early 20th century. Gallitzin Tunnels Park (.5–1 hour) and Allegheny Portage Railroad National Historic Site (1 hour) complete the circle of railroad history. But don't miss the Altoona Railroaders Memorial Museum (2–3 hours), a celebration of all rail workers.

The Civil War Historic Trail (2 hours–all day) in the Cumberland Valley visits the sites of three major Confederate cavalry raids and several skirmishes. Small evidence remains of the heated battles that took place in this farm country, but the modern pavement that covers dirt roads echoes the marching feet of thousands of ghostly horses and foot soldiers. The Gettysburg campaign of 1863 began in Franklin County; Gettysburg National Military Park (all day) is not to be missed. A significant event in American history is memorialized in a beautiful park, dotted with monuments to the soldiers of both sides who fought there.

The Commonwealth is well known among those who live there as a paradise for outdoor activities. Visitors who seek out spectacular vistas will be thrilled just about *anywhere* in the state in spring or autumn. Winter is an especially fine time to visit the country. Outdoor sports such as downhill and cross-country skiing, ice fishing, snowmobiling, and snowshoeing are available everywhere, often accompanied by local festivals and celebrations. Summer is high season for camping, hiking, and cycling.

THE POCONOS AND BLACK DIAMOND COUNTRY

In the Poconos, see the Delaware Water Gap National Recreation Area—especially on a fall day. If you're planning getaway time, try Ricketts Glen State Park, one of the top 20 parks in the state, chosen for wildlife and natural beauty.

ENDLESS MOUNTAINS

The Grand Canyon of Pennsylvania, set in the spectacular Pine Creek Gorge, is a surprise to those used to Pennsylvania's gentle hills. Visit the Pennsylvania Lumber Museum for insights into the area while enjoying Susquehannock State Forest's scenic drive. Also in the area are Cherry Springs State Park, a "dark park" that attracts stargazers, and Ole Bull State Park, known for hiking trails and views.

RAILROAD AND CIVIL WAR COUNTRY

South-central Pennsylvania's natural wonders, limestone and coral caves, are unique to the area, whether you choose to visit Indian Caverns, Lincoln Caverns, Coral Caverns, or all three. The views from the peak in Blue Knob State Park are spectacular, due to its location on a spur of the Allegheny Front overlooking the Allegheny Ridge and valleys below.

LAKE ERIE AND THE ALLEGHENIES

Lake Erie is among the smallest of the inland seas

known as the Great Lakes, but it's an impressive body of water, especially viewed from Presque Isle State Park. The Drake Well Museum chronicles the petroleum industry from its beginnings to present day, among other exhibits. In the area, spend some time in lovely Oil Creek State Park. The gigantic Allegheny National Forest is a beautiful sight, whether you choose to explore all of its 500,000 acres by foot, boat and bike, take the scenic drive, or chug across the fourth-highest railroad trestle in the world on the Knox & Kane Railroad. Cook State Forest has stands of virgin forest that began growing in 1644. Some of these over-300-year-old trees stand 200 feet tall.

on the way to the Grand Canyon

© JOANNE MILLER

WESTERN AMISH COUNTRY

Scenic **McConnell's Mill State Park** follows the path of Slippery Rock Creek and contains a former water-driven gristmill turned into a museum. A Howe truss covered bridge, Kildoo Bridge, marks the northern boundary of Slippery Rock Gorge, a favorite of rock climbers and whitewater enthusiasts. One of the first rails-to-trails established in America, the **Ghost Town Trail** derives its name from the once-thriving coal mining communities along its path, Wehrum and Braken. Little remains of these settlements other than one original house and the foundations of several mine buildings. The 16-mile-long Ghost Town Trail passes by the Eliza Furnace near Vintondale, one of the best-preserved hot blast iron furnaces in existence.

LAUREL HIGHLANDS

Both **Bushy Run Battlefield** and **Fort Necessity National Battlefield** are loaded with history, but the real reason to go there is scenic beauty, especially in spring and fall. The dramatic 1,700-foot-deep Youghiogheny Gorge cuts through the Laurel Ridge Mountains in southwestern Pennsylvania. Nearly 19,000 acres of this area, including more than 14 miles of the Youghiogheny River, form the basis for **Ohiopyle State Park**. The Yough, as it's commonly referred to, is a popular spot for white-water rafters and kayakers.

The Poconos were made for those with a variety of interests – this is an area that is at once wild and civilized. Ease and modern luxury prevail at the full-service resorts; or you may prefer picking and choosing from a number of parks and recreation areas for day trips or overnight camping, such as Frances Slocum State Park in the Scranton area, Delaware Water Gap National Recreation Area (plenty of fishing, hiking, and scenery, no camping), Promised Land State Park, Locust Lake State Park, Ricketts Glen State Park, or the town of Jim Thorpe (which offers a variety of hotels and B&Bs).

If your pleasures require diversity, the Poconos will provide; in addition to anthracite mining history, the area is pocketed with unique little museums, tiny villages, shopping opportunities (especially around Tannersville and Marshall's Creek), and plenty of gorgeous scenery.

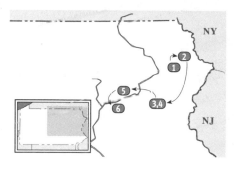

DAY 1:

In Scranton, take the Lackawanna Coal Mine Tour (2 hours) and visit the Anthracite Heritage Museum (2 hours) in the morning, and after lunch, spend some time at Steamtown National Historic Site (2-3 hours) and the Lackawanna Trolley Museum (1 hour).

DAY 2:

Hop in the car, and take a driving tour of the Delaware Water Gap (2 hours–all day) and Zane Grey Museum (1 hour). Stop off for lunch in Hawley, then go on to the Dorflinger Glass Museum (1–2 hours) in White Mills.

© JOANNE MILLER

library in Jim Thorpe

DAYS 3 AND 4:

Move on to Jim Thorpe for an overnight, and follow the Black Diamond Trail to the Ashland Coal Mine and "Lokie" Steam Train (2 hours), the Museum of Anthracite Mining (1–2 hours), Eckley Miner's Village (1–2 hours), Yuengling Brewery (1–2 hours), and The No. 9 Mine Wash Shanty and Anthracite Coal Mining Museum (1–2 hours). The driving tour could take up to three days, depending on how much time you plan to spend at each location.

DAY 5:

The pretty college town of Bloomsburg is centrally located for touring the area east of the Susquehanna, or stay in Ricketts Glen State Park. Take the Covered Bridge Tour: Bloomsburg to Elysburg (2 hours–all day).

DAY 6:

Spend the day or longer (they have camping and trailer facilities) at Knoebels Amusement Park.

Explore Pennsylvania

Philadelphia

Philadelphia is America's first city in many ways. It's an elegant town, but also a tough town, rife with paradox. The phone book lists chandelier cleaners, cheesesteak vendors, firearms dealers, and Friends (Quaker) sanctuaries. It was Philadelphia that produced Grace Kelly—this daughter of a high-toned Main Line family grew up to become an American movie icon and married into European royalty. But it was also Philadelphia that, in 1985, bombed one of its own neighborhoods to eliminate a perceived paramilitary movement and destroyed more than 60 homes in the ensuing fire. It wasn't meant to be this way.

Founded by William Penn in the late 17th century, the city quickly became the keystone not only of the Keystone State, but also of the colonies. When Philadelphia's leaders spoke, America listened.

©JOANNE MILLER

Must-Sees

If you're only in the city for a short time, these are the top attractions, unique to Philadelphia— choosing among the many wonderful sights is a real challenge.

⋈ **Independence National Historical Park:** If you can, see all of the park including the highlights (Liberty Bell, Independence Hall, and the Second Bank) as well as the historic homes and churches. The **Liberty Bell** continues to be the ultimate symbol of the ideal of American freedom; **Independence Hall** is where the colonies united, and the constitution was signed into law by the quill pens of Ben Franklin and Thomas Jefferson; and the **Second Bank of the United States** portrait gallery gives an idea what those famous colonials really looked like (page 39).

⋈ **The U.S. Mint:** A visit here requires planning ahead, but it's a singular, fun, and informative experience. And all that shiny money. . . (page 46).

⋈ **Masonic Temple:** This unusual building offers unparalleled architectural eye-candy in a multicultural, multiera mix (page 46).

⋈ **The College of Physicians of Philadelphia/Mütter Museum:** What you'll see here won't be found anywhere else—guaranteed! Fascinating visual "symptom specimens" helped 19th-century doctors diagnose diseases (page 51).

⋈ **Philadelphia Museum of Art:** This world-class museum attracts major exhibitions to supplement a mind-boggling collection of fine and decorative arts (page 53).

⋈ **Pennsylvania Academy of Fine Arts:** The collection spans the history of American painting; the building, a royal beauty of a Victorian, is worth the trip in itself (page 53).

⋈ **Eastern State Penitentiary:** Another type of history all together—America's first penitentiary gives new meaning to "solitude" (page 59).

⋈ **The Barnes Foundation:** Walls covered with art—this collection stands out as the world's premier private collection of French modern and postimpressionist paintings. Don't miss it (page 77).

castle-like towers of the Eastern State Penitentiary

© JOANNE MILLER

PHILADELPHIA

The Barnes Foundation ⋈

Philadelphia Museum of Art
Eastern State Penitentiary

⋈ Pennsylvania Academy of Fine Arts
⋈ ⋈ Masonic Temple
Independence National Historical Park
U.S. Mint

The College of Physicians of Philadelphia/Mütter Museum

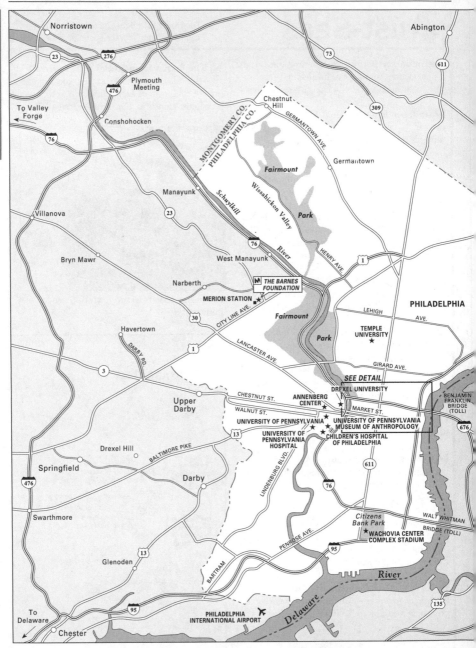

Norristown

Abington

23

276

Plymouth Meeting

476

73

611

To Valley Forge

Conshohocken

Chestnut Hill

309

GERMANTOWN AVE.

MONTGOMERY CO.
PHILADELPHIA CO.

76

Fairmount

Germantown

Manayunk

Schuylkill

Wissahickon Valley

Park

Villanova

23

76

River

Bryn Mawr

West Manayunk

HENRY AVE.

1

PHILADELPHIA

Narberth

30

CITY LINE AVE.

M THE BARNES FOUNDATION

MERION STATION ★★

LEHIGH

AVE.

Havertown

1

DARBY RD.

LANCASTER AVE.

Fairmount

Park

TEMPLE UNIVERSITY
★

3

GIRARD AVE.

SEE DETAIL

DREXEL UNIVERSITY

Upper Darby

CHESTNUT ST.

ANNENBERG CENTER
★

MARKET ST.

BENJAMIN FRANKLIN BRIDGE (TOLL)

676

WALNUT ST.

UNIVERSITY OF PENNSYLVANIA ★

★ UNIVERSITY OF PENNSYLVANIA MUSEUM OF ANTHROPOLOGY

13

UNIVERSITY OF PENNSYLVANIA HOSPITAL

★ CHILDREN'S HOSPITAL OF PHILADELPHIA

Drexel Hill

BALTIMORE PIKE

Springfield

LINDENBURG BLVD.

611

476

Darby

76

Swarthmore

Citizens Bank Park

WALT WHITMAN BRIDGE (TOLL)

★ WACHOVIA CENTER COMPLEX STADIUM

13

PENROSE AVE.

95

Glenoden

BARTRAM

River

To Delaware

95

PHILADELPHIA INTERNATIONAL AIRPORT ✈

Delaware

135

Chester

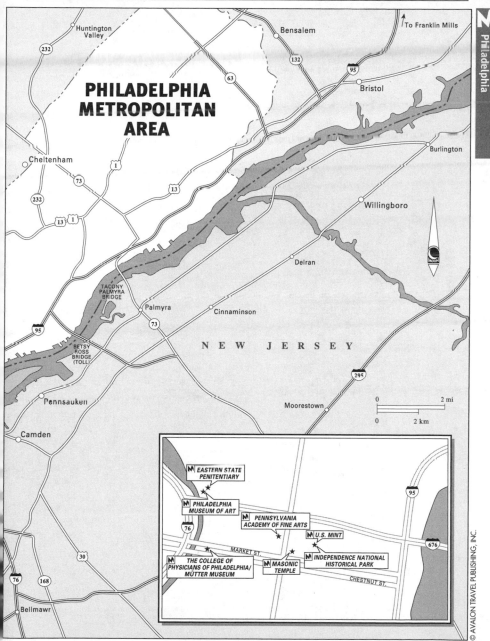

PHILADELPHIA
METROPOLITAN
AREA

Huntington
Valley

Bensalem

To Franklin Mills

Bristol

Cheltenham

Burlington

Willingboro

Delran

TACONY
PALMYRA
BRIDGE

Palmyra

Cinnaminson

BETSY
ROSS
BRIDGE
(TOLL)

N E W   J E R S E Y

Pennsauken

Moorestown

Camden

0   2 mi

0   2 km

EASTERN STATE
PENITENTIARY

PHILADELPHIA
MUSEUM OF ART

PENNSYLVANIA
ACADEMY OF FINE ARTS

U.S. MINT

MARKET ST.

THE COLLEGE OF
PHYSICIANS OF PHILADELPHIA/
MÜTTER MUSEUM

MASONIC
TEMPLE

INDEPENDENCE NATIONAL
HISTORICAL PARK

CHESTNUT ST.

Bellmawr

Philadelphia

Philadelphia

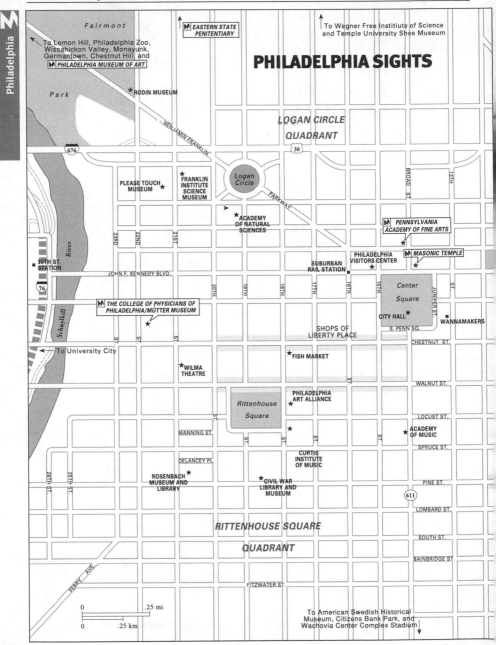

Fairmont

To Lemon Hill, Philadelphia Zoo,
Wissahickon Valley, Monayunk,
Germantown, Chestnut Hill, and
Ⓜ PHILADELPHIA MUSEUM OF ART

Ⓜ EASTERN STATE PENITENTIARY

To Wagner Free Institute of Science
and Temple University Shoe Museum

PHILADELPHIA SIGHTS

Park

★ RODIN MUSEUM

BENJAMIN FRANKLIN

676

LOGAN CIRCLE QUADRANT

30

PLEASE TOUCH MUSEUM ★

FRANKLIN INSTITUTE SCIENCE MUSEUM ★

Logan Circle

PARKWAY

BROAD ST

13TH

★ ACADEMY OF NATURAL SCIENCES

Ⓜ PENNSYLVANIA ACADEMY OF FINE ARTS

23RD   22ND   21ST

36TH ST. STATION

River

JOHN F. KENNEDY BLVD.

76

PHILADELPHIA VISITORS CENTER ★

Ⓜ MASONIC TEMPLE ★

SUBURBAN RAIL STATION ■

Center Square

JUNIPER ST

Schuylkill

Ⓜ THE COLLEGE OF PHYSICIANS OF PHILADELPHIA/MÜTTER MUSEUM
★

20TH   19TH   18TH   17TH   16TH   15TH

CITY HALL ★

S. PENN SQ.

WANNAMAKERS

SHOPS OF LIBERTY PLACE

CHESTNUT ST.

To University City

★ WILMA THEATRE

★ FISH MARKET

WALNUT ST.

PHILADELPHIA ART ALLIANCE

Rittenhouse Square

LOCUST ST.

MANNING ST.

ST.

★

★ ACADEMY OF MUSIC

SPRUCE ST.

DELANCEY PL.

26TH ST.   25TH ST.

ROSENBACH MUSEUM AND LIBRARY ★

CURTIS INSTITUTE OF MUSIC

★ CIVIL WAR LIBRARY AND MUSEUM

PINE ST.

611

LOMBARD ST.

RITTENHOUSE SQUARE

QUADRANT

SOUTH ST.

BAINBRIDGE ST.

FERRY AVE.

FITZWATER ST.

0   .25 mi

0   .25 km

To American Swedish Historical
Museum, Citizens Bank Park, and
Wachovia Center Complex Stadium

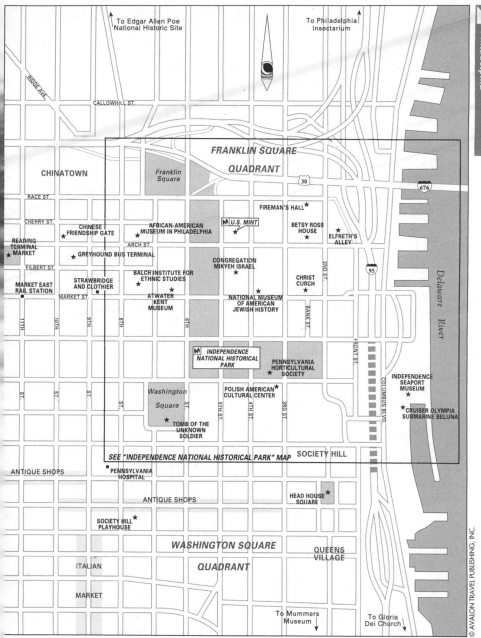

To Edgar Allen Poe National Historic Site

To Philadelphia Insectarium

RIDGE AVE.

CALLOWHILL ST.

FRANKLIN SQUARE QUADRANT

CHINATOWN

Franklin Square

30

676

RACE ST.

FIREMAN'S HALL ★

CHERRY ST.

CHINESE FRIENDSHIP GATE ★

AFRICAN-AMERICAN MUSEUM IN PHILADELPHIA

Ⓜ U.S. MINT

BETSY ROSS HOUSE ★

ELFRETH'S ALLEY ★

READING TERMINAL MARKET ★

GREYHOUND BUS TERMINAL ★

ARCH ST.

FILBERT ST.

CONGREGATION MIKYEH ISRAEL ★

BALCH INSTITUTE FOR ETHNIC STUDIES ★

CHRIST CURCH ★

MARKET EAST RAIL STATION ■

STRAWBRIDGE AND CLOTHIER ■

ATWATER KENT MUSEUM

NATIONAL MUSEUM OF AMERICAN JEWISH HISTORY ★

MARKET ST.

BANK ST.

2ND ST.

11TH

10TH

9TH

8TH

6TH

FRONT ST.

Ⓜ INDEPENDENCE NATIONAL HISTORICAL PARK

PENNSYLVANIA HORTICULTURAL SOCIETY ★

COLUMBUS BLVD.

INDEPENDENCE SEAPORT MUSEUM ★

Washington Square

POLISH AMERICAN CULTURAL CENTER ★

CRUISER OLYMPIA SUBMARINE BELUNA ★

5TH ST.

4TH ST.

3RD ST.

TOMB OF THE UNKNOWN SOLDIER ★

SEE "INDEPENDENCE NATIONAL HISTORICAL PARK" MAP

SOCIETY HILL

ANTIQUE SHOPS

PENNSYLVANIA HOSPITAL ■

ANTIQUE SHOPS

HEAD HOUSE SQUARE ★

SOCIETY HILL PLAYHOUSE ★

WASHINGTON SQUARE QUADRANT

QUEENS VILLAGE

ITALIAN

MARKET

To Mummers Museum

To Gloria Dei Church

Delaware River

95

As you might expect of a city named for brotherly love, Philadelphia has attracted major influxes of different ethnic and lifestyle groups. Like all of America, the mix hasn't always been a happy one, but the city is eager to ease strained relations. Because it offered opportunity to the oppressed early on, nearly half the population is African-American, but virtually every race and sexual orientation is well represented—American dreamers, trying to make it in the promised land.

As birthplace of the United States, Philadelphia is a microcosm of radiant beauties and deep-seated problems. Fortunately, its people share the solid sense of place that permeates the state. For that reason, Philadelphia has what it takes to resolve challenges and grow ever greater.

Today, Philadelphia is Pennsylvania's largest city, with one and a half million residents. Venerable colonial-era buildings share narrow streets with modern steel and glass towers. Landmarks of American history—the Liberty Bell, Independence Hall, Carpenters Hall—anchor a renovated city center that draws visitors from around the globe. Philadelphia offers its guests every kind of amusement: the Philadelphia Museum of Art; the Mummers Museum; restaurants that serve the cuisine of Spain, Vietnam, Italy, and a hundred other countries; comfortable, classic hotels and cozy bed and breakfasts reminiscent of Europe; a lively nightclub and gallery scene; and much, much more.

It offers Old World charm on the same platter as a booming marketplace. The city's historic landmarks coexist with high-tech modernity, especially in the field of Western medicine; Philadelphia has more teaching medical hospitals than any other city in the world, and many of the world's major pharmaceutical houses, including Astra/Merck, Bristol-Myers Squibb, DuPont Merck, and Johnson & Johnson. Over 150 premier biotechnology research centers do business here; many of which have pioneered new prescription drugs and genetic-research breakthroughs.

Philadelphia can claim to represent the best in many categories. Seven of America's Top 50 restaurants, according to *Condé Nast Traveler* reader's surveys in the last decade, were in the city—Le Bec-Fin was number one, The Fountain at Four Seasons was number two. Le Bec-Fin took top honors in 2000, when *Food & Wine* magazine chose it as Best Restaurant. Culturally, Philadelphia's wealth of fine art museums is an embarrassment of riches. In addition to the vast panoply available for viewing at the Philadelphia Museum of Art, the Barnes Foundation art collection of postimpressionist paintings and sculpture has been called the best in the world and is one of many places to view fine art.

The Avenue of the Arts, a $300 million project, added new venues for opera; ballet; popular, jazz, and symphonic music; drama; and musical theater to Broad Street. New properties such as the Wilma Theater, Arts Bank for theater companies, and Orchestra Hall were added to landmarks such as the Academy of Music. Even the venerable Ritz hotel was reborn and rebuilt on the Avenue.

The future of Philadelphia is up to the people, and the people are the real treasure of this city. Genuinely friendly faces of every hue welcome visitors on the street, and local leaders work continuously to patch holes in the social fabric. When a radical leader of the Nation of Islam, Louis Farrakhan, joins with Jewish former mayor Edward G. Rendell to appeal to the people of Philadelphia for tolerance and peace, it's time, once again, for America to listen.

ORIENTATION

Philadelphia is very easy to navigate; it's laid out entirely on a north-south (numbered streets), east-west grid. William Penn planned a neat town with five squares anchoring it. City Hall (Center Square) is in the center between the two rivers; radiating out from this square are the main cross streets: Market (east-west) and Broad/Avenue of the Arts (north-south). Franklin Square (Northeast Square/Old Town) and Washington Square (Southeast Square) are closer to the Delaware, and Logan Circle (Northwest Square) and Rittenhouse Square (Southwest Square) are nearer

WHERE TO FIND IT

Franklin Square Quadrant/Old Town
African American Museum of Philadelphia
Atwater Kent Museum
Betsy Ross House
Chinatown
Edgar Allan Poe National Historic Site
Elfreth's Alley
Fireman's Hall Museum
Independence National Historical Park
Lights of Liberty
Masonic Temple
National Constitution Center
Reading Terminal Market
U.S. Mint

Washington Square Quadrant
Antique Row/Pine Street
Gloria Dei Church
Head House Square
Independence Seaport Museum
Italian Market (9th St.)
Mario Lanza Museum
Mummer's Museum
Physick House (INHP)
Polish American Cultural Center

Powel House (INHP)
Society Hill
South Street
Swedish Historical Museum

Rittenhouse Square Quadrant
City Hall
Civil War Library and Museum
College of Physicians of Philadelphia/
Mütter Museum
Philadelphia Art Alliance
Rosenbach Museum

Logan Circle Quadrant
Academy of Natural Sciences
Eastern State Penitentiary
Fairmount Park
Franklin Institute
Pennsylvania Academy of Fine Arts
Philadelphia Museum of Art
Philadelphia Zoo
Please Touch Museum
Rodin Museum
Temple University
Wagner Free Institute of Science

the Schuylkill River. The entire center of Philadelphia now fills the area between the Delaware and Schuylkill rivers.

This chapter is divided into sections, based on the city's directional squares. Franklin Square Quadrant/Old Town, the colonial-era city of Philadelphia, extends roughly 13 blocks west from the Delaware River and south from the square down to Walnut Street (east-west), the north border of Washington Square; it includes Independence National Historical Park excepting two historic homes, Powel House and Physick House.

Washington Square Quadrant/South Street includes all of the territory south of Old Town and west to the city's center line, Broad Street (Ave. of the Arts).

The Rittenhouse Square Quadrant covers all the area south of Market Street and west of Broad Street to the Schuylkill River.

Logan Circle Quadrant takes in the territory north of Market Street and west of Broad Street, and includes Fairmount Park.

Greater Philadelphia includes areas beyond the boundaries of Center City: University City (west of the Schuylkill River), the Wissahickon Valley (at the north end of Fairmount Park), and the villages of Manayunk and Chestnut Hill.

PLANNING YOUR TIME

How do you choose from the best? To see everything in Philadelphia at a comfortable pace would take a month. If you have only a week, think about adapting the One Week in Philadelphia tour (see the Discover chapter). You can select additional or substitute activities from Pennsylvania for Art Lovers and History Highlights (also in the Discover chapter), as well as from the categories that follow, by area and the amount of time it takes to see each venue. Since eating on a regular schedule is a pleasurable must, we'll assume you'll fit that in between attractions. All the sights (with the exception of the Barnes Foundation) are accessible via an easy walk, cab ride, or public transport. Add the amount of time it takes to get from one attraction to another—anywhere from five minutes to 45 minutes—and pick and choose.

Old Town Plus: These ethnic museums, cultural centers, and galleries add additional interest to Old Town: the **African-American Museum in Philadelphia** (1–2 hours), the **National Museum of American Jewish History** (1–2 hours), the **Polish American Cultural Center** (1 hour), the **Lights of Liberty** show (2–3 hours), the **Masonic Temple** (2–3 hours), the **U.S. Mint** (by reservation only, 1–2 hours), and **Old Town Art Galleries** (1 hour–all day).

Rittenhouse Square: In the Rittenhouse Square Quadrant, stops might include the **College of Physicians of Philadelphia** (2 hours) and the **Rosenbach Museum and Library** (.5–2 hours).

Family Fun: The **Franklin Institute Science Museum** (2 hours–all day) and **Academy of Natural Sciences** (2 hours–all day) both pride themselves on making learning fun, and everyone will enjoy the **Philadelphia Zoo** (all day); all are in the Logan Circle Quadrant. The **Philadelphia Mummers Museum** (1–2 hours, Washington Square Quadrant) and **Fireman's Hall Museum** (1–2 hours, Franklin Square Quadrant) combine history with great visuals. The **University of Pennsylvania Museum of Archaeology and Anthropology** (1–2 hours, Greater Philadelphia) will appeal to older children, while **Please Touch Museum** (3 hours–all day, Logan Circle Quadrant) is for those under 12 years of age.

Outdoor Recreation: Fairmount Park is the ultimate destination, with enough trails and points of interest to keep you occupied for three or more days. The **Wissahickon Valley** (all day), on the north end of Fairmount Park, is a hiker's paradise.

Day Trips: Take SEPTA out to spend a day wandering around either **Manayunk** and/or **Chestnut Hill.** The **Morris Arboretum of the University of Pennsylvania** in Chestnut Hill (2 hours–all day) is a lovely place to walk.

HISTORY
First Contact

During prehistoric times, migratory hunting groups roamed the densely wooded banks of the Delaware River. After A.D. 1000, the tribal families that sought game in the area started to supplement their diet by planting maize and squash; they began wandering less and called themselves the Lenape, "original people" (the more recognized name, Lenni Lenape, uses Lenni as a verbal enhancement, roughly meaning Absolutely Original People). There were approximately 10,000 living in the Philadelphia area at the time of first contact with European explorers in 1524.

The initial European settlers were Swedes, who founded New Sweden in 1638 for the Swedish West India Company. By 1655, Peter Stuyvesant, director general of New Amsterdam (New York), seized the small colony's holdings and supplanted them with a Dutch colony. After the British defeated the Dutch in 1673, the colony became British. Settlers in the New World ran into a major problem: the natives were well organized and could easily defeat the invading colonists. The Swedish and the Dutch both overran their agreed-upon boundaries, and the Lenni Lenape attacked them. The Lenni Lenape conducted a brisk real estate business by leasing use of the land—but not the ownership of the land itself—to each new set of Europeans. By the time of English settlement, the remaining Lenni Lenape were so weakened by smallpox, tuberculosis, and measles that they began leaving the area permanently for healthier climates.

Native susceptibility proved to be both a blessing and a curse. As was common at the time, each wave of European invaders (especially the British) had intended to conquer the indigenous population and enslave them. The Lenni Lenape's susceptibility to European diseases made them even less desirable as working property. While this may have let them off the hook as slaves, it also created a great need for *imported* slaves, who came via the Middle Passage—the trade route between Africa and Jamaica that was the stopover of many ships between Europe and the colonies.

The Quaker Takes Over

William Penn was both a realist and an idealist. He envisioned his New World colony as a place of personal freedom for all men. Strongly adhering to his religious principles, he dealt fairly and honestly with the remaining Lenni Lenape. Unlike the painting commissioned by William Penn's son Thomas (*Wm. Penn's Treaty with the Indians*, by Benjamin West), there was no great single treaty, but rather a series of meetings concluding in lease agreements. Penn laid out the town between the Delaware and Schuylkill Rivers, and the majority of it was constructed between 1730 and 1765. The city exported lumber, furs, wheat, and flour to the West Indies in return for rum, sugar, and molasses. These, along with locally made bar iron and Lancaster County wheat, were then exported to England. Philadelphia became the fastest-growing city in the colonies; in 1683, there were 80 families in Philadelphia; by 1699, there were 4,500.

Expansion

Welcoming immigrants at dockside were inns and ordinaries such as the Blue Anchor, the Crooked Billet, and the Pewter Platter. Ben Franklin moved from his hometown of Boston in 1729 to open a print shop there. The energetic printer instituted the first library in town, organized a volunteer militia, hospital, and fire company, and became the postmaster general of the colonies. Franklin was one of several innovators who made Philadelphia their home, among them John Morgan, father of medical education; David Rittenhouse, astronomer and mathematician; John Bartram, botanist; John James Audubon, naturalist; Benjamin Rush, the leading physician of the day; and Benjamin West, one of the world's most influential painters.

So many immigrants entered the American colonies at Water and Market Streets—200,000 Scotch-Irish alone, a third of all the Scotsmen then in Ireland—that it was called "the most historic highway in America." By the beginning of the American Revolution, Philadelphia had a population of nearly 24,000. At that time, Philadelphia was lauded by author Gabriel Thomas: "It has in it Three Fairs every Year, and Two Markets every Week. They kill about Twenty Fat Bullocks every Week, in the hottest time in Summer, for their present spending in that City, besides many Sheep, Calves, and Hogs." Philadelphia was the colonies' undisputed hot spot, the leading city in the British colonial empire.

The First Capital

In 1774, 12 colonies sent 56 delegates to the First Continental Congress, in Carpenters Hall. Protests over Britain's taxation policies were met by the Congress's attempts to negotiate a peaceful settlement with the mother country. Provoked by the battles of Lexington and Concord, the Second Continental Congress, in 1775, named George Washington commander-in-chief of the new Continental Army. In July of 1776, Thomas Jefferson drafted the Declaration of Independence. A year later, defeats of the Continental Army in surrounding areas forced the Continental Congress to flee to York for a year. The end of the war in 1783 saw the states unite from a loose confederation into a single nation. Philadelphia remained the capital of the United States until 1800, when political wrangling transferred the capital to Washington, D.C. The Revolutionary War signaled the decline of Quaker influence in Philadelphia and Pennsylvania; many Quakers refused to support the war on religious principles and lost property and prestige as a result.

Yellow Fever and the Triumph of Industry

After the Revolutionary War, the city was plagued by yellow-fever epidemics. One of the worst occurred in 1793—the populace died at the rate of 12–18 people per day. At the time, there was no idea that the disease was carried by mosquitoes,

THE SUM OF ITS SQUARES

William Penn was interested in order, and in towns laid out with an abundance of greenery. The original plan for Philadelphia, drawn up in 1682, created the city on a simple grid based on five squares, all crossed diagonally by streets radiating from Center Square. Philadelphia still has its original squares, though the names have changed, and each maintains a unique personality. The grid pattern of the town is easy to navigate—ideal for visitors—although not everyone finds this pleasing: of his visit, Charles Dickens wrote, "It is a handsome city, but distractingly regular."

Center Square, at Broad and Market Streets, was the largest of the squares. Early residents preferred to live along the Delaware River, leaving Center Square to the weeds. In the late 18th century, epidemics of yellow fever motivated the city's caretakers to purify the water supply, and the square became the site of Philadelphia's first waterworks. Within 20 years, Philadelphia required a larger waterworks on the Schuylkill, and the first was demolished. By the late 19th century, the city grew to encompass Center Square; construction began on City Hall, designed by John McArthur Jr. in French Second Empire style, similar to the Louvre. The ornate building took 30 years to complete and is the tallest masonry-bearing structure in the world. Sculptor Alexander Milne Calder—who seemed to hold the license for ornamentation of government projects at the time—created more than 250 works of art for the

building. The most famous is the 36-foot-tall William Penn on top of the building, which faces northeast toward Penn Treaty Park, site of a legendary treaty between Penn and the Lenni Lenape. Until 1986, no building in Center City rose higher than the brim of Penn's hat. On the tower below Penn's feet are four large bronzes representing Native Americans and early Swedish settlers and four American eagles. The sidewalks surrounding City Hall feature a number of statues of local and national heroes, from Civil War generals John Reynolds and George McClellan to the king of general shopping, John Wanamaker.

Before 1815, **Northeast Square** provided livestock pasture and a site for cattle markets; a section was leased as a burial ground (most of the graves were moved in 1835). During the Revolutionary War and War of 1812, the square was used for powder storage and military drills. The area changed from residential to industrial during the early 20th century, and the square became increasingly isolated. Now known as Franklin Square, bordered by Vine, Race, 6th, and 7th Streets, it has evolved into a park with a playground, baseball diamond, and benches among the shade trees—a seldom-used and welcome retreat close to Independence Mall.

Southeast Square became the burial ground for 2,000 Continental servicemen and British prisoners (many of whom had died in a nearby prison) during the Revolutionary War. Within the next

and many wealthy families moved out of the city to the Fairmount Park area to get away from the "bad air"; some of these mansions still stand.

From 1800 to 1820, Philadelphia became a center of sea trade, especially with China. The wealthy city's newest buildings were the Fairmount Waterworks, created to pump water from the Schuylkill River to the city, Eastern State Penitentiary, and Laurel Hill Cemetery, all of which still stand.

New York surpassed Philadelphia in population in 1820 and, with the building of the Erie Canal, created a ready access to the wealth of the continent's interior. Philadelphia's growth

was slowed by a familiar obstacle: the Allegheny Mountains to the west. The Pennsylvania system of state-financed canals, roads, and railways couldn't match New York's transport power. Instead, Philadelphia became a leading manufacturing center. Textiles, apparel, shoes, machinery, tools, iron, steel, locomotives, and shipbuilding provided new sources of wealth for the city.

In the 1830s, the antislavery debate heated up. The overwhelming desire of the city was to protect its lucrative trade with the South. Though a large segment of the population was opposed to slavery, it wasn't necessarily in favor of negroes—or even immigrants. The popula-

four decades, the ground would hold victims of the city's yellow fever epidemics. Trees planted in 1815 by French botanist François André Michaux still stand. The square was renamed for George Washington, and by the late 19th century, law firms and Philadelphia's publishing ventures moved into the area. *The Ladies' Home Journal,* for one, made its debut from Washington Square. In 1952, a remodeling of the square included construction of a life-sized, life-modeled statue of Washington, a crypt that holds the remains of an unknown Revolutionary War soldier, and a memorial flame. In one corner of the park, the Bicentennial Moon Tree spreads its boughs; it's a sycamore grown from a seed carried to the moon by Apollo astronaut Stuart Roosa.

Northwest Square, renamed for William Penn's secretary, James Logan, was a full-service plot—used both for public executions and burials. During the Civil War, a fair was held on the grounds to raise funds for the Union wounded, and temporary buildings held 3,000 convalescing soldiers. In 1919, a parkway plan was adopted, based on the Place de la Concorde in Paris. A traffic circle was built into Logan Square (a.k.a. Logan Circle), linking Center City and Fairmount Park. The Philadelphia Fountain Society, in honor of its late president, Dr. Wilson Swann, commissioned architect Wilson Eyre Jr. to create a monument. The *Swann Memorial Fountain of the Three Rivers* has become one of the city's best-known land-

marks, Eyre and Alexander Stirling Calder designed a central geyser that sends a 50-foot stream of water into the air, surrounded by figures representing the Delaware River as a majestic male Native American surrounded by leaping fish; the Schuylkill River as a mature woman, recalling the Lenni Lenape's reference to the river as "mother"; and Wissahickon Creek as a maiden, reclining against the back of a water-spouting swan. Calder's use of swans was undoubtedly a reference to its namesake, but the fountain also features frogs and turtles—perhaps another allusion to Dr. Swann, president of the Pennsylvania Society for the Prevention of Cruelty to Animals.

Southwest Square, originally used as a pasture and a dumping spot for chamber pots, was christened Rittenhouse Square in 1825, honoring Philadelphia astronomer David Rittenhouse. Although it was once surrounded by brickyards, an 1850 building boom transformed the neighborhood into the most fashionable residential section of the city. Rittenhouse Square has remained a popular local park; trees, landscaping, and small fountains were donated by benefactors. Eventually, all the early fountains were removed; the excess of water had turned the park into a mudhole. In 1913, French architect Paul Phillippe Cret redesigned the square's current layout: the reflecting pool, classical sculpture, ornamental lampposts, and carefully tended planter beds contribute to the peaceful atmosphere of gentilesse.

---

tion, drawn by manufacturing jobs, doubled between 1840 and 1860. Riots over massive Irish immigration from the potato famine were common. When the Civil War finally began, Philadelphia's manufacturing businesses grew exponentially, creating a new level of wealth—and a new draw for immigrants.

Making Modern Philadelphia

Between 1876 and 1900, immigrants from Eastern Europe and Italy flooded into the city. During the late 19th century, Philadelphia was America's premier manufacturing center, turning out everything from Stetson hats (yes, the cowboy hat orig-

inated in Philadelphia; the Stetson Hat Company named it "The Boss of the Plains") to Disston saws. Philadelphia was the largest refiner of sugar in the U.S., and the city boasted 200 confectionery shops, including Whitman's (of Sampler fame). The International Exposition of 1876 characterized Philadelphia as the Electric City. John Wanamaker opened his department store, operating on a policy of "one price only, clearly marked—money back"—thereby revolutionizing the retail business by eliminating haggling with single pricing for all. He furthered the appeal of shopping at Wanamaker's by promising cash in exchange for returned purchases.

Between 1900 and 1930, the city's population doubled to two million. The African-American population alone doubled as jobs beckoned. World War I invigorated the sagging industrial base, but between 1930 and 1945, the Depression wiped out the economy. Fifty banks failed. The citizens relied on their neighbors, churches, and local charities to stay afloat. Philadelphian Charles Darrow invented a game he called Monopoly during the Depression but couldn't sell enough copies of it to make a living. He sold the design to Parker Brothers, and it became the best-selling board game of all time.

World War II pulled the economy out of the doldrums, but the face of Philadelphia had already changed. The advent of mass transportation, which had begun with trolleys in the 1890s, had initiated first a trickle and then an flood of middle-class workers and their families from the city center to the suburbs. Today, Philadelphia consists of a downtown filled with tall buildings, interspersed with a few wealthy neighborhoods such as Society Hill and Rittenhouse Square; a few mixed-income, multicultural neighborhoods, such as West Washington Square and University City; and outlying residential districts segregated by income, race, and ethnicity.

Renewal

After WWII, the city's leaders launched an ambitious plan of urban renewal. A coalition of citizens, civic groups, city planners, and businessmen joined forces to re-create Center City, preserving the historic buildings of the Old Town area while providing an atmosphere that encouraged business. To a great extent, the redevelopment has slowed the flow of people, businesses, and industry out of the city and removed and replaced some of the worst of Philadelphia's slums. A run-down area of food-production facilities where Society Hill now stands was relocated to south Philadelphia; a commuter tunnel linking the region's rail lines was built; the shabby waterfront was transformed into Penn's Landing. In the 1950s, Philadelphia's image was at an all-time high, its sports teams were winning, and the city experienced a true renaissance. In 1952, radio station WFIL began to broadcast popular music. In 1956, 27-year-old Dick Clark took over a dead-air mid-afternoon spot on local television with a program that consisted of local kids dancing to pop music and, lo, *American Bandstand* was born (it would take several more years before the show became integrated, finally reflecting the real population of Philadelphia). Between 1960 and 1985, South Street was almost obliterated by a crosstown freeway. It was saved by residents and merchants.

Urban redevelopment, sometimes contested, often debated, continues. The most recent controversy has been over the redesign of Independence Mall and the best way to showcase Philadelphia's unique heritage. Over the years, the city has won national acclaim and served as a model used by other American cities. West of city hall, in Dilworth Plaza (named for activist mayor Richardson Dilworth, who served 1956–1962), stands an aluminum sculpture that sums up the hopes and ideals of Philadelphia: *Phoenix Rising,* by local artist Emlen Etting.

Franklin Square Quadrant/Old Town

Old Town is the original waterfront of Philadelphia—where all the action took place during the early years of the United States, and where our most historic buildings remain. There's plenty more happening here beyond Independence Mall, the centerpiece of Old Town, however; just take a look.

INDEPENDENCE NATIONAL HISTORICAL PARK

Independence National Historical Park (information: Superintendent, Independence Historical Park, 143 S. 3rd St., Philadelphia, PA 19106, TTY/TDD 215/965-2305, www.nps.gov/inde),

locally referred to as Independence Mall, covers several blocks of old-city Philadelphia. All of the park buildings and sites are associated with colonial Philadelphia, and many are specific to the American Revolution. Primary park sites include the Independence Visitor Center, the Liberty Bell Center, Independence Hall, the Great Essentials, Congress Hall, Old City Hall, Franklin Court, Christ Church, the Second Bank of the United States, City Tavern, Philosophical Hall and the National Constitution Center. Other significant park buildings are Carpenter's Hall, the new Hall Military Museum, and several historic homes and churches within the boundaries of the mall: the Bishop White

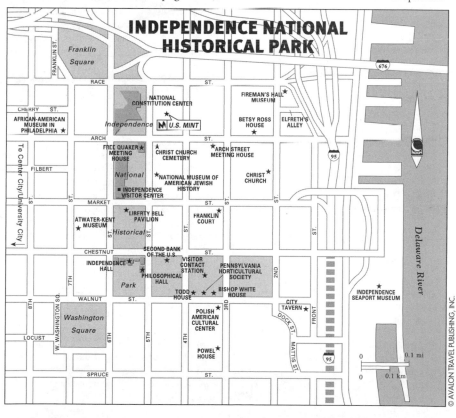

House, Todd House, Declaration House, Deshler Morris House, and Mikveh Israel Cemetery. Two other historically preserved homes, the Powel House (3rd between Spruce and Walnut Sts.) and the Physick House (4th between Spruce and Delancy Sts.), are in the Washington Square Quadrant.

Visitors may start at the visitors center on 6th and Market. The center shows a 28-minute film, *Independence,* and provides maps, services for non-English-speaking visitors, and fee-based tickets to the Todd House and the Bishop White House (restored middle- and upper-class dwellings), which may be seen by guided tour only. Visitors will be directed toward a security-screening facility between 5th and 6th on Market, then on to the Liberty Bell Center and the rest of the park.

Unless noted, there is no admission fee for any Independence Park building and most are open 9 A.M.–5 P.M. daily, with later hours June–Aug. March–Dec., tickets to Independence Hall should be obtained at the Visitors Center or by calling 800/967-2283 for an advance purchase of $1.50 by credit card. Excellent maps of Independence Mall complete with explanatory notes are available in each building. For more information or an accessibility pamphlet for those with special needs, call 215/597-8974 for a recorded message or contact the address above.

Liberty Bell Center

The Liberty Bell hangs in a glass-walled pavilion directly north across the park from Independence Hall. Visitors may enter the building and see the bell, crack and all. The new Liberty Bell Center offers a video presentation and exhibits about the Liberty Bell, focusing on its origins. Park personnel tell the story of the bell and its significance to our nation. The Center is open daily 9 A.M.–5 P.M., longer in summer.

Independence Hall

Independence Hall (Chestnut St. between 5th and 6th Sts., 215/597-8974), lies in the center of Independence National Historical Park. The building must be toured with a guide, daily

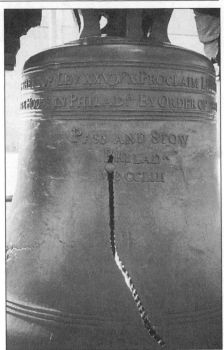

© JOANNE MILLER

Liberty Bell

9 A.M.–5 P.M. Visitors sign up for tours on a first-come, first-served basis Jan.–Feb.; from March–Dec., free timed-reserved tickets must be obtained at the Visitors Center on 6th and Market or in advance with a credit card purchase for a fee of $1.50 by calling 800/967-2283.

The tour is well worth it. Park guides tell the story of the drafting of the Declaration of Independence, pointing out the seats from which Ben Franklin, Thomas Jefferson, and others debated the wording of the revolutionary document. The west wing of the building holds the Great Essentials exhibit, featuring many of the original documents. Independence Hall is flanked by Congress Hall, meeting place of the congress 1790–1800, and Old City Hall, home of the U.S. Supreme Court during the same period of time. The knowledgeable guides and careful restoration of these buildings make history come alive.

Franklin Court and the Franklin Post Office

Rather than rebuilding Benjamin Franklin's home on the original site between 3rd and 4th and Chestnut and Market Streets, designer/architect Robert Venturi created the "Ghost House," a white-painted frame of the small dwelling. It stands in the middle of a garden behind a set of row houses once owned by Franklin. Beneath the building, an underground museum features a film on Franklin's life (215/597-8974, open March–Dec. daily 9 A.M.–5 P.M., Jan. 2–Feb. 29 Mon.–Fri. 10 A.M.–4 P.M., Sat.–Sun. 10 A.M.– 5 P.M., free admission). Restored buildings surround the garden and include the *Aurora* newspaper office, a 1785 press shop and bindery, and an archaeological exhibit.

A branch of the U.S. post office (316 Market St., 215/592-1289) is in one of the row houses. The cancellation stamp is a reproduction of Franklin's hand-canceled signature, "B Free Franklin" (thought to be Franklin's reference to the struggle for independence), and is a collector's item for philatelists. On the second floor of the building is a postal museum featuring displays of postal history, domestic and foreign postage stamps, and other memorabilia (free). The Franklin Post Office is open March–Dec. daily 9 A.M.–5 P.M., Jan. 2–Feb. 29 Mon.–Sat. 10 A.M.–4 P.M.

Christ Church and Christ Church Cemetery

Christ Church (2nd and Church Sts., 215/922-1695), completed in 1754, was a place of worship for many principals of the Revolutionary War such as George Washington and the ubiquitous Ben Franklin (brass plaques mark their customary pews). The cemetery, three blocks away on 5th and Arch Streets, contains the grave of Benjamin Franklin and his wife, among other notables. The church is open March–Dec. Mon.–Sat. 10 A.M.–4 P.M., Sun. noon–4 P.M.; Jan.–Feb. Sat.–Sun. noon–4 P.M., weather permitting. Guided tours of the cemetery are available starting at 10:15 A.M.

Second Bank of the United States

If you've ever wondered what George Washington *really* looked like, this is an opportunity to see his life portrait along with that of nearly every person of colonial historical significance. The Second Bank is at 420 Chestnut St., 215/597-8974. Portraits of women are in short supply in the gallery, but a tour through this masculine repository of American big shots makes the tales of their exploits all the more real.

City Tavern

The tavern is a reconstruction of the original, in which delegates from the First and Second Continental Congresses bellied up to the bar for grog and discussion. City Tavern (2nd and Walnut Sts.) is still a refreshing place to stop for a drink; it serves full meals, too (see Philly's Finest under Food and Drink).

Philosophical Hall

The hall (104 S. 5th St. behind Old City Hall) was the headquarters of the American Philosophical Society, founded by Benjamin Franklin in 1743 for "promoting useful knowledge among the British plantations in America." The members were an early who's-who list of colonial doctors, lawyers, clergymen, merchants, artisans, and rabble-rousers like George Washington, John Adams, Thomas Jefferson, and Alexander Hamilton. The society explored the intersections of history, art, and science, and is a national repository for scientific instruments, patent models, natural history specimens (including painter Charles Willson Peale's plant and animal specimens and mastodon bones), and documents such as Thomas Jefferson's hand-written Declaration of Independence.

National Constitution Center

Though not officially part of the park, the center (525 Arch St., Independence Mall, 215/409-6600, www.constitutioncenter.org, Mon.–Fri. 9:30 A.M.–5 P.M., Sat.–Sun. 9:30 A.M.–6 P.M.) is an associated partner. Admission costs $6 adults, $5 children 12 and under and seniors 62 and better, children under 4 free. The theme of the center is the U.S. Constitution, from 1787 to the present day. The tour begins with a

Philadelphia

multimedia presentation featuring a live actor, film, and video, followed by interactive family-oriented exhibits that show the significant role the Constitution has played throughout history. You can vote for your all-time favorite president, take the Presidential Oath of Office, or become a Supreme Court justice. The center also offers a number of special events throughout the year.

OTHER HISTORIC SITES

Elfreth's Alley

This tiny colonial street is considered to be the oldest continuously occupied residential street in the nation (between Front and 2nd Sts. and Race and Arch Sts.). A small museum at No. 126 (215/574-0560, Thurs.–Sat. 10 A.M.–5 P.M., Sun. noon–5 P.M., admission $2 adults, $1 children 6–18, children 5 and under free) gives tours. The last tour of the day begins at 4:30 P.M. Some of the alley's homes have been converted into shops.

Arch Street Meeting House

Christ Church cemetery is across from another historic building, the Quaker Meeting House (320 Arch St., 215/627-2667, Mon.–Sat. 10 A.M.–4 P.M., closed holidays except Memorial Day, July 4, and Labor Day, donation), built in 1783. Though no longer in use as a place of worship, the meetinghouse was the gathering place for "the fighting Quakers," such as Betsy Ross, who broke from their pacifist brethren to support and enlist in the Revolution. Exhibits and a videotape explain the history of the Society of Friends (Quakers).

Pennsylvania Horticultural Society

This organization, founded in 1827, is the oldest of its kind in America. The original building occupied by the society (325 Walnut between 3rd and 4th Sts.) no longer houses the horticultural society offices (now at 100 N. 20th St.), but the site features a garden that is a pleasant place for a peaceful amble. It's open Mon.–Fri. 9 A.M.– 5 P.M. For more information, call the Horticultural Society (215/988-8800).

Edgar Allan Poe National Historic Site

This building (532 N. 7th Street, 215/597-8780, www.nps.gov/edal, Wed.–Sun. 9 A.M.–5 P.M. Closed Jan. 1, Thanksgiving, Dec. 25 and Jan. 1, free) was the rented home of Edgar Allan Poe, his wife Virginia, and his mother-in-law during Poe's years (1837–1844) in Philadelphia. Because of the Park Service's insistence on accuracy, the rooms have been kept bare, due to the lack of information about their contents during Poe's residence there.

Abandoned as a baby, Poe had a foster family that supported him into his late teens and then became estranged due to his gambling debts. From then on, Poe led a life of poverty and struggle; his dream was to publish his own literary journal, a goal that he realized only intermittently. In his time, Poe was widely admired more for his literary criticism and intellectually detailed methods of crafting poems and stories than for his actual fictional work. However, Poe's prolific pen was a major source of support for his family; "The Fall of the House of Usher," "The Tell-Tale Heart," and "The Murders in the Rue Morgue" were among the works Poe sold during his time in Philadelphia. He singlehandedly recreated the murder-mystery genre, and works such as "A Descent into the Maelstrom" became models for future science-fiction writers Jules Verne and Isaac Asimov. Poe's contemporary, the French writer Charles-Pierre Baudelaire, so admired Poe's methods and stories that he spent 14 years translating the tales into French.

The park features an exhibit on Poe's history and work. Though the house is empty, a visit to the basement will give Poe fans some deeply satisfying creeps—is someone scratching behind that brick wall?

Betsy Ross House

Betsy Ross, who may or may not have worked on the first American flag in 1776, may or may not have lived in this colonial-era home (239 Arch St., 215/686-1252, $5). Even if she didn't, the period restoration is an interesting exploration of 18th-century Philadelphia life, and the price is right. It's open Oct.–March, Tues.–Sun. 10 A.M.–

5 P.M. and all holidays that fall on a Mon.; April–Sept., daily 10 A.M.–5 P.M.

CULTURAL HERITAGE SITES

The African-American Museum in Philadelphia

This collection is nicely balanced between displays that chronicle black heritage in Pennsylvania, and artwork, both contemporary and classic, by African-American artists. The museum (701 Arch St., 215/574-0380, www.aampmuseum.org, Tues.–Sat. 10 A.M.–5 P.M., Sun. noon–5 P.M.; closed major holidays; admission $6, senior citizens and students with ID $4) offers a heavy schedule of classes and workshops.

One exhibit combined a photographic history of neighborhood sports organizations and their impact on African-American youth in Philadelphia with a display of the work of three generations of women sculptors. The sports exhibit emphasized the development of sports heroes such as champion boxer Joe Louis and tennis player Althea Gibson (who went on to excel in golf after winning both the Wimbledon and Forest Hills competitions twice), as well as those who excelled in life using their early sports training, exemplified by Dr. Eric Mitchell and Judge Raymond Pace Alexander. Other exhibits have explored sacred and utilitarian objects from Africa, the Haitian revolution through artist's eyes, and the history of Lincoln University. Sculptural works, displayed in a separate room and placed throughout the multilevel galleries, are exceptional.

National Museum of American Jewish History

Established in 1976, this sophisticated museum (55 N. 5th St.—the entrance is in the middle of the block, along a walkway between 4th and 5th Sts., 215/923-3811, www.nmajh.org), is the only one in the nation dedicated to collecting, preserving, and interpreting artifacts pertaining to the American Jewish experience.

The museum shop features an well-selected collection of Judaica and decorative objects. Both museum and shop are open Mon.–Thurs.

© JOANNE MILLER

citizens outside the African-American Museum

10 A.M.–5 P.M., Fri. 10 A.M.–3 P.M., Sun. noon–5 P.M.; admission is free.

There is no permanent display on Jewish history; the focus here is on issues of American ethnic identity and culture revealed through art. The museum exhibitions have included "Theatrical Realism: the Art of Inez Storer, " featuring 30 paintings, prints, artist's books and assemblages by the California-based artist, and *Art Spiegelman: The Road to Maus,* which chronicled Spiegelman's 13-year exploration of his father's past and his own Jewish/Holocaust identity, which eventually led to the creation of his best-selling books. The exhibit featured Spiegelman's early drawings on the subject, including the ideas he rejected—a unique and emotionally charged experience for the viewer. *Too Jewish? Challenging Traditional Identities* raised compelling questions about ethnic identity, marginality, and stereotyping through the work of 18 contemporary artists.

AFRICAN-AMERICAN PHILADELPHIA

By 1847, in Philadelphia, African-Americans owned a half-million dollars' worth of real estate, supported 19 churches and 106 beneficent societies, and maintained their own insurance societies, cemetery associations, labor unions, and financial organizations. The city was the site of the first antislavery revolts and the earliest educational systems for African-American youth. Today, Philadelphia is a treasure for those who wish to explore the historic roots and cultural heritage of African-Americans.

Many great personages in U.S. history were born or practiced their artistry here. The Union Baptist Church financed the early music studies of Marian Anderson, the first African-American to star at the Metropolitan Opera. Jazz pioneer John Coltrane began his professional career in Philadelphia—his former home is the current site of the **John W. Coltrane Cultural Society** (1511 N. 33rd St.). Singer Billie Holiday was born in the city in 1915. Actor, scholar, lawyer, and civil rights activist Paul Robeson lived at 4951 Walnut Street. Architect Julian Abele, designer of the Philadelphia Museum of Art and the Free Library of Philadelphia, on Logan Circle, was the first black to graduate from the University of Pennsylvania School of Architecture. Crystal Bird Fauset was the first African-American woman elected to the state legislature; she became a member of the U.S. House of Representatives in 1938.

Several cultural institutions promote the work of local African-Americans. **Bushfire Theater of Performing Arts** (224 S. 52nd St., 215/747-9230, box office 215/747-9230) and **Freedom Theater** (1346 N. Broad St., 215/765-2793) encourage, train, and showcase the work of young performing artists and writers. Other locally based organizations feature some of Philadelphia's best black performing artists: **Philadanco** (9 N. Preston St., Philadanco Way, 215/387-8200) the internationally acclaimed dance company, conducts performances, lectures, and demonstrations, and **Philadelphia Clef Club of the Performing Arts** (736–38 S. Broad St./Avenue of the Arts, 215/893-9912, www.clefclubofjazz.8m.com) presents Sunday Jam Sessions with various jazz artists all over the city.

Several tour companies specialize in African-American history. **David Tours** (800/328-4395) offers daylong and longer tours in several cities. The **Greater Philadelphia Tourism Marketing Corporation** (30 S. 17th St., Suite 1710, 888/467-4452, www.gophila.com) can suggest several free walking tours.

MUSEUMS AND COLLECTIONS

The Atwater-Kent Museum

Atwater-Kent (15 S. 7th St., 215/685-4830, www.philadelphiahistory.org, Wed.–Mon. 10 A.M.–5 P.M.; closed major holidays; adults $5; over 54 and ages 3–17 $3) is the official museum of the history of the city of Philadelphia. Its exhibits, which depict daily urban life over the last three centuries, draw upon artifacts selected from the museum's collection of more than 75,000 items. The museum displays a model of Elfreth's Alley, with information on different residents who lived at various addresses over the years. Bits and pieces of Philadelphia's industrial past are featured, including information on the production of paint, tobacco products, printing, lithography, and publishing. Philadelphia-based J.B. Lippincott and Company was the largest publisher in the world in 1870, and the *Saturday Evening Post* originated in Philadelphia. Pharmaceuticals and patent medicines such as Rattlesnake Bill's Liniment ("This preparation may irritate the skin, particularly if applied by rubbing. . . .") were big sellers, even though the main ingredients were snake fat and kerosene. William Penn's wampum belt (the shell belt he received from the Lenni Lenape peoples) is part of the permanent collection, and recent special exhibits have included *Will We Ever Forget: Baseball in Philadelphia,* which explored more than a century of baseball history in the city.

Fireman's Hall Museum

The history of firefighting and contemporary firefighting procedures are the subjects of this museum (147 N. 2nd St. above Arch St., 215/923-1438, www.mfrconsultants.com/pfd /museum, admission free). It's open Tues.–Sat. 10 A.M.–4:30 P.M., and until 9 P.M. the first Fri. of every month. Donations are appreciated. Exhibits include artifacts, graphics, film, a gorgeous stained-glass window, and fire-fighting equipment including 10 antique fire trucks. The building housing the museum is a firehouse, built in 1876.

Philadelphia Insectarium

In a burst of professional pride, the owner of Steve's Bug-off Exterminator Company began showing the "catch of the day" in an outdoor display case at his place of business (8046 Frankford Ave., 215/338-3000, www.insectarium.net, Mon.–Sat. 10 A.M.–4 P.M., $5). The display grew so popular that it expanded to three floors, and has become a favorite destination of local schoolchildren. Madagascar hissing cockroaches, Mexican tarantulas, glow-in-the-dark scorpions, a working beehive, and collections of exotic butterflies—some live, some mounted—give kids and adults a thrill. Little ones can burn off steam crawling through the bungee-cord spider web. Moms and dads will appreciate the Cockroach Kitchen—tips on what *not* to do. Hungry? You may have a chance to try the barbecued baby beetles, cricket taffy, or chocolate-covered mealworms. Or not.

OTHER POINTS OF INTEREST NEAR OLD TOWN

Lights of Liberty

Only in America— the time warp fusion of Philadelphia's 200-plus-year-old historic buildings with a high-tech sound-and-light walking tour (877/GO-2-1776, www.lightsofliberty.org, May–Oct., $17.76, students with ID and seniors $16, children 12 and under $12; family packages are available) that dramatizes the events of 1776. There are 5–7 shows nightly at dusk. Reservations are required.

Lights of Liberty was created by three-time Tony Award winner David Mitchell and assorted Broadway writers and composers, with help from George Lucas and Skywalker Sound, using the voice talents of Walter Cronkite, Claire Bloom, and Whoopi Goldberg (on the children's version) among others. The one-hour show requires participants to meet at the PECO Energy Liberty Center (6th and Chestnut Sts.) don headsets, and walk to each of five sites where they see images projected off the buildings and hear the story, complete with background sounds, of Colonial America's fight for independence.

Reading Terminal Market

When the Philadelphia and Reading Railroad cleared space for its new terminal in 1892, it leveled two older farmers' markets; the Reading Terminal Market (12th and Filbert St., www.readingterminalmarket.org) was created underneath the train shed as a compromise solution. So modern was the market in its time, people came from as far as the New Jersey shore

© JOANNE MILLER

the Reading Terminal Market early in the morning

to buy fresh Lancaster County produce and meats. During the Depression and subsequent exodus out of the inner city, the market declined and was nearly destroyed in the 1970s. Visionary management coupled with the recent demand for fresh local produce and meats has given the market new life. Greengrocers and purveyors of meat and fish vie for space with sellers of barbecued ribs and Greek foods, and Mennonite-run quick-breakfast stands.

The U.S. Mint

Money, and plenty of it! Visions of shiny silver and copper will replace the sugar-plum fairies dancing in your head, but a visit requires advance planning. It's well worth it, especially since the mint has been closed to the public since 9/11. Tours of the mint (5th and Arch Sts., 215/408-0114, www.usmint.gov) must be arranged by your congressional representative for groups of six or less. Contact your senator at www.senate.gov/senators/senator_by_state.cfm or your representative at www.house.gov/house/MemStateSearch.shtml. Reservations should be made at least two weeks in advance. Groups of more than six, such as veterans, military, K–12, and other youth groups may schedule a reservation by phone (215/408-0112). Forms for both types of tours may be downloaded from the Web (www.usmint.gov/downloads/mint_programs/ToursFormsPhilly).

The Philadelphia mint makes the majority of the coins Americans use every day and also produces uncirculated coins, commemorative coins, gold bullion coins, and national medals; most of the U.S. Congressional Gold Medals awarded since 1776 were created in this facility. The mint features bronze copies of the medals awarded to George Washington, actor John Wayne, fighter Joe Louis, aviator Charles Lindbergh, and others. A heroic-sized set of Tiffany mosaics created in 1901 depicting coinage from ancient times to the present is in the lobby.

One of the most interesting parts of the mint is the coin factory. Twenty-four hours a day, five days a week, hundreds of machines and operators in a room the size of a football field can be observed from a glassed-in gallery above; they blank,

anneal, wash, riddle, strike, count, and bag millions of dollars worth of shiny quarters, dimes, and pennies.

Kids will especially appreciate the lobby store (215/408-0230), where a medal press will turn out a Philadelphia mint medal as a souvenir, and all types of collector's coins are available. The store cannot be accessed without permission to enter the mint.

Masonic Temple

The temple (1 N. Broad St., 215/988-1917, www.pagrandlodge.org, $3) was dedicated in 1873 as the Grand Lodge of Free and Accepted Masons of Pennsylvania. An architectural jewel, this remarkable building contains a number of large meeting halls in different styles: Corinthian, Renaissance, Ionic, Egyptian, Norman, and Gothic. The meeting halls, still in use, were built to honor the building trades; all are exemplifications of each style, consistent in architecture, coloring, wall decorations, paintings, and furniture.

tower of the Masonic Temple

THE BROTHERHOOD

Freemasonry, a guild organization once restricted to stonecutters, opened membership to men of wealth, social status, and noble birth after the completion of the cathedrals in the 17th century; the organization became especially popular in England during the Reformation. The Masonic ideals of religious toleration and the basic equality of all people were in keeping with the growing spirit of liberalism during the 18th century. Freemasons upheld ideals such as fraternity, equality, and peace, and their meetings became social rather than business occasions. Four guilds, called lodges, united in London on June 24, 1717, to form a grand lodge for London and Westminster, which became the Grand Lodge of England. This body is the "mother" grand lodge of Freemasons in the world.

One of the basic tenets of the Masonic orders has been that religion is the concern solely of the individual. Because of that tenet, the Roman Catholic Church objected to the organization. As a result, the Freemasons have never been permitted in some strictly Roman Catholic countries, such as Spain. In France, however, following the atheistic and Protestant trend of the French Revolution, the order flourished.

The earliest of the U.S. lodges, founded by authority of the Grand Lodge of England, were the First Lodge of Philadelphia, established in 1733, and one in Boston, established about the same time. Freemasonry is the largest and most widely established fraternal order in the world; American Freemasons make up about three-fourths of the total number of all members.

One of our nation's most famous Masons, George Washington, is commemorated by his Masonic apron, hand-embroidered by Madame Lafayette and given to Brother Washington by fellow Mason the Marquis de Lafayette in 1784. Washington wore the apron when he laid the cornerstone of the Capitol building in Washington, D.C. The apron is on display with other Masonic rarities in the library and museum on the first floor of the Philadelphia Masonic temple.

The Masonic Temple may be viewed by guided tour only. Tours are available Tues.–Fri. at 11 A.M., 2 P.M., and 3 P.M. On Sat., tours are scheduled at 10 A.M. and 11 A.M. only. The temple is closed Sat. during July and Aug., and on major holidays.

The Oriental Hall, decorated in 1896, contains coloring and ornamentation copied from parts of the Alhambra in Granada, Spain. The Corinthian Hall features Grecian classical architecture, with columns and capitals modeled after the monument of Lysicrates in Athens. The Renaissance Hall, decorated in 1908 in an Italian Renaissance motif, contains paintings of Hiran, King of Tyre; Joshua, the High Priest; and John, the Evangelist. The Ionic Hall was inspired by Greek architecture found in Asia Minor. The Egyptian Hall, finished in 1889, takes ornamentation from the Temples of Luxor, Karnak, and Philae. The Rhenish Romanesque-style Norman Hall, 1891, features the rounded bays and arches common to that style. The high arches, pinnacles, and spires of Gothic churches create the Gothic Hall, down to the cross-and-crown emblem of Sir Knights ("Under this sign you will conquer"), which hangs over the commander's throne, a replica of the archbishop's throne in Canterbury Cathedral. One interesting aspect of the meeting rooms is that much of the marble, stone, and tilework is faux-finished—another attestation to the skill of the workmen who created the structure.

The Grand Entrance Gate, Grand Foyer, and Grand Staircase live up to their big names; each is elaborately carved and marbled, and details are often burnished with gold leaf. Every room in this palace of varied architectural styles honors the origin of the Freemasons, the cathedral builders of the Middle Ages.

Art Galleries

Philadelphia's thriving art scene revolves around a compact area in Old Town. More than 40 galleries, including collaborative Space 1026, and Nexus Foundation, a showplace for experimental and innovative contemporary art, can be found in the area bordered roughly by Vine and Walnut Streets, and Front and 4th Streets. The best time to tour is on the first Friday of each month, when the galleries are open in the evening, 5–9 P.M. More information is available from First Friday, Old City Arts Association (230 Vine St., 800/555-5191, www.oldcityarts.org). Old City is the northern boundary of the National Historic District. The neighborhood has seen better days,

and many places are boarded up and covered with graffiti; expect to step over a few sleeping bags in doorways. Like New York's SoHo, it's precisely the kind of place that attracts artists and their patrons. The area has a number of hip cafés and restaurants in which to recharge.

Washington Square Quadrant

Philadelphia south of Washington Square contains some of the city's best-known destinations: South Street, the Italian Market (for more information on both, see Shopping), and the residential neighborhood of Society Hill, in addition to two historic homes maintained by Independence National Historical Park: the Powel House and the Physick House (see Independence National Historical Park).

© JOANNE MILLER

fancy wrought iron on Society Hill steps

HISTORIC WALKS
Society Hill

Perhaps the most elegant collection of early-19th-century houses in Philadelphia, the shady streets of Society Hill, from Delancey to Lombard between Front and 4th, provide the walker with a verdant reminder of what life was like for the wealthy traders and business owners of early Pennsylvania. This is prime real estate, and all the homes are privately owned—please respect the owners' privacy.

Queens Village/Headhouse Square

Queens Village was the site of the original Swedish settlement in Philadelphia in the mid-17th century, and Headhouse Square, established nearly a century later, was the city's first market. Start at the square, then stroll down Kenilworth, Monroe, Pemberton, and Fitzwater Streets between Front and 2nd Streets. Though little is left of the Swedish settlement, the homes represent layers of architectural styles and different eras, beautifully preserved.

HISTORIC SITES
Gloria Dei Church

Before William Penn, there was New Sweden Colony (1638–1655). Gloria Dei Church is located on Christian Street and Christopher Columbus Boulevard, at the south end of the Delaware River port. The church (215/389-1513) is open to the public Sat.–Sun. 9 A.M.–5 P.M. and by appointment. Swedes were among the first groups to settle in Pennsylvania and were responsible for building this, the state's oldest house of worship, in 1700. (For an extensive overview of New Sweden—and an examination of many things Swedish—combine a trip to Gloria Dei with an excursion to the American Swedish Historical Museum.)

MUSEUMS

Independence Seaport Museum

A stunning modern building houses this 100,000-square-foot museum on Penn's Landing, on the city waterfront (211 S. Columbus Blvd. at Walnut St., 215/925-5439, www.phillyseaport.org, 10 A.M.–5 P.M. daily, closed Jan. 1, Thanksgiving, and Dec. 25). Independence Seaport Museum collects, preserves, and exhibits art, artifacts, and archival materials related to the maritime history and tradition of the Chesapeake Bay and the Delaware River and its tributaries.

A special combination pass that includes admission to the Independence Seaport Museum, the Riverbus Ferry (which runs across the Delaware River to Camden, New Jersey), and the New Jersey State Aquarium at Camden is available mid-April to Sept. It costs $22.50 for adults, $16.50 for children 5–12; call the museum for specifics. Admission to the museum plus both historic ships is $9; visitors over 65 and students with ID $8; ages 3–12 $6. Free Sun. 10 A.M.–noon.

Displays combine hands-on computer games, large-scale models, and audio-visuals to entertain and educate. A three-and-a-half story replica of the Ben Franklin Bridge straddles a walkable model of the Delaware River. Visitors can manipulate a miniature crane to unload cargo from a container ship and weld and rivet a ship's hull.

Workshop on the Water, an active boat shop and gallery, allows visitors to watch boat-making in progress as artisans build traditional wooden 19th-century boats. Next to the museum, the USS *Olympia*, Admiral Dewey's historic vessel, and the submarine the USS *Becuna* are open for tours.

The Philadelphia Mummers Museum

Unable to make the Mummers Parade on New Year's Day? The next best thing is the Mum-

MARDI GRAS NORTH

Philadelphia's Mummer tradition is Mardi Gras in the north, with a twist. First of all, the annual Mummer's Parade takes place on New Year's Day rather than the beginning of the Lenten season. To acknowledge visitors who choose not to brave the icy winds whipping down Broad Street, a summer version of the parade and a concert of music and costumes are also held. The Mummers Parade evolved from a unique mix of ethnic celebrations, chiefly the shooting off of rifles and noisemaking on New Year's, African-American-inspired dances and spirituals, and medieval German *mumme* (masquerade) plays.

Mummers come in three basic varieties: String Bands, which march and play instruments (often banjos); Fancies, who dance to a hired band; and Comics, who dress as clowns, wenches, or dudes (a takeoff on the old-fashioned dandy). Mummers groups are organized much like their New Orleans counterparts, as private social clubs. Each club selects its own theme and prepares for the 12-hour parade all year, sewing and gluing millions of feathers and pasting jewels into place.

The "strut"—a jerky, high-stepping bouncy dance similar to the old cakewalk—is the movement of choice down Broad Street, usually performed with parasol in hand to the tune of "Oh, Dem Golden Slippers," the African-American spiritual that is the theme song of the parade.

mers Museum (1100 S. 2nd St. at Washington Ave., 215/336-3050, http://riverfrontmummers.com/museum, Tues.–Sat. 9:30 A.M.–5 P.M., Sun. noon–4:30 P.M.), which features elaborate costumes from years past and a hands-on history of the Mummer spectacle. Admission is $3.50 for adults, $2.50 for seniors, students with ID, and children 2 and up; children under 2 are free.

Kids and adults have an opportunity to learn the "strut" with prop parasols in front of a wall of mirrors. String-band concerts are given Tues. evenings at 8 P.M. May–Sept. Many of the parade participants come down to "Two Street" (2nd Street) after the formal parade on New Year's to continue the celebration.

Mario Lanza Institute and Museum

Though his name might be unfamiliar to some today, his story—of a poor immigrant boy who grew up to be an international singing sensation—is still inspiring. The museum was formerly located was the Settlement Music School, where opera star Lanza received his early musical education. The museum was rededicated (on Mario Lanza Day, Nov. 3) in its new location, the first floor of Columbus House (712 Montrose St., 215/238-9691, www.mario-lanza-institute.org, Mon.–Sat. 10 A.M.–3 P.M., free) next to St. Mary Magdalen de Pazzi Church in South Philadelphia. The displays depict his life and career, including his flirtation with Hollywood films, told in photographs, paintings, and newspaper clippings.

CULTURAL HERITAGE SITES NEAR WASHINGTON SQUARE

Polish American Cultural Center

This one-room museum (308 Walnut St., 215/922-1700, www.polishamericancenter.com) celebrates Polish history and the world-class contributions of Poles such as composer Frederick Chopin and scientist Marie Sklodowsky Curie. The center is open Jan.–April, Mon.–Fri. 10 A.M.–4 P.M. and May–Dec., Mon.–Sat. 10 A.M.–4 P.M. Closed holidays; admission is free. Examples of Polish art and crafts line the walls, and a display of goods made in Poland is for sale. Of particular interest are the examples of *wycinanki* (vi-chi-NON-kee), intricate paper cutouts that are traditionally given as gifts during Christmas and Easter, to be placed over doors to bless the house. The center carries issues of the *Polish American News,* published by the Polish American Congress; the newsletter lists local and national heritage-related events and articles on traditional culture.

American Swedish Historical Museum

This museum (1900 Pattison Ave., south of Center City, near the sports stadiums in Franklin Delano Roosevelt Park, 215/389-1776, www.americanswedish.org) devotes three galleries to the New Sweden Colony, plus several more to Swedish immigration, famous Swedes (such as singer Jenny Lind), and Swedish decorative arts. "Nobel: Celebrating a Century of Nobel Prizes" is one of the permanent exhibits. It's open Tues.–Fri. 10 A.M.–4 P.M., Sat.–Sun. noon–4 P.M., and closed legal holidays. Admission is $5, over 60 and students with ID $4, under 12 free.

Though out of the way, this interesting little museum is worth the trip. The museum building is modeled after Eriksberg Castle, a 17th-century manor house; each gallery is an outstanding example of Swedish interior design of the mid-20th century. The rooms and their furnishings were created by Swedish artists and craftspeople; one room is patterned after an art deco smoking lounge on a 1930s Swedish ocean liner. The museum sponsors celebrations of traditional Swedish holidays year-round as well as temporary art and craft exhibits.

Rittenhouse Square Quadrant

Rittenhouse Square continues to be a very elegant quarter of the city. The tasteful townhouses on the streets that surround the square reflect centuries of care, as do the shops and restaurants that cater to local clientele and visitors alike.

MUSEUMS

The Civil War Library and Museum

Founded in 1888, this research library and museum (1805 Pine St., 215/735-8196, Thurs.–Sat. 11 A.M.–4:30 P.M., closed holidays; adults $5; over 61 $4; students with ID $3; ages 3–12, $2) collects and preserves historical material and artifacts from the Civil War era. The museum was endangered, the subject of a new battle between North and South—it almost moved to Richmond, Virginia. However, it remains in Philadelphia with an expanded section on the Underground Railroad. Items on display include weapons of all types and articles that belonged to Generals Grant, Sherman, and Meade, as well as plaster life casts of Abraham Lincoln's hands and face.

The Rosenbach Museum and Library

Characterized by one scholar as "the bestest of the mostest," this collection of printed works and art was amassed by Dr. A.S.W. Rosenbach, a dealer in rare books and manuscripts, and his brother. The museum is close to Rittenhouse Square (2010 Delancey Pl., 215/732-1600, www.rosenbach.org/home, Tues.–Sun. 10 A.M.–5 P.M.) Admission is $8 adults, $5 for students with ID, seniors over 65, and children ages 5 and up. Children under the age of 5 are free.

Selected holdings include John Tenniel's original drawings for Lewis Carroll's *Alice in Wonderland* and Carroll's personal copy of the book; the literary archive and library of modernist poet Marianne Moore; and Maurice Sendak's original artwork for such books as *Where the Wild Things Are*. Rosenbach holdings also include the largest collection of oil-painted miniatures in the world and examples of fine silverwork, furniture, and paintings. A new highlights gallery displays the best of the best.

The College of Physicians of Philadelphia/Mütter Museum

The 2,000-member-strong College of Physicians (19 S. 22nd St., 215/563-3737, www.phillyhealthinfo.org, Mon.–Sun. 10 A.M.–5 P.M., closed Jan. 1, Thanksgiving, and Dec. 25) was founded in 1787 for the "advancement of the science of medicine." Admission to the Mütter Museum is $9 for adults, $6 for children, free under the age of 6.

Continuing a strong emphasis on public health issues over the years, the college has recently opened the C. Everett Koop Community Health Information Center (www.collphil.org); a circulating library of more than 500 books, videocassettes, journals, two online databases, and pamphlets covering a wide spectrum of health issues are available at no charge. Hours are Wed.–Sun. 10 A.M.–5 P.M. Admission to the C. Everett Koop Community Health Information Center and library is free.

The Mütter Museum, a collection of examples of various pathologies, is also available for viewing. The wax figures, papier-mâché models, preserved specimens, and skeletal constructions were originally used for educational purposes in the mid-19th century, when diseases and genetic defects were identifiable only by their physical manifestations. There is a huge variety of specimens, from enlarged organs to diseased body parts preserved in fluid, along with illustrations of the normal. A 7'6" skeleton and the death cast of Chang and Eng, the original "Siamese Twins," are among the highlights. A caution: the museum depicts some afflictions that are quite grotesque and may not be suitable for small children or those who tend to queasiness. Teenagers love this place.

Philadelphia

OTHER POINTS OF INTEREST NEAR RITTENHOUSE SQUARE

City Hall

City Hall, once the exact geographical center of Philadelphia (Broad and Market Sts.) was designated by Mr. Penn for a "building of publick concerns." His statue now looks out from the top of the 510-foot French second-empire style building. All of City Hall may be toured for free Mon.–Fri. at 12:30 P.M.; don't miss the additional tour of the tower that starts every 15 minutes. There's a grand view from just under William Penn's dainty feet.

Philadelphia Art Alliance

Just off Rittenhouse Square in the Wetherill mansion (251 S. 18th St., 215/545-4302, www.philartalliance.org, Tue.–Sun. 11 A.M.–5 P.M., donation) the alliance offers an eclectic variety of exhibits of photography, painting, sculpture, and crafts year-round. The mansion is the former home of philanthropist Christine Wetherill Stevenson, and was designed by architect Frank Miles Day, who also provided buildings for Yale and Princeton. The Art Alliance has a long history of association with luminaries such as architects LeCorbusier and Frank Lloyd Wright; painter Andrew Wyeth had his first solo exhibition on these walls, and in 1937, Martha Graham inaugurated her modern dance lecture series here. The alliance continues to provide a home for all

© JOANNE MILLER

view from the top of City Hall

the arts: musical concerts, literature readings, and dramatic works are also on the schedule.

Logan Circle Quadrant

Probably the most visited area of the city after Old Town thanks to Fairmount Park and the large number of science, art, and history sites, Logan Circle is the watery highlight in the direct sightline from city hall to the Philadelphia Museum of Art on the Benjamin Franklin Parkway.

ART MUSEUMS

Philadelphia Museum of Art

Forever immortalized as a prizefighter's stone Stairmaster in the film *Rocky*, the Parthenon-like museum stands at the terminus of the Benjamin Franklin Parkway in Fairmount Park (26th St. and Benjamin Franklin Pkwy., 215/763-8100, www .philamuseum.org, Tues.–Sun. 10 A.M.–5 P.M.; Wed. and Fri. until 8:45 P.M.). A world-class museum, it attracts major exhibitions to supplement a mind-boggling variety of artworks ranging from 15th-century illuminated manuscripts to ultra-modern Brancusi sculpture.

Admission is $10 for adults, $7 for seniors, students with ID and children; Sun., pay by donation.

The full-scale medieval cloister courtyard and fountain on the second floor is a favorite, as are the French Gothic chapel and a pillared temple from Madura, India. Computerized stations offering more information on the exhibits and artists are scattered throughout the museum. An extensive collection of Pennsylvania Dutch and American decorative arts including furniture and glasswork adjoins galleries featuring paintings by American artists such as Thomas Eakins. The impressionists have their own place, with works by Picasso and Du Champ on display—if this style is a favorite of yours, however, make a trip out to the Barnes Foundation to immerse yourself.

Pennsylvania Academy of Fine Arts

The collection of this museum, founded in 1805, spans the history of American painting. The Victorian Gothic architecture of the museum build-

ing (118 N. Broad St. at Cherry St., 215/972-7600, www.pafa.edu, Tues.–Sat. 10 A.M.–5 P.M., Sun. 11 A.M.–5 P.M.) is worth the trip. Designed by Frank Furness and George W. Hewitt in 1876, the over-the-top decor—characterized by the grand stair hall with its gold leaf, silver stars, intricate carvings and ornaments—is a superb setting for the wonderful artwork. Adult admission is $2.50; seniors and students with ID $2, under 12, $1.50.

Works by some of the art world's most well-known denizens are found in the galleries: Mary Cassatt, Georgia O'Keeffe, Benjamin West, and Richard Diebenkorn, among many others.

Rodin Museum

This collection, the largest outside Paris (Benjamin Franklin Pkwy. and 22nd St.; 215/763-8100, www.rodinmuseum.org, Tues.–Sun. 10 A.M.–5 P.M., donation), displays 124 original and cast sculptures by the French master sculptor, August Rodin. A taped tour is available for $3. Guided tours are on Sun. at 1 P.M.; it's closed legal holidays. The collection was presented to the city in the name of Jules Mastbaum, a Philadelphia film exhibitor, after his death in 1929. The work is housed in an elegant building surrounded by a formal garden and reflecting pool—all designed by Jacques Greber and Paul Philippe Cret, who created the Benjamin Franklin Parkway.

Rodin's most popular works are here, in their bold and chunky glory—*Eternal Springtime, The Gates of Hell, The Burghers of Calais, The Thinker,* and many more.

SCIENCE AND NATURAL HISTORY MUSEUMS

The Franklin Institute Science Museum

The Franklin Institute (Benjamin Franklin Pkwy. and 20th St., 215/448-1200, www.fi.edu) pioneered the development of hands-on science exhibits in the 1930s. Originally called the Franklin Institute for the Promotion of the Mechanic

Arts, in 1824 it was dedicated to Philadelphia's famous citizen, inventor, and scientist and is the site of the Benjamin Franklin National Memorial.

The Franklin Institute and Mandell Center are open daily 9:30 A.M.–5 P.M.; the Tuttleman IMAX theater is open until 9 P.M. Fri.–Sat. It's closed Jan. 1, Thanksgiving, and Dec. 24–25. The Science Park, an outdoor exhibit, is only open May–Oct. Base adult admission (includes Hall of Science, Science Center, Mandell Center, all demonstrations, and one show at the Fels Planetarium) is $12.75 (plus IMAX, $16.75); seniors over 62 and children ages 4–11, $10 (plus IMAX $14). The Tuttleman IMAX Theater only is $8.

The institute comprises two main branches. A research and educational component, the Center for Innovation in Science Learning is one of a network of American science centers that work together to educate schoolteachers in the use of telecomputing to support science learning, among other outreach programs. The Science Center is the public branch of the museum, with hundreds of interactive exhibits in all endeavors of scientific study.

The Science Center explores several aspects of scientific study through the use of interactive exhibits. Bioscience features a walk-through human heart among its displays; transportation displays include a 350-ton Baldwin steam locomotive, a T-33 Air Force jet trainer, and a flight simulator (there's an entire section on aviation science). The communications section spans history from the colonial screw press to video technology, while the geology and earth sciences section features a puzzle that, when put together, forms the earth from core to crust. In electricity and electronics, static electricity rings bells, repels balls, and makes your hair stand on end.

Computer programs demonstrate mathematics and physics principles. In the largest public observatory in the U.S., visitors can search the heavens with two telescopes, and the indoor physics playground features rope swings and other demonstrations of mechanics. Science Park, a joint effort of the Franklin Institute and the Please Touch Museum, is a 38,000-square-foot outdoor exhibit open May–Oct. More than 30 hands-on activities involve fam-

ily members in learning, from a miniature-golf course to periscopes.

Also part of the Science Center, the Fels Planetarium features the Digistar computer-driven planetarium projection system, with several public shows per day. The four-story Tuttleman IMAX Theater contains a 79-foot-wide screen and shows a 30- to 40-minute film throughout the day, preceded by a short film on Philadelphia. The Mandell Center displays special exhibits such as "Titanic: The Artifact Exhibit."

Academy of Natural Sciences

Founded in 1812, the academy (1900 Benjamin Franklin Pkwy., 215/299-1000, www.acnatsci.org) is the oldest continually operating natural science research and education institution in the country. It's open Mon.–Fri. 10 A.M.–4:30 P.M., Sat.–Sun. 10 A.M.–5 P.M.; it's closed Jan. 1, Thanksgiving, and Dec. 25. Adult admission is $9, seniors 65 and over $8.25, and children over 6 $6.

The Academy conducts environmental research around the world and supports its work partly through the admission fees charged to visitors. Dioramas, talks that showcase live animals, a geology hall with gems and minerals, hands-on experiments, and *Outside-In*, a touchable exhibit focused on local habitats, are part of what's available to visitors. This family-friendly museum showcases the star of Dinosaur Hall, a fully constructed Giganotosaurus, one of the largest meat-eating dinosaurs. Small visitors can climb inside a tyrannosaurus rex skull and dig for fossils. A recent museum-wide show explored the world of dinosaurs and included a full-size, animated (and very scary) apatosaurus. A walk-through tropical rain forest houses hundreds of live butterflies from Kenya, Costa Rica, and Malaysia.

Wagner Free Institute of Science

This natural history museum and educational institution (1700 W. Montgomery Ave., 215/763-6529, www.wagnerfreeinstitute.org, Tues.–Fri. 9 A.M.–4 P.M., free) remains nearly unchanged from the 19th century. Incorporated in 1855 and named for its founders, William Wagner and Louisa Binney Wagner, the institute continues to follow the founder's vision to provide free educational resources, the oldest program devoted to free adult education in the United States. In addition to the museum's extensive collections that span the natural world, the institute offers free public education courses on science, and a library with an astounding array of books, treatises, studies and illustrated texts from all over the world. There's also a special children's section.

SPECIAL-INTEREST MUSEUMS

Temple University Shoe Museum

Part of the School of Podiatric Medicine's Center for the History of Foot Care and Footwear, the collection consists of more than 900 pairs of shoes, with roughly 250 pairs on display on the sixth floor of the college building (8th St. between Race and Cherry Sts., 215/625-5243, http://podiatry.temple.edu, free). Visits must be scheduled in advance by calling the listed number.

Grouped in cases and along walls, the collection pays homage to foot coverings from every era and location. Many of the unusual shoes in the museum's collection were made for women; the extreme is represented by tiny "lily shoes": following a 1,000-year-old Chinese custom that existed into the early 20th century, young girls' feet were tightly bandaged from the age of five, forcing the arch upward and the toes under. This produced a foot about half the normal size; the ideal was the three-inch "Golden Lotus."

There are shoes from first ladies, a size-18 pair from a woman who found employment as a circus giant, Egyptian burial sandals dated 200 B.C., Ringo Starr's white shoes with black stars, Reggie Jackson's five-home-run World Series shoes, Ella Fitzgerald's gold boots, Joan Rivers's Manolo Blahnicks—the displays are fascinating, and made more so by the inclusion of a bit of historical information: ". . . platform shoes were introduced to Europe in the 16th century. Originally known as chopines, these 'stilt' shoes reached dizzying heights of up to two-and-one-half feet. The wearer needed the help of two servants to walk, reinforcing both social status and the image of a woman as frail and dependent." I'll take flats, thanks.

Please Touch Museum

Conceived and created especially for kids under 7, the Please Touch Museum (210 N. 21st St., 215/963-0667, www.pleasetouchmuseum.org, 9 A.M.–4:30 P.M. with extended hours July 1–Labor Day) is completely hands-on. Play is combined with learning experiences, such as an investigation of where food comes from, how public transportation works, and how the sound of horses' hooves is made for television and radio shows. Admission is $8.95 per person, free under the age of 1. Every four children must be accompanied by an adult. Strollers are not permitted, but may be left in a safe, designated area.

This award-winning children's museum is so fun-filled, adults have a great time, too. Each area has a different theme, such as "Alice's Adventures in Wonderland," where kids can play croquet with the queen and sip tea with the Mad Hatter, and Maurice Sendak's "Where the Wild Things Are" and other classics provide props to become part of the stories. During the summer, the Science Park (in conjunction with the Franklin Institute) delights little ones with 20 exhibits ranging from a radar detector to a "Transfer of Energy" swing.

FAIRMOUNT PARK

This 8,900-acre greenway—about 10 percent of Philadelphia's geographical area—is the nation's largest landscaped park and lies to the northwest of Logan Circle. The park encompasses, among other things, the Philadelphia Museum of Art, the Philadelphia Zoo, a historic waterworks, a group of early American houses, dozens of sculptures, a Japanese-style house and gardens, and the Mann Music Center (summer home of the Philadelphia Orchestra).

The Schuylkill River divides the park into east and west, and the grounds are laced with automobile roads and hiking, biking, and bridle trails. (For more information on hike-and-bike trails, see Outdoor Recreation.) Detailed maps are in short supply in the park itself but are available at the visitors' center (John F. Kennedy Blvd. and N. 16th St., 215/636-1666, www.phila.gov/fairpark) or at downtown hotels. The park may be toured

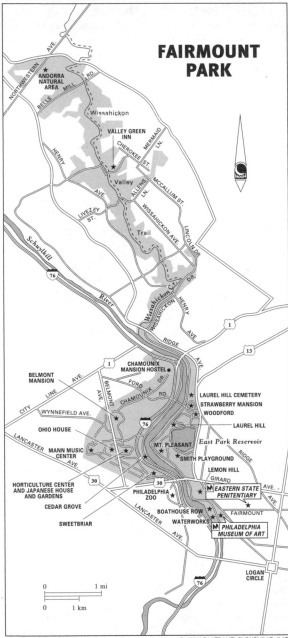

FAIRMOUNT PARK

by auto along either Kelly Drive or West River Drive. One of the easiest ways to enjoy the greenery and river views is the Fairmount Park Trolley bus tour, which takes visitors on a 17-mile loop. For a small fee, the trolley may be boarded at any of the historic houses on the east side of the river, or the zoo.

Fairmount Waterworks
Innovative for its time, the waterworks was designed and built in 1840 to pump water from the Schuylkill to holding tanks on the present site of the Philadelphia Museum of Art. From there, water was gravity-fed to homes and businesses in the growing city. The building and surrounding landscaping are still impressive.

The Philadelphia Museum of Art
Philadelphia features world-class art museums, and this is one of the best. Read more about it in Art Museums.

Boathouse Row
Sculling—rowing on shallow-draft boats that skim the water like so many water beetles—has long been associated with Philadelphia and the Schuylkill River. Nine rowing clubs occupy 10 Victorian boathouses on the river. The boathouses are turreted, gabled, and decorated with coats of arms; at night, viewed from West Fairmount Park shore, the houses are outlined in fairy lights and reflect magically on the river.

Historic Houses
All of the following historic houses are decorated in period style and,

except Orniston, are open to the public year-round (www.philamuseum.org/collections/parkhouse). Most are open Tues. through Sun. 10 A.M. to 4 P.M. (some until 5 P.M.); Sweetbriar and Lemon Hill are open Wed. through Sun. There is a $2.50 fee for a self-guided tour of each home. (Since the homes are set within park boundaries and most have no street addresses, the easiest way to locate them is on the map provided.)

On the east side of the park, Federal-style **Lemon Hill** is an 18th-century mansion noted for its unusual oval rooms. The name came from the greenhouses, stocked with lemon trees, which once adjoined the property.

John Adams was one of many visitors at **Mt. Pleasant,** completed in 1764. The home, an exquisite example of Georgian symmetry, was purchased (though some say not occupied) by Benedict Arnold, who was given a death sentence in absentia for treason by his old friend George Washington.

Ormiston, built after the Revolution, may be viewed May–Aug. by appointment only (215/763-2222).

Laurel Hill, former home of a pacifist Quaker during the Revolutionary War, was confiscated by pro-revolutionary forces and used by General Joseph Reed as a summer home. Loyalists David Franks and his daughter Rebecca entertained British General William Howe during the same period at **Woodford.**

Strawberry Mansion, the largest stately home in the park, is the northernmost mansion on the east side. Strawberries, an exotic fruit imported from Chile, were cultivated there by one of its owners. It was once the site of a meeting between Daniel Webster and a group of northern and southern democrats prior to the Civil War; Webster toasted the strawberries and reputedly avoided the rowdy political argument that followed by escaping through one of the windows. Once a steamboat landing site, the mansion also served as a restaurant serving strawberries and cream.

Across the Strawberry Mansion Bridge, in West Fairmount Park, is **Belmont Mansion,** which showcases an exhibit of the contributions of African-American women to Philadelphia and the United States; the house once entertained George Washington, John Adams, Ben Franklin, and others.

Chamounix Mansion (800/379-0017), an AYH hostel since 1964 (see Accommodations), offers elegant period furnishings on the lower level; it's somewhat isolated, but may be reached by the Fairmount Park Trolley.

The **Ohio House** (Belmont Ave. and States St.) is the home of the Philadelphia Ranger Corps and is built with native Ohio stone. It was a state exhibition building during the 1876 Centennial Exhibition.

Cedar Grove was built as a Quaker farmhouse and retreat in 1748. It was moved from another section of the city and still retains many of its original furnishings.

Built in 1797, **Sweetbriar** features floor-to-ceiling windows that overlook the Schuylkill and the waterworks. During its heyday, the owners welcomed foreign dignitaries such as the Marquis de Lafayette and Charles Talleyrand.

Smith Playground

A delightful anachronism, Smith Playground was given to the children of Philadelphia by wealthy manufacturer Richard Smith in memory of his son in 1894. (Many people assume that Smith's son died young. In fact, he was in his 40s when he died—Smith was simply grateful for having him.) The playground, behind the golf driving range at 33rd and Oxford Streets, is open Mon.–Sat. 9 A.M.–4:45 P.M., free to all children under the age of 12. Standard playground toys such as muscle-powered merry-go-rounds and swings dot the park. Smith Playground also features a renovated mansion, and inside, the Playhouse—open only to children under five, no big kids permitted. There are rooms filled with sturdy toys for toddlers including little tables for tea parties; one room is dedicated to a make-believe village (Smithville) with painted streets, a working traffic light, parking meters, and old-fashioned pedal cars to get around in. The most memorable feature of the playground is the Giant Slide, built in 1908. This enclosed structure can accommodate six or seven children at once on its 12-foot width.

Laurel Hill Cemetery

A vast "park within a park," 99-acre Laurel Hill Cemetery was once such a popular picnic and strolling spot in the late Victorian age that admission was by ticket only. Laurel Hill Cemetery, on the east side of Fairmount Park, is open Mon. through Fri., 8:30 A.M.–4:30 P.M., Sat. 9:30 A.M.–1:30 P.M. Closed on Sun. Maps are available near the main entrance (3822 Ridge Ave. at Huntingdon St., 215/228-8200).

Created in 1836, the carefully tended cemetery is the final resting place for many prominent Philadelphians. It's dotted with obelisks, classic Greek mausoleums, and statuary of enduring beauty. Lambs and crosses, children at play, and *putti* on the wing decorate many tombs; a stone angel stands at philanthropist William Warner's sarcophagus, welcoming his soul to heaven.

Horticulture Center and Japanese House and Gardens

Horticultural exhibits, working greenhouses, and an arboretum are features of the center (off Montgomery Dr. on Belmont Horticulture Dr., 215/685-0096; 9 A.M.–3 P.M. daily). An authentic 17th-century-style Japanese *shoin* mansion and surrounding garden are on the grounds of the Horticulture Center. The Japanese House, originally exhibited at the Museum of Modern Art in New York City in 1957, is closed Nov.–April; admission is $2.50. (Open after April 15 for group tours only.) During the spring and summer, the Japanese House offers special events such as tea ceremonies and flower arranging (call 215/878-5097 for an event update).

Philadelphia Zoo

Founded in 1859, this is the oldest zoo in America—and one of the most pleasant to get around. Though the collections are extensive, the zoo (N. 34th St. and Girard Ave., 3400 W. Girard Ave., 215/243-1100, www.philadelphiazoo.org) has a walkable, intimate feel. The zoo is open Feb.–Nov. daily 9:30 A.M.–5 P.M., Dec.–Jan. 9:30 A.M.–4 P.M.; it's closed Thanksgiving, Christ-

Flamingos preen at the Philadelphia Zoo.

mas Eve, Christmas Day, New Year's Eve, New Year's Day, and June 10 (for the annual fundraising event). March 27–Oct., adult admission is $15.95, children 2–11 $12.95; Nov.–March, adult admission is $9.95 per person; children under the age of 2 and zoo members are free year-round.

A petting zoo with farmyard animals and a plastic cow that can be "milked," plus a play area, the Treehouse, are additional features for families with younger children. The grounds are interspersed with statuary, and the animals are varied, easily viewed, and are often of unusual species. Rare bicolored tamarin monkeys from Brazil, with striking white muffs, are found only in one other U.S. zoo, and the mammal collection includes the only bamboo lemurs (bamboo-eating) and Madagascar giant jumping rats in the U.S. (though day visitors will most likely see giant *snoozing* rats). Long known as a leader in animal conservation and captive breeding programs, the Philadelphia Zoo maintains the "studbook" for Geoffroy's marmosets—more have been born here than at any other zoo.

An exceptional walk-through giant otter habitat shows off the water-based animals at their playful best. Dark rooms displaying nocturnal animals feature an extensive naked mole rat tunnel, and Rodrigues fruit bats, which look like upside-down squirrels until they unfold their three-foot wings. Uncaged finches and hummingbirds zip past your nose in the open bird house. The magnificent big cats, lions, clouded leopards, tigers (including rare whites), and jaguars are kept in near-natural habitats or inside the Carnivora House; the weather-protected cages of the house provide a thrilling close-up view. Visitors stand only a few feet away from the ground-shaking roar of the jungle king.

Roger Conant, co-author of *Peterson's Field Guide to Reptiles*, was the zoo's first reptile curator. The reptile house, appropriately dark and slithery, features a family of alligators in the back, basking in their own tropical paradise. Rainy afternoons are a good time to visit; all of the reptiles are especially active on days when fewer visitors are in attendance.

A tragic fire caused by aged wiring in the ape house on Christmas Eve 1995 resulted in the smoke-inhalation deaths of whole families of lowland gorillas, orangutans, gibbons, and lemurs—23 animals in all. The loss proved extremely traumatic to all the zoo's personnel, especially those in direct daily contact with the animals. A monument dedicated to the victims stands on the site where the ape house has been rebuilt. A new 2.5-acre reserve features 11 primate species, including western lowland gorillas, Sumatran orangutans, and the country's only blue-eyed lemurs. The reserve includes spacious indoor and outdoor areas, barrier-free trails, interactive videos, and the impressive Gorilla Theatre.

OTHER POINTS OF INTEREST NEAR LOGAN CIRCLE
Eastern State Penitentiary

The House, as it was called by inmates and guards, was completed in 1829 and was a revolutionary concept in criminal justice (Fairmount Ave. at 22nd St., 215/236-3300, www.easternstate.com). Prior to that time, criminals were thrown together in despicable conditions and punished by physical brutality; the idea of a penitentiary, a place where a criminal could be alone to ponder and become penitent for his actions, was considered a much more effective and humane solution by the Quakers who proposed it.

The prison offers self-conducted tours, as well as guided, hard-hat tours (the latter is recommended), and holds several art exhibits each year and symposiums on contemporary crime and punishment in our society. Eastern State is open April–Nov., Wed.–Sun. 10 A.M.–5 P.M. Guided tours depart on the hour. The House is closed during winter; call 215/236-5111 for special winter tours for groups of 15 or more. Admission is $9; over 64 and students with ID $7; ages 7–17 $4; children under 7 are not permitted on tours. The neighborhood that surrounds the prison has a number of trendy restaurants—brochures are available in the gift shop.

© JOANNE MILLER

Eastern State Penitentiary hallway

HOPELESS SOLITARY CONFINEMENT

Charles Dickens visited Eastern State Penitentiary in the early 19th century; it was not to his liking: "The system here is rigid, strict, and hopeless solitary confinement. I believe it, in its effect, to be cruel and wrong." Though Dickens conceded that the intention was kind, humane, and meant to reform the criminals it held, he commented that "very few men are capable of estimating the immense amount of torture and agony which this dreadful punishment, prolonged for years, inflicts upon the sufferers."

Dickens saw the prison in its original form: long corridors, lined with cells accessible by small double doors. Those who dwelt in the cells were identified only by numbers above each door.

Prisoners were led to their confinement wearing black hoods. During their stays, they saw no one but the prison officers who passed them food and water. Each prisoner was given a bible, a slate and chalk, and sometimes a pencil and paper and other books. They were permitted to weave cloth, cobble shoes, and spin yarn, but never to see another living face until their sentences were served.

To the Quakers, this solitude provided an ideal opportunity for each prisoner to come to know God and repent past behavior. To Dickens, every prisoner was "a man buried alive; to be dug out in the slow round of years; and in the meantime dead to everything."

The prison was designed with one entrance, 30-foot-high outside walls, and a central hub with "spokes" radiating out. The spokes contained the thick-walled individual cells. Each solitary cell had a private outdoor exercise yard contained by a 10-foot wall. During incarceration, with sentences seldom less than five years in length, the prisoner literally never saw or heard another human being. The cells were double-doored to prevent contact with those who delivered meals and performed sanitary services.

Before the prison was completed, the original design had to be modified to contain more prisoners, though the ideal of isolation was maintained. Eastern State Penitentiary became a model of progressive punishment for the world. In the century after it was built, more than 300 prisons in the United States, South America, northern Europe, Russia, China, Japan, and the British Empire were modeled on it. There were also opponents to the "Pennsylvania Penal System"— Charles Dickens among them—who were fired up by tales of inmates driven to insanity by solitary confinement.

Eastern State's most famous guests included Al Capone, in for a year on a concealed weapons charge, and bank robber Willie Sutton (the original "Slick Willie"), who managed to escape for a few hours with fellow plotter Freddie "Angel of Death" Tenuto. The pair was captured but successfully escaped from another prison some time later. The most peculiar inmate of the prison was Pep, a dog sentenced to life by Governor Gifford Pinchot in 1924 for killing his wife's cat.

The prison was closed in the late 1960s, when repairs and upgrading proved too expensive. Eastern State Penitentiary is now run by the Pennsylvania Prison Society in conjunction with three other organizations, including the National Park Service. The walls may be crumbling, but the extraordinary quiet and solitude, the sense of desperation and redemption that permeates the structures, make this one of the most interesting destinations in the city. World Monuments Watch, a grants organization funded in part by American Express, agrees; Eastern State was recognized as one of five crucial U.S. sites, both for its international architectural importance and for the severity of the threat to its future.

Entertainment and Recreation

PERFORMING ARTS

Full-price and half-price day-of-show tickets to theater, musical, ballet, and other performances are available from the Upstages ticket cart in the Shops at Liberty Place (2nd floor, 17th and Chestnut Sts., 9:30 A.M.–7 P.M.).

Dance: The Pennsylvania Ballet (1101 S. Broad St., 215/551-7000, www.paballet.org) is the premier classical ballet company in the Philadelphia region. They frequently appear at the Academy of Music (Broad and Locust Sts.). The Philadelphia Dance Company, or Philadanco (9 N. Preston St., Philadanco Way, 215/387-8200), performs all over the world, and often in the Annenberg Center (box office 215/898-3900, www.annenbergcenter.org) while in Philadelphia.

Music: The schedule of Concerto Soloists Chamber Orchestra performances is available by phone (215/545-1739). The Philadelphia Chamber Music Society may be reached at 215/569-8587. The Bach Festival of Philadelphia has schedules available at 215/247-4020. Philadelphia Pops performs light classics, Broadway tunes, and popular music. There are a number of places to purchase tickets (888/590-9090, 888/496-4444, and 888/849-9663). For jazz performances, call the Philadelphia Clef Club (215/893-9912).

The Curtis Institute of Music (215/893-5252) features many different musical events throughout the year. Mann Music Center in Fairmount Park (215/893-1999) presents the Philadelphia Orchestra and other musical guests during the summer.

Theater: The Philadelphia Theatre Company (215/985-1400) won a Tony award in 2000 for its presentation of *Master Class*. The Philadelphia Festival Theater for New Plays, at the Annenberg Center located at the University of Pennsylvania (above), and the Prince Music Theater (215/972-1000); both premier new works. The Arden Theater Company (215/922-8900), Wilma Theatre Company (215/546-7824), and

Society Hill Playhouse (215/923-0210) are acclaimed regional theater companies.

The Walnut Street Theater (215/574-3550, www.wstonline.org), Freedom Theatre—Philly's top African-American venue (215/765-2793), and Hedgerow Theatre (Wallingford, 610/565-4211, www.hedgerowtheatre.org) all present stage works by new and familiar authors.

Vocal Performances: The Opera Company of Philadelphia (510 Walnut St., 215/928-2100), Philadelphia Boys' Choir and Chorale (215/222-3500), and the Choral Arts Society of Philadelphia (215/545-8634) schedule numerous performances during the year.

NIGHTLIFE

Philadelphia has a lively after-hours scene with everything from established nightclub/restaurants to every kind of dance music. For current information on jazz clubs and bands, try www.phillyjazz.org, www.citypaper.net, and www.philadelphiaweekly.com.

Comedy

Comedy clubs usually offer two shows a night, roughly 8 P.M. and 10 P.M.; ticket prices vary with the performer. Call for current schedules and prices.

The PlayGround at the Adrienne (2030 Sansom St., 877/98-LAUGH) presents COME-DYSPORTZ, competitive improvisational comedy every Sat., 7:30 P.M. and 10 P.M.

The Laff House (211 South St., 215/440-4242, www.laffhouse.com) is one of the oldest comedy clubs in the area and features local and national names on the comedy scene, such as David Brenner.

Comedy Cabaret (at the Best Western Hotel, 11580 Roosevelt Blvd., 215/676-5653, www.comedycabaret.com, Wed.–Sat.) offers comedy nights that display the talents of many performers seen on Showtime and HBO comedy specials, and big names such as Jay Leno.

THE SCHUYLKILL NAVY

Philadelphia is one of the world's most prominent centers for the training of novice and veteran team-racing rowers and single scullers. Boathouse Row on the Schuylkill is home to many of the most accomplished rowers in the nation. For more than a century, Philadelphia has been a key training point for America's rowing teams. At least one representative from Boathouse Row has been present on nearly every U.S. Olympic team since the late 19th century.

The rowing clubs at the historic landmark boathouses—Fairmount Rowing Association, Vesper Boat Club, University Barge Club, and Crescent Boat Club, among others, collectively known as the Schuylkill Navy—carry on the sport's time-honored traditions along Kelly Drive, named in honor of Olympic sculler, brick contractor, and politician Jack Kelly, father of Grace Kelly. Philadelphian members of U.S. Olympic Rowing Teams included a variety of contenders in different formations and boat types: Theresa Bell, women's lightweight double; Bill Carlucci, men's lightweight four; Jeff Pfaendtner, men's lightweight four; Monica Tranell Michini, women's openweight eight; Kris Kerber, men's lightweight spare; Adam Holland, men's pair; Jennifer Devine, women's double; and Michele Knox-Zalloom, women's double.

Dinner/Music Clubs

All the following clubs feature full menus and live bands.

Zanzibar Blue (intersection of Broad and Walnut Sts., 215/732-5200, www.zanzibarblue.com) is reputed to be the best in the city for live international jazz. Dinner is served daily, from 5:30 P.M.; a streamlined version of the menu is served Sun.–Thurs. until midnight, and Fri.–Sat. until 1 A.M. On Sun., brunch (11 A.M.–2 P.M.) is accompanied by jazz. Prices range $12–20.

For a blues and acoustic fix, try **Warmdaddys** (4 S. Front St., 215/627-2500, www.warmdaddys.com), a popular local rhythm, blues, and soul food spot seven days a week ($16). **Tin Angel Café/Serrano** (20 S. 2nd St., 215/928-0770, www.tinangel.com) showcases a variety of world-music acoustic performers from Irish to country. Serrano serves an equally eclectic menu with middle eastern mezze plates and potstickers among many other dishes ($16).

Brasil's (112 Chestnut St., 215/413-1700, www.brasils.com) offers live and recorded Latin rhythms Wed.–Sat., along with a Brazilian menu featuring entrees such as shrimp sautéed with pineapple chunks, cream, garlic, and fresh herbs ($19).

Dancing

Rock Lobster (221 N. Columbus Ave., 215/627-7625) is a favorite among visitors to the city. It features world beat and alternative rock, both live and recorded. There's no seating, but it draws enough people so that you can lean in any direction for a rest. It closes during the winter.

Philly's best DJs are showcased at **Silk City** (5th and Spring Garden Sts., 215/592-8838, www.silkcitylounge.com). It draws the hip crowd, and is next to the 24/7 Silk City Diner, in case you feel a sudden need for mom's home cooking.

Egypt (520 N. Columbus Blvd., 215/922-6500, www.egypt-nightclub.com) lets you dance among the sphinxes on a split-level dance floor Tues.–Sun. It features a special dance party weekly for 14–18-year-olds.

Glam (52 S. Second St., 267/671-0840) is for those dress-up-and-boogie nights. This downtown hotspot attracts an upscale crowd, and snob appeal is served via an upstairs VIP lounge. The music is house and hip-hop, and an American-Asian-fusion menu is available early in the evening.

SPECTATOR SPORTS

Many sporting events and schedules are listed in the **Greater Philadelphia Tourism Marketing Corporation** Calendar of Events (888/GO PHILA, www.gophila.com). A popular way to get to both Citizens Bank Park and Wachovia Center Spectrum is via SEPTA's Broad Street subway line.

Baseball: The 1993 National League champion Philadelphia Phillies play at The 43,500-

seat, state-of-the-art Citizens Bank Park, on a 21-acre site in South Philadelphia (on the north side of Pattison Avenue, between 11th and Darien Sts., 215/463-1000, http://philadel-phia.phillies.mlb.com).

Basketball: Philadelphia 76ers bounce the ball around at the Wachovia Center Complex Stadium (3601 S. Broad St. and Pattison Ave., 215/339-7600).

Football: The NFL's Philadelphia Eagles play at the Wachovia Center Complex Stadium (Broad St. and Pattison Ave., 215/463-5500). The city also now has Philadelphia Soul (888/ PHIL-AFL, www.philadelphiasoul.com), a team in the Arena Football League, a winter-spring indoor diversion for football fanatics. The team counts rock 'n' rollers Jon Bon Jovi and Richie Sambora among its owners.

Golf: Bell Atlantic Classic is the major senior PGA Tour event in the region. It's usually held around the third week in May; see the website for specifics (www.bellatlanticclassic.com).

Hockey and Soccer: National Hockey League team The Philadelphia Flyers (215/755-9700), American Hockey League team the Phantoms (215/465-4522), and the National Indoor Soccer League's Kixx (888/888-5499) all play home games at the Wachovia Center Spectrum (Broad St. and Pattison Ave.).

Intercollegiate Athletics: All institutions of higher learning in the Philadelphia area have athletic programs for men and women. For schedules of upcoming events, call the following schools: Drexel University (215/895-1999, www.drexeldragons.com), LaSalle University (215/951-1516, www.GoExplorers.com), Temple University (215/204-8499, www.owlsports.com), and University of Pennsylvania (215/596-8800).

OUTDOOR RECREATION

Laced with hiking, biking, and bridle trails, massive **Fairmount Park** (www.phila.gov/fairpark) has plenty to keep outdoor enthusiasts content. Contiguous pathways form a four-mile hike-and-bike trail along the east side of the Schuylkill River paralleling Kelly Drive from the Museum of Art to Lincoln Drive (City Line Ave.) above East Falls. The Wissahickon Valley Trail may be picked up at that point and taken out to the Montgomery County line, an additional five to eight miles. Hike-and-bike paths also parallel West River Drive. From April to October, West River Drive is closed to auto traffic 7 A.M.–noon, providing a very pleasant and scenic four-mile journey.

For more information about Fairmount Park, see the Logan Circle Quadrant section, earlier.

Shopping

Antiques

Two areas in the Washington Square Quadrant are famed for their antique shops, with merchandise ranging from furniture to vintage clothing. The first is **Pine Street** between 9th and 13th Streets; the other is between **Lombard and Fitzwater Streets** between 3rd and 10th Streets. A few of the shops in that area include: **Book Trader** (501 South St.,215/925-0219), with thousands of used books, records, CDs, and cassettes; and **Gargoyles** (512 S. 3rd St., 215/629-1700), a warehouse filled with antiques and reproductions.

Department Stores

The department stores in Philadelphia are not just chains; they were the models for department stores across the nation. Wanamaker's (13th and Market Sts.) began in the late 19th century, trading up from a tiny shop to an institution. Though the actual store is a thing of the past—the national retailer **Lord & Taylor** (215/241-9000) now occupies the main floor of the building—the Grand Court, the Wanamaker Organ, and the Eagle where shoppers meet still anchor several floors of quality merchandise and service. The building has won a National Historic Preservation Trust Award for its renovation. John Wanamaker himself, immortal in bronze, stands on the east side of city hall, gazing fondly in the direction of the family business.

Around even longer than Wanamaker's (since the 1860s), **Strawbridge & Clothier** (8th and Market Sts., 215/629-6000) has developed into a full-service store with old-fashioned panache. It has a food hall, a deli and café, and the Philadelphia Shop for mementos of the city's historical sites.

Malls and Discount Outlets

The Shops at Liberty Place (17th St. between Market and Chestnut Sts.) offer mainly upmarket chain stores such as **Benetton** and **The Coach Store.** The mall itself is modern in design and brightly lit; it has a large food court on the second floor with dozens of food choices at low prices. Underground parking is available.

When it opened in 1895, the **Bourse** (5th St. between Chestnut and Market Sts.) was the home of Philadelphia's stock exchange in addition to business offices. Now it houses specialty shops and restaurants surrounding a 10-story garden atrium.

A section of Philadelphia's old **Chinatown** (on the 100 block of N. 11th St.) has been made over into a shopping district with an emphasis on Asian goods.

Twenty minutes east of the city, **Franklin Mills** is a massive discount outlet mall with lots of big names: **Filene's Basement, Last Call from Neiman Marcus, Nordstrom Rack,** and **Saks Clearinghouse,** among others. This, along with King of Prussia, is where Philadelphians go for bargains. To reach Franklin Mills (Franklin Mills Blvd., 215/632-1500) from Center City, take I-95 north to Exit 24 (SR 63), Woodhaven Road. Franklin Mills is off Woodhaven Road. SEPTA goes direct to Franklin Mills from the Frankford Terminal daily on route numbers 20, 67, and 84.

SHOPPING NEIGHBORHOODS

The fanciest stores and shops in the city surround **Rittenhouse Square.** Chains such as **Borders Books, Talbots, Cache,** and **Jones New York** share street space with upscale boutiques.

The shopping area on two parallel streets above Rittenhouse Square, **Walnut Street and Chestnut Street,** start at 20th Street and extend several blocks to the east. Discount women's clothiers such as **Daffys** share street space with national retailers like **Urban Outfitters.**

South of Washington Square, the area of **Pine and Locust Streets** between 10th and 12th Streets features small cafés, eateries, retro clothing shops, purveyors of handcrafted items, and bookstores such as **Russakoffs Books and Records** (215/592-8380), a small bookshop with mostly used books.

© JOANNE MILLER

wall of an art house on South Street

Starting at **Headhouse Square,** then moving two blocks south to **South Street** and west to 9th Street, the streets are filled with restaurants, cafés, bars, shops—and shoppers. On Friday and Saturday night, South Street continues to be a destination for young Philadelphians. Tourist-oriented shops and those that cater to youth abound on South Street, but there are also quite a few gems. Headhouse Square is surrounded with chain restaurants such as T.G.I. Friday's, but smaller, locally owned bars and cafés abound. South Street literally has an international flavor, with Middle Eastern, Japanese, Moroccan, and Italian restaurants all within a few blocks of each other. Interspersed among the dozens of eateries and cafés are a comedy club, a hat shop, a retired surfer's bar with lurid wall murals, music sellers, craft stores, and several suave-to-funky clothing shops. You'll never be at a loss for holo-gram-heeled platform boots.

Specialty Stores

The Tiffany's of Philadelphia, **J.E. Caldwell,** is another shop that started small in 1839, though unlike Wanamaker's and Strawbridge & Clothier, its clientele has always been the carriage trade. The elegant shop (119 Chestnut St., 215/864-7800) features one of the country's premier jewelry and watch collections, plus gifts by Waterford, Orefors, Lalique, and others.

You can tour the **Lagos** factory (441 N. 5th St., 215/965-1693) and see the crafting of individual pieces of jewelry, or visit the retail store (1735 Walnut St., 215/567-0770).

Accommodations

Philadelphia is one of those rare big cities that actually offers a variety of price ranges and decent less-expensive places to stay. Bed-and-breakfasts in the Center City area are good buys for those planning to stay more than a night, since the comforts of home—kitchen and laundry facilities—are often on the premises, and the price is less than the big hotels. Another option for a quality overnight is to stay out in Chestnut Hill or University City—see Accommodations under Greater Philadelphia.

All hotels, even those in the luxury class, offer some packages to lure customers during slow times; be sure to inquire when you're thinking of booking a place to stay.

UNDER $50

Old Town

Bank Street Hostel (32 S. Bank St., between Market and Chestnut Sts. and 2nd and 3rd Sts., 215/922-0222 or 800/392-4678) is a renovated 19th-century building in the middle of Independence Mall. This AYH hostel has 70 beds, but no family rooms. At $18 a night for members, $21 a night for non-members and a $2 bed-sheet rental if you do not bring your own, it's a great deal for a convenient location, but dropping in is risky—reservations are recommended July–Sept.

Logan Circle Quadrant

⋈ Chamounix Mansion Hostel, converted into an AYH hostel in 1964, is a dream made real, especially in a city with few budget accommodations. The Chamounix mansion and adjacent carriage house were built in 1802 in the middle of what is now Fairmount Park. The dormitory rooms are air-conditioned, and a limited number of smaller dorms are available for families. Parking is nearby, and the SEPTA 38 bus runs to and from the hostel to downtown Philadelphia. For a hostel, it's pricey—$15 for AYH members, $18 for non-members; $2 bed-sheet rental; for Philadelphia, it's amazing. Book as far ahead as

possible. Write or call for reservations (Chamounix Mansion, West Fairmount Park, Philadelphia, PA 19131, 215/878-3676 or 800/379-0017).

$50–100

Washington Square Quadrant

Antique Row Bed and Breakfast (341 S. 12th St., 215/592-7802, www.antiquerowbnb.com) rests among a friendly mix of antique shops, retro-clothing stores, bookstores, and restaurants. Like most bed and breakfasts in the heart of the city, this isn't a Victorian fantasy, but more of a home: clean, quiet, and pleasant (and quite inexpensive for the area). The lower floor has its own bed and bath, and an attached kitchen. The upper floor offers two rooms that share a bath. Innkeeper Barbara Pope, who makes a great breakfast and conversation to match, also offers the services of "the distressed gentlewoman's network"—if she can't put you up, she can probably find someone who will. Sometimes, she can even ferret out parking spaces in a notoriously tight neighborhood. Rates range $65–110.

$100–150

Washington Square Quadrant

Fitzwater Bed and Breakfast (218 Fitzwater St., 215/829-8951) was built in 1874 for Jonathan May, a sea captain. This charming inn rests comfortably in the heart of historic Queens Village, the oldest area of Philadelphia. Comfortable, eclectically decorated rooms echo 19th-century Italy, England, France and early Philadelphia. All rooms have unique furnishings, private baths and lovely views. It's a short walk to Independence Hall, the Liberty Bell, Penn's Landing, South Street and Antique Row. Rates average $95–125.

Rittenhouse Square Quadrant

⋈ The Latham (17th St. at Walnut St., 215/563-7474 or 800/LATHAM-1, www.lathamhotel

.com), decorated in an attractive Italian-contemporary style, is a gracious smaller hotel ensconced in the middle of one of Philadelphia's most popular shopping districts. All amenities, including health club privileges at a nearby facility, are extended to guests. Fifteen of the Latham's 100 employees have worked at the hotel since it opened in 1970, and are an excellent source of information on the hotel and on Philadelphia in general. Rates range from $109–219, with special packages offered online.

$150–250

Franklin Square Quadrant/Old Town

M Omni Independence Park (4th and Chestnut St., 215/925-0000 or 800/843-6664, www.omnihotels.com), one of the newer mid-size hotels in Philadelphia, is located on the boundary of Independence Park Historic District. For comfort and convenience, it's unrivaled. The rooms are spacious and attractive, service is impeccable, and there's a full-size pool in the basement. Parking, as with most lodgings in the city, is available either at a nearby garage or on the street. The Omni offers special packages on weekends and for specific city events. Rates vary according to the occupancy of the day. They normally start at $209 but can often go as low as $139.

Logan Circle Quadrant

Wyndham Franklin Plaza (17th and Race Sts., 215/448-2000 or 800/822-4200, www.wyndham.com/hotels/PHLFP), with 758 rooms and 23 suites, is one of the largest hotels in town. Its good location, along with a glassed-atrium lobby, health club, restaurants, and parking garage make it a favorite among conventioneers and visitors. The deluxe rooms feature a curved wall of glass that overlooks the city for stunning views of the skyline and Swann fountain at night. The Wyndham offers special packages with reduced prices, especially during the summer. Rates range $175–300. Visit the website for Web rate offers.

OVER $250

Franklin Square Quadrant/Old Town

Is it possible to be In love with a hotel? The name Ritz has been around since 1898, when hotelier Cesar Ritz, a shepherd's son from Neiderwald, Switzerland, opened the original Ritz on Place Vendome in Paris. The hotel became synonymous with luxury, so much so that the slang terms "putting on the ritz" and "ritzy" have become part of everyday parlance. The Ritz name has legally changed hands a few times, but the **M Ritz-Carlton Philadelphia** (10 Ave. of the Arts, 215/735-7700 or 800/241-3333, www.ritz-carlton.com) absolutely lives up to its reputation for luxe, quality, and service.

Condé Nast Traveler readers named the Ritz number seven in the top 25 U.S. hotels in the 1990s, and the top hotel in Philadelphia, and in Zagat's *U.S. Resort, Hotel and Spa Survey* the Ritz shared the number-one rating in Philadelphia with the Four Seasons for best overall hotel, best rooms, dining, and service. However, this isn't the same hotel that won the accolades—it's better. The Ritz was rebuilt on Avenue of the Arts in 1997–1998 to symbolically declare the revitalization of the area. To that end, the hotel has refashioned the basis of its reputation into even more sterling surroundings and service.

The hotel is elegant without pretension: brilliant Waterford-crystal chandeliers, deep-toned wood paneling, original 18th- and 19th-century paintings and antiques, Italian marble bathrooms, and hand-woven carpets, and a 24-hour health club on the third floor. If this sounds too heady, the staff quickly brings it down to earth—everyone is interested in your well-being and happiness (money *can* buy love). If you've felt neglected lately, this is the place to regenerate.

The Ritz offers two types of accommodations: rooms and suites. Both are available throughout the hotel, and on the club floors (two floors of the hotel, accessible by a special key). Club floor rooms have access to a private club, which serves five complimentary food and beverage presentations daily: continental breakfast, light lunch, afternoon tea, cocktails and hors d'oeuvres, and

Philadelphia

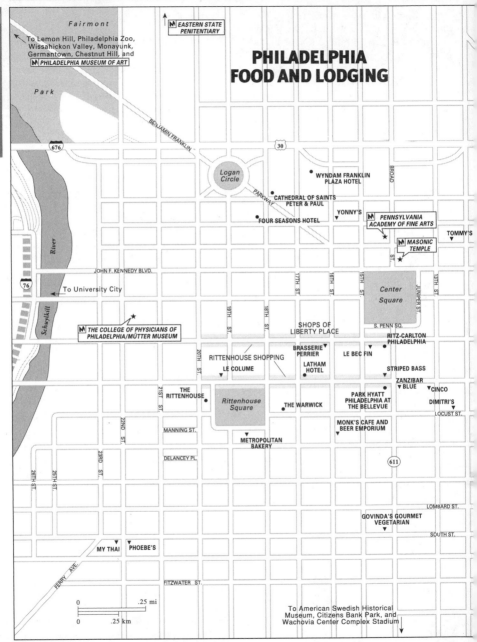

Fairmont

To Lemon Hill, Philadelphia Zoo,
Wissahickon Valley, Monayunk,
Germantown, Chestnut Hill, and
Ⓜ PHILADELPHIA MUSEUM OF ART

Ⓜ EASTERN STATE PENITENTIARY

Park

PHILADELPHIA FOOD AND LODGING

BENJAMIN FRANKLIN

676

30

Logan Circle

PARKWAY

WYNDAM FRANKLIN PLAZA HOTEL

BROAD

CATHEDRAL OF SAINTS PETER & PAUL

YONNY'S ▼

FOUR SEASONS HOTEL

Ⓜ PENNSYLVANIA ACADEMY OF FINE ARTS

★

Ⓜ MASONIC TEMPLE

TOMMY'S ▼

JOHN F. KENNEDY BLVD.

River

76

To University City

Schuylkill

Ⓜ THE COLLEGE OF PHYSICIANS OF PHILADELPHIA/MÜTTER MUSEUM

★

17TH ST.

16TH ST.

15TH ST.

Center Square

JUNIPER ST.

13TH ST.

19TH ST.

18TH ST.

SHOPS OF LIBERTY PLACE

S. PENN SQ.

RITZ-CARLTON PHILADELPHIA

BRASSERIE ▼ PERRIER

LE BEC FIN

20TH ST.

RITTENHOUSE SHOPPING

LATHAM HOTEL

LE COLUME ▼

STRIPED BASS

ZANZIBAR ▼ BLUE ▼CINCO

21ST ST.

THE RITTENHOUSE ●

Rittenhouse Square

●THE WARWICK

PARK HYATT PHILADELPHIA AT THE BELLEVUE

DIMITRI'S ▼

LOCUST ST.

22ND ST.

MANNING ST.

MONK'S CAFE AND BEER EMPORIUM ▼

▼ METROPOLITAN BAKERY

23RD ST.

DELANCEY PL.

611

26TH ST.

25TH ST.

LOMBARD ST.

GOVINDA'S GOURMET VEGETARIAN ▼

SOUTH ST.

▼ MY THAI

PHOEBE'S ▼

FERRY AVE.

FITZWATER ST.

0   .25 mi

0   .25 km

To American Swedish Historical
Museum, Citizens Bank Park, and
Wachovia Center Complex Stadium ▼

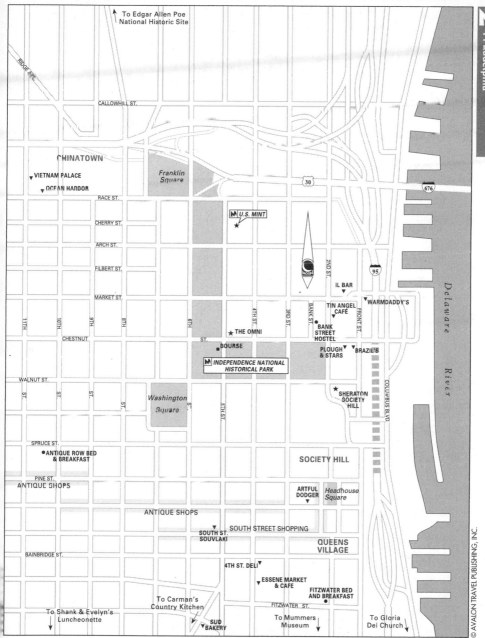

To Edgar Allen Poe
National Historic Site

RIDGE AVE.

CALLOWHILL ST.

CHINATOWN

Franklin
Square

▼ VIETNAM PALACE

▼ OCEAN HARBOR

RACE ST.

CHERRY ST.

ARCH ST.

FILBERT ST.

MARKET ST.

30

676

95

2ND ST.

FRONT ST.

Ⓜ U.S. MINT
★

Ⓜ MOON

IL BAR
▼

TIN ANGEL
CAFÉ
▼

▼ WARMDADDY'S

4TH ST.

3RD ST.

BANK ST.

★ THE OMNI

BANK
STREET
HOSTEL

PLOUGH ▼
& STARS

▼ BRAZIL'S

■ BOURSE

Ⓜ INDEPENDENCE NATIONAL
HISTORICAL PARK

11TH

10TH

9TH

8TH

7TH

6TH ST.

5TH ST.

CHESTNUT

ST.

WALNUT ST.

ST.

ST.

ST.

ST.

Washington
Square

★ SHERATON
SOCIETY
HILL

COLUMBUS BLVD.

SPRUCE ST.

● ANTIQUE ROW BED
& BREAKFAST

PINE ST.
ANTIQUE SHOPS

SOCIETY HILL

ANTIQUE SHOPS

ARTFUL
DODGER
▼

Headhouse
Square

SOUTH ST.
SOUVLAKI
▼

SOUTH STREET SHOPPING

BAINBRIDGE ST.

QUEENS
VILLAGE

4TH ST. DELI ▼

▼ ESSENE MARKET
& CAFE

FITZWATER BED
AND BREAKFAST
●

To Carman's
Country Kitchen

FITZWATER ST.

To Shank & Evelyn's
Luncheonette

▼ SUD
BAKERY

To Mummers
Museum

To Gloria
Dei Church

Delaware River

Philadelphia

chocolates and cordials. We are not talking stale peanuts and mongrel bottles of white wine—all of the meals are prepared by the hotel's exceptional foodservice staff. Cocktail service includes Absolut vodka and other fine liquors, locally brewed beers, and vintage wines complemented by fresh jumbo shrimp, crab claws, and fancy tidbits such as shrimp and avocado in endive. It's conceivable to graze all day in the club room, reading the newspapers, and forget the outside world exists.

Such beauty and bounty comes at a price, but overall, the Philadelphia Ritz is one of the great values in accommodations. You'll get more than you pay for. Though rack rates run from $320 per night all the way up to $3,500 for the Ritz-Carlton two-bedroom suite, and $420 per night to $470 for executive suites in the club levels, the hotel offers a number of packages and special getaways for weekends. For a special occasion, and to experience what a fine hotel is all about, the Ritz-Carlton is a superior choice.

Washington Square Quadrant

Sheraton Society Hill (One Dock St., 215/238-6000 or 800/325-3535, http://sheraton-philadelphia.felcor.com), a modern full-service hotel, perches atop Society Hill between Independence Park and South Street, conveniently near I-95, Penn's Landing, and the waterfront. The large brick complex, with its four-story atrium, provides a contemporary touch to Society Hill's elegant residential neighborhood, the oldest in the city. The hotel features an enclosed pool and health club, and a restaurant and pub. Parking is available at the hotel. Rates average $250–290. Special package rates are also available.

Rittenhouse Square Quadrant

Park Hyatt Philadelphia at the Bellevue (Broad and Walnut Sts., 215/893-1776 or 800/233-1234, www.hyatt.com) is one of the oldest hotels in Philadelphia, and the very name ignites a particular nostalgia among those who live here. The hotel has undergone a grand facelift, with flattering results. High tea in the powder-blue Barrymore Room is an elegant event. Rooms are spacious and beautifully decorated. Use of a full-service health facility next door—the Sporting Club—is available at no charge to guests; the café in the club is a budget stop for healthy sandwiches and snacks, too. One caveat—the hotel occasionally books events in the Palm Court, which serves as the window side for interior rooms. The events are over at 10 P.M., but if a low-noise environment is a must, book rooms in the outside, western section. Rates start at $255. Special packages are available.

Logan Circle Quadrant

Rivaling the Ritz, the **M Four Seasons** (One Logan Circle, 215/963-1500 or 800/819-5053, www.fourseasons.com/philadelphia) holds its own in the luxury department. Visitors may feel the need to don sunglasses after being exposed to the glare of hand-rubbed polished wood and rose-tinted marble in this much-celebrated hotel. The American Automobile Association has awarded the Four Seasons its top rating 16 years in a row; *Condé Nast Traveler* Reader's Choice surveys named it one of the top 11 hotels in America. The rooms are spacious and elegant, decorated in the Federal style, with personal safes in each closet, but it's its public areas that give the Four Seasons its unique beauty. The hotel is adjacent to its own fountain and sculpture garden; the grounds are at the base of the Parkway, next to Swann Fountain, with a view toward city hall.

The Four Seasons is home to two justifiably famous restaurants in a town notable for its eateries: The Fountain and the Swann Lounge (see Philly's Finest under Food and Drink). A fully equipped health center with swimming pool, and a beauty salon with spa services are available to guests; the hotel also maintains a nearby parking garage. The Four Seasons offers accommodation packages. One of the best is the Spa Experience, which includes a guest room overnight, valet parking for one automobile, breakfast in the Fountain Restaurant (or room service), and any two spa services such as a one-hour massage, facial, a manicure/pedicure, haircut and style, or makeup application and lesson. The package starts at $480–570, and several other choices range $295–575 per night. Average room rates range $320–425.

Food and Drink

Check out Greater Philadelphia for additional places to eat and play.

BAKERIES AND CAFÉS

Cafés tend to be open around 8 A.M. and close around 3 P.M.

Carbohydrates, how do I love thee? You can count the ways at **Metropolitan Bakery,** which has seven locations: 51 N. 12th Street, 215/829-1797; 262 S. 19th Street, 215/545-6655; 1036 Marlborough Street, 215/634-4100; 126 Market Street, 215/928-9528; 1114 Pine Street, 215/627-3433; 8607 Germantown Avenue, 215/753-9001; and Reading Terminal, 215/829-9020. The breads are fresh beyond compare, and for a quick lunch, nothing beats a hot cup of coffee, a crusty onion roll or two, and a container of olive tapanade or one of the other spreads. The Metro is no secret; it's often sold out of some items by noon. Expect to pay $5 for coffee and a snack.

Washington Square Quadrant

Sud Bakery (801 E. Passyunk Ave. at Catharine St., 215/592-0499) has a tiny café where visitors can stop for coffee and possibly the best Italian cookies and pastries in Philadelphia. Sud provides a convenient rest stop while shopping at the Italian market three blocks away. It's open Wed.–Fri. 5 P.M. to 10 P.M., Sat. brunch 9 A.M. to 3:30 P.M., Sat. dinner 5:30 P.M. to 10 P.M. Sun. brunch 10 A.M. to 4 P.M.

Rittenhouse Square Quadrant

The building that contains **La Colombe Torrefaction** (130 S. 19th St., 215/426-2011) was also once the site of La Colombe's roasting facility—owners Carmichael and Iberti had to move the roasting operation to a larger building due to the well-deserved popularity of their coffees. The attractive café still serves snacks along with cups of La Colombe's custom-roasted coffee. If you miss the smell of those baking beans, the new production facility is at

2600 E. Tioga Street. Prices are typical. $5 for coffee and snacks.

DELIS AND BARBECUE

Washington Square Quadrant

The **Famous 4th St. Delicatessen** (4th and Bainbridge Sts., 215/922-3274, Mon.–Sat. 7:30 A.M.–6 P.M., Sun. 7:30 A.M.–4 P.M.) is something of a legend, and like all legends, it's a bit of a letdown in real life. This part of south Philadelphia, in one of its incarnations, was a Jewish neighborhood, and the 4th St. Deli is a holdover from those days. There are good things, there are bad things. On the good side, the sandwiches and free-with-a-meal famous chocolate chip cookies are all as tasty as advertised. On the bad side, the restaurant has the ambience of a bus station, right down to the flimsy paper plates, argumentative staff, and messy floors. You'll enjoy the food best by taking it out. An average price is $8.

Rittenhouse Square Quadrant

Now this is 'cue! **Phoebe's Bar-B-Q** (2214 South St., 215/546-4811) is a busy takeout stand that makes pit-barbecued ribs, beef, and pork, and rotisserie-cooked chicken; all are served with either mild or hot sauce (the hot sauce, however, is benign enough that the menu promises, "It won't hurt you"—ask for a taste). It's open Tues.–Sat. noon –10 P.M., Sun. noon–8 P.M. Entrées plus cornbread and one side dish average $8. Also on the menu are sandwiches and skillet-baked cornbread (both plain and jalapeño).

BREWPUBS, BREWERIES, AND TAVERNS

Franklin Square Quadrant/Old Town

Plough and the Stars (123 Chestnut St. 215/733-0300) consistently pours one of the best Guinness pints in town, and the rich and hearty shepherd's pie will stick to your ribs. The name is a reference to the original Irish flag, symbolizing the earth and the sky. It's

Philadelphia

open for lunch Mon.–Sat. 11.30 A.M.–2:30 P.M. and dinner Mon.–Thurs. 5–10 P.M., Fri.–Sat. 5–10:30 P.M., Sun. 5–9 P.M.; brunch Sun. 11 A.M.–3:30 P.M.; and afternoon tea Mon.–Fri. 2:30–4:30 P.M. Average prices for lunch are $10–15; dinner, $18–28. The menu sticks to Western European pub-style food with an Irish twist, shaken in with Old City Philadelphia attitude. The building is the old Corn Exchange, which has been lovingly preserved.

Il Bar in Panorama Ristorante (14 N. Front St. at Market, 215/922-7800) is a quiet and cozy wine bar in Penn's View Hotel near the waterfront. Il Bar is recommended by many people for its excellent by-the-glass wine list and fireplace overlooking the river. Ristorante Panorama has the largest custom-built wine preservation and dispensing system in the world; the wine bar is able to keep 120 open bottles of wine for an extended period of time. The Ristorante serves Italian specialties (dinner daily $15–20).

Washington Square Quadrant

The service is friendly, the pub food is above average, and the location on Headhouse Square make the historic watering hole **The Artful Dodger** (400–402 S. 2nd St., 215/922-1790), open noon–midnight daily, a convenient lunch or late-afternoon drink stop. The spicy chicken wings will set you afire! Lunch and dinner menus are the same; average prices $6.95–18.

Rittenhouse Square Quadrant

If brew is calling you, **Monk's Café & Beer Emporium** (264 S. 16th St., 215/545-7005, www.monkscafé.com, daily 11:30 A.M.–2 A.M.) is the place to find it . In addition to an astonishing array of beer on tap from all over the world, the café produces Belgian specialties and pub food such as rabbit terrine (rabbit, dried fruit, and pistachios with whole-grain bread, capers, and hunter's sauce made with Belgian ale, $8) and grilled sourpuss—octopus braised in Flemish sour ale, marinated in citrus and spices, then grilled ($9). Prices average $10.

DINERS AND LUNCHEONETTES

Washington Square Quadrant

Carman's Country Kitchen (1301 S 11th St., 215/339-9613, Thurs.–Mon. 8 A.M. to 2 P.M.), a little South Philly corner shop, serves hearty breakfasts and lunches. Dishes range $5–20. Carman herself greets you, sits you down at the linoleum-topped diner counter, and dishes out the gossip as well as her home-cooking. You may have to wait for a seat during high-traffic brunch time.

Shank & Evelyn's Luncheonette is a friendly family-owned local hangout (932 S. 10th St., above Carpenter St., 215/629-1093) that makes decent fresh soups and sandwiches. You'll see plenty of local color among the big plates of Ital-

SAY CHEESESTEAK

A cheesesteak sandwich is something that rightfully belongs on the frozen Montana range, toasted over an open fire by a bundled-up cowboy. If only he could get the bread right! A proper cheesesteak, with layers of sliced, fried meat—preferably beef—onions, and green peppers, on a crusty roll with cheese is the perfect midwinter dogie-driving food. Why it was invented in Philadelphia is anybody's guess.

Cheesesteak wars come with the territory; several places claim theirs is the best: Jim's Steaks (4th and South Sts.); Pat's King of Steaks (1237 E. Passyunk Ave.); archrival Geno's (1219 S. 9th St.); D'Alessandro's Steaks (in Roxborough); and Leo's (1403 Chester Pike, Folcroft, in Delaware County)—I've heard more than one person claim the suburban cheesesteaks here are tops.

If cheesesteaks aren't for you (if you, for example, are one of those who deride the cheesesteak as a "heart attack on a roll"), perhaps another Philadelphia culinary institution would interest you: the hoagie, the original submarine sandwich, named for the Hog Island shipyards and stuffed with whatever pleases you. Two popular hoagie stops are Lee's (1334 Walnut St.) and Philadeli (410 South St.). Good eatin'!

ian specialties. Prices are in the $7 range, and it's open Tues.–Sat. 8 A.M.–5 P.M.

Logan Circle Quadrant

Vonny's (1531 Cherry, 215/665-0407, Mon.–Sat. 6 A.M.–3 P.M.), another neighborhood luncheonette, is a convenient stop while wandering around the northwest side of central Philadelphia. Breakfast or sandwich, cup of soup, and coffee runs around $8.

INTERNATIONAL

Franklin Square Quadrant/Old Town

Vietnam Palace (222 N. 11th St. in Chinatown, 215/592-9596, Sun.–Thurs., 11 A.M.–9:30 P.M., Fri.–Sat., 11 A.M.–10 P.M.) started out as a storefront in the early 1990s, and it's a testimonial to quality and service to see it blossom into a larger, elegant eatery. All the traditional dishes are on the menu including extra-crispy spring rolls and vegetarian dishes, and a variety of pho—noodle soup with rich, beef broth, rice noodles, minced scallions and cilantro ($4.50 each). The prices are very reasonable: entrees average $8, and many of the appetizers are big enough to serve light eaters.

Big, bright, and filled with families, **Ocean Harbor** (1023 Race St., 215/574-1398, http://oceanharbor.citysearch.com, Mon.–Thurs. 11 A.M.–midnight, Fri. 11 A.M.–1 A.M., Sat. 10 A.M.–1 A.M., Sun. 10 A.M.–midnight) serves a standard Hong Kong menu plus "special dinners" that show off the chef's skills. Plates run about $8, and special dinners with several courses average $15 per person.

Washington Square Quadrant

M South Street Souvlaki (509 South St., 215/925-3026), a busy, lively Greek eatery, was recommended by several Philadelphians, with good reason. It's open Tues.–Sun. 11:30 A.M.–9:15 P.M., Sat.–Sun. noon to 10:15 P.M., closed on Mon. The Greek specialties—gyros, souvlaki, grilled swordfish, roasted chicken, and kebabs—are delicious and well priced. It's often crowded, especially on Sun. night, when musicians play Greek

Restaurants surround the Chinatown gate.

© JOANNE MILLER

tunes. The menu features lots of choices; prices average $10 for lunch and $14 for dinner.

Rittenhouse Square Quadrant

Winner of multiple awards in Philadelphia for Thai cuisine, **My Thai** (2200 South St., 215/985-1878) serves fresh dishes, including steamed egg noodle with crabmeat and four comrades—a vegetarian dish. It's open 5 P.M.–10 P.M. daily during weekdays and 5 P.M. to 11 P.M. weekends. Expect to spend about $12 for dinner. This small, languid restaurant is decorated with Oriental wall hangings. My Thai has a full bar.

MARKETS AND FOOD COURTS

Franklin Square Quadrant/Old Town

The **M Reading Terminal Market** (12th and Filbert St., www.readingterminalmarket.org) is a place to find groceries, dry goods, and/or a restaurant. It's open 8 A.M.–6 P.M. Food prices range

Philadelphia

widely among the eateries, but expect to spend $5–10. Local favorites are the **12th Street Cantina** (215/625-0321) for Mexican food and **Delilah's** (215/574-0929) for soul food (Oprah Winfrey said Delilah's serves the best macaroni & cheese in the country).

Washington Square Quadrant

An area, as opposed to a place, the **Italian Market** is on 9th Street, extending roughly from Christian Street to Wharton Street. Year-round, merchants sell produce and goods on the sidewalks; in the winter, flaming trash cans warm hands all along the street. The Italian market was founded around the time of the Civil War, making it one of America's oldest outdoor ethnic markets. The shops on 9th Street are nothing special—it's the surrounding neighborhood that makes this area unique. One local retailer, **Cellini's** (1710 E. Passyunk Ave., 215/389-2244, www.cellinisgiftbaskets.com), was established in the 1920s as a family-owned grocery store and does a thriving business in gift baskets. Cellini's features a mind-boggling assortment of coffee, candies, nuts, and Italian foods in addition to a well-stocked deli.

Rittenhouse Square Quadrant

An upscale version of a shopping-mall food court, **Downstairs at the Bellevue** occupies the lower floor of the Bellevue Hotel (Broad and Walnut Sts.) and features a variety of eateries. It's possible to eat your way around the world in one afternoon. There's **Rocco's Famous Italian Hoagies** (877/846-2443, www.roccoshoagies.com) and **Asahi Sushi** (215/893-1211), among others. Prices vary widely, depending on the eatery.

PHILLY'S FINEST

The following restaurants are of note not only because several have been nationally recognized as the best in the country, but also because of their unusual ambience.

Franklin Square Quadrant/Old Town

Food at the Ritz (10 Ave. of the Arts) has embraced a more contemporary point of view with the move to Avenue of the Arts. **The Pantheon** (215/523-8000) serves an à la carte brunch and breakfast, featuring fresh American cuisine in an atmosphere conducive to business as well as a pleasant break from shopping or gallery hopping (daily 7–11:30 A.M., weekend brunch noon–2:30 P.M.; $16).

The Ritz Grill (215/523-8211) serves lunch (Mon.–Fri. 11:30 A.M.–2:30 P.M.) and dinner (Sun.–Thurs. 5:30–10 P.M., Fri.–Sat. 5:30–11 P.M.); the menu focus is on organic ingredients and Continental/American style. Patrons can expect such dishes as free-range chicken with papaya and red pepper salsa, and salads of pesticide-free mixed greens. The grill, keeping with the times, offers both heart-healthy and macrobiotic menus. Dining here is everything you'd expect from the Ritz—top service, elegant food, and beautiful presentation. Prices start at $23 and go up to $36.

M City Tavern (138 S. 2nd St., 215/413-1443, www.citytavern.com) is an accurate reconstruction of the 1773 original in which glasses were raised to celebrate the completion of the U.S. Constitution. Lunch is served beginning at 11:30 A.M., and dinner runs 4 P.M. (3 P.M. Sun.) until 10 P.M.

John Adams once called it the most genteel tavern in America. The servers wear colonial garb but keep amateurish attempts at period conversation to a minimum (the words "Hear Ye" and "libation" are infrequently used). The menu, based on authentic recipes, features dishes such as West Indies pepper-pot soup, roast duck with peach chutney, and English trifle. Loaves of the freshly baked and highly addictive cranberry nut, apple walnut, and pumpkin breads are available for takeout. Dishes average $15 for lunch and go as high as $38 for dinner.

Rittenhouse Square Quadrant

Philadelphia is well known for its restaurants, and **M Le Bec-Fin** (1523 Walnut St., 215/567-1000, www.lebecfin.com) is consistently the top-rated restaurant in the city (the Fountain in the Four Seasons Hotel is its most prominent rival). It's open Mon.–Fri. for lunch, 11:30 A.M.–2 P.M. and Mon.–Sat. for dinner 5:30 P.M.–10 P.M. by reservation only.

So what makes the experience of eating so special that the kitchen and chef that produce it unfailingly win a five-star rating from food critics and patrons alike?

The setting, a jewel box of a room the color of antique coral, could have been plucked from Versailles. Dining here is an event, but an oddly intimate one. Family groups out for a special celebration are seated beside businesspeople in suits, and tables of ladies who lunch; unlike "scene" restaurants, patrons are here to be with each other and share a wonderful meal. Waitstaff refer to patrons as monsieur, madame, or mademoiselle. Though this may sound like the kind of place that induces "am I using the right fork?" anxiety, the effect is just the opposite.

Owner/chef Georges Perrier is notoriously finicky in his own kitchen, so the ingredients and preparation are the best available. Perfectly cooked, artfully presented, thoughtfully served, and so delicious, each dish stays in the memory. Le Bec-Fin is an experience that I would recommend to everyone. The restaurant seats guests by reservation only. All meals are prix fixe and include all wines, meal courses, and a dessert trolley that's guaranteed to make a pig out of you. Both lunch and dinner feature a variety of appetizers and main courses to choose from. Lunch features an abbreviated menu (wine, selection of appetizer and main course, and dessert trolley and coffee or tea) and is one of the world's best values at $45, and a tasting platter for $70. Dinner is an extended six-course extravaganza of difficult choices and delightful wines, priced at $135, and a tasting menu at $155 (per person, available for the entire table only). Plan a long and luxurious evening at the table.

Downstairs from Le Bec-Fin, **Le Bar Lyonnais,** a separate bistro and bar, features several of Le Bec-Fin's famous signature dishes and a few innovations à la carte including the *galette de crabe* (crab cake) and grilled sirloin with white pepper sauce.

Perrier's other establishment, **Brasserie Perrier** (1619 Walnut St., 215/568-3000) features a very social bar and a sophisticated menu in a more relaxed atmosphere. The average entrée is

$30–45. It's open Mon.–Fri. 11:30 A.M.–midnight, Sat. 6 P.M.–1 A.M.

Logan Circle Quadrant

Both **The Fountain** and the **Swann Lounge,** inside the Four Seasons hotel (1 Logan Circle, 215/963-1500), have won multiple awards from *Food and Wine* and *Condé Nast Traveler* magazines, among others. Swiss-trained executive chef Jean-Marie Lacroix has innovated on the usual French-influenced menu by introducing a Japanese breakfast and late-night Viennese buffet. The Fountain is open for breakfast Mon.–Fri. 6:30 A.M.–11 A.M., Sat. 7 A.M.–11 A.M., Sun. 7 A.M.–10:30 A.M. (brunch served until 2 P.M.); lunch Mon.–Sat. 11:30 A.M.–2:30 A.M.; and dinner daily 5:45–10 P.M.

The more casual Swann Lounge is open for lunch daily 11:30 A.M.–2 P.M., high tea Mon.–Sat. 3 P.M.–4:15 P.M.; live entertainment, dancing and a Viennese dessert buffet Fri.–Sat 9 P.M.–1 A.M.; and Sun. brunch 10 A.M.–2 P.M. Both restaurants are elegant, yet intimate—the Fountain is the more formal of the two, filled with expensively attired men and women all through the day. Prices are similar to the Ritz.

VEGETARIAN

Washington Square Quadrant

In business since 1969, **Ⓜ Essene Market & Café** (719 S. 4th St., 215/922-1146, www.essenemarket.com, Sun.–Tues., Thurs., and Sat. 9 A.M.–8 P.M., Wed. and Fri. 9 A.M.–9 P.M.) has provided the area's largest selection of organically grown produce and natural products. A multiple "Best of Philly"–winning natural foods café serves gourmet delights every day, including dairy-free, refined-sugar-free sweets from its on-site bakery.

Rittenhouse Square Quadrant

Govinda's Gourmet Vegetarian (1408 South St., 215/985-9335, Wed.–Mon. 11 A.M.–9 P.M., $9) offers tasty vege versions of your favorite Indian foods, including several varieties of curries and dosas (stuffed pancakes).

Greater Philadelphia

There's much to be found beyond the borders of Center City. University City, so named because it is the home of several of Philadelphia's academies of higher learning, lies west just across the Schuylkill River. The incomparable Barnes Foundation is on the city line just outside Fairmount Park in Merion Station. Wissahickon Valley, the northern extension of Fairmount Park, is a wild place close to the city. Close by, Manayunk, Germantown, and Chestnut Hill, once independent townships, are now also listed under Philadelphia addresses.

UNIVERSITY CITY

The University of Pennsylvania Museum of Archaeology and Anthropology

This museum (33rd and Spruce Sts., University City, 215/898-4001, www.museum.upenn.edu) covers the cultural history of the world with artifacts ranging from Egyptian mummies to American Indian kachinas. It's open Tues.–Sat. 10 A.M.–4:30 P.M. and Sun. 1–5 P.M., closed Memorial Day–Labor Day. Admission is $8; over 52, students with ID, and children over 6, $5; free on Sun.

Some of the sculptural pieces are stunning, such as the head of Ramses II in the Lower Egypt gallery, and Buddha flanked by the Bodhisattvas of Wisdom (astride a lion) and Goodness (riding an elephant) in the Buddhism gallery. There are sections on Biblical and Islamic archaeology, the ancient Greek world, Africa, Polynesia, and the American Southwest, as well. Temporary exhibits have included artifacts from the royal tombs of Ur (Mesopotamia/Iraq) and mystical Huichol yarn paintings (Mexico).

The Institute of Contemporary Art

Located at the University of Pennsylvania, the institute (118 South 36th St. at Sansom, 215/898-7108, www.icaphila.org) is open Wed.–Fri. noon–8 P.M., Sat.–Sun. 11 A.M.–5 P.M., closed Mon.–Tues.; admission is $3 adults, $2 children over 12 and senior citizens; free on Sun. 11 A.M.–1 P.M. ICA is *the* local venue for well-known modern artists such as Andy Warhol and Bruce Connor. Exhibitions bring together painters, photographers and sculptors to explore a theme or an idea.

Shopping

Next door to the White Dog Café, the **Black Cat** (3426 Sansom St., 215/386-6664) sells a wide and thoughtful selection of objects for the home, handicrafts, and paper goods.

Accommodations

The exception to the plain-but-comfortable B&B rule: **The Gables Bed and Breakfast** (4520 Chester Ave. at S. 46th St., 215/662-1918, www.gablesbb.com). This beautifully renovated Victorian mansion, a former Jesuit boarding home, is located south of the University of Pennsylvania campus in University City. The interior is as authentic and elegant as any of the destination lodgings out of town. Two of the rooms share a bath, and eight have private baths—all are comfortable and pretty. Visitors wake up in the treetops in the Christmas Room on the third floor; the decor carries the theme down to the starry sheers on the windows and Victorian ornaments on the room's permanent tree. Parking is easier here than in Center City, and a local trolley line runs right outside the front door. The neighborhood is a comfortable mix of races and income levels, students and families. A bountiful breakfast is included. Prices range $85–135.

Food

A University City gem, **Dahlak Restaurant** (4708 Baltimore Ave., 215/726-6464) serves foods from Eritrea and Ethiopia. It's open daily, 4 P.M.–10:30 P.M.; dinner entrées average $11. Dahlak is a dark little place, and the tables are filled with all nationalities, chatting in a dozen languages, enjoying selections from the singular menu. The restaurant is easy to miss from the street; only the address above the door and a menu placed casually inside the front glass window confirms that this is indeed Dahlak.

Yemisir alicha, lentils in mild sauce; *kay watt,* beef in berbere sauce; and *shro,* garbanzo beans in Dahlak sauce, are a few of the unique stew-like dishes. All are served with a thin, spongy pancake-like bread, a perfect complement to soak up the flavorful sauces. The tastes are unusual and uniformly delicious; try one of the mixed plates to get a feel for this special cuisine.

The White Dog Café (3420 Sansom St., 215/386-9224, www.whitedog.com) is an exceptional college café, socially conscious and sophisticated. It's open Mon.–Sat. 11:30–2:30 for lunch; Mon.–Thurs. 5:30–10 P.M. and Fri.–Sat. 5:30–11 P.M. for dinner (the grill is open from 2:30 until closing). The bar is open daily until 2 A.M. Lunch prices are around $8–12, dinner prices range $15–26.

The unusual name comes from an event that took place in 1875, involving a former resident of the building, Madame Helena P. Blavatsky. Madame B., an eccentric spiritualist who founded the Theosophical Society, became ill with an infection in her leg. After dismissing the surgeon who advised amputation, she cured herself in a few days by making her white dog lie across the infected area at night.

The restaurant hosts many community-focused special events such as lecture/breakfasts, Tuesday-night storytelling, and a Native American Thanksgiving dinner. The menu is wide-ranging, from hamburgers and Chinese chicken salad for lunch to artfully prepared fish, meat, and vegetarian entrées for dinner; there is also a piano parlor for late-night dinners.

For a quick snack and a great view, go to the **30th Street Station** (Market St. between 29th and 30th Sts.), the largest existing and second most-active railway station in America. There are dozens of fast-food shops, and the soaring ceiling of this eight-story building, on the National Register of Historic Places, will give you a new concept of "big." Built in 1934, this stately landmark is the home of the corporate offices for Amtrak.

THE BARNES FOUNDATION

In a city known for the quality of its art, the Barnes Foundation (300 N. Latch's Lane, Merion Station, Montgomery County, 610/667-0290, www.barnesfoundation.org) stands out as the world's premier private collection of French modern and postimpressionist paintings. The foundation is open to the public on a reservation-only basis Sept.–June Fri.–Sun. 9:30 A.M.–2 P.M., July and Aug. Wed.–Fri. 9:30–2 P.M. Admission is $5 per person, ages 3 and up; non-refundable. Admission is by reservation only; 30-day advance recommendation; no walk-ups.

Expect to see 180 works by Renoir, 69 by Cezanne, 60 by Matisse, and hundreds more by Picasso, Seurat, Modigliani, van Gogh, Rousseau, and every other notable painter during the period—a total of 800 paintings in all. The collection also displays works by Dutch, Italian, French, Spanish, German, Flemish, Chinese, Persian, Greek, Egyptian, and American artists; African sculpture; antique furniture; ceramics; and hand-wrought ironwork. Prepare to be overwhelmed—these are first-quality works, many of which have been seen only in reproduction.

The art is not displayed in a traditional museum manner. Apparently unrelated works of art, sculpture, and craftsmanship are grouped into 96 wall ensembles. Because the artwork was (and is) used as a teaching tool, the walls illustrate Dr. Barnes's specific educational theories.

The foundation was chartered as a privately endowed, nonprofit education institution by the Commonwealth of Pennsylvania in 1922 and continues to offer a two-year course. Requirements for admission are democratic indeed: no prior knowledge of art is necessary, but students must attend lectures and seminars regularly and on time and complete assignments. Annual tuition is $200 per year (students enrolled in secondary schools or college are exempt), and scholarships are available. Letters of application should be sent to Acting Director of Education, Art Department of the Barnes Foundation, Merion, PA 19066. The Barnes Foundation also includes a 12-acre arboretum, used in a horticultural education program established by Mrs.

THE VISIONARY DR. BARNES

Albert Barnes, son of a butcher, grew up in the working-class Philadelphia neighborhood of Kensington and graduated from the University of Pennsylvania medical school in 1893 at the age of 21. He worked his way through not one but two internships, finally acknowledging that the active practice of medicine was not for him. Instead, he studied pharmacology in Heidelberg, Germany, where he met his future business partner, Herman Hille. With Hille, and later on his own, Dr. Barnes amassed a considerable personal fortune through the manufacture and marketing of pharmaceutical products. Argyrol, a silver-based antiseptic developed by Hille and Barnes, was widely used before the discovery of penicillin, particularly in the treatment of eye inflammations in newborns.

The art collection that today bears Barnes's name came about not through a desire to collect or an emotional attachment to the work, but rather through the doctor's lifelong interest in education and his convictions that educational deficits were the root cause of personal and social problems and that an educated society was the cornerstone of democracy. Barnes cut the work schedule of his employees to six hours a day and established classes for them in his Argyrol factory—classes that discussed the works of American philosopher/psychologist William James, among other things.

Collaborating with like-minded thinkers such as Bertrand Russell and John Dewey, Dr.

Barnes developed a course based on the study of aesthetics:

[The] course comprises an objective study of the great traditions of painting, from the Byzantines to the work of the leading contemporaries, thus showing the continuity of the traditions and how the great artists of each period utilized the contributions of their predecessors as points of departure for their own creative work.

Barnes sought to promote an objective analysis of each work rather than provoking an emotional response. He summed up his thoughts on art as a teaching tool:

If the creative impulse leaves its mark in a material that generates similar feelings in other people, the work of art is a human document of permanent work. Its degree of worth is determined by the extent to which the artist has enriched, improved, humanized, the common experience of man in the world in which he lives.

Dr. Barnes died in 1951, leaving stewardship of the still-active foundation to Lincoln University, the country's first African-American university. Through this act, Barnes hoped to realize his original dream for the foundation—to educate people from all walks of life.

Barnes in 1940. Classes are given once a week for three years. For admission information, write to Arboretum of the Barnes Foundation, 300 N. Latch's Lane, Merion, PA 19066.

The Barnes Foundation remained a private educational institution until 1961, after a lawsuit brought by the attorney general requesting public access was settled out of court. The buildings were closed between 1993 and 1995 for renovation, and a selection of the paintings was displayed in various art museums around the world for the first time.

The foundation is just over the Philadelphia city line. There is on-site parking for $10. Driving is easier, as transportation from Center City requires at least one transfer via SEPTA bus plus 15 minutes of walking, or two transfers via bus and light rail—and about 15 minutes of walking. If you're planning to take public transportation, look up the route on the SEPTA website (www.septa.org/inside/travel.html) or call 215/580-7800 and press 0 to speak to a travel information agent during normal business hours.

WISSAHICKON VALLEY

Most of Wissahickon Valley's 1,400 rural acres are part of the northwest extension of Fairmount Park. The valley separates the densely packed communities of Manayunk and Chestnut Hill, among others, and is home to the Andorra Natural Area, off Northwestern Avenue. Forbidden Drive (accessed from Wissahickon Drive), a five-mile dirt path, is open to recreational use but not automobiles. Numerous paths connect with Forbidden Drive, winding through the area. Wissahickon Creek bisects the entire length of Fairmount Park. Parking is available on Lincoln Drive, Valley Green Road, and Bell's Mill Road.

Food

The **Valley Green Inn** (Wissahickon Dr. at Springfield Ave., 215/247-1730, www.valley-greeninn.com) looks over Wissahickon Creek and a stone bridge, and the three dining rooms in the 1850s-built edifice are decorated with old photos and antique clocks. It's open Mon.–Fri. noon–4 P.M. for lunch; 5–9 P.M. (10 P.M. on Fri.) for dinner; Sat., lunch 11 A.M.–4 P.M., dinner 5–10 P.M.; Sun. brunch 10 A.M.–3 P.M., dinner 5–9 P.M. The bar is open Sun.–Thurs. until 11 P.M., Fri.–Sat. until midnight. Prices average $8 for lunch, $25 for dinner. The food used to be standard American, but the kitchen has gotten an influx of new talent, and the menu features dishes such as farm-raised Chilean sea bass, coated with a crunchy pistachio breading, topped with a gingered roast pepper, cilantro-lime butter, with seasonal vegetables and homemade mashed potatoes ($23) and grilled wild boar tenderloin with cherry-apricot compote, served with sweet potato ($32)—so it's not just the setting that brings people out to eat here anymore.

MANAYUNK

Manayunk, translated as "where we go to drink" in Lenni Lenape, still carries meaning for many Philadelphians. The town, within the boundaries of suburban Philadelphia, is the site of former textile mills on the Schuylkill River northeast of the city. It has found new life as an all-inclusive getaway destination (find out the latest at www.manayunk.com), capturing several "Best of Philly" awards for both shopping and food from readers of *Philadelphia Magazine*.

There's plenty of public parking, and SEPTA (Southeastern Pennsylvania Transportation Au-

thority) runs the 61 bus direct from Center City to Manayunk. The R6 train (Norristown line) is another easy option from Center City.

Shopping

Main Street is lined with a wide variety of shops. A few of the specialty shops found in downtown Philly, such as **Indigo** crafts and **Maidie Franklin** jewelry, have opened branches here, but most stores are boutiques.

Home design is well represented by members of the **Manayunk Design District,** 20–30 different shops and showrooms on Main Street and its side streets (for a map, click on www.manayunkdesigndistrict.com). Three members are **Charles Tiles** (4401 Main St., 215/482-8440), featuring hand-painted tiles from Italy for the home, the **Owen/Patrick Gallery** (4345 Main St., 215/482-9395, www.owenpartick.com), fine art and furniture, and **Ligne Roset** (4131 Main St., 215/487-2800), featuring an ultramodern furniture line.

Fine art is covered by **ArtForms Gallery Manayunk** (106 Levering St., 215/483-3030, www.artforms.org), a 25-artist cooperative gallery, among others. Shoe and clothing shops, import shops, and bath and body shops abound.

Manayunk Farmers' Market takes place during the warm season at the end of Lock Street, Wed.–Sat. 8 A.M.–7 P.M., Sun. 9 A.M.–6 P.M.

Food and Nightlife

There's no lack of places to eat. On the low end, **Manayunk Coffeehouse** (4311 Main St., 215/487-3927) serves local Buck's County Coffee, along with light sandwiches and baked goods.

M Manayunk Brewery (4120 Main St., 215/482-8220, www.manayunkbrewery.com) is in one of Manayunk's original buildings, Krook's Mill, one of several textile mills in the area during the 1800s. An antique scale in the downstairs pub was used to weigh wool brought into the factory. The comfortable dining room is an option, but in fine weather, choose the outside deck. The menu offers sushi as well as rotisserie-grilled meats and poultry, plus a full selection of their own handcrafted beers and ales and a full bar. For lunch, try the grilled meatloaf ($10), served with mushroom demi-glace, beer-battered fries, and cole slaw; or rotisserie chicken pot pie ($9), served with field greens. Dinner might include St. Louis Ribs ($13 or $20), dry-rubbed with special seasonings, hickory smoked in-house, and served with or without BBQ glaze; or Harry's cedar plank salmon filet grilled, then roasted on an aromatic cedar plank, with Bing cherry glaze, served with basmati rice pilaf and sautéed fresh vegetables ($18). Lunch entrees average $10, dinner $22. Open for lunch Mon.–Sat. 11 A.M.– 5 P.M., Sun. 1–5 P.M., dinner Mon.–Thurs. 5–10 P.M. (late fare served until 11 P.M.), Fri.–Sat. 5–11 P.M. (late fare served until 2 A.M.), Sun. 5–9 P.M.; the sushi bar is open during dinner hours. The Sunday brunch buffet is accompanied by live jazz 10:30 A.M.–2:30 P.M.

Jake's (4365 Main St., 215/483-0444, www .jakesrestaurant.com) has been a local favorite for several years. House specialties from the dinner menu include port-glazed pan-roasted quail with sweet pepper and cabbage stuffing, sweet potato and frisee salad ($24); and sautéed jumbo lump crab cakes with green beans and fried yams ($27.50). Lunch averages $11, dinner $24. Open Mon.–Thurs. and Sun. 11:30 A.M.–2:30 P.M. and 5:30–9:30 P.M. (until 10:30 P.M. Fri.), Sat. 11:30 A.M.–2 P.M. and 5–10:30 P.M.

Since 1993, the nightly drink specials at **Bayou Bar and Grill** (4245 Main St., 215/482-2560, www.thebayoubar.com, Mon.–Fri. 4 P.M.–2 A.M., Sat.–Sun. noon–2 A.M.) bring in a big after-work crowd, which stays for the restaurant's Cajun-influenced tavern-style menu. You'll find jambalaya, gumbo, Creole chili, hard-shell crabs, big burgers, and "Best of Philly" spicy buffalo wings. Dinner averages $8.

Though it looks more like a funky stone tavern than a princely dwelling, **Castle Roxx** (105 Shurs Ln., 215/482-9000, www.castleroxx.com, Tues.–Thurs. 6 P.M.–2 A.M., Fri.–Sat. 5 P.M.– 2 A.M., Sun. noon–2 A.M., closed Mon.) delivers on its original concept of serving good American food in a low-key and casual local setting. It serves an eight-ounce filet Mignon with home fries and spinach rabe for $18.50, a rack of ribs for $11 or $18, and Italian specialties such as

eggplant Parmigiana ($15). There's also a kid's menu, but expect the bar scene to liven up later in the evening. Prices average $15.

GERMANTOWN

Germantown is all about history; Revolutionary War, history to be exact (or the First Civil War, as Britons refer to it). The Battle of Germantown was fought on October 4, 1777, between Colonial forces under the command of General George Washington and British and Hessian troops under Sir William Howe. The British had occupied Philadelphia since September and their army was encamped in Germantown. Washington launched a surprise attack against the encampment, and at dawn in the midst of a heavy fog, advanced into Germantown by two roads, with General Nathanael Greene leading the detachment on the left and General John Sullivan on the right. Sullivan's forces were successful at first, forcing the enemy back; a group of British soldiers took refuge in the Chew mansion (Cliveden, below), and a colonial detachment attempted to dislodge them. Mean-

THE PENNSYLVANIA POET

Francis Daniel Pastorius, founder of Germantown, was considered one of the finest poets of the late 17th century. This verse is from his manuscript *The Beehive:*

If thou wouldest Roses Scent
Mend, and make more excellent,
Then thou formerly hadst them;
Plant but Garlick to their Stem;
Likewise, if a Friend of thine
Should to Goodness so incline,
As to lead a Vertuous life,
Let him take a Scolding Wife;
Thus Natura works, you see
Sometimes by Antipathy.

Philadelphia

while, a detachment under the command of Greene had been drawn too far toward the right wing, and in the confusion, mistook the firing in the vicinity of the Chew house for an enemy attack, they opened fire on their own troops. This incident threw the Colonial forces into a panic and forced a retreat. Although the attack itself had failed, Washington's ability to take the offensive so soon after his defeat at Brandywine encouraged the colonies in their efforts to free themselves and led to the decisive alliance with France.

Germantown Historic District

The Germantown Historic district extends for more than 20 blocks along Germantown Avenue between Upsal Street and 18th Street. It encompasses nearly 500 small-scale commercial and residential buildings. Within the district boundaries there are over 50 important early American sites, which document a full range of the social, political, and architectural history of early Germantown. Most well known among the district's buildings are the Colonial and Federal houses, especially the palatial and largely restored mansions such as Cliveden (below), and others—Upsala, Wyck, Vernon, and Loudon among them—that reflect the most advanced architectural design of the period. Those that are open to the public are noted. For an excellent map and information on more historic sites in the area, visit the website www.ushistory.org/Germantown.

The original back part of **Upsala** (6430 Germantown Ave., across from Cliveden, 215/842-1798) was built around 1740, the remainder in 1797. An excellent example of Federal architecture, the house has been partially restored. Of note are the graceful and seemingly unsupported staircase to the third floor, splendid wooden mantels, delicately carved and faced with Pennsylvania marble, and Sheraton and Hepplewhite period furniture.

Wyck (6026 Germantown Ave., 215/848-1690, www.wyck.org, April–mid-Dec. Tues. and Thurs., noon–4:30 P.M., Sat. 1–4 P.M.; adults $5, students and seniors $4, families $10) was home to nine generations of a Quaker family, the

Haines. The oldest home in Germantown, this colonial house sports alterations from 1824, historic gardens including beds of old roses from the 1820s, and several outbuildings used on the original farm. Visitors will view original family furnishings, 18th- and 19th-century furniture, ceramics, and needlework.

Vernon Park (on the west side of the Germantown Ave. just north of Chelten Ave.) contains a variety of buildings and monuments including **Vernon,** the Wister Mansion (not currently open to the public). The house was built in 1803. At one time part of the park was owned by Melchior Meng, a horticulturalist whose gardens were noted for their rare trees and shrubs. During the Battle of Germantown, the house was occupied by injured soldiers, selected as a hospital because of numerous barrels of vinegar in the cellar, which were used to stanch the flow of blood.

Loudoun (4650 Germantown Ave.) is one of the Federal glories of Germantown (it's currently closed due to damage from a fire). Built about 1801, the house was named after Loudoun County, Virginia, where the original owner first settled when he came to America from England. Five generations of one family are reflected in the changing styles and fashions in the decorative arts, including furniture and paintings of the 18th and early 19th centuries, the later Victorian period, and the 20th century. Had Philadelphia remained the nation's capital, the capitol itself would have been built where Loudoun now stands.

Rittenhousetown

The historic mansions of Germantown are in stark contrast to the setting, scale, and lack of embellishment of the modest stucco and wood-trim tenant houses of the era, such as the John Rittenhouse houses (5900 Germantown Ave. at Rittenhouse St.). Nearby, in Fairmount Park, at the end of Harvey Street in Germantown, is the site of the Rittenhouse family's wealth (206 Lincoln Dr., 215/438-5711, www.rittenhousetown.org; May–Sept. Sat.–Sun. noon–4 P.M.; Oct.–April by appointment only; adults $5, children and seniors $3): the first paper mill in

North America (1690), built by William Rittenhouse, leader of a Mennonite community. His son, David Rittenhouse, mathematician, astronomer, and first president of the United States Mint, was born at the site in 1732. The Rittenhouse family continued to live on the site for over 150 years.

By the early 19th century, the mill had developed into Rittenhousetown, a small self-sufficient industrial community including homesteads, workers' cottages, the paper-mill complex, a church, a school, and a firehouse. The 30-acre site was declared a National Historic Landmark District in 1992. Five of the original buildings are open to the public.

Cliveden of the National Trust

The musket burns are still in evidence at this, the home of Benjamin Chew (6401 Germantown Ave., 215/848-1777, www.cliveden.org, April–Dec. Thurs.–Sun. noon–4 P.M.; adults $8, students $6, free under age 6). Mr. Chew was not a colonial patriot; though he signed the colonies' nonimportation agreement protesting King George's taxes, he refused to relinquish his crown-appointed position as chief justice of colonial Pennsylvania's Supreme Court. Chew spent his youth in England, and Cliveden is named after the country estate of Frederick, Prince of Wales.

Considered a Loyalist threat to the American cause, he was absent from the house during the Battle of Germantown, under house arrest in New Jersey; he wisely laid low through the remainder of the war. Chew returned to public life in federal Philadelphia by the late 1780s. Though forced to sell the house at one point, he repurchased it, and his family remained in Cliveden for eight generations.

German craftsmen built the house of local stone, carefully cut in blocks that got progressively shorter from foundation to roof to exaggerate the building's height. Cliveden's interior reflected its owner's wealth and aspirations. The entrance hall, with its screen of four Doric columns and elaborate woodwork, echoed Chew's court chambers in the Pennsylvania State House (now Independence Hall). The parlor's

decorative carving was produced by the same master craftsmen responsible for Philadelphia's finest Chippendale furniture. Although alterations occurred over the years, Benjamin Chew's eighteenth-century house remains remarkably intact thanks to deliberate efforts by the family to preserve furnishings and architecture.

Germantown Historical Society and Museum

A good place to soak up three centuries of history (5501–03 Germantown Ave., 215/844-0514, www.germantownhistory.org, Tues. and Thurs. 9 A.M.–5 P.M., Sun. 1–5 P.M.; adults $5, seniors and students $4, children $2), the museum's extensive collections include furniture such as 17th-century German trunks, Colonial highboys, tall case clocks, and Victorian chairs, plus Peale family paintings, and quilts, coverlets, and bedspreads dating from the 18th century, hundreds of varieties of needlework, dye cards from Germantown textile mills, and hundreds of Germantown and Quaker samplers dating from the early 1700s. The Society's costume collection is comprised of more than 8,000 pieces of clothing for every age and sex. Researchers for period films could make a home here. Call and try to join a tour (arranged for groups of 10 or more) between March–Dec. The $10-per-person fee includes guides and admission to several historic buildings in the Germantown/Chestnut Hill area.

CHESTNUT HILL

Chestnut Hill (www.chestnuthillpa.com) is an anglophile's dream. When the Pennsylvania Railroad extended service to this small farm village in the mid-1850s, the railroad commissioned architects George and William Hewitt to design and construct an elegant planned community. The Hewitts' tastes ran to English Gothic, and, as a result, Chestnut Hill has a London-by-way-of-the-Berkshires feel. The entire town is now a National Historic District. Many of the homes, businesses, and churches were built by Italian stoneworkers around 1900 and still stand tall on this, the highest point in the city. The cobbled streets offer a pleasant stroll during sunny weather, and the variety of shops and eateries make this a day-trip destination.

Parking lots are abundant, and parking is free with a validated purchase from local merchants. The town is an easy rail ride from Center City on R8, Chestnut Hill West, or R7, Chestnut Hill East.

Morris Arboretum of the University of Pennsylvania

This fascinating park (100 Northwestern Ave., 215/247-5777, www.business-services.upenn .edu/arboretum) is a 92-acre center that showcases more than 4000 trees and shrubs. It's open April–Oct. Mon.–Fri. 10 A.M.–4 P.M., Sat.–Sun. 10 A.M.–5 P.M., and Nov.–March daily 10 A.M.– 4 P.M. Admission is $8 adults, seniors 65 and better and students with ID $6, children 3–12 $3; children under 3 are admitted for free.

The grounds feature statuary, "follies"—fanciful garden buildings—a Victorian house fernery, and a pint sized railway complete with miniature building displays that change annually. The Garden Railway operates mid-June–first week in Oct. June Aug., on Thurs., the arboretum remains open until 8:30 P.M. (the display is open until 8 P.M.). The railway is free with admission to the arboretum.

Guided tours for the public are held on Saturday and Sunday year-round at 2 P.M. These tours are free with admission. Other tours are available by reservation (215/247-5777 ext. 157).

The Morris Arboretum began in 1887 as "Compton," the summer home of two Quakers, brother and sister John and Lydia Morris. As heirs of an iron-manufacturing firm, the Morris siblings were able to travel the world, bringing artwork, crafts and plants back to Compton. They established a tradition of placing sculpture in the garden that continues today. Listed on The National Register of Historic Places, the grounds are recognized as the official arboretum of the Commonwealth of Pennsylvania. Thousands of rare and lovely woody plants, including many of Philadelphia's oldest, rarest, and largest trees, are set in a romantic Victorian landscape garden of winding paths, streams, flowers, and special garden areas.

The Garden Railway Display is set in the splendor of the summer garden, featuring tunnels, overhead trestles, and historic buildings created entirely of natural materials, each meticulously detailed with leaves, bark, vines, and twigs (one exhibit celebrated lighthouses). Families and horticultural enthusiasts should not miss the opportunity to enjoy this special garden.

Woodmere Art Museum

A local stop to enjoy regional artists (9201 Germantown Ave., 215/247-0476, www.woodmereartmuseum.org), Woodmere's permanent collection includes over 300 paintings and sculptures in addition to prints and drawings. Expect to view artwork by Philadelphia-based artists of every style and era, such as Daniel Garber, Thomas Pollock Anshutz, Edward Moran, Violet Oakley, Nelson Shanks, Benjamin West, and N. C. Wyeth. The museum is open Tues.–Sat. 10 A.M.–5 P.M., Sun. 1–5 P.M., closed Mon. and major holidays. Admission is adults $5, seniors and students $3; children under 12 get in free.

Shopping

Though the architecture in itself is reason for visiting, a variety of smart shops and cafés line the main street, Germantown Avenue. The shops, like the town, are elegant and upscale, and prices reflect it.

There are candle shops, bath and body shops, and all manner of small and charming places to wander through. A few of note:

The **Antique Gallery** (8523 Germantown Ave., 215/248-1700) features an assortment of antique furniture, and decorative arts. Prices and quality vary at **Bird in Hand Consignments** (8419 Germantown Ave., 215/248-2473), but you'll also find a large assortment of collectibles, china, crystal, pictures, jewelry, linen, and small furniture.

The **Philadelphia Print Shop** (8441 Germantown Ave., 215/242-4750, www.philaprintshop.com) handles a wide selection of antique prints, maps, and rare reference books.

O'Doodles Toy Store (8335 Germantown Ave., 215/247-7405) carries delightful toys for children up to age 12.

Chestnut Hill also has a small **farmers' market** behind the Chestnut Hill Hotel (8229 Germantown Ave.). It's in full swing Thurs.–Fri. 9 A.M.–6 P.M. and Sat. 8 A.M.–4 P.M. A peaceful place to enjoy a takeout lunch is Pastorius Park, two blocks south of Germantown Ave. on Hartwell Lane.

Accommodations

M Silverstone Bed & Breakfast (8840 Stenton Ave., 215/242-1471, www.silverstonestay.com) is set in a 19th-century mansion in a residential neighborhood. Rooms are equipped with cable TV, VCR and private bathrooms, and a kitchen and laundry room are available for the use of guests, as are the back yard and kitchen garden. This is a family-friendly B&B, within walking distance of Chestnut Hill. Rooms and suites range $60–140 per night, and Silverstone also lets out modern two- and three-bedroom apartments nearby in Chestnut Hill ($110–130 per night, less for longer stays).

Anam Cara Bed & Breakfast (52 Wooddale Ave., 215/242-4327, www.anamcarabandb.com) is in an attractive, quiet home just off Germantown Avenue. The comfortably decorated rooms all have private baths, and long-term-stay apartments are also available. Overnight rates range $105–125 and include breakfast.

An old favorite for all the right reasons, the **M Chestnut Hill Hotel** (8229 Germantown Ave., 215/242-5905, www.chestnuthillhotel.com) offers the charm of a B&B (and the breakfast, too) with the convenience of a modern hotel. Twenty-eight rooms and suites, all with private bath and modern amenities, are decorated in 18th-century style. The location affords easy access to Chestnut Hill; choose a room in the back if you're a light sleeper. Rooms range $109–149, suites $140–179.

Food

For a morning coffee break or light snack at lunch ($10 or less), try the **French Bakery & Café** (8624 Germantown Ave., Rear, 215/247-5959), known for baked goods, and the **Labrador Café** (8137 Germantown Ave., 215/248-5190), for a variety of snacks and heartier fare served in a lovely garden. Also of note, **Roller's Expresso** (8341 Germantown Ave., 215/247-7715) serves salads, sandwiches, and ice cream.

The **M Trolley Car Diner** (7619 Germantown Ave., 215/753-1500, www.trolleycardiner.com, Mon.–Fri. 7 A.M.–9 P.M., Sat. 7 A.M.–10 P.M., Sun. 8 A.M.–9 P.M.) has everything you're looking for, including good food, prices, and a real trolley-car entrance. Breakfast averages $5, and you'll find cornmeal-fried fish and grits with two eggs ($7) on the menu, along with conventional favorites. For lunch ($6) you can order a roasted vegetable grinder ($7), or lump crab cake sandwich ($7.50). Dinner ($10) might include pot roast with roasted vegetables with mashed potatoes and gravy ($11) or vegetarian chili ($9). A good place for the family, anytime.

The **Cresheim Cottage Café** (7402 Germantown Ave., 215/248-4365, www.cresheimcottage.com, lunch Mon.–Sat. 11:30 A.M.–2:30 P.M., dinner Sun.–Thurs. 5–9 P.M., Fri.–Sat. 5–10 P.M., Sun. brunch 10 A.M.–2 P.M.) is not only set in an historic and pretty stone building, but the food is good, too. The property was built by German settlers from the Rhine Valley on land purchased from William Penn in 1683. Lunch averages $12, and the menu features such delights as jumbo lump crab and avocado fritatta ($12) and seafood stew with shrimp, scallops, and mussels over risotto in a saffron tomato broth ($16). Dinner averages $16, and menu items include eggplant rolls (eggplant stuffed with ricotta cheese, roasted peppers and arugula, $12) and organic chicken and dumplings ($16).

Unpretentious **Roller's** (8705 Germantown Ave., 215/242-1771, www.rollersrestaurants.com) sits in a small shopping plaza behind Border's Bookstore at the corner of Germantown Avenue and Bethlehem Pike. It's been a local favorite for several years. Lunch (average price $8) is served Tues.–Fri. 11:30 A.M.–2:30 P.M. and Sat. noon–

2:30 P.M.; dinner (average price $20) is Tues.–Thurs. 5:30–9 P.M., Fri.–Sat. 5:30–10 P.M. and Sun. 5–9 P.M. July–Sept. the restaurant is closed on Sun. The menu features American food with a twist: a veggie burger with tomato, grilled Vidalia onions and jalapeno jack cheese on multigrain bread ($7.25), and broiled filet of beef with Roquefort butter and a grilled Vidalia onion cake ($24.75). There are daily lunch specials ($6) and dinner specials ($11). A caveat—this is a cash-only restaurant.

M Stella Notte Steakhouse & Trattoria (8229 Germantown Ave., 215/247-2100, www.stellanotte.com, Sun. and Tues.–Thurs. 5–9 P.M., Fri.–Sat. 5–10:30 P.M.), inside the Chestnut Hill Hotel, has long been a local favorite for moderately priced Italian food, brick-oven pizzas and steaks. Entrées average $16.

Information and Services

Tourist Services

For a recorded message and to request printed materials on the city (Philadelphia Trip Planner), call the **Greater Philadelphia Tourism Marketing Corporation** (30 S. 17th St., Suite 1710, Philadelphia, PA 19103, 888/GOPHILA, www.gophila.com). You'll reach a live person (eventually) at 215/599-0776—but it's much faster to download the trip planner from the Web, and the site is full of good information. In town, the Independence Visitors Center (6th and Market Sts., 215/965-7676 or 800/537-7676) is a treasure trove of information and brochures. **Philadelphia Convention & Visitors Bureau** (1700 Market St., Ste. 3000, Philadelphia, PA 19103, 215/636-3300, www.pcvb.org) is another resource.

Another useful website is www.digitalcity.com/Philadelphia, AOL's cityguide with lots of useful information on venues.

Emergencies

Ambulance, firefighters, and police may be reached in emergencies by dialing 911. For dental emergencies, call 215/925-6050 for a referral; for medical emergencies, call 215/563-5343. The Poison Control Center may be reached at 215/386-2100; the rape/crisis hotline number is 215/985-3333.

Newspapers

The Pulitzer Prize–winning *Philadelphia Inquirer* has a local/world focus and is published daily. It has a Weekend section in the Friday edition that chronicles upcoming events. The *Philadelphia Daily News* is published Mon.–Sat., emphasizing city news and sports.

Specialty: *The Philadelphia Tribune*, with editions on Tuesday, Thursday, and Friday, is aimed toward the city's African-Americans. *Business Philadelphia* chronicles happenings in the business community, and *PGN (Philadelphia Gay News)* caters to gays and lesbians.

Free: The *City Paper*, found in bookstores, record shops, and hotels all over town, is an excellent source of nightlife and entertainment listings for the current week. The *Forum* bills itself as a marketplace for ideas and opinions, and also carries advertising and event listings. *Metrokids* and *Parents Express* feature monthly listings of family-oriented events. Historic Philadelphia, Inc. publishes *The Town Crier* six times a year, listing a wide variety of history-related events, most of them free.

Personal Safety

Downtown Philadelphia, despite its notoriety for shaky race relations, presents a well-integrated and friendly face to the traveler during the day, at least in Old Town, Center City, and University City, where visitors are most likely to be. That face may quickly turn unfriendly in north, west, and southwest Philly to strangers who don't know where they're going. Don't wander about aimlessly in these residential areas.

Generally, the attractions away from Center City—Manayunk and Chestnut Hill, for example—are more benign. However, wherever tourists gather, there's always an open invitation for opportunists. In Center City, it's wise to follow standard city procedure, both day and night:

GAY PHILADELPHIA

Philadelphia has a large gay and lesbian population, catered to by its own lodgings, restaurants, and nightclubs. The epicenter of gay life is Carmac Street between Locust and Pine Streets, but the heart is **Giovanni's Room** (on the corner of Pine and 12th Sts., 215/923-2960, www.giovannisroom.com). Giovanni's is one of the largest gay- and lesbian-oriented bookstores in America. Ed Hermance, founder and guiding spirit, said that the name Giovanni's Room was a code word for homosexuality among gay men during the early 1970s, inspired by one of the few gay-themed novels published at that time.

"You say 'Giovanni's Room,'" says Hermance, "and straight people associate it with pizza. We get orders for pizza. But times have changed so much—most lesbians and gays don't even know what Giovanni's Room [was]."

The bookstore serves as a resource (the *Gay Yellow Pages, Northeast Edition* is there, among many other publications), a meeting ground, a posting site for community-based flyers, a clearinghouse for information, and sometimes even a crisis hotline—for both the gay community and the southwest Philadelphia community at large. It's a good place to ask for referrals and recommendations.

Carmac Street has been a gay "scene" since the late 1800s, with many bars and restaurants. In the surrounding area (and please note that straights are equally welcome), **Uncle's Upstairs Inn** (1220 Locust St., 215/546-6660) offers accommodations for men; **Ten Eleven Clinton Street** (215/923-8144) is a bed-and-breakfast that welcomes women couples; **Judy's** (3rd and Bainbridge Sts., 215/928-1968) draws a friendly mixed crowd for cocktails and dinner; **Bump** 13th and Locust Sts., 215/732-1800) features an after-hours restaurant and juice bar on Friday and Saturday nights.

Outfest (215/875-9288, www.phillypride.org), which takes place in June, is the one of the nation's biggest outdoor parties celebrating the gay and lesbian community.

keep purses shut and strapped to the body, wallets in an inside pocket, and fancy jewelry to a minimum. Big tourist draws such as the Liberty Bell and Reading Terminal Market attract pickpockets like iron filings to a magnet. Fortunately, the city has made an exceptional effort to help out visitors by hiring unarmed, first-aid-trained community service representatives (CSRs) to act as extra eyes and ears for the police, and to answer questions. Public transportation is safe and convenient all over the city during the day.

After 7 P.M., public transportation undergoes a not-too-subtle transformation; the crowd thins out, and riders take on a slightly more ominous look. Cabs are a terrific alternative for activities such as nightclubbing and late dinners, unless you plan to spend the evening on South Street, which is filled with people at all hours. Other areas that attract a lot of people in the evening are the Washington Square West neighborhood, and Rittenhouse Square/Walnut Street. Muggings and street crimes against both locals and visitors are a reality in Philadelphia, even in "good" neighborhoods—however, compared to Rome and Rio, Philadelphia is tame. Use your street smarts. If you feel unsafe walking into an area, avoid it; if a commotion on the street is diverting everyone's attention, it could be a ploy to make a pickpocket's work easier.

SERVICES

Medical Services

There are 123 hospitals and clinics in Philadelphia, including 24 teaching hospitals and seven medical schools. Pennsylvania Hospital (9th St. between Pine and Spruce Sts., ER 215/829-3358) and Hospital of the University of Pennsylvania (Spruce St. on campus, ER 215/662-3920) are two of the best known. There's also Children's Hospital (215/590-1000), next to the university hospital.

Money

The following banks make cash advances against Visa or MasterCard credit cards (call for the branch nearest you): Mellon PSFS (215/553-3000) and Wachovia (800/222-

2150). For bank ATM cardholders with Cirrus and Plus system symbols, contact these numbers for information on additional automated tellers that will service your cards: Cirrus Network (800/424-7787) and Visa Plus Systems (800/843-7587).

Foreign money exchanges are available at the airport and also at various branches of American Express (215/587-2300), Thomas Cook Currency Services (1800 JFK Blvd., 215/492-1723), Mellon PSFS (Broad and Chestnut Sts., 215/553-2145), and Wachovia Bank (16th and Market Sts., 215/985-6000).

Post Office

The U.S. Postal Service maintains drop stations every four to six blocks in the downtown area, with mailboxes in between.

Transportation

GETTING THERE

By Air

Philadelphia International Airport (www.phl.org) benefitted from a $1 billion improvement program and is served by all major airlines. The airport is eight miles out of town, but SEPTA (Southeastern Pennsylvania Transportation Authority) offers a convenient direct service line (R1) between the airport and downtown, with stops at University City Station, 30th Street, Suburban Station, and Market East. It operates every half-hour 5:30 A.M.–midnight; the fare is $5.50 one-way. The entrance is on the pedestrian bridges and commercial roadway; for directions, stop at one of the information booths in any of the airport terminals or call 215/937-6800. Cabs are readily available at the airport, and the flat fee set by city regulations from there to any destination in Center City is $20 (if you're unsure whether your destination comes within the $20 rule, ask your driver).

A number of downtown hotels offer their own shuttle service to and from the airport; check with your hotel when making reservations. Several independent shuttle services operate on a regular basis to and from the airport. Information is available at the Centralized Ground Transportation Counters in all baggage claims or by phone (215/937-6958).

Car-rental agencies available at the airport are Alamo (215/492-3960 or 800/327-9633, www.goalamo.com), Avis (800/331-1212, www.avis.com), Budget (800/527-0700, www.drivebudget.com), Dollar (800/800-4000, www.dollar.com), Hertz (215/492-7200 or 800/654-3131, www.hertz.com), and National (800/227-7368, www.nationalcar.com).

By Auto

Philadelphia's major access routes are I-276 and I-95 (east-west) and US 1 and I-76 (north-south). The interstates provide smooth four-lane travel, while US 1 is mainly two-lane and littered with stoplights. In the center of the city, an automobile is more of a hindrance than a help; parking is difficult and expensive (up to $18 an hour). For a stay of less than a week, try leaving your auto in a secured airport parking lot and taking public transportation.

By Bus

The Greyhound terminal (10th and Filbert Sts., 800/231-2222, www.greyhound.com) is the destination for daily arrivals and departures from all over America, including New England and New York, and transcontinental buses via Chicago and St. Louis.

By Rail

SEPTA operates regional rail lines from Chester, Delaware, Montgomery, and Bucks Counties to Philadelphia. SEPTA (215/580-7800, www.septa.org) also runs trains from Trenton, New Jersey, and Wilmington, Delaware. To receive SEPTA schedules by mail, call 215/580-7777.

Amtrak (800/872-7245, www.Amtrak.com) connects with the city at its 30th Street station. Both the Capitol Limited and the Pennsylvanian stop there, and both interconnect with Amtrak trains throughout the United States.

Philadelphia

GETTING AROUND

Ferry

The Riverlink ferry (215/925-5465, www.river-linkferry.org) is the easy way to get from Penn's Landing (Walnut St. and Columbus Blvd.) to the New Jersey State Aquarium (Federal St. and Delaware Ave., Camden, NJ) and other nearby New Jersey attractions. Service begins from 9:20 A.M. in Philadelphia and the final ferry leaves Camden at 5:40 P.M. Round-trip fares are $5 adults, $3 children under 12 years.

Bus and Rail

Excellent public transportation is one of the many pluses of Philadelphia. SEPTA (215/580-7800, www.septa.org) maintains **regional rail service** between the city and the suburbs (such as Chestnut Hill and Manayunk) and schedules frequent subway service and a fleet of buses and streetcars

in transit at the 30th Street Station

throughout the urban area. SEPTA's three main rail stations are Market East (11th and Market Sts.), Suburban (16th St. and JFK Blvd., near the main visitors center)—commonly known as Center City—and the attractive art-deco 30th Street Station (across the Schuylkill River on 30th and Market Sts.). Fares on the commuter trains are determined by distance traveled.

SEPTA offers two **subway** lines with frequent stops; the Market-Frankfort (east-west) and Broad Street (north-south) divide the city into quadrants. **Buses** run everywhere in the city, with reliable frequency. Bus and subway schedules and maps are available at the regional rail stations and most subway stops. Fare on both buses and subways is $2 exact change, or you can purchase a token for $1.30 each. Seniors ride all city transportation free with a SEPTA card. The easiest way to travel is with a $5.50 DayPass, which is good until midnight, and may be purchased at most of the stations or at the SEPTA store at 15th and Market, and at many Rite-Aid drugstores. Most SEPTA buses and all trains are equipped to handle wheelchairs.

Cabs

Philadelphia has plenty of cabs—1,400-plus registered—and they're easy to spot and catch on the street. Many hotels and all the transportation systems often have cabs available nearby. Drop charge is $1.80, $1.80–2.30 per mile thereafter, and Center City is so small that this is a quick, easy, relatively inexpensive alternative to driving your own car. Most point-to-point destinations cost less than parking in a garage for three hours.

On Foot and Bicycle

The easiest and best way to see Philadelphia is on foot. It's possible to walk from one end of Center City to the other in less than an hour; one favorite walk that traverses dozens of architectural styles and interesting stops is Pine Street, from the Delaware River to 24th Street. Bikes are a different story. Streets are narrow, traffic is dense, and traveling on a bicycle is hazardous. For a good bike workout and fabulous scenery, try Fairmount Park.

© JOANNE MILLER

Delaware River Valley

Like all cities of any size, Philadelphia has expanded exponentially since its founding. The surrounding territory is made up of upscale suburban and rural towns and villages that grew thanks to the riches and transport of the Delaware River; over time, the areas gave the vast Delaware River Valley new names. To the west of Philadelphia, the Brandywine River flowed into the Delaware and the area came to be known as the Brandywine Valley. Residents of Bucks County and environs northeast of Philadelphia can wave to New Jerseyites across the Delaware. Upriver to the north, near the Delaware Water Gap, the

Lehigh Valley was an industrial giant, once home to America's largest steel mills, aflame on the Lehigh River—another Delaware tributary.

The Brandywine Valley contains a number of manicured manses for the horsey set; in fact, one of the du Pont heirs willed his home and extensive horticultural planting to the public, creating the beautiful Longwood Gardens. Not far, the Brandywine River Museum displays the works of a few of America's most well-known and loved illustrators and painters, the Wyeths. This area is also home to American history, with Valley Forge and Brandywine Battlefield.

Must-Sees

M **Longwood Gardens:** If time permits only one option, make it this world-class pleasure garden with expansive glass-enclosed conservatories and many rare and unusual trees—a great destination year-round (page 95).

M **Valley Forge National Historical Park:** This is the site of Washington's headquarters and encampments during one of the bitterest periods of the Revolutionary War (page 97).

M **Brandywine River Museum:** The museum offers one of the largest collections of notable works by three generations of the Wyeth family, including classic illustrator N. C. Wyeth, plus works by other well-known artists (page 100).

M **Pennsbury Manor:** Another must-see in the area is the well-preserved country estate of William Penn (page 105).

M **Washington Crossing Historic Park:** This park includes colonial buildings and a museum dedicated to Washington's daring crossing of the river during the Revolutionary War (page 105).

M **The Pearl S. Buck House:** On the Delaware River, stop by the evocative home of this Nobel Prize-winning author and children's advocate (page 106).

M **Moravian Pottery and Tile Works:** In Doylestown, visit this "castle" to view a revived art form in action and pick up beautiful tiles (page 108).

M **Fonthill Museum:** Also in Doylestown, be sure to see Henry Mercer's art collection and unusual self-designed architecture (page 109).

M **Bowman's Hill Wildflower Preserve:** Located in Washington Crossing Historic Park, this 80-acre site is covered with Pennsylvania's native flora (page 112).

M **The Crayola Factory and Museum:** This is a colorful and fun place for the whole family in Easton; interactive exhibits will entertain the kids (page 118).

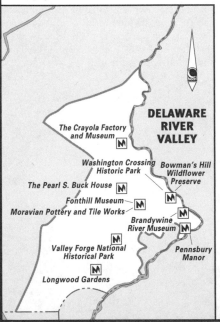

Pearl S. Buck House at Christmas

© JOANNE MILLER

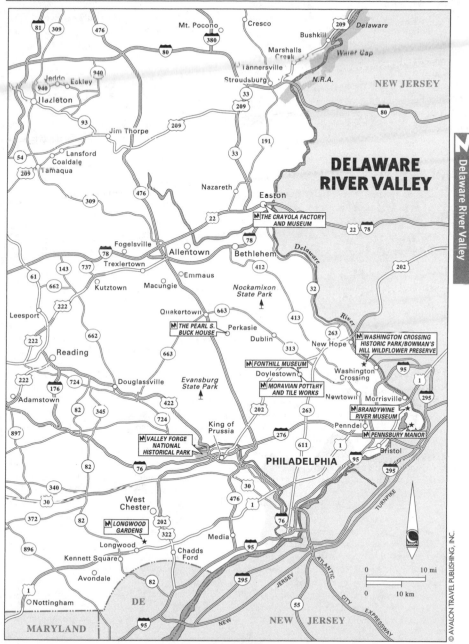

DELAWARE RIVER VALLEY

Bucks County and Doylestown offer a different experience. The bucolic surroundings offer a fun getaway for families, good shopping, and a pleasant history lesson set in William Penn's "country house."

In the Lehigh Valley, Allentown, Bethlehem, and Easton remain commercial centers, though their museums and historic sites are a worthy draw. Bethlehem, in particular, has become the "Christmas City," a great place to stay over the holidays.

PLANNING YOUR TIME

The Brandywine Valley offers a number of day trips from Philadelphia, or longer stays in the area. Plan on an entire day at **Longwood Gardens** and another at **Valley Forge National Historical Park**. The **Brandywine River Museum** (3 hours) is another must-see—**Brandywine Battlefield** (1–2 hours) is nearby. For relaxed touring, spend a day at historic **Newlin Grist Mill Park**, or **Mill Grove/Audubon Sanctuary**.

Bucks County is also suitable for day trips. The one-day driving tour **Cruising the Delaware** takes visitors past several points of interest to choose from: **Pennsbury Manor** (2 hours–all day), **Washington Crossing Historic Park and Bowman's Hill Wildflower Preserve** (2 hours–all day) and the **Pearl S.**

THE MAIN LINE: PENNSYLVANIA'S CANAL SYSTEM

Dense forests and the nearly insurmountable passage of the Allegheny Ridge made transport of people and goods a difficult undertaking during the first 150 years after the founding of Pennsylvania. Fortunately, nature had provided a solution to all, except the Appalachian barrier, in the form of water gaps—passes carved through the mountains by streams and rivers.

Pioneers and traders had used the navigable waterways for some years before the first manmade canal link was built, in 1797. The Conewago Canal, on the Susquehanna River, bypassed the rocks and rapids of Conewago Falls and linked the Columbia with the turnpike that led to Philadelphia.

Canal building experienced a growth spurt after the state of New York completed the Erie Canal in 1825. The Pennsylvania Assembly gave authorization, and by 1834, the publicly funded Pennsylvania Canal—the Main Line—was built, giving access to Pittsburgh from Philadelphia. A major feat of engineering, the great waterway required an elaborate system of 94 lift-locks (changes in water level), aqueducts, canal basins, towing paths, and tow bridges in addition to the portage railroad—a gravity system that lifted boats from the canal port near Hollidaysburg more than 2,000 feet over the ridge and then dropped them more than 1,000 feet to the canal in Johnstown.

The same year, publicly owned canals opened up the Delaware River from Bristol to Easton and paralleled the two great branches of the Susquehanna to Lock Haven and Nanticoke. Private projects made the Lehigh and Schuylkill Rivers navigable. The Delaware and Hudson Canal linked the coal mines of the Lackawanna Valley with the Hudson River and New York City. In the western section of the state, canals connected the Beaver, Youghiogheny, and Monongahela Rivers with Pittsburgh. By 1840, the Pennsylvania Canal System totaled 726 miles and connected railways and waterways—and another 208 miles were under construction.

Travel and transport moved at a leisurely pace on canal boats, which were often drawn by mules or horses along the towpaths and had to be raised and lowered in the many lift-locks. Steam tugs and side-wheelers powered the boats down the rivers. Four miles per hour was considered standard speed for cargo boats. By mid-1850, competition from state and privately funded railroads rapidly made the canal system, after being in business for less than 25 years, obsolete.

Many of the public canals were sold to the railroads, and the Pennsylvania Railroad Company bought the Main Line. Today, west of Philadelphia, the Main Line refers to the popular commuter

Buck House (1 hour). The **Village of New Hope** or Doylestown and vicinity are good alternatives to base from in the area. Plan on two days in Doylestown to see the **Moravian Pottery and Tile Works** (1 hour), **James A. Michener Art Museum** (2 hours), **Mercer Museum** (2 hours), and **Fonthill Museum** (2 hours)—each one offers so much visual overload that you'll need to take time out for shopping, dining etc. **Sesame Place** (all day) and **Carousel Village at Indian Walk** (1 hour–all day) also must be planned into the mix for families with younger children. If camping or outdoor recreation is your aim, **Nockamixon State Park** offers a nearby getaway.

The Lehigh Valley, particularly around Bethlehem, offers a lot to see and do. Bethlehem's historic buildings and museums that are part of the **Historic Bethlehem Partnership** are a full day. Add on any other attractions such as the **Delaware and Lehigh Navigation Canal** (1–2 hours), **Liberty Bell Shrine** (1 hour), **Hugh Moore Historical Park** (2 hours or more) or **Dorney Park and Wildwater Kingdom** (all day). Though close together, the **Crayola Factory and Museum** (2 hours), **Easton Museum of PEZ Dispensers** (1 hour), **National Canal Museum** (1–2 hours), and **Allentown Art Museum** (2 hours) all appeal to a variety of tastes and interests. You can choose to make a day or two (or three) of it.

railroad that was built on canal property. Within a few years, the western division of the Main Line, from Johnstown to Pittsburgh, was abandoned. East of the Allegheny Ridge, canals remained profitable because of the movement of coal and stayed in operation until 1931, when the Lehigh Coal and Navigation Company, owners of the Lehigh and Delaware Canals, ceased operation.

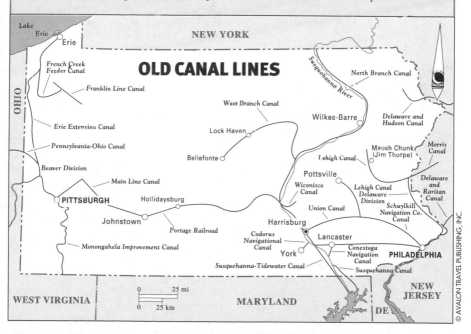

GETTING THERE AND GETTING AROUND

By Air and Bus

The closest major airport to the Delaware River is Philadelphia. Greyhound (800/229-9424, www .greyhound.com) travels between all the major cities in the area including Doylestown, Easton, Bethlehem, and Allentown, with stops in between.

By Auto

The major north-south route in the area is SR 476. In the Brandywine Valley, I-76 (toll) and US 202 run east-west. US 22 and I-78 traverse the area around Allentown.

HISTORY

The Lenni Lenape

Though most of the lower Piedmont was largely uninhabited, members of the Lenni Lenape tribe occupied the area along the Delaware River well before Europeans began to erect colonies and forts there. When the river was renamed for British Baron De La Warr, the first governor of Virginia, explorers commonly referred to the Lenni Lenape as "Delaware River Indians," then simply Delawares, a name they carried even though their eventual migrations took them far north and west of the river.

The Lenni Lenape the first colonists came to know were a peaceful, settled people who lived in individual family huts in small unfortified villages. They depended largely on the cultivation of corn, beans, and squash for their food and supplemented their diet by hunting. Though the villages along the river were permanent, they were occupied only during the spring and summer of the year; families would move to other established dwellings during different seasons. In *pooxit*, "time of the falling leaves," men, sometimes accompanied by their families, would travel to a traditional hunting ground to harvest deer and larger game animals in preparation for *winigischuch*, "time of the falling snows." In February—*mechankhokque,* "when the cold makes the trees crack"—whole families would move to sugar maple country

to set up sugar-boiling camps. In early spring— *anixi gischuch,* "when the ground squirrels run"—tribal members would return to their riverside villages to plant, renewing the annual cycle. The arrival of the Europeans, with their sophisticated implements for hunting and endless desire for fur pelts, changed the lives of the Lenni Lenape forever.

Losing the Land

By the time William Penn arrived on the scene, the natives had had 40 years of experience dealing with land leases, starting with an agreement with Swedish colonist Peter Minuit in 1638. Though their initial understanding of "purchase" referred to the right to use the land versus a complete transfer of a specified piece of property, confusion over the extent of ownership was not an issue by Penn's time. It appears from records that much of the land transferred from the Lenape *was* for use rights only, since it was "resold" to Penn's representatives ("the Proprietors") several times. Many Lenni Lenape chose to leave the immediate area where colonies were established because the sparsely populated Delaware Valley offered any number of choice spots to relocate, and the natives did not find the colonists to be compatible neighbors. After Penn's death, the remaining Lenni Lenape were forced by the diminishment of their hunting territories and their own dependence on trade goods to part with their land permanently. By 1737, all of the land of the Lenni Lenape, from the Delaware River to the Susquehanna, was owned by Europeans.

Settled Valleys

In the late 18th century, while wars and recriminations raged in the Wyoming Valley to the north, the Brandywine Valley west of Philadelphia, and the Lehigh Valley (containing Allentown and Bethlehem), were settled peacefully. With easy access by water from Philadelphia— due in large part to the expanding canal systems that laced the region together—the area attracted prosperous farmers and those seeking a place for a country respite. The Moravians were among the first Germans to establish a foothold there.

Bethlehem became the center of the Moravian Church in America, as it remains today.

Lehigh Industry

The Brandywine Valley and Bucks County remained rural and agricultural during the Civil War, but as demand for coal and iron increased, the Lehigh Valley met the need. Disgruntled, injured, and dead miners in the anthracite fields to the north were replaced by recently immigrated Germans, Irish, Welsh, Slavs, Poles, Ukrainians, Lithuanians, and Czechs, all eager for the steady work below ground and in newly built factories. A thriving quarry and stone dressing industry attracted Italians who had worked with marble in the old country. These immigrants came in through Philadelphia, and settled in the Lehigh Valley and points north. The wives and children of these recent émigrés found jobs in the silk mills strategically placed near the mines and foundries. By 1885, the Lehigh Valley was the most productive iron-making region in America, closely followed by Scranton. In the 1880s,

Bethlehem Iron—later Bethlehem Steel—erected the first heavy steel forging plant in the U.S., producing plate and cannon for the prototype steel warships of the burgeoning national navy.

The Brandywine Builds

By 1832, the Pennsylvania Railroad had taken over the canal routes, and the main line heading west from Philadelphia sprouted a series of small, elite towns that catered to vacationing city dwellers. The mnemonic device "Old Maids Never Wed And Have Babies. Really Vicious Retrievers Snap Willingly, Snarl Dangerously. Beagles Don't. Period." is still useful when recalling the towns westward from Philadelphia: Overbrook, Merion, Narberth, Wynnewood, Ardmore . . . all the way to Paoli.

The Brandywine retains its combination of rural and suburban roots, as does Bucks County, though the latter is more tourist oriented. The Lehigh Valley's heavy industrial days are past, but the area remains a commercial center with some interesting attractions for visitors.

Delaware River Valley

The Brandywine Valley and Environs

The Brandywine Valley is the affluent extension of Philadelphia's western communities. Second-home farms and horse-breeding facilities abound; the duPont family built an estate here that was to become Longwood Gardens. Because of its proximity to the colonial capitol, the Brandywine Valley was also the site of some of the decisive events of the American Revolution.

SCENIC SPOTS

Longwood Gardens

Longwood Gardens (US 1, Kennett Square, 610/388-1000, www.longwoodgardens.org) was bought in 1906 by Pierre du Pont and his wife in order to save the large number of rare and unusual trees on the property. The visitors' center and outdoor gardens are open 9 A.M.–5 P.M.; conservatories are open 10 A.M.–5 P.M. Hours are extended in the warmer months and at Christmas. Admission is $12.

Visitors enjoy dancing waters at Longwood Gardens.

COURTESY LONGWOOD GARDENS

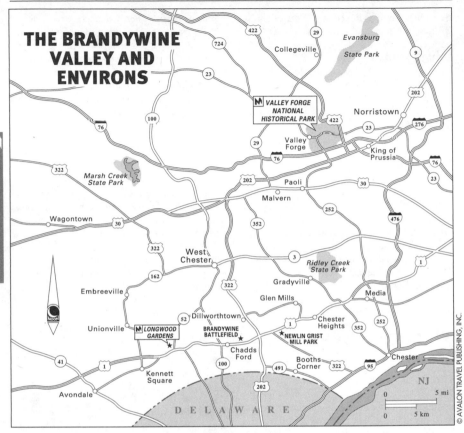

THE BRANDYWINE VALLEY AND ENVIRONS

The land originally had been owned by a Quaker family, the Peirces, for more than 200 years prior to the purchase. They had planted a great variety of trees and flowers, giving "Peirces's Park" a local reputation as a notable pleasure garden. In the later years, the property became severely run down and was sold to a lumber business before Pierre du Pont offered to buy the grounds.

Great-grandson of the founder of the Du Pont chemical company, and a millionaire financier and industrialist in his own right, Pierre du Pont had a lifelong interest in botany and landscaping. In his late teens, when his studies at Massachusetts Institute of Technology were complete, he began to travel extensively throughout Europe, where an interest in fountains and formal gardens

was kindled. He bought Longwood in order to develop those interests and provide a place of entertainment for his family and friends.

Longwood eventually became the family home. As Pierre du Pont wished, the extensive gardens with over 11,000 varieties of plants including colorful year-round seasonal displays, whimsical topiaries, dancing fountains, and a pint-sized children's garden were posthumously opened to the public. Numerous theme gardens set within the more than 1,000-acre park change with the seasons, and the massive main greenhouse and conservatory are engineering marvels that shelter an evolving array of exotics. Artistically placed fountains rise above the treetops or shape-shift among colored lights and fireworks.

For sheer beauty at any time of year, Longwood is unmatched; this may be the finest public garden in the United States. In keeping with Pierre du Pont's desire to have the gardens be a place of visual delight and entertainment, Longwood sponsors numerous musical and theatrical events year-round.

Mill Grove/Audubon Sanctuary

The first American home of John James Audubon, Mill Grove (Audubon and Pawlings Rds., Audubon, near Collegeville, 610/666-5593) features examples of every one of his major published works, including the rare *Double Elephant Folio Birds of America*. Audubon conducted his first experiments with bird banding here. The home is surrounded by a 175-acre nature preserve with numerous trails. It's open Tues.–Sun. 7 A.M. to dusk, and the museum is open Tues.–Sat. 10 A.M.–4 P.M. and Sun. 1–4 P.M. Admission is free.

HISTORIC SIGHTS

Valley Forge National Historical Park

The park (610/783-1011), which covers the area to the east of the village of Valley Forge, was the site of Washington's headquarters and the encampments of 16 of the brigades that followed him to the Schuylkill River after the defeat at Brandywine. The park is open year-round; the visitors' center at N. Gulph Road and SR 23 shows an 18-minute film on life in the camp. The Museum of the Valley Forge Historical Society is on the park grounds. The park offers a bus tour with taped narration Fri.–Mon. May–Sept. The park, museum, and visitors' center are free; admission to Washington's headquarters is $3. The park has three picnic areas, a six-mile hike-and-bike trail, and 10 miles of horse paths.

One of many interesting facts about the Continental Army and the encampment at Valley Forge was the physical and class separation between officers and fighting men. Officers were frequently companioned by their wives over the winter; two of the camp's feminine inhabitants were Mrs. Washington and the wife of General Greene. The women and their husbands dwelt in comfortable homes around the camp and held parties for other officers and their wives. Officers seldom set foot in the tiny log cabins and drilling areas of the soldiers. In contrast, Baron von Steuben, the Prussian mercenary who was responsible for creating an efficient fighting force from a ragged bunch of frontier volunteers, earned the respect of the men by working directly with them, on their own grounds, every day.

Brandywine Battlefield

This battlefield at Chadds Ford (off US 1, Chadds Ford, 610/459-3342, www.ushistory .org/brandywine) was the site of a painful and difficult defeat in the American War for Independence. Deceived by British general Howe's military ploy of splitting his troops, General

VALLEY FORGE

The winter of the French alliance was a time of suffering at Valley Forge. The men built and were quartered in 14- by 16-foot log huts, 12 men to a hut. As many as 2,000 died of typhus, typhoid, dysentery, pneumonia, and deprivation. Many deserted, returning to their homes in disgust.

The Continental Army's guardian angel came in the form of a dandified Prussian mercenary, Baron von Steuben (who created his upper-class mystique from humble beginnings). His colorful uniforms and blustering style amused the ragtag army, but his years as a soldier of considerable prowess proved invaluable to the outcome of the American Revolution. Writing in French and using translators to convert his words into English, he literally wrote the master training manual for the Continental Army; von Steuben's organized approach to training and personal drilling of the troops at the encampment resulted in an army fortified with much higher levels of tactical knowledge and cohesiveness. With knowledge of the French Alliance, the colonials were inspired with a sense of purpose and destiny, and the Continental Army was reborn into a formidable fighting force.

Newlin Grist Mill Park

Washington lost the battle, as well as a number of his troops—not to death or injury, but to attrition. Howe went on to take Philadelphia while Washington, fighting as he retreated, marched his remaining troops to Valley Forge. The property has a small museum dedicated to the implements and weaponry of both sides, and Washington's headquarters and Gideon Gilpen's house, which quartered the young French volunteer Marquis de Lafayette, are also available for touring. The small museum and park are free. Admission is charged ($5) to tour Washington's headquarters and Lafayette's quarters. The park is open Tues.–Sat. 9 A.M.–5 P.M., Sun. noon–5 P.M.

Newlin Grist Mill Park

Newlin Grist Mill Park (intersection of US 1 and S. Cheyney Rd., east of US 322, 610/459-2359) features a water-powered gristmill built in 1704 by Nathaniel Newlin, a Quaker who moved to the area from Ireland in 1683 to escape religious persecution. The mill is restored and operational; visitors can watch it grind corn. An accompanying exhibit illustrates various aspects of 18th-century colonial life. Adjacent to the mill is a miller's house, which was built in 1739 and contains furniture of the period. Other historic buildings include a barn, log cabin, springhouse, and functioning blacksmith shop.

In addition to the historic complex, the park's 150 acres of rolling countryside offer nature walks, fishing ponds and streams, and picnic areas. Three miles of walking trails follow the millrace and stream, winding past native tree species to the original dam constructed by Newlin for redirecting water to the gristmill. The fishing ponds are well stocked with trout and especially popular with children.

The Newlin Grist Mill Park is open daily 8 A.M. to dusk, office hours 9 A.M.–4 P.M. Admission to the park is free, and guided tours of the mill and

BY THE OLD MILL STREAM

O ne of the first necessities required by settlers in a farming area was a grinding mill. Mills had to be situated by certain rock formations; a hard porphyritic granite with a clean crystal face was necessary to provide the sharp cutting surface required for a millstone. The fashioning of millstones was a specialization in the settlements, and millstone cutters were journeymen in demand.

Each fall, local farmers brought in their crops of wheat or corn. After unloading the crop from the wagon, the farmer would channel it, with the miller's help, under the millstone. One hour was required to grind a bushel of corn. Some mills had a second set of coarse-surfaced millstones to grind the "chop," or chaff, which was used to make "mash," a coarse bran, for winter livestock feed.

Though occasionally driven by mules, most mills were powered by water channeled into a heavy single flow—usually the plunging torrent of a narrow mountain stream. Water-ground flour or cornmeal was considered the best to be had. As the wheels turned, the miller carefully controlled the flow of grain and felt the flour with his fingers to be sure of the desired texture. Overheating of the milled grains was considered ruinous to the taste. Some millers "bolted" their flour by sifting it through a sieve to remove the coarser fragments (bran). Bolted flour was sold at a premium, usually taken by the miller as one-tenth of the amount of flour that was ground. Millers were among the wealthiest residents of a new settlement, and their honesty was often a matter of grumbling dispute.

COURTESY OF NEWLIN GRIST MILL

dam at Newlin Grist Mill Park

the miller's house are available at midday or may be arranged in the office or by calling in advance. Trout fishing in the ponds is available weekends only March–Oct., 9 A.M.–4 P.M. The fishing fee is $3, plus $3 per fish caught. No license is required, and there is no releasing. Group and educational tours are also available.

OTHER POINTS OF INTEREST

Kennett Underground Railroad Center

Located in the History Station (505 S. Broad St., Kennett Square, 610/347-2237, http://undergroundrr.kennett.net), this information exhibit keeps alive Kennett Square's past as a hotbed of abolitionist activity (almost always by Quakers) prior to the Civil War. The center is open May–Sept., Sat.–Sun. 1–3 P.M. Visitors can also call to arrange for individual appointments throughout the year. Admission is free.

The Kennett Underground Railroad Center documents over two dozen underground railroad sites or "stations" within an eight-mile radius of Kennett Square, possibly the largest concentration of underground railroad stations in the nation. Click on their website for an excellent map of sites.

Herr Foods Factory Tour

After viewing a film starring Chipper, Herr's chipmunk mascot and chief sales representative, visitors can tour the plant and see how the family-owned factory (Herr Drive in Nottingham, 800/63-SNACK, www.herrs.com) produces its wide variety of snack foods, from potato chips to cheese curls.

Delaware River Valley

"THERE WAS SUCH A GLORY IN EVERYTHING"— QUAKERS AND SLAVERY

Though individual freedom was one of the tenets of the Quaker religion, and the Philadelphia Yearly Meeting of 1776 refused membership to slaveholders, not all who followed the faith agreed that slavery should be abolished. In 1854, the Longwood Meeting of Progressive Friends was formed by Quaker abolitionists who had been barred from their own meetings for their outspoken stand against slavery. From the beginning, the meeting was a center of radicalism and offered a place for leaders of the abolitionist movement to speak publicly.

Sojourner Truth, Susan B. Anthony, and Lucretia Mott, among others, spoke to overflow crowds on the lawn of the meetinghouse, while Quaker families in the Kennett Square area kept the Underground Railroad running smoothly—albeit illegally—through their barns and lofts. John and Hannah Pierce Cox, owners of Longwood (later to become Pierre duPont's Longwood Gardens) and ardent abolitionists, built the meetinghouse on their property. Their homestead still stands along US 1 at the entrance to Longwood Gardens, and the meetinghouse now houses the Brandywine Valley Tourist Information Center.

Harriet Tubman, a freed slave who lived and worked in the Kennett Square area, aided local Quakers in transporting hundreds of former slaves to freedom. When she first set foot over the Mason-Dixon boundary into the free state of Pennsylvania, she said, "When I found I had crossed that line I looked at my hands to see if I was the same person. There was such a glory in everything."

To reach the factory from US 1, take PA 272 south and follow signs. After the tour, visitors are plied with trays of whatever is being produced that day: still-warm potato chips, popcorn, flavored chips, or pretzels. Call to schedule a free tour Mon.–Thurs. 9 A.M.–3 P.M. and Fri. 9–11 A.M.

Herr foods was founded in 1946, when a young Mennonite farmer, Jim Herr, bought two iron kettles, a three-potato slicer, a peeler that held 10 pounds of potatoes, and a 1938 Dodge panel truck. Jim and his young wife Mim (Miriam Hershey) built the business in spite of setbacks including a fire in the 1950s that destroyed the chip factory and a hurricane that injured Jim Herr and collapsed some of the plant structures.

All of the Herrs' five children continue to work for the company. Current production, distributed in 11 eastern states, also produces considerable waste, which is recycled on the Herr property—potato peels and imperfect products become cattle feed for the family's Angus cattle. Once you go through the tour and load up on fresh samples, you'll understand why Chipper is

the perfect spokes-rodent—chipmunks have food pouches that extend to their shoulders.

Chaddsford Winery

Chaddsford (on US 1, Chadds Ford, 610/388-6221, www.chaddsford.com) grows and presses its own varietals. Winemaking facilities are housed in an 18th-century barn that frequently hosts special events including festivals and concerts. The winery is open daily noon–6 P.M.

MUSEUMS
Brandywine River Museum

The Brandywine River Museum (on US 1 in Chadds Ford, 610/388-2700, www.brandywinemuseum.org) is home to one of the largest collections of works by N. C. Wyeth, Andrew Wyeth, and Jamie Wyeth, three generations of world-class artists from one family. The museum, which has a café on the lower level, is open daily 9:30 A.M.–4:30 P.M.; Jan.–March, the café closes Mon.–Tues., but the museum remains open. Admission is $8.

holiday decor at the Brandywine
River Museum

Regularly changing exhibits showcase N. C.'s familiar book illustrations (notably for *Treasure Island*), Andrew's landscapes (unfortunately, Andrew Wyeth's famous *Christina* in her wheatfield resides in New York City), and Jamie's distinctively modern mix of subjects, as well as rarely seen works. The Civil War-era gristmill-cum-museum also shows the works of other artists and illustrators of the Brandywine area such as Maxfield Parrish, Rockwell Kent, and Rose O'Neill.

Christian C. Sanderson Museum

Pennsylvania seems to have a high proportion of wealthy and eccentric collectors, and the Christian C. Sanderson Museum (on SR 100, 300 feet north of US 1 in Chadds Ford, 610/388-6545) stands tall as an example of the genre. It's open Sat.–Sun. 1–4:30 P.M.; admission is by donation.

Eight rooms in his former home contain Revolutionary War and Civil War items, sand exca-

vated from the Panama Canal, melted ice from the South Pole, and a beautiful portrait of Sanderson painted in 1937 by close family friend Andrew Wyeth, and many other interesting and curious items. Much of the collection was brought to Sanderson by friends from all over the world.

SHOPPING

Antiques

The town of Kennett Square has several antique shops, including **McLimans** (940 West Cypress St., 610/444-3876, www.mclimans.com), which has been in business since 1976. With two floors and 13,000 square feet, they have one of the largest inventories of antique, reproduction, and traditional furniture in the area. It's open July–mid-Sept. Wed. 10 A.M.–7 P.M. and Thurs.–Sat. 10 A.M.–5 P.M.; mid-Sept.–June Wed.–Sat. 10 A.M.–5 P.M. and Sun. noon–5 P.M. **Pennsbury-Chadds Ford Antique Mall** (640 East Baltimore Pk., Chadds Ford, 610/692-6311) has 120 dealers offering furniture, jewelry, china, sterling, books, dolls, oriental rugs, clocks, military items, and more. It's open Thurs.–Mon. 10 A.M.–5 P.M.

Malls and Outlets

Glen Eagle Square, in Chadds Ford, features more than 30 specialty stores such as Banana Republic and Ann Taylor. **MOMM's** (Manufacturer's Outlet Mall, Morgantown) offers 55 outlet stores such as Bass shoes and Levi-Strauss.

The real magnet for shoppers in the area is the town of King of Prussia, with 280 specialty shops and six major department stores in two huge covered malls, **The Court** and **The Plaza,** between I-275, I-76, and US 202.

Farmers' Markets and Orchards

Linvilla Orchards (137 W. Knowlton Rd., Media) has been selling produce and specialty items out of its octagonal barn since 1914. There are animals for the kids to visit and many seasonal special events year-round.

Booth's Corner Farmers' Market (1362 Naamans Creek Rd., Boothwyn) has been going strong since the mid-1940s. Amish and other local merchants travel to this market to sell home-baked goods, produce, meats, and cheeses. Crafts are also displayed and sold.

OUTDOOR RECREATION

Golf

Wyncote Golf Club (Avondale, 610/932-8900) is a semiprivate Scottish-style facility that was named one of the top 25 "Places to Play" by *Golf Digest* in the 1990s. Another option is **Hartefield National Golf Course** (Avondale, 610/268-8800).

Canoeing and Tubing

The **Northbrook Canoe Company** (West Chester, 610/793-2279) offers escorted canoe trips on the Brandywine River and rents canoes, kayaks, and rubber "tube" boats to those who wish to go it alone.

ACCOMMODATIONS

Under $50

Evansburg State Park Hostel is located within the state park (837 Mayhall Rd., Collegeville, 610/409-0113); this year-round AYH hostel offers 12 dormitory beds and family rooms. Reservations are essential Sept. 15–May 15. The rate is $15 per night.

$100–150

It's the way of the world—in 1997, Chadds Ford was nothing more than a cluster of buildings at a crossroads, but now, a number of "instant historic-look" buildings had sprung up, and Philadelphia's suburbs extended west into the formerly quiet valley. The upside is, there's more to do for visitors, and newer hotels have a lot to offer. A case in point is the **Brandywine River Hotel** (intersection of US 1 and DE 100, 610/388-1200). It offers every amenity of a big-

TRAVELING BY WATER

In the mid-19th century, before railroads linked the elements of the nation, travelers making their way west had two choices: the dusty wagon roads via horse or horse-drawn vehicle, or the speedier canal boat. The newly built Main Line from Philadelphia shortened the trip to Pittsburgh, the Mississippi River, and points west by some days and allowed the traveler to proceed in relative comfort—or, more accurately, with a different set of discomforts.

Traveling by road was slow, rough, and filthy, but conditions aboard the canal boats were crowded and equally unhygienic. A bucket of water drawn from the canal was set out on deck in the morning for those who wished to wash. Breakfast, lunch, and dinner all consisted of the same unvarying meal: tea, coffee, bread, butter, salmon, shad, liver, steak, potatoes, pickles, ham, pork chops, black puddings, and sausages.

Privacy was rare. In 1840, Charles Dickens, accustomed to the plusher confines of continental travel, made a disconcerting discovery at the beginning of his canal boat trip:

I have mentioned my having been in some uncertainty and doubt, at first, relative to the sleeping arrangements on board this boat. I remained in the same vague state of mind until ten o'clock or thereabouts, when, going below, I found suspended, on either side of the cabin, three long tiers of hanging bookshelves, designed apparently for volumes of the small octavo size. Looking with greater attention at these contrivances (wondering to find such literary preparations in such a place), I descried on each shelf a sort of microscopic sheet and blanket; then I began dimly to comprehend that the passengers were the library, and that they were to be arranged edgewise on these shelves till morning.

city hotel (including secretarial services and golf privileges) but retains comfort in the guise of Colonial style. Even George Washington would have appreciated a fireplace and whirlpool tub after a long muddy ride. Rates range $125–169 and include a Continental breakfast and afternoon tea. Packages are available.

An elegant three-story Georgian mansion built in 1734 and expanded in 1815, **Ⓜ Sweetwater Farm** (50 Sweetwater Rd., Glen Mills, 610/459-4711 or 800/793-3892, www.sweetwaterfarmbb.com) offers seven cozy guest rooms with private baths and four-poster beds; rooms in the 1815 wing all have fireplaces. In addition, there's a swimming pool and hot tub and five additional cottages away from the main building, three with fireplaces, three with kitchens. Space in the cottages ranges from a bed with sitting area to two bedrooms with private kitchen. Sweetwater is surrounded by 50 acres of peaceful farmland filled with frolicking horses and grazing sheep in an area of undisturbed rural beauty. It's so quiet it's easy to forget you're only minutes away from the major attractions of the Brandywine Valley. Rates range $100–250. Midweek rates are discounted.

The menu includes dishes such as Colorado rack of lamb with whipped potatoes, eggplant caviar, apple and zucchini chutney with thyme jus ($36) and pan-seared diver scallops over carrot curry risotto and lobster cream sauce ($28). Entrees average $30.

A good value and good food, the **State Street Grille** (115 West State St., Kennett Square, 610/925-4984, www.streetgrille.com; lunch Tues.–Fri. 11:30 A.M.–2:30 P.M., dinner Tues.–Thurs. and Sun. 5–9 P.M., Fri.–Sat. 5–10 P.M.) serves up specialties such as a North Carolina barbeque pork sandwich ($6.50) and a Chesapeake crab cake sandwich ($6.95) for lunch (average: $7). Dinner is prixe fixe at $29.50, and includes three courses with entrees such as grilled loin pork chop in orange chipotle glaze with roasted garlic potato mousse, and pan-seared breast of duckling in dried cherry and green peppercorn demi-glace and caramelized endive on a bed of vanilla sweet potato mousse. Parking is free on the metered streets after 5 P.M., and also free in the Linden Street parking garage on the corner of Linden Street and SR 82, 500 feet from the restaurant.

FOOD AND DRINK

The **Ⓜ Dilworthtown Inn** (1390 Old Wilmington Pike, West Chester, 610/399-1390, www.dilworthtown.com) is open Mon.–Fri. 5:30–9:30 P.M., Sat. 5–9:30 P.M., Sun. 3–8:30 P.M.). It's a special-occasion dining experience; lighting is strictly by candlelight, in keeping with its colonial character. Long a Philadelphian favorite for out-of-town celebratory dinners (and winner of *Wine Spectator Magazine*'s "Best Award of Excellence"), the inn's food is carefully chosen for freshness and served with attention to visual appeal. The historic building serves as a perfect setting to share Australian lobster tail for two.

INFORMATION

Contact the **Chester County Visitors Center** (300 Greenwood Rd., Kennett Square, PA 19348, www.brandywinevalley.com, 610/388-2900 or 800/228-9933) and the **Brandywine Conference and Visitors Bureau** (One Beaver Valley Rd., Chadds Ford, PA, 19317, 610/565-3679 or 800/343-3983, www.brandywinecountry.com) for more information. Specifics on the Audubon Sanctuary at Mill Grove may be sought from the **Valley Forge Convention and Visitors Bureau** (600 W. Germantown Pike, Ste. 130, Plymouth Meeting, PA 19462, 610/834-1550, www.valleyforge.org).

Delaware River Valley

Bucks County and Environs

Northeast of Philadelphia, directly on the Delaware River, Bucks County has developed its own style and attractions, catering to the sophisticated tastes of New Yorkers and others from the big cities to the east and south.

Centrally located **Doylestown,** the Bucks County seat, offers numerous attractions. The historic downtown area is a charming hodgepodge of boutique-style shops interspersed with cafés and restaurants; a major fine arts museum, several eclectic collections, and a variety of accommodations make the town valuable for a day trip or as a base from which to see all of Bucks County.

SCENIC TOURS

Cruising the Delaware

The peaceful drive along SR 32 will lull visitors away from urban cares. Alongside the two-lane road, the old Delaware Canal parallels the Delaware River down the eastern edge of Pennsylvania from Easton to Washington's Crossing, passing through tiny villages and forests. An occasional restaurant or snack bar pops up along the route; sometimes during the warmer months, a farmer will sell tomatoes or other produce from a shack on the side of the road. During winter,

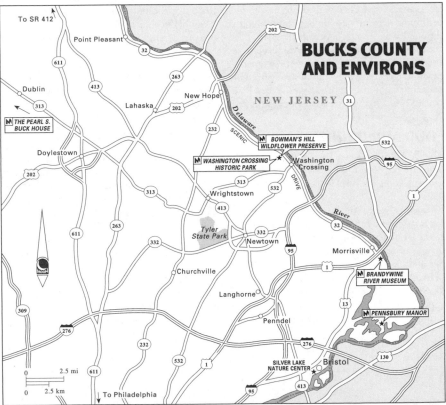

BUCKS COUNTY AND ENVIRONS

© AVALON TRAVEL PUBLISHING, INC.

the trees thin out to give a full view of sunlight sparkling on the river.

HISTORIC SIGHTS

 Pennsbury Manor

This 43-acre site was the country estate of William Penn, originally built in the late 17th century. Pennsbury Manor (400 Pennsbury Memorial Rd., Morrisville, 215/946-0400, www.pennsburymanor.org) is open Tues.–Sat. 9 A.M.–5 P.M., Sun. noon–5 P.M. The hours are subject to change, depending on the weather, so call before you go. Admission is $5 adults, $3 children 6–17.

An extremely well-preserved manor house, workers' cottage, smokehouse, bake-and-brew house, and other outbuildings as well as farm animals and kitchen gardens complete the portrait of the Pennsylvania founder's home-away-from-home. There are many reconstructed colonial

river entry to Pennsbury Manor

© JOANNE MILLER

dwellings in Pennsylvania, but this one is special; Penn retreated here to escape the intrigues of Philadelphia and carry on his own politicizing away from the maddling crowd. In his time, the only way to reach the isolated country dwelling was an arduous journey by water; as a result, the farm has remained intact and unviolated. You can almost feel the Quaker gentleman walking through the unadorned rooms of the manor house.

Costumed guides escort groups through the property. The tours are informative and interesting, and a special effort is made to include little ones.

Washington Crossing Historic Park

George Washington was not a military strategist; in fact, the only battle he decisively won was here, when he rallied what few colonial troops remained to cross the icy Delaware in the middle of a fierce winter storm before dawn on Christmas Day 1776. The Washington Crossing Historic Park (215/493-4074) is on River Road, also known as SR 32; the Thompson's Mill Section is near the intersection of Lurgan Road, and the McConkey's Ferry Section is 3.5 miles south on SR 32, near the intersection of SR 532. The park is open Tues.–Sat. 9 A.M.–5 P.M., Sun. noon–5 P.M. Though entry to both sections of the park is free, six of the park's buildings including the Bowman Hill Tower and several dwellings in McConkey's Ferry require an admission ticket, $5.

Though General Washington expected to be supported by two divisions of troops crossing to the south, he ended up on the shores of Trenton with only his division. Fortunately, the element of surprise was so strong that the Continental soldiers managed to overwhelm and capture the Hessian mercenaries of the British.

Victory in the Battle of Trenton was fortuitous; many revolutionaries, fired up at the beginning of the war, had deserted or given up, expecting the British to reestablish themselves in the colonies. Washington's decisive win pumped new life into the colonial forces and reversed the fortunes of war.

Delaware River Valley

HOW WE WON THE REVOLUTION

In the late 18th century, Britain was a superpower, with the greatest navy in the world and a formidable army; however, the colonies had distinct advantages. Unlike the British forces, which had to wait for both replacements and supplies to arrive by sea, the Continental Army could draw upon a vast reservoir of manpower (though supplies were often scarce). The Continental Army permitted short-term enlistments; many who served came for only a few weeks or months (it is estimated that more than 200,000 men participated on the colonists' side). As frontiersmen, Americans owned guns and knew how to use them. And they were fighting on their own soil and consequently could be more flexible in their military operations.

Washington and other Continental Army commanders usually followed the principle of concentration, meeting the enemy in force wherever British armies appeared. In the interior, however, against bands of loyalists and isolated British outposts, the American militia frequently employed guerrilla tactics with marked success.

In spite of colonial advantages and initial victories, strategic initiative was taken by the British beginning in the summer of 1776; they moved against what they perceived as the real core of the insurrection, New England and New York. British Major Gen. William Howe captured New York City. Washington himself lost the battle, defeated by Howe's troops on Long Island. General Howe pursued the retreating Washington across New Jersey until the Americans managed to escape over the Delaware River into Pennsylvania on December 7, 1776.

With the Revolution at its lowest point, Washington rallied his forces and struck back, showing the persistence that would make him a popular hero during the 8.5-year war—the longest in American history before Vietnam. Washington noted that Howe, in characteristic European fashion, preferred to avoid winter campaigning and had divided his army between New York City and various New Jersey towns. Collecting scattered regulars and militiamen, Washington crossed the Delaware on Christmas Day of 1776 and captured a garrison of German mercenaries at Trenton, and then routed another enemy contingent at Princeton just after the new year.

Led by the words of firebrand Thomas Paine in his highly influential pamphlet *Common Sense,* the third Continental Congress had voted on July 4, 1776, to separate the American colonies from

The park consists of two main areas: the McConkey's Ferry section, a small settlement including the visitors' center, an inn, several dwellings, a general store, and a boathouse—the original boats were launched from here; and the Thompson's Mill section, containing Bowman's Hill State Wildflower Preserve (see Outdoor Recreation), a 100-acre area devoted to native plants of Pennsylvania and laced with trails; an operating gristmill; soldier's graves; and Bowman's Hill Tower, a 110-foot observation tower built in 1930 to commemorate the lookout of the American Revolution. The tower offers a panoramic view of the Delaware River and surrounding countryside.

OTHER POINTS OF INTEREST

The Pearl S. Buck House

The beautiful stone farmhouse (520 Dublin Rd., Perkasie, 215/249-0100 or 800/220-2825, www.pearlsbuck.org) has been left much as it was when author Pearl Buck and her husband lived there with eight adopted children. Proceeds from the $6 admission fee support the Pearl S. Buck Foundation, a child assistance agency that facilitates international adoptions and aids displaced children. Tours are given Tues.–Sat. at 11 A.M., 1 P.M., and 2 P.M. and Sun. at 1 P.M. and 2 P.M. It's closed Jan.–Feb.

Britain, adopting the words of Thomas Jefferson in the Declaration of Independence.

General Howe, meanwhile, was winning small victories along the Pennsylvania border; he chose not to advance up the Hudson to aid his comrade General Burgoyne nor march directly on Philadelphia by land. Instead, he landed his forces on upper Chesapeake Bay, 57 miles from Philadelphia, and marched north to capture the Continental capitol.

Washington hurried south from Morristown, New Jersey, and positioned his army astride Brandywine Creek to block Howe's progress. But on September 11, after several hours of furious fighting, Washington's right flank collapsed, and he withdrew. Howe entered the patriot capitol, causing Congress to flee to York. Washington's troops failed in a night assault on the enemy's advance base at Germantown and withdrew to Valley Forge.

France's King Louis XVI, eager to settle an old score with Britain, funneled secret aid to the patriots in 1776 and 1777. Munitions, arms, and clothing were passed to the playwright Caron de Beaumarchais and his fake Hortalez and Company, who, with the aid of Benjamin Franklin and other patriots, shipped the goods across the Atlantic. Baron von Stueben, a former Prussian

Army officer who was to prove invaluable in training the colonial troops at Valley Forge, was also sent through the secret French-American connection.

Once France was convinced that the rift between the colonies and Great Britain was irreconcilable, formal treaties of commerce and alliance were signed. France became the first nation to recognize the United States; it renounced all claims to North America east of the Mississippi River and made an agreement with the Continental Congress that neither country would lay down arms until American independence was achieved.

Battles between the Continental Army and British troops continued. In 1783, the war in America ground to a halt; neither side had the resources to obtain victory. England had sent 60,000 soldiers across the Atlantic to fight a prolonged war against a people who were numerous and well armed. The Americans were unable to win a clear-cut military victory, since they couldn't drive out the British completely. British emissaries worked with Benjamin Franklin to secure Parliament's recognition of American independence and to declare the territory from the Appalachians to the Mississippi River as part of the United States.

Pearl Buck, who penned *The Good Earth* and numerous other books and publications, settled on this Bucks County farm in 1934. Raised in China by missionary parents, Buck's legacy of humanitarianism and love of the Orient shines through in the eclectically decorated rooms. One chamber is given over to the numerous honors she received, including both the Nobel and Pulitzer Prizes.

National Shrine of Our Lady of Czestochowa

A gathering place of central importance for Polish Catholics in America, the shrine (Ferry Road west of SR 313, north of Doylestown, 215/345-

0600) contains a duplicate of the icon Our Lady of Czestochowa (shay-STOSH-a-va, or alternately, shays-toe-SHOW-va), the patron of Poland. The original, thought to be painted by St. Luke the Evangelist, was brought to Poland in 1382, and numerous miraculous healings and events are attributed to it. The prototype remains in the Shrine of Jasna Gora in the town of Czestochowa. Many Polish immigrants carried a copy of the icon with them when they traveled from their homeland to remind them of their faith and country.

Thousands of pilgrims come each year to the soaring structure that houses the American icon, especially during the summer months, when the feast day of Our Lady of Czestochowa is celebrated around August 26. Nearby, a chapel made of stained glass houses a replica of the icon surrounded by racks of flaming votives (free).

Village of New Hope

A mecca to visitors for many years, the village of New Hope (www.newhopepa.com) has a little of everything: history, scenery, a multitude of shops, and a variety of places to eat and stay. The **New Hope and Ivyland Rail Road,** on W. Bridge Street, offers a nine-mile ride along the Delaware River, and the **New Hope Mule Barge Company,** on New Street, lets visitors experience canal life as it was 150 years ago, drifting down the Delaware Canal on an old-fashioned mule-drawn barge. **Farley's Bookshop** (S. Main St.) is one of a number of small shops that sell souvenirs, fine art, antiques, and collectibles. **Scarlett** (S. Main St., 800/862-2311) offers a bounty of beauty products and makeup. New Hope is on the Delaware River, just before US 202 crosses over into New Jersey.

 Moravian Pottery and Tile Works

During the early 20th century, the tile works (130 Swamp Rd., Doylestown, 215/345-6722) successfully revived a forgotten industry, rekindling an interest in the use of local materials and handcrafted ceramics. The tile works is open for tours daily 10 A.M.–4:45 P.M. The Tile Shop keeps the same hours. The shop is free, but admission is $3.50 to tour the tile works.

Created by the eclectic Henry Mercer following his graduation from Harvard, the Tile Works became a major force in the Arts and Crafts movement (see Mercer Museum and Fonthill, below). The distinctively designed tiles (many based on whimsical animals or fruits) are available for purchase at the gift store. The building itself, constructed of reinforced concrete, resembles a Moorish castle in the south of Spain.

MUSEUMS

James A. Michener Art Museum

Internationally known author Michener (*Hawaii, Poland,* and many others) was raised in Doyles-

town and is a major benefactor of this museum, set in the reconstructed buildings of the Bucks County prison. The museum (138 S. Pine St., Doylestown, 215/340-9800, www.michenerartmuseum.org) is open Tues. and Thurs.–Fri. 10 A.M.–4:30 P.M., Wed. 10 A.M.–9 P.M., and Sat. 10–5 P.M., and Sun. noon–5 P.M. Admission is $6.50.

The museum's collections focus on 20th-century American art and sculpture. A permanent exhibit, *James A. Michener: A Living Legacy,* celebrates the prolific author's career and lifelong commitment to racial harmony. Three residents of Bucks County—Edward Redfield, who pioneered the Pennsylvania School of landscape painting (Pennsylvania impressionism); Daniel Garver, who settled in Bucks County in 1907 and taught at the Pennsylvania Academy; and internationally recognized designer/architect George Nakashima—are also featured.

The Mercer Museum

Henry Chapman Mercer built the seven-story-high Mercer Museum (84 S. Pine St., Doylestown, 215/345-0210; $6), with the help of eight laborers and a horse. A pioneering archaeologist,

© JOANNE MILLER

Moravian Pottery and Tile Works

anthropologist, and ceramicist, Mercer made a serious study of then-neglected American folkways and single handedly regenerated local craftsmanship; he left behind three uniquely designed structures: two museums—Mercer Museum and Fonthill Museum—that house thousands of artifacts and artworks, and a ceramics studio that continues to produce distinctive tiles (the Moravian Tile Works).

The Mercer Museum houses H.C.M.'s mind-boggling collection of artifacts. His fondness for tools of trades such as metalworking, textile weaving, and dairy farming is well represented, as are Native American implements dating from 6000 B.C. to 8000 B.C. Beware of visual overload. The museum is open Mon.–Sat. 10 A.M.–5 P.M. (until 9 P.M. on Tues.), Sun. noon–5 P.M.

ferocious tiger carved by the Dentzel Carousel Company

Fonthill Museum

Every inch of this 44-room, tile-filled palace (E. Court Street, Doylestown, 215/348-9461) was designed "room by room" by Henry Chapman Mercer. It's open for guided tours (by reservation only) Mon.–Sat. 10 A.M.–5 P.M., Sun. noon–5 P.M. The last tour is given at 4 P.M. Admission is $7. Eighteen fireplaces, 32 stairwells, and more than 200 windows grace the interior, showing off his collection of over 900 prints and art objects. Ever mindful of leaving a cultural legacy for the future, Mercer dubbed Fonthill "a concrete castle for the New World," which he left as "a museum of decorative tiles and prints." Henry Mercer also called this particular castle home until his death in 1930.

AMUSEMENT PARKS

Sesame Place

This amusement park (Oxford Valley Rd., Exit 29A off US 1 in Langhorne, 215/752-7070, www.sesameplace.com) is as cute as the *Sesame Street* characters that provide its theme. It's open May Fri.–Sun. and mid-Sept.–Oct. Sat.–Sun. 10 A.M.–5 P.M.; June–Aug. daily 10 A.M.–8 P.M. Call for a current schedule. General admission is $38.95. There is a $10 charge for parking.

Bert, Ernie, Oscar the Grouch, Big Bird, and others from the TV show stroll through the activity areas, perform in a musical revue, and lead an alphabet parade to the delight of everyone. Sesame Place is definitely aimed towards active children, rather than passive thrill riders. Physical activities for kids of all ages are a constant: little ones can swim through a sea of plastic balls and slide on gentle slopes throughout the park. Everyone can stroll through Twiddlebug Land, where flowers are as big as trees and a wave pool is the result of a giant leaking garden hose. Older children can leap, climb, and jump to their heart's content in the park's 50 physical play areas. Sesame Place also has several water slides and water play areas that the whole family can enjoy. If it rains continuously on the day of your visit for an hour or more, Sesame Place will give you a free ticket to come back to the park another day during the current operating season.

Giggleberry Fair

This combination fast-food restaurant/fun center (SR 263, Lahaska, 215/794-8960), part of

PENNSYLVANIA'S CAROUSELS

Exhibits, displays, and theatrical presentations are among the amusements that give amusement parks their name, but rides have traditionally been the favorite attraction. The oldest of these is the carousel, or merry-go-round (called a roundabout in England). The name derives from the Italian word *carosello* (little war), which originally referred to games of skill played by cavalrymen. In the mid-1700s, the French court of King Charles VIII frequently held "carousels," festivals that included demonstrations of horsemanship and skill. In one such competition, a horseman would ride full speed at a suspended ring and attempt to spear it—a game adapted from the Moors. Horsemen practiced for this event by sitting on wooden horses suspended from a rotating device powered by servants or draft animals.

European craftsmen began to produce similar devices for amusement parks and traveling shows—one of the earliest was in Tivoli Gardens in Copenhagen. With the addition of steam power, amusement parks and fairs began to feature as many as 15 whirling rides, mounted with gondolas, carts, buggies, and, most popular, farmyard animals such as pigs, roosters, and horses. Most of the carousels were portable. Manufacturing competition grew keen among carousel makers in England, France, and Germany.

Crude carousels have been made and used in the United States since 1825. In 1867, the industry began to flourish when Gustav Dentzel opened his cabinet shop in Philadelphia. Dentzel's father had carved carousel horses in Alsace, and Dentzel himself carved a small portable carousel and took it from town to town, selling tickets to supplement his income. Carousels soon became his main business. Dentzel founded the first of three primary schools of carousel carving in America—the Philadelphia style, characterized by highly realistic animals. The other styles are Coney Island (richly decorated and ornate) and country fair (simple folk representations of animals). Dentzel's shop hired some of the most gifted carvers in the world, Daniel Muller and Salvatore Cernigliaro among them. Dentzel's success spurred competitors; in Pennsylvania, the Philadelphia Toboggan Company (PTC) also hired several of Dentzel's carvers. Daniel Muller and his brother, who had been raised by the Dentzels as foster children, formed their own company for a time, causing Gustav Dentzel to disown them. They were welcomed back into the company by Dentzel's son after his father's death. It was common for master carvers such as Muller, Cernigliaro, Charles Carmel, Charles Illions, Leo Zoller, and John Zalar (a former carver of church interiors) to work for more than one company, including those in Coney Island, New York.

Carvers were artists as well as highly trained craftsmen—even with advanced skills, it took 40

---

the Peddler's Village complex, is aimed at all ages. It's open Sun. 10 A.M.–7 P.M. Mon.–Tues. 10 A.M.–6 P.M., Wed.–Thurs. 10 A.M.–8 P.M. A ticket to all exhibits is $6.95 adults, $9.95 children. The Grand Carousel is $1.95 per ticket. Video games, a rock-climbing wall, a "foam mountain" to climb, and an old-fashioned carousel are a few of the attractions.

Carousel Village at Indian Walk

A rare 1890 Dentzel carousel is the showpiece of this small local park (591 Durham Rd., Wrightstown, 215/598-0535) that also features a rideable one-third-scale replica of a C.P. Hunt-

ingdon Locomotive–powered train and a farm with animals. The garden-like park is three miles north of Newtown on SR 413. There is a $1.50 charge to enter the park.

SHOPPING

Peddler's Village and Penn's Purchase

The village (junction of US 202 and SR 263, Lahaska, 215/794-4000), which contains 70 specialty shops, six restaurants, and accommodations, grew from a family innkeeping business started in the mid-1700s. Earl Hart Jamison, the

hours to create an average jumping horse. Apprentice carvers began as small children by sweeping sawdust and sharpening tools; by the age of 18, they were fast and precise woodworkers. The styles of different carvers are often easily detectable. Salvatore Cernigliaro became famous for his Cherni figures, embellishments to the saddle in the forms of flying cherubs and standing female figures, and his cats, which always carry prey (fish or birds) in their mouths. Daniel Muller's saddles were frequently decorated with precise military paraphernalia.

Horses have always been the most popular animals in the menagerie. Decoration took many forms, from medieval chargers in chain mail to Indian ponies, complete with flying feathers and woven saddle blankets, all made of wood. Parrots, eagles, monkeys, imps, and puppies peeked out from the backs of saddles.

A menagerie of other animals also joined the ranks of horses: camels, giraffes, the hippocampus (part horse, part sea serpent), lions, tigers, and bears. The outer row of animals—usually stationary—was frequently the most ornate. Intricacy decreased the closer the carvings were set to the center post, just as the side that faced out—called the romance side—was always more detailed.

By the Depression, the demand for handcrafted carousel animals was over. Most companies ceased production or began creating animals with molded aluminum parts. The PTC bought

Dentzel's factory and continues to refurbish old carousels and manufacture other amusement park rides. The works of master carvers today bring thousands of dollars from eager collectors at auction.

In Pennsylvania, several intact and operating carousels include the following.
- **Bland Park,** in Tipton, has a three-row Coney Island style Herschell/Spillman.
- **Bushkill Park,** a small park in Easton, has a carousel that features work by Muller, Dentzel, and Carmel.
- **Dorney Park,** in Allentown, has a three-row Dentzel.
- **Hersheypark,** in Hershey, has one of the finest carousels operating today. It's a four-row PTC with exceptional work by John Zalar.
- **Kennywood Park,** in Pittsburgh, has a four-row Dentzel.
- **Knoebel's,** in Elysburg, has two exceptional carousels: a four-row Coney Island style with work by Carmel, and a two-row Stein and Goldstein, also in the Coney Island style.
- **Waldameer Park,** in Erie, has a three-row Dentzel with some lovely carvings by Muller.
- **Weona Park,** a small park in Pen Argyl, features a 1900 three-row Dentzel with original paint, a stationary menagerie, and brass rings. This is a favorite among devotees of Dentzel's work.

scion of the family, built the Golden Plough Inn and became inspired to create a village around it after a trip to the scenic town of Carmel, California, in 1962. Now visitors can shop, ride a carved horse on the carousel, eat, and sleep, all within six acres. Shops sell paper goods, country crafts, leather goods, gourmet foods, clothing, and much more. The village is open Mon.–Thurs. 10 A.M.–6 P.M., Fri.–Sat. 10 A.M.–8 P.M., and Sun. 11 A.M.–6 P.M.

Penn's Purchase (US 202 between Lahaska and New Hope, 215/794-0300) offers 50 factory outlets such as Etienne Aigner and Jones New York.

Doylestown Shops

The downtown historical district of Doylestown, centered on the intersection of Main and State Streets, is lined with older buildings housing boutiques and shops featuring new and antique goods. **Cyborg One Comic Books,** 5 S. Main St., features a full line of comics, plus toys, trading cards, and games. Across State Street, at 7 N. Main St., **Kind Earth** sells a variety of environmentally safe goods, aromatherapy materials, and skin and hair care products. **Dragon's Den of Antiques,** 135 S. Main St., just north of the SR 202 bypass, is an upscale 4,000-square-foot antique co-op. Restaurants and cafés provide resting places along the way.

OUTDOOR RECREATION

ⓜ Bowman's Hill Wildflower Preserve

Established in 1934 to preserve Pennsylvania's native flora, Bowman's Hill consists of woods, meadows, ponds, and special manmade habitats. Twenty-six trails wind through 80 acres of wildflowers, ferns, trees, shrubs, and vines. The Preserve building houses nature displays and an observation area overlooking the bird-feeding station. Bowman's Hill is located on SR 32 in Washington Crossing Historic Park, 1.6 miles north of the intersection of SR 32 and SR 532. For more information, contact Bowman's Hill Preserve (P.O. Box 103, Washington's Crossing, PA 18977, 215/862-2924, www.bhwp.org). It's open daily 8:30 A.M.–sunset. Admission is $5.

Silver Lake Nature Center

This 235-acre protected coastal plain off US 13 in Bristol features a wheelchair-accessible walkway over a marsh and a visitors' center with a number of exhibits on woodlands, wetlands, fields, and bogs.

Nockamixon State Park

Several Lenni Lenape historic sites are documented in the park (1542 Mountain View Dr., Quakertown, 215/529-7300, www.dcnr.state.pa.us/stateparks/parks/nockamixon). The name Nockamixon comes from the Lenni Lenape phrase "nocha-miska-ing" ("at the place of soft soil"). Boating, fishing, biking, and horseback riding are popular here in the warmer months (inquire at the park for nearby equine rentals); the trails adapt well to winter sports. Swimming is not permitted in the lake, but a pool is available. Some picnicking areas, fishing areas, trails and cabins open year-round. Most of the park is open sunrise to sunset. Fishing and boating is permitted 24 hours a day in designated areas.

Bicycle and Equestrian Trails: The 2.8-mile bicycle trail and 20 miles of equestrian trails are available for riding in the park. Off-road biking is not permitted.

Boating: Power boats of up to 20 hp motors are permitted on 1,450-acre Lake Nockamixon; there are four public launching areas. The Marina and Tohickon launch ramps are popular with sailboat, catamaran and windsurfing enthusiasts (the Marina has docking facilities for boats up to 24 feet in length). Three Mile Run and Haycock launch facilities are favored for motorboats, canoes and inflatable watercraft. Launching facilities are open 24 hours a day. A boat rental concession offers canoes, motorboats, rowboats, sailboats, paddleboats and pontoon boats during the summer season.

Hunting and Fishing: About 3000 acres are open to hunting, trapping and the training of dogs during established seasons. Common game species are deer, pheasant, rabbit and turkey.

The lake is a warm-water fishery. Commons species are walleye, muskellunge, pickerel, smallmouth and largemouth bass, striped bass hybrids, channel catfish, carp and various types of panfish. A fishing pier is at the midpoint of the lake. Fishing is prohibited in the marina and boat rental areas. Pennsylvania Fish and Boat Commission laws apply.

Swimming: The swimming pool complex includes a one-half acre main pool, separate diving well equipped with one meter boards, dressing rooms, first aid station and snack bar. The swimming pool is operated by a concession and an admission fee is charged. The swimming pool is open Memorial Day weekend-Labor Day daily 11 A.M.–7 P.M., weather permitting.

Winter Sports: Ice skating and ice fishing are permitted on the frozen lake surface when conditions are suitable. Cross-country skiers may use the bicycle trail and the roads in the closed day use area are open for cross-country skiing. There are also steeper hiking trails in the environmental study area. The area above the marina is used for sledding and tobogganing.

Park Camping and Cabins: Ten modern cabins are available for rentals throughout the year. Each cabin contains a furnished living area, kitchen/dining area, toilet/shower room, two or three bedrooms and are equipped with electric heat. One cabin is handicap-accessible. To reserve a cabin, call 888-PA-PARKS, 7 A.M.–5 P.M. Mon.–Sat. In addition, the park operates a youth hostel (see Accommodations).

Getting There: Nockamixon State Park is along SR 563, just off of SR 313, five miles east of Quakertown and nine miles west of Doylestown.

ACCOMMODATIONS

Eleven Bucks County Inns have bonded together to form the Bucks County Bed and Breakfast Association of Pennsylvania (P.O. Box 154, New Hope, PA 18938, www.visitbucks.com).

Under $50

The **Weisel Youth Hostel,** along the Tohickon Creek in the southwest corner of Nockamixon State Park, offers overnight accommodations for hikers and bicyclists for $15–25 per night. For reservations, contact the house parents (Weisel Youth Hostel, 7347 Richlandtown Rd., Quakertown, PA 18951, 215/536-8749).

Tyler Hostel (off SR 232 near Newtown, 215/968-0927), an AYH hostel in Tyler State Park, offers 25 beds and a few family rooms. Because of its central location, reservations are essential. The hostel is in an old farmhouse; to get there from the intersection of SR 332, take SR 232 north half a mile, turn right on Twining Ford Road, and continue into the park on the dirt road. The road will veer to the left; travel 300 feet beyond the left turn and bear right on White Pine Trail, then left at the first intersection onto Covered Bridge Trail. The hostel is at the end of the trail. The rate is $15 per night, family rooms are higher.

$100–150

In the 1930s, "Pop" and Ethel Reading ran a small sandwich shop in downtown New Hope and lived with their five children in this brick-and-clapboard house (one of the children's drawings still enhances a wall). The current bed and breakfast, **Porches on the Towpath** (20 Fisher's Alley, New Hope, 215/862-3277, www.porchesnewhope.com) is situated next to the canal

(the Ivyland train station is on the other side of the water); guests will enjoy sitting on the porches and living, if only temporarily, in slower, more friendly times. A two-day stay is required on weekends, three days on holidays. Breakfast is included, and all rooms have private baths. Rates are $95–135 Mon.–Thurs., $140–195 on weekends.

Arianna Miles Bed and Breakfast (243 Old Bethlehem Rd./North Lake Nockamixon, Quakertown, 215/529-1587, www.ariannamiles.com) offers six uniquely different guestrooms based on French Country inspired decor. This country stay is close to Nockamixon State Park and 18 miles from Doylestown on the back road. Two rooms share a bath, four have private baths, $85–185. A full breakfast is included.

Wednesday–Sunday by reservation, the B&B serves dinner. The New York/French Culinary Institute–trained chef produces exotic dishes such as a lamb stuffed artichoke appetizer ($12) and spicy chipotle grilled shrimp with jasmine rice and bell pepper relish ($22). Dinner averages $22.

Over $150

The **Golden Plough Inn** (US 202 and SR 263, Lahaska, 215/794-4004) is located in the heart of Peddler's Village (a combination entertainment center/shopping mall). This modern luxury inn features every amenity—private bath, cable TV, complimentary champagne, and in-room refrigerators.

Some rooms have kitchens and fireplaces. A complimentary breakfast is served in the nearby Spotted Hog restaurant. Special rates are available for children under 12, and the Golden Plough offers cost-conscious package plans year-round. Rates range $130–380.

FOOD

Looking for a decent place to eat in New Hope that won't cost the aphoristic arm and leg? The **Eagle Diner** (US 202, New Hope, 215/862-5575) won't be found on any tourist promotion brochures—this is where the locals eat. The bread is fresh-baked, the upscale diner entrées delicious, and the surroundings pleasant. It's all-American, with a salad bar, full bar, and children's menu. It's open daily 24 hours. Lunch averages $6, dinner $10.

The watering hole of choice for locals and visitors, **Martine's** (7 E. Ferry St., New Hope, 215/862-2966) is a cozy English pub housed in a 1752 tollhouse. The fireplace crackles in winter and there's an outdoor dining section for the warmer months. The menu is French-inspired American. Martine's is open daily 11 A.M.–2 A.M. and closes early on Sunday. Expect to pay around $20 for dinner.

Odette's (S. River Rd., 215/862-2432) has been a New Hope landmark since it was built as a tavern for boatmen in 1794. Parisian stage and screen star Odette Logan turned it into a first-class French restaurant during the 1960s, and the current owners continue to offer a piano bar and cabaret shows along with the European-inspired menu. The restaurant serves lunch Mon. and Wed.–Sat. 11:30 A.M.–3 P.M., dinner Mon.

and Wed.–Sat. 5–9 P.M. and Sun. 4–9:30 P.M. Sunday brunch is offered 10:30 A.M.–1:30 P.M. Dinner averages $22.

Conveniently located in the center of Doylestown's boutique-filled shopping district, **Chong's Garden** (22 N. Main St., Doylestown, 215/345-9444) is a popular lunch stop for shoppers and their families. Luncheon specials under $5 are offered Mon.–Sat., and all the food is MSG-free. Both Cantonese (mild) and Hunan (spicy) dishes are on the menu. Takeout is available anytime. Chong's is open Tues.–Thurs. 11:30 A.M.–9:30 P.M., Fri. 11:30 A.M.–10:30 P.M., Sat. noon–10:30 P.M., and Sun. noon–9:30 P.M.

INFORMATION

The **Bucks County Conference and Visitors Bureau** (3207 Street Rd., Bensalem, PA 19020, 215/639-0300 or 800/836-2825, www.experiencebuckscounty.com) offers an excellent booklet that details the towns in the county.

The Lehigh Valley

The towns of **Bethlehem, Emmaus,** and **Nazareth,** settled in the early 1740s, were created as private communal enclaves and bases for the missionary work of the Moravian Church, a Protestant sect. For the first 100 years of Bethlehem's existence, habitation within city limits was restricted to church members. The Moravian Museum and God's Acre cemetery in Bethlehem's historic district reveal the story of the settlement. The church choir, founded in 1900, still performs glorious renditions of Bach and other composers today, especially during the Christmas season. Bethlehem, decked out in 65,000 tiny white lights and one giant star that can be seen for 25 miles, celebrates the birth of Christ with a Christkindlmarkt (gift market) and numerous special events.

Founded by William Penn's son Thomas, the city of **Easton** has a number of colonial-era buildings around its main square. Easton is also home to the Canal Museum and the Crayola Factory and Museum. The industrial city of **Allentown,** with its excellent art museum, lies west of Bethlehem.

SCENIC TOURS

Moyer Aviation (Easton, 610/258 0473 or 800/321-5890, www.moyeraviation.com) offers a glimpse of the wonders of the Delaware River area and Poconos via aircraft. Tours vary in length of time from 10 minutes to 45 minutes, and from $15 to $50. One trip flies south on the Delaware River, circles Lake Nockamixon and returns past Historic Bethlehem and Easton.

HISTORIC SITES
Historic Bethlehem Partnership

This organization (459 Old York Rd., Bethlehem) operates the Colonial Industrial Quarter and HistoryWorks!, 1810 Goundie House, the Burnside Plantation, the Kemerer Museum of Decorative Arts, and the Moravian Museum of Bethlehem. Its purpose is to interpret the cultural, religious, and industrial heritage of Bethlehem and chronicle the changes that occurred in

The Moravian Star is the symbol of Bethlehem.

Bethlehem's first 250 years. The Colonial Industrial Quarter and Goundie House are open intermittently; for information on which sites are open and when, call 610/691-0603 (the Partnership Department of Education). Burnside Plantation is open for self-guided walking tours daily. Guided tours for groups of more than 10 may be scheduled at any time for any of the sites above. The Kemerer and Moravian museums are open Feb.–Dec. In the past, the Partnership has offered a "5&10 Pass" ($5 for students and $10 for adults) that may be used at any and all of the sites above for a full year.

The **Colonial Industrial Quarter** is, at present, only open at specific times of the year: Saturday, July 1–Aug. 26; and weekends during the Christmas season. Entry fee is $3; self-guided walking tour brochures are available at the Mill desk. HistoryWorks! is open weekends noon–4 P.M. and some holidays, and requires a separate entrance fee of $2.

In 1741, members of the Unitas Fratrum (Moravian Church) immigrated to the New World to bring the Gospel to Native Americans. Operating under a communal plan called the "General Economy," these early Moravians founded Bethlehem, Pennsylvania, and quickly developed a unique complex of trades, crafts, and industries. By 1748, when Bethlehem's population stood at only 395, 38 industries were in

full swing, many of them along the banks of Bethlehem's Monocacy Creek. Today, the quarter, a short walk from Main Street down Ohio Road (immediately below the Hotel Bethlehem) contains the restored 1761 Tannery, the 1762 Waterworks (oldest pumped waterworks in America), and the 1869 Luckenbach Mill with the HistoryWorks! children's interactive gallery located on the first floor.

The **Goundie House** (501 Main St.) is a Federal-style 1810 building, Bethlehem's first brick residence; it's the only present-day house museum in the historic district. John Sebastian Goundie (1773–1852) was a prominent Moravian brewer and community leader. His home, built in 1810, has been restored to its early 1800s appearance. Its period rooms tell the story of life in Bethlehem in the 1820s. This home is included in the entry fee to the industrial quarter, and is open during the same times, plus additional hours not yet finalized.

Burnside Plantation (1461 Schoenersville Rd.), a farm spread over seven acres within the city, lies within the shadow of the imposing Martin Tower, world headquarters of Bethlehem Steel Corporation. In 1748, Moravian missionary James Burnside and his wife, Mary, built the first single-family house in Bethlehem on 500 acres adjacent to the Moravian settlement. It was a move of historic proportions since all other Moravians of that period lived communally in houses especially built for single men, single women and married people. Today, seven acres of that original farm are being developed as a living history museum to interpret farming between 1748 and 1848, a time of great change in agricultural methods. It's open year round; self-guided walking tours may be taken during daylight hours (be aware that the road to the plantation is unpaved). Tour brochures are in a protected box along the fence nearest the corn crib.

The collection at the **Kemerer Museum of Decorative Arts** (427 N. New St., Bethlehem, 610/868-6868) represents fine examples of 18th- and 19th-century decorative furniture, silver, glass, textiles, china, paintings, and toys from the Lehigh Valley. It's in the historic district; the museum is open Tues.–Sun. noon–4 P.M.

Delaware River Valley

MORAVIAN LIFE

Early Moravians were distinctive in dress, adopting the plain style of other religious sects. Little Moravian girls wore net caps tied under the chin with pink ribbons. Older girls wore white linen caps with red ribbons after they became church members. Married sisters wore caps tied with light blue, and widows' ribbons were white. Unmarried members lived separately and were expected to practice celibacy.

Some of the early Moravian outer settlements were memorably named—the Society of the Woman in the Wilderness, for one (so called because in the Book of Revelation, the church is described as a woman). The members of this settlement expected the arrival of the reincarnated Jesus in 1694 and watched for signs of his

coming at night with telescopes placed on the roof of the church.

As a group, Moravians sought to retain some of the values of monastic life—altruism, self-denial, meditation, industry, frugality, and self-discipline—while living in a communal, familial society. They refused to take an oath or to bear arms. Instead of religious services, Moravians periodically held "love feasts," with shared food and drink. In all their congregational deliberations, the Moravians sought direct guidance from God, in the form of lots. They would submit their questions in prayer, then choose from three ballots—marked "yea" or "nay" or blank (which meant that the question was unanswerable). Once drawn, the lot's answer was accepted.

Admission fee for special guided tours and entry into self-guided special exhibits is $6, $3 for children ages 6–12 and free for children under the age of 6; for self-guided exhibits only, admission is less. Discounts for AAA members and seniors are offered.

The **Moravian Museum of Bethlehem, Inc.** (66 W. Church St., Bethlehem, 610/867-0173) is located in a *gemeinhaus* (meetinghouse) built in 1741 and depicts the early Moravian community in a series of exhibits featuring art, musical instruments, and furnishings. The museum is open Tues.–Sun. noon–4 P.M. Guided tours are scheduled every half hour 12:30–3:30 P.M. and there is a charge for admission of $6, $5 for AAA members of seniors, $3 for children ages 6–12. Children under 6 are free. Set in the historic district, the building is Bethlehem's oldest. Grave markers in God's Acre, the cemetery dating from 1742 on the hill behind the museum, bear testimony to the faith of the early Moravian community.

Delaware and Lehigh Navigation Canal/Lehigh Section

Easton is the midpoint of the National Historic Corridor, which follows the 150-mile path of the former Delaware and Lehigh Canal from

Wilkes-Barre to Bristol, east of Philadelphia. The upper section of the canal, from White Haven to Jim Thorpe, was destroyed in a flood in 1862 and never rebuilt. The roads that parallel the Lehigh River south from Jim Thorpe through Allentown, Bethlehem, and Easton to the Delaware River are easily accessible.

Thirty-two miles of the Lehigh Towpath are designated National Recreational Trails, and one of the most popular sections is the Towpath Bike/Hike Trail. It extends 7.8 miles from the village of Bethlehem near SR 378 and Lehigh Street along the Lehigh River to the Delaware River in Easton.

Liberty Bell Shrine

A full-size replica of the Liberty Bell, a 46-foot mural depicting events that took place in the area during the American Revolution, maps, guns, Revolutionary War uniforms, and a "Betsy Ross" flag made by her granddaughter are on display in the basement of Zion Reformed Church (622 Hamilton Mall, Allentown, 610/435-4232). The shrine is open May–Oct. Mon.–Sat. noon–4 P.M.; Nov.–Dec. and Feb.–April Thurs.–Sat. noon–4 P.M. Admission is by donation.

In 1777, George Washington retreated from the city of Philadelphia and withdrew his troops to

Valley Forge. The capital of the new nation was about to fall into British hands. Washington knew that the British were short of ammunition and it was likely they would melt down the city's available iron—including its church bells for musket and cannon balls. The Liberty Bell, the symbol of the new nation, was likely to share this fate.

A wagon train was organized to carry military stores to Bethlehem; several church bells and the Liberty Bell were hidden among the goods. The bells were hauled to Allentown, where they were hidden under the floor of old Zion Reformed Church. When the British evacuated Philadelphia nearly a year later, the bells were restored to their rightful places.

Hugh Moore Historical Park

The park (200 S. Delaware Dr., off Glendon Ave., Easton, 610/250-6700), named for Dixie cup founder and museum supporter Hugh Moore, has hiking trails, a 3.5-mile paved bike path, and picnic areas that wind among locks, canal structures, and 19th-century industrial ruins. A restored locktender's house is nearby, and during warmer weather, visitors can take a ride on a mule-drawn canal boat operating on a restored section of the Delaware and Lehigh Canal. Canal boat rides take place May 3–Sept. 28, Mon.–Sat. 11 A.M.–4:30 P.M. and Sun. 1:15–4 P.M. Rides are 40 minutes. From Aug. 31–Sept., rides are offered on weekends only. Combination admission fees to both The Locktender's House and the canal boat ride are $6, $5.50 for seniors, and $4 for children. Canoe and paddleboat rentals are available.

OTHER POINTS OF INTEREST

Dorney Park and Wildwater Kingdom

Dorney Park and Wildwater Kingdom (3830 Dorney Park Rd., Allentown, 610/398-7955, www.dorneypark.com) have separate hours. Dorney Park's are as ornate as Oprah's datebook. Roughly, it's open May–Oct., 10 A.M.–7 P.M. (with extended hours mid-June–Aug., and some early closings for private parties—make sure to call and confirm). Wildwater Kingdom operates daily June–Aug., weekends only Sept., 10 A.M.–

10 P.M. The ticket price for those 48 inches or taller varies by season: Early Season (May, when the Waterpark is closed) is $21. Spring season, May 29–June 11 is $29.95. Summer season, June 12–Labor Day weekend, weekends only is $35.75. Late season, select dates in late Aug.–mid-Sept. Those less than 48 inches tall in shoes pay $16. Entry includes unlimited access to all rides, slides, and daily entertainment; kids age 2 and under are free. Parking is $7 per vehicle. Two-day, starlight (after 5 P.M.), and season passes sometimes go for bargain rates.

In 1860 Solomon Dorney opened his Fish Weir and Summer Resort, featuring eight trout ponds and shady picnic groves. In the next 25 years, the park added bowling-on-the-greens, quoits, archery, and safety swings, along with a miniature zoo. As tastes changed, rides such as a scenic railway and Ferris wheel were added. In 1901, the Allentown-Kutztown Traction Company bought the park and started daily trolley service from Allentown.

Today, Dorney Park is spread over 200 acres and includes a Dentzel four-abreast carousel; ThunderHawk, the original upgraded wooden roller coaster; Skyscraper, a 90-foot-high Ferris wheel; and a number of thrill rides, such as Hercules, one of the world's tallest wooden roller coasters. Wildwater Kingdom, a water play area within Dorney Park, features Aquablast, one of the tallest, steepest, and fastest waterfall plunge rides in the country; it's the most-visited water park in the nation. Both Dorney Park and Wildwater Kingdom have areas dedicated to small children. The short set can visit Camp Snoopy, where they can play on a variety of interactive attractions with themes from the popular comic strip *Peanuts* (such as a Sopwith Camel biplane ride).

Lost River Caverns

Five chambers of crystal formations provide underground entertainment for visitors at Lost River Caverns (off SR 412, Hellertown, 610/838-8767). The 52°F temperature remains steady year-round. The caverns are open daily 9 A.M.–5 P.M., with extended hours in the summer, 9 A.M.–6 P.M. Admission is $8 for adults and $4 for children ages 3–12.

The Martin Guitar Company

For those with musical interests (including future rock stars) a tour of the venerable Martin Guitar Company (510 Sycamore St., Nazareth, 610/759-2837, www.mguitar.com) is a must. Tours are Mon.–Fri. at 1 P.M. The company, founded in 1833 by Christian Frederick Martin, remains one of the few surviving family-owned and -operated manufacturers of top quality acoustic guitars in the world.

The guitar museum features a priceless collection of unusual and vintage Martins; a luthier supply shop—kits, tools, parts, etc.—is on the premises.

Clover Hill

Clover Hill (9850 Newton Rd., Breinigsville, 610/395-2468) is one of the most popular local wineries in the Lehigh Valley area. Varietals are bottled from grapes produced in its own vineyards in a modern state-of-the-art facility. A scenic picnic area is available. The winery is open Mon.–Sat. 10 A.M.–5:30 P.M., Sun. noon–5 P.M.

MUSEUMS

The Crayola Factory and Museum

The Crayola Factory (30 Centre Square, Easton, 610/515-8000, www.crayola.com)—very colorful and fun with a daily calendar of events—is a combination factory tour and learn-by-play museum. The factory is open Sept.–March, Tues.–Sat. 9:30 A.M.–5 P.M. and Sun. noon–5 P.M. It is closed on most Mondays and in summer there are extended hours. Admission is $9 for adults, $8 for seniors and $3 for children and free for ages 2 and under.

Visitors can see Crayola crayons and markers being made, and there are more than a dozen interactive exhibits to encourage creativity. Some of the highlights are a 3-D sculpture that can be manipulated and scribbled on by participants, a CD-ROM computer studio, a "mold your own" sculpture area with free Model Magic, a color garden for younger kids where they may harvest red apples from a velcro tree, and a glass wall that kids (and adults) can mark up to their heart's content.

Easton Museum of PEZ Dispensers

It's true, there are museums for everything. Close by the Crayola Factory, the Easton Museum of PEZ Dispensers (15–19 S. Bank St., Easton, 610/253-9794 or 888/THE-PEZ1, www.eastonmuseumofpez.com) features 1,500 PEZ dispensers in miniature landscapes. It's open Labor Day–April Tues.–Sun. 10 A.M.–5 P.M., May–Labor Day Mon.–Sun. 10 A.M. to 6 P.M. Admission is $5 adults, $3 children, free for ages 4 and younger.

PEZ, if you'll recall, are little mystery-flavored rectangles of hard candy that are loaded into a dispenser (featuring a multitude of cartoon characters, superheroes, cultural icons—you name it), which pops out the candies one at a time. The handy little lozenge dispensers are grouped together by theme: Disney dispensers sit in a 10-foot-high castle, Halloween-themed dispensers frolic in a haunted house; psychedelic dispensers (yes, they exist) are set beside a real Volkswagen Beetle that appears to be crashing through the wall. It's pretty cute, and something anyone who grew up on PEZ will enjoy. There's also a gift shop where you can load up on PEZ merchandise.

National Canal Museum

The Canal Museum (30 Centre Sq., Easton, 610/559-6613) offers an opportunity to step back in time to the period when America's waterways were the main (and often only) transportation routes. The museum features displays on the building and use of the canals.

The museum is open year-round, Tues.–Sat. 9:30 A.M.–5 P.M., Sun. noon–5 P.M.; hours are extended during the summer. April 1–Labor Day, it's also open on Mon. Admission is $9 for adults and seniors, Children under 2 are free.

Allentown Art Museum

The Allentown Art Museum (5th and Court Sts., Allentown, 610/432-4333) was founded by a group of citizens in 1939 and is dedicated to working artists in the area. In the late 1950s, the Samuel H. Kress Foundation made this small museum into a major player. It's open Tues.–Sat. 11–5 P.M., Sun. noon–5 P.M. The Museum is closed on Monday and major holidays.

© JOANNE MILLER

Delaware Canal and the river beyond

Kress was born in Cherryville, nine miles north of Allentown. He amassed a fortune though his eponymous five-and-dime stores and became a collector of paintings by old masters. Samuel Kress and his brother Rush were two of the founding benefactors of the National Gallery of Art in Washington, D.C., among others. The Kress gifts to the Allentown museum were selected from Samuel Kress's personal favorites and represent an impressive survey of Italian Renaissance art, and Dutch and German paintings.

In addition, the Allentown Art Museum features a broad-based collection of European and American fine prints, drawings, photographs, paintings, and sculpture, including many modern works. A library designed by Frank Lloyd Wright for a Prairie-style private home was reinstalled in the museum and has become a popular attraction. Visitors are encouraged to use the room and to take advantage of the books related to Wright's work that line the walls.

Saylor Cement Museum

David Saylor emigrated from Great Britain and received the first U.S. patent for liquid rock—Portland cement—in 1871. In 1893, his company erected the Schoefer kilns at 245 N. 2nd St., Coplay, and made industrial history. The kilns, looking vaguely like giant beehives or misplaced towers from Angkor Wat, still stand. The museum and kilns are open May–Sept. weekends 1–4 P.M. Admission is free.

SHOPPING

Bethlehem

Downtown Bethlehem is a bustling shopping district with a variety of upscale stores. One particularly good one is the **Moravian Book Shop** (428 Main St., 610/866-5481 www.moravianstar.com), which has been in business for 250 years. The bookshop has a lot more than books: gifts, cards, herbs, crafts, and a small deli make this an entertaining stop.

Christkindlmarkt (corner of Main and Spring Sts., 610/861-0678, www.fest.org) is in full swing Nov. 24–Dec. 17, Thurs.–Sun. in Bethlehem; both the phone number and website are for Artsquest, which handles most events in Bethlehem. This wildly popular outdoor market has things to see—ice sculptures, more than 100 créches (Christian manger scenes) from around the world, strolling entertainers, artwork—and things to buy, such as a variety of foods, ornaments, paintings, and crafts.

OUTDOOR RECREATION

Downhill Skiing

Fifteen slopes, seven lifts—including three doubles and one triple—and non-ski amenities make **Bear Creek Ski & Recreation Area** (101 Doe Mountain Land, Macungie, 610/682-7100, www.skibearcreek.com) the most popular place for skiers and snowboarders of all experience levels in the Allentown area; snowboarders have their own runs. There are plenty of events and special discounts to keep the whole family entertained. To get there from the town of Macungie, go west on Church Street for five miles.

THE LEHIGH AND THE DELAWARE

The same two men who bought up coal land in the infancy of the anthracite boom, Josiah White and Erskine Hazard, also took it upon themselves to improve the Lehigh River by adding a working transportation corridor of locks, dams, rail connections, and inclined planes. The Lehigh Navigational System stretched from White Haven, high up in the Poconos, to the Delaware River in Easton. During the same period, 1817–45, the Delaware Canal was being built in stages from Easton to Bristol. Both waterways were built by local farmers and Irish immigrants, using picks, shovels, and wheelbarrows. Mauch Chunk (now Jim Thorpe), in Carbon County, began to send coal to Philadelphia and beyond via its novel switchback railroad, which transported coal directly from the mine over a hill down to a waiting canal boat.

The heyday of the canal system was between the 1830s and the 1860s. Competition from railroads and road transport spurred the decline, as did flooding. Mauch Chunk's switchback railroad became the first tourist thrill ride, the model for modern roller coasters. In recent years, it's become a hiking/biking path. The Upper Grand section of the Lehigh System, between White Haven and Mauch Chunk, was destroyed by flood in 1862 and never rebuilt; the lower section continued to operate until 1942. The Delaware Canal, though still usable, ceased operation during the Depression.

Lift ticket rates vary by the day (lower on weekdays and non-holidays) and time (lower after 1 P.M.). Ski rentals and many special programs are available. The resort is open daily 9 A.M.–10 P.M. during cold weather.

Biking

The **Lehigh Valley Velodrome** (LCV; at the junction of SR 100 and SR 222 in Trexlertown, 610/967-7587, www.lvvelo.org) is one of 20 velodromes (graded bicycle racing tracks) in the United States. Originally built on land owned by the Rodale family, it was modeled after the 1960 Olympic facility in Rome and attracts riders from the world over. The LCV has hosted more than 100 riders who have represented 20 different countries at the Olympic Games; 30 have gone on to become Olympic medalists. The velodrome was the site of the 1996 U.S. Olympic Cycling Team trials.

The track sponsors a number of spectator racing events and classes. It's open to the public at no charge when not used for racing meets; amateur racers can bring their own bikes and helmets and ride the track at their own pace. The LCV also has one of the largest bicycle flea markets on the East Coast each October. Call for a schedule of events and open track times.

Pool Wildlife Sanctuary

This 72-acre sanctuary, once privately owned farmland, features a nature center, trails, a bird blind, beehives, ponds, and an arboretum. All of the trails are under a mile in length, and the sanctuary is a good place to observe native trees and floodplains. From Allentown, take SR 29 to Riverbend Road. Turn left onto Riverbend Road, and right onto Orchid Place across the white bridge into the sanctuary. Admission is free.

ACCOMMODATIONS

Most major chains have hotels/motels in the Lehigh Valley.

The Lafayette Inn (525 W. Monroe St., Easton, 610/253-4500, www.lafayetteinn.com) was originally constructed as a private residence in 1895. It went through several reincarnations, including that of fraternity house. The College Hill neighborhood in which the inn is located is one of the prettiest in Easton. All rooms are attractively decorated and have private baths; suites with kitchenette units are available. A continental breakfast is served in the Taylor room downstairs. Rates range $105–180.

Glasbern (2141 Pack House Rd., Fogelsville, 610/285-4723, www.glasbern.com) is the ultimate in luxurious country inns. Three renovated buildings, including a 19th-century barn, capture the elegance of a fine hotel. The inn's setting is a secluded 110-acre property, reminiscent of the Scottish highlands. All rooms have private baths, and rooms and suites with whirlpool baths and fireplaces are available. Breakfast is included, and some weekends may require a two-night stay. Glasbern is a welcoming place to dine after a chilly walk through the fields and woods. Rates range $127–$391, higher on weekends and high season.

The giant neon "HOTEL" sign perched atop the north face of the **M Radisson Hotel Bethlehem** (437 Main St., Bethlehem, 610/625-5000 or 800/333-3333) since 1958 is no more, though a replica of the sign on the south side still proclaims "HOTEL BETHLEHEM" to weary travelers, as it has since the hotel was built during the early 1920s. The hotel features 127 rooms available year-round. Rates range $95–180, and packages are offered.

The hotel, a local landmark, was closed in January 1998 when the owners filed for bankruptcy and was purchased by a group of investors who spent nearly $4 million restoring the building to its original 1922 art deco splendor. The property is now managed by Radisson Hotels Worldwide and strives to live up to the elegance and grandeur of the period in which it was built. The open lobby is furnished with plush sofas and wingback chairs that invite guests to sit and relax. Minimal draperies allow the ambience of downtown Bethlehem to be easily viewed. The hotel offers Internet access, a fitness center, and airport shuttle service. The hotel's restaurant, the Colonnade, is decorated with murals dating back to 1937, depicting the history of the city of Bethlehem.

FOOD

Inexpensive

An Allentown institution, **Yocco's "The Hot Dog King"** (625 Liberty St., Allentown, 610/433-1950) has been serving up messy, cheap (under $5), delicious hot dogs since 1922. Yocco's is known for its secret recipe chili sauce. Hamburgers, other types of sandwiches, and piero-

gies are also on the menu. Yocco's has three other locations: 2128 Hamilton St. in Allentown, SR 29 (Buckeye Rd.) in Emmaus, and I-78 and SR 100 south in Fogelsville. Pass the napkins!

Confetti Café (462 Main St., Bethlehem, 610/861-7484) is an attractive little eatery serving soups, salads, and sandwiches for $8 or less.

Moderate

A local favorite, the **King George Inn** (Hamilton and Cedar Crest Blvds., Allentown, 610/435-1723) has been around since 1756 (the building is a National Historic Site). Expect relaxed, casual dining and a varied menu: crab cakes are especially good here, and salads are fresh and delicious. The bar in the cellar is a popular nightspot. It's open at Mon.–Sat. 11 A.M.–10 P.M. Call for Sunday brunch hours. Lunch costs around $8, dinner $20.

M The Sun Inn Restaurant (564 Main St., Bethlehem, 610/866-1758) built by Moravians in 1758, has served such notables as Benjamin Franklin, Martha and George Washington, and the Marquis de Lafayette. John Adams called it "the best Inn I ever saw." The menu features generous portions of American standards. It's located in the heart of downtown Bethlehem; the lower floor of the historic building is available for guided tours, and the restaurant is on the second floor. It's open daily 11:30 A.M.–2 P.M. and 5–8 P.M. Prices average $11 for lunch, $18 for dinner.

Bethlehem Brew Works (569 Main St., Bethlehem, 610/882-1300, www.thebrewworks.com) features a 250-seat restaurant. Signature beers include Fegley's ESB, Valley Golden Ale, and the award-winning Steelworkers' Oatmeal Stout. In addition, three seasonal taps have been frequented, with beers ranging from Pale Ales and Wheats to Pumpkin Ale and a Belgian Lambics. Accompanying the six beers brewed right in the restaurant is a full bar specializing in single malt scotches, small batch bourbons, and fine cigars. Open seven days a week, 11 A.M.–2 A.M., BBW offers lunch and dinner featuring many items with the handcrafted beer incorporated into the recipes. Golden Ale Hummus, Beer and Cheese Soup, Porter Chicken, Diamond Plate Pork, and marinated portabella mushrooms are just a start. Prices run $7–16.

Elegant

A tastefully decorated dining room anchored by a massive fieldstone fireplace enhances the special dining experience of ☒ **Glasbern** (2141 Packhouse Rd., Fogelsville, 610/285-4723, www.glasbern.com/dining). Set on a private farm, this inn and restaurant serves contemporary continental cuisine. A full bar is available. Glasbern serves dinner daily 5:30– 8 P.M. by reservation only; entrees average $25. There is a four-course prix fixe menu for $55 on Saturday.

INFORMATION

The **Lehigh Valley Convention and Visitors Bureau** (P.O. Box 20785, Lehigh Valley, PA 18002, 610/882-9200 or 800/747-0561, www.lehighvalleypa.org) is exceptionally helpful to visitors. The **Bethlehem Visitors' Center** (52 W. Broad St., Bethlehem, PA 18018, 610/868-1513, www.bethlehempa.org) can give additional information on Bethlehem. Easton has information on activities in that city at www.easton-pa.com.

Pennsylvania Dutch Country

When asked to name a place or feature characteristic of Pennsylvania, most visitors would focus on the familiar attributes of Dutch Country, in Pennsylvania's Piedmont region. The gentle valleys of the Piedmont continue to reflect the agrarian interests of the first settlers in the colony. Urban development outside of Philadelphia has taken place in cities that expanded during the industrial revolution, such as Reading, or, like Lancaster, were major stops on the wagon road, the main (canal) line, or the railroad line between Philadelphia and Pittsburgh.

Today, the Amish country of Lancaster County and the Lebanon Valley; the chocoholic's favorite destination, Hershey; and the shopping mecca of Reading arc a few of the attractions that make this one of the most visited in the state. Lancaster remains the center of Dutch Country, surrounded by satellite villages, activities, and amusements celebrating the lifestyle. Nearly 5,000 small farms cover the area; the average farm size is 85 acres, and many of the fields continue to be tilled with horses and mules as they have been since colonial times.

Must-Sees

M Ephrata Cloister: This authentic site affords visitors an insider's look at an 18th-century Pennsylvania phenomenon—the austere village of a religious commune (page 130).

M Landis Valley Museum: This is the largest outdoor collection concentrating on Pennsylvania German rural heritage and farming techniques (page 131).

M The Watch and Clock Museum: One of a kind, the museum displays four centuries of timekeeping devices, miniature to gigantic. Several clocks have multiple moving figurines (page 132).

M The National Toy Train Museum: If you've ever spent a holiday morning putting together tin tracks, this is for you. Many styles, gauges, and models are on display (page 132).

M Railroad Museum of Pennsylvania: Here you'll find plenty of rail lore, and the lure of a really *big* engine—that you can walk under (page 133).

M Farm and Bulk Stores: No visit to the Lancaster area would be complete without visiting its fun and fascinating local bulk food shops (page 137).

M Hershey: It may be a one-industry town, but it offers a documentary on the making of chocolate, a 90-acre amusement park, a zoo with 200 animals of 75 species, and a 23-acre landscaped garden—something for everyone (page 140).

M State Museum of Pennsylvania: An excellent admission-free collection presents a broad perspective of life in Pennsylvania as it was 3.6 billion years ago to the present (page 143).

M Berks County Hex Tour: Decorated barns are a familiar sight along Pennsylvania roads, and this auto tour winds through gently folded farm terrain, passing 14 decorated barns and a covered bridge (page 147).

M Hopewell Furnace: An authentic iron "plantation"—foundry and village—within a park. Nearby, see the Mary Merritt Doll Museum, a wonderful jumble of 1,500 dolls and stuffed toys, and the Merritt Museum of Childhood, filled with whimsical collectibles (page 148).

PENNSYLVANIA DUTCH COUNTRY

Berks County Hex Tour — M

Hershey — M

Hopewell Furnace — M

State Museum of Pennsylvania — M

M — Ephrata Cloister

The Watch and Clock Museum — M

M — Landis Valley Museum

M — Farm and Bulk Stores

M — The National Toy Train Museum

Railroad Museum of Pennsylvania — M

Ephrata Cloister

© JOANNE MILLER

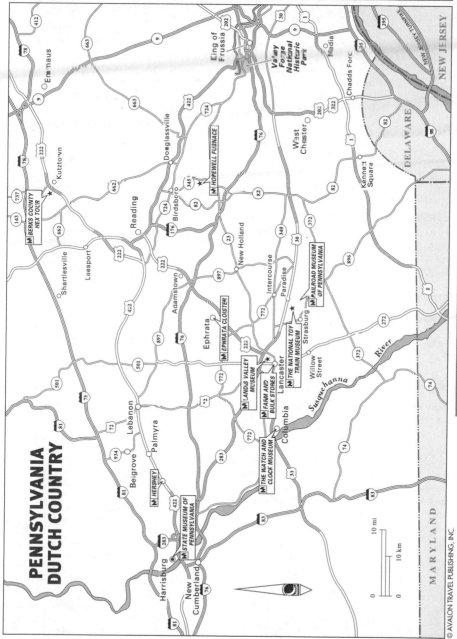

PENNSYLVANIA DUTCH COUNTRY

NEW JERSEY

DELAWARE

MARYLAND

Pennsylvania Dutch Country

NEW TURNPIKE

295

95

82

King of Prussia

Valley Forge National Historic Park

Media

9

30

202

Chadds Ford

Kennett Square

West Chester

202

322

1

82

82

Emmaus

78

412

663

9

9

663

422

724

76

HOPEWELL FURNACE

345

Douglassville

Kutztown

222

78

737

BERKS COUNTY HEX TOUR

143

662

Reading

662

724

Birdsboro

82

176

New Holland

23

340

372

Intercourse

Paradise

RAILROAD MUSEUM OF PENNSYLVANIA

896

30

Shartlesville

Leesport

222

222

Adamstown

897

EPHRATA CLOISTER

Ephrata

222

772

Strasburg

THE NATIONAL TOY TRAIN MUSEUM

272

River

74

422

897

76

501

772

LANDS VALLEY MUSEUM

FARM AND BULK STORES

Lancaster

Willow Street

372

Susquehanna

501

78

Lebanon

72

Palmyra

73

772

Columbia

74

81

Belgrove

934

HERSHEY

283

THE WATCH AND CLOCK MUSEUM

772

33

81

422

STATE MUSEUM OF PENNSYLVANIA

283

83

74

Harrisburg

New Cumberland

76

83

81

10 mi

10 km

0

0

© AVALON TRAVEL PUBLISHING, INC.

Harrisburg, the state capital, remains a relatively small town with a couple of excellent museums. Reading, its industrial life diminished, has rebuilt itself as a discount-outlet capital with several outstanding restaurants. The entire area offers visitors bountiful and varied choices, with something for every taste and budget.

PLANNING YOUR TIME

This area is best divided into three sections, taken one-by-one or together, depending on interests.

If the Dutch Country is your focus, plan three days—one week based in the Lancaster area. On Day 1, historians and those curious about the lifestyle of Amish and other religious groups will want to visit the **Ephrata Cloister** (2 hours) and the **Mennonite Information Center** (1 hour). On Day 2, take in the **Landis Valley Museum** (3 hours–all day), perhaps with a stop in Lititz to enjoy a pretzel. **The Amish Village** (2 hours–all day) is another alternative. Day 3 could include stops at the Lancaster Cultural History Museum (1 hour) or the Lancaster Quilt and Textile Museum (1 hour) downtown before lunch. Then the entire family will enjoy the **National Toy Train Museum** (2 hours) and, after lunch at one of the local favorites, stop by one or more of the crafts and **farm and bulk stores.** The **Railroad Museum of Pennsylvania** (3 hours) will take the better part of Day 4, perhaps followed by a buggy ride. On Day 5, families with young children will want to stop at **Dutch Wonderland** (2 hours–all day) and **The People's Place** (1 hour). If possible, do try to schedule a show at **Sight and Sound** (3 hours). On Day 6, adults and children will enjoy the **Watch and Clock Museum** (2 hours), especially on the hour, when every musical timepiece goes off.

Is Hershey on your must-visit list? Plan at least three days. **Hershey's Chocolate World** and the **Hershey Museum** will take all of one day; **ZooAmerica** and **Hershey Gardens** (1–2 hours each) another, and **HersheyPark** the third—that's if you don't plan to golf or enjoy outdoor recreation in the area. While in the Hershey area, plan an additional 1–2 days visiting Harrisburg. The excellent **State Museum of Pennsylvania** (3 hours) and **Whitaker Center for Science and the Arts** (3 hours) are well worth a visit, and the **Capitol Complex** tour (2 hours) is interesting, too.

In the Reading area, plan on 4–5 days for shopping and sightseeing. The **Berks County Hex Tour** will take all of the first day, and give you an excellent overview of the area. The children (and anyone interested in miniatures) will also want to take in **Roadside America** (1–2 hours), and if it's the holiday season, don't miss **Koziar's Christmas Village** at night. **Hopewell Furnace** (2–3 hours) is a lovely place to spend all or part of a day, and visiting the **Daniel Boone Homestead** (1–2 hours) is a great addition or an alternative. Don't miss the nearby **Mary Merritt Doll Museum** (2–3 hours) and **Merritt Museum of Childhood** (2–3 hours). In Reading proper, catch the view from the **Reading Pagoda** (1 hour) and do a little shopping at the VFOutlet center or **Renninger's.**

GETTING THERE AND GETTING AROUND

By Air, Rail, or Bus

Almost all major airlines fly into Philadelphia International Airport; Lancaster, Harrisburg and Reading may all be reached via connecting airlines.

Amtrak offers frequent service from Philadelphia through Lancaster to Harrisburg on both the Pennsylvanian and Three Rivers trains (also referred to as the Keystone route).

Greyhound buses (800/231-2222) travel through most of the larger cities. Call for bus schedules and fares.

By Auto

Major east-west routes into the area are I-78 along the northern border from Easton to Harrisburg, I-76, and US 30. Routes running north-south are SR 9 (toll), US 422, SR 501, SR 272, and SR 32. All, with the exception of SR 9 and parts of US 422, are two-lane roads.

PENNSYLVANIA "DUTCH"

The "Dutch" in the term Pennsylvania Dutch is a corruption of *Deutsche* (doitch)—that is, German, the native language of the majority of early settlers in Pennsylvania. Over time, the designation has also come to refer to those who speak it.

Though many think of the "Plain People"—Amish and Mennonites—as being representative of Pennsylvania "Dutch" culture, these groups made up only 10 percent of the original German immigrant population and remain in the minority. Approximately 16,000 Amish live within the borders of Pennsylvania today, out of a total population of more than 12 million. Regardless of religious affiliation, most Germans immigrated in groups associated by religion, tended to form their own settlements—preserving their culture, customs, and language—and were often slow to assimilate.

Many German immigrants had adopted agriculture as a means of survival in the Old World.

Some did so by default—religious prejudice in Europe closed the doors of many schools and guilds to members of the sects—turning to farming to feed their families. Southeastern Pennsylvania, consisting almost entirely of fertile land, proved a ready new home. Tobacco and other extremely labor-intensive crops did well in Pennsylvania's early farms. In the 1700s, Lancaster County was the largest producer of wheat in the colonies, and the area continues to thrive in the hands of the descendants of those who were willing to risk the voyage to America.

Today, German surnames such as Peachey, Stoltzfus, and Yoder can be found in every professional directory and telephone book in the state. The "Dutch" lifestyle, expanded from its agricultural roots, continues to offer visitors a Germanic style of design, level of craftsmanship, and hearty cuisine unique to Pennsylvania.

HISTORY

Lost Lands

In 1682, William Penn's characterization of the Lenni Lenape—the "Delaware Indians" who inhabited peaceful villages on the eponymous river—as a people who "never have much, nor want much; Wealth circulateth like the Blood, all parts partake," changed radically over the next century. The Lenni Lenape became dependent on goods and foodstuffs offered to them by European traders in exchange for the beaver pelts they harvested. Their seasonal, agricultural lifestyle eroded.

After Penn's death, in 1718, his heirs purchased tracts of land based on earlier land-lease agreements. The Lenape were powerless to make any other deals by that time; in less than 40 years, their overdependence on European wealth and goods had put an end to their old way of life. Hunting with European rifles had devastated the Delaware River Valley, making the area no longer viable to support the Lenape hunters and their families. With few options, they chose to sell the land and wander, moving north and west into the regions protected by their overlord "uncles," the Iroquois Confederacy.

The Great Migration

William Penn's Quaker brethren poured into the New World, immigrating from Britain and several German-speaking countries. Penn's promise of religious freedom brought followers of the reform churches, such as Presbyterians and Mennonites, and more esoteric Protestant sects—the Moravians, the Amish, and the Ephratans. There was a marked contrast between the religious beliefs of the Puritans, who colonized New York and New England, and those of the Quakers. Puritans saw God as a stern and demanding figure intent on punishing wrongdoing; their churches were led by authority figures who often had the final word on biblical interpretation. Quakers, following the tenets of George Fox, welcomed a generous and loving God who cared for, spoke to, and guided each individual. Because of a fundamental difference in belief systems, Quakers and other minority religions relied heavily on the protection of the British to keep peace among the factions. Though the French and Indian War of the late 18th century and, subsequently, Pontiac's War were fought mainly on the frontiers, touching only the fringes of the Piedmont, settlers' reliance on the power of the crown was absolute.

Roots of Dissent

Colonists in the Piedmont area had little reason to argue with Britain; they did not recognize themselves as Americans, being more likely to describe themselves as British, or Pennsylvanians. The colonies were content with their high wages, cheap land, and almost complete autonomy over their internal political and domestic affairs. The popularly elected lower houses of the assembly served as nurturing ground for such future Revolutionary leaders as John Adams, John Dickinson, Thomas Jefferson, and George Washington.

Britain had left the colonies alone for decades, reaping the benefit of their economic riches in exchange for autonomy. By 1759, though, the mother country began to suspect that its neglect of the colonies might lead to their eventual independence. Britain's actions were immediate and heavy-handed; decisions made in the colonial lower houses of assembly were disputed by British courts. Parliament forbade settlement beyond the Appalachian divide, on the west side of the Piedmont—a decree extremely unpopular with the land-hungry pioneers—and eliminated colonial paper currency as legal tender, among other acts.

These measures were followed almost immediately by Parliament imposing taxes on Americans for the first time. In 1767, the Townshend Acts levied duties on incoming lead, paper, tea, paint, and glass. Besides meeting expenses such as the upkeep of the British army in America, these duties were used to pay the salaries of royal governors and other crown officials. These officials had previously been paid by the colonial assemblies, and this change was seen as a move to shift the appointees' allegiance back to the English, instead of insuring responsiveness to local needs and demands. The result was that many colonials felt their lives and livelihoods threatened and gathered together to air their low opinion of King George.

A few years later, patriots held their own costumed tea party. Dressed as Mohicans, they threw 340 chests of taxable tea overboard from ships in the Boston Harbor. Parliament closed the port of Boston and provided for the quartering of troops there. The other colonies rallied to the defense of Massachusetts in a Continental Congress that met in Philadelphia in September 1774.

The Revolution Begins

Hostilities erupted at Lexington and Concord on April 19, 1775, and, soon afterward, militia contingents throughout New England took up positions outside Boston, putting the city under siege. British casualties came to 42 percent of the 2,500 redcoats engaged—their heaviest losses of the war. The second Continental Congress, then meeting at Philadelphia, took control of the New England forces; as commander of this Continental Army, they chose a 43-year-old delegate from Virginia, a planter by trade and a ranking militia officer in the French and Indian Wars—George Washington.

Quiet Victory

After several years of fighting, both sides, depleted and exhausted, signed the Treaty of Paris on September 3, 1783, which recognized the United States as independent; it was ratified by the Continental Congress on January 14, 1784. Soldiers of the Piedmont returned to their homes and farms to work the rich soil and watch their livestock grow fat for market. Though many settlers in the area had participated in the Revolution, a significant number, including many Quakers, were pacifists who had remained on their farms, quietly producing provisions to support the Continental Army. For the next 70 years, farmers in the fertile valleys continued to function in peace much as they had in war.

The Civil War to the Present Day

Most of the Quakers who dwelt in the Piedmont were staunchly antislavery, and when Pennsylvania was declared a free state, Quaker communities on the newly established Mason-Dixon Line provided a series of safe houses for escaping slaves. Inhabitants of the Piedmont supplied troops and food to the northern army during the War Between the States, and when it was over settled back into their agrarian ways, even as other regions in Pennsylvania were gearing up for the Industrial Revolution.

The waterways and roads of the Piedmont became major transport routes for raw materials and people. In 1792, the rough old wagon road between Philadelphia and Lancaster, often called the Conestoga Road, became the first paved and toll-road in America. The Conestoga Road was the basis for a system of canals and railroads developed to serve the area, the "Main Line of Public Works." Dutch Country remains largely rural, as evidenced by the fact that two-thirds of the land remains agricultural. Tourism plays a big part in keeping the area agrarian.

Lancaster and the Heart of Dutch Country

This is it, the epicenter of Amish country in Pennsylvania. Oddly, this reclusive religion has become a business, due in part to the romantic idea most of us have of the "unworldly" practice of Old Order Amish. The appeal of simplicity and community among the Amish and other religious groups that were drawn to this area is undeniable, and Lancaster and environs gives visitors an opportunity to explore and appreciate the more graceful parts of those who are "in the world, but not of it."

In addition, the area is home to several sites of historical interest, and numerous other attractions including an excellent railroad museum, a truly unique watch and clock museum, and a Broadway-style show. There's something for everyone, and plenty of reasons to visit and stay awhile.

SCENIC TOURS
The Strasburg Railroad
The railroad (SR 741, Strasburg, 717/687-7522) covers the nine-mile track from Strasburg to Paradise and back; the route passes through 14 farms, 11 of which are owned and

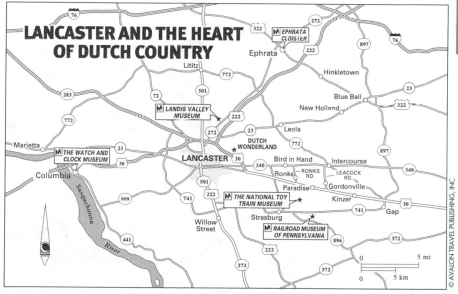

LANCASTER AND THE HEART OF DUTCH COUNTRY

Pennsylvania Dutch Country

worked by Amish or Mennonites. The train itself consists of one of several restored steam engines and a number of early-20th-century wooden passenger cars.

The railroad is open daily mid-Feb.–Nov. and Dec. 26–31; it's open weekends (weather permitting) Dec. 1–24 and Jan. 15–March 27. Excursion fares are $9.50 or less.

Visitors have a choice of seating ranging from the first-class parlor car (the *Marian*), a dining car, or an observation car. Since the ride is short, smaller children can enjoy it without becoming restless.

Ed's Buggy Rides

Ed's stable (Herr Rd. and SR 896, Strasburg, 717/687-0360) lets visitors ride in Amish-style horse-drawn carriages on a three-mile route along the farm roads outside the village of Strasburg. Horse-drawn traffic on the road is almost constant as many Amish are involved in local businesses and travel to and fro by buggy. This is an opportunity to slow down the pace and watch the cars go by. Call to reserve a seat; Ed's will take drop-ins, but there may be a wait. Ed's is open daily, 9 A.M.–5 P.M. The average cost of a ride is $8.

HISTORIC SITES

Ephrata Cloister

The Ephrata (EF-ra-ta) Cloister (632 W. Main St., Ephrata, 717/733-6600, www.ephratacloister .org), founded in 1732, was home to one of America's earliest communal societies. This community of religious celibates practiced an austere lifestyle that emphasized self-denial, spiritual goals, and the artistic use of music and the written word. Excelling in the calligraphic art of *Frakturschriften*, or "broken lettering," reminiscent of illuminated manuscripts, the orders produced numerous decorative books and inscriptions. The cloister consists of a unique collection of medieval-style buildings, surrounded by a park. Visiting hours are Mon.–Sat. 9 A.M.–5 P.M., Sun. noon–5 P.M. Admission is $7.

Wheatland

Wheatland (1120 Marietta Ave. Lancaster, 717/392-8721, www.wheatland.org) is open April–Oct.; one-hour tours depart every 30 minutes daily 10 A.M.–4 P.M. for $5.50. Wheatland was the rural home of Pennsylvania's only successful candidate for U.S. president (and the only bachelor to ever hold office), James Buchanan. To call it "rural" would be misleading; this 1828-built Federal-style mansion came complete with servants and all the outbuildings necessary for a luxurious retreat "as contrasted with the troubles, perplexities, and difficulties" of public life, according to Buchanan. Guides lead tours in period costume, and candlelight tours are available during the first two weeks of December.

Hans Herr House

In 1719, when southeastern Pennsylvania was wilderness, Hans Herr built a stone house (1849 Hans Herr Dr., Willow St., 717/464-4438, www.hansherr.org) on his fields to serve as a gathering place for his Mennonite brethren. It

Ephrata Cloister

© JOANNE MILLER

was the first Mennonite meetinghouse in America, and it is the oldest structure in the county. Outbuildings on the property are examples of the necessity of self-sufficiency: a blacksmith's shop, farm sheds, orchards, and gardens. Andrew Wyeth, a descendant of Herr, painted pictures of the medieval Germanic stone structure a number of times. It's open April 1–Nov. 30, Mon.–Sat. 9 A.M.–4 P.M. A $5 admission fee is charged to enter the property.

MUSEUMS

Lancaster Cultural History Museum

Set in a Masonic Lodge Hall dating from the 1790s, this museum (corner of King and Queen Sts., next to the Lancaster market, 717/299-6440, www.lancasterheritage.com) displays regional decorative and fine arts produced by generations of Lancaster County craftsmen. It is open year-round Tues.–Sat. 10 A.M.–5 P.M., Sun. noon–5 P.M.; admission is free. The well-preserved wall and ceiling

paintings of the former Masonic meeting room are a colorful backdrop to the display of folk art, quilts, silver, and furniture.

Lancaster Quilt and Textile Museum

Run by the folks at the Lancaster Cultural History Museum, this collection (37 N. Market, Lancaster 717/299-6440, www.lancasterheritage.com, same hours as above, $6) specializes in the famous needlework of the region. Displays change regularly, and often have themes.

ⓜ Landis Valley Museum

This living museum (2451 Kissel Hill Rd., Lancaster, 717/569-0401, www.landisvalleymuseum.org) is the largest outdoor collection concentrating on Pennsylvania German rural heritage. The museum is open year-round Mon.–Sat. 9 A.M.–5 P.M., Sun. noon–5 P.M. Admission is $9. Brothers George and Henry Landis, born just after the Civil War ended, collected more than 75,000 objects and artifacts of cultural significance from the 1700s to the 1800s. The

Pennsylvania Dutch Country

THE EPHRATAN COLONY

The communists of Ephrata interpreted the biblical description of Solomon's temple—which was built without hammers, axes, any iron tools, or nails—as a prohibition against the use of metal. All tools and utensils were ingeniously fashioned of stone and wood. The group also followed the biblical injunction that "Narrow is the way which leadeth unto life": all entrances and doorways in their structures were a diminutive five feet in height and 20 inches in width. In fact, suffering of all sorts was considered desirable—stone pillows and coarse woolen garments were common accoutrements, and a regimen of near-starvation and prayer every few hours throughout the day and night was strictly followed. The community survived rumors of sexual scandal by its leaders and members and even attracted a number of scholars as adherents. One commune member was commissioned by the newly formed governing body of the United States to translate the Declaration of Independence into seven languages.

Noted for their exquisite manuscript illumination and *fraktur,* a style of fancy lettering based in medieval illuminated texts, the Ephratans also established one of the first printing presses in the area and proceeded to publish books, broadsides, and tracts for a century. The most ambitious work produced by the Ephratans' press was the largest book ever printed in colonial America, the 1,200-page *Martyrs Mirror,* commissioned by and produced for the Mennonites. The press also turned out copies of countless hymns, penned by Johann Conrad Beissel and others, exalting the spiritual life. The Ephratans love of the written word and music carried over into other areas of life: the cloister choir followed strict dietary rules to purify their voices and sang in an unusual falsetto.

Landis brothers established a small museum to display the collection during the 1920s on the grounds of their Landis Valley homestead. The museum was acquired by the state in 1953 and expanded to include structures original to the Landis Valley farm, new exhibit buildings, a crossroads village, and an adjoining farmstead with traditional breeds of animals and heirloom plants. The collections, together with demonstrations of traditional crafts and skills such as sheepshearing and tinsmithing, serve to demonstrate rural life as it was lived by German immigrants new to the rich Piedmont region.

Exhibits include a print shop and leather workshop, a log farmhouse, a blacksmith shop, school, country store, firehouse, and tavern, among others—all authentically re-created and stocked. The buildings are connected by pleasant paths along lanes and through orchards and fields.

The museum offers a number of special tours (self-guided or with guides) that address different aspects of colonial life; a children's tour of farm animals introduces livestock, and Women's Farm Work during the 1700s gives a taste of the effort and hours necessary to keep a farm family fed and clothed.

Landis also has an exceptional museum shop, the Weathervane, and an heirloom seed saver program. Through time, many heirloom seeds have been lost because of hybridization and large-scale agricultural production. The project seeks to protect and expand the pool of sturdy and adaptable survivors, thereby providing diversity for the future. The Seed Project won Pennsylvania's highest history preservation award. Landis Valley offers a catalog of heirloom seeds for sale. For information, contact Heirloom Seed Project (Landis Valley Museum, 2451 Kissel Hill Rd., Lancaster, PA 17601).

⋈ The Watch and Clock Museum

One of a kind, this unusual museum represents four centuries of horological developments, from early pocket sundials to the latest Philippe Patek. The Watch and Clock Museum is west of Lancaster on the Susquehanna River (514 Poplar St., Columbia, PA 17512, 717/684-8261, www .nawcc.org/museum). It's open April–Dec.

Tues.–Sat. 10 A.M.–5 P.M., Sun. noon–4 P.M.; Jan.–March, it's open Tues.–Sat. 10 A.M.–4 P.M. Admission is $6.

Among the 8,000 items in the thoughtfully arranged collection are American railroad watches, 19th-century ormolu French mantel clocks (the kind that protrude from a shepardess's belly), a room full of German cuckoos, and a Stephen Engle Monumental clock with several independent groups of figures that appear at different times during the hour—Father Time swings his scythe after a group of Revolutionary War soldiers march around a woman on a balcony (Betsy Ross? Molly Pitcher?). Clocks such as this were transported from town to town during the 19th century and exhibited for an admission price.

After viewing this collection, it's impossible to not appreciate the precision, dedication, and occasional whimsy that is the life of a clockmaker. All of the clocks are set on different times, and it's worth spending an hour to watch and listen to different timepieces show off their artistry. The helpful staff will direct you to whatever rings your chimes.

The museum is the home of the NAWCC, the National Association of Watch and Clock Collectors, and the source for its bulletins and market publications. For membership information, contact the museum.

⋈ The National Toy Train Museum

There's a memory from everyone's childhood in this museum (Paradise Lane between US 30 and SR 741, east of Strasburg, 717/687-8976, www.traincollectors.org); locomotives and cars created by manufacturers such as Lionel, American Flyer, and others from the 1800s to the present are on display, along with specialty trains and other types of tin toys. The museum is open weekends in April and Nov.–mid-Dec., 10 A.M.–5 P.M.; May–Oct. 31 it's open daily 10 A.M.–5 P.M. Admission is $3.

On display are a 1920s standard gauge model with tin-plate trains, 1940s O gauge models and S gauge American Flyers. Five operating layouts, standard gauge to G gauge outdoor trains (gauge measures the width of the distance between the two tracks), are on view. This museum is the headquarters of the Train Collectors Association (P.O. Box 248, Strasburg, PA 17579, 717/687-8623).

Ⓜ Railroad Museum of Pennsylvania

Founded in 1995, this railfan mecca (SR 741, Strasburg, 717/687-8628, www.rrmuseumpa.org) was clearly created out of love. It's open Mon.–Sat. 9 A.M.–5 P.M., Sun. noon–5 P.M.; closed Mon. Nov.–March. Admission is $7. Visitors enter through a reconstructed 1915 railroad depot and move from there into the shop, where a stairway leads down to the pit, a repair area. There, they may walk beneath the massive underside of a 62-ton freight locomotive (imagine a blue whale gliding over you).

The core of the museum's holdings is the Pennsylvania Railroad Collection, originally loaned to the state by the Pennsylvania Railroad. Most of the collection was designed and built at either the Pennsylvania Railroad's Juniata shops in Altoona or Baldwin Locomotive Works in Philadelphia. The collection consists of a motley assortment of 24 locomotive and passenger cars from different eras. Included are the *Tahoe* from 1875, a wood-burning locomotive that hauled silver ore from the Comstock Lode mine in Virginia City, Nevada, and the sleek GG1 class, number 44935 electric locomotive from 1943, used to move passenger cars.

Many of the beautifully preserved locomotives and rail cars are housed in the enormous Rolling Stock Hall. The hall, 150 feet by 320 feet, has four railroad tracks down the center. In addition to viewing exhibits, which line either side of the hall, and reading individual information plaques on each locomotive and car, visitors may step up to a second-floor balcony to get a wider perspective. A statue of Alexander Johnston Cassatt, seventh president of the Pennsylvania Railroad and brother of impressionist painter Mary Cassatt, stands at the entrance of the hall. Behind the Rolling Stock Hall is the yard, where more locomotives and cars are kept. The museum also has a complete rail lore library, which you can see by appointment.

OTHER POINTS OF INTEREST

Dutch Wonderland

This amusement park (2249 US 30 east, Lancaster, 717/291-1888, www.dutchwonderland .com) features a 44-acre landscaped park with 20 rides that appeal to children up to about age 12—a reasonably scary roller coaster, steamboat, train, paddleboats, and the like—plus a high-diving show with an Acapulco cliff diver who plunges 40 feet into a shallow pool of water. The park is open weekends Easter–Memorial Day 10 A.M.–6 P.M.; Memorial Day weekend Aug., it's open daily 10 A.M.–8:30 P.M.; Labor Day weekend–Columbus Day (weather permitting), it's open weekends only 10 A.M.–6 P.M. Admission for adults is $26.95, $21.95 kids to age 6.

New Holland Livestock Auction

Wear shoes that are easy to wash and assume a liberal attitude toward intense farmyard odors when visiting this authentic livestock sale. Two flights of stairs from the street lead up to a wooden gallery crowded with local farmers and ranchers cruising for new heifers or a fancy colt to break to harness. Straw hats and felt hats mix with caps bearing logos from farm equipment companies in the gallery as trotting livestock on the floor below are inspected and bid upon in this fast-moving, fast-talking spectacle. The auction, held in the auction building on the west end of Fulton Street, New Holland, begins weekdays at 7:30 A.M. and lasts until all the livestock are sold (2–3 P.M.).

The People's Place

The People's Place (Main St., Intercourse, 800/390-8436) is a cluster of related sites that functions as a commercial Mennonite and Amish cultural center. A slide documentary, *Who Are the Amish?* gives a pleasant history lesson; Amish World displays artifacts; the film drama *Hazel's People* is an Amish fable; and the Book Shoppe specializes in books about Amish, Mennonite, and Hutterite (another branch of the Mennonites, largely based in the great plains) life and thought. The best part of the complex is the Quilt Museum across the street from the

LIFE AMONG THE AMISH

The basic social unit of an Old Order Amish community is the congregation—usually no more than 40 families (families tend to be large—eight or 10 children is not unusual). The congregation meets at a member's home every other week for a three-hour service. Within a community, an Amish sect may be as small as a single congregation. Though most Amish look similar to outsiders, sects differ from each other by their practice of edicts handed down by their community elders. One sect may share a telephone for outgoing business calls, for instance, while another may avoid telephones completely. Sect members sometimes refer to themselves as being "Yellow-top," "Black-top," or "White-top" Amish. This is a colloquial reference to the color of the tops of the horse-drawn carriages each family owns and actually refers to a sect.

The church has no control over unbaptized members (usually those under the age of 20), so "wild behavior"—violation of standards of modest dress, racing buggies, driving cars, wearing wristwatches—is not uncommon among Amish teens. However, when given the opportunity to be baptized, four out of five children raised in the Old Amish way do choose a lifetime commitment to the church.

One thing true of all Amish is that the religious basis of their lives demands that they be aware of the larger world but not participate in it. Because their lifestyle is so attractive to outsiders, visitors occasionally step over the line of polite interaction. Some Amish have a standard parody of a pushy outsider—much like the "ugly American" Europeans joke about. The most frequent comment made by their non-Amish neighbors is, "They're just people, with the same problems as anyone else."

Faith shapes the lives of the Amish; their core values, based on the teachings of the New Testament, are submission, self-surrender, humility, and obedience. They consider the joys of individualism to be illusory—identity, meaning, and belonging are found by being part of a larger community. Though known for eschewing education beyond the eighth grade and disdaining electricity and telephones, Old Order Amish often, in fact, embrace the new—when it doesn't conflict with the faith. Church leaders judge the long-term consequences of each modern item brought into the fold—namely, will it lead to greater contact with the outside world and violate core values? Higher education is considered to lead to feelings of superiority and competitiveness with other community members. Batteries are acceptable because they're self-contained (providing no conduit to the outside world), as are battery-powered electronic cash registers. Plug and cord electricity is avoided, however, since it's connected directly to the outside and may lead to the desire for a forbidden television or computer, thereby creating dissatisfaction with the simple Amish lifestyle. Automobiles present opportunities for frequent travel and worldly interaction, and telephones endanger the practice of "visiting," the face-to-face contact on which the community thrives.

main building, with a quilting supplies store downstairs and a display area upstairs. The walls are hung with new and antique quilts, many from the Heritage Center Museum of Lancaster County, Lancaster Mennonite Historical Society, or Mennonite Historians of Eastern Pennsylvania. During Christmas, People's Place and the country store next door sponsor a quilting contest, and the winners and best entries are displayed. This is traditional fiber art at its finest. Hours of operation at the different sites vary, but generally, they're open Memorial Day–Labor Day, Mon.–Sat. 9:30 A.M.–5 P.M. Admission varies, depending on selection, averaging $5.

The Amish Village

The Amish Village (SR 896, Strasburg, 717/687-8511) is one of several re-creations of idealized Amish farms in the area. It's open spring, summer, and fall, Mon.–Sat. 9 A.M.–5 P.M. and Sun. 10 A.M.–5 P.M. Admission is $6.50 for adults, $2.50 for kids 5–12. There is a guided house tour (reservations are required in July and Aug.), a smokehouse, blacksmith shop, schoolhouse, springhouse,

© JOANNE MILLER

dairy cattle calves

Pennsylvania Dutch Country

windmill, waterwheel, and livestock—the kids' favorite part—next to the gift shop. Most contemporary Amish are considerably more mechanized thanks to batteries, gasoline engines on tractors, and self-contained generators, but the village effectively re-creates rural life prior to the 20th century.

Sight and Sound

Reminiscent of early stage spectaculars and Broadway shows, Sight and Sound (SR 896, Strasburg, 717/687-7800, www.bibleonstage .com) produces two or more Christian-themed extravaganzas a year to sellout crowds. Slides, special effects, actors, singers, animals—whatever can be used to tell the story appears on the 100-foot-wide stage.

Past productions have included *Noah,* which featured 300 live animals, and *The Joys of Christmas,* with toy soldiers, dancing trees, and the Nativity. Though the somewhat evangelicized stories may not be for everyone, there's also nothing to offend any member of the family.

Shows run nearly continually from March–early Jan. Generally, there are three performances

a day on weekends and two on weekdays; times vary with the show. Reservations are required. Admission depends on the program but averages $30–50.

Mennonite Information Center

Because commercialization of the Amish is so widespread in the Lancaster area, the Mennonite Information Center (2209 Millstream Rd., Lancaster, 717/299-0954, www.mennoniteinfoctr .com) is ideal for those who are curious about authentic Mennonite and Amish beliefs. The real core of these related groups is their strong Bible-based faith. Volunteers at the center will answer questions about both groups, as well as guide visitors around the area. Guides ride in the visitor's car, tailoring the tour to individual interests and budget. The center shows a free film about Mennonite and Amish culture and can also recommend Mennonite homestays and overnight lodging. It's open April–Oct. 8 A.M.– 5 P.M.; Nov., Dec., and March 8:30 A.M.– 4:30 P.M.; and Jan.–Feb. 10 A.M.–3 P.M. The center is always closed on Sun. Admission is free.

Factories and Manufacturers

In 1861, Julius Sturgis opened **Sturgis Pretzel House,** the first commercial pretzel bakery in America, on this site (219 E. Main St., Lititz, 717/626-4354). It's open Mon.–Sat. 9 A.M.– 5 P.M., with tours (Sat. only during winter months); a $2 tour fee is charged. Children of all ages are invited to try their hand at pretzel twisting. The factory tour includes the mechanized bakery for hard pretzels, plus a look at the 200-year-old ovens used for handmade and baked soft pretzels. Pretzel samples are given out after the tour.

The town of New Holland is the site of an innovation that changed modern farming: the hay baler. This machine, which saved many hours of hand labor, was invented by a small local equipment manufacturer several decades ago. The company was subsequently bought by a European firm, but the **New Holland Factory** (Fulton Rd., New Holland, 717/355-1371) still produces balers and gives guided tours through the process (sorry, no samples of hay balers are given). Tours are offered April–Oct., Mon., Tues., Thurs., and Fri. at 1 P.M. Admission is free.

SHOPPING

Quilts and Crafts

Handmade quilts are often sold from homes in the Lancaster area. Two that come well recommended are **Rosa and Elmer Stoltzfus** (102 N. Ronks Rd., Ronks; no phone) and **Witmer Quilt Shop** (1070 W. Main St., New Holland, 717/656-9526). The latter welcomes visitors Mon.–Fri. 8 A.M.–8 P.M. and Sat. 8 A.M.–6 P.M., and is closed on Sun. and religious holidays. Both also take custom orders.

Eldreth Pottery (246 N. Decatur St., Strasburg, 717/687-8445) makes the salt-glazed stoneware most associated with this part of the world. This is the factory, which sells first-quality pottery as well as seconds.

King's Homestead (3518 W. Newport Rd., Ronks, 717/768-7688) sells locally made quilts, candles, and a variety of other country crafts. It's open Mon.–Sat. 8 A.M.–5 P.M.

The Weathervane/ Landis Valley Museum Store

This shop in the Landis Valley Museum (2451 Kissel Hill Rd., Lancaster, 717/569-9312) is worth a special stop for those interested in buying or making authentic country crafts. It features a unique collection of handcrafted gifts modeled after period pieces and reproduced using traditional methods and tools. The Brothers Bookstore, inside the gift shop, offers a wide variety of books, pamphlets, and articles on crafts, antiques, and decorative arts. The Weathervane is open Mon.–Sat. 9 A.M.–5 P.M., Sun. noon–5 P.M. The shop may be visited without paying admission to the museum.

Kaufmann's Hardware and Country Wares, Inc.

Kaufmann's Hardware (201-215 E. Main St., New Holland, 717/354-4606) has been in business since 1779. Its current purpose is to provide all the bits and pieces of hardware and clothing necessary to run a farm. The middle section of the store is given over to an eclectic assortment of antiques and collectibles, all of which surround a glass case featuring melted items from the store's fire some years ago. A collection of sturdy shoes (mostly black—this is Amish country) is upstairs. Kaufmann's is open Mon.–Wed. 6:30 A.M.–5:30 P.M., Thurs.–Fri. 6:30 A.M.–8 P.M., and Sat. 6:30 A.M.–5 P.M.

Lapp's Coach Shop

Though Lapp's (3572 W. Newport Rd., Intercourse, 717/768-8712) no longer restores antique carriages as it did in 1944, it does offer the best-made selection of chests, wagons, and wooden furniture and toys in the area. All of the goods are made by local crafters, and insiders say this is a prime source for quality and price. It's open Mon.–Sat. 8 A.M.–6 P.M. in summer, 8 A.M.–5 P.M. in winter.

Hayloft Candles

Thousands of hand-poured and hand-dipped candles line the aisles in this barnlike outlet (97 S. Groffdale Rd., Leola, 717/656-9463). The candles are made on the premises by the same modestly dressed young women who work the cash register. A free petting zoo with farm animals will entrance little kids while big kids inside the store decide on pink or purple tapers. Hayloft sells its own ice cream, too. In winter it's open 9 A.M.–5 P.M. Mon.–Sat.; May–Aug. hours are Mon.–Wed. plus Sat. 9 A.M.–7 P.M. and Thurs.–Fri. 9 A.M.–8 P.M.

Outlets

Rockvale Square (intersection of SR 30 and SR 896, Lancaster) has all the big names: Jones New York, Levi's, and Lenox, among others. **Tanger at Millstream** (US 30 near Millstream Rd., Lancaster) features Izod and Ann Taylor.

⚅ Farm and Bulk Stores

Every Friday, 400 local growers, merchants, and craftspeople participate in the indoor/outdoor **Green Dragon Farmers' Market** (955 N. State St., Ephrata). Look for the fat green dragon flying through the air by the side of the road.

W.L. Zimmerman & Sons (downtown Intercourse, 717/768-8291) is ostensibly a grocery store (it carries a lot of bulk items on the lower floor), but it also carries a plethora of dry goods on the upper floor. A trip up the narrow stairway will reveal clothes, dish towels, umbrellas, notebooks, and souvenirs of uncertain vintage. If you want it and are willing to dig, you'll probably find it at Zimmerman's. It's open Mon.–Sat. 7 A.M.–9 P.M.

When shopping at **Centerville Bulk Store** (3501 B Scenic Rd., Gordonville), chances are good that your vehicle will be parked among a bunch of black-topped buggies. This Amish-run dry goods and grocery store specializes in pre-packaged bulk ingredients and candy; it's often filled with farm neighbors in to pick up a few things. Don't try to call—like all "plain" businesses in the area, there's no phone on the premises. The store is open Mon.–Thurs. 7 A.M.–5 P.M., Fri. 7 A.M.–9 P.M., Sat. 7 A.M.–4 P.M.

The **Leola Produce Auction** (Brethren Church Rd., Leola, 717/656-9592) is the place to buy or sell seasonal fresh fruits and vegetables. The auction is set up along the lines of a flea market; farmers bring their produce loose or bagged in varying quantities. Prices and quality are exceptional, and the auction has a festive air,

enjoyable whether buying or just looking. It's open from 8:30 A.M. during fruit/vegetable season from early spring to late fall. Hours and days may vary; It's wise to call to before you go.

ACCOMMODATIONS

$50–100

The **Inns at Doneckers** (318–324 N. State St., Ephrata, PA 17522, 717/738-9502 or 800/377-2206) is a tiny empire consisting of three bed-and-breakfast inns: The **Guesthouse** (318–324 N. State St.), The **1777 House** (301 W. Main St.), and **The Homestead** (251 N. State St.), all with different room styles and prices ($65–150; suites are $155–210). Doneckers also offers a department store with men's, women's, and home fashions (409 N. State St.); a restaurant (333 N. State St.); an art gallery, the Artworks (100 N. State St.); a farmers' market (100 N. State St., Thurs.–Sat.); and a mail-order catalog.

tobacco in the drying shed, Cherry Crest Tourist Farm

© JOANNE MILLER

Pennsylvania Dutch Country

$100–150

The Alden House Bed and Breakfast, an 1850 brick Victorian house, is located in the center of the charming and historic town of Lititz (62 E. Main St., 717/627-3363 or 800/584-0753). Sturgis Pretzel House and a number of other attractions, shops, boutiques, and dining establishments are nearby. Each of the attractively decorated rooms and suites has a private bath, and breakfast is included. Corporate rates are available. Rates range $90–135.

A modern home built in the colonial style, **Flowers and Thyme** (238 Strasburg Pike, Lancaster, 717/393-1460) offers the advantages of a quiet overnight stay that's only 10 minutes away from the city of Lancaster. The suite has its own hot tub and shower; all rooms have a private bath. The Gathering Room, where breakfast is served, has a vaulted ceiling, which creates a sunny atrium effect—it's a cheery spot to begin the day and enjoy the complimentary breakfast. Rates range $89–159.

The Railroad House, a 12-room bed-and-breakfast, is an artfully restored hotel built between 1820 and 1823 to service travelers on the Pennsylvania Main Line Canal. Cozy with Victoriana, the rooms are individually decorated and have private baths. The Railroad House (corner of W. Front and S. Perry Sts., Marietta, 717/426-4141) is close to the Susquehanna River and has its own full-service restaurant on the premises. Rates range $99–350 and include breakfast.

This is a family vacation that will please everybody. Each of the two guest suites at **Ⓜ Cherry Crest Tourist Farm** (150 Cherry Hill Rd., Ronks, 717/687-6843) consists of several sleeping spaces and a kitchen. Both suites are in a duplex a short distance from the silo, cattle, and barns of this working dairy farm. Any member of the family who can get down to the "parlor"—the milking shed—by 5 A.M. can help with the milking; there are swings, horseshoe pits, and a farm-animal menagerie in the yard near the guest

KOMM ESSE: EATING, DEUTSCHE STYLE

The Pennsylvania Piedmont's steady output of grains and vegetables supplies the area's markets with some of the cheapest and best produce in the world—a bounty of corn, wheat, rye, and grain-fattened livestock. The numerous dairies yield rich supplies of butter, cheese, and cream.

Fear of fat or the sugar blues have never concerned the average Pennsylvania Dutch farm cook. "Dutch" cooking (which actually refers to *Deutsche* or German ethnicity, and includes the Amish) is, at its heart, the ultimate American comfort food. Huge helpings of meat (often pork in some form), starches, home-baked bread, several kinds of vegetables, hot and cold salads, and a multitude of dessert choices make up an average meal. Typically, the menu at local family-style restaurants consists of an all-you-can-eat spread of chicken, ham, beef, sausage, pot pie, chicken salad, mashed potatoes, gravy, sweet potatoes, lima beans, dried corn, garden peas, pickled beets, pepper cabbage, chowchow, pickles, mustard beans, applesauce, tapioca pudding, dried apricots, sugar cookies, five kinds of pie (in-cluding cherry and apple), ice cream, apple butter with cottage cheese, bread, butter, milk, tea, and coffee. This feasting is a year-round phenomenon, its origins being to meet the needs of strenuous farm work (even though this is only a memory for some) and cold winters—both of which require a lot of calories.

To be stingy on ingredients such as butter, eggs, and sugar would brand a woman a bad cook. Church gatherings, weddings, or any other celebrations that call for potluck often bring together seven sweets and seven sours (savories), the putative ingredients of a good meal. Sometimes, sweet and sour combine—three-bean salad made with equal amounts of white vinegar and sugar, for example, or Schnitz und Knepp, a combination of dried apples, brown sugar, ham, and dumplings. Other dishes give one or the other an exclusive starring role, such as the toothache-sweet, molasses-based shoo-fly pie. Not all is tradition, however. The new rage in Amish kitchens is pizza—made with plenty of cheese, of course.

quarters. Kids can gather their own eggs in the morning from the chicken house or get lost in the corn maze. Cherry Crest's guest book is filled with grateful letters from young visitors; with so many activities available, a farm vacation like this one is easy on parents, too. It's a unique experience, especially for city dwellers. Cherry Crest requires a two-night minimum stay July–Oct. 28. The rate is $120 per night.

FOOD

N The Lancaster Malt Brewing Company (Plum and Walnut Sts., Lancaster, 717/391-6258) is a hip, contemporary addition to the city of Lancaster. It's open Sun.–Thurs. 11:30 A.M.–midnight, Fri.–Sat. 11:30 A.M.–2 A.M. The restaurant serves innovative pub food; it has the usual burgers and buffalo wings, but is also working hard to provide some heart-healthy dishes to its patrons. Full lunches and dinners ($5–20) include steak and pasta entrées, and the beer is excellent (all on draught, of course). The microbrewery makes its fresh-tasting lagers, ales, porters, and seasonal beers on the premises. Free brewery tours are offered on Sat. from 5–8 P.M.

N Dienner's Country Bar-B-Q (2855 Lincoln Hwy. E, Ronks, 717/687-9571) was highly recommended to me by a local farm couple, and it really is worth a stop. The name is a little misleading: Dienner's (named after the Mennonite couple who started the restaurant) is much more than a barbecue place. All types of basic American meals are served, and the food is fresh, inexpensive (under $3 for breakfast to $9.85 for a dinner buffet), and delicious. Portions are meant to fill farm appetites, which is common in the family eateries around Lancaster. The breakfasts are especially good. A hearty breakfast buffet is served 7–10:30 A.M. There's a lunch buffet 11 A.M.–

3 P.M. daily and a dinner buffet 3–6 P.M. Mon.–Thurs. and Sat., and 3–8 P.M. Fri.

Yep, it's a diner, and a good one At **Lapp's Family Restaurants** (2270 Lincoln Hwy. East, Lancaster, 717/394-1606), enjoy inexpensive but filling dishes such as fried chicken and hot ham sandwiches (smaller servings of the same items are available for more petite appetites). Even the smaller portions are hefty, so plan accordingly. Lapp's dishes out goodies Tues.–Sun. from 7 A.M.–9 P.M. and Mon. 7 A.M.–8 P.M.; during the winter, hours are Tues.–Sun. 7 A.M.–8 P.M. Expect to pay around $8 for lunch, $15 for dinner.

A pleasant homey atmosphere distinguishes **Stoltzfus Farm Restaurant** (one mile east of Intercourse on SR 772, 717/768-8156), a German family-style eatery. The dining room is in a country farmhouse, and Stoltzfus sausage, ham loaf, and other meats come from its own farm butcher shop. The restaurant is open weekends in April and Nov., daily May–Oct., Mon.–Sat. 11:30 A.M.–8 P.M. Prices average $12–20, all you can eat.

For something completely different, try the **Nav Jiwan Tea Room** (10,000 Villages Gift Shop, SR 272, Ephrata, 717/721-8400). It features cuisine from a different country each week and serves breakfast and lunch Mon.–Fri., dinner on Fri. evenings, and brunch on Sat. from 10 A.M.–3 P.M. Dinner prices average $10.

INFORMATION

Contact the Pennsylvania Dutch Convention and Visitors Bureau (501 Greenfield Rd., Lancaster, PA 17601, 717/299-8901 or 800/PA-DUTCH, www.padutchcountry.com) and ask for the informative brochure, map of the area, and bargain coupons. It also offers a pamphlet, *Farm Vacations at Lancaster County Bed and Breakfasts.*

Hershey, Harrisburg, and Environs

The Lebanon Valley is a rural area studded with bucolic small towns and villages—Hershey, the chocolate city and a destination in itself, is one of them—the region is also home to Harrisburg, the state capital. Harrisburg was established in 1718 as Harris Ferry—named for John Harris, the English trader who operated a post there. The town became the state capital in 1812. Due to its central location, Harrisburg became a transportation center, especially during the heyday of the Main Line canal and, later, for the railroads. Harrisburg remains a relatively small town, with a population around 52,000, and the state government is the largest employer in the area.

N HERSHEY

Hershey (US 422, east of Harrisburg, 717/534-4900 or 800/437-7439, www.hersheypa.com) has just one industry—but its products are recognized the world over. This factory town has become a major tourist destination with several attractions. Milton Hershey operated candy-manufacturing businesses in New York and Philadelphia before returning to his hometown, in the heart of Pennsylvania's dairyland. He made a success of the caramel business, then decided to revamp his factory into a chocolate processing plant.

Hershey was a shrewd businessman. His plant grew to employ most of the local workforce, and he bought or created quite a few supply businesses, such as butcher shops and groceries, thereby making the town of Hershey not too different than the coal patch towns farther north. To his credit, Hershey was reputed to be a decent and benevolent landlord.

If current publicity is any clue, Milton Hershey wanted to be remembered as a paragon of humanity; he founded a school for disadvantaged (Caucasian male) children that now has more liberal entry requirements. However, Hershey, the man and the town, were, above all, about making money; that's the unfortunate impression that time spent in Hershey may leave with some visitors—something is for sale around every

corner, from Hershey candy bars to Hershey Christmas ornaments. Hershey's business heirs appear to be following in the dubious footsteps of the merchandising masters of Disneyland. Bring a fat Hershey wallet.

Since the grounds have become so vast, visitors can get around on the Hershey Trolley while being entertained by singing conductors ($7, including multiple stops).

Hershey's Chocolate World

Chocolate World, the original attraction for visitors to Hershey, offers a free 15-minute amusement-park-style ride through a series of animated tableaux revealing Hershey's chocolate-making process. A free sample awaits at the end of the tour, and the remainder of Chocolate

downtown Hershey "kiss" streetlamp

World is a series of shops that sell various souvenir items and every Hershey product made. Chocolate World is next to the amusement park, and the town that surrounds both really does have streetlights shaped like Hershey's Kisses. Chocolate World is open Jan.–Feb. Mon.–Sat. 9 A.M.–5 P.M., Sun. 11 A.M.–5 P.M.; March–mid-April daily 9 A.M.–5 P.M., mid-April–May Mon.–Thurs. 9 A.M.–5 P.M., Fri. and Sun. 9 A.M.–8 P.M. Sat. 9 A.M.–10 P.M.; June daily 9 A.M.–10 P.M.; July and Aug. Sun.–Fri. 9 A.M.–10 P.M. and Sat. 9 A.M.–11 P.M.; Sept.–Oct. Mon.–Fri. 9 A.M.–5 P.M., Sat. 9 A.M.–10 P.M., Sun. 9 A.M.–8 P.M.; Nov. daily 9 A.M.–5 P.M.; mid-Nov.–Dec. 31, call for special holiday hours. Admission is free.

HersheyPark

This 90-acre amusement park has 50 rides and attractions, including five water slides, four roller coasters, and one of the finest Philadelphia Toboggan Company four-row carousels in existence today. Years ago, ride operators would let visitors' pets accompany them on some of the rides, though that doesn't seem likely nowadays, especially with newer rides like Lightning Racer, a dual-track roller coaster that pits one set of cars against another (literally "against" on part of the track). HersheyPark is open weekends and holidays in late April and Sept., weekends mid-Oct.–Dec., daily June–Aug. Gates open at 10 A.M.; closing hours vary from 6 P.M. midweek in May and Sept.

IT'S ALMOST LIKE BEING IN LOVE

Hernán Cortés brought the fruit of the cacao tree to Spain in 1519, after learning its secrets from the Aztecs during his invasion of South America. Originally, the cacao beans were prepared by crushing and mixing with water and a touch of chili pepper—a bitter beverage indeed. The Spanish, who liked their brews strong, spread the use of chocolate throughout Europe. The British weren't the first to add sugar, cream, or milk, but they spread the use of the flavoring throughout their far-flung empire, and the first chocolate manufactured in the United States was near Dorchester, Mass., in 1765. Rumors that Paul Revere fed it to his horse to keep him happy during his midnight ride are unsubstantiated.

Nowadays, Ghana, Côte d'Ivoire, Nigeria, and Cameroon produce about two-thirds of the world's raw beans. Most of the remainder comes from South American countries, chiefly Brazil and Ecuador.

Getting from the tree to the shiny foil wrapper is not a pretty process. In today's manufacturing, the fruit that contains the cocoa beans is crushed and fermented for three to nine days, during which the heat kills the seeds and turns them brown. The enzymes activated by fermentation do the magic: they give the beans their characteristic chocolate flavor later during roasting. The beans are sun-dried and cleaned before they are roasted. They are then shelled in a crushing machine and ground into chocolate. During the grinding, the fat melts, producing a sticky liquid called chocolate liquor, which is used to make chocolate candy (à la Hershey's) or is filtered to remove the fat and then cooled and ground to produce cocoa powder (for the drink). Small percentages of various unappetizing substances may be added, such as starch to prevent caking, or potassium bicarbonate to neutralize the natural acids and astringents and make the cocoa easy to dissolve.

The good news is, chocolate has a high food value, containing as much as 20 percent protein, 40 percent carbohydrate, and 40 percent fat. Memorize those percentages (except the last one) the next time you ask for another chocolate bar. It's mildly stimulating because of theobromine, an alkaloid closely related to caffeine; there's also evidence that chocolate consumed mimics the sensation of being in love. Though it didn't seem to have that effect on Hernán Cortés, we knew there was a good reason for its worldwide popularity. Here in America, we eat more than 11 pounds per person, per year.

COURTESY HHC C&VB

view of Harrisburg from across the Susquehanna River

to 11 P.M. on weekends July–Aug. The admission price of $37.95 includes all rides and is also good for a same-day visit to ZooAmerica, the Hershey Museum, and Hershey Gardens.

ZooAmerica

ZooAmerica North American Wildlife Park features more than 200 animals of 75 species, including buffalo and several varieties of deer. It's open year-round Sept.–May, 10 A.M.–5 P.M.; mid-June–Aug., daily 10 A.M.–8 P.M. Entrance is included in the HersheyPark package, or separate admission is $7.

Hershey Museum

Upon entry, a display details the chocolate-coated story of the founding of Hershey, with some charming photographs of the early days of the town. The visitor then has an opportunity to explore a good collection of Pennsylvania German art and cultural artifacts; clocks, including a monumental Apostolic clock with moving figures; and Hershey's broad personal collection of Native American artifacts. The museum is open

Memorial Day–Labor Day, 10 A.M.–6 P.M.; during the rest of the year, it closes at 5 P.M. A $7 admission is charged when not part of the HersheyPark package.

Hershey Gardens

From mid-April to Sept., 9 A.M.–6 P.M. (and Oct., 9 A.M.–5 P.M.) this 23-acre botanical garden is in bloom and open to the public. Milton Hershey's original "nice garden of roses" has expanded to include spring flowering bulbs such as daffodils and forsythia in May, 450 varieties of roses June–Aug., a butterfly house with 400 North American species, and chrysanthemums and fall foliage in Sept. If not part of the HersheyPark package, admission is $7.

Other Attractions

Hershey also features five golf courses; an upscale hotel, lodge, and campground (below); an ice hockey team, the American Hockey League Hershey Bears, playing in the HersheyPark arena; and a special shopping area, Candylane, during the Christmas season.

Pennsylvania Dutch Country

SCENIC SPOTS

Fort Hunter Mansion and Park

This 35-acre park and mansion (5300 N. Front St., Harrisburg, 717/599-5751, www.forthunter.org), north of the urban section of Harrisburg on the Susquehanna River, offers picnic pavilions, play equipment, and several trails including a Pennsy Canal trail and riverfront paths. The restored mansion may be toured with a guide. Fort Hunter is open May–Dec. 23, Tues.–Sat. 10 A.M.–4:30 P.M., Sun. noon–4:30 P.M. In December, it's specially decorated. Admission is $4 to tour the mansion.

MUSEUMS

M State Museum of Pennsylvania

This excellent museum (3rd and North Sts., Harrisburg, 717/787-4979, www.statemuseumpa.org) presents a broad perspective of life in Pennsylvania as it was 3.6 billion years ago to the present. The displays in different galleries imaginatively animate dry topics; in the Hall of Geology, the museum staff has created a walk-through Carboniferous Period forest. The Hall of Pennsylvania Mammals brings beavers and bears up close for study. Archaeological diggings in the Hall of Anthropology reveal the remains of prehistoric dwellers, and a re-created 16th-century Lenni Lenape village shows life from birth to death. There are displays and paintings on the Civil War, including Rothernel's much reproduced painting *Battle of Gettysburg*. Complete dining rooms and parlors from different homes and periods in history show how Pennsylvanians lived. The *Market, Shop, and Home* exhibit is a small re-created town. There is a planetarium on the top floor that offers shows on the weekends, and on weekdays during the summer months. The museum is open Tues.–Sat. 9 A.M.–5 P.M., Sun. noon–5 P.M.; admission is free, but there's a $3 charge for planetarium shows.

Whitaker Center for Science and the Arts

The center (222 Market Street, Harrisburg, 717/214-ARTS, www.whitakercenter.org) includes the Harsco Science Center (Mon.–Sat.

9:30 A.M.–5 P.M., Sun. 11:30 A.M.–5 P.M.; adults $7.75, children 3–12, students, and seniors $6.25); an IMAX theater ($6–8); and the Sunoco Performance Theater, featuring Doc Watson and a variety of other entertainers (admission varies according to shows and times). Combination tickets are available for the science center and IMAX theater.

The science center offers three floors with more than 240 exhibits that explore physical

Pennsylvania Dutch Country

HOME SWEET HOME

Like all pioneers, the early Pennsylvania Dutch settlers built their homes with available materials. Walls were constructed of adzed timbers or woven rushes (wattle) covered with heavy mud (daub). The major advantage of this type of dwelling is that it could be built by unskilled laborers with no tools except an ax and an adze. Seventy to 80 trees were needed to make a log house. The early houses were small, usually about 16 by 20 feet; working steadily, six men could build one in a week. To chink against bad weather, moss and mud were stuffed into cracks between the logs. Roofs were covered with wide boards, then chinked with clay or covered with skins. Masonry foundations and chimneys were mortared with clay. The houses offered little protection against rain or snow, and many pioneers slept fully dressed during the winter.

Because of iron's scarcity and expense, builders learned to work without nails or screws. The houses were framed and joined with mortises, tenons, and wood plugs; doors swung on wood pegs. Small window openings, which offered better protection against attack by hostile Indians, were covered with greased paper; the paper could be easily pierced when the openings were used as gunports. The floors were either of pounded earth or rough-sawn wood. A ladder led up to an unventilated sleeping room above a single main room. The most luxurious mattresses were made of homespun stuffed with chaff, pine needles, or moss—which seldom discouraged fleas and other varmints from sharing the warmth of the bed with homesteading families.

science, natural science, life science, mathematics, and technology. This is where you'll find Stuffee, a nine-foot-tall doll that opens up to show internal organs and the remains of his peanut butter and jelly sandwich (not as gross as it sounds). Big Science Theatre, an "infotainment" feature of the Harsco Science Center, offers performances throughout the day.

Stoy Museum

Of interest for both its historical collections and its building, the Stoy Museum (924 Cumberland St., Lebanon, 717/272-1473) has plenty to offer the visitor. The museum is open Sun. 1– 4:30 P.M., Mon. 12:30–8 P.M., and Tues.–Fri. 12:30–4:30 P.M. Admission is by donation.

Originally the home of a prominent Revolutionary War physician, the upper floor of the building was used as Lebanon County's first courthouse in 1813. James Buchanan practiced law here before he became President of the United States. The comprehensive collection contains many examples of Pennsylvania German craftsmanship in furniture, *fraktur,* and quilting, and re-creations of the interiors of early shops and offices in Lebanon county; the permanent-wave machine for ladies looks like it could cause permanent damage. Railroading and firefighting paraphernalia, toys, a general store, and Babe Ruth's baseball uniform are all under one roof.

OTHER POINTS OF INTEREST

Capitol Complex

The capitol of the Commonwealth of Pennsylvania (State and 3rd Sts., Harrisburg, 717/787-6810) covers two acres in a 13-acre park and has more than 600 rooms. A 272-foot-high dome (reminiscent of St. Peter's Basilica in Rome), bronze doors, murals, and stained glass frame a broad marble staircase inspired by the Paris Grand Opera House. Sculptural works by Pennsylvanian George Barnard flank the main entranceway. It's open Mon.–Fri. 7 A.M.–6 P.M., Sat., Sun., and holidays 8 A.M.–4:30 P.M. (rotunda only). Guided tours available on weekdays every half-hour from

8:30 A.M.–4 P.M. and weekends at 9 A.M., 11 A.M., 1 P.M. and 3 P.M. Admission is free.

Factories and Manufacturers

Pennsylvania German cookery is world-famous for its cured meats and sausages. Lebanon Valley is home to several smokehouse facilities that make, among other things, a particular type of spicy-sour bologna that looks like salami but is much less salty. One of the oldest and most famous manufacturers is **Original Seltzer's Lebanon Bologna** (230 N. College St., Palmyra, 717/838-6336 or 800/282-6336), where towering wooden smokehouses add an authentic touch to the tour of this family-owned sausage company. The special secret family recipe has been cooked up, smoked, and sold since 1902. The sales outlet next door is open Mon.–Fri. 7 A.M.–5 P.M., Sat. 7 A.M.–1 P.M.

Another old-timer, **The Daniel Weaver Company** (15th Ave. and Weavertown Rd., Lebanon, 717/274-6100 or 800/932-8377) has been in business even longer than Seltzer's—since 1885. The company produces both Lebanon and Sweet Lebanon bolognas, as well as a variety of other meats, including ham, bacon, and beef. Cold smoking is part of the unique process. An outlet is open Mon.–Fri. 8 A.M.–4:30 P.M.

OUTDOOR RECREATION

Stony Valley Railroad Grade

A rails-to-trails route, this 17.4-mile trail runs along the old railbed of the Schuylkill (SKOO-kul) and Susquehanna Railroad and passes through the remains of five coal rush towns: Rausch Gap, Yellow Spring Gap, Gold Mine, Rattling Run, and the former resort, Cold Springs. Very little is left of the towns, but the surrounding forest of oak, white pine, hemlock, beech, and maple is so thick, it's hard to believe that it's second growth—the lumber industry had stripped the area by 1944. Moravian missionaries who settled in the region in 1742 named Stony Creek St. Anthony's Wilderness. It became the first area protected under Pennsylvania's Wild and Scenic Rivers program in 1980.

Heading from east to west, the trail follows several upgrades, with an opportunity for a steep

2.5-mile side trip to a vista (Stony Mountain Fire Tower) about three miles from the Stony Valley Road western terminus. To reach the western terminus, travel on US 22/322 about 15 miles north of Harrisburg, and turn right (east) on Stony Creek Valley Road. A sign directing you to state game lands leads down a five-mile-long dirt road to the gate that marks the railroad grade. The eastern terminus is north of Lickdale. Take SR 72 north to SR 443 to Gold Mine Road, which veers off SR 443 to the left. Follow Gold Mine Road to the state game lands entrance on the left.

Canoeing Swatara Creek

The **Union Canal Canoe Rental** (off Black's Bridge Road, west of the town of Bellegrove, 717/838-9580) rents canoes and assorted equipment for paddling down Swatara Creek. There are several pickup and delivery points along the creek from Pine Grove all the way down to the Susquehanna River, and distances between the points vary from two to 25 miles. Swatara Creek has two permanent dams, which must be portaged, but passes under several scenic bridges and by Bindnagle's Church, a brick structure dating from colonial times. The Union Canal, in use 1791–1857, parallels the creek.

ACCOMMODATIONS AND FOOD

The **Hotel Hershey** (Hotel Rd., Hershey, 717/533-2171 or 800/533-3131) was conceived by Milton Hershey as a project to provide employment for local construction workers during the Great Depression; it was modeled after European hotels Hershey and his wife had visited. This lodging has won several awards for service, quality, and cuisine. In addition to luxurious amenities and spa services, Hotel Hershey offers indoor and outdoor swimming, cross-country skiing, tobogganing, lawn bowling, horseback riding, hiking, golf, and tennis. An elegant restaurant and more casual dining room are on the premises. A number of room/activity packages are available throughout the year. Rates range $198–360 for two, per night, depending on day and season.

Considerably more casual but still quite nice, the **Hershey Lodge and Convention Center** (W. Chocolate Ave. and University Dr., 717/533-3311 or 800/533-3131) allows guests access to the golf courses and restaurants at the Hotel Hershey. Free shuttles run to the hotel and Hershey-Park. Rates range $199–229 per night, and packages and specials are frequently offered.

The most economical alternative in the Hershey galaxy is the **Hershey Campground** (1200 Matlack Rd., Hummelstown, 717/534-8999). The 300-site campground offers electricity and water, but no access to hotel amenities.

An 11-room limestone farmhouse, **Farm Fortune Bed and Breakfast** (204 Limeklin Rd., New Cumberland, 717/774-2683) sits high on a hill overlooking Yellow Breeches Creek. It's conveniently close (but not too close) to a major route. New Cumberland is just across the Susquehanna River from Harrisburg. Visitors luxuriate in the cozy great room with its walk-in fireplace and in the antique-filled guest rooms. All guest quarters have private baths, and a cottage with living room, fireplace, and kitchenette has been added. The surrounding three acres are dotted with old trees and provide a peaceful setting to fish, float down the Yellow Breeches, or just relax. Overnight rate includes breakfast, $95 and up.

Probably the most popular small restaurant in the area, **N Pete's** (401–403 Market St., New Cumberland, 717/774-7273) is crowded with happy families chowing down on bountiful entrées (the seafood is especially recommended). Dinner prices hover between $12 and $15, and smaller portions are available. Reservations are advised every night of the week. Open Tues.–Fri. 11 A.M.–10 P.M., Sat. 3–11 P.M.

INFORMATION

The **Hershey Capital Region Visitors Bureau** (208 Harrisburg Transportation Center, Fourth and Chestnut Sts., Harrisburg, PA 17101, 877/PA-PULSE or 717/231-7788, www.hersheycapitalregion.com) will send information and answer your questions.

Pennsylvania Dutch Country

Reading and Environs

Founded by two of William Penn's sons and named for their ancestral home in England, Reading became a supply base for forts along the Blue Mountains during the French and Indian War. The first Civil War regiment mustered in Pennsylvania came from Reading; between the end of the conflict and the beginning of the 20th century, the city grew into a major industrial force. Reading contains a wealth of 18th- and 19th-century buildings, but its current fame—and fortune—stems from the modern use of its abandoned industrial buildings. When the 1950s brought economic depression to the town, Reading boosters ushered in the outlet craze by offering beneficial site deals to a number of retailers. Several of the old factories and the train station are now home to major-name retailers who offer merchandise at discounts of 20–80 percent off re-

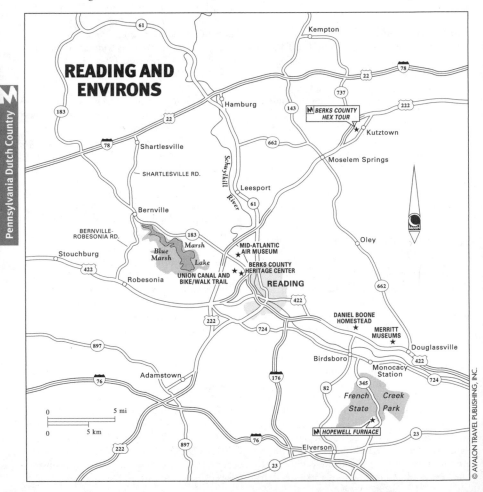

tail price. Nearby **Adamstown** offers some shopping specials of its own in antiques and collectibles. History buffs will enjoy a visit to Hopewell Furnace and Daniel Boone's birthplace, both a short drive from the city; and no Christmas could be complete without a trip to Koziar's Christmas Village, a fantasy in lights.

SCENIC TOURS
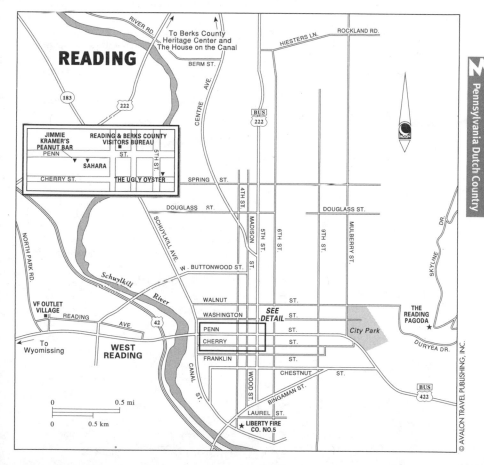

Berks County Hex Tour

Decorated barns are a familiar sight along Pennsylvania roads. The meaning of the geometric "hex" signs is disputed; many Pennsylvania Germans do not believe that the symbols are connected to protection from witches *(hexen)* and the black arts. In Europe, similar barn decorations are associated with religious and holy symbolism.

This 30-mile backroads loop winds through gently folded farm terrain and passes 14 decorated barns and a covered bridge. It's suitable for either bikes or autos; all distances are approximate. Take the Kutztown exit off US 222, and continue to Crystal Cave Road. Set your odometer at the intersection of Kutztown Road and Crystal Cave Road, and drive west toward Crystal Cave (3.3 miles).

On the right (5.2 miles) is the Stutzman Farm, and at 5.7 miles on the left is the Dreibelbis Farm. At 6.2 miles, turn left onto SR 143 (south). At 6.8 miles, you will pass a decorated barn on the left, and at 7.3 miles, another on the right. At 8.5 miles, turn right (west) onto SR 662.

At 8.8 miles and 12.6 miles, look for barns on the right. At 12.7 miles, turn right (north) onto Windsor Castle Road. At 12.8 miles, the Christman Farm barn is on the right. At 14.3 miles, turn right (east) onto Virginville Road.

This road has several decorated barns, all on the left (at 14.4, 14.5, 14.6, 15.5, and 15.6 miles). At 17.0 miles, turn left (north) onto SR 143. Look for two barns on the left, the Sunday Farm (17.3 miles) and the Leiby Farm (17.8), then the Dreibelbis Covered Bridge on the right at 19.0 miles. At 20.6 miles, you will reach old US 22. A right (east) turn on old US 22 leads to Kempton/Kutztown Road (turn right, south),

then to SR 737 (26.0 miles); a right turn (south) on SR 737 will return you to Kutztown.

HISTORIC SIGHTS

Ⓜ Hopewell Furnace

Hopewell Furnace (SR 345 and Hopewell Rd., Elverson, 610/582-8773, www.nps.gov/hofu) was one of the largest coal-fired iron plantations in Pennsylvania. The plantation and surrounding grounds are open 9 A.M.–5 P.M. Admission is $4, free during Jan. and Feb. Founded in 1771, one of the first tasks of this pig-iron production facility was to produce cannonballs and shot for the Continental Army. The "plantation" was actually a village, complete with foundry, outbuildings, ironmaster's mansion, and workers' housing. Hopewell Furnace closed its doors in the summer of 1883, a casualty of advancing technology. The site hosts many special events during the year

D. BOON CILLED A BAR

Daniel Boone got around. A beech tree on the Wataugh River in Tennessee bears this inscription:

D. Boon

cilled A BAR on

The Tree

in YEAR

1770

Daniel Boone was the first of a series of folk heroes who exemplified the romantic ideal of the frontiersman. In his time, he became known through his own writings and through newspaper and pulp accounts of his exploits.

Born into a Quaker family east of Reading in 1734, Boone would disappear into the forests for weeks at a time as a young man. He became a trapper and wilderness guide, and served as a wagoner in Gen. Edward Braddock's ill-fated expedition to dislodge the French from Fort Duquesne in 1755. A year later, Boone married Rebecca Bryan and

attempted to settle down on a farm in North Carolina. His halfhearted venture into agriculture was short-lived.

Boone had heard tales of a westward gap that Native American tribes used to pass through the supposedly impenetrable Cumberland Mountains at the juncture of Virginia, Tennessee, and Kentucky. With five companions, Boone walked from Castle's Woods in Virginia through the newly named Cumberland Gap into the Kentucky wilderness. He wrote:

We found everywhere abundance of wild beasts of all sorts, through this vast forest. The buffaloes were more frequent than I had seen cattle in the settlements, browsing on the leaves of the cane, or cropping the herbage on those extensive plains, fearless, because ignorant, of the violence of man. Sometimes we saw hundreds in a drove, and the numbers about the salt springs were amazing.

In May of 1769, Boone led the first of many expeditions of settlers through the gap. A North

and is an excellent opportunity to learn about an industry that was crucial to the survival of the young United States.

Daniel Boone Homestead

Woodsman Daniel Boone was born on this site in 1734. The 579-acre homestead (500 Daniel Boone Rd., Birdsboro, 610/582-4900, www .danielboonehomestead.org), which encompasses several buildings including the log house built by Daniel's English Quaker parents, is the largest state-run historic site in Pennsylvania. In 1750, Daniel's parents had been reprimanded by their meeting's elders for allowing Daniel's older brother to marry a non-Quaker. As a result of this censure, and partly for economic reasons, the family moved to North Carolina, where Daniel began his career as a frontiersman. The homestead and park are open Tues.–Sat. 9 A.M.–5 P.M., Sun. noon–5 P.M.,

© JOANNE MILLER

Boone family cabin

Pennsylvania Dutch Country

Carolina lawyer, Col. Richard Henderson, acquired 20 million acres in Kentucky from Cherokee chiefs and persuaded Boone to build a wagon road through the Cumberland Gap in exchange for 2,000 acres for himself and smaller tracts for each of his 30 workers. An anonymous road builder in Boone's party wrote:

I must not neglect to give honor to whom honor is due. Col. Boone conducted the company under his care through the wilderness with great propriety, intrepidity, and courage, and was I to enter an exception to any part of his conduct, it would be on the grounds that he appeared void of fear and its consequence—too little caution for the enterprise. But let me, with feeling recollection and lasting gratitude, ever remember the unremitting kindness, sympathy, and attention paid to me by Col. Boone in my distress. He was my father, my physician, and friend: he attended me as his child, cured my wounds by the use of medicines from the

woods, nursed me with paternal affection until I recovered, without the expectation of reward.

Boone's company finished the wilderness road ahead of schedule and pushed on to build a fort at Boonesborough. The gap road became a major route for pioneer migration. Thomas Lincoln and his wife, Nancy, were among those who ventured west through the gap; they settled and gave birth to a son, Abraham. Davy Crockett was the child of another couple who emigrated shortly after the road was built.

The onset of the French and Indian War proved disastrous to the unprotected settlers on the western side of the gap. The Cherokee, regretting the loss of their land, joined with the British against the colonials. They continued to rampage during the Revolutionary War, burning new settlements in Kentucky to the ground and destroying the wilderness road. The Cherokee were defeated when their British allies were driven out. Daniel Boone, then 61, asked to be placed in charge of the rebuilding of the wilderness road. He lived to the age of 86, after successfully resettling Kentucky.

with a reduced schedule in Jan. and Feb. Admission to the park is free, but a $4 fee is charged to view the homestead.

Berks County Heritage Center

The heritage center (2201 Tulpehocken Rd. off SR 183, Reading, 610/374-8839, www.berksparkandrec.org) consists of three parts: the Gruber Wagon Works, the C. Howard Hiester Canal Center, and the Deppen Cemetery. It's open May–Oct., Tues.–Sat. 10 A.M.–4 P.M., Sun. noon–5 P.M. Admission is $3.

The Gruber Wagon Works, begun as a hand-crafting business in 1870 by Franklin Gruber, grew to become a major manufacturer of wooden wagons and sleighs. His sons continued the business until World War I brought about a decline in demand for wooden wagons; they finally closed their doors in 1972. The wagon works, completely intact with tools and machinery, was moved five miles from its original location to the heritage center site.

C. Howard Hiester rescued many items of his extensive collection of canal memorabilia from the Schuylkill Navigation Company canal bed; when the company closed operations in Reading around 1927, everything stored in and around the building—tools, patterns, photos, ledgers, and more—was thrown into the canal bed for fill. An authority on the canals of Berks County, Hiester collected thousands of items, among them steamboat whistles, anchors, a pilot house, post lights, tickets, and a coal scow, *Mildred,* rebuilt into a houseboat. At Hiester's bequest, the heritage center has arranged the collection into displays that show the significance of the canals in Berks County and what life was like for people who drew their livelihood from the water roads.

When Blue Marsh Lake was created, the newly risen water level threatened to flood the Deppen Cemetery. Descendants of the interred were given three choices: each family could request a new burial plot at the federal government's expense; 10 feet of ground could be placed on top of the cemetery, raising the elevation above the waterline; or, the cemetery could be relocated to the heritage center. Respondents opted for the latter, ensuring a permanent and respectful home for the graves of Reading's pioneers. Among the approximately 67 marked and unmarked grave sites dating from 1808 are those of several Irish immigrants who died while digging the Union Canal; local history attributes their deaths to "canal fever," a strain of dysentery.

MUSEUMS

Mary Merritt Doll Museum

Over 1,500 dolls ranging in age and origin from 7th-century Egypt to 20th-century America are on display in this unique and wonderful museum (843 Ben Franklin Hwy./US 422, west of Douglassville, 610/385-3809, www.merritts.com). The museum is open Mon. and Wed.–Sat. 10 A.M.–4:30 P.M., Sun. 1–5 P.M. Admission is $3. The admission price covers both the doll museum and the Museum of Childhood next door.

One favorite is an antique French "Fortune" doll, whose voluminous skirts were made of folded paper fortunes; peddlers would carry the dolls through the streets, where, for a centime, children could tear a fortune from the skirt. The museum also features dozens of mechanical dolls that wave, blow kisses, or dance. The center space in the museum is taken up by a dollhouse with more than 40 miniature period rooms. An enchanting and irresistible toy shop with vintage and modern toys is on the premises.

Merritt Museum of Childhood

This museum, next door to the Mary Merritt Doll Museum (907 Ben Franklin Hwy., 610/385-3408, www.merritts.com) contains a staggering collection of (to name a few) rare tin and iron toys, pottery, porcelain, baby carriages, Native American relics, paperweights, life-size wax figures in costume, and cigar-store advertising figurines. Mary and Robert Merritt devoted their lives to buying and selling antiques, and this museum houses less than one-seventh of their mind-boggling personal collection. In an urban area, these items would be displayed in precious settings; here, the effect is one of stumbling on a magical treasure trove in grandma's attic. Open hours are the same as the doll museum, and one admission of $3 covers both.

© JOANNE MILLER

antique German bears at the Mary Merritt Doll Museum

Mid-Atlantic Air Museum

This museum at the Reading Regional Airport (Van Reed Road off SR 183, Reading, 610/372-7333, www.maam.org) is dedicated to the preservation, restoration, and operation of historic aircraft. The museum's collection includes military trainers, transports, bombers, helicopters, and experimental aircraft, such as a 1935 Kellett Autogiro. Aircraft-related exhibits complement the collection. A P-61B "Black Widow" night fighter, one of only four remaining in the world, is on display. The museum is open daily except major holidays 9:30 A.M.–4 P.M. Admission is $6.

OTHER POINTS OF INTEREST

Reading Pagoda

It's Old Japan high above the town of Reading! Originally built as part of a resort in the early 1900s, the red-brick and yellow-tile pagoda (610/375-6399, noon–5 P.M. daily) was modeled after a Shogun dynasty castle was graced by a dolphin and a Torii gate. The resort was never developed, but the pagoda remains; at one time,

it was used as a signal center. Flashing lights corresponded to a code published in the newspapers to inform the citizenry of current events.

Over the years, weather and fire took their toll. In 1969, a group of Reading residents formed an organization to renovate the pagoda; the exterior remains much the same, though the interior now consists of a snack bar on the first floor, a gift shop on the second floor, display areas featuring local wildlife on the third, fourth, and fifth floors, and an observation deck on the sixth floor. Cherry trees encircle the building, and there are walking trails throughout the adjacent park. Exact replicas of the original dolphin were created and once again crown the pinnacle. A bonsai island with Oriental bridge, gazebo, stone lantern, and landscaping have been added. The views of the surrounding countryside are the best available, especially in fall and spring. The pagoda may be reached via Skyline Drive.

Liberty Fire Company No. 5

Organized by a group of concerned citizens in 1854, the Liberty Fire Company still works out of the oldest fire department building in Reading

(501 S. 5th St., 610/375-6482). The company bought its first piece of motorized apparatus in 1914 over protest—many of the older firefighters felt that horses were far more reliable than motorized equipment and were reluctant to replace their equine partners.

Part of the station is a museum; glass cases upstairs contain memorabilia from the department's long history, and visitors can take a look at the old meeting room, still in use. Ring the bell near the glass door on the street, and a fireman will take you up to look around, though he or she will warn you that the visit may be cut short—they're on duty. Admission is free.

Roadside America

The lifelong work of two brothers, Laurence and Paul Gieringer, Roadside America (610/488-6241, www.roadsideamericainc.com) is a vast landscape of villages, churches, and history lessons laid out much like a small-gauge railroad display. The brothers became fascinated by miniatures in their youth—Laurence, at age five, became lost in the woods overnight when he went in search of the "toy" building he had seen on a distant mountain. The boys began to re-create buildings they had seen as a hobby. Over the years, the collection grew. In 1935, Laurence set up part of the miniature world for his children. Some years later, the collection of miniatures was moved to Shartlesville on I-78 (Exit 23) for public display; it continues to be maintained by Laurence Gieringer's family. It's open July–Labor Day Mon.–Fri. 9 A.M.–6:30 P.M., Sat.–Sun. 9 A.M.–7 P.M.; Sept.–June, it's open Mon.–Fri. 10 A.M.–5 P.M., Sat.–Sun. 10 A.M.–6 P.M. Admission is $5 for adults, $4.50 seniors, and $2.50 children 6–11.

The scenes and buildings are varied and highly detailed; many of the buildings depicted are accurate representations of existing architecture. The Locust Summit coal breaker and a replica of a church in Bolzano, Italy, share space with an early gristmill, covered bridges, Pennsylvania German farms, a replica of the town of Fairfield, a zoo, and much more. The scenes are populated with people, animals, cable cars, trains, and cars, all to scale. If you like models and miniatures, you'll spend hours here.

Koziar's Christmas Village

Bill Koziar began decorating his home (Christmas Village Rd., Bernville, 610/488-1110, www.koziarschristmasvillage.com) with multicolored lights during the holiday season in 1948; he expanded the display every year since then. Now, every building on the farm from barn to silo is covered with brilliant lights. From Nov. 3–Thanksgiving Day, it's open Fri. 6–9 P.M., Sat.–Sun. 5:30–9:30 P.M.; Thanksgiving–Jan. 1, it's open Mon.–Fri. 6–9 P.M. and Sat.–Sun. 5:30–9:30 P.M. Admission is $6 adults, $5 seniors, kids 6–12 $4.

The spectacular light show glows on the dark backcountry road like a fairy city. Special on-site displays feature stuffed animals posed in vignettes (Christmas in the Jungle, Santa's Post Office), and cardboard cutouts illustrate various

© JOANNE MILLER

Koziar's Christmas Village at night

cartoon characters and fairy tales. This is really a holiday treat for children of all ages.

Rodale Institute Research Center

The Rodale Institute (611 Siegfriedale Rd., Kutztown, 610/683-1428, www.rodaleinstitute.org) is the country's leading facility for organic farm and garden research. Tour guides take visitors through the institute's gardens and explain organic techniques such as the use of predator insects to control pests. The Rodale Institute, which has an extensive publishing facility, features its discounted publications in the bookstore. The public is welcome to stroll the grounds Mon.–Sat. during daylight hours for an admission fee of $6.

SHOPPING

Outlet Capital of the World

In 1892, Ferdinand Thun and Henry Janssen built a textile machine works on Cedar Street in Reading. Eventually, they expanded into several more manufacturing businesses, including a full-production knitting mill. The mill was to become the largest in the world—The Berkshire Knitting Mill—producing silk hosiery and other dainties under various brand names, including Vanity Fair. Thun and Janssen curtained off part of the mill to be used as a sales area where employees could purchase overruns and irregulars. The shop was such a success that it was opened to the public. When nylon and new manufacturing techniques made the old Berkshire mill and others in the area obsolete during the 1930s, the mills were converted to factory outlets for a number of manufacturers.

Since then, the original outlet stores have been fancied up into a modern cluster of buildings that house hundreds of brands, including London Fog, Woolrich, Osh Kosh, Dooney and Bourke, Oneida, Gund, and many others—including the manufacturer who started it all, Vanity Fair. **VF Outlet Village** (801 Hill Ave.) includes the original Vanity Fair Factory Outlet plus 90 more stores. Hours in the outlet stores vary, but they're generally open Mon.–Thurs. and Sat. 9 A.M.–7 P.M., Fri. 9 A.M.–9 P.M., Sun. 10 A.M.–5 P.M.

Renninger's Antiques and Farmers' Market

Renninger's (740 Noble St., Kutztown, 610/683-6848) in Lehigh Valley's largest and liveliest antiques sale and flea market, ongoing every Saturday year-round, weather permitting. A Pennsylvania Dutch farmers' produce market is also on the premises on Friday and Saturday, beginning at noon. Perhaps the biggest events of the year are the three Collectors' Extravaganzas: over 1,200 dealers from all over the United States converge during the last weekends of April, June, and September. The antique market is open every Sat. 10 A.M.–7 P.M.; the farmers market is open Fri.–Sat. 8 A.M.–4 P.M.

Bollman Hat Company

This is the Mad Hatter's vision of paradise. Bollman (SR 272, Adamstown, 717/484-4615) manufactures many of the hat styles seen in department stores. Here you can pick up berets, shaped felt hats, velvet toppers, cowboy hats, Stetsons, and hunter's caps for a fraction of the retail price. The outlet shop is open Mon.–Fri. 9 A.M.–5 P.M., Sat. 9 A.M.–4 P.M.

OUTDOOR RECREATION

Downhill Skiing

Ski Blue Marsh Lake in Bernville (610/488-6399, www.skibluemarsh.com) is a learn-to-ski facility that offers several classes a day for all age groups. Ski slopes are mostly intermediate, with two bunny runs and two black diamond (most difficult) runs. There's a T-bar, beginner chairlift, pommel lift, and a triple chairlift. It's open Oct.–Feb. and has 100 percent snowmaking capability.

Hiking

Blue Marsh Lake, west of Reading on SR 183, is a dammed recreation area maintained by the U.S. Army Corps of Engineers. Boating and fishing are available on the lake, and an extensive system of linked hiking trails follows the east and south shores. The separate trails vary from under half a mile to over 2.5 miles in length—the total trail is 14.7 miles long. The trail begins at the Dry Brooks day-use area off Plum Creek Road, though some of the links wander off the main path—a map is available from Blue Marsh Lake Project, U.S. Army Corps of Engineers, Philadelphia District (RD #1, Box 1239, Leesport, PA 19533, 215/376-6337).

Union Canal Bicycle and Walking Trail

This 4.5-mile trail follows the old path of the Union Canal from Reber's Bridge Road (there's a parking area next to the road on the north side of Tulpehocken Creek) to Stonecliffe Recreation Area. The Union Canal was 79.5 miles in length and ran from the Schuylkill River in Reading to Middletown on the Susquehanna River. Completed in 1827, the canal was never a commercial success due to the narrow channel and locks.

The trail passes several points of interest, including the Van Reed Paper Mill, the Berks County Heritage Center, and several old bridges and locks in varied states of repair. A detailed map is available from Berks County Park and Recreation Department (2083 Tulpehocken Rd., Wyomissing, PA 19610, 610/372-8939).

French Creek State Park

So named because of its proximity to a French fort during the French and Indian War, this park surrounds the Hopewell Furnace National Historic Site and features several lakes and streams plus a number of unusual recreational opportunities. For maps detailing hiking trails and the park, and to make reservations for the camping areas, contact DER, French Creek State Park (RR 1, Box 448, Elverson, PA 19520, 610/582-9680 or 888/727-2757).

Boating and Swimming: Non-powered and electric power boats are welcome on Hopewell and Scotts Run Lakes, with proper permits. Swimming is allowed at the guarded swimming pool at Hopewell Lake Memorial Day–Labor Day, Wed. 10 A.M.–6 P.M., Thurs.–Tues. 11 A.M.–7 P.M.

Disc Golf: A challenging 18-hole Frisbee-golf course is near the public boat launching area at

Hopewell Lake. Scorecards are available from the park office.

Hiking: The park offers more than 32 miles of hiking tails with a variety of terrains, and the Horseshoe Trail (a 120-mile trail that runs from Valley Forge to Rattling Run Gap, near Hershey) passes through the park for a distance of 6.5 miles.

Hunting and Fishing: 1,000 acres of the 7,000-acre park are open to hunters in season. Scotts Run Lake is stocked with trout for both winter and spring fishing. Hopewell Lake contains several species of warm-water fish such as black crappies, yellow perch, bluegills, and largemouth bass.

Orienteering: Considered by some as the orienteering capital of North America, French Creek Park has a permanently marked self-guided course that can be followed with map and compass.

Camping: The park offers 260 tent, trailer, and RV sites by reservation. Drinking water and pit toilets are available in each of the three camping areas. Winter season access may not be available; call the park office for information, or 888/PA-PARKS (888/727-2757) to make a reservation.

Getting There: The park is 14 miles southeast of Reading via US 422 and SR 82, SR 724, and SR 345. From I-76, take Exit 298 (Morgantown Interchange) and drive north on SR 345.

ACCOMMODATIONS

$50–100

The Little House in Oley Valley (675 Covered Bridge Rd. in Oley, 610/689-4814) is a restored 18th-century stone house with three rooms including a kitchen, in an area known for its surviving prerevolutionary homes; $80 a night.

$100–150

M The House on the Canal (4020 River Rd., Reading, 610/921-3015), a magnificent home on the banks of the Schuylkill River, seems light years from the city of Reading, yet is only a few minutes by auto from shopping outlets and the airport. Fishing, bike paths, and walking trails are also nearby. The farmhouse, built in the

ORDINARIES

During the colonial years, taverns, inns, and public houses were commonly called ordinaries, most consisted of small dwellings with extra rooms, far removed from populous places. Ordinaries were an integral part of the early life of the colonies. Many served as rest-and-refreshment stops along the wagon roads. Because of the remote but necessary services they provided, ordinaries frequently charged exorbitant prices for "lodging in clean sheets, one in a bed," and portions of food. Home-brewed peach brandy, a libation found in nearly every ordinary, was considered cheap at four shillings a gallon. "A warm diet with small beer," for example—bacon and eggs with fry-bread (also known as Indian hoecake), served with a cup of peach brandy or whiskey—fetched up to nine pence, the equivalent of a day's pay for some.

Ordinaries often specialized in specific clientele. There were drovers' inns, packhorses' inns, and wagoners' inns. Noisy singing, card-playing, and barroom brawls were common in the drovers' and wagoners' inns, which the gentry avoided.

A great number of ordinaries operated in the heavily traveled 63 miles between Philadelphia and Lancaster. Frequently run by German settlers, these inns were famed throughout the colonies for hearty meals that included traditional German dishes such as *sauerbraten, apfelklose,* bratwurst, and fruit pies.

Most ordinaries proclaimed themselves with brightly painted roadside signs, often with a portrait or symbol to illustrate the tavern's name for the benefit of the illiterate. The Black Horse, The Ball, The Ship, and Widdow Caldwell's Hat were among southeastern Pennsylvania's taverns and inns. Some ordinaries survive to this day; the Historic General Warren Inne, in Malvern, had its origins in the dust of the wagon roads. Once owned by William Penn's loyalist grandson John Penn, the General Warren was an infamous meeting place for those who remained loyal to the British crown during the Revolution.

In Lancaster, York, Gettysburg, and other towns, the presence of the inn dictated the location of a county seat. On court days, the ordinaries would swarm with lawyers and litigants. Often, county farmers came to town on those days to trade livestock and produce. Contests of strength and skill, such as wrestling, foot racing, horseshoe pitching, and bowling were played, and many a lawyer took pride in these sportive pastimes. Towns grew around the ordinaries—one, the General Paoli Inn, even gave the township of Paoli its name.

1700s, is filled with antiques, period furniture, and fine decorative details. Both suites and guest room have private baths and fireplaces, and a gourmet breakfast is included. Rates range $125–150.

Minute attention to detail is one of the hallmarks of the **N Adamstown Inn Bed and Breakfast** (62 W. Main St., Adamstown, 717/484-0800 or 800/594-4808, www.adamstown .com), a pretty Victorian home located near the antique shops on Adamstown's Miracle Mile (US 222). Featured in *Country Victorian* magazine, the inn displays the exceptional decorating and antique-collecting talents of its owners. Each room has a private bath, and the inn is situated on the main street of a pretty, quiet village. Breakfast is included in the package. Rates range $79–159.

The Amethyst House Bed and Breakfast (144 W. Main St., Adamstown, 717/484-0800 or 800/594-4808, www.adamstown.com), a Victorian "Painted Lady," is named for the surprisingly subtle color combinations (two shades of purple and red) on the exterior. Large rooms, carefully chosen antiques, warm decor, and fireplaces and baths with Jacuzzi double tubs in all rooms promise a luxurious stay. The innkeepers, refugees from the corporate world in Baltimore, have worked hard to create an attractive, comfortable setting for their guests. Breakfast is included. Rates range $139–199.

The **Hawk Mountain Inn** (610/756-4224) is a bed-and-breakfast with private baths near the Hawk Mountain Sanctuary in Kempton. It's $85–170 per night.

FOOD

Reading used to be the sort of place that you'd go knowing you'd never be far from a burger or a pizza. Recently, there's been a foodie revolution in town. The best of the old American menu places have stayed, and a new wave of international and specialty restaurants have sprouted up.

American with a Twist

Jimmie Kramer's Peanut Bar (332 Penn St., Reading, 610/376-8500 or 800/515-8500, www.peanutbar.com) is a hyper-diner; it serves the usual hamburgers, sandwiches, and salads, but it also has Middle Eastern vegetarian entrées, grilled meats and fishes, and a full bar. Kids will love the opportunity to litter the floor with peanut shells (the peanuts are free)—that is, if they're not too busy tucking into the frozen chocolate-covered pretzel pie. It's good American food served in a friendly setting. The Peanut

---

TWO-DAY DUTCH SLAW

Dutch slaw is one of the basic dishes found in Pennsylvania Dutch–style family meals. A good pepper slaw is sweet, crunchy, and piquant, and you may find yourself craving it on a hot summer day. This recipe makes six servings.

3 cups shredded green cabbage
3 large green or red bell peppers, cored, seeded, and thinly sliced
2 tablespoons salt
2–3 tablespoons cider vinegar
2 tablespoons sugar
$1/2$ cup sour cream (or unflavored yogurt)

1. In a large colander set over a pan, combine the cabbage and peppers. Sprinkle with salt, and drain for one hour. Press down on the cabbage and peppers with a wooden spoon to extract any excess liquid. Set aside.
2. In a large serving bowl, mix vinegar, sugar, and sour cream together until blended. Add the cabbage and peppers and toss with the dressing. Add fresh ground pepper to taste, cover, and chill overnight.

Bar is open Mon.–Thurs. 11 A.M.–11 P.M., Fri.–Sat. 11 A.M.–midnight. Prices range from under $5 to over $15.

A local favorite, **Dan's Restaurant** (1049 Penn St., Reading, 610/373-2075) serves up an American menu with a Continental twist for lunch Tues.–Fri. and dinner Tues.–Sat. Reservations recommended. Prices average $8–15 for lunch and $19–29 for dinner.

Haag's Hotel (old US 22 and 3rd St., Shartlesville, 610/488-6692) is a family-owned traditional Pennsylvania Dutch restaurant. The Haag family has owned the hotel and the adjoining 125-acre farm that supplies it for five generations. Shartlesville's 300 residents are mostly direct descendants of the original German settlers. Though Haag's serves breakfast, lunch, and dinner 7 A.M.–7:30 P.M. daily, the restaurant is especially proud of its Sunday dinners featuring chicken, ham, beef, sausages, several kinds of potatoes, gravy, corn, peas, cabbage, beets, apple sauce, and home-baked desserts, among other things. Come eat—this is farm country! Sunday dinner prices are in the $20 range, but you can order à la carte from the menu for much less.

Haag's also has hotel rooms with private baths in case you can't drag your stomach back to the parking lot.

Brewpubs and Microbreweries

The Ugly Oyster (21 South 5th St., Reading, 610/373-6791), a once-ordinary workingman's tavern, is now a brewpub that out-greens the Irish. Live traditional Irish music rings out on Thursday, and when Penn State or Notre Dame plays. Chicken wings are 10 cents apiece and Yuengling lager is a buck a glass. The pub food averages $6.

The **Stoudt Brewing Co.** (SR 272, Adamstown, 717/484-4387) brews a wide range of pilsners and ales and has won several awards, notably for Stoudt Gold, a smooth, full-bodied lager. All brews are on tap, and specialty beers such as Holiday Spice Ale are available seasonally. Stoudt's Brewery is next to the Black Angus, an upscale beef-and-spuds restaurant (entrees average $15) owned and operated by the Stoudt family, and a large antiques mall with 200 antiques dealers.

Beer by the case is sold on the premises, and there's also a gift shop, open Mon.–Thurs. 9 A.M.–5 P.M., Fri. 9 A.M.–6 P.M., Sat. 2–6 P.M. Tours of the brewery are given Sat. at 3 P.M. and Sun. at 1 P.M.

International

You can have lunch Mon.–Fri. and dinner Mon.–Sat. in a tented Middle Eastern fantasy. **Sahara** (334 Penn St., Reading, 610/374-8500) serves specialties such as sujok (a spicy homemade beef sausage) and all the familiar foods associated with the Mediterranean and Middle East: hummus, falafel, and tabbouleh, among others. The prices are comfortable: around $5 for appetizers, $9 for entrees.

Borelli's Family Restaurant and Pizzeria (US 422 East, Birdsboro, 610/385-7900) serves Italian food and pizza. It's open Sun. and Tues.–Thurs. 10:30 A.M.–8 P.M., and Fri.–Sat. 10:30 A.M.–9 P.M.

INFORMATION

Talk to the **Berks County Chamber of Commerce** (601 Penn St., Suite 101, Reading, PA 19601, 610/376-6766, www.berkschamber.org). They'll be happy to send you what you need and answer your questions.

The Poconos and Black Diamond Country

The mountains in this area were once a wilderness of pine-shrouded roundtops floating in an early morning haze and marching to the horizon. The image still exists, though the land here has been a vacation and second-home destination for a century and has therefore been modified with a couple of sprawling cities, fancy resorts, fast-food outlets, and lots of ways to enjoy both nature and peculiarly American amusements.

This section of the Appalachian Plateau is commonly called the Poconos, the legendary destination for lovers who come to loll in heart-shaped tubs. Now dotted with ski and sports resorts, the Poconos began to attract visitors when travel by rail became a reality.

The Poconos and all of northeastern Pennsylvania sit upon one of the rarest geological phenomena in the world—underground anthracite coal fields. The coal, so valuable it's sometimes referred to as black diamonds, has created its own mystique, a brotherhood, and an industry that shaped the cities and lands that grew to embrace it.

Scranton and Wilkes-Barre are commercial centers, though their museums and historic sites are a worthy draw. Some Pocono resorts have become legendary for their pull-out-all-the-stops honeymoon getaways, complete with star-studded ceilings and hot tubs shaped like champagne glasses. Others offer great skiing, hiking, river-rafting, or plain old-fashioned relaxation. The coal-mining region remains true to its rough roots—and for that reason is one of the most interesting places in America.

PLANNING YOUR TIME

What's your pleasure? If it's skiing, one of the Poconos' many ski resorts is waiting for you. Outdoor adventures, hiking, and camping? White-water rafting is popular near Jim Thorpe, and **Frances Slocum State Park** in the Scranton area, **Delaware Water Gap National Recreation Area, Promised Land State Park, Locust Lake State Park,** or **Ricketts Glen State Park** could all be on your list of great places to visit for two days or two weeks.

To see all the urban pleasures of Scranton would take a minimum of four days: the **Lackawanna Coal Mine Tour** (2 hours) and **Anthracite Heritage Museum** (2 hours) on Day 1; **Steamtown National Historic Site** (3 hours–all day), **Lackawanna Trolley Museum** (1 hour), and **Scranton Iron Furnaces** (drive-by or picnic there for lunch) on Day 2; **The Everhart Museum** (2 hours–all day) and the **Lion Brewery Tour** (1 hour) on Day 3; and the **Houdini Museum** (2 hours) and a little harness racing at **Pocono Downs** on Day 4. Add a couple of days for sightseeing outside of town, particularly the **Delaware Water Gap, Dorflinger Glass Museum,** and **Zane Grey Museum.** Basing in Scranton or in pretty Hawley or south of Wilkes-Barre is a great idea.

If you'd like to snap your fingers and have your vacation at your fingertips, think about spending time at one of the **Caesar's Resorts**—like a cruise on dry land.

Jim Thorpe is a good central location for exploring Black Diamond Country, including the historic sights of the **Black Diamond Trail: Ashland Coal Mine and "Lokie" Steam Train** (2 hours), the **Museum of Anthracite Mining** (1–2 hours), **Eckley Miner's Village** (2–3 hours), **Yuengling Brewery** (1–2 hours), **The No. 9 Mine Wash Shanty and Anthracite Coal Mining Museum** (1–2 hours), and more. The driving tour may take up to three days, depending on how much time you plan to spend at each location.

The pretty college town of Bloomsburg is centrally situated for touring the area east of the Susquehanna, or stay in **Ricketts Glen State Park.** Make sure to enjoy the **Covered Bridge Tour: Bloomsburg to Elysburg** (all day) and **Knoebels Amusement Park** (all day–3 days).

GETTING THERE AND GETTING AROUND

By Air, Rail, and Bus

Scranton is served by a major metropolitan airport that is accessible directly as well as through Pittsburgh and Philadelphia.

Amtrak rail connections are through Harrisburg; both the Pennsylvanian and Three Rivers trains offer service to Harrisburg with continuing service to Scranton on a Capitol Trailways bus.

Greyhound (800/231-2222) offers bus service to many towns and resort areas in the Poconos. Call for schedules and fares.

By Auto

Major east-west routes are I-78, I-80, and I-84. North-south routes are I-81 and I-380. State Route 9, a two- to four-lane highway, also runs north-south from Scranton to Allentown. The remainder of those black lines on the map are two-lane roads, slow but scenic.

HISTORY

Pre-European History

The Unami Delaware (Lenni Lenape of the Turtle tribe) and other tribal units of the widespread Lenni Lenape nation hunted in the Poconos, chiefly along the rivers. The area, an Iroquois protectorate, was largely unsettled, though it was crossed by numerous hunting trails. Water travel on the rivers was unreliable, since floods and ebbs frequently made them impassable. The Lenni Lenape's claims to the Wyoming Valley,

The Poconos

Must-Sees

Look for **M** to find the sights and activities you can't miss and **N** for the best dining and lodging.

M Lackawanna Coal Mine Tour: A journey to the center of the earth—well, not quite, but you'll experience life underground in a maze of tunnels (page 164).

M Steamtown National Historic Site: No rail fan would want to miss this opportunity to see the multitude of locomotives and cars from all eras (page 164).

M Dorflinger Glass Museum: The delicate and beautiful pieces here are enhanced by their simple presentation; the museum is surrounded by a lovely wildlife sanctuary (page 173).

M Delaware Water Gap National Recreation Area: Even if you only drive through, see the gap, especially on a fall day (page 176).

M The Black Diamond Trail: Speaking of driving, this trail is an excellent way to see the territory and visit the highlights of this unique area (page 186).

M Eckley Miner's Village: This is the real deal: a coal patch town where people lived, worked, worshipped, and went into debt at the company store (page 187).

M Yuengling Brewery: The oldest in the state, and still going strong—tour and get the story (page 187).

M Covered Bridge Tour: Bloomsburg to Elysburg: Another auto-tour option is the beautiful scenery in this bucolic area, and the variety of original covered bridges (page 191).

M Knoebels Amusement Park: This is one of the most magical of the older parks—visitors can camp nearby and cross a covered bridge into the park (page 192).

M Ricketts Glen State Park: If you're planning getaway time, try this, one of the top 20 parks in the state, chosen for wildlife and natural beauty (page 193).

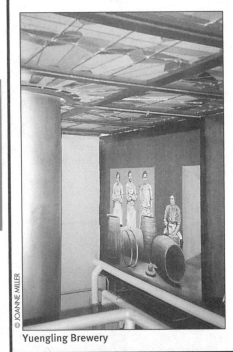

© JOANNE MILLER

Yuengling Brewery

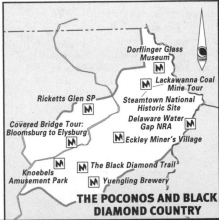

THE POCONOS AND BLACK DIAMOND COUNTRY

The Poconos

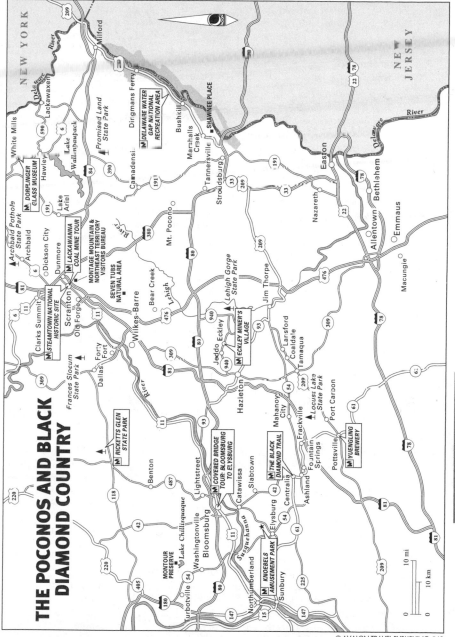

THE POCONOS AND BLACK DIAMOND COUNTRY

The Poconos

© AVALON TRAVEL PUBLISHING, INC.

the present site of Scranton and Wilkes-Barre (WILKS-bahr), were honored until the death of William Penn, when German and Scotch-Irish squatters began moving into the area. In 1754, Mohawk Chief Hendrick, representing the Iroquois Confederacy and the Lenape, declared:

We will never part with the Land at Shamokin and Wyomink; our Bones are scattered there, and on this Land there has always been a great Council Fire. We desire You will not take it amiss that we will not part with it, for We reserve it to settle such of our Nations upon as shall come to us from the Ohio, or any others who shall deserve to be in our Alliance. Abundance of Indians are moving up and down, and We shall invite all such to come and live here, that so We may strengthen ourselves.

In that same year, agents of the Susquehannah Company tricked several tribal members into putting their marks on paper, authorizing the dubious Wyoming Purchase. The sale was never approved by the Onondaga Council, and prospective settlers were warned that

whosoever of the white should venture to Setle any land on Wyomock or thereabout, belong hitherto to the Indians, will have his Creatures killed first, and then If they did not desist they them self would be Killed, without distinction.

The Colonial Wars

Frustrated by the continuous abuse of their land agreements, the Wyoming Valley Lenni Lenape joined with the French against the English in the French and Indian War. Raids, ambushes, and kidnappings became frequent, and settlers, leaving the area for their own safety, dubbed it "The Bloody Ground." Shawnees and Nanticokes joined the Lenni Lenape and French raiders to terrorize the tiny unprotected settlements. Many pioneers left, never to return. Attacks continued through Pontiac's War and the Revolution, when the Wyoming Valley Lenni Lenape sided with the British.

To complicate matters, the area was the center of a dispute known as the Yankee-Pennamite

Wars. The colony of Connecticut claimed ownership of the valley and sent colonies of "Yankees" to settle there; Wilkes-Barre was laid out New England–style, with a town square and river park commons on the Susquehanna. Connecticut families took up residence in the valley and were the victims of the first massacre of Wyoming when, in 1763, a Lenni Lenape raiding party swept through, destroying white settlements. Pennsylvania and Connecticut fought over ownership of the territory 1769–1785, when Congress ruled in favor of Pennsylvania (though Connecticut did not relinquish its claims until 1800).

Early Settlement

The importance of the area as a source of grain during the American Revolution led to repeated attacks by British-sympathizing Tories. In the Battle of Wyoming, in 1778, a force made up of renegade Native Americans and British-affiliated colonists defeated a much smaller group of frontiersmen near Forty Fort, leaving the settlements in the Wyoming Valley unprotected. The triumphant force passed up and down the valley after the defeat, laying waste to the area in a series of raids that became known as the Wyoming Massacre. Though the consequent fury of the colonies was aimed at the Indians, they had simply carried out a plan that had been developed months before by the British, using tactics modeled on the Battle of Bushy Run in western Pennsylvania. Reprisals for the massacre—in the form of expeditions led by Gen. John Sullivan and others, destroyed 40 Indian towns and thousands of acres of cornfields belonging to the Iroquois Confederacy. The Seneca, far from being defeated, united in their aggression until the United States made grudging peace in a series of treaties. In 1795, Pennsylvania's Indian wars finally ceased.

Old King Coal

The Poconos, ever rich in resources, remained poor in accessibility. From the Lenni Lenape early settlers learned about anthracite, the long-burning hard coal that resembled opaque obsidian; however, the difficulty of igniting it made it almost useless in the average home. Two enterprising Philadelphians, Josiah White and Erskine Hazard, secured rights to thousands of acres of coal land, and through the use of a new ignition system convinced the public of the viability of the shiny black rock.

Engineering innovations such as incline planes and the newly built canal system began to haul black diamonds out of the collieries—mines and processing plants—and the patch towns that surrounded them. Northeastern Pennsylvania expanded further when, in 1840, the first anthracite-fueled iron smelter opened, in Catasauqua. Rural furnaces, factories, and forges multiplied along the canal route.

The demand for hard coal and the iron and steel it produced extended the railroads into the formerly inaccessible Pocono Plateau. The Philadelphia and Reading Railroad (P&R) maintained two large locomotive repair facilities in Pottsville; the shops also built lokies, small steam engines that pulled cars of culm (refuse) from the deep pit mines. Philadelphia & Reading Coal and Iron Company, a sister organization of the railroad, became one of the major players in the coal business, organizing its own police force—a necessity since laborers were beginning to rebel against mine conditions. Acts of terrorism and strikes became common.

Mining for Tourist Dollars

Conditions in the deep mines continued to fuel discontent. One strike closed down the entire industry in 1902. The winter strike of 1925–1926 signaled the decline of deep mining. Companies began to dismantle the collieries, leaving the mines to bootleggers, who would sink illegal shafts on the property and carry off whatever coal they could raise. Strip-mining, begun in 1909, revitalized the industry for a time, even as it devastated the beautiful hilly country of the Pocono Plateau. But interest in anthracite as a fuel source declined in recent times; oil was cheaper to extract. Oil embargoes can always be relied on for a surge in strip-mining. Today, however, tourism is giving the old natural resource economic base a run for its money. And the real value of the Poconos—their scenic beauty—has become the focus.

Scranton and Environs

As the epicenter of the anthracite industry, Scranton eventually became the destination for 36 separate ethnic groups, most of whom came to work in the vast coalfields nearby, the textile industry, or Scranton's massive iron furnaces. Iron was the cornerstone of Scranton's wealth.

William Henry and the Scranton brothers built their first iron furnace in 1840. Iron and steel production exploded seven years later, along with the demand for high-quality rail. The foundries produced rail for the trains, railroads transported the coal, and Scranton became a city. This wealth translated into civic and technological innovation. Prominent architects such as Edward Langley (who, with Kenneth Muchison, created the elegant Lackawanna Train Station and the Houlihan-McLane Performing Arts

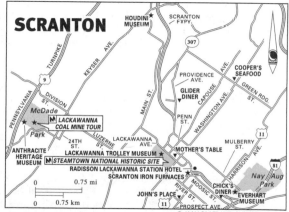

© AVALON TRAVEL PUBLISHING, INC.

The Poconos

THE ROCK THAT BURNS

Coal was crucial to the economic development of the state of Pennsylvania, which sits on vast veins of this prehistoric fuel. In spite of its hardness, coal isn't a mineral but rather an organic substance made of decomposed plant material. This material compresses and forms peat. Through pressure, heat, and time, the chemical and physical properties of peat are changed into several "types" of coal—the most familiar being bituminous and anthracite—distinguished mainly by solidity and composition.

Most people are familiar with bituminous coal, also known as soft coal or clinker, the Christmas-stocking trick every "bad" child feared. Most coal in western Pennsylvania is bituminous, contains a relatively high percentage of volatile minerals, sits close to the surface in flat-lying or slightly folded beds, and can be extracted by pick and shovel.

Anthracite—hard coal—is found in very few places on earth; northeastern Pennsylvania has three of the largest fields in the world. The peat deep under the surface was highly pressurized, heated, and deformed to produce anthracite, a clean-burning material with increased carbon content relative to the volatile minerals. In appearance, it resembles a shiny, sparkling black rock.

Introduced by Native Americans to "the rock that burns," early settlers searched for the stands of white birch trees that signaled subterranean veins and started digging. In spite of the fact that anthracite burns hotter and longer than soft coal, it was hard to mine, difficult to ignite, and, until a forced-air system for reliable ignition was invented, in 1810, impossible to sell.

Anthracite is extracted from the deep mines in only one way—blasting. Miners followed tarry veins deep into the earth, setting explosives, shoring tunnels, and making rooms (a mining space blasted off to the side of a tunnel). Because a short room—often only two to three feet in height—was much less likely to cave in than a tall room, the miners often wound up passing the coal out hand over hand while lying on their backs. Miners sometimes referred to this method as "monkey mining."

On-site deaths of deep miners between 1870

Center, at 346 Jefferson Ave.) led a citywide building expansion. The first commercially successful electric streetcar system graced Scranton in 1866.

Today, Scranton's heritage is manifest in its architecture. The Lackawanna Coal Mine Tour and Anthracite Museum, the remains of the Scranton (Lackawanna) Iron Furnaces in the park at 159 Cedar Ave., and Steamtown, the rail museum, actively tell the story of this commercial and industrial center of the mid-Atlantic.

HISTORIC SIGHTS

☒ Lackawanna Coal Mine Tour

The mine (in McDade Park off N. Keyser Ave., Scranton, 570/963-6463 or 800/238-7245) is next to the Pennsylvania Anthracite Heritage Museum. Daily mine tours are scheduled April 1–Nov. 30 every hour to 1.5 hours between 10 A.M. and 3 P.M. (you must be there by 3 P.M. for the last tour of the day). Admission is $7 for adults, $5 for children, and $6.50 for seniors.

A wide yellow transport car slides visitors backward 300 feet down into the darkness of the Lackawanna mine. As the circle of light that was the tunnel's entrance disappears from view, another world opens. Former mine workers lead walking tours from that point into three veins of the underground city that served as home for hundreds of miners—and it was a city, complete with offices, stables, and hundreds of rooms. This entertaining tour gives an authentic feel of life in the mines and illuminates the camaraderie that grew among the men and boys who worked there.

The mine temperature hovers around 50°F; jackets are provided at no charge if you've forgotten yours. Visitors must be able to walk half a mile.

☒ Steamtown National Historic Site

Steamtown (150 S. Washington Ave., 570/340-5200, www.nps.gov/stea) had a difficult birth—it was hailed as a boon to the city's economic growth at its inception, but rumors of political pork barrels and illicit profit-taking nearly halted

and 1949 totaled 30,060. Invisible dangers such as flash damp (methane gas) and black damp (carbon dioxide) were ever-present dangers, as was the more visible risk of cave-in. Ventilation in the mines was controlled by soggy burlap curtains that were pulled back as needed. The Black Mariah, a black-plumed, horse-drawn hearse carrying a dead or dying miner to the back steps of his home, was a common sight in the isolated coal patch towns.

Everyone in a coal town worked. Disabled miners and boys ages 7–12—considered too young to go below safely— worked on the surface as breaker boys, sorting rocks and debris from the mine tailings. Below the surface, the boys graduated to mule tending, wearing rubber boots to combat the watery

ditches in which they walked while guiding the animals. Women and children spent their days picking through the mine tailings for coal to heat their own homes, and then came home to feed and care for their families.

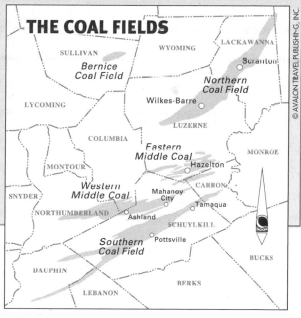

THE COAL FIELDS

the project before completion. Difficulties aside, it celebrated its grand opening in the summer of 1995 and remains a popular destination.

The Steamtown Museum is open daily 9 A.M.–5 P.M. year-round. Admission is $6 for adults, $5 for seniors 62 and over $3 for children ages 6–12 and free for children under 6. There are several tours and programs during the day; Steamtown offers three excursions on the Great Steam Shuttle, pulled by the largest steam locomotives operating in the United States today. Excursions are offered only in the summer and it's wise to make reservations. Fare is between $15 and $75.

The beating heart of Steamtown is a group of 29 standard-gauge steam locomotives and 90 freight and passenger cars, originally brought together in the 1950s and '60s by collector F. Nelson Blount. When the national historic site was created, the yard and collection became part of the National Park System.

Steamtown occupies 40 acres of the Scranton railroad yard of the Delaware, Lackawanna, and Western Railroad (DL&W), one of the earliest rail lines in northeastern Pennsylvania. The yard itself was built during the Civil War. The National Park Service has restored a section of the original roundhouse; mechanics perform daily running repairs on several operational steam locomotives. The NPS has also created a visitors' center, 250-seat theater, history museum, and technology museum—all tell the story of steam railroading.

The theater shows an 18-minute movie every half hour, *Steel and Steam,* which recounts one man's career as a worker on the DL&W. The history museum features an example of a gravity railroad (similar to the incline planes of

The Poconos

Pittsburgh and Johnstown), four passenger station waiting rooms, and exhibits on rail history. The technology museum, partially located in a restored section of the roundhouse, tells the story of the technical aspects of steam locomotive design and operation, railroad architecture, and engineering, and it features an operating model of the DL&W Scranton Yards as they appeared in 1937. The best show of all, though, may be outside the museum on the tracks next to the parking lot, where operational engines puff away in all their metallic glory.

Scranton Iron Furnaces

Before there was a city, there was an iron industry. Scranton's earliest settlers built the massive stone pig iron furnaces that remain in place on Cedar Avenue, and the city grew up around them. One of the Anthracite Heritage Museum sites (information: R.D. 1, Bald Mountain Rd., Scranton, PA 18504, 570/963-3208 or 570/963-4804), the furnaces are on view year-round at 159 Cedar

A locomotive lets off steam at Steamtown National Historic Site.

© JOANNE MILLER

Avenue. The furnaces may be a little tricky to spot if you don't know where to look (or what to look for), so call the listed numbers or get directions at www.phmc.state.pa.us/bhsm/toh/scranton/scrantoniron.

OTHER POINTS OF INTEREST
The Lion Brewery Tour

This facility (700 N. Penna Ave., Wilkes-Barre, 570/823-8801, www.lionbrewery.com), which produces beers and nonalcoholic beverages, is proud of its heritage—the original brewery was founded in 1901. The 11th-largest distributor in the nation, Lion uses the traditional English method of upward infusion mashing to create lagers and ales inspired by old-world values, but with modern quality and consistency. The brewery merges rustic architecture with state-of-the-art brewing technology. Tours are available Sat. at 1 P.M. by reservation (call 570/823-8801, ext. 346, or email infor@lionbrewery.com, subject line: Tour Request). Open-toed shoes, spike heels, and sandals are not permitted in the brewhouse; sneakers or shoes that cover the entire foot are necessary. The tour involves climbing several flights of steps. A light jacket is recommended, as some areas are very chilly. Lion Brewery Root Beer is always on tap for visitors under 21.

Harness Racing

Pocono Downs (1280 SR 315, Wilkes-Barre, 570/825-6681, www.poconodowns.com) shows off some of the finest harness-trained trotters from all over the world. It also offers year-round simulcast wagering, and special events.

MUSEUMS
Anthracite Heritage Museum

The museum (Bald Mountain Rd. in McDade Park, Scranton, near the Lackawanna Coal Mine, 570/963-4804) is a great double bill with the mine tour; it's open year-round, Mon.–Sat. 9 A.M.–5 P.M., Sun. noon–5 P.M. Admission is free for children under the age of 6, $2 for ages 6–17, $4 ages 18–59, and $3.50 for those over 60.

The Poconos

Immigration and industry: this clever museum chronicles the lives of Scranton's citizens, from prehistory through modern times. Native American artifacts, pioneer quilts, a replica of a patch town saloon (which swings into action via a hidden sound machine when a visitor enters), a church altar, and a mechanical lace-making machine are a few of the exhibits that educate visitors on life in the hard coal region.

Lackawanna Trolley Museum

More than 100 years ago, Scranton became the site of the first commercially viable, all-electric trolley system in America. This museum, on the Steamtown National Historic Site in a resplendently restored late-19th-century mill building, celebrates one of America's most beloved forms of transportation. It's open 9 A.M.–5 P.M. year-round. Closed Mon. and Tues. during the winter but open daily after April 1. Excursion rides are Wed. through Sun. Admission is $3.50 for adults, $3 for seniors, and $2.75 for children. For information, call 570/963-6590.

The museum tells the story of electric traction systems and the impact they had on the development of the Lackawanna Valley, Northeast Pennsylvania, and the industrial northeast. Interactive exhibits and displays include vintage trolleys; Trolleys Exposed, an intriguing under-the-skin view of a restored trolley; and Electric City, a kids' exhibit that puts children in the driver's seat as they drive a model trolley on a suspended track. Young visitors and their parents will also have the opportunity to build their own anthracite-region communities on a 24-foot-long platform that represents the Lackawanna Valley and beyond—complete with historic trolley lines. There's also a 50-seat theater and a Trolley Restoration Shop, offering visitors an opportunity to see and learn about ongoing restoration of the museum's collection from a rare turn-of-the-20th-century "open" car to sleek, aerodynamically inspired interurbans.

Houdini Museum

The Houdini Museum (1433 N. Main Ave., Scranton, 570/342-5555, www.houdini.org) is the work of two dedicated fans of the great escape artist: Dorothy Dietrich and John Bravo. Both are professional magicians: Dietrich is also an escape artist, and Bravo is former editor of *Hocus Pocus* magazine. The museum is open Memorial Day weekend, Mother's Day, Father's Day, weekends in June, July–Oct. daily 12:30–6 P.M. The museum and magic show may be viewed at other times by reservation. Admission is $12 adults, $9.95 for children.

The museum itself is a combination of film clips, framed paintings, memorabilia, write-ups, and photos—slick, it's not. What it *is* is a love letter to one performer who grabbed the attention of the world, and to magicians everywhere.

Houdini never lived in Scranton, but he did perform here, in a series of stunts that would make the most jaded public relations executive's jaw drop in envy. Many of his stunts were sponsored by local companies: the workers of J. B. Woolsey & Co. of Scranton nailed Houdini into one of their own packing crates, along with seven pounds of nails; he escaped in six minutes. Standard Brewery of Scranton sealed Houdini in a keg of Tru-Age beer, and he escaped with the keg intact and still full of beer (the keg, not Houdini—though it's possible that he was as well).

These and other escapades are chronicled in a two-hour tour that usually includes a magic show by Dietrich and Bravo (call for show schedules). This quirky, very personal museum and its resident prestidigitators bring back the days of vaudeville.

Everhart Museum

Set in Nay Aug Park (1901 Mulberry St., Scranton, 570/346-7186, www.everhart-museum.org), Everhart is the regional center for natural history, science, and art exhibits. It's open Wed.–Sun. noon–4 P.M., Thurs. noon–8 P.M. Admission is $5 for adults, $3 for seniors, and $2 for children. There's plenty of variety at Everhart: the museum has a dinosaur room, American folk art displays, and a permanent collection of Dorflinger glass. The Folk Art Collection, with more than 500 pieces on display, is especially strong; it includes Pennsylvania-Dutch *fraktur* pieces, painted furniture, mourning pictures, whirligigs, trade signs, and more.

Pieces of this collection are exhibited in the Abby Aldrich Rockefeller Museum of American Folk Art in Williamsburg, Virginia. The Maslow Collection of modern art is also worth viewing. In the permanent collection are 130 artists and 500 works, and new works are added at each exhibition by artists such as Martin Mull and Francesco Clemente.

SHOPPING

In 1884, two Wilkes-Barre merchants, F. M. Kirby and F. W. Woolworth, opened a new kind of retail establishment. Packed with gadgets, gifts, and small necessities, the "5 and 10 cent store" made shopping fun. Woolworth stores are long gone, but shopping is not a lost art.

Carriage Barn Antiques (1550 Fairview Rd., Clarks Summit, 570/587-5405, www.carriage-barnantiques.com) is the largest antique store in northeast Pennsylvania and was featured in *Country Living* magazine. It also offers custom building and refinishing workshops. Hours are Mon.–Fri. 9 A.M.–5 P.M., Sat.–Sun. 10 A.M.–5 P.M. The Carriage Barn can arrange worldwide shipping of your purchase.

Malls

Steamtown Mall, adjacent to Steamtown National Historical Site in downtown Scranton; **Viewmont Mall,** US 6 in Scranton; and **Wyoming Valley Mall,** off Business SR 309 in Wilkes-Barre, are all covered malls that offer big-name stores such as Sears, JC Penney, and Bon-Ton.

OUTDOOR RECREATION

Hiking and Biking

For more than a century, trains traveled through Scranton along the Central Railroad of New Jersey, also known as the Jersey Central. Beginning in 1871, Jersey Central acquired this branch line from the former Lehigh and Susquehanna Railroad, and its trains carried anthracite coal and passengers from Northeastern Pennsylvania to other cities. The Jersey Central remained in operation until the floods of 1972 and was acquired by Conrail in 1976.

The line remained dormant for nearly two decades until the Lackawanna River Corridor Association and, later, the Lackawanna Heritage Valley Authority developed the abandoned railroad into the **Lackawanna River Heritage Trail,** part of a regional hiking/biking recreational trail that may eventually extend 60 miles through Taylor, Scranton, Carbondale, Forest City, and other communities. The Jersey Central passenger station once stood at the corner of Lackawanna and 7th Avenues in Scranton, and the Central New Jersey segment of the trail begins there.

Winter Sports

Montage Mountain (1000 Montage Mountain Rd., Scranton, 570/969-7669, www.skimontage.com) features 20 trails, snowmaking capability, five chairlifts, two pommel lifts, and a separate Snowboard Fun Park. Montage offers lessons and packages. It's south of Scranton, off I-81. For snow conditions, call 800/468-7669 (800/GOT-SNOW).

Montage is also open in the summer and is a favorite for its 3,000-foot-long alpine waterslide. Montage sponsors a big-name music series in the summer, showcasing entertainers such as Bob Dylan, Britney Spears, and others. Call the resort for the entertainment lineup.

Seven Tubs Natural Area

A bit of terrain rife with potholes is the Seven Tubs Natural Area. Glacial meltwater eroded the bedrock and created a series of potholes in Whirlpool Valley. Owned by Luzerne County, Seven Tubs can be reached at Exit 47 off I-81. Follow SR 115 south for 2.5 miles; the park is on the right. For information, contact the Luzerne County Parks Department, 570/477-5467.

Archbald Pothole State Park

This is the world's largest glacial pothole, 38 feet deep and up to 42 feet across—sounds dramatic, doesn't it? Actually, pulling off the road and looking at the fern-covered hole may be a bit of a disappointment unless one is pothole-savvy. You'll find it about 12 miles north of Scranton off I-81 near Carbondale.

POCONOS GOLF COURSES

Scranton Area

Fox Hill Country Club, 18 holes, West Pittston, 570/654-9242
Glen Oak Country Club, 18 holes, Clarks Summit, 570/586-0946
Lehman Golf Club, nine holes, Dallas, 570/675-1686
Nine Flags Golf Course, nine holes, Clarks Summit, 570/254-9933
Scranton Municipal Golf Course, 18 holes, Lake Ariel, 570/689-2686
Twin Oaks, nine holes, Dallas, 570/333-5933
Wemberly Hills Golf Course, nine holes, Olyphant, 570/472-3590
Wilkes-Barre Golf Club, 18 holes, Wilkes-Barre, 570/472-3590
Blue Ridge Trail Golf Club, 18 holes, Wilkes-Barre, 570/868-4653

The Poconos

Glenmaura National Golf Course, 18 holes, Moosic, 570/343-4642
Jean's Run Golf Course, nine holes, Hunlock Creek, 570/256-3444
Pine Hills Country Club, 18 holes, Taylor, 570/562-0138
Aberdeen Golf and Country Club, nine holes, Mountaintop, 570/868-4653
Four Seasons Golf Course, 18 holes, Exeter, 570/655-8869
Cricket Hill Golf Club, 18 holes, Hawley, 570/226-4366
Lakeland Golf Course, nine holes, Fleetville, 570/945-9983
Elmhurst Country Club, 18 holes, Moscow, 570/842-7691
Hollenback Golf Course, nine holes, Hollenback, 570/821-1169
Marjon Golf Course, nine holes, Moscow, 570/842-7922
Shadowbrook Resort, 18 holes, Tunkhannock, 570/836-5417
Skyline Public Golf Course, 18 holes, Carbondale, 570/282-5993
Woodloch Springs, 18 holes, Hawley, 570/685-1200

Black Diamond Area

Arnold's Golf Course, 18 holes, Nescopeck, 570/752-7022
Edgewood in the Pines, 18 holes, Hazleton, 570/788-3149
Rolling Meadows Golf Course, 18 holes, Ashland, 570/875-1204

The Poconos

A pothole is worn into the bedrock of a stream at the base of waterfalls or in strong rapids. The moving water spins sand, gravel, and rock fragments in any small indentation in the bedrock. After enough time, the sand and stones carve out an elliptical hole. Potholes may also form under or near the edge of glaciers by the action of glacial meltwater.

Archbald Pothole was formed during the Wisconsin Glacial Period, between 30,000 and 11,000 years ago. A meltwater stream flowing on top of the glacier probably broke through a crevasse (a crack in the glacier) and fell to the bedrock hundreds of feet below. There was enough force generated by the falling water to begin a whirling motion of rock fragments in a small depression. The rock fragments eventually were reduced to tiny particles, but new rock fragments continually tumbled into the hole, enabling the grinding process to continue. As the glacier moved, so did the crevasse and the waterfall. Sand, gravel, and rounded stones filled in the pothole, and the waterfall moved off to make a new pothole. At Archbald Pothole, the water first wore away the top layer of bedrock, which is sandstone. The bottom layer of bedrock is black anthracite coal.

Preserved underground by nature for around 13,000 years, the pothole was discovered in 1884 by coal miner Patrick Mahon while extending a mineshaft. Mahon fired a blast of explosives, and water and stones came rushing out. The miners fled, fearing that the mountain was falling on them. Edward Jones, the manager of the mining company, investigated and ordered the area cleared of debris. Archbald Pothole was briefly used as a ventilation shaft for the mine. A large fire was kept burning in the bottom, and the pothole functioned like a chimney, drawing air out of the mine. In 1887, Colonel Hackley, the landowner, built a fence and retaining wall around the hole. Edward Jones gave many tours of the pothole to local citizens and to noted geologists. The pothole became a popular tourist attraction. With the addition of 150 acres, Archbald Pothole became a Lackawanna County Park in 1940. Hiking trails are available on the park grounds, and more than 100 acres of Archbald Pothole State Park are open to hunting during established seasons. (For information, contact the park c/o Lackawanna, Dalton, PA 18414-9785, 570/945-3239 or 888/727-2757.)

Getting There: Archbald Pothole State Park is easily accessible off I-81. Take Exit 191A to Route 6 east towards Carbondale. The park entrance is six miles on the right.

Frances Slocum State Park

The park (565 Mt. Olivet Rd., Wyoming, PA 18644-9333, 570/696-3525, or Pennsylvania Bureau of State Parks, 888/727-2757, www.dcnr.state.pa.us) is named for Frances Slocum, one of nine children of a Quaker family that lived on what is now North Street in Wilkes-Barre. On the night of November 2, 1778, Lenni Lenape braves entered the Slocum home and carried away Frances, who was then five years old. The first night after her abduction was spent in a crude shelter under a rock ledge along Abraham Creek, within the state park boundary. Frances tried to escape but was taken along as the American Indians moved westward.

Her brothers never gave up searching for her. Fifty-nine years after her abduction they found her living on a reservation in New Reserve, In-

diana. She had been married twice and had four children. Frances refused to return to Pennsylvania; she died in New Reserve in 1847 at the age of 74.

Frances Slocum Lake was created to control flooding. Picnicking areas and the dam were constructed and opened in the spring of 1968. Natural and cultural history programs are conducted by a park environmental educator from March through November, and picnicking is available throughout the year in the picnic areas.

Hiking: Hiking here is a trail network of nine miles, made up of five trails varying in length from less than one mile to three miles. One is the Frances Slocum Trail, .7 mile, a loop trail that begins and ends at the boat rental parking lot. This forest trail passes the rock shelter where American Indians held Frances Slocum captive.

Water Sports: Boats may use electric motors. Nonpowered boats must have one of the following: state park launching permit or state park mooring permit, which are available at most state park offices, or current Pennsylvania boat registration. Motorboats must display a current boat registration. Motorboats registered in other states must display a Pennsylvania state park launch permit or mooring permit in addition to their current registration. Two boat launches and courtesy docks are provided. A boat concession rents rowboats and canoes.

The swimming pool is open from Memorial Day weekend to Labor Day daily 11 A.M.–7 P.M., unless posted otherwise.

Hunting and Fishing: Approximately 300 acres are open to hunting, trapping, and the training of dogs during established seasons. Common game species are deer, rabbit, and squirrel. Hunting groundhogs is prohibited. Dog training is permitted only from the day after Labor Day to March 31 in designated hunting areas. The Department of Conservation and Natural Resources and the Pennsylvania Game Commission rules and regulations apply. Contact a park manager for hunting information.

Fishing enthusiasts will find a wide selection of warm-water species: crappie, bluegill, perch, catfish, muskellunge, pickerel, smallmouth bass, largemouth bass, and walleye.

Winter Sports: Ice skating is permitted on the lake; be sure the ice is at least four inches thick and carry safety equipment. A two-acre dedicated ice-skating area is near the fishing pier Ice fishing is permitted on the entire lake except in the ice-skating area.

A five-acre slope for sledding and tobogganing is west of the swimming pool.

The park has a seven-mile trail system that snowmobilers can use. Snowmobiles must be registered and operated in accordance with Pennsylvania law. Snowmobiles may be used only on designated snowmobile trails.

Camping: A 100-site campground, with 15 walk-in tent sites and 85 tent or trailer sites (some with electric hookups), is available from the second Friday in April through the third Sunday in October. Each site contains a picnic table and fire ring. Flush toilets, showers, drinking water, and a sanitary dump station are available. For reservations, call 888/PA-PARKS (888/727-2757).

Getting There: From Exit 170B of I-81, take Route 309 north approximately seven miles. Turn right (east) on Carverton Road and go approximately four miles. Turn left (north) on 8th Street Road and go approximately one mile. Turn left (west) onto Mt. Olivet Road and go one mile. The park entrance is on the left.

ACCOMMODATIONS

$50–100

Scranton has a number of reasonably priced national hotels, all around $70 a night. Among them are the Courtyard by Marriott, 800/321-2211, Knights Inn, 800/662-4084, and the Ramada, 800/2-RAMADA (800/272-6232).

An alternative to hotels, the **Ponda-Rowland Bed and Breakfast Inn** (RR 1, Box 349, Dallas, 888/855-9966, www.pondarowland.com, $90–115) offers six rooms with private baths, air-conditioning, fireplaces, and a full breakfast. The house was originally built in 1850. Dallas is about 10 miles west of Wilkes-Barre and is a good location for outdoor activities such as canoeing and hiking in nearby Frances Slocum Park. Children are welcome.

$100–150

The **M Radisson Lackawanna Station Hotel** (700 Lackawanna Ave., Scranton, 570/342-8300 or 800/333-3333, $99–169) is the reborn queen of the Delaware, Lackawanna, and Western railroad stations and is listed on the National Registry of Historic Places. Fueled by the tremendous prosperity of the rail industry, the station was built at the behest of William Trusdale, the president of DL&W, in 1908. When it was converted to a hotel in 1983, the original Italian marble lobby and stained-glass atrium ceiling were complemented by a full-service health club, two dining rooms, and a bar. In addition, the Lackawanna offers modern conveniences such as valet parking and free airport shuttle service.

Built in the late 1970s and renovated in the late 1990s, the pleasant **Woodlands Inn and Resort** (1073 SR 315, Wilkes-Barre, 570/824-9831 or 800/762-2222, $79–200) is set on 40 acres of lush greenery and meticulously landscaped grounds threaded by Laurel Run Stream. The inn features 200 well-appointed guest rooms and suites, private cottages with kitchen, an indoor pool, whirlpool bath, health and fitness center, and tanning, steam, and sauna rooms. Among other specials, the Woodlands offers excellent Ski and Stay Packages for those visiting Montage Mountain during the winter: overnight accommodations, full breakfast, and an all-day lift ticket run approximately $155–195 per night. Cottages are available by the month only.

In addition to lodging, Woodlands features the Tyme Restaurant, the 25th Hour Night Club, the Left Bank Lounge (with an open hearth fireplace), and the Executive Lounge, all featuring DJ or live music.

M Bischwind (directly off SR 115 south of Wilkes-Barre in Bear Creek, 570/472-3820, www.bischwind.com, $125–235) is an elegant Tudor-style manor house and farm that once sheltered former Presidents Theodore Roosevelt and William Howard Taft within its walls. A stay includes breakfast. The Tiffany transoms, Austrian crystal chandeliers, and French antiques might be intimidating in lesser hands than those of Barbara and Alfred von Dran. Instead, the feeling is one of warmth and welcome. All rooms have gracious appointments and private baths, and the property is laced with walking trails that wind through the von Drans' equine breeding stables and extend out into the picturesque countryside.

FOOD

Quick Stops and Late-Night Runs

Agostini Bakery (1216 S. Main St., Old Forge, southwest of Scranton, 570/457-2021, Mon.–Fri. 8 A.M.–3 P.M., Sat. 8 A.M.–1 P.M.) is a local destination for baked goods and fresh bread. Family-owned and operated, Agostini's has added take-and-bake pizzas to its menu. The Agostinis taught one of their daughters so well she moved to the big city and became a pastry chef at the Philadelphia Ritz-Carlton.

It's smoky, it's crowded, it's the **Glider Diner**—a Scranton institution for decades. Breakfast is available anytime, and dinner prices average $8 for a full meal, which would include an entrée such as stuffed pork chops, potato, two fresh vegetables, and homemade bread. The Glider (890 Providence Rd., Scranton, 570/343-8036, Mon.–Fri. 24 hours, Sat. until 3 A.M., closed Sun.) also has daily specials and free delivery in Scranton 10 A.M.–2 P.M. with a $20 minimum.

French fries and gravy? Go to **Chick's Diner** (1032 Moosic Ave./Rt. 307, Scranton, 570/344-4156, open daily, 24 hours). Chick's has been in the same family for two generations (the family also owns the Hawley Diner). A meal is around $7.50.

A Little Fancier

John's Place (702 Prospect Ave., Scranton, 570/961-9299) is a casual restaurant with home cooking and a comfortable atmosphere combined with reasonable prices (dinner Mon.–Sat. 4:30–10 P.M., Sun. 3–9 P.M., $10–$15).

At **Mother's Table** (117 Penn Ave., Scranton, 570/969-0260) the pasta bar and great bread make this eatery a local favorite for breakfast and lunch (Mon.–Fri. 7 A.M.–3:30 P.M., Sat. 7 A.M.–3 P.M., Sun. 7:30 A.M.–2 P.M., $6–15).

Carmen's (Radisson Lackawanna Station Hotel, 570/342-8300) is the hotel restaurant, but the food is much better than average hotel fare. Prices are high for the area: breakfasts are in the $7 range, lunch (the best value) is around $8, and dinners average $22. The Italian-influenced cuisine is delicious and artistically presented. It's open daily 6:30 A.M.–2:30 P.M. for lunch, and 5–10 P.M. for dinner.

What kid wouldn't want to eat in a place that looks like Noah's Ark? **M Cooper's Seafood House** (701 N. Washington Ave., Scranton, 570/346-6883) has been the seafood house of choice for visitors and locals since the flood receded and Noah set foot on dry land. The front of the building is a ship decorated with life-sized denizens of the deep; inside the decor is over-the-top nautical kitsch. A children's menu is available. Though the place is big, it's well managed (you won't have to wait long) and serves every finny dish ever invented, plus "landlubber specials" such as steak platters and Reuben sandwiches. Open every day 11 A.M.–midnight except Sun., when it opens at noon. The Ship's Pub (bar) is open until 1 A.M. on Sat. Cooper's has another location (Adams Ave. on the waterfront in Pittston, 570/654-6883). Early-bird dinners run $6.95–16.95, regular dinners are $12–26.95.

Other Restaurants in the Vicinity

Scrantonites recommended these restaurants within an easy drive of the city's urban area: **Ragnacci's Family Restaurant and Lounge** (507 S. Blakely, Dunmore, 570/346-3330, Mon.–Sat. lunch 11 A.M.–2 P.M., dinner 5 P.M.–10 P.M.), a great place for lunch, fine Italian food, and cute waitresses.

Tiffany's Tap and Grill (291 Main St., Eynon, near Archbald, 570/876-0710, lunch Tues.–Fri. 11:30 A.M.–2 P.M., dinner Mon.–Thur. 4–10 P.M., Fri.–Sat. 4–11 P.M., closed Sun.) offers a beautiful setting, with good food and prices.

Several people recommended **Bella Roma** (1500 Main St., Dickson City, just north of Scranton, 570/383-8966, Mon.–Fri. 5 A.M.–9:30 P.M. Sat.–Sun. 7 A.M.–9:30 P.M.); Vinny and Rico run this small Italian-style restaurant and pizzeria serving delicious food at very reasonable prices—almost all entrees are under $12.

INFORMATION

The **Northeast Territory Visitors Bureau** (99 Glenmaura National Blvd., Scranton, PA 18507, 570/963 6363 or 800/229-3526, www.visit-nepa.org), has specifics about Scranton and the northeastern counties. There's also a Scranton-Lackawanna home page: www.pocono.org.

Wilkes-Barre and Luzerne County information is available from the **Wilkes-Barre Convention and Visitors Bureau** (56 Public Sq., Wilkes-Barre, PA 18701, 888/905-2872, www.tournepa.com).

Happenings magazine (www.happenings-magazinepa.com) is a free what-to-do, where-to-go magazine that's available all over the Scranton area.

The Poconos

Pohoqualine, "a river passing between two mountains," was the name given to the Delaware River by the indigenous Lenni Lenape. The wildly beautiful area has long been a recreational mecca for overurbanized escapees from New York City and Washington, D.C.

Home to wildlife sanctuaries, environmental learning centers, more than 100 varieties of trees, nine state parks, and 21 game lands, the Poconos have been declared one of the "Last Great Places" by the Nature Conservancy to point out the need for protection of the area. Though dotted with the occasional tourist attraction, golf course, and ski resort, the Poconos retain their intrinsic value—and a drive along the narrow roads (especially in the fall) reveals a visual thrill literally around every curve.

Wildlife takes on a new meaning at some Pocono resorts. Morris B. Wilkins created the heart-shaped bathtub for two for his Cove Haven property in 1963 and made honeymoon history. Now several resorts in the area compete for the title of "Honeymoon Capital of the World" with activities and innovations that appeal to romantics of all ages.

SIGHTS

Grey Towers National Historic Landmark

Gifford Pinchot, the first chief of the U.S. Forest Service and "father of modern conservation," developed his love of natural beauty as a child while exploring the grounds of the Pinchot family home, Grey Towers. This stunning rock-faced, turreted castle in Milford, and the grounds on which it rests, are now a National Historic Landmark. Look for the signs for Grey Towers off US 6 on the west end of Milford; the turnoff is just before the Apple Valley Restaurant. The U.S. Forest Service offers tours of the mansion during the warmer months, and the extensive grounds are open year-round 9 A.M.–5 P.M. Call for tour hours: 570/296-6401. The grounds are free, but there is an admission charge of $3 to tour the mansion.

Claws 'N' Paws Wild Animal Park

Since 1973, this small local park has displayed exotic and common animals in a natural setting. The park (on Ledgedale Rd./SR 590, four miles east of Hamlin, Lake Ariel, 570/698-6154, www.clawsnpaws.com) is open May 1–Oct. 22, 10 A.M.–6 P.M. Admission is $10.95 for adults and $7.95 for children ages 2–11.

Where else could you see a white tiger, giraffe, timber wolf, lion, snow leopard, bear, otter, monkeys, birds of prey, tropical birds, reptiles, and farm animals in one place? There are two different live animal shows May 1 through Labor Day (no shows in the fall), and a petting zoo (no tigers allowed). A popular feature of the park is the Dino Dig, where kids get to search an excavation area for "dinosaur bones."

MUSEUMS

Dorflinger Glass Museum

This remarkable small museum (on Long Ridge Rd., P.O. Box 356, White Mills, PA 18473, 570/253-1185, www.dorflinger.org) is surrounded by the pristine beauty of the

Dorflinger-Suydam Wildlife Sanctuary. It's open mid-May to the beginning of November, Wed.–Sat. 10 A.M.–4 P.M., Sun. 1–4 P.M. Admission is $3 for adults, $2.50 for seniors over 55, and $1.50 for students ages 6–18.

During the later part of the 19th century, Alsatian artisan Christian Dorflinger and his eponymous glassworks company produced exquisite crystal pieces for eight American presidents, including Abraham Lincoln and Woodrow Wilson, and for wealthy patrons the world over.

Dorflinger first opened his glass company in New York state, was enormously successful to the point of strain, and moved to White Mills at the age of 35 to recover his health. His country idyll proved short-lived; within a few years of his "retirement," he decided to start a new business in the then-remote area and began inviting master craftsmen to join him. By Dorflinger's death at age 87 in 1915, inexpensive mass-produced glassware and a falling demand for the elite product created in his shops had decimated the business. It closed shortly thereafter.

Superbly refined cut glass, engraved, etched, gilded, and enamel pieces are carefully displayed by natural and artificial light in this museum. Dorflinger glass was never value-priced. All the pieces produced by the factory were for the high-end consumer. Contemporary manufacturers fall short of the level of quality on view here; the cut pieces seem to radiate light rather than catch and reflect it. The Dorflinger museum is a must-see for anyone interested in art glass.

Zane Grey Museum

This former home of the author of hundreds of Western classics includes photographs, books, and personal belongings of Grey and his wife, Dolly. In the past, the museum (on Scenic Dr. in the village of Lackawaxen, 570/685-4871) has been open daily Memorial Day–Labor Day Thurs.–Sun. 10 A.M.–5 P.M.; from Labor Day to mid-October, it's open weekends only 10 A.M.–5 P.M. Admission is $2. However, call first: volunteer staffing sometimes leaves holes in the schedule.

Though the bucolic Pennsylvania setting may seem strange inspiration for the creator of such tumbleweed-strewn hoof-pounders as *Heritage of the Desert* and *Riders of the Purple Sage*, the lovely old house and the placid section of the upper Delaware River that it overlooks is inspiring indeed. Local legend has it that Grey is buried on the hill across from the house so that he may see the mist rising from the river forever.

Pennsylvania Fishing Museum at Peck's Pond

Fishing equipment and memorabilia from the 1700s through the 1950s is on display at this appropriately laid-back museum (Dingmans Ferry, 570/775-7237, www.peckspond.com). Visitors can pore over tackle, ice-fishing gear, rods, reels, lures, and flies, and fishing-related folk art and decoys. The museum is open daily 9 A.M.–6 P.M. Call ahead during the winter to check hours of operation. The gift shop should interest avid anglers; you can buy fishing antiques and unusual items related to the sport.

SHOPPING

Outlets and Discounters

Equip yourself with a combination wallet/flotation device—you're about to enter the Bermuda Triangle of shopping. Options include: **Crossings Factory Stores** (Crossings Outlet, Tannersville, 570/629-4650); **Pocono Outlet Complex** (9th and Ann Sts., Stroudsburg, 570/421-7470); the **Foxmoor Village Outlet** (2 Fox Run Lane, East Stroudsburg, three miles north of Marshalls Creek on US 209, 570/223-8706); and nearby, the **Odd-Lot Outlet** (US 209, Marshalls Creek, 570/223-1844).

Antiques and Crafts

The town of Milford is a pleasant place to spend a day. It retains much of its old-fashioned charm in dozens of antique shops and craft stores. Among them, **Elizabeth Restucci Antiques** (214 Broad St., 570/296-2118) features period jewelry; **The Craft Show** (120 E. Harford St., 570/296-5662) is a gallery of fine arts and crafts; and **Gerola Art Gallery** (201 Sawkill Ave., 570/296-6388) shows fine modern art. The **Upper Mill Complex** (Water and Mill Sts., 570/409-0051) is home to a variety of shops, including booksellers, clothing stores, and gift shops.

In Stroudsburg, stop by **Carroll & Carroll Booksellers** (740 Main St.); it's a great outlet for new, used, and rare books.

OUTDOOR RECREATION

Hiking

You'll find more than 116 maintained hiking trails throughout the Poconos, including 25 miles of the Appalachian Trail in the Delaware Water Gap. **Bushkill Falls** is made up of a series of cascades, including the 100-foot-high main falls. Trails varying from less than .25 mile in length to a more strenuous two miles wind over rustic bridges though thick forest. Picnicking, boating, and fishing are permitted; there's a small shopping and eating area nearby. To get there, take Bushkill Falls Road off US 209 between Dingmans Ferry and Bushkill.

Horseback Riding

Carson's Riding Stables (one mile south of the village of Mt. Pocono on SR 611, 570/839-9841) is open all year, with rides leaving on the hour. Carson's features more than 60 acres of trails winding through the local woodlands. Reservations are appreciated.

Boating and Fishing

Lake Wallenpaupack, on the border of Wayne and Pike Counties via I-84, is the third-largest body of water in the state. It's maintained by Pennsylvania Power and Light, which installed a 44,000-kilowatt power plant in 1926, when the lake was created by damming "the stream of swift and slow water." The 5,700-acre lake has a 52-mile shoreline and has become a favorite recreational spot for boaters and fishermen.

Rafting and Canoeing

The Delaware Water Gap offers a scenic background for water travel. **Adventure Sports** (in Marshalls Creek, 800/487-2628) rents canoes, rafts, and camping equipment and guides one-to three-day trips down the Delaware. Another company that features kayak, canoe, and raft rentals is **Kittatinny Canoes and Rafts** (Dingmans Ferry, 800/356-2852). **White-water Challengers** (800/443-8554) guides white-water rafting trips on five rivers in Pennsylvania and New York, runs a kayaking school, and rents rafts, kayaks, and bikes.

Swimming

Shawnee Place water park (off US 209 north, 570/421-7231) is next to Shawnee ski resort; follow the signs. The park is designed for families with children between ages 2 and 12 to play together. There are plenty of slides, pools, and tubes. It's open June 19–Labor Day; admission is $19 for ages 3–59. Seniors are $10.

Camelbeach Waterpark (Exit 299, I-80, Tannersville, 570/629-1661, http://camelbeach.com) is on the site of Camelback ski area and offers 22 waterslides and a variety of other wet pleasures. It actually runs heated water through the attractions. It's open May 29–Sept. 6 10 A.M.–6 P.M., mid-June–Sept. 10 A.M.–7 P.M. One-day general admission (ages 12–64) is $26.95, one-day child age 3–11 and seniors age 65 and better $22.95, spectator $11.95, under age 2 free.

Winter Sports

The Poconos have more than a dozen downhill ski facilities; the Pocono Mountains Vacation Bureau (1004 Main St., Stroudsburg, PA 18360, 570/424-6050 or 800/762-6667 for brochures only) has a basic listing of facilities. Two of the most popular resorts are Camelback and Shawnee.

Camelback (Exit 299, I-80, Tannersville, 570/629-1661, www.camelbackski.com) is one of the largest and best-equipped ski resorts in the Poconos. With 13 lifts (including two high-speed quad lifts) and 33 trails, a halfpipe, two terrain parks, night skiing, and 100 percent snowmaking facilities, Camelback has something for the whole family (including learn-to-ski programs for all ages and a supervised full-day session especially for children). Camelback is northeast of Tannersville. Weekend and holiday lift passes are slightly higher than those for midweek skiing. Lift tickets are also available in breakdowns of morning, afternoon, day, twilight, and night.

Higher holiday rates are in effect Dec. 25–Jan. 1, Jan. 15, and Feb. 19. Camelback has packages available. The resort opens at the first snowfall and closes at the beginning of spring; in summer, it reopens as Camelbeach, a water park. For a ski condition report, call 800/233-8100.

Shawnee (off US 209 north, 570/421-7231) offers 23 trails and nine chairlifts, and it is the closest major Pocono ski area to metropolitan New York and New Jersey. Children's programs, snowmaking, night skiing, and snowboarding lessons and trails are part of the package. The picturesque village of Shawnee-on-Delaware is close by. Lift ticket prices vary by age, day of the week, and time of day. The resort is open weekdays 9 A.M.–5 P.M., weekends 8 A.M.–5 P.M. The snow condition number is 800/233-4218.

The Dorflinger-Suydam Wildlife Sanctuary

Dorothy Grant Suydam (glassmaker Christian Dorflinger's granddaughter) designated this property a wildlife sanctuary upon her death. The isolated grounds are among the most beautiful in the state; hiking trails disappear into the forests, and rolling hills surround a small lake. Music and art festivals take place on the grounds in the warmer months. The sanctuary is on Long Ridge Road in White Mills and is open year-round to hikers and cross-country skiers. Admission is free.

Hickory Run/Lehigh Gorge Complex

John James Audubon explored the pine swamps of Hickory Run and fished along the Lehigh River; perhaps he helped blaze a few of the more than 30 miles of hiking trails through the area. One highlight is Boulder Field, a 12-foot-deep, valley-filling collection of rough boulders left behind by a glacier 20,000 years ago.

Remnants of the Delaware Lehigh Canal can also be found along the Lehigh Gorge. The complex is off SR 534 and SR 9 (the turnpike) and offers 400 campsites. For reservations, call 888/PA-PARKS (888/727-2757). For trail maps and more information, contact Hickory Run State Park, RR 1, Box 81, White Haven, PA 18661, 570/443-0400.

The Lacawac Sanctuary

Once surrounded by Lenni Lenape villages, this sanctuary 18 miles east of Scranton contains one of the least-disturbed glacial lakes in America. Because of the long-term research being done on the lake, and the purity of its environment, the area is closed to the public except during the summer, when a full schedule of programs, walks, lectures, workshops, and history tours take place. Reservations are necessary. For a schedule, contact Lacawac Sanctuary, RR 1, Box 518, Lake Ariel, PA 18436, 570/689-9494.

Cranberry Bog Nature Preserve

Another natural area accessible by reservation only, this Nature Conservancy–owned property is a relict boreal bog, the southernmost of its kind along the eastern seaboard. The bog is in the Tannersville area and features a 1,450-foot floating boardwalk. For information, contact Tannersville Cranberry Bog, Environmental Education Center, 8050 Running Valley Rd., Stroudsburg, PA 18360, 570/629-3061.

Ⓜ Delaware Water Gap National Recreation Area

The 70,000-acre Delaware Water Gap follows the Delaware River on both the Pennsylvania and New Jersey shores from Milford south to Portland. Visitors may stop for park information at Bushkill visitors' center (SR 209, Bushkill, 570/588-7044) or Kittatinny Point visitors' center (on the New Jersey side of the park, off I-80, 908/496-4458). Popular walks include a hike up Mt. Tammany on the New Jersey side, Dingmans Falls, and the George W. Childs Recreation Site, a .8-mile trail with three waterfalls.

The Appalachian Trail is on the New Jersey side of the water gap, though both sides are laced with smaller trails. A map of selected hiking trails is available at either visitors' center or by contacting Delaware Water Gap, National Park Service, River Rd., Bushkill, PA 18324. The park headquarters can be reached at 570/588-2451, dewa_interpretation@nps.gov, www.nps.gov /dewa. There are also a number of lakes, beaches, and picnic areas open to the public, though camping is not available within the park boundaries.

Pocono Environmental Education Center: Pocono Environmental Education Center, off US 209 south of the Dingmans Falls visitors' center, offers six different loop trails of varying lengths and levels of difficulty. Trail maps are available at the center.

The five-mile Sunrise Trail wanders through oak and hickory forests, old fields, and wetlands; there is one steep descent. Tumbling Waters Trail, three miles in length, leads the hiker up two challenging grades, but its rewards include scenic vistas and a side trip to the falls. Scenic Gorge Trail is two miles long and winds through moderately hilly terrain with a few stream crossings. The 1.25-mile Fossil Trail travels down a few steep grades on its way to a bedrock outcrop of marine fossils.

Two Ponds Trail, 1.5 miles long, features a blind for observing wildlife; it follows streams, ponds, and logging roads. The Sensory Trail, .25 mile, is intended to be a nonvisual experience. A rope guides the user around the loop; pick up blindfolds at the main office, if you like. All trails are open year-round, weather permitting, dawn to dusk.

Promised Land State Park

Approximately 3,000 acres, the park tops the Pocono Plateau, 1,800 feet above sea level, and is surrounded by 12,350 acres of state forest and a natural area. The deciduous forest, two lakes, and several small streams add to the park's outstanding scenic beauty.

Local tradition holds that the land was "promised" to the Shakers, a fundamentalist religious group from New York state. After clearing the land, the Shakers found that it was unable to support farming. They departed, leaving the land to wilderness. The Commonwealth of Pennsylvania bought the land in 1902. Since the departure of the Shakers, the area had been clear-cut. With the loss of trees came erosion, forest fires, and migration of wildlife from the area. The commonwealth worked to protect and reclaim the area, and the forest and wildlife began to return. The first park facilities were opened to the public in 1905. Additional facilities were built in the 1930s by the Civilian Conservation Corps (CCC), which also built roads, bridges, and dams and planted thousands of trees. Environmental programs on a wide variety of topics and levels are offered spring through fall, and picnicking is available.

Hiking and Biking: There are more than 30 miles of hiking trails in Promised Land State Park and the surrounding state forest. Bruce Lake Road leads to a natural glacial lake, and the East Branch of Wallenpaupack Trail skirts a series of little waterfalls.

A 6.5-mile bike trail runs around Promised Land Lake. Bicycles are not permitted on hiking trails. Mountain biking is permitted on adjacent Delaware State Forest Land.

Water Sports: Boats may use electric motors. Nonpowered boats must have one of the following: state park launching permit or state park mooring permit, available at most state park offices; or current Pennsylvania boat registration. Motorboats must display a current boat registration. Motorboats registered in other states must display a Pennsylvania state park launch permit or mooring permit in addition to their current registration.

Five mooring areas offer a total of 240 mooring spaces, rented seasonally. There are five boat-launching areas. A boat rental concession is on Promised Land Lake across from Main Beach. Rowboats, canoes, and paddleboats may be rented.

Swimming: In the day-use area, the main beach is guarded and open from Memorial Day weekend to Labor Day 11 A.M.–7 P.M. unless otherwise posted. A small beach is at Pickerel Point.

Hunting and Fishing: Approximately 450 acres of Promised Land State Park are open to hunting, trapping, and dog training during established seasons. Common game species are deer, bear, and turkey.

Both lakes offer great opportunities for fishing, including ice fishing. Some of the common species of fish are largemouth and smallmouth bass, pickerel, muskellunge, yellow perch, sunfish, and catfish. Lower Lake is approved trout waters and is stocked with brook, brown, and rainbow trout.

Winter Sports: Registered snowmobiles may be used on more than 27 miles of designated snowmobile trails. The trails, which are on both state park and state forest lands, are open daily after the end of the antlerless deer season in late December, weather permitting. Snowmobile maps are available at the park office.

Bruce Lake Natural Area and Conservation Island are set aside for the slower, quieter winter sports such as snowshoeing and cross-country skiing. Conditions permitting, ice fishing is popular on both lakes, and an ice-skating area is maintained on Promised Land Lake.

Camping and Cabins: Four tent and trailer camping areas feature 487 campsites. The maximum stay in all camping areas is 14 days during the summer season and 21 days during the off-season. Campers must vacate the park for 48 hours before setting up again. Pets and alcoholic beverages are not permitted in overnight areas. For reservations, call 888/PA-PARKS (888/727-2757).

Nestled in hemlocks, adjacent to Lower Lake, the Bear Wallow Cabin Colony contains 12 rustic rental cabins constructed by the Civilian Conservation Corps. These primitive cabins each have a fireplace, electricity, and an adjacent private bath.

Getting There: Promised Land State Park is in Pike County, 10 miles north of Canadensis, along SR 390. Call 570/676-3428 for more information.

Camping

Pennsylvania Power and Light Campground, next to Lake Walunpaupak, has both tent and trailer sites (318 total), a dump station, electric/water hookups, a store, and a laundromat. It's near Hawley and is open year-round. For campsite availability and reservations, contact PP&L Camp (P.O. Box 122, Hawley, PA 18428, 570/226-3702).

Hickory Run State Park (off SR 534 and SR 9 (the turnpike), RR 1, Box 81, White Haven, PA 18661, 570/443-0400) allows camping, with 400 sites in the park.

Several commercial campgrounds are also in the area; call ahead for reservations, information, and individual campground policies: **Sandy Valley Campground** (I-80 Exit 40, SR 940 west—follow signs, 570/636-0770); **Moyer's**

Grove Campground (I-80 Exit 38, SR 93 north—follow signs, 570/379-3375); **W. T. Family Campground** (I-80 Exit 43, SR 115 south, 570/646-9255); **Fern Ridge Campground** (I-80 Exit 43, SR 115 north, 570/646-2267); and **RV Park and Kampground** (I-80 Exit 39, SR 309 north, 570/788-3382).

ACCOMMODATIONS

The Poconos are famous for sports resorts, honeymoon resorts, and small country inns. **B&Bs of The Endless Mountains** (712 Rte. 6 east, Tunkhannock, 570/836-5431) is a referral service for all types of stays, be they farmhouses, Victorian mansions, or town bungalows.

$100–150

Academy Street Bed and Breakfast (528 Academy St., Hawley, 570/226-3430, www.academybb.com) is a well-located Civil War–era Victorian featuring 11 rooms, four with private baths. A full breakfast and afternoon tea are included in the room rate, $95–105, double occupancy. An additional person is $10 extra. There's a two-night minimum on holiday weekends.

Built in 1870, **M Roebling Inn** (Scenic Dr., Lackawaxen, 570/685-7900) was once home and office to Judge Thomas J. Ridgeway, superintendent and tallyman for the Delaware and Hudson Canal Company. The building is shaded by huge maple trees, nestled beside a bend in the road right on the Delaware River close to the Zane Grey Museum—this is really a beautiful setting. Rooms have private baths, and rates range $79–119 midweek, $95 to $145 on weekends. Add an additional $10 to rates in July and August (the most expensive room has a kitchen and fireplace).

The **Country Inn at the Old Mill Stream** (120 Falls Ave., Hawley, 570/226-1337, www.oldmillstreaminn.com), near the Lake Wallenpaupack recreational area, is a hotel with modern guest rooms and two- and three-bedroom suites with kitchens, next to a lovely old mill above the village of Hawley. The craggy limestone-lined creek that runs nearby adds ambience and a bit of history. The hotel slows down at the end of summer, but

OF HOT WATER AND ROMANCE

Ah, the Poconos in June: mountain laurel blooming pink in the hills, quaint little towns, two-story champagne-glass-shaped hot tubs for two. Yes, those honeymoon resorts writer D. Keith Mano described in *Playboy* a few years ago as "half brothel cloud chamber, half Houston mission control" are still bubbling strong, tickling the knickers off newlyweds, olderweds, and lovers lacking legal definition. Caesars resorts were the first to have heart-shaped swimming pools. Now, according to Morris B. Wilkens, designer of the first valentine-style soaker, they're everywhere. The fantasy-glass hot tub is another product of his fecund brain:

I hit on the idea of a jacuzzi in the shape of a champagne glass. Champagne . . .

says romance and marriage more than any other liquid I know. So I built a prototype, made it seven feet tall, and used the same material that's used for helicopter bubbles. To test them for strength, I filled them with water and banged them with sledgehammers for three weeks.

Now, Wilkens reports, Caesars' champagne tower suites "are booked up six months in advance." For a group of revamped rustic camps that never achieved their hoped-for status as gambling casinos, the Caesars Pocono resorts have gurgled their way to major profitability, thanks in part to Wilkens's innovations; the sound of giant glasses filling must be champagne music to his ears.

---

rooms are still available. Rates range $75–170 per night with reduced rates for longer stays.

A restored Tudor-style manor house, **The Settler's Inn** (4 Main Ave., Hawley, 570/226-2993 or 800/833-8527, www.thesettlersinn.com) is warmly decorated in a British country theme. From the rustic lobby to the 20 cozy bedrooms (all with private baths), this getaway in the Poconos is a unique treat. The restaurant is celebrated, with good reason. An overnight stay includes breakfast. There is a popular restaurant on the premises; it offers a room/dinner special rate. Lodging ranges $110–$180 during the week and $120–200 on the weekends.

Over $200

M **Caesars Pocono Palace** (on US 209 near the village of Marshalls Creek, 570/226-4506 or 800/233-4141, www.caesarspoconoresorts.com) is *the* Poconos honeymoon destination. Caesars takes conspicuous consumption to a grand scale with copious food, two-story love chambers, and abundant pseudo-Roman decor. This legendary target zero for lovers is as plush as advertised: all rooms are designed for maximum intimacy and privacy. To the uninitiated, the whole concept may seem tacky, but Caesars manages to wed the peculiar to the sublime; the place is filled with deliriously happy people having fun.

Each of the four Caesars Pocono resorts in the area is different in layout and focus: Pocono Palace draws sports enthusiasts; Brookdale welcomes families; Cove Haven, the largest facility, features the widest range of sports activities; and Paradise Stream is woodsy and traditional.

Buffet meals are served morning and evening in the common areas and, like most onsite activities, are part of the package. Sports facilities at Pocono Palace include ball courts, swimming pools, a health club, and a lake for waterskiing and sailing. However, guests at any of the four Caesars resorts in the area are free to use facilities at the other resorts. Evening entertainment (included) is a big part of the draw. The Palace's resident masters-of-ceremony in the Gladiator Lounge, Dawn and Anthony, do a masterful job of balancing low-reaching sexual innuendo with good clean yuks. Big names such as Jay Leno and Howie Mandel put in appearances at Cove Haven. In all of the resorts, prices start at $215 per couple per night, all-inclusive, and go up to $460 per couple per night depending on season and choice of resort.

FOOD

The Apple Valley Restaurant and Pub (US 6, Milford, 570/296-9905) is an upscale country-style eatery where local businesspeople meet for lunch and families come for a nice dinner. The menu includes a thick Chicago-style skillet pizza; barbecue; deli sandwiches; and poultry, beef, and seafood entrées. A full-service bar is on the premises. Apple Valley is open weekdays 11 A.M.–9 P.M., Fri.–Sat. 11 A.M.–10 P.M. (in winter, the restaurant closes at 8:30 P.M.). Lunch averages $8, dinner $12.

Philadelphia magazine dubbed the food at the Ⓜ **Settlers Inn** (4 Main Ave., Hawley, 570/226-2993 or 800/833-8527) "the best in the Poconos." The dining room offers a wide variety of quality local produce, including organic fruits and vegetables; breads and desserts are made in the inn's own bakery. The Settlers Inn serves daily lunch noon–2:30 P.M. and dinner 5–8:30 P.M. Dinners run about $18, less for lunch.

The restaurant at the **Old Mill Stream** (120 Falls Ave., Hawley, 570/226-1337) is in the Country Inn of the old mill. The indoor dining room serves formal meals such as steak au poivre and chicken breast in a puff pastry. There's a full bar, and the outdoor deck is open in warm weather. The restaurant is open for dinner only 6–10 P.M. Though the hotel is open all year, the warm months tend to be busy (reservations, especially on weekends, are a good idea). During the winter, the dining room draws a small, local crowd. Prices range $8–22.

INFORMATION

The Poconos have a well-oiled publicity machine that is very helpful to visitors. The **Pocono Mountains Vacation Bureau** (Box NG, 1004 Main St., Stroudsburg, PA 18360, 570/424-6050 or 800/762-6667, for brochures only, www.800poconos.com) will provide general and specific information.

If the natural beauty of the area is a specific interest, ask for *The Poconos Nature Guide,* which gives a little information on several places to visit.

Jim Thorpe and Environs

This well-preserved Victorian town has drawn tourists for more than 100 years, since it was known as "The Switzerland of America." Today, its former heritage as two separate and competitive coal-transport towns—Mauch Chunk (bear paw) and East Mauch Chunk—and the dramatic story of how it came to be named after a famous Olympic champion is well told through exhibits at the local museum (for more, see the sidebar "The Saga of Bright Path"). The clean mountain air continues to bring visitors who enjoy outdoor recreational opportunities, and quaint shops line the main street.

SCENIC TOURS

Over the Blue to Hawk Mountain Sanctuary

A series of back roads winds from the charming town of Jim Thorpe over alternating ridges and fertile plateaus that make up the southern edge of the Alleghenies. Small whitewashed churches, neat farms (with some amusing modern-style barn paintings), and dense forest are interspersed with tiny villages. This 45-mile drive ends on the summit of Hawk Mountain, in the sanctuary (I-78 is less than 15 miles away).

From Jim Thorpe, take US 209 north to Lehighton (the road is marked north, but you're actually heading south). Take SR 443 west, and make a left turn (south) on Ashfield-Mountain Road to the village of Ashfield. Turn right (east) on Ben-Salem Road (SR 895 west) through the village of Andreas to the village of Snyders. Turn left (southeast) on SR 309 over Blue (Kittatinny) Mountain to New Tripoli. Turn right on SR 143 (southwest). Watch for the Albany/Eckville /Hawk Mountain turnoff on the right (west). Make the turn and follow the road up the mountain to the sanctuary. To reach I-78, continue west on the mountain road to SR 895. Turn left (south) to SR 61, then left again (south).

The sanctuary itself was established in 1934 as a private nonprofit conservation organization to stop the shooting of hawks as they migrated along the Kittatinny Ridge. From September through

©JOANNE MILLER

hex signs painted on a barn near the
Hawk Mountain Sanctuary

November (the most popular—and crowded—
time to visit), more than 24,000 raptors of 16
species cross over the north lookout; however,
the park is worth visiting year-round for its trails,
wildflowers, and songbirds. Hawk Mountain
Sanctuary is on the summit of the Albany-Eckville
Road near the hamlet of Eckville, between SR
895 and SR 143, about five miles north of I-78.
For information, contact Hawk Mountain Sanctuary Association (1700 Hawk Mountain Rd.,
Kempton, PA 19529-9449, 610/756-6000,
www.hawkmountain.org). Trails are open dawn to
dusk year-round. The visitors' center is open daily
9 A.M.–5 P.M.; Sept. 1–Nov. 30, it's open 8 A.M.–
5 P.M. Admission for trails is $5, $4 for seniors
ages 65 and up, $3 for children ages 6–12.

Rail Tours

Rambles through the flaming fall foliage are
the most popular tour on this scenic passenger
train that schedules varied eight- to 18-mile
trips through the mountains around Jim
Thorpe. Trains leave from the former Central
Railroad of New Jersey passenger depot—now

the visitors' bureau—on US 209 across from
the Carbon County courthouse in downtown
Jim Thorpe. Trips are scheduled for various destinations on holidays, and during summer and
autumn. For more information contact Rail
Tours (P.O. Box 285, Jim Thorpe, PA 18229,
570/325-4606, www.railtours-inc.com). An excursion fee is charged, and the amount depends
on the trip.

SIGHTS

Mauch Chunk Museum and Cultural Center

This small regional museum (41 W. Broadway,
570/325-9190) covers the history of the area
from the original Lenni Lenape inhabitants
through the discovery of coal along the Lehigh
River, beyond its industrial golden age. It's open
year-round, Tues.–Sun. 10 A.M.–4 P.M. Admission is $4. The museum also features rare pho-
tographs of Jim Thorpe and a display on his life
and career.

Asa Packer Mansion

Once the home of Victorian industrialist Asa
Packer, this mansion (on Hazard Sq. Extension,
Jim Thorpe, 570/325-3229) remains much unchanged on the inside, though the outside has
been renovated through the years. The well-preserved interior gives an accurate idea of the high-
Victorian taste for copious decoration—the
chandelier in the west parlor served as a model for
Tara's in the film *Gone With The Wind*. It's open
April–May, Nov., and the first two weekends of
Dec., weekends only 11 A.M.–4:15 P.M.; open
daily May 29–October. The mansion is closed
third week of Dec.–March. Group tours of 10 or
more can be arranged. General admission is $7;
seniors 55 and over pay $6; students 13–18 years
of age are $5; children 6–12 are $3 and under the
age of 5 are free.

Packer's fortune came from transporting coal by
rail from mines in nearby towns to larger markets.
Jim Thorpe (then Mauch Chunk) escaped much
of the pollution that was the fate of coal towns because of its role as a transport center. Asa Packer
went on to serve two terms in the United States

The Poconos

Congress and became the unsuccessful Democratic nominee for president in 1868. He lived in the mansion until his death in 1879.

The Old Jail

This fortresslike structure, built in 1871 and continuously occupied since then, played a major role in America's labor movement. The jail (128 W. Broadway, 570/325-5259) is open weekends Memorial Day–Labor Day; free. In 1877, four men accused of being Molly Maguires—members of a secret society that avenged mistreatment of coal miners with murder and sabotage—were hanged on the gallows inside the jail. Before the executions, several bystanders swore to the innocence of the accused men. Before he was executed, one of the prisoners placed his hand on the concrete wall of Cell 17—the jailkeepers claim that the handprint is still visible today.

Old Mauch Chunk H.O.-Scale Model Train Display

The train display (second floor of the old Hooven Mercantile Building, Hazard Sq., Jim Thorpe, 570/325-2248) is open Jan.–May and national holidays noon–5 P.M.; June 1–15 and day after Labor Day–Oct. Sun. and Wed.–Fri. noon–5 P.M., Sat. 10 A.M.–5 P.M.; June 16–Labor Day, Sun.–Fri. noon–5 P.M., Sat. 10 A.M.–5 P.M.; and Nov.–Dec. Sat.–Sun. noon–5 P.M. The last show of the day starts at 4:30 P.M. Hours are subject to change without notice. The Mercantile Building is free to enter, but there is a $3 charge to see the train display.

The lower floor of the Mercantile Building is a merchandise-packed, fun place to visit. Upstairs in the train display, little ones and railroad buffs will especially enjoy the miniature town laced with more than 1,000 feet of track. The display has more than 200 structures; a favorite is the burning building, complete with smoke, flames, and fire trucks.

SHOPPING

Antiques, handmade clothing, stained glass, jewelry, collectibles, books, fine art, and sculpture—

the town of Jim Thorpe has everything to entertain and fulfill a browser's whimsy. Both Broadway and Race Street are lined with unique shops and restaurants in the original mid-19th-century buildings.

West Broadway, farther up the hill, is lined with art galleries, craft displays, and more shops. All of the shops and galleries have different hours, but most are open weekdays and Sat. 10 A.M.–5:30 P.M., Sun. 11 A.M.–5 P.M. Many are open during the evening in summer.

OUTDOOR RECREATION

White-Water Rafting

White-water rafting is one of the most popular activities in the scenic Lehigh River Gorge area. Spring often has the fastest water, because of snowmelt; summer and early fall are less challenging and more appropriate for families. **Jim Thorpe River Adventures** (570/325-2570) is one of several companies that offer equipment and guided trips—it also rents mountain bikes by the hour and day. Call for trip types, prices, and schedules. A 12- to 18-mile white-water tour through the Lehigh River Gorge is the most

a quiet morning in Jim Thorpe

frequently booked excursion; other trips are available, including weekend outings that feature a cookout. Another local outfitter is **Pocono Whitewater Adventures** (570/325-8430), which also offers bike tours, bike rentals, and free trail maps.

Biking

In addition to the companies above, **Blue Mountain Sports** (34 Susquehanna St., 570/325-4421 or 800/599-4421) rents bikes, camping equipment, and winter sports equipment. Blue Mountain offers a shuttle service and free trail maps.

Hiking

The **Switchback Trail,** an 18-mile rails-to-trails route, follows the path of America's second operating railroad, the gravity-powered Switchback. When it opened in 1827, the railroad had one purpose: to haul coal from Summit Hill to the Lehigh Canal in Mauch Chunk. When steam-powered railroads rendered the Switchback obsolete, it was turned into a tourist attraction, only to be put out of business by the Great Depression. It became a multiuse trail in the early 1980s.

The Switchback is not an average rail-trail. The trail starts at the Opera House (Hill Road) on Broadway in Jim Thorpe. The first mile is roughened by tree roots, mud, and chunks of rock. The trail smooths out alongside Mauch Chunk Creek and passes Mauch Chunk Lake Park, a possible stop for swimming, fishing, picnicking, or camping (and cross-country skiing in winter). Beyond the lake, the trail crosses Lentz Trail Highway to a crossroads marked by stonework—an old stone trestle that once crossed overhead.

The trestle marks two choices: continue straight, and the path leads gradually uphill for 3.5 miles until it reaches Summit Hill. Return on the same path. A sharp turn to the right at

THE MOLLY MAGUIRES

The secret society known as the Molly Maguires was formed in Ireland in 1843, during the great potato famine. They organized to fight the oppressors of the poverty-stricken population—rent collectors, landlords, and their agents. The origin of the society's name is disputed; it's an homage to a widow who either killed several hated agents or was herself killed because she was unable to pay her debts.

The organization was brought to the Pennsylvania coalfields by Irish immigrant miners who were poorly paid for dangerous work and often deeply in debt to the owners' company stores. From the mid-1860s to 1877, the society's members initiated coal strikes and worked to form a union but also committed acts of sabotage and attacked, intimidated, and murdered mine owners, superintendents, and police officers. Many deaths were attributed to the Mollies, but when arrested, they could always produce large groups of "witnesses" who would swear to the truth of their alibis.

In 1874, a group of mine owners hired James McParlan, an agent of the Pinkerton Detective Agency, to infiltrate the society. He posed as a miner, became a member of the Molly Maguires, and gathered sufficient evidence to testify against, convict, and execute 11 of the society's members in a series of sensational trials lasting 1875–1877. In 1877, Michael Doyle, Edward Kelly, Alexander Campbell, and John "Yellow Jack" Donohue were arrested and brought to the Mauch Chunk jail, where they were hanged. Six more Mollies were sent to Pottsville and died on the gallows there. A few years later, English author Arthur Conan Doyle pitted Sherlock Holmes against the Molly Maguires in his story "The Valley of Fear."

The Molly Maguires apparently ceased to exist. McParlan and his agency subsequently became notorious as a private police force for wealthy owners to use against the unions that were forming in industrial areas across the state. Some historians claim that the actions of the Molly Maguires were conscionable, given the oppression fostered by the all-powerful mine owners, and that the Mollies were targeted more out of anti-Irish sentiment and mine owners' self-interest than a sense of justice.

The Poconos

THE SAGA OF BRIGHT PATH

His Sac and Fox name was Wa Tho Hjck (Bright Path) but as Jim Thorpe, he became known as one of the world's greatest all-around athletes. In the 1912 Olympics, he broke world records in both the decathlon and the pentathlon. The King of Sweden called him "the greatest athlete in the world"; a month later, his medals were taken away when Olympic officials determined that he had damaged his amateur status before the competition by accepting a small salary for playing exhibition baseball.

He played for the New York Giants in the 1913 World Series and went on to play for two other major league baseball teams in the next six years. He then began a 15-year career in professional football. In 1920, Jim Thorpe became the first president of the American Professional Football Association (now the National Football League). Known for his moodiness and violence on the field, Thorpe was an uneven player and ended his career in the shadow of Red Grange, sitting out his last season on the bench. Following promises of fame and stardom, Thorpe went west to Hollywood, only to end up working as a laborer during the Depression. In 1953, he died, apparently from an alcohol-related illness.

Thorpe's widow wanted to honor his remarkable athletic career with a memorial, but neither the state of his birth—Oklahoma—nor Carlisle, Pennsylvania (where he attended school), was willing to finance the monument. Two small towns in Pennsylvania—Mauch Chunk and East Mauch Chunk—caught Mrs. Thorpe's attention through a series of newspaper articles. Residents there had been donating a nickel a week toward a development fund, struggling to entice new industry to their failing towns. When approached, the Mauch Chunks agreed to join together and be reborn as the town of Jim Thorpe. Though the area had been a tourist destination around the turn of the last century, the Mauch Chunks were in economic distress. The name change had a solidifying, invigorating effect on the communities.

Now a major tourist destination, Jim Thorpe counts a variety of accommodations, restaurants, shops, and outdoor activities among its attractions. The Jim Thorpe Memorial, a crypt on SR 903, is in a park on the edge of the town named in his honor. Jim Thorpe's Olympic medals were returned to the family nearly three decades after his death.

the trestle leads to a steep and strenuous four-mile ascent to Mt. Pisgah; take this alternative only if you're in good shape and steady on your feet (or pedals). The Mt. Pisgah trail connects with a wagon road just before the summit that leads (again, steeply—it's a 10 percent grade, so bikers may have to walk all or part) down to Pine Street. Go right on Pine one block to Center Avenue; make a left and follow the road into Jim Thorpe.

ACCOMMODATIONS

$50–100

M Broadway Guest House (W. Broadway, two blocks from Market Sq., 877/412-3247) features eight guest rooms with private baths, air conditioning, cable TV, garage parking, and a continental breakfast. It also has a bicycle-storage-and-cleaning facility. This late-1800s dwelling is operated by the Mauch Chunk Museum and Cultural Center; rates are $69–$109 during the week and $89–149 on the weekends—possibly the best deal in town.

$100–150

A pretty house on the corner of North Street and Broadway, **Cozy Corner** (504 North St., 570/325-2961) is filled with antiques. Visitors may stay in any of three bedrooms, with either shared or private baths, or the suite; all include a continental breakfast. Rates range $100–120, less during slow season.

M Inn at Jim Thorpe (24 Broadway, Jim Thorpe, 570/325-2559, 800/329-2599, or 888/370-9170, www.injt.com) is one of the busiest lodgings in town; book early, especially for the spectacular autumn leaf-turning display. This two-story brick Victorian building blends period decor with modern amenities—all the rooms have private baths and cable TV. A continental breakfast is included. The inn also has a suite with fireplace, whirlpool bath, and kitchen. Rates range $85–250.

The **Gilded Cupid** (40 W. Broadway, 570/325-5453) was built in the mid-1800s. It was once owned by Mary Packer and has large rooms, rounded windows, an upstairs porch, and an outside sitting area where you can hear the stream that runs beneath the fenced courtyard. Each bedroom has a private bathroom, complete with claw-foot tub. All rooms cost $140 per night all year.

$150–200

A century after its construction, **M** The Harry Packer Mansion B&B (Packer Hill, 570/325-8566, www.murdermansion.com) is completely restored while maintaining original features and appointments of detailed Minton tiles, bronze and brass chandeliers, Tiffany windows, intricate carved wood mantels, and period antique furnishings. The accommodations in the Harry Packer Mansion and the adjacent carriage house are as elegant as the decor, and the prices reflect it: rates range $135–$250. The mansion has Murder Mystery weekends throughout the year; guests participate in costume (provided). Prices, which include some meals, are $495–650.

FOOD

Folks who live in Jim Thorpe name the **Black Bread Cafe** (47 Race St., 570/325-8957) as one of their favorites. All items are homemade, and the menu changes frequently according to the whims of the chef. Sandwiches, soups, and baked goods come highly recommended. The café is open Thurs.–Tues. 11 A.M.–9 P.M. Lunch is around $8, dinner $12.

The **Sunrise Diner** (3 Hazard Sq., 570/325-4093 for takeout): Settle in on a stool or slide into a booth and hunker down to the finest of bacon-and-egg sandwiches, hamburgers, or meatloaf platters, whatever your diner-heart desires. It's open every day, early to late. Expect typical diner prices of $3–12.

The Behan family, from Dublin, runs **M** The Emerald Restaurant (24 Broadway, Jim Thorpe, 570/325-8995) with warm Irish hospitality. The Emerald serves lunch and dinner daily (11 A.M.–9 P.M., later on summer weekends). Christmas is the only day it closes. Lunch averages $10, dinner $22. The restaurant menu reflects the Behans' heritage but goes beyond to include European-style favorites such as pasta and bouillabaisse. The **Molly Maguires Pub** (adjacent to the restaurant) is a late-night hot spot. The pub is open until 1:45 A.M. and serves a sandwich menu that averages $6.

INFORMATION

Contact the **Jim Thorpe Network** (P.O. Box 90, Jim Thorpe, PA 18229, 570/325-3673, www.jimthorpe.net) or **Pocono Mountains Vacation Bureau** (Box NG, 1004 Main St., Stroudsburg, PA 18360, 570/424-6050 or 800/762-6667, for brochures only, www.800poconos.com) for specifics on accommodations, events, and activities.

Black Diamond Country

The fortunes of many of the towns in northeastern Pennsylvania were built on the coal industry. The heart of that industry lay roughly between the forks of the Susquehanna River and the city of Scranton. (Later, iron and steel and the rails made from them carried the natural wealth of the area to the boundaries of the state and beyond. The first commercial railroad in America was built in 1829 by the Little Schuylkill Coal and Iron Company and ran south 15 miles from Tamaqua to Port Clinton, on the Schuylkill River.) In 1886, the town of Tamaqua, rolling in dollars gritty with coal dust, was the third municipality in the country to get electric streetlights—three years before New York City.

At one time, this area supplied anthracite for more than 80 percent of the nation. Though the coal industry is no longer as active, its legacy is a trail of workingmen's towns separated by forests and mounds of shining black slag in this forested hill country.

stands are interspersed with enormous hills of shining black waste from the coal mines. Look for deserted wooden buildings (coal breakers, where coal was sorted into different sizes), which signal the presence of collieries.

Leave Centralia on SR 42 south to Ashland. While there, be sure to make time to explore the Museum of Anthracite Mining and the mine tunnel there. From Ashland, follow SR 54 and SR 61 south and east through Fountain Springs to SR 61 south, which leads to Pottsville, home of the oldest brewery in America.

From Pottsville, take US 209 east through Tamaqua to Lansford, and visit the No. 9 Mine wash shanty.

Continue east on US 209, then go east on SR 54 to SR 93. Turn north on SR 93 to the town of Hazleton. Take SR 309 north to SR 940 east. Pass through the village of Jeddo, watching for the small signs that will direct you past cinder-filled coalfields to Eckley Miner's Village.

SCENIC TOURS

⚄ The Black Diamond Trail

The approximately 90-mile route from Centralia—where underground mines still erupt in occasional fires—through Ashland, Pottsville, Lansford, and Eckley follows a trail of patch towns through northeastern Pennsylvania. Birch

HISTORIC SIGHTS

Ashland Coal Mine and "Lokie" Steam Train

Kids will get a few thrills out of this mine tunnel tour—visitors are transported 1,800 feet into a horizontal drift mine (the tunnel follows the horizontal drift of the coal vein) dug out

MINERS AND LABORERS BENEVOLENT ASSOCIATION

Low wages and few safety standards antagonized miners and laborers, who were also often in debt to the company. Most mining companies set up a colliery, which included a deep pit mine; a breaker, a tall wooden structure used to sort coal; assorted outbuildings for mine processing; and a company town. All the buildings and dwellings were owned by the company, including the store. Miners had few options, since many of them were paid in scrip rather than real dollars, and scrip was redeemable only at the company store. Several workers' groups attempted to unionize, but few succeeded. One that did was the Miners and Laborers Benevolent Association, which became today's United Mine Workers Association.

of Mahanoy Mountain (mah-NOY). The tunnel and steam train (Oak and 19th Sts., Ashland, 570/875-3850, www.pioneertunnel.com) are next to the Museum of Anthracite Mining. The museum is open during the week starting April 1, 10 A.M.–6 P.M.; daily after Memorial Day. Mine tours are at 11 A.M., 12:30 P.M., and 2 P.M. The mine tour and steam train ride also operate during May, Sept., and Oct., and are open weekends 10 A.M.–6 P.M.; during the week, mine tours are limited to 11 A.M. and 2 P.M. Admission to the mine tour is $7.50 and children 2–11 are $5; the train ride is an additional $5.50 for adults and $4 for children ages 2–11.

To say that mining coal by hand is a difficult way to make a living is an understatement, and this tour gives some insight into the dirty, dangerous business of underground mining. The mine's temperature never rises above 52°F— bring a jacket or sweater.

The gleaming restored steam engine **Henry Clay** pulls a trainload of visitors on a .75-mile track over the surface of the mountain past Mammoth Stripping, a vein scraped from the surface of the earth by massive steam shovels. The 150-foot-high wall that remains extends far to the west and is an impressive testament to the days when Ashland and its neighboring towns were the backbone of America's coal industry.

inside Yuengling Brewery

© JOANNE MILLER

Eckley Miner's Village

A fascinating stop on any tour of coal country is Eckley Miner's Village (570/636-2070), comprising the entire town of Eckley. The village sponsors a number of lectures and special events; it's open Mon.–Sat., 9 A.M. to 5 P.M., Sun. noon–5 P.M. Admission is $4 for adults, $3.50 for seniors, $2 for children, and free for children under six. It was one of hundreds of company patch towns built during the 19th century.

In 1854, the mining firm of Sharpe, Leisenring, and Company leased the land and began work on a colliery and the village. Miners' homes, stores, schools, and churches were built and run by the company; it owned and controlled every aspect of the workers' lives. The village covers 100 acres and has 58 buildings.

Over the years, strip mining replaced underground mining, and the work force and population of Eckley gradually declined from over 1,000 in 1870 to 20 today. The coal vein that initially made the area a desirable spot for a village continues to be mined. Though the original colliery is gone, the village remains and is still home to miners and their wives, widows, and children.

Village structures may be seen from the outside at any time. Interiors of churches, laborers' homes (with the exception of private homes), a company store, and a doctor's office are open to visitors accompanied by a tour guide. The visitors' center provides guides on request for a small additional charge (calling ahead is a good idea) and presents an orientation slide show and exhibits on the history of Eckley and life in the mining towns.

Yuengling Brewery

Yuengling is America's oldest brewery (5th and Mahantongo Sts., Pottsville, 570/628-4890). It's

The Poconos

open Mon.–Fri. 10 A.M.–1:30 P.M., and tours are given Mon.–Fri. at 10 A.M. and 1:30 P.M. The brewery does not operate Sat.; however, it's open 10 A.M.–3 P.M. and tours are given at 11 A.M., noon, and 1 P.M. Admission is free.

When Andrew Jackson was president, German immigrant David G. Yuengling founded the Eagle brewery in Pottsville; it burned down three years later, in 1831. Yuengling moved up the hill, rebuilt, and renamed the brewery after himself; those fireproof brick buildings and cooling tunnels still stand today. The brewery survived Prohibition by producing near-beer, a low-alcohol version of the real thing. Now owned and operated by the fifth generation of Yuenglings, the brewery is the 15th-largest in America.

Yuengling offers a fun and enlightening tour plus a charming museum of old advertising materials and artifacts, including a certificate that thanks the brewery for its participation in raising funds to restore Abraham Lincoln's log cabin—signed by Mark Twain and President William Howard Taft, among others.

At tour's end, visitors age 21 and over have an opportunity to taste four out of five beers that Yuengling produces. Beer cannot be purchased on the premises, but tour guides will direct you to the nearest outlet. Warning: the gift shop items are hard to resist.

OTHER POINTS OF INTEREST

Jerry's Classic Cars and Collectibles Museum

Jerry's (394 S. Centre St., Pottsville, 570/622-9510) houses a number of classic automobiles from the 1950s and '60s. The collection includes a wide variety of artifacts from Schuylkill County and America's past. It's open the end of May through the end of Oct., Sat. Sun. noon to 5 P.M. Admission is $8, $6 for seniors and students, and free for children under the age of six.

Oheb Zedack Synagogue and Jewish Museum of Eastern Pennsylvania

Wave after wave of Eastern European miners, Celtic workers, and German farmers entered Schuylkill County during the early days of the mines. All built at least one monument to the religious ties that held them together; the region has a Lutheran church, a Russian Orthodox church, a Lithuanian church, a Roman Catholic church, and a synagogue—Oheb Zedack in Pottsville. After the coalfields played out, families left the area for work elsewhere, and many of the smaller congregations of each of the faiths disappeared.

Oheb Zedack Synagogue (2200-B Mahantongo St., Pottsville, 570/622-5890) has a small

JOHN O'HARA: POTTSVILLE'S FAMOUS NATIVE SON

At 606 Mahantongo St., just across from the Yuengling Brewery, stands a marker highlighting the home of Pottsville's most famous son, writer John O'Hara. The author of 14 novels and more than 400 short stories, O'Hara began his career as a newspaperman and then turned to fiction. In his own words, he wanted "to record the way people talked and thought and felt and to do it with complete honesty and variety." This tall, big-shouldered son of Irish immigrants who wrote about "Gibbsville" (a fictionalized representation of Pottsville), O'Hara was one of the first authors to depict the coal region using real-life stories and authentic local dialect. After winning acclaim for his

work, he counted several contemporaries as friends, including Ernest Hemingway, F. Scott Fitzgerald, and William Faulkner.

Pottsville, a multicultural city of wealthy entrepreneurs, struggling workers, and down-and-outers, provided rich raw material for O'Hara's work. His "Pennsylvania protectorate" remains much the same as it was when he wrote *An Appointment in Samarra*. Visitors can walk up the hill past the luxurious mansions of former coal barons on Mahantongo and picture fictional character Julian English driving along "Lantenango Street" on his way to the club to drink and insult snobbish members of the city's upper class.

MY SWEETHEART'S THE MULE IN THE MINES

My sweetheart's the mule in the mines,
I drive her without reins or lines,
On the bumper I sit,
I chew and I spit
All over my sweetheart's behind.

When mules were the main source of power in the pit mines, a variation of this song was sung in colliery saloons and at work in the tunnels by mule drivers (who made up their own ribald versions). Until an Act of the Legislature in 1965 halted the practice, some mules spent their entire lives without ever seeing the sun. They were kept in large stables below the surface, watered in troughs that drained excess water from the shafts, and fed from bins that lined the stable. Until they were replaced by steam power, the animals hauled carts between the mine's rooms and up to the surface. Horses proved unsuitable for mine work; only oversized Percherons and Clydesdales had the re-

quired strength to pull the large, heavy carts, and those horses took up too much space in the confines of the mines. Mules, unlike horses, weren't easily frightened—a necessary attribute in close quarters, where explosions were an everyday part of the process of anthracite mining.

Mules were extremely valuable in mine culture. After the mines were electrified, mules often wore leather hats to protect them from possible electrocution when they bumped into wires strung against the wall. Boys who had grown old enough to go below the mine surface became mule tenders. The mules were considered more valuable than the child, and if an animal died, the mule boy had to replace it from his own wages. If an adult driver was responsible for the animal's death, he would be fired immediately. Many of the drivers pampered their animals, sharing sweets, plug tobacco, or beer with them at the end of a shift.

display dedicated to the memory of Schuylkill County's lost Jewish congregations. The museum in the building features a quality collection of paintings and artwork. It's open Mon., Tues., and Wed. 10 A.M.–1 P.M. Services are Sat. at 9 A.M.

MUSEUMS

The Museum of Anthracite Mining

The major focus of this museum is the mining and processing of anthracite, including miners' tools and machinery, which show the formation, cleaning, and grading of the mineral. The museum is next to a pleasant park (17th and Pine Sts., Ashland, 570/875-4708, www.phmc.state .pa.us). It's open Mon.–Fri. 10 A.M.–4 P.M., Sat.–Sun. and holidays noon–4 P.M.; closed in winter. Adult admission is $3.50, seniors $3, youth $2. Visitors walk through a timbered structure, which illustrates mine shaft support, and view models, photographs, and charts showing exploration and extraction methods.

The No. 9 Mine Wash Shanty Anthracite Coal Mining Museum

The No. 9 Mine opened in 1855, and it was the world's oldest operating anthracite deep mine when it closed in 1972. The museum (Dock St., Lansford, 5/0/645-7074) gathers the odds and ends of a dangerous and difficult line of work; it's open Wed.–Sun. noon–3:30 P.M. Admission is $3. Mine tours are the same days and times between mid-May and mid-Sept. only. Admission for the museum and the mine tour is $7.

On display are tools, mine models, and a kitchen from a typical miner's home. Clothes in wire baskets hang on chains from the ceiling at the Wash Shanty, just as they did when as many as 450 miners worked the tunnels below.

The village of Lansford not only produced strapping miners but a couple of internationally known musicians, too. It was the long-time residence of brothers Tommy and Jimmy Dorsey, who, in their youth, appeared frequently at a nightclub called the Ballroom in the Clouds above the town of Jim Thorpe.

The Poconos

SHOPPING

Tamaqua Farmer's Market

Every Wednesday in fair weather, the **Hometown Farmers' Market** (.25 mile west on SR 54 from the intersection of SR 54 and SR 309 in Tamaqua, 570/668-2630), welcomes buyers and sellers. On sale are baked goods, fresh vegetables, meats, crafts, toys, clothing, and more.

OUTDOOR RECREATION

Locust Lake State Park

This park covers 1,144 acres, including a 52-acre lake, adjacent to the 600-acre Weiser State Forest, Schuylkill County. For camping reservations or trail maps, contact Locust Lake State Park/Tuscarora State Park (RD 1, Box 1051, Barnesville, PA 18214, 570/467-2404).

Boating and Fishing: A campstore/concession on Locust Lake Road rents rowboats and canoes. Only nonpowered or electric-powered boats with current registration are permitted.

Locust Lake is a high-intensity fishing area and receives several stockings of brown and brook trout each year. Pickerel, bass, and panfish are also available. Night fishing and ice fishing during the winter are permitted.

Hiking: Ridge Trail, .75 mile in length, winds through a mature forest, along a creek, and through a younger woodland area. Hemlock Trail, two miles, is blazed through a mature hemlock stand and along Locust Creek. Oak Loop Trail, the longest trail at four miles, circles a ridge covered by a mature deciduous forest.

Hunting: Approximately 1,045 acres of parkland are designated for hunting from fall to March 31, Sunday excepted. Common game species found in the park are white-tailed deer, rabbits, squirrels, turkeys, woodcocks, doves, ruffed grouse, and ring-necked pheasants.

Swimming: Lifeguards are on duty Memorial Day–Labor Day 11 A.M.—7 P.M. on the west side of the lake. The swimming area is marked with buoys and has a maximum depth of 5.5 feet.

Camping: Circling the lake are 282 tent and trailer sites; tent sites are on the north side of the lake and trailer facilities are on the south side. Conveniences include comfort stations, wash houses with showers, and a sanitary trailer dump station. Two playgrounds are in the trailer area, and an additional playground is in the tent area. A number of walk-in sites away from the main campgrounds are available by reservation. Call 888/PA-PARKS (888/727-2757) to make reservations.

Getting There: The park is three miles south of Mahanoy City via SR 54 east, then I-81 south; or take SR 1006 (St. Clair Road) south from Mahanoy City. It's seven miles north of Pottsville via SR 61 north, then SR 1006 east from St. Clair.

ACCOMMODATIONS

$100–150

The Kaier Mansion (729 E. Centre St., Mahanoy City, 570/773-3040, $75–185) presides over the old anthracite-mining town of Mahanoy City, a reminder of the boomtown prosperity that once graced the area. Charles Kaier opened a brewery in 1862, which enjoyed great success even after his death in 1899. He and his wife built a magnificent mansion for themselves, and it stands today, once again welcoming guests to the black diamond region. The mansion is in a continual process of restoration and renovation; a two-bedroom suite and double suite have private baths, and two rooms share a bath. Breakfast is included, and a two-night minimum is required on holidays. Kaier Mansion is close to two state parks, Tuscarora and Locust Lake.

If sports stories fill a large part of your verbal repertoire, the **Butterfly and Bee Bed and Breakfast** (just off SR 61 N on Sculpshill Rd., Deer Lake, 570/366-6365) is the place to stay. Muhammad Ali trained here in the 1970s, though it's hard to tell that this little collection of cabins was once the getaway of champions. Now, the views, forested surroundings, and horse stables are the draw. The location is distraction-free, between Pottsville and Reading on Sculpshill Mountain. The three cabins range $100 per night, and a two-night stay is preferred.

The Angel Rose Bed and Breakfast (616 W. Market St., Pottsville, 570/628-4850, www.geocities.com) in downtown Pottsville near Garfield Square, is only two blocks from the Yuengling Brewery. The 1911 Victorian offers three bedrooms that share two baths. To give you some idea of the authenticity of the setting, the national retailer Urban Outfitters chose this setting for a photo shoot. Prices are $90 with breakfast, $80 without.

INFORMATION

The **Schuylkill County Visitors Bureau** (P.O. Box 237, Pottsville, PA 17901, 570/622-7700 or 800/765-7282, www.schuylkill.org) has information about sights and events on the Black Diamond Trail. The **Pottsville Commission on Tourism** (570/628-4647, www.easternpa.com) is another good contact.

East of the Susquehanna

Though the economy of the region was largely dependent upon the extraction of anthracite, the area where the Susquehanna River branches east and west was built instead on lumber and agriculture. That rural past (and present) is reflected in the auto tour from Bloomsburg to Elysburg.

SCENIC TOURS

M **Covered Bridge Tour: Bloomsburg to Elysburg**

This auto route starts in the pleasant college town of Bloomsburg, winds through sunlit forests, and crosses streams, lakes, and patches of cleared fields to end at Knoebels Amusement Park in Elysburg. The 16-mile one-way route (30 miles round-trip, if the return is taken on SR 42 and SR 487) explores the backroads from Bloomsburg to Elysburg. Cyclists in good shape will find the hilly terrain a challenge.

Set your odometer at the intersection of US 11 and SR 42, south of the town of Bloomsburg. Turn south on SR 42 and drive .1 mile to the "Y." Veer to the left (CR 4001; follow signs for Indian Head Campground). At .3 mile, look left to see Rupert Bridge. Continue on CR 4001.

Cross an old plank bridge and rejoin SR 42 by turning left (south).

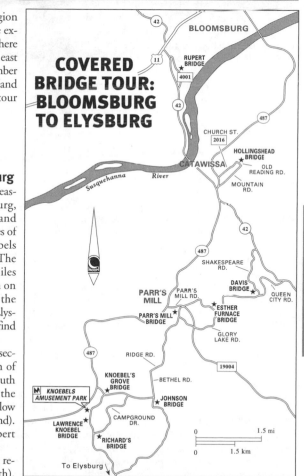

COVERED BRIDGE TOUR: BLOOMSBURG TO ELYSBURG

The Poconos

© AVALON TRAVEL PUBLISHING, INC.

Cross the tracks and a bridge over the Susquehanna River into the village of Catawissa. Continue south on SR 42/SR 487. At the first light, turn left (east, on Church Street, CR 2016). You'll pass a small cemetery on your left. At 3.8 miles, make a very sharp right (south) onto Old Reading Road, and follow it down to the Hollingshead Bridge. Turn right (west) on Mountain Road (4.2 miles). You'll dead-end on SR 42/SR 487.

Turn left (south) on SR 42/SR 487. At the "Y" (five miles), veer left onto SR 42 south. Drive over the hill, and on the downgrade, look for the first right turn (west), Queen City Road (7.6 miles). Turn, and follow the stream. The Davis Bridge will be on your right, on Shakespeare Road (8.5 miles). Continue on Queen City Road. At 9.5 miles, make a right (west) at the "T"; you're now on Glory Lake Road.

At 9.6 miles, make a right (north) just before Glory Lake and pass through the Esther Furnace Bridge. You'll pass a small church and cemetery as you drive up the hill; at the crest (11.9 miles), turn left (southwest). Cross the next intersection after the stop sign, and you'll come to the Parr's Mill Bridge (Parr's Mill Road, 12.4 miles). Drive through and stay on Parr's Mill Road.

At the "Y" (12.6 miles), veer right (west). At 13.8 miles, make a right (west) on Ridge Road. Turn left (south) on Bethel Road (14.1 miles). At the bottom of the hill (14.6 miles), you'll see the Johnson Bridge in front of you. Don't cross it—keep on the main road. At Campground Drive (Knoebels Alternate Campground), 15.4 miles, turn left (south). The first part of the road is dirt; follow the road through the Richards Bridge to dead-end on SR 487. A right turn on SR 487 will take you to Knoebels Amusement Park, the Lawrence Knoebel Bridge, Knoebel's Grove Bridge, and eventually to Bloomsburg; a left turn on SR 487 leads to Elysburg.

SIGHTS

 Knoebels Amusement Park

Knoebels is one of the largest free-admission amusement parks in Pennsylvania. There is a charge for rides, but parking, picnic grounds, and nightly entertainment are free. Bands and

off-season at Knoebels

© JOANNE MILLER

musical revues are staples at the Bandshell and at the Roaring Creek Saloon; special children's shows are offered at the Time Machine Theatre.

Knoebels (pronounced *with* the "k"—ka-NO-buls), on SR 487 between Elysburg and Catawissa (P.O. Box 317, Elysburg, PA 17824, 570/672-2572 or 800/487-4386, www.knoebels.com) is set within a forest; it gives the impression of a hybrid fairyland-carnival, especially in the evenings when it's lit up like Philadelphia. It's big, clean, well run, and filled with sprawling families in the summer.

The park is open daily after June, 11 A.M.–10 P.M. In April and May, it's open on the weekends noon–6 P.M. Both Memorial Day weekend and Labor Day weekend have extended hours. Admission is free, and rides are $.60 and up.

Amusements include the extra-large Krystal Pool for swimming, four waterslides, zippy bumper cars, and an antique carousel and carousel museum. The Phoenix, which is rated by

The Poconos

roller-coaster aficionados as one of America's best, tops the list of thrill rides, though there are plenty of tamer rides for children. There's park food galore: hand-dipped ice cream, barbecued chicken, candy apples, and pizza. Knoebels also has a 500-site campground nearby, and cabins for rent by reservation.

Joseph Priestley House

Joseph Priestley, the preeminent Unitarian theologian and chemist noted for his discovery of oxygen and other invisible gases, built his home on the sparkling shores of the Susquehanna River in 1794. Furnished with authentic period objects, the house (472 Priestley Ave., Northumberland, 570/473-9474, www.phmc.state.pa.us) features Priestley's laboratory, as well as exhibits representing his accomplishments and interests. Hours are Tues.–Sat. 9 A.M.–5 P.M., Sun. noon–5 P.M. Admission is $4 adults, $2 children.

SHOPPING
Farmer's Markets

July–Sept., on Tues., Thurs., and Sat., a farmers' market is held on Market Square in the center of Bloomsburg 7 A.M.–1 P.M. For information, call the Chamber of Commerce (570/784-2522).

Rohrbach's (two miles south of the town of Catawissa off SR 487 on Apple Drive, 717/356-7654) features homemade pies, fruits, vegetables, and preserved goods.

To get to Krums Orchards (Orchard Dr., Catawissa, 717/356-2339) continue on Apple Drive past Rohrbach's, turn left at the stop sign (Longwood Road) and go about one mile farther to Orchard Drive. The market also features a bakery, fresh food, bulk groceries, and occasional orchard tours.

OUTDOOR RECREATION
Montour Preserve

This preserve, which is owned and operated by Pennsylvania Power and Light Company, has facilities available for family activities such as picnicking, boating, and fishing on 165-acre Lake Chilisquaque (CHILL-a-sqwak), and nearly 15

miles of nature trails for hiking. The visitors' center offers public programs throughout the year. Take Exit 33 off I-80 (SR 54) to the village of Washingtonville. Follow the signs to PP&L Montour Preserve and Lake Chilisquaque. For information, contact PP&L Montour Preserve (RR 1, Box 292, Turbotville, PA 17772). Trails are open year-round. The visitors' center is open Mon.–Fri. 9 A.M.–4 P.M. The center is also open Sat.–Sun. noon–4 P.M. May–Sept. Admission is free.

Ricketts Glen State Park

This is one of the most scenic areas in Pennsylvania (Ricketts Glen State Park, 695 SR 487, Benton, PA 17814, 570/477-5675, www.dcnr.state.pa.us). The park is named for American

THE BEAR FACTS

This area of Pennsylvania, particularly within the state parks, is black bear country. They appear cute and cuddly; they are not. In fact, they can sprint as fast as Seabiscuit and can ascend a tree as quickly as a cat with a dog pack on its tail. Those big, handy claws tear apart rotting logs for goodies, and will do the same to your cooler, given the chance. They may not see well, and their hearing is only a little better, but the faint scent of that well-wrapped salami in your backpack wafts through the woods and into their shiny black noses, as compelling as a free lunch to a travel writer. Black bears normally avoid people, but just as in Yosemite, bears dependent on eating human food can become slightly aggressive when people get between them and their intended nosh.

Do yourself a favor: store all food items inside a car trunk, or suspend food between two trees, 10 feet in the air and three feet from either tree. If you come in contact with a black bear, try chasing it away by making loud noises such as yelling, honking a car horn, or banging a pot. Do not attempt to make friends; like most wild animals, their food-gathering needs far outweigh a yen for interspecies dating.

The Poconos

Civil War veteran Robert Bruce Ricketts, who controlled more than 80,000 acres of land in this area. His heirs sold 48,000 acres to the Pennsylvania Game Commission, and the area was approved as a national park site in the 1930s, but World War II intervened and development was dropped. In 1942, the Falls and Glens area came under the auspices of the Commonwealth of Pennsylvania. Additional purchases have brought the park to its present size of 13,050 acres in Luzerne, Sullivan, and Columbia Counties. Ninety-four-foot Ganoga Falls is the highest of 22 named waterfalls in the park, set among wetlands, old growth forests, and majestic geological formations. There are two main types of waterfalls: sheer "bridal veil," such as F. L. Ricketts Falls, and cascading "wedding cake," such as Ganoga Falls.

Ricketts Glen is famous for its diversity of bird life, including bald eagles and 23 varieties of warblers. Picnicking, hiking, and wildlife observation are popular uses of the park.

The Glens Natural Area, a registered National Natural Landmark, is the main scenic attraction. Two branches of Kitchen Creek cut through the deep gorges of Ganoga Glen and Glen Leigh, unite at "Waters Meet," and then flow through Ricketts Glen, among giant pines, hemlocks, and oaks. Many of the magnificent trees in this area are more than 500 years old and ring counts on fallen trees have revealed ages as high as 900 years. Four-foot diameters are common and many trees tower to 100 feet. The area is the meeting ground of the southern and northern hardwood types, creating an extensive variety of trees.

Boating: Lake Jean, at 245 acres, has dry mooring and one boat launch. A boat rental concession operates during the summer season and offers rowboats, paddleboats, kayaks and canoes. Nonpowered boats must have one of the following: launching permit or mooring permit from Pennsylvania State Parks, available at most state park offices; or boat registration or launching permit from the Pennsylvania Fish and Boat Commission. Motorboats must display a current boat registration. Motorboats registered in other states must have one of the aforementioned launching or mooring permits.

Hiking: Trails vary from fairly level to very steep hills. The 26 miles of trails are a prime attraction of the park. Following are a few selected hikes:

The **Falls Trail** is 7.2 miles if hiking both the upper and lower sections of the park (difficult). The trails pass 21 beautiful waterfalls ranging in heights from 11 feet to 94 feet. The terrain is rocky, can be slippery, and descends steeply on both the Ganoga and Glen Leigh sides. Hikers should take extra precautions with trail conditions, wear proper footwear, stay on the trail, and be in good physical condition. A shorter 3.2-mile loop that includes most of the waterfalls can be taken by going on the Highland Trail and the Glen Leigh and Ganoga Glen trails.

The **Evergreen Trail** consists of a guided one-mile easy hike through an old growth forest, one of the few stands remaining in all of Pennsylvania. Here you can see a hemlock that stood on this continent before Columbus arrived.

Ganoga View Trail, named after the park's highest waterfall, allows one to walk up to the side of Ganoga Falls without having to hike the Falls Trail (2.8 miles, moderate). Ganoga View along with the Old Beaver Dam Road Trail makes an excellent loop trail for hikers and cross-country skiers.

Grand View Trail (1.9 miles, moderate) takes you to the highest point on Red Rock Mountain (elevation 2,449 feet). In mid-June, the mountain laurel is in bloom, followed late June–early July by the rhododendrons. In mid-July, the high bush blueberries bear fruit, and in the fall, you have an inspiring view of the fall foliage encompassing the surrounding hillsides.

The **Highland Trail** (1.2 miles, moderate) cuts across the top of the Falls Trail and crosses through Midway Crevasse, a narrow passageway between large blocks of Pocono sandstone conglomerates that were deposited throughout this area by glacial movements. At least three times in the last one million years, continental glaciers buried this land under hundreds of feet of ice.

Hunting and Fishing: About 9,000 acres are open to hunting, trapping, and the training of dogs during established seasons. Common game species are deer, turkey, grouse, bear, rabbit, pheasant, and squirrel.

The 245-acre Lake Jean has warm-water game fish and panfish. Fishing is prohibited in the Glens Natural Area.

Horseback Riding: Horse riders may enjoy taking a nine-mile loop by riding the Cherry Run Trail, Fish Commission Road, and Mountain Springs Trail. Sights to see include old railroad grades, Mountain Springs Lake (formerly used to make ice), and an old concrete dam once used to hold back Lake Leigh (now a dry lake).

Swimming: A 600-foot beach is open late May–mid-Sept., 8 A.M.–sunset. Lifeguards are on duty Memorial Day weekend–Labor Day daily 11 A.M.–7 P.M., unless otherwise posted. A food and refreshment concession, boat rental, and picnic facilities are nearby.

Winter Activities: The park offers cross-country skiing, ice fishing on Lake Jean, snowmobile trails, ice climbing, and winter camping. Contact the park office to determine ice and snow conditions in advance of any planned outing.

Camping: There are 120 tent and trailer campsites, some available year-round. The campground features hot showers, flush toilets, shaded sites, gravel parking spurs, and a sanitary dump station. Six campsites are ADA-accessible. Ten modern rental cabins are available year-round. Cabins are furnished and have a living area, kitchen/dining area, toilet/shower room, and two or three bedrooms; one cabin is ADA-accessible. To reserve a campsite, cabin, organized group tenting area, or a picnic pavilion, call 888/PA-PARKS (888/727-2757), Mon.–Sat. 7 A.M. to 5 P.M.

Getting There: The park is 30 miles north of Bloomsburg (Luzerne County) on SR 487. The section of SR 487 from the town of Red Rock to the Lake Jean area of the park is a very steep road. Heavy trailer units should avoid this hill and enter the park by taking SR 487 south from Dushore (Sullivan County).

ACCOMMODATIONS AND FOOD

Latorre House Bed and Breakfast (RR 2, Box 266, Elysburg, 570/672-7243, $75–150) is a good place for couples and families to stay while visiting Knoebels Amusement Resort. It is just off Route 487 and operates seasonally Memorial Day–Labor Day. It features a swimming pool, full breakfast, and four rooms, though only one has a private bath.

Wine Spectator magazine conferred an Award of Excellence on **M Russell's Restaurant** (117 W. Main St., Bloomsburg, 570/387-1332) for its extensive wine list and well-chosen menu. Russell's serves American classics with a gourmet touch: beef Wellington, Cajun tuna, bouillabaisse, and pecan-crusted chicken, among others. There's a special Sunday brunch menu. The **Bistro** next door is the local evening gathering place. Russell's is open daily 10 A.M.–1 A.M. The Bistro is open until 2 A.M. Prices average $7 for lunch and $15 for dinner.

INFORMATION

The **Columbia-Montour Tourist Promotion Agency** (121 Papermill Rd., Bloomsburg, PA 17815, 570/784-8279 or 800/847-4810, www.itourcolumbiamontour.com) is happy to fill you in on events in the Bloomsburg area. More information on the Susquehanna River Valley is available from **Susquehanna Valley Visitors Bureau** (www.visitcentralpa.org).

The Poconos

Endless Mountains

North-central Pennsylvania—once scarred and stripped by logging—is carpeted with lush second-growth forests, a tribute to the strength of nature. This, the least-populated area of the state, contains numerous highlights of America's historic and industrial past; it's also home to the country's largest outdoor recreational area. The region contains more than 30 interconnected state parks and wilderness areas, stretching from the Allegheny National Forest in the west to Pennsylvania's own version of the Grand Canyon in the east. Untracked forests interspersed with lakes, rivers, and caves provide year-round activities for all types of outdoor enthusiasts. The hulks of once-productive lumber mills and iron-production facilities are fading back into the landscape, overgrown by a dizzying variety of hardwood trees. The area is so vast and the population so sparse that most of the time, drivers will pass few cars on the narrow but excellent roads.

US 6 is a two-lane segment of the Grand Army of the Republic Highway, which connects the Atlantic with the Pacific. This high road, scrawled by a shaky hand across the top of the state map, starts near Scranton in Eastern Pennsylvania and ends a few miles south of Lake Erie in the northwestern part of the state. It touches the boundaries of several state parks and passes through a series of all-American small towns, forests of pine and beech, and neat farms, wandering through the Allegheny National Forest, emerging at Youngsville. It's the road less traveled now that high-speed I-80 whisks people along, and for that reason (and others), this is one of the best auto tours in Pennsylvania.

Year-round outdoor sports are highlighted here. During the warm months, the area draws hikers, white-water rafters, canoeists, and anglers. This section of the state is also home to a perennially popular autumn celebration, the Flaming Foliage Festival in Renovo. Cold weather brings hunters, cross-country and downhill skiers, and snowshoe hikers, though the premier recreational pastime in winter here is snowmobiling—most parks are laced with trails. Wellsboro is one of the hubs for the sport, which draws enthusiasts from all over the world.

North-central Pennsylvania is also home to one of America's favorite college football teams. The Penn State Nittany Lions of State College, under coach Joe Paterno, garnered the attention of the nation with their ability to win and win again, inspiring near-religious fervor among their followers. The most urbanized area in the north-central region, State College remains an idyllic small town, referred to by students and residents as "Happy Valley."

PLANNING YOUR TIME

North-central Pennsylvania covers hundreds of square miles. It's best to pick one area or focus to concentrate on at a time.

Those interested in outdoor recreation may choose to spend a week or more camping at **World's End State Park** or downhill skiing at **Elk Mountain** (both on the eastern end of north-central); or camping in **Leonard Harri-**son State Park, Cherry Springs State Park or Ole Bull State Park, or skiing in Sawmill or Denton (all, western end of north-central); or camping in Hyner View/Hyner Run State Parks or Black Moshannon State Park (southern end of north-central).

Driving SR 6 (1–2 weeks) will give you an opportunity to see some wonderful scenery and take in a few of the area's highlights, such as Wellsboro and the Grand Canyon of Pennsylvania, Pennsylvania Lumber Museum, and Susquehannock State Forest.

In the eastern end of north-central, the Mountains, Rivers, Bridges tour (1–2 days) or Old Mill Village (3 hours) and the Starucca Viaduct (driving time) could be taken as day trips from Scranton.

You could spend three days in Williamsport, enjoying the museums and amenities, and drive out to Woolrich for shopping (1 hour plus drive time). Another day could be spent in Renovo for the Flaming Foliage Festival.

Plan on a week in State College to see the surrounding towns of Boalsburg and Bellefonte, visit Penn's Cave, and enjoy the university's museums.

GETTING THERE AND GETTING AROUND
By Public Transportation
Greyhound Bus Lines (800/231-2222) travels I-80 and has regular destination stops at Scranton, Williamsport, and State College. Those cities also have airports, which handle commuter flights from Philadelphia and Pittsburgh. Reaching destinations outside of the major cities becomes a major hassle without a car.

By Auto
Autos are the absolute best way to get around. Because of the sparse population in the area, and also the large amount of public land, there aren't many alternatives. Scranton, State College, and Williamsport all have car rental agencies. The main east-west route through the area is US 6. Running north-south, I-81 in the east, US 220 in Bradford and Sullivan Counties, and US 15 in the west are the through-roads.

Endless Mountains

Must-Sees

Look for **M** to find the sights and activities you can't miss and **M** for the best dining and lodging.

M Mountains, Rivers, Bridges: Much of north-central Pennsylvania's charm is its great outdoors. The 110-mile tour takes you past three of the Endless Mountains prettiest covered bridges and some gorgeous views (page 203).

M The Grand Canyon of Pennsylvania: Set in the spectacular Pine Creek Gorge, this natural phenomenon is a surprise to those used to Pennsylvania's gentle hills (page 207).

M Pennsylvania Lumber Museum: Stop by for insights into the area and its early industry while enjoying the outdoorsy delights of Susquehannock State Forest (page 211).

M Cherry Springs State Park: This is a "dark park" that attracts stargazers (page 213).

M Sugar Valley Loop: This scenic trip includes an 1800s-era gristmill, covered bridge, one-room schoolhouse, log cabin, and a number of old churches and graveyards with tombstones dating back to 1806 (page 215).

M Little League Baseball Museum: Williamsport is the original home of Little League ball, and the museum is a must-see for those with tykes in uniform (page 218).

M Boal Mansion and Columbus Chapel: In the pretty town of Boalsburg, this is an unusual op-

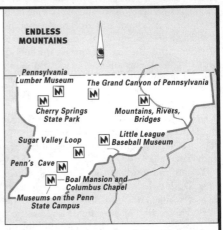

portunity to see contents of the Christopher Columbus family chapel from Spain (page 224).

M Penn's Cave: The watery limestone haunts will appeal to spelunkers and the merely curious (page 224).

M Museums on the Penn State Campus: The Penn State campus in State College offers a number of small, free museums and collections. Of special interest are the **All-Sports Hall of Fame,** where followers of the Nittany Lions and Joe Paterno can walk down memory lane, and the **Palmer Museum of Art,** a must for those interested in fine art (page 226).

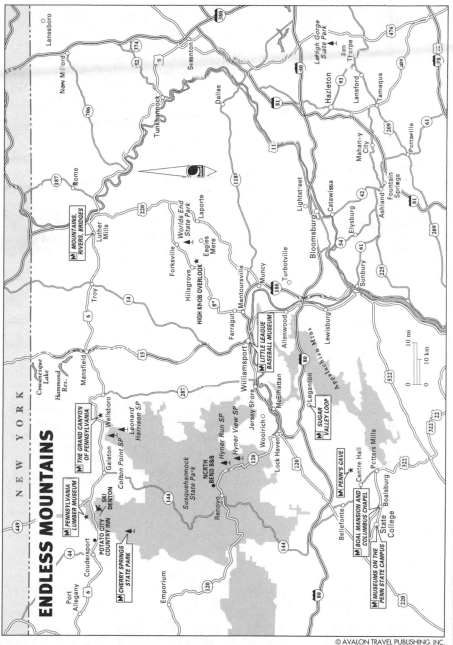

ENDLESS MOUNTAINS

NEW YORK

© AVALON TRAVEL PUBLISHING, INC.

HISTORY

Iroquois Resettlement

Before the 1600s, north-central Pennsylvania was largely unpopulated, used only as hunting grounds by Seneca and Iroquois tribesmen. A war pitting the Iroquois Nation against the Susquehannocks, who occupied the lower Susquehanna River Valley, resulted in victory for the Iroquois but exacerbated another problem—encroachment in the area by European settlers moving west from Philadelphia. The Iroquois' solution was to repopulate the area with members of tribes over which they had domin-

ion. In 1758, Christian Post, a Moravian missionary, wrote:

> . . . they settle these New Allies on the Frontiers of the White People and give them this as their Instruction. Be Watchful that no body of the White People may come to settle near you. You must appear to them as frightful men, & if notwithstanding they come too near give them a Push we will secure and defend you against them.

Delawares traveled through the area and settled around the West Branch of the Susquehanna, and Senecas drifted from the west, but

THE GREAT PEACEMAKERS: SHICKELLAMY AND JOHN LOGAN

Much credit is given to (and deserved by) William Penn for his fair dealings with native dwellers in Pennsylvania, but the wars and uprisings that plagued European expansion could not have been quelled without the cooperation of an Oneida chief, Shickellamy, and his son, John Logan, who became a chief of the Cayuga and is immortalized in the name of Loganton, southwest of Williamsport.

Shickellamy was, in fact, French by birth. He had been captured as an infant and raised by the Oneida tribe. As an adult, he was directed to oversee the resettlement of Shawnees on the Susquehanna. He settled in Shamokin (now Sunbury) and worked with the colonial representative, Conrad Weiser (himself raised by Mohawks), to keep peace on the frontier by developing a policy that strengthened the powers of the neutral Iroquois Confederacy, reinforcing their ability to control the native inhabitants of Pennsylvania.

Shickellamy's half-Cayuga second son, Taghneghdorus—who came to be known as John Logan or simply Logan—also worked with the British to keep the peace. He was instrumental in the creation of the Albany Purchase of 1754, which opened south-central Pennsylvania to European settlement. He became something of a folk legend among the colonials with whom he lived, known for his kindness and personal in-

tegrity. In 1763, several of Logan's peaceful Christian kinsmen near Conestoga were killed by a bloodthirsty mob, the Paxtang boys, but Logan refused to take revenge.

After the Revolutionary War, the new American government held little power over settlers on the edge of the frontier, and the settlers attacked native dwellers wantonly and without provocation. Ben Franklin once observed, "It grieves me to hear that our Frontier People are yet greater Barbarians than the Indians, and continue to murder them in time of Peace." When a raiding party of colonials massacred an undefended group of 13 of Logan's closest family members near the Ohio River, Logan was pushed beyond his limits. He lamented, "There runs not a drop of my blood in the veins of any living creature. . . . Who is there to mourn for Logan—not one!" He organized Shawnee, Mingo, and Lenni Lenape in the area and carried out a series of raids against settlers. The ensuing Shawnee War ended at Mt. Pleasant, where Logan (who was said to have taken 13 scalps) and his warriors fought 3,000 Virginian troops to a draw. Logan agreed to peace, but would no longer share a table with any white men. He died a broken man. Some say he died of drink; in another version, elders of his own tribe ordered his death, which was carried out by his nephew. They claimed he had become presumptuous—"too great a man to live."

the area remained sparsely populated. By 1784, the Iroquois ceded much of the territory to Pennsylvania.

Eurotrickle

The first European to settle legally in the Lawrenceville area was Samuel Baker, who built a cabin on the Tioga River in 1787. Land hungry pioneers moved north from the lowlands of the Piedmont and carved out homesteads and tiny villages from the dense forests of the Allegheny Mountains. The area remained hunting territory for roving bands of Native Americans. Friction was inevitable, and stories of massacres (on both sides) as late as 1876 have been handed down.

River transportation up the Susquehanna was difficult, due to both flooding and shallow water, and creeks and branches beyond the main part of the river were too shallow to navigate. Life's luxuries and any semblance of trade could only be procured by a one-horse wagon on rutted trails or by canoe on the Susquehanna and smaller rivers, requiring days of toil to visit the nearest market town and return. Towns on transport lines faired well. Boalsburg was founded by David Boal, who fought in the Revolutionary War after settling in the area—nine generations of his family have since called it home. A group of Scotch-Irish expanded Boalsburg in 1806, and its convenience as a stagecoach stop on the primitive road ensured its prosperity.

Several overland roads were built between 1796 and the early 1800s; these routes remain as US 15, SR 287, and US 6, all of which follow former Iroquois footpaths. The area was divided into several counties in 1804. At the time, the population of Tioga County was between 500 and 600 residents.

King Pine

The pioneer surge westward and the subsequent need for building materials were prime influences on population growth in north-central Pennsylvania. The entire area was thickly forested in old-growth white pine, the building material of choice. Lumber companies both large and small sprang up, bought up as much property as pos-

sible, and stripped it clean. From Saint Marys to Black Moshannon, Coudersport to Renovo, enormous rafts of white pine were lashed together and sent downriver to transportation centers. Some parts of the plateau and mountains appeared as bare as a Kansas prairie. By 1890—the peak of the lumber boom—the central counties' population peaked at 54,000. Lumber kings used their profits to build massive Victorian mansions in Williamsport (as evidenced by the Victorian mansions in various states of repair and disrepair on Millionaire's Row, downtown) and other towns along the rivers.

The Queen, et al.

When pine was king, other members of the royal family of resources were also producing wealth. Limestone building materials, coal, and iron brought prosperity. Soft coal was hammered out from seams throughout the region.

French statesman Talleyrand, while in exile in America from 1794 to 1796, visited a small village in the center of Pennsylvania. He remarked on "la Belle Fontaine"—what the locals referred to as "Big Spring"—a clear-water source that outflowed 11,500,000 gallons per day. Thereafter renamed Bellefonte, the expanding village bought the spring from Maj. William Reynolds in 1879 for $1. Well known for its stately Victorian mansions, Bellefonte was home to seven of Pennsylvania's governors. Today, the town retains its turn-of-the-century splendor, and homeowners and businesses alike cooperate to maintain its rich appearance.

Farmer's High School

Meanwhile, the area continued to grow as an agricultural center, and the scientific study of effective means for increasing quality and production was an idea whose time had come. In the early 1800s, the abundance of iron and other raw materials in Centre County inspired Moses Thompson and Gen. James Irwin to build and operate the successful Centre Furnace. General Irwin then donated 200 acres of land for the establishment of a school that would educate Pennsylvania farmers in the latest agricultural techniques—the Farmer's High School. It was renamed the Agricultural College of Pennsylvania in 1862 and officially declared Pennsylvania State College in 1874. Since 1953, though, 40,000 annual full-time students, the surrounding town of State College, and all Big Ten football fans have known it as Penn State. The focus of the college continues to be leading the nation and world in agricultural development, though a full curriculum is available and the school is considered one of the best all-around institutions of higher learning in the mid-Atlantic area.

The Iron Horse

Water transport was slow and sometimes unreliable—the rivers often ran too shallow, or flooded, as the Allegheny First Fork River did in 1911, wiping out the mills and budding town of Austin in Potter County. Preliminary surveys for a rail line were made about 1847, and 10 years later the projected road from Sunbury to Erie was begun;

the work commenced in the east and gradually pushed westward. In 1862, a locomotive of the Pennsylvania and Erie Rail Road whistled into Renovo, bringing a "construction train" with material for the road and supplies for workmen to continue building westward. It was a harbinger of prosperity in a poor area and brought with it dreams of wealth and riches.

But all natural resources are finite, and as the area became depleted, it returned to its wild side, where it has remained. Beautiful vistas, serene farms, and deep forests beckon to the sportsman and outdoor enthusiast alike. Close to 50 percent of the area is publicly owned land, open to all year-round. Agriculture remains a major economic factor, and the once-vanquished pine forests have replaced themselves with a variety of trees and undergrowth that form a dense green carpet. In autumn, the maples, sumacs, and oaks provide a color show that is unparalleled.

The High Road/Endless Mountains

Scenic US 6 passes through some beautiful and mountainous territory here, beginning in Clark's Summit north of Scranton. Visitors have an opportunity to enjoy a covered-bridge tour and to see a beautiful Pennsylvania bluestone viaduct, experience elegant shopping, and drive through a number of delightful small towns.

SCENIC TOURS
⋈ Mountains, Rivers, Bridges

This 110-mile round-trip route takes you past three of the area's prettiest covered bridges (the fourth is in Old Mill Village in Susquehanna County). All distances are approximate. You may choose to break up the trip by staying near Eagle's Mere or at World's End State Park.

Begin in the town of Luther's Mills, 11 miles east of Towanda on US 6. Here, Knapp's Bridge, a "Burr-Arch Truss"–type spans Brown's Creek. Head east to Towanda, then turn south on US 220 for 21 miles, past the town of Dushore to SR 87. Turn right (west) and travel 17 miles to Forksville. Turn left (west) on SR 154 (past High Knob) to Hillsgrove (nine miles). The Hillsgrove Covered Bridge is just north of town on SR 87, on Loyalsock Creek. You might want to take a detour here to the High Knob Overlook. Return to Forksville, and take SR 154 south to see the Forksville Covered Bridge, which spans Loyalsock Creek just south of town. Take SR 154 south to the edge of World's End State Park (five miles). Turn right (southwest) on SR 42 to Muncy Valley (you might want to take a detour towards Eagles Mere), about 10 miles. Take US 220 north toward Laporte. Less than two miles up the road is Sonestown. Just south of Sonestown on Muncy Creek, you'll see the Sonestown Covered Bridge. Continue on US 220 back to Towanda (29 miles).

SCENIC SPOTS
High Knob Overlook

You'll have an outstanding view of the mountaintops of seven counties from this overlook.

The best times to come are during the June mountain laurel bloom and the fall foliage period, late September to mid-October. To reach the overlook, take High Knob Road from Double Run Road (CR 3009) or Dry Run Road (gravel/dirt and very bumpy unless you have four-wheel drive) from SR 87 south of Hillsgrove.

Starrucca Viaduct

This beautiful arched structure is also known as the "Lanesboro Bridge of Stone." The bridge was built of Pennsylvania bluestone in 1847–1848 to carry railroad cars full of lumber over the Starucca Valley. Rail fans rate this as one of the most beautiful in the United States. From *Appleton's Journal: a monthly miscellany of popular literature*, April 27, 1872:

> *The structure is of stone, reaching in height one hundred and ten feet, and in length twelve hundred, consisting of eighteen heavy stone piers, with arches of fifty feet span. It is located in a region that includes some of the finest scenery on the Erie [rail] Road.*

You can see it yourself from SR 171, just south of Lanesboro.

OTHER POINTS OF INTEREST
Old Mill Village

This 34-acre living museum (Old Mill Village Museum, 848 Harford Rd., New Milford, PA 18834, 570/465-3448, www.oldmillvillage.com, last weekend in May–Oct.) is dedicated to the preservation of the history and heritage of Northeastern Pennsylvania and the Endless Mountains Heritage Region. Special programs and craft demonstrations are scheduled for weekends ($5–6 adults, $3 ages 6–11). The village is available to see during weekdays by reservation (call and leave a message, 570/465-3448, or email oldmillvillage@epix). Visits during the week are by donation of choice.

⋈ Endless Mountains

mountain cabin in the Alleghenies

Dozens of historical buildings from several different communities were donated beginning in the 1970s, including the Beaven Covered Bridge on SR 848, a one-room schoolhouse, cobbler shop, dress shop, post office, gift shop, gunsmith's shop, blacksmith's shop, wood shop, and others. People are encouraged to visit each of the buildings at their own pace, using maps available upon arrival. Demonstrators in different buildings answer questions, and there are demonstrations of spinning, weaving, quilting, blacksmithing, gunsmithing, candle-making, leather-making, soap-making, outdoor oven-baking, and more throughout the summer.

In addition, the village sponsors special events such as the folk festival with old-time instruments, an 18th-century living history program with reenactors from all over the United States, and an antique engine display with working engines, a frog-jumping contest (you can bring your own or borrow one), and a hollering contest(!). A recent addition is the antique appraisal show, at which experts give appraisals.

The village is one mile south of New Milford on SR 848 (Exit 223 off I-81).

Christopher Ries Glassworks

The perfect place to be on a summer day (511 Keelersburg Rd., 4.2 miles off SR 29 south, Tunkhannock, 570/836-1142, www.christopherries .com, Mon.–Fri. by appointment, Sat. by chance), this working studio and gallery is in a restored 1830s barn. Christopher Ries is an internationally known sculptor in glass. His large cut, ground, and polished refractive pieces use light as an additional element.

P. P. Bliss Gospel Songwriters Museum

The little hamlet of Rome (Main St., Rome, 570/247-7683 or 570/247-2228, May–Sept. Wed. and Sat. 1–4 P.M. and by appointment, donation) displays music, pictures, letters, and musical instruments associated with 19th-century gospel musicians P. P. Bliss, James McGranahan, and D. B. Towner. Visitors are escorted through the museum, told the story of Bliss, and may ask questions. In mid-July each year the museum sponsors a rousing concert of gospel music near the date of Bliss's birthday.

SHOPPING

The village of **Eagles Mere** blends the Victorian country charm of its late-19th-century heritage with an array of contemporary amenities. Known as *the* resort for wealthy Philadelphians at the turn of the last century, Eagles Mere has been converted into a shopping village that's retained the original architecture. Visitors have a range of choices—quaint shops such as Caravan Book Store and Gallery on the Green in the Victorian Village Shoppes (570/525-3503), and in the vicinity, dining, tranquil country inns, miles of hiking and mountain biking trails, scenic vistas, and Eagles Mere Lake. Eagles Mere sponsors several antique markets and craft fairs during the summer and fall.

OUTDOOR RECREATION

Loyalsock Trail

This 59.21-mile trail passes vistas and waterfalls. It starts on SR 87, nine miles north of Montoursville, and ends at a parking lot on Mead Road, .2 mile off US 220 near Laporte. Trail guide and maps ($4 plus tax and postage) are available from the Endless Mountains Visitors Bureau.

Worlds End State Park

The name of this park (SR 154, Forksville, 570/924-3287, www.dcnr.state.pa.us; information: Worlds End State Park, P.O. Box 62, Forksville, PA 18616-0062) was embroiled in controversy. A map from 1872 called the area Worlds End, though some referred to it as Whirl's Glen, or Whirls End. The first name arose from the topography; seven mountain ranges converge on the point. Others refer to the whirlpool in the Loyalsock Creek and the third name was probably a contraction of the other two. Since the whirlpool had largely disappeared, it was decided that the name Worlds End would be the most appropriate.

Early settlers of the area used two horse trails to cross the rugged highland from Muncy Creek to the forks of the Loyalsock Creek at the town of Forksville. This treacherous road became obsolete in 1895 with the building of SR 154. Pioneer

LEAVES: FALLEN BEAUTIES

A Native American legend holds that celestial hunters slew the Great Bear (Big Dipper) in the autumn, and his blood, dripping on the forests, changed the leaves from green to red. Other trees were turned yellow by the fat that spattered out of the kettle as the hunters cooked the meat.

Today, most people give Jack Frost the credit for spectacular autumn color, but temperature actually has little to do with it. A combination of favorable weather conditions is required for color changes to take place. Cloudy, rainy weather or a very hot, dry summer prevents the pigments from developing; warm days followed by warm nights cause vital plant sugars (the coloring agent) to drain out of leaves and into the woody portions of the plant. Ideal conditions for a spectacular autumn are bright, sunny days followed by cool nights.

As daylight decreases, a layer of cells forms at the stem at the base of a leaf. (The leaf is held in place by woody fibers; the separation layer doesn't permeate the fibers, so the leaf remains on the tree until frost or wind tears it free.) As the separation layer forms, the manufacture of food materials within the leaves slows down, and the cells and veins in the leaf become clogged. Chlorophyll production halts, and the green color disappears.

That allows red, yellow, and other tints to emerge. All leaves contain yellow pigments, owing to the presence of carotene and xanthophyll. Some also have red and purple pigments, caused by anthocyanin. Pigments are formed in cell sap that is sugar rich. Sugar maples, oaks, and sumacs have the most brilliant scarlet and purple colors. To develop high color, they must be exposed to intense sunlight—sugar maples that are heavily shaded by larger trees do not become red and show only yellow coloring.

After the leaf has fallen, the separation layer seals and protects the scar where the leaf was attached to the limb. In some oaks, the separation layer doesn't develop fully, and the leaves remain on the tree all winter.

Pennsylvania's hardwood forests offer a bounty of color each autumn. Trees are easily identifiable by color and leaf shape.

Endless Mountains

Road Trail and Double Run Road follow the path of the old horse trail.

By 1900, logging became big business in the area. The loggers left behind hillsides covered in briars, stumps, and tree refuse that were prone to forest fires and flooding. In 1929, the former Department of Forests and Waters began buying the devastated land to create a state forest park. After 1933, the Civilian Conservation Corps (CCC) performed reclamation and construction projects in the park area.

The park still retains its rustic, natural character, though there are facilities for picnicking, a snack bar, and interpretive programs.

One of the most popular features of the park is the Canyon Vista, reached via Mineral Spring and Cold Run Roads, which provides outstanding views of the Endless Mountains region.

Hunting and Fishing: About half of Worlds End State Park is open to hunting, trapping, and the training of dogs during established seasons. Common game species are deer, grouse, squirrel, bear, and turkey. The Department of Conservation and Natural Resources and the Pennsylvania Game Commission rules and regulations apply (www.pgc.state.pa.us).

Loyalsock Creek is stocked with trout each year by the Pennsylvania Fish and Boat Commission (www.fish.state.pa.us). The cold mountain water provides good fishing most of the year.

Swimming: A small dam on Loyalsock Creek forms a swimming area that is open late May–mid-Sept., 8 A.M.–sunset. This is mountain water, so be prepared to be chilly. Lifeguards are on duty from Memorial Day weekend to Labor Day daily 11 A.M. to 7 P.M., unless otherwise posted.

White-Water Boating: White-water boaters may use the Loyalsock Creek at any time of the year although the area by the swimming beach is closed during the summer. The best water is March–May. Because of rapid fluctuations in water level, kayakers should inquire about conditions before coming to the park. The stream is *not* suitable for open canoes.

Winter Activities: Several miles of park roads are used as joint-use snowmobile trails.

Additionally, many trails have been designated on nearby state forest land. A trailhead is established along the Double Run Road to Eagles Mere, a short distance south of the park. Several park areas are suitable for Nordic skiing. A 20-mile trail network is close by on state forest land.

Cabins and Camping: Nineteen rustic cabins are available for rent year-round. Rentals are for one-week periods during the summer and two-night minimum stays in the off-season. Information is available at the park office. Cabins are equipped with a refrigerator, range, fireplace insert, table, chairs, and beds. A central shower building is available and a recycling center is at the entrance to the cabin area.

A 70-site tent and trailer campground is along SR 154, one mile east of the park office. Half of the campsites have electric hookups. Water and restrooms are within a short distance of all sites. Showers are in both loops. A sanitary dumping station is available for emptying travel-trailer holding tanks. Pets are not permitted, and access is not guaranteed in the winter.

To reserve a campsite, cabin, picnic pavilion, or an organized group tenting area, call 888/PA-PARKS (888/727-2757), Mon.–Sat. 7 A.M.–5 P.M.

Elk Mountain Ski Resort

Elk Mountain (SR 374, Union Dale, 570/679-4400 or 800/233-4131, www.elkskier.com, adult $39–45 all day, children 2–12 $29–34 all day) dates from 1959, when it became one of Pennsylvania's first commercial ski areas.

Through the years, the resort began an ambitious expansion program that included reforesting. More than 13,000 trees—most of them Norway spruce—have been planted since the mid '80s. Now one of the premier ski areas in Pennsylvania, Elk Mountain boasts a 4,000-foot quad lift among several others, snowmaking capability, night skiing, a ski school for children and adults, and 27 slopes and trails with great variety. Its runs are considered the most challenging terrain in Pennsylvania.

Union Dale is north of Scranton on I-81; take the SR 374 east turnoff.

ACCOMMODATIONS AND FOOD

Stone Bridge Inn & Restaurant (R.R. 2, Box 3112, Union Dale, PA 18470, inn 570/679-9200, restaurant 570/679-9500, www.elkmtnarea .com), an updated Swiss mountain–style inn with high beams and warm-toned wood, was constructed in 1979. It's surrounded by 200 acres of woodlands and rolling pastures traced with hiking and ungroomed cross-country ski trails. The inn and restaurant are open year-round; modern, comfortable rooms with private bath run $75–130 depending on season and day.

The restaurant (Wed.–Thurs. 5 P.M.–9 P.M.; Fri.–Sun. 5 P.M.–10 P.M.; average price $22) serves specialties such as herb-roasted rack of lamb with grilled Romano polenta ($25) and roasted duck with roasted beets, sweet potatoes, and a ginger apricot glaze ($19). The candle-lit dining area provides a spectacular view of the surrounding countryside and Elk Mountain. Cocktails and dining are also available on the patio during the summer. The inn's tavern (Wed.–Sun. 4 P.M.– closing) offers a full bar, including a variety of beers, and a tavern menu. Most weekends feature musical entertainment.

The Weeping Willow Inn (308 N. Eaton Rd., Tunkhannock, PA 18657, 570/836-7257, $85–95) offers a true respite, far from the madding crowd. Three rooms with private bath are comfortably decorated in this 1840s farmhouse, and the surrounding countryside offers some of the prettiest views in the Endless Mountains. The innkeepers, Patty and Randy Ehrenzeller, can steer you to several good places to eat. Tunkhannock is an interesting little town—it's attracted a number of New Age devotees of alternative healing along with more typical outdoor sportspeople and hunters.

INFORMATION

The place to find out about the many hidden charms of this area is the **Endless Mountains Tourism Bureau** (712 US 6, East Tunkhannock, PA 18657, 570/836-5431 or 800/769-8999, www.endlessmountains.org).

The High Road/Tioga County

Wellsboro, the central town in Tioga County, could have been Main Street in any movie from the 1950s. This pleasant little town provides many of the more sophisticated amenities for visitors who have come to enjoy the wild beauty of north-central Pennsylvania.

SCENIC SPOTS

Ⓜ The Grand Canyon of Pennsylvania

This surprising geological site (information: Department of Environmental Resources/ Pennsylvania Grand Canyon, 4797 SR 660, Wellsboro, PA 16901-8970, 570/724-3061), set in the spectacular Pine Creek Gorge, was created by ancient Pine Creek. Before glaciers covered the area in the last ice age, the headwaters of Pine Creek, near Ansonia, flowed northeast. As the glacier that sheeted the area began to recede, it left a dam of gravel, sand, and clay that blocked the flow of the creek. The dam forced Pine Creek to reverse its flow to the south, and its reversed flow carved out the canyon, which is designated a National Natural Landmark by the U.S. Park Service. The Grand Canyon is 50 miles long and 1,000 feet deep.

OUTDOOR RECREATION

Covered Wagon Rides

The Mountain Trail Horse Center, 570/376-5561, offers a tour of the canyon by covered wagon. Storm's Horse Drawn Rides, north of Wellsboro (570/376-3481), takes visitors on rides over the nearby mountains and valleys (24-hour notice is required).

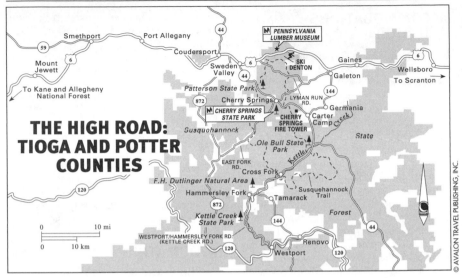

© AVALON TRAVEL PUBLISHING, INC.

THE HIGH ROAD: TIOGA AND POTTER COUNTIES

Fishing

Tioga County boasts five lakes and 40 major streams for every species of warm- and cold-water fish. Fifteen of the streams are stocked. Contact the Tioga County Tourist Visitors Bureau (570/724-0635 or 888/846-4228), for a special brochure with types of fish, locations, and legal seasons for anglers.

Cowanesque Lake and Hammond Lake offer warm-water fishing, boating, and water-skiing. Tioga Lake is open to boaters and water-skiers. Slate Run and Francis Branch Tributary to Slate Run are restricted to fly-fishing. Cedar Run is a trophy trout–fishing area; Hills Creek Lake offers warm-water fishing and restricts powerboats to those with electric motors.

Horseback Riding

Several companies offer trail rides. The Mountain Trail Horse Center (570/376-5561) and Tioga Trail Rides (570/724-6592, www .pavisnet.com) both offer a variety of durations and destinations.

Rafting and Canoeing

Rafting Pine Creek is an exciting and scenic adventure for the whole family. On an average year,

best rafting is in the spring through midsummer. By fall, the water is lower, but still high enough to run.

Chuck Dillon, author of several books on the Pine Creek Gorge and an expert on local flora and fauna, also owns and runs Pine Creek Outfitters, the premier rafting company in the area; he leads many trips himself. Wetsuits and other necessaries are available for rental, as are kayaks and rubber floatboats ("duckies") for those who wish to go it alone. Guided trips start at 8 A.M. Daylong and longer trips are available. Pine Creek Outfitters (570/724-3003, www.pinecrk .com) is on US 6, close to and across from the Coach Stop Inn. Call for a copy of its "Outdoor Adventure Guide," which has lots of information on activities in the region. Pine Creek Outfitters is open daily year-round, with longer hours in the spring.

Snowmobiling

The area has more than 550 miles of joint-use roads, more than 100 miles of snowmobile-only roads, plus private snowmobile club roads and township roads. For a free list and partial map of north-central snowmobile and ATV trails, contact DER, Snowmobile Unit (P.O. Box 1467, Harrisburg, PA 17120). For a schedule of events and information on rentals, contact the Potter County Snowmobile Association (P.O. Box 82, Coudersport, PA 16915, 814/274-7372).

Downhill Skiing

Ski Sawmill Mountain Resort (on the south side of Grego Road, 570/353-7521 or 800/532-7669, www.skisawmill.com) is close to the Oregon Hill Winery in Morris and offers alpine skiing during the winter. During ski season, the resort is open Mon. 10 A.M. –9 P.M., Tue.–Thurs. 1 P.M.–9 P.M., Fri. –Sat. 9 A.M.–10 P.M., and Sun. 9 A.M.–5 P.M. Ski season begins when the temperature drops below 32°F—Sawmill has 100 percent snowmaking capacity. Ski Sawmill Mountain Resort was noted as being "tops in skiing value" by *Snow Country* magazine. Its longest run is more than 3,000 feet, and snowboarders have their own park and runs. Lessons are available for all ages, and package deals are frequently offered. Sawmill has two T-bars, a double chairlift, and a cafeteria. A motel and bunkhouse opened in 2004.

Leonard Harrison and Colton Point State Parks

Leonard Harrison State Park and Colton Point State Park perch on opposing sides of Pine Creek Gorge, and both have hiking trails and dramatic vistas, though Leonard Harrison is slightly easier to get to, particularly in a larger vehicle. Hiking trails are accessible at the end of SR 660 (Leonard Harrison State Park) or Colton Point Road (Colton Point State Park). The parks are on the east and west sides of the canyon, respectively. The area is spectacular year-round, and a rails-to-trails hike/bike path is being extended along the valley floor.

Hiking: The Turkey Path Trail descends one mile to the bottom of Pine Creek Gorge from either Harrison or Colton Point Parks; if the water is low, it's possible to continue to the other side. On the Harrison Park side, a side trial continues to a scenic waterfall, about .75 mile. The Harrison Park Overlook Trail is a .6-mile loop with a southern-facing vista. The trails are rugged but lined with rails.

Camping: Leonard Harrison State Park offers 30 sites for tents or trailers, and Colton offers an additional 25 sites. Both are open mid-April–late Oct. For maps and reservations, contact Leonard Harrison State Park, R.R. 6, Box 199, Wellsboro, PA 16901-8970, 570/724-3061.

ACCOMMODATIONS

$50–100

The Coach Stop Inn (on the north side of US 6, 1.7 miles west of the intersection of US 6 and SR 362, 570/724-5361 or 800/829-4130, www.pavisnet.com), is a former stagecoach stop in service since 1832. Nestled in the heart of Grand Canyon country, the inn is open year-round, has direct access to groomed snowmobile trails, and is a popular meeting place for snowmobilers and river-runners. There are two facilities, the inn itself and a motel. Each of the rooms has a private bath, and the larger rooms

© JOANNE MILLER

Endless Mountains

the Grand Canyon of Pennsylvania

OF HUNTING AND HUNTERS

Hunting—for waterfowl, deer, wild turkey, and bear, using either firearms or hand-drawn bows—is one of north-central Pennsylvania's most popular pastimes. Many youngsters are initiated into hunting by their elders as a rite of passage. Some hunters don't hunt for meat for themselves—a large percentage of the venison that is harvested each year winds up on the dining tables of feeding programs and institutions such as orphanages. Other game, especially bear, is taxidermied into trophies. Different hunters offer different insights into an activity that consumes a large segment of the overwhelmingly but not exclusively male population of Pennsylvania year after year.

The rationales for hunting range from male bonding to Daniel Boone scenarios. No one seems to feel (or will admit to feeling) superiority at besting an inferior opponent; genuine respect for the prey does seem to be the norm. One hunter who lives on a ranch on the outskirts of the Allegheny Forest enjoys the challenge of the hunt. For him, a significant part of the ritual is the research—not only into firearms and their capabilities, but also into the habits of his prey, tracking techniques, and woodsmanship.

A dairy farmer from south of Lancaster joins the same group of buddies every year in their turkey cabin. They spend the night before the hunt absorbing alcohol and dealing hand after hand of poker. They end the evening by promising each other how early they intend to get up to lie in wait for the gobblers, who are notoriously difficult prey. "Every year," he says, "we get up later and later."

Hunting's impact on wild populations in Pennsylvania is controlled through limitations on available hunting areas, seasons, and licensing. Under criticism by some conservationists, hunters are quick to point out that, of the excise taxes on sporting arms and ammunition, handguns, and archery equipment—well over $20 million a year—70 percent is allocated to wildlife preservation projects and hunter education programs. The money from hunting licenses is used to carry out various state programs of wildlife research, habitat acquisition, and restoration.

Since many of the state forests permit hunting, hikers may experience anxiety about accidental injury. All public areas (camping sites, boat launches, etc.) are off-limits to hunters. Hunting seasons (which vary each year) are restricted to the colder months—roughly late Sept.–mid-May. Though becoming an accidental target during these seasons is rare, hikers and snowmobilers can be extra careful by wearing red or neon orange. Also, keep a watchful eye on your dogs, as hunters do.

will accommodate up to five. The units are simply and functionally furnished. Inn rates are $55–63; the newer motel is slightly higher at $65–75. A swimming pool is available for guests. The lower floor of the inn is a restaurant and bar with daily specials and a children's menu.

$150–200

La Petite Auberge, a beautiful bed-and-breakfast (3 Charles St., Wellsboro, 570/724-3288, www.nellesinns.com), is on the gas-lit street that runs through the center of town. Built in 1903 as a wedding present and completely renovated by an artist and her husband in 1998, the five tastefully decorated guest rooms and great room make for a pleasant stay. All of the rooms have a private bath. Rates are $155 per night.

FOOD

A staple for breakfast, lunch, and dinner is the **Laurel Café** (299 Tioga St., Wellsboro, 570/723-2233, daily 6 A.M.–9 P.M.). Start your day with waffles and freshly ground coffee, or stop in for a burger and salad. Prices range from under $5 to around $10.

Early morning cravings may be met at the **Wellsboro Diner** (19 Main St., Wellsboro, 570/724-3992, Mon.–Sat. 6:30 A.M.–8 P.M., Sun. 7 A.M.–8 P.M.; $3–12).

The ☒ **Coach Stop Inn Restaurant** (on the north side of US 6, 1.7 miles west of the intersection of US 6 and SR 362, 570/724-5361) has been serving platters of all-American favorites such as surf and turf and stuffed flounder since the 1800s. It's open in summer Mon.–Thurs. 3 P.M.–8 P.M., Fri.–Sat. 11 A.M.–10 P.M. and Sun. 11 A.M.–8 P.M. In winter, it's closed Tues. There's a specially priced all-you-can-eat Sun. buffet 11 A.M.–8 P.M. Prices average $6 for lunch, $12 for dinner. The inn attracts a diverse crowd local farmers, truck drivers, families, and outdoor types in the area for the rafting, snowmobiling, and hiking.

One of the most popular eateries in town, the ☒ **Steak House** (29 Main St., Wellsboro, 570/724-9092, Mon.–Sat. 5–9 P.M.) is famous for its generous portions of porterhouse steak and pork chops. It also serves poultry and seafood. Reservations are recommended, and dinners average $20.

INFORMATION

Tioga County Visitors Bureau (570/724-0635 or 888/846-4228, www.visittiogapa.com) has information on Wellsboro and the Pennsylvania Grand Canyon.

The High Road/Potter County

In Potter County, the road passes through towns and villages that fulfill their original purpose, as a meeting place for far-flung landowners and occasional visitors. The area offers a wide variety of year-round recreational opportunities—fishing, hiking, skiing, boating, and more—among Pennsylvania's unspoiled forests. A museum, set in an old lumber camp, offers insight into the history of the region.

MUSEUMS
☒ **Pennsylvania Lumber Museum**
Before the 1920s, before clear-cutting devastated the industry, Pennsylvania produced the major part of white pine and hemlock lumber used to build homes and furniture in the expanding United States. The Pennsylvania Lumber Museum (on the north side of US 6, 3.5 miles west of the intersection of US 6 and SR 449, Galeton, Potter County, 814/435-2652, www.lumbermuseum.org), chronicles the lives of "woodhicks" (lumbermen) in a typical lumber camp; the restored buildings are the originals, and you can almost smell the sawdust. The museum is open April–Nov., daily 9 A.M.–5 P.M., and closed Dec.–March. Admission is $4 for adults, $2 for kids, and $3.50 for seniors.

On the peaceful grounds, a bunkhouse, kitchen and dining hall, timekeeper's office, carpenter shop, blacksmith and sawfiler shop, and

stable and tack room share space. The kitchen has a giant coffeepot on the stove that still looks ready to pour for the men who once took their seats at the long plank table. A walk-through coal-powered Shay logging train engine and sawmill further illuminate the lives of these hardworking laborers of the past. The reconstruction of the logging camp is accurate right down to the rough lumber boardwalk between the buildings to keep men and supplies out of the mud and the mud out of the kitchen.

OUTDOOR RECREATION
Fishing and Boating
In Potter County, Lyman Run and Cross Fork Creek offer fly-fishing only. Lyman Run Lake features trout fishing, but powerboats are restricted to electric engines. Kettle Creek is a catch-and-release artificial lure area, and the first fork of Sinnemahoning Creek permits delayed-harvest artificial lures only.

Ski Denton
One of the few downhill ski facilities in the area, Ski Denton (south side of US 6, 3.5 miles west of the intersection of US 6 and SR 449, Potter County, 814/435-2115) is across from the Pennsylvania Lumber Museum. Denton has a Ski-Wee training program for kids and an adult ski

Endless Mountains

outside the village of Port Allegany along US 6

and white pine was cut and the stumps burned, a new forest of trees that needed more light, such as cherry and ash, grew to take its place. The forest continues to be logged on a sustained-yield basis by the state and is managed not only for the timber products it produces, but also for watershed protection, wildlife conservation, aesthetics, and recreation. The forest encompasses several state parks. For more information about the forest, contact the Susquehannock State Forest, District Forester (P.O. Box 673, Coudersport, Potter County, PA 16915, 814/274-3600, state.pa.us), or stop by the district office headquarters, Denton Hill summit on US 6.

Scenic Drive: The western section of the Coudersport-Jersey Shore Pike, SR 44, bisects the forest and passes several dramatic views of the forest and rivers. At the village of Sweden Valley, about six miles east of Coudersport, SR 44 turns south. It passes the Cherry Springs fire tower before intersecting with SR 144/44 at Carter Camp. Turn north on SR 144 to return to US 6 at Galeton.

ATV/Snowmobile Trail: A 35-mile ATV loop, popular with anglers in the warm months, becomes a hot spot for snowmobilers in winter. For a detailed map with access points, contact the state forest.

Hiking: The state forest links together a series of shorter, older trails to form the Susquehannock Trail System, an 89-mile loop for the exclusive use of foot travelers. Most of the trail is flat and well marked, with only a few steep grades. Shorter trails of varying difficulty are accessible from the Susquehannock Trail. The district office on US 6, at the summit of Denton Hill, is the main trail entry point. Others are: forest headquarters on Lyman Run Road; SR 44 near Cherry Springs fire tower or the entrance to Patterson State Park; forest headquarters on SR 144; and East Fork Road, one mile south of the end of the paved road. A long section of the trail passes through the Hammersley Area, a primitive forest that was once the scene of a busy logging industry with railroad grades, logging camps, and a small town. Few traces of the former industry remain.

The F. H. Dutlinger Natural Area, accessible by the Trout Run Ridge Trail or Nelson Hollow

school ("Learn to ski or your money back"). All alpine skiers and snowboarders are welcome, and the resort has 90 percent snowmaking capability. Though the run is shorter than in western ski resorts, night skiing and the extreme drops (the steepest on the eastern seaboard) make it challenging. Two pomalifts, a double chair, triple chair, and handle tow are provided. During the cold months, Ski Denton is open weekends and holidays 9 A.M.–9 P.M.; Mon., Wed., and Fri. 10 A.M.–9 P.M.; Tues. and Thurs. 1–9 P.M. Prices vary, but an all-day pass on weekdays is $20 for adults, $14 for youth; an all-day pass on weekends and holidays is $30 for adults, $20 for youth. Half-day prices are available.

Susquehannock State Forest

The forest, named for the Susquehannock (sus-ka-HAH-nuck) Indians who once claimed the entire region, covers 262,000 acres in McKean, Potter, and Clinton Counties. The original forest was logged during a 40-year period beginning in the 1800s. As the older, dense growth of hemlock

Trail, both off SR 144 between one and two miles north of Hammersley Fork, contains old growth hemlock trees, three to four feet in diameter, which were never logged. The two trails intersect, creating a four-mile loop from the highway. Detailed maps of the Susquehannock Trail are available from Potter County Visitors Association (P.O. Box 245, Coudersport, PA 16915, 888/768-8372, www.pottercountypa.org).

Hunting and Fishing: In-season hunting and fishing are permitted throughout the state forest with the exception of the designated natural areas. The park is surrounded by more than a dozen state game lands.

Cherry Springs State Park

Cherry Springs is 15 miles southeast of Coudersport, Potter County, on SR 44. The park is deep in the midst of the Susquehannock State Forest, 11 miles south of the US 6/SR 44 junction at Sweden Valley. For more information on the park, call 814/435-5010 or 888/PA-PARKS (888/727-2757).

This is a "dark park"—a site that attracts stargazers from all over because of the almost total lack of light from surrounding towns. The local area is dominated by farmland and vast tracts of state forest, so there are very few sources of light pollution. Cherry Springs is also far enough inland from Lakes Erie and Ontario to escape most lake-effect cloud-cover events. On any given dark-of-moon weekend you'll almost certainly find dozens of amateur astronomers enjoying the velvet black skies. The park's facilities include fresh cold-water taps (spring through fall), a primitive camping area with picnic tables and fire rings, a large picnic shelter, well-cared-for pit toilets (no showers) with red lighting, and an approximately 300-foot by 600-foot open observing field. Camping fees for Pennsylvania residents are $10 Sun.–Thurs. and $12 Fri.–Sat.; for non-Pennsylvania residents fees are $12 Sun.–Thurs. and $14 Fri.–Sat.

Ole Bull State Park

Ole (OH-lay) Bull State Park is another area nicknamed "the Black Forest" because of its dense tree cover. The park is surrounded by the Susquehannock State Forest (Potter County) and is divided by Kettle Creek, which runs through the center.

WOODHICKS

Around 1900, two of the largest sawmills in the world were at opposite ends of the Susquehannock State Forest—at Austin and Galeton. Fortunes were made from the hemlock and pines that grew on the hillsides of the northern Appalachian Mountains; Frank and Charles Goodyear, John DuBois, and Elisha Kane all became millionaires on sawdust and sap.

The migrant workers who came to cut and process trees here were called woodhicks. Their work season extended from early spring until late winter and stopped only for heavy rain or deep snow. Crudely constructed logging camps were set up near each new work site. Camp conditions were primitive, often without any bathing facilities, and cursed with an abundance of fleas and lice. Food was hearty, however, since it was meant to fortify each man for a day's worth of heavy labor: hot biscuits, steak, eggs, fried potatoes, oatmeal, cake, doughnuts, prunes or other fruit, and coffee.

The average camp crew consisted of 60 men. A woodhick's day began at 5 A.M. and ended at 9 P.M. with a strictly enforced lights out. Each camp was maintained and disciplined by a foreman, who was responsible for the production and morale of the men.

Before 1910, a work week of six 11-hour workdays was common. However, board and lodging were free, and, depending on the job, earnings ranged $1.50–3 a day. A few months in a logging camp was considered an adventure for a young man and a good way to make money (with little temptation to spend it). The industry didn't see eight-hour days or five-day weeks until 1920, when little was left of the old-growth forest but memories.

Named after Ole Bornemann Bull, a popular Norwegian violinist and composer who toured the United States in the 1850s, the park was the original site of New Norway. Bull, a patriot who chafed under Swedish rule, sought to revitalize the arts in his native country and was the founder of the National Theater at Bergen. He was aided by playwright and stage manager Henrik Ibsen (Ibsen's character Peer Gynt was thought to be modeled on Bull). When the theater failed, Bull set his sights on the New World.

Entranced with America—and especially north-central Pennsylvania—Bull returned to the area, bringing "thirty stalwart sons of Norway" with him; he attempted to settle a colony on the hilltop behind the present park office. After a year of hardship, the colony disbanded and those who remained in America moved west to Michigan and Wisconsin. Just as Bull was returning to Norway, the lumber industry was on the verge of a boom. Lumber companies logged much of the surrounding forests during the next 30 years. New Norway and surrounding park lands were purchased by the state from the lumber companies after their usefulness faded, and they were modernized and improved by the Civilian Conservation Corps (CCC) during the Great Depression.

Hiking: The 89-mile-long Susquehannock Trail passes through the park, becoming the Ole Bull Trail for a short time. The Ole Bull Trail threads its way into the northern part of Ole Bull park, with a short side trail to reach the site of Bull's original home, the castle, with its valley vista. Ole Bull Trail links with the Daugherty Loop Trail, following the old logging and railroad grades to form a two-hour walk into the darkest part of the forest; the trail circles back to its origin. The Beaver Haven Nature Trail is the shortest trail. All are accessible from the visitors' center. Maps are available by contacting Ole Bull State Park (HCR 62, Box 9, Cross Fork, PA 17729, 814/435-5000).

Hunting and Fishing: Most of the park is closed to hunting and trapping, with the exception of 25 acres. Trout fishing is popular along Kettle Creek, and there's a special children's area near the dam.

Swimming: A guarded 150-foot sand beach, in campground area No. 1, is open during the summer 8 A.M.–sunset.

Winter Sports: Snowmobiles are restricted to the access trail only, and ATVs are not permitted. Cross-country skiing and snowshoeing are allowed throughout the park.

Camping: Eighty-one tent and trailer campsites are available early April–Dec. Most sites are primitive, though there are 20 sites with electric hookups. There is one modern cabin, a split-level log structure that sleeps 10 and is open year-round. Make reservations by calling 888/PA-PARKS (888/727-2757).

Getting There: Bull Park is directly south of Denton Hill and the Susquehannock State Forest main offices. Take either SR 44 (approximately 55 miles) or SR 144 (approximately 25 miles) south from US 6.

ACCOMMODATIONS AND FOOD

The barn-red one- and two-bedroom cottages of the **Nine Mile Motel** (on US 6, just over two miles west of the intersection of US 6 and SR 449, Potter County, 814/435-2394, $53) overlook a small pond and are less than five minutes from Susquehannock State Forest and the Lumber Museum. The cottages sleep one to six people, and each has simple decor and a unique personality. The motel is open mid-April–mid-Dec. and offers special rates for longer stays.

Potato City Country Inn, a combination motel/restaurant/lounge (US 6 between Galeton and Coudersport, Coudersport, Potter County, 814/274-7133, www.potatocityinn.com, $60), was originally built to house meetings and other functions related to the flourishing potato industry in northern Potter County. Local resident Dr. E. L. Nixon, former president Richard Nixon's uncle, is credited with breeding and developing potato hybrids that still thrive in the area. Potato City Country Inn continues to be "the hub of Potter County for hungry, thirsty, sleepy people."

The **Ox Yoke Family Inn** (29 US 6 W, Galeton, Potter County, 814/435-2515, www .ox-yokeinn.com, $40) is a clean, comfortable motel. Forty rooms are equipped with air conditioning for the summer, and baseboard heat for the fall and winter. All rooms have cable and color television. Ski and snowmobile packages are available for the winter. Ox Yoke also features a campground on Pine Creek, with 25 permanent camper sites, four tent sites, and two visitor camper/RV sites. All camper sites have water, sewer, and electric. Cable television is available for an extra charge upon request.

The **Ox Yoke Family Restaurant** on the premises features a full menu in a very casual family dining atmosphere (lots of hunters and snowmobilers stay here). The restaurant has homemade breakfast, lunch, and dinner specials, as well as a soup and salad bar, open daily 7 A.M.–9 P.M. The prices are extremely reasonable: $3 for breakfast, up to $12 for dinner. There's also a full bar.

Private Cabins at Ski Denton

There are five cabin chalets situated conveniently on the Ski Denton grounds. Each cabin has wall-to-wall carpeting, two bedrooms (sleeps six), and a generous living room with cathedral ceiling. Every cabin includes a full kitchen and dining area, bath, and electric heat. Call 814/435 2115 for rates and availability, or email skidentn @penn.com.

INFORMATION

Potter County Visitors Association (888/768-8372, www.pottercountypa.org) and **Tioga County Visitors Bureau** (570/724-0635 or 888/846-4228, www.visittriogapa.com) both provide information on the area. Another resource is **Northern Alleghenies Vacation Region** (814/726-1222 or 800/624-7802, www .northernalleghenies.com).

Lycoming and Clinton Counties

In Lycoming County, Williamsport, a compact city with slightly more than 32,000 residents, lies along a 14-mile stretch of the West Branch of the Susquehanna River in the foothills of the Alleghenies. Once a lumber boomtown (as evidenced by the Victorian mansions in various states of repair and disrepair on Millionaire's Row, downtown), Williamsport has continued to hold its own in a changing world.

Williamsport is the home to the Little League Baseball Museum and the annual Little League World Series. The Lycoming County Historical Museum is a must-see for history buffs, and a picnic ride down the Susquehanna on the paddlewheeler *Hiawatha* makes for a pleasant afternoon.

Thanks to the local Amish, the horse and buggy remains a common form of transportation in rural Clinton County. This area features one of Pennsylvania's most popular events, the Flaming Foliage Festival.

SCENIC TOURS

M Sugar Valley Loop

Sugar Valley is a small community named for the many sugar maple trees growing there, a few miles off I-80 in Clinton County. Places of interest include a gristmill built in the 1800s, a covered bridge, a one-room schoolhouse, and a privately owned log cabin. A number of old churches and graveyards are in the valley, some with tombstones dating to 1806. The route is approximately 25 miles long, suitable for driving and for bicyclists in good shape.

Take Exit 185 off I-80 and head south on SR 477 toward Loganton. You'll pass a sulfur spring and picnic area. Loganton was named for James Logan, an Iroquois chief who lived in the area until his death in 1780. Pass through Loganton, turn right (west) on the Carroll/Tylersville Road toward Greenburr (the Carroll/Tylersville Road is

Endless Mountains

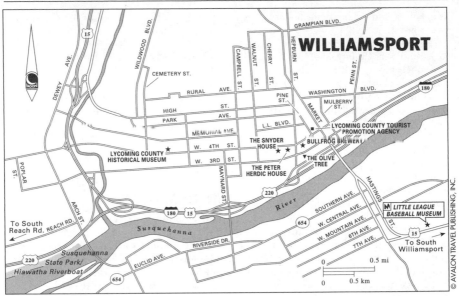

also confusingly labeled SR 477 from here to Tylersville, though SR 477 also makes a jog south). Look for the left (south) continuation of SR 477. Follow it and you'll see the Bull Run School and Lamey Log House (private) within a few miles.

Bull Run School was built in 1899 and contains all its original equipment, including double desks, schoolmaster's desk, recitation bench, and a Waterbury clock. Because of numerous absences caused by the agricultural demands of local farmers, it wasn't unusual for pupils to repeat grades several times. The school served between 10 and 52 pupils a year before it was closed in 1955.

Return to the Carroll/Tylersville Road/SR 477 and continue west. Pass through Greenburr to LR 18026. Turn right (north) on Local Road 18026, go through a 45-foot covered bridge and see the gristmill, which produced flour for the state prison system in the 1840s. This small road dead-ends on SR 880. Turn right (east) to return to Loganton.

OTHER POINTS OF INTEREST

The Hiawatha Riverboat

The *Hiawatha* is a replica of the paddlewheel riverboats of a bygone era that plied trade and passengers up and down the Susquehanna River. The riverboat (Reach Rd., Williamsport, 570/326-2500 or 800/248-9287, ridehiawatha .com) operates May–Oct. In May, Sept., and Oct., trips are scheduled Sat.–Sun. at 1 P.M., 2:30 P.M., and 4 P.M. In June, July, and Aug., you can ride Tues.–Sat. at 11:30 A.M., 1 P.M., 2:30 P.M., and 4 P.M.; Sun. 1 P.M., 2:30 P.M., and 4 P.M. Admission is $7.50 adults, $6.50 seniors, $3.50 kids, with discounts on family night. The cool breeze that comes off the sparkling river is a welcome treat in the warm months. In June, July, and Aug., family cruises are offered Tues. at 6 P.M.—plan a picnic on the river and see the lights of Williamsport the way visitors did a hundred years before. The boat is moored at Susquehanna State Park, on the south bank of the Susquehanna River, off Arch Street just before the bridge crosses the river (take the Reach Road exit off US 15).

Williamsport Trolley

In the mid-1800s, Williamsport was known as the Lumber Capital of the world and a city of millionaires. These millionaires provided the funds and impetus for Williamsport's first form of public transportation—the streetcar. In 1863,

The *Hiawatha* picks up passengers.

the Williamsport Passenger Railway Company was created; the first streetcars were horse-drawn and equipped with a small stove to keep passengers warm in the winter. Electric streetcars were introduced to Williamsport in 1891, one year before those in Philadelphia. They operated in the city until June 11, 1933, when the last trolley rolled to a halt.

Today, Williamsport City Bus re-creates that era with the Peter Herdic, Anne Weightman, and Carl Stotz Trolley Tours of the sights of the city. The Historic Trolley Tour, complete with taped narration, rides through Williamsport's areas of interest, including Millionaire's Row. Other highlights of the tour include Memorial Park, where the first Little League baseball game was played, and Brandon Park, whose entrance is guarded by the magnificent tree sculpture of Chief Waopalanee.

Tickets for the Williamsport Trolley Tour may be purchased from the trolley driver or at the Hiawatha House, Susquehanna State Park, Tues., Thurs., and Sat. beginning at 10:30 A.M. Tickets may also be purchased one day in advance at City Bus between 9 A.M. and 5 P.M.

Passengers may start the trip at any of the three Trolley stops: 3rd Street Parking Garage across from the Trade and Transit Centre in downtown Williamsport; Lycoming County Historical Museum; or Susquehanna State Park/ Hiawatha Riverboat. One fare allows passengers to get on and off once at each trolley stop during that particular day. Call City Bus (570/326-2500 or 800/248-9287) for rates, dates, and other information.

Clyde Peeling's Reptiland

Reptiland (US 15, 15 miles south of Williamsport in Allenwood, 570/538-1869, www .reptiland.com) is a tropical garden filled with tortoises, lizards, and crocodiles. It's open Memorial Day–Labor Day 9 A.M.–7 P.M.; April–May and Sept.–Oct. 10 A.M.–6 P.M.; Nov.–March 10 A.M.–5 P.M. Admission is $9 for adults and $7 for kids 4–11.

Cobras, giant pythons, boas, and vipers are displayed behind glass, and several shows daily give visitors an opportunity to interact with the scaly residents. This is the original Reptiland, built in 1964 (the other is in New York state).

Endless Mountains

MUSEUMS

ℳ Little League Baseball Museum

Williamsport is the original home of little league ball, and the annual Little League World Series is played here in August; highlights from past series are captured on videotape in the museum (US 15, Williamsport, 570/326-3607). It's open Memorial Day–Sept. 30, Mon.–Sat. 10 A.M.–7 P.M., Sun. noon–7 P.M. During the rest of the year, it's open Mon., Thurs., and Fri. 10 A.M.–5 P.M., Sat. noon–5 P.M., and Sun. noon–4 P.M. Admission is $5.

A popular feature are the bat and pitch cages where players (mom and dad, too) can check out their style and speed on video replay. There's also a "message" room about the dangers of drugs and alcohol, and a Little League Hall of Excellence (actor/director Kevin Costner was an inductee). Trophies and equipment related to the game are also on display. The museum is on US 15 (take the Little League Museum turnoff), 15 miles north of the intersection of US 15 and I-80 in South Williamsport.

Lycoming County Historical Museum

Besides having one of the best displays of model trains in the world, this museum (858 W. 4th St., Williamsport, 570/326-3326, www .lycoming.org) is an excellent place to learn about northern Pennsylvania from the days of the earliest inhabitants through the Victorian lumber boom to the present. It's open Tues.–Fri. 9:30 A.M.–4 P.M. and Sat. 11 A.M.–4 P.M.; May 1–Oct. 31, it is also open Sun. noon–4 P.M. Admission is $5 adults, $4 seniors, and $2.50 kids. The museum comes with its own ghost story. In one of the period rooms hangs the portrait of a child who died during the painting of the picture; the portrait refused to stay on the wall until it was placed in a special exhibit—a "parlor" similar to that of the child's home. Lycoming County Museum is one of the state's top 10 museums and genealogical/historical research facilities.

Piper Aviation Museum

The Piper Museum (1 Piper Way, Lock Haven Airport, Lock Haven, Clinton County, 570/748-8283, www.pipermuseum.com) displays models, a flight simulator, and a memorabilia collection and photographs that detail the founding and early manufacture of Piper aircraft, including the famous bright yellow J-3. Museum hours are Mon.–Fri. 9 A.M.–4 P.M.; Sat. 10 A.M.–4 P.M.; Sun. noon–4 P.M. Nov.–Feb., the museum is closed on Sun. Admission is $5 for adults, $4 seniors, $1 for kids 12–18.

WHY "JERSEY SHORE"?

Pennsylvania has its fair share of global place names. You can travel to California, Indiana, Washington, and (the) Yukon, as well as Frisco (with apologies to San Franciscans), Palo Alto, and Nashville without leaving the state. If you're in an international mood, there are always Finland and Egypt, and those cosmopolitan destinations Damascus, Moscow, Bethlehem, Nazareth, and Bath. But why Jersey Shore?

Jersey Shore is nowhere near New (or old) Jersey. In fact, it's also hundreds of miles from any ocean. It lies in north-central Pennsylvania, 10 miles west of Williamsport.

The name stems from the town's very beginnings, when two brothers, Reuben and Jeremiah Manning (from New Jersey) bought the property after the treaty of Fort Stanwix in the late 18th century. On the opposite side of the Susquehanna River a rival settlement begun by a family named Stewart. The Manning brothers dubbed their town Waynesville, and so it remained for a short time on the records of the U.S. Post Office Department. However, the Stewarts on the east side of the river referred to Waynesville derisively as "the Jersey shore" because of the Mannings' origin. The Stewarts must have been big talkers with a lot of contacts—by 1826, the settlers of Waynesville gave up and incorporated their borough under the name Jersey Shore. The Stewart colony disappeared in time, but Jersey Shore remains.

The best time to enjoy the museum (and to see dozens of vintage Piper planes in action) is during the annual Sentimental Journey fly-in, which takes place in June.

PENNSYLVANIA STATE FLAMING FOLIAGE FESTIVAL

For two days each year—the second weekend in October—the small town of Renovo celebrates brilliant fall foliage in the area with an annual old-fashioned parade and crafts festival. Once a strictly local event, word has gotten around, and the parade now draws more than 1,000 spectators. The color-splashed trees on SR 120 this time of year are spellbinding. The small-town celebration comes complete with floats containing the high school homecoming queen and her court. The crafts area features lots of festival food. Get into town before 1 P.M. on parade day (Sat.) and don't plan on leaving before 4 P.M. For specifics, contact the city of Lock Haven (20 E. Church St., Lock Haven, PA 17745, 570/893-5900, www.lockhavencity.org) or check upcoming events on the North Central Pennsylvania Portal (www.mywol.net).

SHOPPING

Woolrich Company Store

The store (570/769-7401) is in the attractive factory town of Woolrich, three miles from US 220 between Williamsport and Lock Haven. Men's and women's sportswear, outdoor wear, blankets, and fabrics are featured at discounts of 20 percent or more. It's open Mon.–Thurs. and Sat. 9 A.M.–6 P.M., Fri. 9 A.M.–9 P.M., and Sun. noon–5 P.M.

OUTDOOR RECREATION

Fishing

Little Pine Dam offers trout fishing, and Rose Valley Lake features warm-water fishing; both restrict powerboats to electric motors only. Big Pine Creek is a haven for trout fishermen from the Lycoming County line near Blackwell to Waterville. Canoes and floatboats are also popular on

THE HENRY FORD OF AVIATION

In 1937, William T. Piper, then the head of the aircraft company that would bear his name, built a new company headquarters in an old silk mill in Lock Haven, Pennsylvania. Piper, an oilman by trade, had hired Walter Jamouneau as chief engineer; together they pioneered the bright yellow J-3, one of the first personal aircraft. Popularly known as the "Cub," the J-3 became synonymous with the Piper name. Over the next 47 years, the Piper Aircraft Corporation would build 77,000 airplanes in Lock Haven. The planes were used as trainers in World War II, and Piper modified a series of J-3s for military use. Nearly 6,000 of these specially equipped planes were built for the armed forces, and four out of five American pilots were trained using the modified J-3.

Many WAFs (Women Air Force pilots, also known as WASPs) who flew during the war became licensed pilots at Piper field in Lock Haven; they would then move on to Sweetwater, Texas, to learn other types of military planes. In the 1984 edition of *Aviation Quarterly*, B. Kimball Baker wrote:

These women earned their wings when flying was considered far too dangerous and unladylike for a woman. But for them, the challenge and excitement of flying—those feelings of getting above it all which every pilot knows but few can describe—were magnets too powerful to resist.

Piper introduced the company's first all-metal twin engine airplane, the Apache, in 1954. With the success of that model, Piper Aircraft built a new year-round research and development facility in Florida, and operations in Lock Haven came to a close.

Piper Aircraft and the birth and growth of an industry remain a fond memory at the Piper Aircraft Museum and at the annual Sentimental Journey Fly-in. In 1995, the fly-in hosted more than 40 of America's most courageous World War II pilots and numerous others in "Honoring the WASP."

this stretch of water March–mid-May. Slate Run and Loyalsock Creek permit fly-fishing only.

Trout and warm-water fishing is available at Alvin Bush Dam (nonpowered or electric motors only). Boating and water-skiing are popular on the West Branch of the Susquehanna River in the vicinity of Lock Haven. The West Branch is also suitable for canoe and floatboat trips mid-March–early May; access is at the village of Keating on SR 120. The Right Branch of Young Woman's Creek, 5.5 miles north of Gleasonton on CR 18020 is a good spot for fly-fishing. A trophy trout section is on Fishing Creek from the Tylersville fish hatchery to Fleming Bridge on CR 2004.

Hyner View/Hyner Run State Parks

Hyner View State Park (Clinton County) is worth a drive to the top to see the Susquehanna River Valley spread out below, especially in the autumn. Hyner View was the original site of the Flaming Foliage Festival, now held in the town of Renovo. Hang-glider pilots have made the place legendary—it draws aficionados from all over the eastern states to its dramatic drop. Hyner Run State Park lines Hyner Creek at the base of the view road, offering a swimming pool, playground, and campsites. It's also a popular cross-country skiing area in winter. Contact Hyner Run State Park (P.O. Box 46, Hyner, PA 17738, 570/753-6001) for information.

Hiking: The parking lot at Hyner Run is the site of the eastern trailhead for the 50-mile Donut Hole Trail system, a moderate to rugged backpacking trail. There is also a short interpretive trail accessible through the picnic area.

Swimming: Hyner Run Park features a 3–5-foot-deep Olympic-sized swimming pool open Memorial Day weekend–Labor Day.

Camping: The park provides 30 primitive campsites for tents and trailers. Contact Hyner Run State Park (P.O. Box 46, Hyner, PA 17738, 570/923-6000 or 888/727-2757) for reservations.

Getting There: Both Hyner Run and Hyner View Parks are accessible from either SR 120 or SR 44, both west of Williamsport.

ACCOMMODATIONS

$50–100

Just before the village of North Bend on SR 120, **North Bend Bed and Breakfast** (570/923-2927, www.northbendpa.com, $56) is a casual home away from home for all sorts of guests, from city folks who've come to see the Renovo Flaming Foliage Festival to hunters, hikers, and hang-glider pilots (Hyner View Park is nearby). The bedrooms share baths (with the exception of a travel trailer that serves as an extra room during the warm months). There's a two-day minimum stay for the Flaming Foliage Festival Weekend and during Pennsylvania's bear- and buck-hunting seasons.

In Lock Haven, Clinton County, the **Victorian Inn Bed and Breakfast** (402 E. Water St., 570/748-8688 or 888/653-8688, $65–95) is close to Piper airfield and is open year-round. It provides transportation to the airport and a shuttle to the Woolrich Store and factory outlets.

$100–150

The Bodine House (307 S. Main St., Muncy, 570/546-8949, www.bodinehouse.com) is about a 10-minute drive from I-80 via I-180, in the old Susquehanna River Valley village of Muncy. The clapboard house was built in 1805, has been authentically restored, and is listed on the National Register of Historic Places. Many of the furnishings throughout the house are antiques.

Guests may relax and enjoy the atmosphere of an age when life moved at a slower pace. Take a short walk to the center of Muncy with its shops, movie theater, restaurant, library, and churches, or borrow one of the bed-and-breakfast's bicycles and ride the quiet tree-lined streets flanked by architecture from the last three centuries. All rooms have private baths. Rates, $75–125 (for the carriage house cottage), include a full breakfast.

The Snyder House Victorian Bed and Breakfast (411 W. 4th St., Williamsport, 570/326-0411, $125) is next door to the Peter Herdic Mansion on Millionaire's Row in downtown Williamsport. Five rooms, all with private bath, are authentically decorated in period style, with elegant dark-wood furnishings especially designed for the house when it was built in the 1890s. There's a two-day minimum stay on weekends, and for safety and health reasons, the inn is completely smoke-free.

FOOD

M The Olive Tree (169 W. 3rd St., Williamsport, 570/326-4493, Mon.–Sat. noon–8 P.M.), a little Greek oasis in a vast territory of American food, makes everything fresh on the premises, including the wonderful honey-soaked hazelnut baklava and oatmeal cookies. Prices vary from a baked snack for less than $2 up to $25 for a full meal. Reservations recommended. The menu is widely varied with both traditional Greek dishes and American-style sandwiches and salads. The baked goods alone are worth the trip!

The elegant **M Peter Herdic House** (407 W. 4th St., Williamsport, 570/322-0165) is the showplace of Millionaire's Row, the former street of manor houses belonging to Victorian lumber barons in Williamsport. Dinner is served Tues.–Sat. 5–9 P.M. Expect prices in the $17 range. Though the neighborhood has faded through the years, the Herdic House continues to carry its reputation as a beautifully restored Italianate villa and a fine continental-style dining establishment. Reservations are necessary.

Bullfrog Brewery (231 W. 4th St., 570/326-4700, Mon.–Wed. 11 A.M.–11 P.M., Thurs.–Sat. 11 A.M.–midnight, Sun. 9 A.M.–10 P.M.), the newest hot spot in downtown Williamsport, is an award-winning microbrewery with a tasty variety of brews on tap and pub food at reasonable prices ($10 for lunch and $15 for dinner). The brewery also offers live entertainment, varying from jazz to Celtic music and everything in between on the weekends.

M Restless Oaks Restaurant (US 220, McElhattan, just off the McElhattan/Woolrich exit, 570/769-7385) serves good American food at reasonable prices for breakfast and lunch; the prices go up substantially for dinner, however, when a local pianist comes in to tickle the ivories. Hours are Mon.–Thurs. 6 A.M.–8 P.M., Fri.–Sat. 6 A.M.–9 P.M., Sun. 7 A.M.–8 P.M. Breakfast and lunch average $6, lunch $7, dinner is around $14. A children's menu is available. The grounds of the restaurant offer special interest. Oaks that have died on the property have been carved by local artists into fanciful animals such as bears, eagles, and mountain lions.

INFORMATION

For information on Williamsport and vicinity, contact the **Lycoming County Tourist Promotion Agency** 848 W. 4th St., Williamsport, PA 17701, 800/358-9900, http://williamsport-pa.com) or **Valleys of the Susquehanna** (210 William St., Williamsport, PA 17701, 877/507-3570, www.pavalleys.com). In Clinton County, try the **Clinton County Economic Partnership** (212 N. Jay St., Lock Haven, PA 17745, 570/748-5782, www.clintoncountyinfo.com). For upcoming events, check the North Central Pennsylvania Portal (www.mywol.net).

State College and Centre County

The town of State College has grown up around the original site of the Farmer's High School (now called University Park) established by Irwin's land grant in 1855. Now greatly expanded, Penn State (officially The Pennsylvania State University, with its main campus at University Park) now enrolls more than 80,000 students at 24 campuses statewide, of which 40,000 are at University Park. It is also home to the wildly popular Nittany Lions football team. For more information, visit Penn State's website at www.psu.edu.

State College itself is a textbook example of the perfect college town: clean, tree-shaded streets lined with sophisticated shops and restaurants that cater to students, professors, and visitors from all over the world. The small towns and hill country that surround State College offer a number of unusual attractions and recreational opportunities.

Boalsburg remains a quaint village with an historic tavern; Bellefonte retains its turn-of-the-20th-century splendor, and homeowners and businesses alike cooperate to maintain its rich appearance. During the Christmas season, all schools, churches, civic and service organizations, cultural groups, and government agencies work together to make the town sparkle with authentic Victoriana. During the summer, Bellefonte hosts its own art festival. Close to State College and other sights in the central region, Bellefonte remains a lovely destination for a stroll through history.

HISTORIC SIGHTS

Curtin Village and the Eagle Ironworks

Visitors who are curious about the lives of ironworkers and the technology involved in early

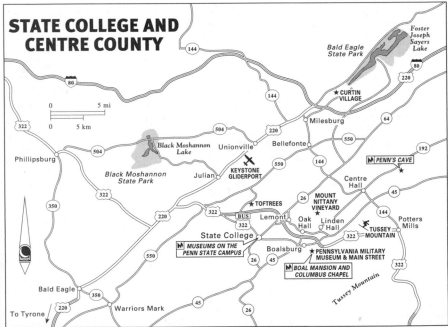

STATE COLLEGE AND CENTRE COUNTY

© AVALON TRAVEL PUBLISHING, INC.

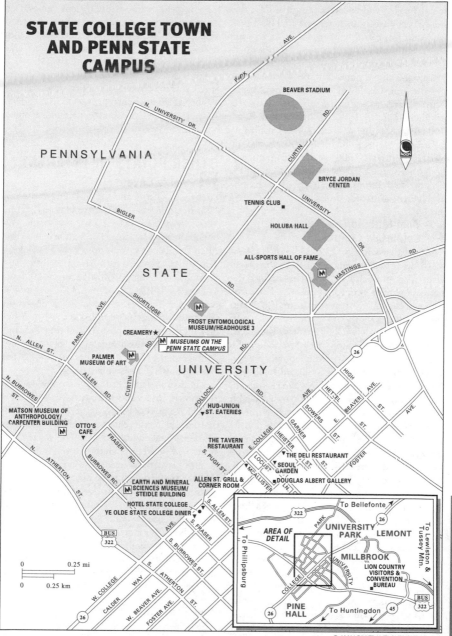

STATE COLLEGE TOWN AND PENN STATE CAMPUS

PENNSYLVANIA

STATE

UNIVERSITY

BEAVER STADIUM

N. UNIVERSITY DR.

BRYCE JORDAN CENTER

TENNIS CLUB

HOLUBA HALL

ALL-SPORTS HALL OF FAME

HASTINGS

SHORTLIDGE

FROST ENTOMOLOGICAL MUSEUM/HEADHOUSE 3

CREAMERY ★

MUSEUMS ON THE PENN STATE CAMPUS

PALMER MUSEUM OF ART

N. ALLEN ST.

MATSON MUSEUM OF ANTHROPOLOGY/ CARPENTER BUILDING

OTTO'S CAFE

HUD-UNION ST. EATERIES

THE TAVERN RESTAURANT

THE DELI RESTAURANT

SEOUL GARDEN

EARTH AND MINERAL SCIENCES MUSEUM/ STEIDLE BUILDING

ALLEN ST. GRILL & CORNER ROOM

DOUGLAS ALBERT GALLERY

HOTEL STATE COLLEGE

YE OLDE STATE COLLEGE DINER

BUS 322

0   0.25 mi

0   0.25 km

W. COLLEGE

CALDER WAY

W. BEAVER AVE.

FOSTER AVE.

26

To Bellefonte

322

AREA OF DETAIL

UNIVERSITY PARK

26

LEMONT

To Lewiston & Tussey Mtn.

MILLBROOK

To Phillipsburg

LION COUNTRY VISITORS & CONVENTION BUREAU

PINE HALL

26

To Huntingdon

45

BUS 322

To Bellefonte

Endless Mountains

© AVALON TRAVEL PUBLISHING, INC.

metal-forging will enjoy walking through the ironmaster's mansion, water-powered blast furnace and forge, and worker's cabin on this restored and rebuilt historical site (County Road 1003, Centre County, 814/355-1982). Curtin Village also hosts a number of special events during the year: Civil War encampments, Apple Butter Day, and crafts and antique shows. To get there from SR 150, take the County Road 1003 turnoff south one-third mile to Curtin Village. From SR 144 in Milesburg, turn east on Water Street (CR 1006, at the war memorial doughboy statue). Follow the road to CR 1003. Call for more information, hours of operation, and current admission prices.

⚋ Boal Mansion and Columbus Chapel

The Boal Mansion (US 322, Boalsburg, 814/466-6210, www.boalmuseum.com) is in the pretty little village of Boalsburg, which has escaped the rampant growth of much of the area. The mansion and chapel are open May 1–mid-June and the day after Labor Day–Oct. 31, Tues.–Sun. 1:30–5 P.M.; mid-June–Labor Day, Tues.–Sat. 10 P.M.–5 P.M.; Sun. noon–5 P.M.; $10 adults, $6 children. Tours are available on request.

The mansion was built by David Boal, who fought in the Revolutionary War after settling in the area; nine generations of his family called it home. The mansion might be merely a threadbare bit of American history if it weren't for the Boals' interesting relatives: the Lees of Virginia, Simón Bolívar (the South American revolutionary leader), St. Bernard de Menthon, and, most notably, Christopher Columbus. The contents of the Columbus family chapel in Spain were inherited by one of the Boal wives (the niece of a direct descendant) and have been transported to the mansion grounds. An altar, religious paintings and statuary, and Columbus's explorer's cross are within touching distance in the stone building; the objects transport the viewer across 500 years of history. Though Columbus did not bring back a cargo of "gold, pearls, and spices," the goal of his enterprise, he remained convinced that China lay just beyond the islands he had claimed for Spain. Thus, the continent that lay directly between Eu-

rope and the riches of the Orient came to be named after the Florentine merchant, Amerigo Vespucci, who recognized that it was "a new world, since our ancestors had no knowledge of it." This is the only exhibit of its kind in the world.

From the Boal Mansion, walk down Church Street, pass the cemetery at which Memorial Day was first celebrated, then turn on to Main Street. There are several gift shops, a restaurant, and a bed-and-breakfast.

OTHER POINTS OF INTEREST

⚋ Penn's Cave

Penn's Cave Farm, the site of Penn's Cave (SR 192, five miles east of Centre Hall, 814/364-1664, www.pennscave.com), was originally bought in 1773 by James Poe, a relative of Edgar Allan Poe. Penn's Cave is open Feb. 15–May 31 daily 9 A.M.–5 P.M., April 1–May 31 daily 9 A.M.–5 P.M., June 1–Aug. 31 daily 9 A.M.–7 P.M.; Sept. 1–Nov. 30 daily 9 A.M.–5 P.M.; Dec. 1–Dec. 31 weekends only 11 A.M.–5 P.M. Tours depart on the hour. In warmer months, the last tour begins on the last hour posted. In spring, fall, and winter, the last tour is one hour before closing. Admission is $11. A 90-minute auto tour of the wildlife preserve is also offered.

The cave on the site had been visited by local Native Americans for some years before the first European visitor, Rev. James Martin, braved the dark and crawled into the entrance in 1795. Penn's Cave has been a public attraction since 1885, the first year boats were poled through the narrow, water-filled cavern. Formations created through hundreds of thousands of years continue to fascinate—a limestone wonderland of curtains, statues, ribbons, and small intricate cities. The farm in which Penn's Cave sits is also a wildlife sanctuary and working Angus beef cattle ranch. Visitors also enjoy a seven-acre picnic area with covered shelters and a small commercial airport, which offers tours by airplane. The cave tour takes place in flatboats; children younger than 11 months are not permitted.

Keystone Gliderport

The Gliderport (on US 220 between Unionville and Julian north of State College, 814/355-2483,

GOING UNDERGROUND

C entral Pennsylvania is riddled with caves and caverns (series of connected caves). The National Speleological Society state database lists more than 1,000 wild caves (those not prepared for visiting) and nine show caves, which are open to the public. Penn's Cave is one of the latter.

Nearly all of Pennsylvania's caves were created, 10–30 million years ago, by the action of carbon dioxide and water working together to slowly dissolve limestone in underground rivers. As the surface land eroded or was pushed up because of geological pressure, the level of the rivers dropped, creating the caves.

When the dissolved limestone material dripped and splashed against a hard surface, formations were created. These natural sculptures were exercises in patience—it takes an average of 120 years for one cubic inch of solidified rock to form. Can't tell a stalactite (points down from the ceiling) from a stalagmite? Impress your friends by using the geological term speleothem, which, helpfully, covers both of those common formations as well as several more exotic types such as bacon, cave grapes, popcorn, cave flowers, soda straws, and flowstone.

The color of a speleothem is determined by its mineral content. Pure calcite (dissolved and reformed limestone) is translucent or white; iron oxides tint some of the formations red and orange. Less common minerals cause shades of blue and green. In Penn's Cave and many other older show caves, what appear to be black formations on the walls are actually formations stained by soot from the lamps and torches of previous explorers. Because of their stable environments, caves preserve evidence of past human and animal activity—providing clues about the lives of American Indians and the early colonists.

In Pennsylvania and throughout the United States, there is much concern about the irreversible damage being done to caves and the underground water system of which they are part. Areas that are rich in limestone (called karst terrain) are characterized by large numbers of caves, springs, sinkholes (collapsed caves), and surface streams which disappear underground. Karst is like a sponge sitting in a bath, and the bathwater is the source of potable water for all who dwell above. When sinkholes are used for dumping waste, or large amounts of pesticides are spread on the surface soil, all pollutants reach the water system in a very short time. Caves, which are full of living organisms, often show the first signs of pollution, since they're on the top layers of the sponge. The National Speleological Society (Cave Ave., Huntsville, AL 35810, 205/852-1300) works to educate the public about the fragile karst ecosystem and can also refer you to grottos (caving clubs) in your area. Grottos often train novice spelunkers in caving techniques and know the locations of wild caves open to exploration.

www.eglider.org) grew out of a club formed in State College in 1964. The area has become famous for superior soaring conditions along the local ridges, and one of the world's longest flights on record took place here—more than 1,023 miles, by pilot, author of *Glider Basics from First Flight to Solo,* and Keystone Gliderport principal Tom Knauff. The Gliderport offers rides, rentals, and lessons.

Mount Nittany Vineyard

Mount Nittany (Centre Hall, 814/466-6373, www.mtnittanywinery.com) uses the crush from its own vineyards as well as other juice sources to produce exceptionally sophisticated varietal reds and whites and some table wines. It's open Tues.–Fri. 1:30–5 P.M., Sat. 10 A.M.–5 P.M., Sun. 12:30–4 P.M. Visitors must be 21 years old to taste wines.

The vineyard's chardonnay, seyval blanc, and red wines are all aged in oak barrels to enhance flavor. The winery has won numerous awards in Pennsylvania wine competitions. To get there, take SR 45 east of Boalsburg; turn north on Linden Hall Road, continue for a half-mile. Veer

Endless Mountains

right on Rock Hill Road for .4 mile. At the intersection with the old church, turn left for .1 mile, then right on Houser Road for .8 mile until it dead-ends at the winery (part of the road is gravel).

Bellefonte Historical Railroad

The restored Pennsylvania Railroad station in Bellefonte on High and Water Streets is home to this two-car diesel train that is maintained and run by volunteers. For tickets and schedules, call 814/355-2917 or visit www.bellefontetrain.com. The railroad operates scheduled excursions over more than 60 miles of track in Centre, Clinton, and Blair Counties, through the Bald Eagle Valley, and over Nittany Mountain. Some trips are combined with rail/bus tours to the Horseshoe Curve near Altoona and the flood museum and inclined plane in Johnstown. Other destinations include Curtin Village and the Eagle Ironworks, Keystone Gliderport, the Coachlite restaurant, and the quaint village of Lemont. The train operates on weekends throughout the summer and fall (dinner excursions are on the last Sunday of each month year-round).

MUSEUMS

Pennsylvania Military Museum

This attractive museum (on US 322 in Boalsburg, 814/466-6263, www.psu.edu), traces the military history of Pennsylvania from Ben Franklin's Associators (the group that met to oppose British rule) through Operation Desert Storm. There are cannons and artillery aplenty among the exhibits, and a highlight is a walkthrough World War I trench complete with exploding mortars. The Pennsylvania Military Museum has achieved a difficult goal: it neither glorifies war nor does it diminish those who have chosen to serve their country in the armed forces. The museum is scheduled to open after extensive renovations sometime in 2005; call for hours of operation and admission fees.

Museums on the Penn State Campus

The Penn State campus offers a number of small, free museums and collections. All are closed on

THE WINNINGEST COACH IN FOOTBALL

Raised by a strict Catholic family in Brooklyn, N.Y., and educated by Jesuits, Joe Paterno planned to become a lawyer. However, a football scholarship to Ivy League Brown University led to an opportunity to coach for an obscure football team in central Pennsylvania—the Penn State Nittany Lions. The Penn State University team was already attracting good players—unusual for a state school, and an agricultural college at that—one of Paterno's first players was Roosevelt Grier.

Paterno became head coach in 1966, and worked with football greats such as Charlie Pittman, Denny Onkoth, Franco Harris, and Heisman Trophy winner John Cappelletti. Through the years, the Lions with Paterno at their head achieved 30 straight wins over three seasons, and became national champions. "To win right," he says, "you cannot be afraid to lose. But God, I hate to lose." Today, following Paterno ("Joe-pa") and the Nittany Lions during the season remains a near-religious experience for thousands of fans; the town of State College is engulfed in a sea of navy and white, Penn State's colors. Go Lions!

university holidays, and hours may vary during summer break—call for information.

Formerly the Football Hall of Fame, the **All-Sports Hall of Fame** (call 814/865-0044 for hours), completed in 2001, exhibits memorabilia of players of the past, including photos of former athletes and several national championship teams, and winners of the Heisman Trophy. At State College through the years, preoccupation with sports—especially football—has taken on an all-consuming fervor; this is the place to fill in those trivia statistics. The museum is a 7,000-square-foot celebration of athletic achievement; it's in the Beaver Stadium expansion, in the Louis E. Lusch Football Building.

The galleries of the **Palmer Museum of Art** (Curtin Rd., 814/865-7672) display selections from a collection that spans 35 centuries of paintings, sculptures, ceramics, and works on paper. It's open Tues.–Sat. 10 A.M.–4:30 P.M., Sun. noon–4 P.M. The building was designed by Charles W. Moore and Arbonies Vlock to showcase the numerous dramatic and sophisticated international works.

The **Frost Entomological Museum** (Headhouse 3, Curtin Rd., 814/863-2863) displays approximately a half-million insect and related arthropod specimens, but the real interest lies in the active beehive set into an artificial tree trunk in one corner of the room. Bees freely come and go through a tube attached to the nearby window, and the hive itself is a maze of honeycomb and dripping honey. It's open Mon.–Fri. 9:30 A.M.–4:30 P.M.

The **Matson Museum of Anthropology** (Carpenter Bldg., 2nd floor, 814/865-3853) features a small but fascinating display of cultural artifacts from around the planet. Archaeological finds by Penn State research teams are also displayed. It's open Mon.–Fri. 9 A.M.–4 P.M.

The **Earth and Mineral Sciences Museum** (112 Steidle Bldg., 814/865-6427) features a variety of crystals, gems, stone carvings, and fossils, and a collection of paintings depicting Pennsylvania's mineral-based industries—oil, coal, and steel. Hours of operation are Mon.–Fri. 9:30 A.M.–5 P.M.

SHOPPING

Douglas Albert Gallery

This shop (McAllister Alley, 814/234-9822) is the showplace of State College guy-about-town and entrepreneur Doug Albert (owner of Uncle Eli's, the oldest art supply house in the area). The gallery is literally crammed with all manner of art glass, paintings, carvings, and art errata varying from kitsch to collectible. Don't turn around too fast—you may find yourself owning the shattered pieces of a unicorn or a fabulous sandblasted lead-crystal vase. The shop is open Mon.–Sat. 11 A.M.–5:30 P.M. McAllister Alley is between Calder Way and College Avenue.

University Creamery

The University Creamery (on campus next to Borland Laboratory, 814/865-7535) sells products of the dairies and growing fields of Penn State, which continues to be, first and foremost, an agricultural school. All types of ice cream (by the cone and boxed), cheese, milk, eggs, and produce in season are available. Everything is very fresh and inexpensive—and dry ice is provided to keep purchases cold up to 12 hours. It's open Mon.–Fri. 7 A.M.–10 P.M., Sat. 8 A.M.–11 P.M., Sun. 9 A.M.–10 P.M.

OUTDOOR RECREATION

Penn State Facilities

Penn State operates two 18-hole **golf courses** (on SR 26 west of State College, reservations and information 814/863-0257, pro shop 814/865-4653), with putting and chipping greens, sand bunkers, and a lighted practice range. All are open to the public.

The **Tennis Club** (on campus next to Holuba Hall, 814/865-1381) offers six clay outdoor courts, six Deco Turf II outdoor courts, and four indoor courts. Lessons and clinics are available. Call to arrange court times.

Stone Valley Recreation Area, on CR 1029/Charter Oak Road, includes a 100-acre lake, year-round cabin rental facilities, boating, fishing, hiking, and an environmental center. For information, contact Stone Valley (110 Housing and Foods Bldg., University Park, PA 16802, 814/863-1164, www.psu.edu). The recreation area is near Tussey Mountain off SR 26.

Tussey Mountain

On US 322, four miles east of the intersection of US 322 and College Avenue, this small, attractive ski center (814/466-6266 or 800/733-2754, www.tusseymountain.com) close to State College offers a number of programs for all levels of ability, including several "instructed playcare" programs for small children (ages 3–6) and those with a little more experience (ages 6–10). The majority of the runs are beginner-intermediate, with a couple of black diamond slopes for the more adventurous. Length of the annual ski season varies with the amount of snow. Prices vary depending on the time and day of the week; a number

BATS

Along with bears, skunks, and moths, bats are trogloxenes, or cave guests, animals that live above ground but often retreat to caves for shelter. Bats are also mammals—the only true flying mammal in the world.

These *chiroptera*, or hand-winged animals, are found in every continent in the world except Antarctica; there are 9–11 species in Pennsylvania, six of which are permanent, nonmigratory residents. Pennsylvania's bats are small; the largest, the hoary bat, is only five inches in length. Eastern Pipistrelles (pygmy bats), the smallest, are only 3–3.5 inches long. All bats in the state are insect eaters and consume more than half their own weight each night; bats are the major predators of night-flying insects in the United States.

All six of Pennsylvania's nonmigratory bats are cave dwellers who spend their winter hibernation hanging from dark ceiling recesses. The high humidity in the air helps slow water loss from their bodies. During hibernation, all bodily functions drop, including temperature, which falls to within one degree of the steady cave temperature. Bats do wake from time to time, but too frequent arousals may deplete their stored body fat to the point of starvation. Many wild caves in the state are being closed to winter exploration so as not to disturb hibernating bat colonies.

Bats, once feared for their apparent inability to outmaneuver hairdos and curtains, and as carriers of rabies, are losing their bad guy image. Most people now know that bats not only have adequate vision but guide themselves precisely by echolocation (bouncing sound off objects). Diseased wild bats, living in a fragile niche in the ecosystem, usually die themselves before they have contact with any other species. In the last 40 years, only 18 people are believed to have been infected by rabid bats—less than 10 percent of the number of people who have been attacked by their own dogs.

And what would we do without that famous bat byproduct, guano? Those après-hibernation droppings scraped from cave bottoms in the spring remain a highly prized fertilizer for our human gardens.

of special packages are offered. During the warm months, Tussey features a par-three golf driving range.

Black Moshannon State Park

Natives named the stream running through this park Moss-hanne, which means "Where the Moose Are," or "Moose Stream." The Black Moshannon area, on SR 504, nine miles east of Philipsburg, was once the site of a small timber town called Antes, which held a hotel, store, and a 10-pin bowling alley—it was a stopover for stagecoaches traveling on the old Erie Turnpike between Philadelphia and Erie.

During the late 1800s, Black Moshannon was one of the greatest pine lumbering areas in the state. The 3,394-acre park was developed courtesy of the WPA and CCC in the 1930s. For more information, camping reservations, and trail maps, contact Black Moshannon State Park (4216 Beaver Rd., Philipsburg, PA 16866-9519, 814/342-5960).

Bicycling: More than 20 miles of bicycle, snowmobile, and auto joint-use roadways thread through the park. There are also several miles of trails exclusively for bike or snowmobile use. Bicycles are prohibited on designated hiking trails. Maps are available from the address above.

Boating: Black Moshannon stream is dammed to form a small lake. Electric power and non-powered boats are permitted, and boat rentals are available in the summer.

Hiking: A 16-mile trail network winds through the park.

Hunting and Fishing: Most of the park is open to hunting in season. The lake provides warm-water game fish, and anglers can cast for trout in several nearby feeder streams.

Camping: Seventy-six primitive tent/trailer camping sites are available mid-April–late Dec. The park also offers 13 rustic family cabins during the warm months. Six modern cabins are also available year-round, by the week in summer and by the day during the rest of the year. Call

814/342-5960 or 888/PA-PARKS (888/727-2757) for reservations and fees.

Getting There: The northern boundary of Black Moshannon State Park runs parallel with I-80, but to reach the center of the park, take SR 504 via US 220 south from Exit 158 off I-80.

Camping

Tent sites, trailer sites with hookups, and cabins are all available at **Fort Bellefonte Campground** (one mile north of I-80 on SR 26, 814/355-9820 or 800/487-9067 for reservations).

ACCOMMODATIONS

State College and the surrounding area offer a number of larger hotels and bed-and-breakfasts. **Rest and Repast** (800/BNB-2655) is a bed-and-breakfast referral service that features a variety of accommodations ranging $75–150. The lower-end accommodations tend to be European-style (shared bath), such as the pretty **Stonehouse** (814/466-6579) a guesthouse with rates ranging $80–250.

$50–100

Hotel State College (100 W. College Ave., 814/237-4350, $30–95) began serving travelers in 1885 under the moniker Jack's Roadhouse. The Corner Room/Allen Street Grill share building space with the hotel, so bacon and eggs are never far away. All rooms have been spruced up to provide simple, inexpensive lodging in the heart of State College. The place is popular with potential students and their families coming to check out Penn State. Weekly rates are available, and longer stays may be arranged.

Kay and Wally Lester built **ⁿ Laurel Ridge Bed and Breakfast** (1673 Mountain Laurel Ct., Warriors Mark, 814/632-6813, www.laurelridgebb.com), their fresh, modern woodland retreat, at the top of Laurel Ridge. It's the place for guests who desire peace and quiet and nicely decorated rooms with a full bath. The location is ideal for businesspeople and other visitors seeking a nearby escape from Altoona or State College, plus a chance to see the Milky Way overhead. Kay and Wally also have infor-

mation on local Native American history and their Amish neighbors. Great people, nice place. The bed-and-breakfast is near the village of Bald Eagle off SR 350; the bridge is sometimes out, so check with the innkeepers ahead of time. There's a two-day minimum stay during Penn State home games and graduation. Rates range from $60–70, but can go as high as $100 per night during Penn State events such as Homecoming and home football games.

$100–150

The Queen (176 E. Linn St., Bellefonte, 814/355-7946 or 888/355-7999, http://bellefonte.com/queen), a Victorian-era bed-and-breakfast, is perhaps more elegant now than at any time in its past. Originally built as an upper-middle-class home in the 1890s, it was the newest of the Victorian styles. Through the years, it was "modernized" by the conversion of one of its eight fireplaces to gas, the removal of its pocket doors, and their replacement with smaller French doors, and the removal and addition of several walls to change room configurations. The elaborate detail in the exterior architecture was hidden under a clean white coat of paint; ceilings were lowered. When the present owners acquired the house in 1972, it had been abandoned for several years. The past 25 years have been spent restoring the home to its former splendor. Two rooms, both with private baths, range $75–$165; a two-night minimum is required for special events.

ⁿ Reynolds Mansion Bed and Breakfast (101 W. Linn St., Bellefonte, 814/353-8407 or 800/899-3929, www.reynoldsmansion.com) was the showplace of a wealthy banker and entrepreneur who completed the building in 1885. A marble vestibule, handcrafted woodwork, stained-glass detailing all contribute to this luxurious bed-and-breakfast. Guests may enjoy a game of pool in the billiard room and a full breakfast by the fire in the dining room. Two of the rooms feature whirlpool baths. Again, there's a two-night minimum on Penn State home-game football weekends and graduation. Rates increase during those times. The mansion sits on the corner of West Linn and North Allegheny. Rates range $115–175.

$150–200

A thoroughly modern adaptation of a Scottish country manor, the ◪ **Carnegie House** (within Toftrees Resort, 100 Cricklewood Dr., 814/234-2424 or 800/229-5033, www.carnegiehouse.com) is a wonderful combination of warmth (thanks to hosts Helga and Peter Schmid) and luxurious amenities. The simplest rooms have many of the qualities of a suite, including elegant decor, a separate seating area, and a separate shower and extra-large tub. The suites have kitchens and well-appointed receiving and sleeping areas. The library and bar for the use of guests and their invitees will transport you to Andrew Carnegie's castle on the Scottish moor. There is also a full-service restaurant on the premises. Expect a two-day minimum stay requirement on Penn State home-game football weekends, graduation, parents' weekend, and the arts festival (and book as far ahead as possible for those events). Rates range $150–210 and $300 for suites.

FOOD

Inexpensive

For a quick, cheap snack or meal, try Penn State University Food Services. One, **Union Street** (ground floor of the HUB-Robeson Center on campus), is an award-winning food-service operation. Eleven different vendors offer a variety of menus—Mexican, Chinese, burgers, coffee and pastries—for low prices. It's fast food, so don't expect linen napkins, but it's a good place to refuel without spending big bucks. It's open Mon.–Fri. 8 A.M.–5 P.M.

Otto's Cafe (in the Kern Graduate Building, across from Rec Hall) is a satellite operation of Union Street (with the same hours). The restaurant serves coffee, pastries, bagels, fruits, and frozen yogurt and features a grab-n-go case, with a variety of deli sandwiches and salads. At the grill, you can order a burger, chicken sandwich, veggie burger, or fries. The grill also serves breakfast in the morning, offering bagel and muffin sandwiches and hashbrowns. There are also daily pasta features, complete with salad and bread and a build-to-order deli.

Ye Olde State College Diner (26 W. College Ave., 814/238-5590) seems to have been around practically since the creation of the earth. Since then, it's been filled with students bemoaning finals and locals grabbing an early breakfast. Not cuisine, just cheap diner food, ready for business any time you are. What more could you ask? The diner is open 24 hours a day, 365 days a year. Meals average $6.

For a cozy breakfast stop in Bellefonte, go where the locals go: the **Waffle Shop** (127 W. Bishop St., Bellefonte, 814/355-7761, Mon.–Sat. 6 A.M.–3 P.M., Sun. 7 A.M.–3 P.M.).

Bonfatto's Italian Restaurant (213 W. High St., Bellefonte, right down the street from the courthouse in the center of town, 814/355-2638, Mon.–Sat. 8 A.M.–9 P.M., Sun. 10 A.M.–8 P.M.) looks like a fairly ordinary pizza joint until you come in and taste the food. Locals regularly eat here for the delicious meat sauce and homemade bread and pizza crust. The Bonfatto family also owns another restaurant of the same name in Bellefonte (1211 Zion Rd., daily 11 A.M.–9 P.M.), and both are operated by family members who cook and wait on tables. Plenty of the food that kids love, with the quality (and prices) adults want. Full meals average $8.

International

◪ **Seoul Garden** (129 Locust Ln., 814/237-7444) is a rare find. Living on the West Coast, I appreciate masterful Asian cooking; I didn't expect to stumble on one of the best (possibly *the* best) Korean restaurants of my noodle-crazed gustatory career. The array of pickles, including kim chee, are all freshly made, as are the noodles used in the soups. If your taste runs to the less-than-fiery, make sure that you ask for mild spiciness—this food is authentic (read: hot!) and absolutely delicious. A jeweled lotus in a sea of sunflowers, the Seoul Garden is open Mon.–Thurs. 11:30 A.M.–9:30 P.M., Fri.–Sat. 11:30 A.M.–10:30 P.M., Sun. noon–9 P.M. Prices average $6 for lunch and $8 for dinner.

Midrange

No need to wonder—it's on the menu at **The Deli Restaurant** (1313 Hiester St., 814/237-

5710), a popular State College eatery. The atmosphere is casual, so whether you're hungry for the high-end (steaks and chops, $15) or sandwiches, burgers, salads, or gyros ($5), the deli can meet your needs without a lot of hoopla.

Ⓜ Allen Street Grill and Corner Room (100 W. College Ave., 814/231-4745, serves healthy food with a nouvelle twist: bruschetta with pesto, mushroom ravioli, jambalaya, and low-fat, "hearthealthy" dishes as well as a good old-fashioned Reuben sandwich with pastrami. The grill is open daily 11 A.M.–2 A.M. and the Corner Room is open Sun.–Thurs. 7 A.M.–10 P.M., Fri.–Sat. 7 A.M.–midnight. Grill prices average $8–12 for lunch, the Corner Room less than $5 for breakfast. The Corner Room downstairs, owned by the same organization, serves inexpensive breakfasts and lunches.

The Tavern Restaurant (220 E. College Ave., State College, 814/238-6116) has been serving dinner daily since 1948. The menu is American, with veal, chicken, fish, and pastas; entrees average $15.

High End

Historic **Ⓜ Duffy's Boalsburg Tavern** (113 E. Main St., Boalsburg, 814/466-6241, www.duffystavern.com, Mon.–Sat. 11:30 A.M.–1 A.M., Sun. 11:30 A.M.–9 P.M.) is divided into two sections, one more formal than the other with dinner offerings such as venison and crab cakes, averaging $19. The bar/tavern serves pub food and has a number of specials throughout the week, including steamed clams on Tuesday and Thursday for $4.99, half-priced hamburgers on Monday, daily lunch specials and a sandwich board with all sandwiches $1.59, and more. Both are open for lunch and dinner daily—the tavern/bar stays open later.

Travel by stage in those days was sufficient to warrant three taverns—one for gentry, one for coachmen and wagoners, and one for drovers.

Duffy's is one of three original taverns in town, built in 1819 by Col. James Johnson to cater to the gentry. The tavern operated continuously from 1819 until 1934, when it was damaged by fire. The tavern has been resurrected, and its 22-inch stone walls are as solid as the day they were built, keeping the inside temperature at 68–70 degrees on hot summer days.

The **Ⓜ Carnegie House** (100 Cricklewood Dr., 814/234-2424) welcomes guests with a roaring fire in cold weather. Lunch is available Mon.–Sat. 11:30 A.M.–1:30 P.M., dinner is served Mon.–Sat. 4:30–8:30 P.M. Lunch is around $12, and dinner is in the $23–40 range. Reservations are required. The dining room, next to the foyer of the inn, has a beautiful view of Toftrees Golf Resort. Filet mignon, venison steak, and soy and ginger roasted duck breast grace the menu, and the atmosphere is dressy casual.

Ⓜ Gamble Mill Tavern (160 Dunlap St., Bellefonte, 814/355-7764) has long had a reputation for sophisticated fine dining in a comfortable and romantic historic atmosphere. Lunch is served Mon.–Sat. 11:30 A.M.–2 P.M. and dinner is served 5–8:30 P.M. Expect to pay $16–25 for dinner. Crab cakes, a vegetarian eggplant-based lasagna, and seafood strudel are among the favorites, and if there's room . . . death by chocolate (the chocolate selection changes daily). Reservations are recommended.

INFORMATION

Central Pennsylvania Visitors and Convention Bureau (800 E. Park Ave., State College, PA 16801, 814/231-1400 or 800/358-5466, www.centralpacvb.org or www.visitpennstate.org) has information on all State College activities, lodging, sights, and the annual football schedule. It will also provide specifics on Boalsburg and Bellefonte.

Railroad and Civil War Country

South-central Pennsylvania is a place of transformation: a transitional area between the relatively flat, fertile farmlands of west Piedmont and the folded mountains and valleys of the Allegheny Plateau; an evolution from buggies and boats to swift machines hurtling on steel rails; the gentling of a country at war with itself into a land of placid farms and sorrowful memories. The eastern part of the area was settled early by German and Scots-Irish farmers and remains farmland today, dotted by towns and villages along the early trade routes. As the land rises, settlements become sparse and the land grows more demanding.

Clacking rails were the ties that bound tiny settlements along the Allegheny Ridge with peaceful farmlands in west Piedmont, and so it remains today. The strategic location of Altoona and its railcar repair facilities and the remarkable efforts by engineers to surmount the Al-

© JO ANNE MILLER

legheny Ridge have created a steely mecca for rail pilgrims. At the Altoona facility, locomotives, pulling dozens of train cars, are strewn like a giant's toys across miles of switching tracks—a Christmas fantasy come to grease-and-metal life.

This peaceful land was also the scene of cataclysmic events in the Civil War; the lives and deaths of more than 50,000 young men, there to defend their own belief in the rights of man, are immortalized in Gettysburg. Slavery is an issue that seems implausible to Americans now; it just shows how far we've come. Gettysburg and the surrounding Civil War Trail are by far the area's most popular attractions.

Outdoor recreation, particularly around Blue Knob State Park, Raystown Lake, and Yellow Breeches Creek, is a big draw for sports enthusiasts. The limestone caves of Huntingdon County provide an opportunity for visitors to explore and enjoy a unique natural feature.

South-central Pennsylvania is also the site of possibly the most authentic and accessible Amish life left in the state today. The Big Valley is far enough from both Philadelphia and Pittsburgh to have avoided the commercialization that taints other areas and friendly enough to welcome a visitor with a handshake instead of an open palm.

PLANNING YOUR TIME

South-central Pennsylvania is made up of distinctive areas that cater to different interests. If you wish to see everything in the area, plan on two weeks.

If you're largely interested in general sightseeing of the area, plan to spend a day on the **Covered Bridge Tour: Hollidaysburg to Bedford** and two days on the **Path of Progress National Heritage Route.**

Blair County will appeal to those with an interest in railroading. Plan on one day in Altoona (a good place to overnight) to see the **Altoona Railroaders Memorial Museum** (2–3 hours) and **Conrail Viewing Platform** (.5–2 hours), plus an additional day each if you plan to add **Lakemont Park** and/or **DelGrosso's Amusement Park.** You'll need two additional days to visit **Horseshoe Curve National Historic Landmark** (1 hour), **Gallitzin Tunnels Park** (.5–1 hour), **East Broad Top Railroad** (2 hours), **Allegheny Portage Railroad National Historic Site** (1 hour), and the **Portage Station Museum** (1 hour).

If your interests tend to the historic, Bedford County is the place to go. The **Southern Bridge Tour** gives a good overview of the rural area. **Blue Knob State Park** offers a superb variety of outdoor activities year-round, from one day to several weeks. Base in Bedford and plan on a full three days to see **Fort Roberdeau** in Blair County (2 hours), the town of **Bedford** (2 hours), **Old Bedford Village** (2 hours), and the **Fort Bedford Museum** (2–3 hours).

In Huntingdon County, outdoor recreation, especially **Raystown Lake** (1 day–several weeks) and the area's limestone caverns, draw visitors. The caves are unique to this part of the United States, and cavers will want to see all three: **Indian Caverns** (2 hours), **Lincoln Caverns** (2 hours), and **Coral Caverns** (near the town of Bedford, 2 hours). If you plan to see all the caves, see each one on a separate day, and base in Bedford or Belleville (especially if you want to see authentic Amish life). While in Mifflin County, stop by the **Mifflinburg Buggy Museum** (1 hour), **Brookmere Winery** (1 hour), and don't miss the **Belleville Market** (2 hours–all day).

The Civil War comes alive on the **Civil War Historic Trail** in the lower Cumberland Valley. The trail will take a day to drive, and ideally will end in Gettysburg (lots of good places to stay). Plan on at least three days in **Gettysburg**—there's so much to see and do there, starting with **Gettysburg National Military Park** (1 day). Shopping is a big pastime in the area, so plan a little time to stop at unique places such as **Boyds Bear Country** and **American Crafters.** For a breath of fresh air, drive north to Biglerville to see **The National Apple Museum** (1 hour) and stop in **The Country Store and Museum** (1–2 hours).

In Perry County, across the Susquehanna River from the state capitol, many folks with an interest in colonial and military history look forward to visiting the **Hessian Guardhouse** (30 minutes) and **Omar N. Bradley Museum** (1–2 hours) at Carlisle Military Barracks and

Must-Sees

Look for **M** to find the sights and activities you can't miss and **N** for the best dining and lodging.

M Horseshoe Curve National Historic Landmark: This is the engineering marvel of the late 19th century that changed the nature of travel from one end of the state to the other (page 243).

M Altoona Railroaders Memorial Museum: An interesting and informative series of life-size tableaus, the museum celebrates all rail workers from brakemen to waiters (page 246).

M Blue Knob State Park: The views from the peak are spectacular, due to its location on a spur of the Allegheny Front overlooking the Allegheny Ridge and valleys below (page 249).

M Belleville Market: Early Wednesday mornings, the roads leading to Belleville are packed nose-to-tail with horse-drawn buggies. The market is the big draw for Amish and other visitors to this unspoiled area (page 254).

M Caverns: Find why cave bacon won't be on the menu. The limestone formations in **Indian Caverns** and **Lincoln Caverns** are equally spectacular (page 255).

M Civil War Historic Trail: This route through the Cumberland Valley visits the sites of three major Confederate cavalry raids and several skirmishes.

The Gettysburg campaign of 1863 began in Franklin County (page 256).

M Gettysburg National Military Park: Don't miss this! A significant event in American History is memorialized in a beautiful park (page 262).

M Land of Little Horses: All animal lovers (especially children) will enjoy an outing here. The tiny horses put on a big show (page 266).

M York Historic Sites: York offers several superb authentic buildings, among them the **Golden Plough Tavern and General Gates House, Friends Meeting House,** and the **Central Market** (page 275).

M Harley-Davidson Final Assembly Plant and Tour Center: Giant presses form steel sheets into fenders while candy-colored motorcycles fly overhead (page 277).

modern conveniences at the Belleville Market

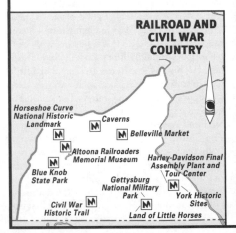

RAILROAD AND CIVIL WAR COUNTRY

Horseshoe Curve National Historic Landmark

Caverns

Belleville Market

Altoona Railroaders Memorial Museum

Blue Knob State Park

Gettysburg National Military Park

Civil War Historic Trail

York Historic Sites

Land of Little Horses

Harley-Davidson Final Assembly Plant and Tour Center

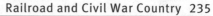

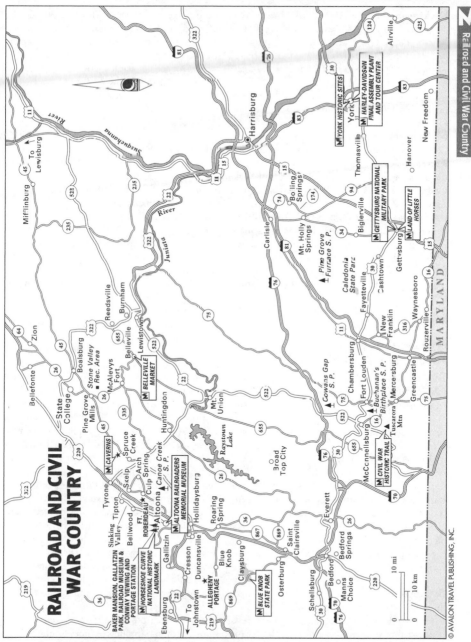

RAILROAD AND CIVIL WAR COUNTRY

BAKER MANSION, GALLATZIN PARK, RAILROAD MUSEUM & CONWAY VIEWING AND PORTAGE STATION

HORSESHOE CURVE NATIONAL HISTORIC LANDMARK

BLUE KNOB STATE PARK

ALLEGHENY PORTAGE

CAVERNS

ALTOONA RAILROADERS MEMORIAL MUSEUM

FT. ROBERDEAU

BELLEVILLE MARKET

CIVIL WAR HISTORIC TRAIL

LAND OF LITTLE HORSES

GETTYSBURG NATIONAL MILITARY PARK

HARLEY-DAVIDSON FINAL ASSEMBLY PLANT AND TOUR CENTER

YORK HISTORIC SITES

MARYLAND

© AVALON TRAVEL PUBLISHING, INC.

0   10 mi
0   10 km

Dickinson College (1–2 hours), one of the original Colonial colleges. **Allenberry Playhouse,** with its plays and musicals, is another big draw in the area (and a good place to overnight). Sportsmen know this area as an excellent place for fly-fishing.

Plan on one to five days in York, depending on interests. Historians will enjoy the **York County Colonial Courthouse** (1 hour), **York Friends Meeting House** (30 minutes), **market houses** (2 hours–all day), **Agricultural and Industrial Museum** (3 hours), **York County Fire Museum** (2 hours), and the **Historical Museum of York County** (1–2 hours). The **Harley-Davidson Final Assembly Plant and Tour Center** (3 hours) is a must-see, and **Bob Hoffman's U.S. Weightlifting Federation Hall of Fame** (1–2 hours) is fascinating, particularly if you're interested in catching up on the history of California's governor Arnold Schwarzenegger. York and environs is also the place for great factory tours: **Wolfgang Candy** (30 minutes), **Stauffer's Bakery** (1 hour), and **Utz Quality Foods** (1.5 hours), to name a few.

GETTING THERE AND GETTING AROUND

By Air, Rail, and Bus

Commercial airports south of Altoona (near Martinsburg), in State College, and on the Susquehanna River south of Harrisburg all connect via commuter airlines to Pittsburgh and Philadelphia.

Amtrak runs two daily train services, the Pennsylvanian and Three Rivers, between New York City and Chicago. The trains stop in Harrisburg, Lewistown, Huntingdon, Tyrone, and Altoona in south-central Pennsylvania.

Greyhound buses (800/231-2222) connect all of the major cities in the area, and many of the smaller ones. Call for schedule and fare information.

By Auto

Since south-central Pennsylvania is primarily made up of long reaches of farmland and forests between towns, the best way to see the area is by auto. If you are traveling east-west, major routes are I-80 in the north and I-70/76 (the toll road) in the south. Two-lane routes include US 22 in the north-central area and US 30 across the southern part of the state; both are better choices for scenic travel. North-south routes are less direct: US 220 in the west, and I-81, US 15, and I-83 in the southern part of the state.

HISTORY

Defeat of the Susquehannock

Before Europeans began flooding into coastal areas to the east, the lower Susquehanna River was populated by a large tribe of farmers/hunters, the Susquehannocks. The French in Canada and western New York were applying pressure on the powerful Iroquois Confederacy to the north in an attempt to break up the six-nation union. The Iroquois themselves were eager to expand their pelt-hunting area to increase profitable trade with the Europeans. Worried about encroachment by the Iroquois, the Susquehannocks allied themselves with the Maryland British and the Hurons of southern Canada, traditional enemy of the Iroquois (and allies of the French). When war broke out over the fur trade, the Hurons were defeated by the Iroquois in 1663, and the Susquehannocks were attacked by the Seneca, members of the Iroquois Confederacy. The state of Maryland declared war against the Seneca, and the war dragged on for a decade, until, in 1674, Maryland reversed its policy and made peace with them. Deserted by their British allies and with their chiefs dead at the hands of Virginia militiamen, the Susquehannocks' resistance diminished; survivors left their settlement on the Susquehanna River to wander. Most were adopted by Iroquois tribes; some created a new village near Conestoga with their former enemies, the Seneca. Six years before William Penn was granted land rights to the territory of Pennsylvania, the Iroquois controlled the land.

To fill the void, the Iroquois invited other tribes under its protection, chiefly the Conoys and the Tuscaroras, to move into the area. They migrated from points south and continued to move north into Iroquois territory for the next 50 years, leaving their legacy in place names.

DICKENS TOPS THE MOUNTAIN

Charles Dickens ventured across America in the mid-1800s, using whatever transportation was available. From Harrisburg to Pittsburgh, he rode the waterways of the Main Line canal. In *American Notes*, he described his trip over the Portage Railroad:

We had left Harrisburg on Friday. On Sunday morning we arrived at the foot of the mountain [the Allegheny Ridge], which is crossed by railroad. There are ten inclined planes; five ascending, and five descending; the carriages are dragged up the former, and let slowly down the latter, by means of stationary engines; the comparatively level spaces between being traversed, sometimes by horse, and sometimes by engine power, as the case demands. Occasionally the rails are laid upon the extreme verge of a giddy precipice; and looking from the carriage windows the traveller gazes sheer down, without a stone or scrap of fence between, into the mountain depths below. The journey is very carefully made, however; only two carriages travelling together; and, while proper precautions are taken, is not to be dreaded for its dangers.

It was very pretty, travelling thus at a rapid pace along the heights of the mountain in a keen wind, to look down into a valley full of light and softness. . . . It was amusing . . . to see the engine . . . come buzzing down alone, like a great insect, its back of green and gold so shining in the sun, that if it had spread a pair of wings and soared away, no one would have had occasion, as I fancied, for the least surprise. But it stopped short of us in a very business-like manner when we reached the canal; and, before we left the wharf, went panting up this hill again, with the passengers who had waited our arrival for the means of traversing the road by which we had come.

By the early 1700s, the only occupants of the area were Shawnee from the south and Lenni Lenape (Delaware) from the east, both living here by permission of the Iroquois. The village of Ohesson (now Lewistown) was home to 100 members of both tribes. European settlers were banned from entering the area until the Albany Purchase of 1754.

Moving West

After the Albany Purchase, frontiersman Arthur Buchanan traded rum and trinkets for land near Ohesson and brought members of his family and others to settle there, in the Big Valley (Kishacoquillas Valley). This so outraged the local Delaware and Shawnee that they burned their own villages and left. During the French and Indian War, nearby Fort Granville was destroyed, and settlers left the area for their own safety. When they attempted to return, they were discouraged by Shawnee Chief Kishacoquillas, who warned them that antisettler sentiment still ran

hot among Shawnee in the area. Though the land was officially purchased from the Iroquois in 1754 at Albany, the agreement stipulated that the land would be settled gradually. Europeans were forbidden to move beyond the Allegheny Ridge until 1763—however, Pontiac's war, which followed immediately, prevented settlement for several more years.

The Canal Connects East and West

Once pioneers began to flow into south-central Pennsylvania, villages and small towns sprang up along the waterways, usually based around pig-iron foundries, grain-milling operations, and lumber mills. Public roads, such as the Huntingdon, Cambria, and Indiana Turnpike, built in 1818, connected some of the villages. With the completion of the Pennsylvania Canal in 1832, Hollidaysburg—at the difficult-to-reach northwestern end of the area—became connected with Philadelphia and the eastern seaboard. Two years later, the Allegheny Portage

Railroad began hauling canal boats over Allegheny Ridge, connecting the midstate area to Pittsburgh, the Mississippi, and beyond.

Pennsy Speeds the Journey

Though the area's rich natural resources drew settlers initially, it was the Pennsylvania Railroad that was responsible for growth and prosperity. The city of Altoona was once the site of the largest railroad repair and manufacturing shop in the world. The Pennsylvania Railroad expanded its track every year, finally dead-ending in Williamsburg in 1873, at one of the area's earliest iron furnaces, the Etna.

The golden age of rail saw the emergence of robber barons—railroad, lumber, and manufacturing tycoons who lived in hulking mansions and lined their pockets with urban gold. Some of their Victorian palaces may still be seen in Tyrone, north of Altoona.

The Conflict

The Pennsylvania Railroad hauled men and munitions throughout the Civil War. The peaceful farming area of the Piedmont is imprinted with our nation's history in Gettysburg and the surrounding towns, which retain vivid memories of the devastating War Between the States. After the war, the natural resources that created wealth were steadily depleted; a change in the industrial needs of America also helped to fuel an economic and population decline in the center of the state.

South-Central Pennsylvania in the 21st Century

South-central Pennsylvania has remained true to its farm-and-forest heritage. Most of the villages have remained small enclaves of family and friends. Combined competition from cars, trucks, and airplanes pushed the railroads—once the lifeblood of the area—to near extinction. By the late 1960s, the Pennsylvania Railroad was headed for bankruptcy. The Staggers Rail Act of 1980 partially deregulated the nation's rail lines and freed companies to set their own routes, rates, and schedules. Overnight, railroads became highly competitive, moving 40 percent of the nation's freight. Larger towns—especially Altoona—have prospered either because of shifts in economic basis or a new emphasis on recreation or history.

Blair and Bedford Counties

Altoona, "Gem of the Mountains," was created as a railroad town in Blair County and remains a major repair facility for Conrail, one of the nation's largest rail-freight companies; visitors to the historic Horseshoe Curve may see more than a dozen trains pass by each hour. Altoona houses the sprawling Juniata Locomotive Repair Facilities and miles of Conrail switching tracks. Home to the Railroaders Memorial Museum, the area is a magnet for rail fans from around the world.

The town is the largest in the county and is surrounded by attractions such as the village of Tyrone, with its Victorian homes built by railway executives; historic Fort Roberdeau, in the peaceful Sinking Valley; and the hamlet of Spruce Creek, with its Indian caverns and massive rock formations. The village of Tipton is the site of Bland's Amusement Park, and south of Altoona lies another, Lakemont Park, near the charming village of Hollidaysburg. Antique shops are only minutes away in Duncansville.

In 1758, troops led by British Gen. John Forbes forged their way through the wilderness to liberate "the forks of the Ohio" (now Pittsburgh) from the French; they paused to build a supply fort at the site of a trading post on the banks of the Raystown Branch of the Juniata River. The present town of Bedford grew from these roots, as settlers traded surplus from their farms via Forbes Road (now US 30).

Though Bedford remains a small town, its rich history is reflected in the downtown walking tour, which includes colonial-era buildings such as the Espy House—George Washington's headquarters during the Whiskey Rebellion. The Bedford area features a complete reconstructed colonial village (Old Bedford Village), as well as a functioning tavern from that era (Jean Bonnet's). The surrounding farmland is a scenic treasure with numerous covered bridges, and Blue Knob State Park, the state's most popular downhill ski area, is easily accessible from Bedford.

SCENIC TOURS

Covered Bridge Tour: Hollidaysburg to Bedford

This route takes visitors past a vintage train station and through some of Pennsylvania's most scenic farm country, beginning in Blair County and ending 48 miles south in Bedford County.

Start from the intersection of SR 36 and US 22 in Hollidaysburg. Turn southeast on SR 36 toward the town of Roaring Spring. After you pass the quarry on the left, veer right at the "Y" to SR 867; follow signs for SR 867 through the town. If the paper mill is operating, you'll be treated to *eau de mill*, reminiscent of cooking sauerkraut. As you journey through this pretty little factory town, you'll pass the only remaining Victorian-era train station in Blair County, built in 1906. The aquifer that supplied the area with water once flowed so copiously that passersby could hear the thunderous outpouring a mile away—hence the name Roaring Spring. It's settled into more of a purr since then. A public park is at the site of the spring (515 Spang St.).

Follow the signs for SR 867 out of town. This road passes through Baker's Summit, Morrison Cove, and a number of Amish and Mennonite farms—you'll see a hazard sign for horse-drawn buggies on the road. Set against misty low mountains to the east, the farms are uniformly beauti-

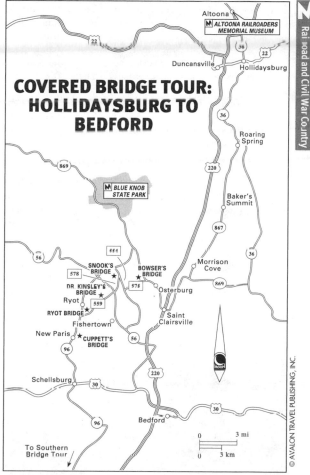

COVERED BRIDGE TOUR: HOLLIDAYSBURG TO BEDFORD

ful, displaying fresh laundry hung on lines outside the houses. There are birds everywhere—painted buntings of orange and blue, yellow and black finches, and red-dotted red-winged blackbirds. The popularity of colorful banners and garden statuary—especially matched buck and doe—remains undiminished in this corner of the world. When you reach the intersection with SR 869, jog west/southwest on SR 869 to pass under US 220 to St. Clairsville. Continue to Osterburg.

Wind through the village of Osterburg. When you come to the "Y," take the left fork toward

Bowser's Covered Bridge (also called the Osterburg Bridge). Less than .1 mile down the road, past a you-pick farm, you'll see the bridge on your left with a road alongside it. Warning—wrong turns off these lanes may land you in the Point, a maze of named and unnamed farm roads between US 220 and SR 96 and US 30. You may be trapped until the Minotaur comes to get you.

Set your odometer to zero at Bowser's Bridge. Make a left (south) on the road next to the bridge, T575. At the stop sign (1.9 miles) make a right (west, T554). At a gray farmhouse (2.6 miles), make a left at the intersection (south, T578). A sign directs you to a One Lane Bridge, Snooks Bridge. At 2.9 miles, pass through the bridge and immediately make a right turn (west, T578). At the stop sign, you've reached SR 56.

Cross over the road to T559. About 300 feet from the intersection on your right is Dr. Kinsley's Bridge, a non-rossable span. Continue straight on this road. At approximately 6.1 miles, you'll come to Ryot Bridge. Turn right through the bridge.

At the next intersection (6.6 miles), you've reached SR 96. Make a left (south). You'll pass through the village of Ryot. At 9.3 miles, behind a grove of trees on your left is Cuppett's Bridge. Just past that is Cuppett's farm and store. Continue on the road until you reach the intersection of US 30 at Schellsburg. Make a left (east) to go to Bedford, about seven miles.

Southern Bridge Tour

This 24-mile auto/bike loop begins at Jean Bonnet's Tavern, at the intersection of US 30 and SR 31; it passes the only coral caverns open to the public in Pennsylvania and several covered bridges. The final leg of the tour bisects beautiful Shawnee State Park. If biking, mountain bikes are recommended because of the number of unpaved (though well-maintained) roads.

Set your odometer at the tavern, and head south on SR 31. At 2.3 miles, make a right turn (west) on Watson Street; drive past the Bridge Out sign, and drive to the end, where you'll see the impassable Herline Bridge. Turn around and return to SR 31, turning right (south). Less than .1 mile south is the Coral Caverns turnoff on the left side of the road (see description under Outdoor Recreation). They're worth a

Turner's Bridge

look, but call first—the hours are capricious and the caverns are on a single-lane dirt road that leads up into the hills. Continue through the village of Manns Choice; you'll come to the SR 96/31 intersection traffic light. A left turn up the hill will lead to the main street (one block) and the friendly Manns Choice grocery, open seven days a week, a good place to pick up picnic supplies. Manns Choice folks certainly have a sense of humor; on the hill above the store in the residential area is a mailbox set on a 14-foot-high post; the box is labeled airmail. Back at the traffic light/intersection, reset your odometer to zero and head west on SR 31 toward Schellsburg.

At 1.8 miles, SR 31 jogs to the left toward West End—follow it. At approximately 3.6 miles, look to your right and you'll see Turner's Bridge. To get to it, take the turnoff on the right onto a dirt road at 3.9 miles. Go through the bridge and continue over the interstate; at the stop sign, 5.1 miles, make a right turn (east) onto the paved road (T432). At the next stop sign, make a left (north) onto SR 96. Follow it to Schellsburg through Shawnee State Park. At 7.3 miles, you'll reach the traffic light (and US 30) in Schellsburg.

Make a left (west). At 7.4 miles, on the left, turn onto the street marked Colwin Covered Bridge (Covered Bridge Road). The impassable bridge is less than a mile down the road; it's next to the Schellsburg Bed and Breakfast. Return to US 30 to continue your journey; a right turn (east) leads back to Bedford, about 10 miles.

Path of Progress National Heritage Route

The Path of Progress is a 500-mile route over the Allegheny Mountains in southwestern Pennsylvania that encompasses nine counties and features hundreds of sites relating to the nation's industrial story. The region was the first place in the country to officially pay tribute to the role of industry in our nation's development. Sites of all aspects of industrialization—canals, railroads, coal and steel development—are visited in the spots where they happened first. Included are the Altoona Railyards, the Johnstown Flood National Memorial and Museum, the steel mills of Johnstown (for more on Johnstown, see the Laurel Highlands chapter), and Horseshoe Curve, a 19th-century engineering marvel built by the Pennsylvania Railroad. Contact Path of Progress National Heritage Route (105 Zee Plaza, P.O.

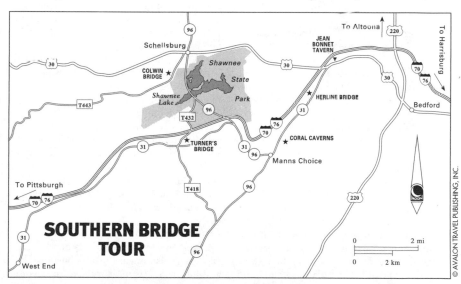

SOUTHERN BRIDGE TOUR

Box 565, Hollidaysburg, PA 16648-0565, 814/696-9380, www.sphpc.org) for a trail map and information.

HISTORIC SITES

Fort Roberdeau

Fort Roberdeau (mailing address R.D. 3, Box 391, Altoona, PA 1660, Blair County, 814/946-0048) is a reconstructed Revolutionary War–era fort that hosts numerous special events, including military reenactments. Picnicking on the grounds is free. The fort, surrounded by a sharpened-log barrier wall, was originally built in 1778 to house men who mined lead for the Army's musket balls. Nature trails lace the property, and a visitors' center with a mineral museum and picnic facilities is available. The fort is open mid-May–mid-Oct., Tues.–Sat. 11 A.M.–5 P.M., Sun. 1–5 P.M. The surrounding park is open 8 A.M.–sunset; admission is $3 to enter the fort. The fort is between the hamlets of Skelp and Culp on CR 1015 east out of Altoona. Where SR 1015 intersects with Kettle Road, turn south onto Kettle Road and follow it about a half mile. A small sign directs you onto the park's access road. This is a very scenic area, lined with Amish and Mennonite farms. A side trip on SR 453 leads past the hamlet of Arch Spring; the wrought-iron arch at the cemetery reads: That Which is So Universal as Death Must Be a Blessing.

Baker Mansion and Museum

Baker Mansion (3419 Oak Ln., Altoona, Blair County, 814/942-3916, www.blaircohistorical society.homestead.com), former home of ironmaster Elias Baker, has been a landmark in Blair County since 1848. The mansion is now home to the County Historical Society and a broad collection of regional memorabilia. A tour of the house allows visitors to discover how past generations lived, worked, and spent their leisure time. Baker amassed a fortune in the iron industry, and the home's furnishings reflect it: Italian marble, hand-carved furniture from Belgium, and a children's room full of antique toys. The mansion is open Memorial Day–Labor Day Tues.– Sun., 1–4:30 P.M.; April–Memorial Day and Labor

Day–Oct. 31 Sat.–Sun. 1 P.M.–4:30 P.M.; admission $4 adults, $2 children 5–12 years.

Allegheny Portage Railroad National Historic Site

A world-class feat of engineering at the time of its inception in 1834, this wasn't a railroad at all (US 22, Blair County/Cambria County border, visitors' center 814/886-6150, www.nps.gov/alpo; Lemon House Museum, daily 9 A.M.–6 P.M.; Staple Bend Tunnel daily sunrise–sunset; $3, under 16 free). It was actually a link in the Main Line, the canal system that ran from the Delaware River outside Philadelphia to the Ohio River in Pittsburgh. The Portage Railroad hoisted passengers, freight, and entire canal boats over the summit of Allegheny Mountain between Hollidaysburg and Johnstown, shortening the trip by several days. The Portage Railroad worked by means of stair-step inclines; canal boats were hauled from one platform to another up one side of the mountain and down the other. Its total length was 36.5 miles, with 10 separate inclines; the trip took five days.

Models of horses and vehicles used to operate the system when it was first devised are in the visitors' center. Of special interest is the Lafayette, a steam locomotive of the type that replaced the horse and pulley mechanism on the inclines. Eventually, more powerful steam engines made the portage railroad obsolete. By 1854, the Horseshoe Curve and Gallitzin Tunnels replaced the Portage Railroad. The canal system disappeared as more passengers and freight crossed the Alleghenies using the faster, more practical railroads.

This park features a film at the visitors' center, forested trails along the Portage Railroad's route, and the Lemon House, an old public house that served those passing through. The historic site and visitors' center is 12 miles west of Altoona and 10 miles east of Ebensburg on US 22 on the Blair County/Cambria County border. Take the Gallitzin exit and follow signs.

City of Bedford

Washington slept here (really). Bedford still contains many of its original colonial buildings. Penn and Juliana Streets meet at the town square set aside by the family of William Penn in 1761 as the center of Bedford. From the square, walking east on East Penn Street, you'll pass the Russell House, built in 1816 by the first burgess of Bedford—a good example of the Georgian style. Turn north on Huntington Avenue, cross Pitt Street, and between West Pitt and the end of Huntington is the Espy House, built in 1771. It was the headquarters of George Washington in 1794, when he came to Bedford to review troops assembled to quell the Whiskey Rebellion. Heading east on East Pitt Street, you'll pass the Anderson House, 1815, on the corner of East Pitt and Richard Streets. The east room of the house was the site of the first bank in Bedford, and it still contains the original vault. Since 1924, the house has been used as a public library and community center. Several miles south of town is the site of the old Bedford Springs Resort, once a leading spa visited by President James Buchanan for the water's healing properties. President Buchanan used the resort as his summer White House while in office.

OTHER POINTS OF INTEREST

Horseshoe Curve National Historic Landmark

The Horseshoe Curve (Altoona, Blair County, 814/946-9457, www.railroadcity.com), which opened in February 1854, changed the nature of travel from one end of the state to the other. A trip from Hollidaysburg to Pittsburgh that once took 20 days by horse had been modified to one week with the Portage Railroad; with the Horseshoe Curve, it became 12 hours. The curve, still considered to be an engineering marvel, rises a foot every 100 feet to conquer Allegheny Mountain, the most severe challenge to the railroad pushing west. A mecca for rail buffs, the curve

RAIL LIFE

During the mid-19th century, iron horses began to gallop over miles of rails, powering the support system for the North in the Civil War, and later pulling carloads of passengers and materials to the West. Industrial transport and travel by rail declined during the first half of the 20th century, but it is booming again. Between 1983 and 1993, rail productivity shot up 157 percent; the nation's seven major freight handlers (Burlington Northern, Santa Fe, Southern Pacific, Norfolk Southern, CSX, and Conrail) each takes in more than a billion dollars in revenue annually.

Conrail, created from sections of the Pennsylvania Railroad and other rail companies, is the largest freight hauler in Pennsylvania. Though today's locomotives have come a long way from the steam-powered contraptions of old, Conrail's car-repair facility in Altoona continues to keep the rails humming. At that facility, cars damaged from carrying rough cargo are rewelded, strengthened, and put back on the tracks. Automated metal lathes the size of pickup trucks trim worn wheels into perfect circles. On average, the shop crew repairs 64 cars a day and turns out at least 10 new ones.

The sprawling locomotive facility performs major services on the company's 2,000 locomotives—no small task when the repair job in question is on a 90-foot-long, 425,000-pound engine. Locomotive skeletons line the walls, waiting to be repowered with rebuilt diesel engines.

Fully computerized contemporary trains carry chemicals, grain, industrial raw materials, mail—everything from auto parts to zucchini. One special place to watch sleek modern locomotives in action (often accompanied by helper engines) is on Horseshoe Curve, a National Historic Landmark. Built on a nine-mile incline through the Allegheny Mountains in 1854, the curve is one of the most beautiful (and busiest) sections of railway in the country.

Massive trains of 200 cars seem to be coming and going at the same time when seen from the curve's central vantage point. The viewing platform is often shared by dozens of rail buffs, some equipped with portable scanners for eavesdropping on the conversations of engineers and switchmen, others with notepads in hand to add locomotive numbers to their collections.

© JOANNE MILLER

The New Jersey mail train rockets around Horseshoe Curve.

handles nearly constant rail traffic. This stretch of track is so important to the U.S. economy that it was the subject of an unsuccessful sabotage attempt by Axis powers during World War II. Horseshoe Curve and visitors' center is approximately eight miles northwest of Altoona, on 40th Street/Burgoon Road. It's open April–Dec., Tues.–Sat. 10 A.M.–4 P.M.; Sun. noon–4 P.M.; admission to Horseshoe Curve and the Railroaders Memorial Museum US $7.50 adults, $5 children under 17. Information is also available through the Railroaders Memorial Museum (814/946-0834 or 888/425-8666). There's a small funicular railway that takes visitors up to the viewing platform; ride tokens are two for $1 (for the energetic, a 194-step stairway is also available).

Gallitzin Tunnels Park

The steep incline of the Allegheny Ridge was only partially solved by Horseshoe Curve. In addition, the Pennsylvania Railroad blasted out a 3,612-foot tunnel (Gallitzin Tunnels Park, Jackson and Convent Sts., Gallitzin, Blair County/Cambria County border, free) under the summit of Gallitzin Mountain. The first tunnel, begun in 1851, eliminated the last 150 ver-

tical feet of the curve, and a second tunnel was added in 1905. The Allegheny Tunnel and the Gallitzin Tunnel are the highest and longest tunnels on what was once the Pennsylvania Railroad. The first of the "Twin Tunnels" completed the railroad west, after passing around the Horseshoe Curve. This factor made the tunnels so valuable that they were guarded by Pennsylvania Railroad Police during war times. Both are still in operation, and traffic through the tunnels can be observed from the park.

Conrail Viewing Platform

This is steel-track heaven for rail fans. The Conrail viewing platform is a raised wooden walkway at the dead-end of 2nd Street, off Chestnut/4th Avenue, in Altoona, Blair County. It's open and free to the public year-round and rises 20 feet above hundreds of miles of track, spanning the width of one of Conrail's main switching facilities. To the south, the platform looks over Conrail's primary repair shops from roughly 1st to 7th Streets along Chestnut Avenue; to the north, the view is of the Juniata Locomotive Repair Facility at 4th Avenue and 2nd Street in Juniata (Chestnut Avenue becomes 4th Avenue when it crosses

Juniata Gap Road into the suburb of Juniata). The yards below are strewn with locomotives and parts. Railroad track crew members (once called gandy dancers), switchmen, and engineers move cars and switch lines continually in the busy yard.

Another nearby viewing area is Turntable Park, at 3rd Avenue and 6th Street in Juniata. Free.

East Broad Top Railroad

The only remaining example of a regional narrow-gauge steam-powered rail system east of the Rockies, this little train (Broad Top City, Huntingdon County, 814/447-3011, www.ebtrr.com, open June–Oct. Sat.–Sun., adults $10, children 2–11 $7) has gotten national attention in *Smithsonian* magazine for its unique character. Cars, locomotives, 33 miles of rail, a roundhouse, and even a company town, much of it from the 19th century, make this National Historic Landmark a rare find. Steam trains depart Orbisonia Station at 11 A.M., 1 P.M., and 3 P.M.

Also in Broad Top City, stop by the **Rockhill Trolley Museum** (814/447-9576, www.rockhilltrolley.org, Memorial Day–Oct. Sat.–Sun. and holidays, 11 A.M.–4 P.M., adults $5, children 2–12 $2) to explore its 25 restored cars; trolleys depart each half-hour. Plan a picnic.

The nearby **Broad Top Coal Miners Museum** (Reality Theatre, Main St., Robertsdale, 814/635-3807, www.angelfire.com/pa3/btcoal, Fri.–Sat. 10 A.M.–5 P.M., Sun. 1–5 P.M.; adults $3; children $2) is another part of the complex. The museum houses coal mining and railroading exhibits and a research library. Broad Top City is on SR 913, southeast of Raystown Lake, and Robertsdale is four miles south of there on SR 913.

Old Bedford Village

This village (220 Sawblade Rd, Bedford, Bedford County, 814/623-1156 or 800/238-4347, www.oldbedfordvillage.com) is made up of more than 40 original log homes and shops, transported from all over Pennsylvania to the Bedford site and reconstructed. The purpose of Old Bedford is to reflect the work and lives of pioneers during the 1790s. It's .75 mile south of Bedford on old US 220 (Business 220), via Exit 11 on I-70/76.

Many of the buildings host craft demonstrations such as broom- and candle-making by costumed interpreters, and the village holds several special events throughout the year, including a Crafts Fest, Bluegrass Festival, and Civil War reenactments. Set on 72 acres, the natural footpaths and roads lend themselves to walking (and are also wheelchair-accessible). The Village is open Memorial Day–Labor Day Thurs.–Tues. 9 A.M.–5 P.M.; Labor Day–Oct. Thurs.–Sun. 9 A.M.–5 P.M.; admission is $8, less for children over 6 through college. Some special events are held during the Christmas season—call for details.

AMUSEMENT PARKS
Lakemont Park and The Island Waterpark

Lakemont Park (700 Park Ave., off the Frankstown Rd. exit from US 220, Lakemont, Blair County, 814/949-7275, www.lakemontparkfun.com) has been around since 1894, when it, like many other East Coast amusement parks, was built at the end of the local trolley line to encourage riders.

During May, the park is open weekends only, noon–8 P.M.; June Sun.–Fri. 11 A.M.–9 P.M.; July–Aug. daily 11 A.M.–9 P.M.; Labor Day weekend noon–8 P.M.; Thanksgiving–Jan. 4, 6 P.M.–10 P.M. Admission to the park is free. The Season Pass (includes unlimited rides and water park, does not include minigolf, go-karts) is $35; All Day Ride & Slide Pass (includes The Island Waterpark) $7.95; Evening Ride Pass (5 P.M.–close) $5.95; Monster Motorway Go-Karts $3; Traintown Miniature Golf $2.50; Mini-Indy Go-Karts $1.50; individual ride tickets $.50. Visitors are welcome to picnic in the park for no charge.

In winter, the 13-acre lake in the middle of the park was open for ice skating, and trolleys would mount special indicator lights—green when it was safe to skate, red for not safe—to advertise the status of the lake along the line. Lakemont is one of only four free-admission amusement parks still in existence—another is Bland's in nearby Tipton.

A haven for families with small children and young teens, the park features many familiar rides—Tilt-a-Whirl and a Ferris wheel—as well as a set of water slides and a clever wading pool with a pirate ship spouting water and minifountains for the smaller set. The "Leap the Depths" roller coaster, which is the oldest existing wooden roller coaster in the world, was originally powered by the same method as the trolleys—a 660-volt electric motor. It's an unusual single-car roller coaster, rather than the more familiar train style. "Leap the Depths" is part of a restoration project by American Coaster Enthusiasts and local groups.

Lakemont Park sponsors several events, such as the Keystone Country Festival in September, with entertainment, arts and crafts, and an ethnic food village.

DelGrosso's Amusement Park

This is another turn-of-the-20th-century park (old US 220 between the Bellwood and Grazierville exits in Tipton, Blair County, 814/684-3538, www.delgrossos.com), originally called Bland's after the family farm on which it was built. Fred DelGrosso (of the famous spaghetti sauce) bought the park in 1946, and in 2000, after 50 years of management, the family finally changed the name to its own (perhaps the tasteful DelGrossos didn't find the name piquant enough). The park is open daily mid-June–Aug. Tues.–Sun. 11 A.M.–10 P.M.; May–mid-June and September, it's open on weekends only. Admission and parking are free; individual ride tickets are $.50 each. A season pass is $70 (all-park, all-ride admission). An all-day ride pass with Waterworks is $11; an all-day, all rides, waterworks, and rapids pass is $14; live ponies, golf ($3.50), and Speedway ($3) are not included in All-Day Passes.

DelGrosso's features more than 30 rides (including its trademark carousel), miniature and full-sized golf links, and its special attraction, the Speedway. The Speedway features separate tracks for go-cart and Naskart racing. The waterworks offers rapids, slides, and the "big bucket" (which dumps gallons of water on the "unsuspecting"), among other water play features. The park also promotes a free summer concert series starring classic rock 'n' roll stars such as the Guess

Who, America, and Peter Noone of Herman's Hermits, and a country stars series. Of note for families with young children, Tyrone Hospital sponsors an infant/family care center in the park, with free diapers, baby food, and a quiet atmosphere for time out.

MUSEUMS

Altoona Railroaders Memorial Museum

The former Pennsylvania Railroad Master Mechanics building (1300 9th Ave., Altoona, Blair County, 814/946-0834 or 888/425-8666, www.railroadcity.com; houses the Railroaders Memorial Museum, founded to honor the men and women who labored in various capacities to create the American rail system. Exhibits focus on the uniforms, tasks, and folklore surrounding those who built the tracks and trains as well as those who served on them as technical and service personnel, including switchmen, engineers, conductors, and food-service workers. The museum is open April–Dec., Tues.–Sat. 10 A.M.–4 P.M.;

Juniata Locomotive Shop entrance sign near the Conrail viewing platform

Sun. noon–4 P.M.; admission to Horseshoe Curve and the Railroaders Museum is adults $7.50, children under 17 $5.

Portage Station Museum

The two-story brick structure that houses this small museum (400 Lee St., Portage, Cambria County, 814/736-9223, www.portagestation-museum.org, March–Dec., Wed. and Sat.–Sun. 11 A.M.–4 P.M.; free/donation) was a station on the Pennsylvania Railroad until 1954, when it was sold for commercial use. It is now the permanent home of the Portage Area Historical Society; in addition to exhibits on local life, mining, and railroading, the national award-winning video *63 Men Down* (the story of the Sonman Mine disaster of 1940) is shown during museum hours. Donations for upkeep are appreciated—this is an all-volunteer operation.

Fort Bedford Museum

The original Fort Bedford (end of N. Juliana St., Bedford, Bedford County, 814/623-8891 or 800/259-4284, www.bedfordcounty.net) was built by the British in 1758 as a supply station for troops on their way to recapture Fort Duquesne from the French (the next link in the chain was Ligonier). In use for only a few years, Fort Bedford was manned by a skeleton force. Around 1765, Capt. John Smith deserted his British commission and formed a gang of like-minded locals into a colonial rebel group, the Black Boys. Smith was captured by the British, and the Black Boys attacked and held the fort overnight to successfully regain their leader. After that, British troops deserted the fort; it fell into disrepair and was taken apart piece by piece for use in other buildings.

The blockhouse that encloses the museum is a reproduction of the original. The collection concentrates on the history of Bedford; one highlight is the Transportation Room, which features a number of horse-drawn vehicles, including a Conestoga wagon, milk wagon, wheeled cannon, and carriages. The museum is open June–Aug. and Nov.–April, daily 10 A.M.–5 P.M.; May, Sept.–Oct., Wed.–Sun. 10 A.M.–5 P.M.; admission $4.

SHOPPING

Duncansville Antique Depot

The Duncansville Depot (intersection of SR 764 and US 22, Duncansville, Blair County, 814/696-4000, www.antiquedepots.com; daily 9 A.M.–5 P.M.) is a warehouse-sized building that is home to hundreds of small antique dealers. The booths are patrolled by floorwalkers who can open any cabinet and answer questions. Every type of antique item and collectible is available here, from rare to kitsch—hours of fun for hard-core shoppers. Part of the building is an indoor flea market, which is open on weekends. In the summer, an outdoor flea market is held in the parking lot Thurs. and Labor Day weekend 8 A.M.–4 P.M.

Benzel's Pretzel Factory

Benzel's (5200 6th Ave., Altoona, Blair County, 800/344-4438, www.benzels.com, Mon.–Fri. 10 A.M.–5 P.M.,Sat. 10 A.M.–1 P.M.) produces five million pretzels daily in a 100,000-square-foot bakery. Grandpa Adolf Benzel emigrated from Germany in the late 1800s and started out with a 75-square foot bakery in 1911. The company has been passed from grandfather Benzel to his son, and then to his son's sons. Factory operations are on view through a series of large windows. A brief walking tour gives a little history on Altoona and the pretzel-baking business, and an outlet offers well-priced munchies.

Boyer Candy Company

This manufacturer on the 17th Street bridge between 9th and 10th Streets in Altoona (821 17th St., 814/944-9401, Tues.–Fri. 9 A.M.–4:30 P.M., Sat. 9 A.M.–4 P.M.) welcomes visitors to its outlet with very reasonable prices for its own brand of chocolates (including the venerable Mallo Cup) and other candies. An ownership dispute in 2001 put the company in jeopardy, but the popularity of its products has brought it back to health. Boyer also manufactures for a number of other labels, including Schrafts.

Hollidaysburg, Blair County

This small town has a fine restored downtown diamond on Allegheny Street between Penn and

Juniata Streets. Among the shops that surround the diamond are a number of cafés and eateries. Hollidaysburg hosts a weekly farmers' market on the diamond July–Oct.

The Slinky originated in Hollidaysburg, and the factory is still here, though tours are not offered. There is an outlet in nearby Canal Basin Park, but hours are irregular. Call 814/696-0544 to see if it's open.

OUTDOOR RECREATION

Bicycling

Bedford County has excellent bike routes that combine paved and nonpaved roads, and vary from easy to expert. The visitors' bureau (see Information) has put together a series of maps and routes for all tastes and skill levels—the routes are also available online at www.bedfordcounty.net. **Grouseland Tours** (467 Robinsonville Rd., Clearville, 814/784 5000, www.grouseland.com) offers rentals and complete package tours (also kayaking, swimming, camping—it does it all). **Fat Jimmy's** (Breezewood, Exit 12 off I-70, 814/735-2453, www.fatjimmys.com) rents bikes, canoes, and ski equipment.

Fishing and Water Sports

Shawnee, Koon, and Gordon Lakes, Yellow Creek, and Bob's Creek all have native and stocked trout. The lakes also offer warm-water varieties such as bass and walleye. Yellow Creek has an area designated for fly-fishing. **Adventure Marine** (Whetstone Rd., Bedford, 814/623-1821, www.bedford.net) rents bikes, canoes, kayaks, and camping space, and also outfits trips. To get there from Breezewood (Exit 12 off I-70), take SR 30 west .5 mile to CR 1011; turn right onto CR 1011 at the Graceville sign and LaMalot farm sign. Go north for 2 miles and turn left onto CR 1010; go west on CR 1010 for 2.2 miles and turn right onto Whetstone Road, which is between a house trailer and a farmhouse.

Golf

Bedford Springs (Bedford Springs, 814/623-8700), 18 holes/par 74, was designed by greens architect Donald Ross. The **Down River Golf Course** (in Everett, 814/652-5193), 18 holes/par 72, is next to the Juniata River. **Blue Knob State Park** (R.R. 1, Box 449, Imler, PA 16655-9407, 814/239-5111) offers a nine-hole/par 35 golf course.

Coral Caverns

The caverns (outside the village of Manns Choice, Bedford County, 814/623-6882, www.coralcaverns.com; Memorial Day–Labor Day daily 10 A.M.–5 P.M.; May–June and Sept.–Oct. weekends 10 A.M.–5 P.M., $8) are seven miles west of Bedford on SR 31. One of the most distinctive features of this cave is the coral reef, a towering fossil wall containing the fossilized remains of coral and other sea-creatures buried more than 400 million years ago when Pennsylvania was partially covered by the Appalachian Sea. A large rock and fossil shop is on the premises.

The Lower Trail of the Pennsylvania Canal

This converted Pennsylvania Railroad bed is an 11-mile recreational trail along the Frankstown Branch of the Juniata River (Blair County). The trail is one of the oldest transport routes in the region—it was first used by Native Americans as part of the Kittanning Trail, then by pioneers moving west. In the early 1880s, this section of the river was part of the rail-canal link between Philadelphia and Pittsburgh and became part of the Main Line, which brought growth and abundance to the area. The trail passes through forest and farmland, as well as parts of canal locks, channels, lock-tender house remnants, and the Mt. Etna Furnace, where iron ore was smelted. The ironmaster's residence and related buildings are nearby. Start at the Alexandria trailhead, along SR 305 about a mile off US 22, midway between Huntingdon and Water Street, or the Williamsburg Trailhead, at the pavilion corner of First and Liberty Streets in Williamsburg. Williamsburg is lalong SR 866, about four miles south of US 22, midway between Hollidaysburg and Water Street. For more information contact Rails-to-Trails of Blair County (221 High St., Williamsburg, PA 16693, 814/832-2400).

STATE PARKS

Canoe Creek State Park

This modern day-use park 12 miles east of Altoona (mailing address R.R. 2, Box 560, Hollidaysburg, PA 16648-9752, 814/695-6807, www.dcnr.state.pa.us) offers 958 acres with a panoramic view and a 155-acre lake for fishing, boating, and swimming. Fields and woodlots are managed to provide diversified habitat for small game species and a variety of wildlife. Geologic formations in and around the park are rich in limestone. The park has several old quarry operations, including two calcining plants (limekilns): the Hartman kilns site and the Blair Limestone Company kilns site, which are the focus of historical and interpretive programs and displays.

The park is the home of the largest nursery colony of little brown bats in Pennsylvania. On warm summer evenings, thousands of bats can be seen exiting the old church sanctuary. Education programs about bats are scheduled regularly during the warm months of the year.

Hiking: An extensive hiking and bridle trail system has been developed for people to explore the park on foot or by horseback. Riding horse rentals are not available in the area.

Hunting and Fishing: Approximately 550 acres of Canoe Creek State Park are open to hunting, trapping, and the training of dogs during established seasons. Common game species are deer, pheasant, and rabbit.

The lake has been stocked with walleye, muskellunge, bass, trout, chain pickerel, catfish, crappies, and other panfish. Pennsylvania Fish and Boat Commission laws apply. Ice fishing is a popular winter activity during the extended trout season.

Boating and Swimming: Boats may use electric motors only. Nonpowered boats must have one of the following: state park launching permit or state park mooring permit, which are available at most state park offices; or current Pennsylvania boat registration. Motorboats must display a current boat registration. Motorboats registered in other states must display a Pennsylvania state park launch permit or mooring permit in addition to their current registration. Boat launching

areas are provided on both sides of the lake. Boat mooring spaces are available along the eastern shoreline.

The swimming beach is open Memorial Day Weekend–Labor Day unless posted otherwise. The regular hours are 11 A.M.–7 P.M. A bathhouse, complete with showers and dressing booths, is available for bathers at the beach. The sand beach is 350 feet long. It has a grass sunning area and sand play areas.

Winter Activities: The park is open year-round. Winter activities include ice skating on two ponds next to the Beaver Dam Road Boat Launch, and also sledding, cross-country skiing, ice fishing, and ice-boating.

Camping and Accommodations: The park does not have campsites, but eight modern cabins overlook the lake. They are within walking distance of the swimming area and are available for year-round rental. The rental period in the summer is one week. During the remainder of the year, they may be rented for a minimum of two days. Call 888/PA-PARKS (888/727-2757) for reservations.

Getting There: Travel on US 22 until you arrive at the small village of Canoe Creek (seven miles east of Hollidaysburg), then turn north on the Turkey Valley Road for .5 mile to the main park entrance road.

ⓜ Blue Knob State Park

At 3,146 feet, Blue Knob (124 Park Rd., Imler, PA 16655-9207, border of Bedford and Blair Counties, 814/276-3576, www.dcnr.state.pa.us) is the second-highest peak in Pennsylvania, after Mt. Davis. The views from the peak are spectacular because of its location on a spur of the Allegheny Front overlooking the Allegheny Ridge and valleys below. Since much of the park is wild, visitors are warned to supervise young children closely. Blue Knob offers year-round recreational opportunities and is a favorite of many downhill skiers because of its high vertical drop.

Biking: Several of the park's multiuse trails have been designated for mountain bike use. For the beginner, Chappel's Field Trail is a good challenge. For the more experienced, Three Springs Trail is an intermediate ride. Note: Three Springs

Trail is also open to horseback riding. For the expert mountain biker, Crist Ridge Trail, Rock 'N' Ridge Trail, and parts of Mountain View Trail are available.

Fishing and Hunting: Trout-fishing enthusiasts enjoy Bob's Creek and its tributaries—the waters contain native brook trout and stock trout. Fishing is good April–June and again in the early autumn.

More than 5,000 acres of this 5,614-acre park are open to hunting in season. Wild turkey, deer, squirrel, and grouse are abundant. The park is adjacent to 12,000-acre State Game Land No. 26.

Golf: Blue Knob offers a nine-hole/par 35 course.

Hiking: There are 18 miles of trails through the park, winding through many acres of rugged, forested land, and occasionally passing overgrown pioneer homestead sites. A hike along the Mountain View Trail, accessible from either the Willow Springs picnic area or Group Camp 1, provides a southwestern view along the Appalachian Plateau from the Pavia Overlook. Contact the park (R.R. 1, Box 449, Imler, PA 16655-9407) for maps.

Lost Turkey Trail, constructed in 1977 by the Youth Conservation Corps, is a 17-mile trail traversing state park, state forest, game, and private lands. Distance markers have been installed at one-kilometer intervals. Hikers are advised to secure maps and information on parking areas, trail conditions, and regulations. Many people use sections of this trail for day hikes.

Swimming: A swimming pool with lifeguard on duty is open Memorial Day weekend–Labor Day. The pool is 3–5 feet deep.

Downhill Skiing: The downhill skiing area, leased to Blue Knob Recreation, is one of the finest and most challenging ski resorts in the state—a vertical drop of 1,050 feet. The ski area provides snowtubing, day and night skiing, snowmaking capabilities, and four chairlifts. For information, call 800/458-3403 or visit www.blueknob.com.

Other Winter Sports: Snowmobiles are permitted on marked trails only, for a total of eight miles of routes. The routes are open daily after the end of hunting season in December. Park roadways are not open for snowmobile use. No other off-road vehicles are permitted on state park lands.

Expert cross-country skiers will be challenged by the Sawmill Loop Trail; while for beginners, the Chappel's Fields area, off Knob Road, its adjacent campground, and traffic-restricted roads and campgrounds are recommended. Intermediate skiers may choose the service roads, closed roadways, and open areas. Weather conditions on the trails are usually ideal but skiers should use expert or mountain ski equipment.

Blue Knob Recreation features an outdoor ice rink.

Camping: Forty-five rustic tent and trailer sites are open to the public mid-April–mid-Oct. Sites are in open fields and wooded areas. Twenty-five sites have electric hookups. Two sites are walk-in only. Call 888/PA-PARKS (888/727-2757) Mon.–Sat., 7 A.M.–5 P.M. to reserve campsites. During the winter, the nearest accommodations are within the Blue Knob ski area; the resort offers fully equipped condos, with a two-night minimum.

Getting There: Blue Knob (the village) is at the intersection of SR 164 and Knob (Newry/Pavia) Road; the state park, however, is five miles farther south on Knob Road. The ski resort is off Tower Road, which splits off from Knob at the north end of the park. South access to the park is via SR 869.

ACCOMMODATIONS
Under $50
Living Waters Hostel (300 Campliving Waters Rd., Schellsburg, PA 15559, 814/733 4212, one mile west of the center of Schellsburg, Bedford County, on US 30), an AYH branch, is operated by an active church group, so reservations are necessary to make sure space is available. The hostel itself is a large white building within beautifully landscaped grounds, next to the western edge of Shawnee State Park. Meal packages may be arranged. Rates are around $15 per night.

$50–100

M Jean Bonnet Tavern (6048 Lincoln Hwy./intersection of US 30 and SR 31, Bedford, 814/623-2250, www.jeanbonnettavern.com, $85–120) was licensed as a public house in 1780, though it has been in service since it was built in the 1760s; it's listed on the National Register of Historic Places. The tavern offers a unique experience: a genuine colonial setting with thick fieldstone walls, huge fireplaces, warped plank floors, and chestnut beams. The guest rooms—once minimal at best—have all been pleasantly decorated in a colonial style with updated private baths. The rooms are on the second floor, a small bar is situated on the first floor, and a full-service restaurant (where breakfast is served for overnight guests) is in the authentically dark tavern in the lower level. I spent a misty fall morning on the upstairs porch watching a woodchuck prepare for winter on the lawn below. One caveat: though the roads that border the tavern appear to be quiet country two-lane roads, the considerable noise from trucks rumbling through during the night will be a distraction to light sleepers.

The **Golden Eagle Inn** (131 E. Pitt St., 814/624-0800, www.bedfordgoldeneagle.com, $79–119) is in a recently renovated 1790 building, in downtown Bedford with shops and eateries just a few steps away. The inn offers dining on the premises with full bar service, along with 16 rooms (two with working fireplaces), all with private bath, TV, phone, and air conditioning. Rates include breakfast.

The tranquil **M Covered Bridge Inn** (north of Shawnee State Park on Covered Bridge Rd., Schellsburg, Bedford County, 814/733-4093, $80–110) has long been a favorite for newlyweds (at least one couple was married under the arches of the Colvin Covered Bridge next to the house) and those wanting a quiet getaway. The property was expanded from a log cabin built by pioneer Jacob Schell around 1800; the cabin remains part of the main house today. In addition to the pleasant rooms in the house, all with private bath, there is a fully equipped cottage next to the bridge. Catch-and-release fishing spots and hiking trails are nearby.

$100–150

M Cedar Hill at Spruce Creek Bed and Breakfast (SR 45, Spruce Creek, Huntingdon County, 814/632-3804 or 888/764-9790, www.cedarhillsprucecreek.com, $85–125) is a 42-acre working farm managed by three generations of the Vance family. The 1820 stone house and early 20th-century addition provide comfortable living areas. Each of the six guest rooms has a special theme that sets it apart from the others and allows visitors plenty of space for personal relaxation. Four rooms have private baths, and two of the rooms may be connected with one bath between them. There is a minimum two-night stay for weekends during any special Central Pennsylvania events. Rates include a full breakfast while staying at Cedar Hill, use of comfortable leisure areas, and a light evening refreshment. The bed-and-breakfast is 11 miles east of Tyrone on SR 45 between Water Street and State College, a little over two miles from Indian Caverns.

Spruce Creek Bed and Breakfast (SR 45, within the village of Spruce Creek, Huntingdon County, 814/632-3777, www.sprucecreekbnb.com, $60–170) is nestled next to a thriving trout stream and is popular with hikers, cyclists, and nature lovers of all types. It consists of two homes, next door to each other: the Edward Bell House (1877), four rooms with shared bath, and the John Stockdale Isett House (1833), four rooms with private bath. The homes have been restored to offer comfort and convenience and provide a country getaway from either Altoona or State College.

The **Bedford House** (203 W. Pitt St., Bedford, Bedford County, 814/623-7171, www.bedford county.net, $90–145) was a latecomer by local standards—built about 1788, 40 years after the founding of Fort Bedford. Situated on the edge of town, this two-story brick home is within easy walking distance to the downtown historical area and the Bedford Museum. All rooms have a private bath, though some require a few steps down the hall (robes are provided). Some rooms have gas fireplaces and private entrances; reservations are encouraged. All rooms for the first two weekends in October require a two-night minimum at double occupancy rates.

$150–200

Pine Cone Condos (contact Sheryl Bradley, 2513 Lark Ave., Altoona, PA 16602, 814/949-5927, www.bedfordcounty.net, $150–185) are privately owned homes in Blue Knob Resort, Claysburg, Blair County, that include one-bedroom/one bath, and two-bedroom/two-bath units. Both offer fully equipped kitchens, queen beds, TV, and fireplaces in the living room, as well as a private balcony or patio. The resort's indoor pool and hot tub areas and tennis courts are available for guests to use at no charge. Spring, summer, and fall, two-night getaway packages are available.

FOOD

Casual/Inexpensive

M The Dream (1510 Allegheny St., Hollidaysburg, Blair County, 814/696-3384, www.thedreamrestaurant.com, Sun.–Thurs. 8 A.M.–9 P.M., Fri.–Sat. 8 A.M.–9 P.M.) is a popular restaurant that serves mountainous plates of old favorites such as fried chicken and stuffed pork chops at decent prices. A children's menu is available, and the Sugar and Spice Bakery on the premises produces all the restaurant's baked goods. On weekends, reservations are suggested to avoid a wait—breakfast, lunch, and dinner are all equally well attended at this former diner. Prices average $5 for breakfast and lunch, $10 for dinner, and there are lunch and dinner specials on the menu every day.

M Ed's Steak House (4476 Business Route 220, 814/623-8894, Mon.–Thurs. 7 A.M.–9 P.M., Fri.–Sat. 7 A.M.–10 P.M., sometimes Sun.), a family-owned operation since 1954, is an updated diner with pleasant serving rooms (including a nonsmoking area) and a broad menu that will please everyone with its quality and low prices. This is a good place to stop with the family for a meal or light snack. The chef shows genius in preparing that ultimate diner dinner, liver and onions with bacon; expect mountains of potatoes with gravy. Ed's is on the Bedford exit off I-70/76. Prices are reasonable—breakfast and lunch $8 or less; dinner averages $10.

The Landmark (647 E. Pitt St., Bedford, 814/623-6762) with two locations in Bedford

(the other is on S. Juliana St.), is where many Bedfordites stop for coffee and a slice of pie. Its proximity to downtown makes it a convenient stop for visitors as well—the prices are low, $3–10, and the menu is American diner-style.

Midrange

M The U.S. Hotel (401 S. Juniata St., Hollidaysburg, Blair County, 814/695-9924, www.theushotel.com, brunch Sun. 10 A.M.–2 P.M., lunch Mon.–Fri. 11 A.M.–2 P.M., dinner daily 4:30 P.M.–close, tavern 11 A.M.–1 A.M.), built during the canal heyday of central Pennsylvania, went through a devastating fire and several changes of hand to become a popular bar and restaurant for today's visitors. The tavern, with a hand-carved mahogany backbar, beveled mirrors, and stained-glass windows, still boasts a water-trough spittoon that flows beneath the brass foot rail (a limited menu is served here also—averaging $6). The restaurant serves continental-style dishes with some unique additions, such as boar and buffalo. Expect to pay around $7 for lunch, $17 for dinner, served daily.

One step beyond the heavy wood doors of the **M Jean Bonnet Tavern** (6048 Lincoln Hwy., intersection of US 30 and SR 31, Bedford, 814/623-2250, www.jeanbonnettavern.com, lunch daily 11 A.M.–5 P.M., dinner weekdays 5–9 P.M. and Fri.–Sat. until 10 P.M., Sun. 10 A.M.–8 P.M.), and visitors swear that they've time-traveled back to the days of the old Forbes Road. This remarkably preserved 200-year-old-plus public house, with its wood fires and candle-powered lighting, is an unusual experience. The colonial-style restaurant in the basement has lightened up the menu and added a variety of chicken, fish, and beef dishes with fresh vegetables. Lunch averages $7, and dinner is in the $15 range. If subterranean dining isn't on your agenda, go upstairs to the actual tavern, on ground level. The entire menu is also served here during the day.

Formal/Expensive

M The Allegro Restaurant (3926 Broad Ave., Blair County, 814/946-5216 or 800/372-5534, www.allegro-restaurant.com, lunch

Thurs.–Fri. 11:30 A.M.–1 P.M., dinner Mon.–Thurs. 4–9 P.M., Sat. 4–10 P.M.), situated in a nondescript building outside of downtown Altoona, has built an outstanding reputation since 1978, winning several central Pennsylvania Premier Restaurant awards through the years for its Italian twist on old favorites: veal, steaks, chops, and seafood. Pricewise, it's a special occasion restaurant—averaging $9 for lunch, $25 for dinner—but well worth the splurge.

INFORMATION

Find out more about Altoona and the surrounding area by contacting **Allegheny Mountains Convention and Visitors Bureau** (1 Convention Center Dr., Altoona, PA 16602, 814/943-4183 or 800/842-5866, www.alleghenymountains.org).

Contact the **Bedford County Conference and Visitors Bureau** (141 S. Juliana St., Bedford, PA 15522, 814/623-1771 or 800/765 3331, www.bedfordcounty.net) for information on the area.

Huntingdon County and the Big Valley

Huntingdon County is celebrated for its outdoor recreational opportunities, particularly Raystown Lake, the largest natural body of water in the state. It's also the site of two of central Pennsylvania's most well-known caverns.

Try writing out "Kishacoquillas Valley" a few times and you'll understand why folks around here just call it Big Valley. Along with the Juniata Valley, it encompasses large sections of Mifflin, Juniata, and Perry Counties and is almost entirely covered with farms. Lewistown, the 197-year-old seat of Mifflin County, is the economic hub of the area, with a thriving small-town main street. This city of 9,500 residents was once an industrial center; several large manufacturing sites were permanently damaged during Hurricane Agnes in 1972, but only one year later it was named an All-American City for its successful recovery.

The Big Valley has a long-standing Amish and Mennonite population base. Unlike "Amish Country" in south-east Pennsylvania, the culture remains unspoiled, an integral part of the landscape. People in the valley told me that when young, uncommitted (i.e., unconfirmed in the faith) Amish want to experience the world, they take an apartment in the big city of Lewistown. Most return to the fold within a year.

GOOSE DAY

Goose Day is colloquial central Pennsylvania-speak for the religious holiday Michaelmas, the feast day of St. Michael the Archangel. The actual date on which Michaelmas falls, September 29, has been celebrated in England since the 5th century. The custom on that day was to present one's debt holder with a fattened goose along with payment to ensure good relations. Legend has it that central Pennsylvania Dutch acquired the custom just after the end of the Revolutionary War, when a local farmer hired a former British sailor to help him and agreed to the young man's insistence that they "settle all debts on September 29." On that day, the young man appeared at the door with the best goose from his flock and related the Michaelmas story (including the proverb "Eat goose on Michaelmas Day, you'll never want for money"). Today, many central Pennsylvanians feast on the birds just for luck on September 29, either at home or at one of the dozens of area restaurants, hotels, fire stations, or fraternal orders that serve goose dinners

POINTS OF INTEREST
Mifflinburg Buggy Museum
A century ago, the entire economy of Mifflinburg was based on its production of horse-drawn wagons—so much so that it was referred to as Buggy Town. The museum (523 Green St., Mifflinburg, Union County, 717/966-1355, www.lycoming.org/buggy, May–Sept. Thurs.–Sun. 1–5 P.M.; weekends only in Oct. 1–5 P.M., $4) is inside the buildings of the original William Heiss Coach

Works and features a restored home as well as the necessary work areas, tools, and a number of vehicles.

Purity Candy

In 1907, Henry Ford was getting the first Model-T into production, the Wright Brothers were launching the aviation age at Kitty Hawk, and in Lewisburg, Ford G. Burchard was starting the Purity Candy Company (422 Market St., Lewisburg, Union County, 800/821-4748, www.puritycandy.com). He used all natural ingredients, simple machines, and carefully tested recipes. He believed that making small batches by hand contributed to Purity's outstanding reputation for quality. The Burfeindt family continues to use the same recipes and techniques as the company's founder, and you can sample for yourself at either of Purity's two locations, the retail shop (above) or the factory/store on SR 15 in Allenwood. It offers a variety of filled chocolates and its best-seller, the milk-chocolate covered pretzel.

Brookmere Winery

Brookmere (5369 SR 655, Belleville, Mifflin County, 717/935-5380, www.brookmerewine .com), five miles west of the intersection of SR 655 and US 322, produces a large number of table wine blends and a few varietals. The winery is open year-round Mon.–Sat. 10 A.M.–5 P.M., Sun. 1–4 P.M. The wines are notable for their artistic labels—one (Valley Mist, a blend of white varietals) portrays an Amish carriage on a local road. An art gallery is on the upper level of the tasting room. Tours are available on request, and visitors must be age 21 to taste.

SHOPPING
Belleville Market

Early Wednesday mornings, the roads leading to Belleville, Mifflin County, are packed nose-to-tail with horse-drawn buggies. Once at the market site, two blocks south of Main Street, the same steaming horses lounge in front of their now-empty carriages and crop the roadside grass

as their passengers buy and sell at one of the best country markets in Pennsylvania. There's a flea market that sells the usual T-shirts and junk, plus plenty of fresh produce and baked goods. The real eye candy here, though, is the people, and a way of life that's been blasted into history by high-speed thruways and supermarkets. One of the big draws for the Amish is the livestock auction, which takes place later in the day.

Peighty's Store

Peighty's (Apple House Road, Belleville, no phone) sells touristy souvenirs of the Amish. It's a good place to pick up cheap items, but if it's authenticity and quality you're after and you're staying in the area, ask your host (or people at the restaurants) if they know of anyone who's selling handmade goods, such as straw hats and clothing. A number of Amish women make goods for sale; they're generally more expensive (the hats I saw ranged $12–45), but they're worth it. Don't think

bargaining at the Belleville Market

the Amish are naive about the worth of their labor in any way. The women I dealt with may turn away from modern society, but they were shrewd traders; set a fair limit on what you want to pay before you start to negotiate, respect your-self and the person you're dealing with, and you'll both walk away happy.

OUTDOOR RECREATION

Raystown Lake

Raystown, the largest lake totally within the bounds of the state of Pennsylvania, is maintained by the U.S. Army Corps of Engineers (mailing address Raystown Lake, R.D. 1, Box 222, Hesston, PA 16647, 814/658-3405, http://raystown.nab.usace.army.mil). It's a central recreation area and offers every commercial service: tour boats, tent and trailer camping (mid-May–mid-Sept., reservations:www.reserveusa .com), hiking, lodging, and eateries. This body of water is famous for its enormous striped bass, and several guide services are available. Contact the Huntingdon County Visitors Bureau (R.D. 1, Box 222-A, Seven Points Rd., Hesston, PA 16647, 814/658-0060 or 888/729-7869, www.raystown.org) for a list of service providers and a map of the area.

Stone Valley Recreation Area

Owned and operated by Penn State University, Stone Valley (mailing address: Stone Valley Recreation Area, 108 Business Services Bldg., University Park, PA 16802-1002, 814/863-1164, www.psu.edu) is open year-round. It features 11 cabins for rent, boat rentals, and fishing on the lake, 25 miles of hiking and cross-country ski trails, and ice skating and ice fishing in the winter. In addition, Shavers Creek Environmental Center is within the recreation area; here you'll find hummingbird, bee, and butterfly gardens, exhibits, and a birds of prey education center. Stone Valley is on SR 26, between Pine Grove Mills and McAlevys Fort, Huntingdon County. For information and cabin reservations, call 814/863-1164. Three state parks are also accessible off SR 26 between Pine Grove Mills and

McAlevys Fort: Whipple Dam, Greenwood Furnace, and Penn Roosevelt.

CAVERNS

Indian Caverns

Used by Native Americans more than 400 years ago as a winter shelter, council chamber, and burial ground, Indian Caverns (SR 45, Spruce Creek, Huntingdon County, mailing address Indian Caverns, Indian Trail, Spruce Creek, PA 16683, 814/632-7578, www.indiancaverns.com; May 30 Labor Day, daily 9 A.M.–6 P.M.; April–May and Sept.–Oct. daily 9 A.M.–4 P.M.; adults $9, children 6–12 $4.50) also served as a hideout for local bandit David Lewis 1816–1820. The cavern—the largest limestone cave in Pennsylvania—features several unique formations, including an enormous sheet of flowstone larger than a two-story building, a "musical rock," and the Star Room grotto. More than 500 Native American relics are on display. Concrete and gravel walkways make this tour a good choice for those who have difficulty with rocky terrain. Dress in layers: the air is a constant 56°F (13°C) all year. Indian Caverns is three miles northeast of the village of Spruce Creek; look for directional signs on SR 45.

Lincoln Caverns

A one-hour tour winds through both Lincoln Caverns and Whisper Rocks Cave (US 22, Huntingdon, Huntingdon County, 814/643-1358, www.lincolncaverns.com). The caverns are open Memorial Day weekend–June 30 daily 9 A.M.– 5 P.M.; July–Labor Day daily 9 A.M.–6 P.M.; March–May and Sept.–Nov. daily 9 A.M.–4 P.M.; and Dec. Sat.–Sun. with tours at 11 A.M., 1 P.M. and 3 P.M. Tours are available in January and February by appointment. Admission is $9.50 with an additional charge to pan for gems.

The passageways and rooms are lined with ornate formations and contain flowstones, limestone stalactites (formed by mineral-rich water dripping from the ceiling), and white calcite and quartz crystals. Lincoln Caverns is 2.1 miles west of the US 22/SR 26 intersection.

ACCOMMODATIONS AND FOOD

Alas, Esther Studer no longer takes on boarders at her Farview Farm, but she recommends **Mercer & Bratt Bed & Breakfast** (3782 W. Main St./SR 655, 717/935-2327, $55–65) on the edge of the village of Belleville. Elaine (Mercer) and Mike (Bratt)'s lovely white Victorian features three guestrooms; all share a bath on the second floor and a half-bath on the first floor. The views of Big Valley are gorgeous from here, and a full country breakfast awaits in the morning. West Main Street is actually SR 655, and trucks sometimes rumble through in the middle of the night, so if you're a light sleeper, request a room away from the street.

M A. J. Peachey and Sons Restaurant (at the intersection of Barrville Rd. and SR 655 near Belleville, 717/667-2185) is Mennonite-owned (no tipping) and employs a number of its Amish neighbors, many of whom stop in for the buffet or dinner. A gut-stretching farm meal costs so little one would swear that the menu is misprinted. This is real Pennsylvania country cooking: plain food, great prices, and an experience you won't soon forget. Next to the restaurant is a store featuring fresh produce, meats of all kinds, and bulk foods. Peachey's is closed Sun. and all Christian holidays. It's open Mon.–Thurs. and Sat. 6 A.M.–7 P.M., Fri. 6 A.M.–8 P.M. A full meal costs around $6. Friday—seafood day—the price goes up to $8.65.

INFORMATION

Huntingdon County information is available from **Huntingdon County Visitors Bureau** (R.D. 1, Box 222-A, Seven Points Rd., Hesston, PA 16647, 814/658-0060 or 888/Raystown, www.raystown.org).

The **Juniata River Valley Visitors Bureau** (152 E. Market St., Ste. 103, Lewistown, PA 17044, 717/248-6713 or 877/568-9739, www.juniatarivervalley.org) has information on Mifflin, Perry, and Juniata Counties.

Civil War Country

Leaning over from west to east like a wind-blown cedar, the Allegheny Ridge rises from the Big Valley to mark the first and final mountainous boundary that separates the flat and fertile Piedmont of southern Pennsylvania from the rest of the state. This area is home to history, being the site of more military activity during the Civil War than any other area in the north. Fulton, Franklin, and Adams Counties make up Civil War Country.

M CIVIL WAR HISTORIC TRAIL

The Cumberland Valley in Franklin County was the target of three major Confederate cavalry raids—Stuart in 1862, Jenkin in 1863, and McCausland in 1864—as well as several skirmishes. A full-scale Confederate invasion, the Gettysburg campaign of 1863, began in Franklin County. The route starts on US 30, at the top of Tuscarora Mountain. The forested crest offers a spectacular view of McConnellsburg to the west and the gentle hills of the Piedmont to the east. The entire route will take at least one full day, depending on your interests.

Head east on US 30, turn south on Fort Loudon Road, then right (southwest) on to Mountain Road, CR 28051, which dead-ends in Cove Gap, the birthplace of James Buchanan, 15th president of the United States. A pyramid, fronting an 18-acre park, serves as a marker. Turn left (south) on SR 16 to Mercersburg.

Mercersburg

The Mansion House, a popular hotel in 1852, was the site of a speech by James Buchanan. Ten years later, recruiting rallies were held in front for Company C, the 126th Pennsylvania Infantry. The hotel is on the southwest corner of the Mercersburg diamond.

This picturesque town also saw frequent action during the war by Confederate raiding parties, including Mosby's and McNeill's Rangers. During the first Chambersburg Raid of 1863 by Gen. J. E. B. Stuart, rebel forces took over the Steiger family home, a stone house (120 N. Main St.) where General Stuart took his lunch.

In 1863, nearly 700 wounded Confederates captured by Union cavalry were brought here; many buildings became makeshift field hospitals. One was the Reformed Church, now the United Church of Christ (129 E. Seminary St.). Also used was the Reformed Church Seminary. Two of the original seminary buildings stand today, known as North and South Cottage, in the Mercersburg Academy off Academy Lane. The cabin in which James Buchanan was born is also on the campus grounds. At the end of Bennet Avenue in Mercersburg lies the Black Cemetery, which contains the graves of numerous veterans of the United States Colored Troops (USCT).

Greencastle

Continue west on SR 16 to Greencastle. In June of 1863, most of the Army of Northern Virginia—more than 65,000 men, 200 cannons, 2,000 vehicles, and 10,000 horses and mules—passed through Greencastle. The first Union soldier to die in Pennsylvania during the war, William Rihl, met his fate at what is now the intersection of US 11 north of Greencastle and Mason Road.

Rouzerville

Continue west on SR 16 through Waynesboro to the intersection of SR 16 and old SR 16 near Rouzerville. The brick house at the intersection is Stephey Tavern, where Gen. Robert E. Lee and his staff took food while retreating from Gettysburg. This area, the Monterey Pass, was also the site of Kilpatrick's Union cavalry attack on Lee's troops. Union forces captured more than 1,000 prisoners and many supply wagons. Much of the original roadway lies beneath Old SR 16 as it extends down the mountainside to Rouzerville. The area south of the intersection of SR 16 and old SR 16 saw heavy fighting.

Return west through Waynesboro and make a right turn on SR 316 (Wayne Road, north) toward Chambersburg. Turn right (east) on New

Franklin Road; the stone farmhouse just east of the railroad tracks on the left is the Snyder farm, in New Franklin.

New Franklin

After the battle of Gettysburg, farmer Jacob Snyder wrote this account:

After 10 or 11 o'clock on the night of Saturday, July 4, 1863, we heard a great noise . . , along the road. . . . I at once arose, struck a light, opened the door and went out, and in less than fifteen minutes the large hall of my house and the yard in front were filled with wounded Confederate soldiers. They at once set up a clamor. . . . "Water! Water! Give us water!" They also begged to have their wounds dressed. O, what a sight!

Return to Wayne Road and continue north. At the "Y," take the left fork and look for Bowman Road (it may also be signed as Country Road), then turn left (west). Make the first left on to Country Road.

Confederate stragglers murdered farmer Isaac Strite when he refused to tell where his money was kept. His house and barn still stand, slightly modernized, at 2999 Country Road. Follow Country Road west to the end, and turn right (northwest) on Guilford Springs Road to US 11. Take US 11 north to Chambersburg.

Chambersburg

In 1859, abolitionist leader John Brown—using the name Isaac Smith—rented a room at 225 E. King St. in Chambersburg and began planning his famous raid on Harper's Ferry. After the raid, John Cooke, an associate of Brown's, was held in the Franklin County Jail at 175 E. King Street. Today, the jail is the home of the county historical society.

In 1861, Union Gen. Robert Patterson encamped in Chambersburg before his unsuccessful assault on Confederate forces in the Shenandoah Valley to the south.

In the aftermath of the Battle of Antietam, September 1862, Chambersburg became an important supply and hospital center for the Union.

ROOTS OF THE CONFLICT

Since America's colonial period, individual states insisted on their right to oppose the demands and impositions of federal government, particularly in the areas of taxes and tariffs; pro and antislavery elements existed in America since Europeans landed on the nation's shores. Tariff arguments often pitted northern manufacturing interests against southern planters and slaveholders, favoring the former. This friction increased during the half-century following the formation of the Union, when America expanded through several large purchases of territory. The combination of these elements formed the basis for the Civil War.

Politics and economics became linked during the first half of the 19th century, with the passage of the Missouri Compromise (1821), which prohibited slavery in the majority of the Louisiana Purchase territory. Southern states feared that their power in the House of Representatives would dwindle as new free states came into being. To appease them, the Fugitive Slave Act of 1850 was drafted, permitting slaveholders to locate and capture slaves who had fled to free states. The act was challenged by slave Dred Scott, who sued his master in court for his freedom after they had resided for a period in a free state. The court case dragged on for several years, and Scott's petition was finally denied by the Supreme Court in 1857.

New controversy arose over the status of the Kansas and Nebraska Territories, which were supposedly covered by the Missouri Compromise.

Moneyed Northerners wished to run the transcontinental railroad through the territories (rather than farther south, as had been planned originally). In order to garner Southern support for the route, Sen. Stephen A. Douglas of Illinois proposed that the principle of popular sovereignty be applied, allowing the settlers in each territory to decide for themselves. The resulting act repealed the Missouri Compromise and led to a flight of pro- and antislavery settlers—and violence—into "bleeding Kansas."

Businessman and abolitionist John Brown, along with five of his sons, became embroiled in the struggle between proslavery and antislavery forces for control of the territorial government in Kansas. By the spring of 1855, civil war had broken out in the state and Brown had assumed command of a local Free-Soil militia. In less than a year, proslavery forces had sacked the Free-Soil town of Lawrence, an event that triggered a bloody retaliation by Brown. During the night of May 24, 1856, Brown, four of his sons, and two other followers invaded the Pottawatomie River country and killed five helpless settlers, hacking them with sabers.

Brown, who was never caught, took full responsibility for the act. From then on, Brown became even more preoccupied with abolition by slave insurrection and was responsible for a raid on the federal arsenal at Harper's Ferry, an event that fueled the Civil War. Though not representative of the majority of abolitionists, Brown and

Four hundred wounded soldiers were brought to recover or die in private homes in the town.

On October 10, 1862, Confederate Gen. J. E. B. Stuart's cavalry destroyed the Cumberland Valley Railroad warehouses and shops. Stuart's raiders approached Chambersburg from the west on what is now Radio Hill on US 30. The outstanding view of the town helped Stuart plan an effective attack.

In June 1863, Gen. Robert E. Lee and 65,000 Confederate troops camped in and around Chambersburg. Lee and Gen. A. P. Hill strategized on the town diamond. In Messersmith's Woods, on Lincoln Way East at Coldbrook Avenue, a Confederate scout named Harrison reported that the Army

of the Potomac was marching into Pennsylvania, prompting Lee's decision to move east to Gettysburg. A historical marker lies on the south side of the intersection, though recent research suggests that the encampment was north of the highway.

Chambersburg was held for ransom in 1864 by Confederate Gen. John McCausland and his cavalry. McCausland issued his ultimatum in front of the Franklin County courthouse, on the northeast corner of Memorial Square: pay $100,000 in gold or the city would burn. Confederate artillery fired a warning shot, and the cannonball's entry is marked by stars on the west wall of the building. When the ransom went unpaid, citizens of Cham-

others like him roused the deep-seated fear of a slave uprising among Southerners. By mid-1855, the spirit of accommodation which had held the Union together began to erode.

In the early 1830s, slaveholding states claimed the largest number of antislavery societies in the United States. During the next 20 years, northern abolitionists stopped attacking slavery in the state legislatures and began morally condemning all those who lived in the South. In defense, Southerners who had been ambivalent about the slavery question up to that time developed a philosophy of positive good, arguing that slave holders provided shelter, food, and care for a race unable to compete in the modern world. Threatened economically by the developing North, and satirized and condemned in popular culture (Harriet Beecher Stowe's *Uncle Tom's Cabin* was wildly popular), slaveholding states in the South began to draw together. By the mid-1850s, there were no antislavery societies south of the Mason-Dixon line.

In the U.S. election of 1860, the Democratic party shattered over the issues of slavery and states' rights, spreading its influence among several candidates. Republican Abraham Lincoln captured the election through the electoral college (180 against 123), though he lost the popular vote by nearly one million ballots. Proslavery states were anti-Lincoln—they referred to him as "the black Republican." The South was in a strong position, economically, and many thought that the threat of secession alone would force acceptance of Southern demands. Popular sentiment overwhelmed temperance, however, and on December 20, 1860, South Carolina voted to secede, followed within the year by Mississippi, Florida, Alabama, Georgia, and Louisiana. Virginia, North Carolina, Tennessee, and Arkansas followed the next year, though West Virginia broke off from the rest of the state to remain in the Union. Jefferson Davis became president of the Confederate States of America and set about protecting Fort Sumter in Charleston Harbor—the symbol of the Confederate states' sovereignty. Eleven Confederate states, containing nine million people (including three million slaves), few railroads, poorly organized manufacturing and agricultural networks, and no more than $27 million in funds, stood against 23 northern states, 22 million people, well-oiled transportation and manufacturing systems, and diplomatic relations with foreign nations offering unlimited international credit.

Jefferson Davis, an able and effective politician, made several attempts to negotiate with Lincoln's cabinet. But when a Union expedition came to Fort Sumter on April 12, 1861, Confederate cannons opened fire. Lincoln did not declare war; he officially denied the existence of the Confederacy and asked for volunteers to put down "combinations too powerful to be suppressed by the ordinary course of judicial proceedings." Within days, fighting broke out and the Civil War had officially begun.

bersburg took refuge in the Cedar Grove Cemetery on King Street. The Masonic Temple on 2nd Street near Queen Street and surrounding buildings were among the few that escaped the razing—spared, legend has it, by Confederate brother masons.

From Chambersburg, travel east on US 30 to Fayetteville.

Fayetteville
In 1863, General Hill's 3rd Corps, Army of Northern Virginia, bivouacked here in preparation for the move to Gettysburg. General Hill stayed at Font Hill, a brick home north of US 30 on Woodstock Road (.4 mile).

Ahead of advancing rebel forces, Confederate Gen. Jubal A. Early ordered his raiders to burn the Thaddeus Stevens Iron Works in June 1863. The blacksmith shop remains, now a museum, on US 30, nine miles east of Fayetteville at the Caledonia State Park entrance. The troops continued to Gettysburg.

STATE PARKS
Cowans Gap State Park
Cowans Gap (vicinity of Richmond Furnace, Fulton County, mailing address Cowans Gap State Park, 6235 Aughwick Rd., Fort Loudon, PA

17224-9801, 717/485-3948, www.dcnr.state .pa.us) was named after Maj. Samuel Cowan, a British officer during the Revolutionary War. He fell in love with the daughter of a Boston merchant, but being a British officer he was rejected by his lover's father. After the war he returned to Boston and the two eloped to Chambersburg. After a few years, they decided to move to the Bluegrass Region of Kentucky. Their wagon broke down en route, and they traded their wagon to a Native American chief for the tract of land that later became known as Cowans Gap. Forbes Road Trail passes through the park. This historic frontier path was made by General Forbes in 1758 to relieve a siege at Fort Duquesne (Pittsburgh) during the French and Indian War. The first park facilities were opened in 1937. The cabin colony was listed in the National Register of Historical Places in 1987.

Hiking: There are 10 miles of hiking trails in the park and many more trails in the adjacent state forest land. Because of the terrain some of the trails are not for beginners, especially sections of Cameron, Horseshoe, and Three Mile Trails. Information on individual trails can be obtained at the park office.

The 105-mile Tuscarora Trail in Pennsylvania and Maryland connects to the Big Blue Trail that starts in northern Virginia. The Tuscarora Trail runs parallel to the Appalachian Trail and junctions with it and the Darlington Trail near Deans Gap, north of Carlisle. The Tuscarora Trail is marked with rectangular blue blaze marks painted on trees.

Forbes Road Trail is not a state park hiking trail. The section through Cowans Gap State Park is on the Stumpy Lane and Allen Valley Roads.

Hunting and Fishing: Approximately 630 acres are open to hunting, trapping, and the training of dogs during established seasons. Common game species are deer, turkey, and squirrel. Dog training is permitted only from the day following Labor Day to March 31 in designated hunting areas.

Cowans Gap Lake offers excellent trout fishing and also has bass, perch, and panfish. The South Branch of Little Aughwick Creek offers good trout fishing.

Swimming: The 500-foot beach offers excellent swimming and sunbathing. The beach is open Memorial Day weekend–Labor Day daily 11 A.M.–7 P.M. unless otherwise posted.

Boating: There are two boat launches and 68 mooring spaces on 42-acre Cowans Gap Lake. Boats may use electric motors. Nonpowered boats must have one of the following: state park launching permit or state park mooring permit, which are available at most state park offices; or current Pennsylvania boat registration. Motorboats must display a current boat registration. Motorboats registered in other states must display a Pennsylvania state park launch permit or mooring permit in addition to their current registration.

Ice Fishing: All of the lake is open for ice fishing except the ice-skating area. For your safety, be sure the ice is four inches thick and carry safety equipment.

Ice Skating: A section of the lake is available exclusively for ice skating. It is recommended that skaters contact the park office to check the ice conditions. During the winter, ice conditions are monitored only in the ice-skating area. Be aware of "Unsafe Ice" signs posted throughout the lake area.

Cross-Country Skiing: Closed park roads and some of the hiking trails are suitable for cross-country skiing.

Camping and Cabins: Cowans Gap has 233 campsites with a sanitary dump station, modern comfort stations with flush toilets, and hot showers. The campsites will accommodate campers from the smallest tent to 30-foot motor homes. Seven walk-in tent sites are adjacent to Camping Area B. An overnight courtesy boat mooring area is provided for registered campers during their stay at the park. The camping area is open from the second Friday of April until the day following the antlerless deer season in December.

The park has 10 rustic cabins available during the spring, summer, and fall. The three-room cabins have a four-person overnight capacity. They contain a refrigerator, stove, inside fireplace, and two bunk beds. There is no indoor plumbing; a water faucet is outside and a central comfort station has showers and flush toilets. Make reservations by calling 888/PA-PARKS (888/727-2757), Mon.–Sat., 7 A.M.–5 P.M.

Getting There: The park is in the foothills of the Tuscarora Mountains on the western side of the Cumberland Valley just south of US 30 between Chambersburg and McConnellsburg. From US 30, take SR 75 north at Fort Loudon to Richmond Furnace and follow signs. Cowan's Gap sits in the 70,242-acre Buchanan State Forest; for information and maps contact Buchanan State Forest, Department of Conservation and Natural Resources (R.D. 2, Box 3, McConnellsburg, PA 17233).

Buchanan's Birthplace State Park

This 19-acre day-use park (mailing address Buchanan's Birthplace State Park, c/o Cowans Gap, Fort Loudon, PA 17224-9801, 717/485-3948, www.dcnr.state.pa.us) marks the birthplace of James Buchanan, 15th president of the United States and the only Pennsylvanian to ever occupy the office of president. A stone monument surrounded by majestic conifers stands on the site of the Buchanan cabin. The park is nestled in the gap of Tuscarora Mountain; Buck Run, a native brook trout stream, skirts the perimeter. The park is on SR 16, about six miles north of Mercersberg.

ACCOMMODATIONS AND FOOD

M Cashtown Inn and Restaurant (1325 Old US 30, Cashtown, 717/334-9722 or 800/367-1797, www.cashtowninn.com), at the west end of Cashtown village, one mile south of US 30, eight miles northwest of Gettysburg, has been serving travelers by candlelight since 1797. Now managed by innkeeper Dennis, Eileen, and Jason Hoover, the inn served as the first stagecoach station west of Gettysburg. It housed Confederate Gen. A. P. Hill and his headquarters staff before and during the Gettysburg campaign. Civil War fans will recognize the inn from its appearance in the TV miniseries *Gettysburg*, featuring actor Sam Elliott.

All rooms have four-poster or canopy beds and private baths; the inn's decor reflects the Civil War period. A two-night stay is required on all holidays and weekends from Memorial Day through October. Rates, which include a full breakfast, range $100–150.

Restaurant specialties (lunch Tues.–Sat. 11:30 A.M.–3 P.M., dinner Tues.–Thurs. and Sun. 5–8 P.M., Fri.–Sat. 5–9 P.M.; lunch $10, dinner $19) include gruyere of veal ($18.50), and an Angus beef filet mignon ($23), plus a number of seafood specialties. Reservations are recommended. The adjacent tavern, open until 2 A.M., is a local favorite.

INFORMATION

The **Fulton County Tourist Promotion Agency** (112 N. 2nd St., McConnellsburg, PA 17233, 717/485-4064) and **Cumberland Valley Visitors Council** (1235 Lincoln Way E, Chambersburg, PA 17201, 717/261-1200) both have information on sites and events on the Civil War Trail.

Gettysburg and Adams County

Is there anyone who hasn't heard of Gettysburg? Before the Civil War, this tiny, isolated farming community was one of dozens of villages eking out an existence on the lower Piedmont. After the eponymous three-day battle, both the Union and Confederate armies filled every shelter with wounded and dying soldiers. Gettysburg became a symbol of the stubborn horror in the American Civil War. Almost immediately, reporters and artists were dispatched from New York and London to tell the story of what happened in the quiet fields and orchards. The village achieved celebrity—and kept it. The only really surprising aspect is that Gettysburg hasn't become an industry, a historical Disneyland. There are indeed wax museums (some quite good), documentaries, and plastic souvenirs, but somehow Gettysburg has remained true to itself. The town, with a variety of shops and restaurants, is pleasant, though crowded during the warmer months. Above all, the battlefield, memorialized by the regiments that fought there, still stirs the soul and memory.

Adams County, in which Gettysburg is the jewel, also offers a few interesting side trips, especially to Biglerville's Apple Museum and country store.

HISTORIC SITES

Ⓜ Gettysburg National Military Park

Gettysburg National Military Park lies immediately south of the town of Gettysburg. There is no charge to view the battlefield and enter the visitors' center (97 Taneytown Rd./SR 134, 717/334-1124, www.nps.gov/gett, Sept.–May daily 8 A.M.–5 P.M., June–Aug. daily 8 A.M.–6 P.M.). Inside the visitors' center, a giant electronic relief map chronicles the battle (30 minutes, $4 adults, $3 seniors and children). The center also contains a vast museum that features the George Rosensteel Collection of original artifacts, uniforms, and weapons of the Civil War

(free). The Eastern National Park and Monument bookstore is also here.

It's difficult to emphasize how moving a tour of the battlefield sites of Gettysburg can be. A visit to Wheatfield, Peach Orchard, Big and Little Roundtops, and the "Confederacy's highwater mark"- its farthest-won point—brings the painful reality of more than 23,000 Union and 27,000 Confederate dead and wounded (many under the age of 20) to a human level. Monuments honoring regiments from both the North and South are placed throughout the fields and forests. Though the Civil War continued for two years beyond Gettysburg, it's rightfully called the turning point; the losses shocked and deeply wounded both sides of the shattered United States.

The Gettysburg Cyclorama

The Cyclorama (in Gettysburg National Military Park, 717/334-1124) dramatically recounts the story of Pickett's charge using a rare art form that was considered the epitome of entertainment when it made its debut in Boston in 1884. French artist Paul Philippoteaux, with the help of five assistants, produced the giant (originally 50 feet high and 400 feet long) circular mural that is the basis of the cyclorama show. Philippoteaux's only other cyclorama on display is *The Crucifixion of Christ* at St. Anne-de-Beaupre near Québec.

The painting was stored for nearly five decades before the National Park Service began restoration work, which was completed in 1962. Richard Dreyfuss narrates the accompanying light and sound show. The cyclorama is across from the Gettysburg National Military Park visitors' center and is open daily 9 A.M.–5 P.M. Admission is $4 adults, $3 for seniors 62 or better and children under 16.

Gettysburg National Cemetery

The cemetery is across the road from the visitors' center on SR 134 in Gettysburg National

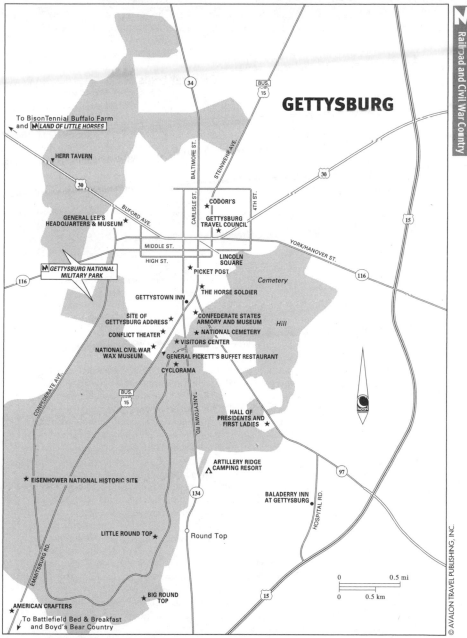

GETTYSBURG

To BisonTennial Buffalo Farm
and ⓜ *LAND OF LITTLE HORSES*

HERR TAVERN

GENERAL LEE'S
HEADQUARTERS & MUSEUM ★

CODORI'S ★

GETTYSBURG
TRAVEL COUNCIL
★

BALTIMORE ST.

STEINWEHR AVE.

CARLISLE ST.

4TH ST.

BUFORD AVE.

30

30

34

BUS.
15

15

MIDDLE ST.

HIGH ST.

LINCOLN
SQUARE

YORK/HANOVER ST.

ⓜ *GETTYSBURG NATIONAL
MILITARY PARK*

116

116

★ PICKET POST

Cemetery

★ THE HORSE SOLDIER

GETTYSTOWN INN ●

SITE OF
GETTYSBURG ADDRESS ★

CONFLICT THEATER ★

NATIONAL CIVIL WAR
WAX MUSEUM ★

★ CONFEDERATE STATES
ARMORY AND MUSEUM

★ NATIONAL CEMETERY

★ VISITORS CENTER

▼ GENERAL PICKETT'S BUFFET RESTAURANT
★
CYCLORAMA

Hill

CONFEDERATE AVE.

TANEYTOWN RD.

BUS.
15

HALL OF
PRESIDENTS AND
FIRST LADIES ★

MOON

ARTILLERY RIDGE
△ CAMPING RESORT

97

★ EISENHOWER NATIONAL HISTORIC SITE

134

BALADERRY INN
AT GETTYSBURG ●

HOSPITAL RD.

EMMITSBURG RD.

LITTLE ROUND TOP ★

Round Top

15

AMERICAN CRAFTERS
★
To Battlefield Bed & Breakfast
and Boyd's Bear Country

★ BIG ROUND
TOP

0   0.5 mi

0   0.5 km

© AVALON TRAVEL PUBLISHING, INC.

Military Park. The cemetery is open daily dawn to dusk (free). When the armies marched away from Gettysburg on July 5, 1863, they left behind a destroyed community. Soldiers immobilized by wounds, many beyond recovery, were crowded into makeshift hospitals, and many of the dead lay in shallow graves or no graves at all. Then-Governor Andrew Curtin commissioned the purchase of a burial ground; the cemetery was dedicated on November 19. The principal speaker, Edward Everett, delivered a two-hour oration, followed by President Abraham Lincoln's two-minute-long Gettysburg Address. The president's words of sorrow and unity gave meaning to the sacrifice of the dead and hope to the living. Through the years and wars, United States veterans continue to be buried in the Gettysburg National Cemetery.

General Lee's Headquarters and Museum

This stone farmhouse (401 Buford Ave., 717/334-3141, mid-March–Nov. 30, it's open daily 9 A.M.–5 P.M., $3) dates to the 1700s; it became the headquarters of Confederate Gen. Robert E. Lee during the Battle of Gettysburg. Displays include Union and Confederate military equipment, photographs, and documents.

THE TURNING POINT

The Battle of Gettysburg, July 1–3, 1863, marked the northernmost point reached by Confederate forces during the Civil War—and also the end of rebel supremacy on the battlefield. Confederate Gen. Robert E. Lee had crossed the Mason-Dixon line into Pennsylvania for strategic and logistical reasons. As a student of Napoleon's use of audacity by small forces against larger ones, Lee's interest in engaging the much larger northern army was keen. Some historians say it began with a search for shoes—a need to provision the Southern army—while others claim that the battle took place because Lee, emboldened by his recent victory over Union Gen. Joseph Hooker at Chancellorsville, in Virginia's wilderness, wished to engage the blue forces on their own turf.

After passing through Chambersburg to the west, the rebel army of 75,000 men circled back through Gettysburg and unexpectedly met the forward column of Union General George Meade's cavalry, whom they pursued. During the night, Meade sent reinforcements from the Army of the Potomac, assembling a force of 90,000 soldiers. Battle lines were drawn—Union soldiers were forced into tight formation between Big Roundtop, Little Roundtop, and Culp's Hill, south of Gettysburg. In a battle of considerable movement, Lee tested first the Union right (July 1) and then, in an assault led by Gen. James Longstreet, the left (July 2). Confederate bombardment on the second day proved fruitless.

On July 3, against the Union center, Gen. George Pickett led one of the most famous charges in American military history. As the third day of battle dawned, Lee, dismissing the concerns of his generals, ordered General Pickett to send 12,000 men across an open field toward the enemy line. In 50 minutes, 10,000 of them were killed. Distraught, Lee withdrew the remainder of his army (and confessed, "It is all my fault"). A military leader of considerable experience and prowess, he never again attempted a massive offensive. General Meade chose not to pursue the defeated Confederates, drawing criticism from President Lincoln, who thought that immediate action would have shortened the war. Though the conflict continued for another two years, Gettysburg proved to be the battle that determined the victor—and also amassed the most devastating roster of casualties: 51,000, North and South combined.

The Civil War ended on April 26, 1865. Six weeks after the assassination of President Lincoln at Ford's Theater, Gen. Joseph Johnston surrendered what little remained of the Army of Tennessee to William Tecumseh Sherman in Durham Station, North Carolina.

Eisenhower National Historic Site

Former President Dwight D. Eisenhower and his wife, Mamie, called this 231-acre farm (97 Taneytown Rd., Gettysburg, 717/338-9114, www nps gov/eise, daily 9 A.M.–4 P.M., adults $7, less seniors and children, includes shuttle) home both during and after their Washington years. The premises have been carefully preserved, including original furniture and photographs, as well as many of the president's own paintings, gifts, and memorabilia. A visit to this site is a unique opportunity to see a national figure's home life. The farm has been visited by Nikita Khrushchev, Charles De-Gaulle, and Winston Churchill. Only 1,100 visitors are allowed per day. Shuttle buses to the site depart frequently from the Gettysburg National Military Park Visitor Center, one mile south of Gettysburg on SR 134 (Taneytown Road), and US 15 business route (Steinwehr Avenue).

© JOANNE MILLER

Tammany Regiment memorial, one of Gettysburg's many monuments

BATTLEFIELD TOURS

There are several different ways to tour the battlefield. Here are a few popular options:

GNMP Self-Guided or Guided Tour

Gettysburg National Military Park offers a free map/brochure for a self-guided tour by auto. A few of the stops have "talking history" kiosks. If you'd prefer to have a customized tour with a live guide, the park trains and licenses guides who will walk or ride along with visitors. Tours last two hours. The guides are assigned from the visitors' center desk on a first-come, first-served basis beginning daily at 8 A.M. Guides may be reserved for bus groups by calling 717/334-4474 or 877/438-8929. Special-needs visitors who require a guide with foreign language skills should call ahead for information and reservations for a guide with a language specialty. The tariff for 1–6 people is $40.

Auto Tape Tours

Another alternative is the Gettysburg Auto Tape Tour, published by CCInc.; this audiocassette offers fascinating snippets of history and information as it tells the story of the three-day battle. Sound effects and music combine with facts, legends, and stories to increase enjoyment of the park tour for all ages. The CCInc. Gettysburg Auto Tape Tour is available, for rent (with cassette player) or to own, from the National Civil War Wax Museum (717/334-6754) during the museum's regular hours, and at many other businesses in town. The price is $12 to rent the tape and player for several hours, $12.95 to own the tape.

Ride into History

The **Artillery Ridge Camping Resort** (see Camping; 717/334-1288) offers a unique way to see the battlefield. A horseback tour, led by a licensed battlefield guide, rides over forested Cemetery Ridge past Little Roundtop into the Pickett's charge area and back. Though only part of the battlefield is covered, the guide recounts historic events associated with the area and answers questions pertaining to the Battle of Gettysburg. This is an unusual way to view the park and an opportunity to see the battleground from a cavalryman's point of view. Rides are by reservation only, and Artillery Ridge requests that reservations are made well ahead of the expected date of arrival (at least three weeks). Tours may be scheduled April–Oct. at 9 A.M., noon, and 3 P.M., for either one hour ($33) or two hours ($58).

OTHER POINTS OF INTEREST

The Battle Theater
In this small theater (571 Steinwehr Ave., 717/334-6100, June–Aug. 9 A.M.–9 P.M., April–May and Sept.–Oct. 9 A.M.–7 P.M., March and Nov. 9 A.M.–5 P.M., entrance to theater: adults $6, children 6–12 $3.50, live show $7) across from the entrance to the Cyclorama, sections of a 50-foot diorama are lit in sequence to highlight the history of the battle during a program that includes human-interest vignettes. On select days, actor Jim Getty portrays Abraham Lincoln in an hour-long, one-man show; reservations are required.

Gettysburg Diorama
Another version of the battlefield in miniature, it's at the Artillery Ridge Campground (610

Taneytown Rd., 717/334-6408). This is also a good way to get an overview of the events at Gettyburg—particularly if you're planning a horseback tour. The diorama is open seasonally, April–Oct. 9 A.M.–5 P.M.; adult admission is $4.50.

Land of Little Horses
The Land of Little Horses (Glenwood Dr., west of Gettysburg off US 30, 717/334-7259) features several performances per day by cleverly trained Fallabella miniature horses from Argentina. At maturity, the horses reach a height of three to four feet at the shoulder. The farm is open weekends April–Aug. Mon.–Sat. 10 A.M.–5 P.M., Sun. noon–5 P.M., Sept.–Oct. Sat. 10 A.M.–5 P.M., Sun. noon–5 P.M. The charge for admission is $7 adults, $6 children. The show includes a short, hilarious segment starring the ranch's family of rebellious Jack Russell terriers, which is worth the price of admission. You'll also see miniature donkeys, cows, and sheep.

Begun some years ago by a couple of merchant seamen, the Land of Little Horses retains its origins in the names of the stallions—they all begin with the word "Sea." This clean, well-kept

getting ready for a star turn at the Land of Little Horses

© JOANNE MILLER

farm is also home to llamas, sheep, and dozens of other animals, which can be viewed and often petted by visitors. Before the shows, the performing horses are paraded through the barn and introduced to their fans. The new owners have succeeded in their desire to make the Land of Little Horses a fun place for families to visit and a good place for animals to live.

To get there, take US 30 west approximately three miles from Gettysburg, turn south on Knoxlyn Road, then north on Glenwood Drive. Follow the signs. Call for show times.

MUSEUMS

American Civil War Museum

Though some children may label this classic wax museum (297 Steinwehr Ave., 717/334-6245) too low-tech, the 30 separate tableaux and 200 life-sized figures effectively illustrate vignettes from throughout the Civil War. It's open mid-April to mid-June daily 9 A.M.–7 P.M., mid-June–Labor Day daily 9 A.M.–9 P.M.; day after Labor Day–Dec. 31 and March 1–mid-April Sun.–Thurs. 9 A.M.–5 P.M., Fri.–Sat. 9 A.M.–7 P.M.; rest of the year Sat.–Sun. 9 A.M.–5 P.M.; admission is $5.50 adults, less for children.

A battle room auditorium re-creates Pickett's charge through a light-and-action show, and a figure of President Lincoln delivers the Gettysburg Address at the National Cemetery. If your memory of Civil War history has gaps, some of the museum's tableaux will either fill it in or confuse you further.

Confederate States Armory and Museum

The main thrust of this small museum (529 Baltimore St., 717/337-2340) is weaponry. It's open June 2–Sept. 14, Wed.–Mon. 10 A.M.–8:30 P.M.; mid-April–June 1 and mid-Sept.–Nov. 30, Wed.–Fri. and Mon. 1–8 P.M., and on Sat., Sun., and holidays 11 A.M.–8 P.M. Admission is $4. Displays reveal the construction, manufacture, and purpose of various blades and arms used during the Civil War. Memorabilia from the Confederacy is on display as well as an assortment of Union weapons.

Hall of Presidents / Hall of First Ladies

The lower level of this museum (789 Baltimore St., 717/334-5717) features life-sized wax figures of each of America's presidents; an audiotape plays segments of speeches given by each of the men, revealing the history of America through their words. It's open April–May and Sept.–Oct. 9 A.M.–7 P.M.; March and Nov. 9 A.M.–5 P.M.; June–Aug. 9 A.M.–9 P.M. Admission is adults $6, children 4–11 $3.50. A section of the museum is devoted to the life of President Dwight D. "Ike" Eisenhower.

On the upper level, the charming display of America's first ladies is reproduced roughly one-third normal size. Several of the "dolls" resemble each other because the women's likenesses were unavailable—however, each wears a carefully reproduced and detailed inaugural gown. From Martha Washington in pink brocade through Jackie Kennedy in white satin to Hillary Rodham Clinton and Laura Bush, the Hall of First Ladies is a delight. The Hall of Presidents is wheelchair-accessible; the upper level is not.

The National Apple Museum

This little museum (154 W. Hanover St., Biglerville, Adams County, 717/677-4556, late April–Oct. Sat. 10 A.M.–5 P.M., Sun. noon–5 P.M.; $2) is a project of the Biglerville Historical and Preservation Society. It honors the founders of the apple industry in the area, one of the most intensive fruit culture regions in America. An intact old-fashioned country store was donated to the museum by the owners of the country store and museum (see Especially for Families under Shopping), Marion Thomas Harbaugh and Jean E. Thomas. A gallery display of antique items, apple industry paraphernalia, and exhibits varying from information about the lives of farm families to the importance of honeybees are followed by apple juice and cookies and the 18-minute video *Apples, Apples, Apples*. Tours are available anytime by appointment.

SHOPPING

Arts and Crafts

Codori's (on the square, downtown Gettysburg, 717/334-6371) specializes in European gifts, including woodcarvings, fine Russian art and gifts, nesting dolls, icons, ornaments, glass, lacquer work, and fine jewelry. The selection is of unusual quality. It's open daily Jan.–March, 10 A.M.–6 P.M., and April–Dec. 9 A.M.–9 P.M.

American Crafters (1919-B Emmitsburg Rd., 717/337-9186) displays thousands of handicrafts from more than 100 local and national artists. The items range from the usual (quilt potholders) to the extraordinary (pierced tinwork and imaginative ceramics), and the prices are exceptional. This is a great place to pick up gifts for yourself and others. Emmitsburg Road is also known as Business US 15 south. Except for Easter, Thanksgiving, Christmas Eve and Christmas, and New Year's Eve and New Year's Day, it's open Jan–May Thurs.–Mon. 10 A.M.–6 P.M., July–Sept. daily 10 A.M.–6 P.M., Oct.–Nov. Thurs.–Tues. 10 A.M.–6 P.M., Dec. daily 10 A.M.–6 P.M.

Civil War Goods

Those completely entranced with Civil War military memorabilia and times shouldn't miss the **Picket Post,** 341 Baltimore St., 717/337-2984. Picket Post provides the real thing (antiques) and the reproduction thing (Civil War–era style clothing for men, women, and children), gifts, and souvenirs. It's open Mon.–Sat. 10 A.M.–5 P.M.

The Horse Soldier (777 Baltimore St., 717/334-0347, www.horsesoldier.com, Thurs.–Tues. 9 A.M.–5 P.M. except Sun. 10 A.M.–5 P.M., longer hours in summer) unconditionally guarantees all of its merchandise—Civil War firearms, edged weapons, documents, soldier letters, autographs, relics, more than 1,000 unique items—to be genuine. It also carries books, historical art, and prints. Check its website for an excellent online catalog of items.

Especially for Families

It doesn't get cuter than **Boyds Bear Country** (75 Cunningham Rd., Gettysburg, 717/630-2600 or 866/367-8338, www.boydsbearcountry.com, daily 10 A.M.–6 P.M.). Adorable Boyd's Bears (and hares, tabbies, moose, mice, and other stuffed friends) inhabit displays such as Kringle's Yuletide Hideaway and Land of Liberty guaranteed to make you laugh or sigh. The building features a three-story

© JOANNE MILLER

straw donkey in Biglerville

atrium, a baby bear nursery, and a collection of antique farming equipment. This is a must-see for families; it's not possible to walk away without a Boyd's buddy of your own, so be prepared.

The Country Store and Museum (at the intersection of SR 34 and SR 234 in Biglerville, Adams County, 717/677-7447, Mon.–Sat. 10 A.M.–5 P.M., closed Sun.), is packed—50,000 items on three mazelike floors—and sells everything from penny candy to wedding gowns. Handmade goods, an antique sled exhibit, and more than 1,000 prom gowns are featured. (Biglerville is a small town, so the Country Store is a prom-gown mecca for the entire area.) Every nook and cranny is worth exploring, just to get a look at the original (antique) store fixtures and the hodgepodge, varying from trinkets to the highest quality; the store carries Pendleton wool suits, too. President Eisenhower and his wife Mamie loved the store and stopped in often; it's been running since 1909, started by Ner and Netti Thomas, former schoolteachers who built the country emporium. Their daughters, Marion and Jean, took over; Jean passed away a few years ago, but Marion continues to run the shop and is a font of great stories about the area.

Farm Stores

Hollabaugh Bros. (481 Carlisle Rd., Biglerville, Adams County, 717/677-9494, late spring–Oct., hours vary), a family-owned and -operated fruit farm and market, specializes in quality home-grown fruits, farm tours, and shipping fruit gifts.

CAMPING

Artillery Ridge Camping Resort (610 Taney-town Rd., Gettysburg, 717/334-1288) offers 113 trailer campsites (16 have water, electricity, and sewer, 36 have sewer hookups only, 26 are horse camping sites, and the remainder are pull-in sites with no hookups) and 40 tent sites. It's open April–Oct., and runs $22–33 per night.

Gettysburg Campground (2030 Fairfield Rd., Gettysburg, 717/334-3304, www.gettysburgcampground.com, April–Thanksgiving) features 250 sites (150 electric and water, 50 full hookup, and 19 tent sites), camping cabins, and a cottage. There's a pool, minigolf course, play-ground, and creek on-site (the staff also repairs RVs). It's three miles west of Gettysburg on SR 116. Rates are $27–34 for RV sites, $5 for tents, and $53–109 for cabins and cottage.

ACCOMMODATIONS

$100–150

Gettystown Inn (89 Steinwehr Ave., 717/334-2100, $75–160) is a tranquil Civil War–era home adjacent to the spot where Lincoln gave the Gettysburg Address; the inn is centrally located on one of the main streets in town. All eight rooms have private baths and antique furnishings (five standard rooms, three suites), and a hearty country breakfast is served in the Dobbin House Tavern next door. As with most historic buildings, this one is two stories, no elevator. Prices rise slightly during special event times.

Baladerry Inn at Gettysburg (40 Hospital Rd., Gettysburg, 717/337-1342, www.baladerry

inn.com), a quiet, renovated 1812 inn on the edge of the battlefield, once functioned as a military hospital. Eight rooms, all decorated in period style, come with private baths and a full breakfast. As with most historic buildings, this one is two stories, no elevator. Rates range $130–155. A one-bedroom suite is also available ($185).

Over $150

M Battlefield Bed and Breakfast (2264 Emmitsburg Rd., 717/334-8804 or 888/766-3897, $150–250) isn't just a place to stay—it's an experience, and an exceptional one. In this beautifully decorated stone farmhouse, all rooms come with private baths. The main building was built in 1809 and witnessed the Battle of Gettysburg at close range. Innkeepers Charles and Florence Tarbox and their staff dress in period costume and present a historical demonstration (selected by the guests) after breakfast. A ride in the carriage, pulled by the inn's handsome matched bays, is included in the stay (a big hit with the whole family), and adults and children can dress in Civil War duds and fire an unarmed musket while host and military scholar Charles answers questions on Gettysburg and the Civil War. Even the littlest visitors are entertained—Florence provides a hefty box of toys for those more interested in Minnie Mouse than "minnie balls." As with most historic buildings, this one is two stories, no elevator.

Battlefield Bed and Breakfast offers a number of historical and special-interest packages all through the year—call for more information. The inn is on a quarter-mile-long private road on the South Cavalry Battlefield; look for the sign and turnoff from Emmitsburg Road, three miles south of the visitors' center near Big Roundtop.

FOOD

Casual and Inexpensive

Though some might question the wisdom of naming a restaurant after the reluctant leader of a massacre, **General Pickett's Buffet Restaurant** (571 Steinwehr Ave., 717/334-7580, lunch Mon.–Sat. 11 A.M.–3:30 P.M., dinner Mon.–Sat.

4:30 P.M.–close, and Sun. 11 A.M.–close) remains popular with big families and big eaters. Basic diner fare is perked up by freshly baked bread and homemade soup and desserts, and the buffets for lunch ($6–8, including a 50-item salad bar and seasonal fruits) and dinner ($10–12, carved top round of beef and ham, Southern-style fried catfish, barbecued spare ribs, baked chicken, and a variety of fresh vegetables) offer a good selection of dishes.

Midrange and Up

The same year that Napoleon fought the Battle of Waterloo (1815), Thomas Sweeney built **⚑ Herr Tavern and Publick House** in Cumberland Township, Pennsylvania, operating it as a tavern and "Publick House . . . for travelers and strangers" who required sojourn along the turnpike from Gettysburg to Chambersburg. The building (900 Chambersburg Rd., Gettysburg, 717/334-4332 or 800/362-9849, Mon.–Thurs. 11 A.M.–9 P.M., Fri.–Sat. 11 A.M.–3 P.M. and 5–9 P.M., Sun. 5–9 P.M.) changed hands through the years but kept its identity as a place of respite. That tranquility was shattered during the Civil War; the Battle of Gettysburg virtually began in the fields around the tavern buildings. Within minutes of the opening rounds, the barn, house, and outbuildings of Herr's Tavern began filling with Confederate wounded. A shell from a Union cannon crashed into the second floor of the building, destroying most of the outside wall. Today, the Herr Tavern has been faithfully restored to the "publick house"

it once was, offering overnight accommodations and serving lunch Mon.–Sat. and dinner daily. The menu is sophisticated American—a chicken and pecan salad served in a pineapple, prime rib au jus sandwiches—and the lunch is a good value, averaging $8. Dinner prices are around $20.

The **Dobbin House Dining Room and Springhouse Tavern** (89 Steinwehr Ave., 717/334-2100, www.dobbinhouse.com, dinner daily 5–9 P.M., $23) is a home converted into a suite of six renovated colonial rooms (including one in which you can dine in bed!). Featured is a continental menu plus one or more dishes based on authentic Civil War–era recipes per night; the service is sometimes slow (perhaps because of the period garb the servers wear—it's hard to hurry in baggy breeches), but the food is worth the wait. Take a moment to look at the one-room museum, which houses a re-creation of the Underground Railroad shelter on the second floor of the house.

The more casual (and less expensive) Springhouse Tavern, next door, serves deli sandwiches and lighter fare for lunch and dinner (daily 11:30 A.M.–10 P.M., $12).

INFORMATION

Contact the **Gettysburg Convention and Visitors Bureau** (P.O. Box 4117, Gettysburg, PA 17325, 717/334-6274 or 800/337-5015, www.gettysburgcvb.org) for brochures and information on Gettysburg and Adams County.

West of the Susquehanna

In Cumberland County, across the Susquehanna River from Harrisburg, the rural/suburban mix of New Cumberland and Camp Hill spreads to the west. Beyond, the old town of Carlisle proudly displays its collection of Revolutionary War–era buildings. Farther south, bucolic Yellow Breeches Creek hosts sportfishing and other recreational opportunities.

HISTORIC SITES

Hessian Guardhouse

The Hessian Guardhouse, also known as the Powder Magazine, was built by German mercenaries fighting for the British who were captured by George Washington at the Battle of Trenton in 1777. The guardhouse, at the intersection of Gibner Road and Garrison Lane (Carlisle, Cumberland County, 717/245-3971, late May–early Sept. daily 10 A.M.–4 P.M., free) is on the grounds of Carlisle

© JOANNE MILLER

corncrib outside Boiling Springs in Cumberland County

Military Barracks in the town of Carlisle. This historic structure, built of rock and wood, may be viewed from the outside any time of year. This military installation was chosen by Washington in 1757 to house the country's first arsenal and is one of the nation's oldest active military posts.

Dickinson College

Founded in 1773, Dickinson College (W. High and College Sts., Carlisle, Cumberland County, 717/243-5121, www.dickinson.edu) is one of the original 14 colonial colleges. Its buildings have been around for everything from Revolutionary War marches to Civil War shelling. Dickinson is a popular and busy campus; most buildings are open Tues.–Sat. 10 A.M.–4 P.M. during the academic year, sporadically during the summer. Pick up a map at the college bookstore (in the centrally located Holland-Union Building), and visit the former chapel in which George Washington worshipped.

On campus, the **Trout Gallery** (West High St., Emil R. Weiss Center for the Arts, 717/245-1344, during the academic year Tues.–Sat. 10 A.M.–4 P.M., free) features nearly 6,000 works of art on display, varying from antiquities to 20th-century pieces.

OTHER POINTS OF INTEREST

Omar N. Bradley Museum

Carlisle Military Barracks is the site of the U.S. Army War College as well as a museum featuring memorabilia from the career of celebrated five-star Gen. Omar N. Bradley. The Bradley Museum (Carlisle, Cumberland County, 717/245-3971, late May–early Sept. daily 10 A.M.–4 P.M., free) displays a wealth of information on all military subjects; it's in one of the college buildings, Upton Hall, on Ashburn Drive on the barracks post. For those interested in military strategy and minutiae, this is a rare opportunity to see the inner workings of American armed forces in one of the oldest arsenals in our history.

GETTING TO KNOW COLONEL WASHINGTON

George Washington was not a military strategist. In fact, he lost every battle he fought except one, the Battle of Trenton. His success was due more to a combination of qualities that made him a good leader: he was steadfast, uncomplaining, and took his time assessing a situation—basing his decisions on sound information. Colonel Washington was able to supply strength when others were weak, faith and decisiveness when others were uncertain. Reserved, rigid, and self-disciplined, Washington was merciless to those under his command who did not display the same qualities.

During the first days of the French and Indian War, fear pervaded the frontier when news of Gen. Braddock's defeat filtered through the colony. A settler wrote:

One terrifying message after another came in that General Braddock had been completely beaten with all his men by the French and Indians, raising such alarm and horror among the people that it is hard to express while we daily fear to be fallen upon by the Wild Men.

Washington, serving as Braddock's aide, regrouped the surviving troops and took responsibility for training them and others during the spring and summer of 1756. He maintained firm discipline, which instilled both loyalty and fear in the rowdy-spirited troops under his command. When it was needed, he literally whipped the reluctant soldiers into fighting condition. For drunkenness, they received 100 lashes; for profanity, 25 on the first occasion, and more on the next offense; for malingering, 50 strokes with a cat-o'-nine-tails. The second time a sergeant was found guilty of "running away with his party" before the enemy, the man was hanged. Washington recorded that he timed such hangings so that "the newly draughted recruits for the regiment may be here by that time to see it executed, and it will be good warning for them."

Though some historians paint Washington as a plodder, he was both ambitious and clever. His ambition was most evident in his traitorous turn against his former employers (the British) during the Revolution; Washington's declared motives for switching sides may have been lofty, but the emerging colonies also presented much greater opportunity for becoming a big fish in a small pond. As commander in chief of the Revolutionary forces, Washington cleverly opted to be reimbursed for expenses only, rather than accepting the $500 monthly salary offered him. From 1775–1783, he came out $400,000 ahead. When he accepted the presidency, he once again offered to work for expenses, but a somewhat more experienced Congress insisted on paying him an annual salary, of $25,000.

Allenberry Playhouse

Set within the Allenberry Resort (Boiling Springs, Cumberland County, playhouse 717/258-3211, www.allenberry.com), the 420-seat modern Allenberry Playhouse began as a summer theater program in 1949. Because of its popularity, the playhouse expanded the original 10-week season to more than 30 weeks, and it now attracts professional casts who perform everything from Agatha Christie mysteries to original Broadway-style musicals. I enjoyed a very professional performance of *Ten Little Indians* there, in a full house with people of all ages. Tickets to the performances are sold individually, and they're also offered in conjunction with a good-quality lunch or dinner buffet, served in one of the adjoining lodges. The playhouse is midway between SR 34 and SR 74 on SR 174.

Performances run year-round. Show schedules vary throughout the year; call for titles, schedules, and special packages. Ticket prices vary with the show, season, and type of package (price for the play alone is about $27; play plus dinner is about $50 for an adult).

OUTDOOR RECREATION
Pine Grove Furnace State Park

The park (mailing address 1100 Pine Grove Rd., Gardners, PA 17324, 717/486-7174, www.dcnr

.state.pa.us) is named for the Pine Grove Iron Furnace that opened in 1764 and operated for more than 100 years. Visitors can explore the remains of the furnace. During its century of operation, the furnace manufactured cast-iron products including tin-plate stoves, fireplace backs, iron kettles, and military supplies. Slate and brick works were also in the area in the late 1800s. Other buildings dating to the charcoal iron community still stand and include the ironmaster's mansion, clerk's office, stable, gristmill (now the visitors' center), the inn (now the park office) and several residences. Remnants of raceways, charcoal hearths, and related man-made features are still discernible.

Fuller Lake was the major ore quarry from which iron ore was mined for Pine Grove Furnace. The quarry filled with groundwater when mining ceased. Laurel Lake once supplied water power to Laurel Forge. Laurel Forge reheated and hammered the cast iron ingots from Pine Grove Furnace to produce wrought iron. In 1977, Pine Grove Furnace was entered in the National Register of Historic Places.

Hiking and Biking: The park offers three miles of easy-to-moderate trails. A more challenging trail is the six-mile Buck Ridge Trail; it winds through the Michaux State Forest and connects Kings Gap Environmental Education and Training Center and Pine Grove Furnace State Park. The trailhead is across from the park office and is marked with orange paint blazes.

The 2,000-mile Appalachian Trail is marked by white blazes and goes from Mt. Katahdin in central Maine to Springer Mountain in northern Georgia. The trail is popular with day hikers as well as backpackers. Begin your Appalachian Trail experience along Quarry Road by the furnace. A parking area near the furnace pavilion and a comfort station are available for trail users. Please visit the park office to register your car and intended destination and/or time of return.

All park roads and service roads are open to bicycles unless posted otherwise. A two-mile section of the Cumberland County Bike Trail connects the Furnace Stack Day Use Area with Laurel Lake Day Use Area. Bicyclists are advised to use caution because all trails are shared with pedes-

trian traffic and some are open to motor vehicles. Pennsylvania state law requires all bicyclists under the age of 12 to wear an approved helmet. A bicycle rental concession is available at the boat launch at Laurel Lake.

Swimming: Two guarded beaches are available from Memorial Day weekend to Labor Day. The regular hours are 11 A.M. to 7 P.M. Laurel Lake has accessible swimming. Swimmers at Laurel Lake and especially at Fuller Lake are advised to exercise caution because of the extreme depths and cold subsurface waters. In the summer season, a snack bar is available at each beach.

Boating: Electric motors only; boating is permitted only on Laurel Lake. Nonpowered boats must have one of the following: state park launching permit or state park mooring permit, which are available at most state park offices; or current Pennsylvania boat registration. Motorboats must display a current boat registration. Motorboats registered in other states must display a Pennsylvania state park launch permit or mooring permit in addition to their current registration. Laurel Lake has a boat launch, 85 mooring spaces, and a boat rental facility.

Hunting and Fishing: More than 75 acres are open to hunting, trapping, and dog training during established seasons. Common game species are deer, turkey, rabbit, pheasant, and squirrel.

The chief species of fish in Laurel and Fuller Lakes are pickerel, perch, and stocked trout. Mountain Creek, which flows through the park, is stocked with brown, brook, and rainbow trout. Pennsylvania Fish and Boat Commission regulations apply.

Winter Activities: At Laurel Lake, a small area by the boat launch is maintained for ice skating. Ice fishing is permitted in the rest of the lake. Ice thickness is not monitored except in the designated skating area. Be sure the ice is at least four inches thick and carry safety equipment. Ice sports are not permitted on Fuller Lake.

Cross-Country Skiing: Nordic skiers can enjoy the use of the railroad grade when snow conditions allow. Although no trails are specifically designated for cross-country skiing, numerous opportunities exist, especially during winters with heavy snowfalls, both within the park and on the surrounding state forest lands.

Snowmobiling: A trailhead parking area on nearby state forest land provides parking for vehicles and snowmobile trailers, and access to many miles of trails on state forest lands. Maps of the trails are available at the park office.

Camping and Accommodations: The park features rustic campsites, some with electricity; 74 tent and trailer sites are available year-round. Access cannot be guaranteed in severe winter weather. The campground offers drinking water, nonflush toilets, and a sanitary dump station. A camp store is .25 mile from the campground. For reservations, call 888/PA-PARKS (888/727-2757), Mon.–Sat. 7 A.M.–5 P.M. (See Accommodations under $50, for the Ironmaster's Mansion hostel.)

Getting There: Pine Grove Furnace State Park is off I-81 south, Exit 11, eight miles south on SR 233 in southern Cumberland County.

ACCOMMODATIONS

Under $50

The **A.Y.H. Hostel/Ironmaster's Mansion** (717/486-7575) is a renovated historic brick structure operated by the American Youth Hostel in Pine Grove Furnace State Park, Cumberland County. It was built in 1827 as the home of the owner of the Pine Grove Furnace Ironworks, which manufactured cannonballs during the Revolutionary War. The hostel has 46 beds, a hot tub, and is on the Appalachian Trail. Biking, fishing, swimming, and cross-country skiing are nearby. Overnight, dormitory-style lodging and cooking and dining facilities are available for about $20. For more information, contact the hostel manager.

$100–150

Built in 1790 and named by its first Innkeeper, **Jacob's Resting Place Bed and Breakfast** (1007 Harrisburg Pike, Carlisle, Cumberland County, 717/243-1766 or 888/731-1790, www.bedand breakfast.com, $75–120) was a colonial inn 1801–1835. Decorated with period antiques and

historical displays, each room reflects a unique period of history from the 1700s to the 1900s. The grounds include a large in-ground pool and patios, a hand-hewn log pool house with hot tub, colonial gardens, and a classic limestone trout stream on three acres. Five guest rooms come with private bath; a gourmet breakfast in the original Tavern Room is included.

Over $150

A once-private estate, **🅽 Allenberry Resort Inn** (Boiling Springs, Cumberland County, 717/258-3211 or 800/430-5468, www.allenberry .com) features 57 acres of groomed grounds along Yellow Breeches Creek (excellent catch-and-release trout fishing), a full-sized swimming pool, and lighted tennis courts. Many come to Allenberry for its activities combined with special packages—a weekend getaway, trout-fishing seminars, or Allenberry Playhouse theater/dinner specials. Prices include up to three excellent buffet-style meals a day, and accommodations and service are tops (the Pine Lodge is especially gracious). Families may rent their own cottage—kids have the run of the facilities, and parents can enjoy freedom and grown-up amenities (including two cocktail lounges) on the property. The resort is on SR 174, midway between the intersections of SR 34/SR 174 and SR 74/SR 174. Kids under 17 are free; rooms range $110–415 per night, but take advantage of the many package deals—one offers dining, a show, lodging, and breakfast.

FOOD

The **Sunnyside Restaurant** (850 N. Hanover St., Carlisle, 717/243-5712, Mon.–Sat. 11 A.M.–10 P.M., lunch $7, dinner $15) has been owned and operated by the Mallios family since 1948. The menu includes Mediterranean specialties, seafood, and western-cut steaks.

INFORMATION

For more information on Cumberland County, contact **Cumberland Valley Visitors Center** (1700 Harrisburg Pike, Carlisle, PA 17013, 717/249-4801 or 800/995-0969).

York and York County

The town of York, laid out in 1741, was the first Pennsylvania settlement west of the Susquehanna River. The main business of this rural outpost was to serve the flow of pioneers to the west—as may be inferred from the fact that of the town's limited population, 59 were licensed as tavern-keepers. York's most glorious historical moment occurred in 1777, when the second Continental Congress retreated there during the invasion of Philadelphia. Articles of Confederation were drawn up, linking the colonies together as a single entity, and for nine months York reigned as the first capital of the United States.

In the years that followed, York prospered; tobacco and cigar-making employed more people than any other industry. By 1900, manufacturing became the main source of income. One company, Pullman Motor Car, built and sold a horseless carriage for $2,000. Though rocked by the Depression, and later by civil unrest in the 1960s, York became known for its superior athletes: NCAA champion swimmer Bill Groft and Vern Weaver, a Mr. America who trained with locally manufactured York barbells.

York boasts several outstanding attractions, including colonial-era buildings, the Harley-Davidson factory/museum, and agricultural and industrial museums, as well as several historic public markets. Several of the attractions (Golden Plough Tavern, Gates House, Bobb Log House, York County Colonial Court House, Bonham House, the Historical Society Museum, Fire Museum, and Industry and Agricultural Museum) are maintained by the York County Historical Trust (YCHT); one admission covers entry to all these sites (adults $6, seniors and children 12–18, under 12 free).

N HISTORIC SITES

Golden Plough Tavern and General Gates House

This rustic tavern (157 W. Market St., York, c/o York County Heritage Trust, 717/848-1587, Tues.–Sat. 10 A.M.–4 P.M., YCHS site $6) built in

1741, was in service when York was an outpost of civilization; the interior is restored so carefully that it looks as if travelers have just risen from the table. General Gates's house, built next door, was the dwelling place of the hero of Saratoga as he attended the Continental Congress, held in the nearby courthouse. The second floor, with its unique swinging wall, is the site of Lafayette's famous toast in support of General Washington, a signal to the conspirators who met there that the French would support Washington —not Gates—as commander of the Continental Army. The 1800s frontier-style Bobb log house is also on this site.

York County Colonial Courthouse

On November 15, 1777, the United States of America first came into being as a sovereign independent nation by action of the second Continental Congress on this site (W. Market St. at Pershing Ave., York, 717/848-1587, March–Dec. Mon.–Sat. 10 A.M.–4 P.M., Sun. 1–4 P.M. and by appointment; YCHS site $6). The congress, consisting of representatives from all 13 colonies, moved to change the "free and independent states" into one nation. The adoption of the Articles of Confederation made York (however fleetingly) the nation's first capital. The courthouse building is a re-creation that contains artifacts from the original. A sound-and-light show dramatizes the debates and decisions that forged the United States.

The Bonham House

Not many families can claim they lived in a house for almost 100 years like the Bonham family (152 E. Market St., York, 717/843-0464, www.yorkheritage.org, March–Oct. Sat. 10 A.M.–4 P.M., YCHT site $6). Through a guided tour, visitors learn about life for a upper-middle class family in the late 19th and early 20th centuries. Horace and Rebekah Bonham moved with two daughters into this townhouse in 1875. Horace trained as a lawyer but spent most of his life as a painter of portraits, landscapes, and genre scenes, many of which can be seen in the house. One daughter, Elizabeth, continued to live in the house until her death in 1965. A 1920s library room, 1870s bedroom, and other rooms in this genuine three-story family home reflect the period from the 1850s to the 1930s.

York Friends Meeting House

This Friends (Quakers) meetinghouse, constructed in 1769—several years before the Continental Congress met down the street—is the oldest house of worship in York. It has changed little since it was built (the benches were replaced with even older ones from another meetinghouse that was dismantled). There is a tiny cemetery in back. William Penn, who founded Pennsylvania on Quaker principles, would feel right at home. The meetinghouse (135 W. Philadelphia St., York) is available for viewing anytime. The Friends meet Sun. at 11 A.M. for about an hour. All are welcome to the meeting and to view the meetinghouse interior afterward.

Market Houses

York has a wealth of covered public markets, all of which date from the 19th century; all continue to feature the bounty of local farms and a diversity of baked goods and prepared foods.

Since 1888, **Central Market** (34 W. Philadelphia St., York, 717/848-2243, www.centralmarkethouse.com, Tues., Thurs., and Sat. 6 A.M.–3 P.M.) has been the place to go for local fresh produce, flowers, and meats. There are also plenty of diverse, inexpensive eateries and bakeries in

FOLLOW THE NORTH STAR

When the United States Constitution was created in May 1787, some of those present wished to remove the clause that sanctioned slavery. The objections were due to religious beliefs, incompatibility with the phrase "all men are created equal," and the principles of free government. Nonetheless, the majority of our forefathers who signed the document were slaveholders, and the clause was included.

This government sanction, combined with the Fugitive Slave Law (1850), which permitted slave owners and their agents to enter free states (which discouraged slave ownership) to recapture runaways, led to the creation of the Underground Railroad, which was established to aid fugitive slaves to freedom.

Until the mid-1830s, the North was, by vast majority, in favor of slavery. Abolitionists were individually reviled and persecuted, even by churches, and country meetings were frequently broken up by ruffians. The Board of Aldermen of Boston refused to rent Faneuil Hall, the so-called "Cradle of American Liberty," to abolitionists for a convention; the building was commonly used for proslavery purposes. Northern merchants, who profited greatly from Southern trade—particularly in cotton—could not afford to allow abolitionists to overthrow slavery.

In this atmosphere, Northerners who wanted to help escaping slaves move successfully from town to town, prevent captures, and avoid their own arrest and punishment required great courage and conviction. Almost all of those involved in southern Pennsylvania were members of the Society of Friends (Quakers). As a free state, Pennsylvania drew escaping slaves from Virginia, Maryland, and points south. Slave owners and their bounty hunters would track their quarry, often following the trail into the town of Columbia (near York), a principal center of activity on the edge of the Susquehanna River. After several incidents of kidnapping and shooting of fugitive slaves in the town, a group of Columbia residents, most of whom were Friends, took action to protect the runaways who came into the area. The most scrutinizing inquiries and searches failed to turn up knowledge of the runaways, and slavehunters decided that "there must be an underground railroad somewhere."

"Stations" were established southward from Columbia to the Maryland line, and north, west, and east at distances about 10 miles apart. Slaves moving up from the South would "follow the North Star" along the Susquehanna River from Maryland to Gettysburg, York, and Columbia, where they would be hidden by various members of the group and eventually spirited away to other safe houses, then north to Canada, free from U.S. law.

this brick building. The market really bustles on Saturday mornings.

The oldest (1866) public market in town is **Farmer's Market** (380 W. Market St., 717/848-1402); it's more casual and also offers great produce and meats. It operates Tues., Fri., and Sat. 7 A.M.–3:30 P.M.

The **New Eastern Market** (201 Memory Ln., York, 717/755-5811) features its own blend of produce and crafts; it's open Fri. 8 A.M.–7 P.M.

OTHER POINTS OF INTEREST

Ⓜ Harley-Davidson Final Assembly Plant and Tour Center

Giant presses form steel sheets into fenders while candy-colored motorcycles fly overhead during this carefully controlled walk through the Harley-Davidson factory (1425 Eden Rd., York, 717/848-1177, ext. 5900). Eden Road is off US 30; look for an American flag the size of a battleship.

Tours of the factory are free and last approximately one hour; tickets are distributed on a first-come, first-served basis, so arrive early to make sure you get a space. Tours begin on a regular basis Mon.–Fri. between 9 A.M. and 1 P.M. The tour center is open Sat. 10 A.M.–2 P.M. June–Aug. (except when a Saturday falls on either July 3 or 4). The plant closes for several days during retooling for new models, usually March–Aug.; call for availability of plant tours. The factory tour schedule is subject to change; call 877/883-1450 (toll free) or 414/343-7850 before your visit for up-to-date tour information.

The plant is easily the size of two football fields, and just as noisy and colorful. In one section, each new bike is "road tested" for speed and control on a rolling road much like a treadmill.

Visitors 18 and over must present a valid government-issued photo ID and complete a registration card. No children under 12 are allowed on the factory tour, and no cameras are permitted in the factory; all visitors must wear closed-toe shoes. The factory and museum are wheelchair-accessible.

The tour center offers an education on Harley-Davidson history, covering the company's founding as a motorized bike company in 1903

through the use of motorcycles in World Wars I and II to the present. Forty motorcycles are on display, including special police bikes and Malcolm Forbes's favorite personal touring model.

Bob Hoffman's U.S. Weightlifting Federation Hall of Fame

The Hall of Fame (3300 Board Rd., Exit 11 off I-83, York, 717/767-6481, Mon.–Fri. 8 A.M.–6 P.M., Sat. 10 A.M.–5 P.M., free) is devoted to the strong: Olympic lifting, competitive powerlifting, bodybuilding, and history of the strongman. Barbells, photos, and statues of physique immortals are on display (yes, George "Superman" Reeves and Arnold Schwarzenegger have their own display areas), as are background data on international competitions, trophies, and awards garnered by the sport's elite—including women—since 1923. There is also a small Baseball Hall of Fame adjunct.

The York Barbell Company developed from an iron foundry business during the 1920s into an internationally known weightlifting gear and athletic equipment manufacturer (the first in the United States) under owner Bob Hoffman. The first national powerlifting contest was held in York in 1964, giving the small city the moniker Muscletown.

Naylor Wine Cellars

The winery (two miles north of Stewartstown off SR 24 south of York, 717/993-2431 or 800/292-3370, www.naylorwine.com, daily Mon.–Sat. 11 A.M.–6 P.M., Sun. noon–5 P.M.) offers tours of its cellars and tasting of current releases. Using fruit grown on 30 acres of surrounding vineyards, Naylor produces a number of varietals and blends unique to the microclimate of the growing area.

MUSEUMS

The Agricultural and Industrial Museum

Once part of the George F. Motter printing complex, this beautiful museum (217 W. Princess St., York, 717/848-1587, www.york heritage.org, Tues.–Sat. 10 A.M.–4 P.M., YCHT site $6) now houses exhibits on York's industries. Displays on weightlifting equipment, welding, pottery, casket manufacturing (!), woodworking, mineral processing, refrigeration, piano and organ manufacturing, auto body manufacturing, and the making of artificial teeth—among others—give visitors a taste of York's past and present.

Other exhibits document three centuries of agricultural history, from plowing and cultivating to cigar manufacturing. Locally made wagons, sleds, tractors, steam engines, and other farm tools are on display.

York County Fire Museum

All 69 fire companies of York County are represented in this museum (757 W. Market St., York, 717/843-0464, www.yorkheritage.org, March–Oct. Sat. 10 A.M.–4 P.M., YCHT site $6); some date to pre-Revolutionary days. Currier and Ives prints, early firefighting equipment (including leather buckets and hand-drawn hose carts), and memorabilia are featured in a 1903 firehouse built by the Royal Fire Company and presided over by a stone representation of its symbol, the lion of

firefighter's statue, York County Fire Museum

© JOANNE MILLER

Judah. One display shows a few mascots used by other companies, such as roosters and owls.

Among the artifacts on display are firefighter's rattlers—an enlarged version of a toy noisemaker, used by hotel clerks to wake patrons in case of fire—and firefighter's trumpets, used to yell out orders during a fire fight. When fire captains would march in parades, they carried flowers in the upended trumpet. Outside the museum is a memorial dedicated to the "noble horse of the rescue," and a statue of a firefighter and child, facing the setting sun.

The Historical Museum of York County

This museum (250 E. Market St., York, 717/848-1587, www.yorkheritage.org, Tues.–Sat. 10 A.M.–4 P.M., YCHT site $6) features a street of shops, with printing, apothecary, and toy shops plucked from the past. The transportation gallery displays Conestoga freight wagons and early examples of York's automobile industry, as well as Harley-Davidson motorcycles. The adjunct library and archives comprise one of the region's best genealogical research collections; all are open to the public.

Indian Steps Museum

One mile south of the Otter Creek Recreation Area off SR 425 near Airville (4923 Pleasant Valley Rd., 717/755-3777, mid-April–mid-Oct. Thurs.–Fri. 10 A.M.–4 P.M., Sat.–Sun. 10 A.M.–5 P.M., $1), this small museum is a local favorite. It's named for something no longer visible: ancient steps worn into the rocks along a walking path now covered by water. The museum, on more than nine acres of land, contains Native American artifacts dating from 2000 B.C. found on or near the site.

SHOPPING AND FACTORY TOURS

Founded in 1921, **Wolfgang Candy** (50 E. 4th Ave., P.O. Box 226, York, 800/248-4273, www.wolfgangcandy.com, tours Mon.–Fri. 10 A.M. and 2 P.M., free) is one of the oldest family-owned and managed candy companies in the United States. Four generations of Wolfgangs have added their expertise to manufacturing millions of pounds of seasonal (Christmas and Easter) candies for schools, clubs, churches, associations, and other groups. The visitors' center and museum features illustrations of old-time American candy craftsmen. Display cases are filled with wooden sugar molds, glass candy jars, and many other priceless antiques. You'll also see a video of the Wolfgang candy-making process, along with a history of the Wolfgang family, who made their candy-making dream come true in the founding of "Das Sweeten Haus."

In 1871, David F. Stauffer baked five barrels of crackers each day for his customers in York, then delivered the finished goods door-to-door in a wheelbarrow. Around 1900, Stauffer's began baking its best-known product, Animal Crackers. Today, the main plant in York (there are two others, one in Pennsylvania and one in New York) turn out millions of pounds of cookies and snacks. The York cookie outlet of **Stauffer's Bakery** (Belmont and 6th Aves., 717/843-9016, Mon.–Sat. 9 A.M.–5 P.M.) offers samples and bargain prices on Stauffer products.

Pfaltzgraff (Bowman Rd., Thomasville, 717/792-3544, www.pfaltzgraff.com, Mon.–Fri. 10 A.M. tour, free), the famous pottery manufactory, invites visitors to walk through the factory to see the creation, firing, decorating, and glazing of thousands of cups, saucers, plates, and specialty items made there. It's necessary to call the factory to let someone know you're coming at least one day ahead. Tours are for those over six years old, in closed-toe, flat-heeled shoes (spikes will get caught in the grating). The Pfaltzgraff outlet store is in York (Village at Meadowbrook shopping center, 2900 Whiteford Rd., 717/757-2200). All Pfaltzgraff products are on sale, including factory seconds and discontinued lines.

Chips, pretzels, and popcorn are a few of the products of the well-known east coast manufacturer **Utz Quality Foods** (900 High St., Hanover, 717/637-6644 or 800/367-7629, www.utzsnacks.com, Mon.–Thurs. 9 A.M.–4 P.M., free). This family-owned business began in 1921 and now turns out 14,000 pounds of chips in one hour. Grab a free bag of chips on your way out of the self-guided tour, and stop by the outlet store (861 Carlisle St./PA 94) to pick up more (the Bay Seasoning chips are the best!). Reservations are not necessary.

While in Hanover, check out **Snyder's** (1350 York St., 800/233-7125, ext. 8592, www.snydersofhanover.com, Tues.–Thurs. 10 A.M., 11 A.M., and 1 P.M., free). This is another business that began as a chip manufacturer in 1921, but Snyder's gained fame for its sourdough hard pretzels. The tour includes a video and guided walk through the plant, and samples of whatever's being processed that day. The outlet store is on the premises and offers discounts on many items. You must make reservations for the tour at least one day ahead.

OUTDOOR RECREATION

Heritage Rail Trail County Park

York County maintains this 21-mile paved multi-use trail (717/840-7440, www.york-county.org) that extends from the historic district of downtown York to the Maryland border south of New Freedom, where it connects with Maryland's Northern Central Rail Trail. Popular with hikers, runners, horseback riders, cross-country skiers, and snowshoers, the trail is most frequently used by bicyclists. Most of the trail is level (the highest point is at New Freedom), and restrooms and picnic tables are placed along the route. It meanders through rolling countryside and passes the New Freedom Railroad Station, Hanover Junction Railroad Station, and Howard Tunnel, the oldest operational tunnel in America. To get to the trail from York city, take West Philadelphia Street to Pershing Avenue, go left on Pershing Avenue, then look for signs for the trail parking lot. This trail is next to an active railway, so be aware that trains may come along to startle your steed.

ACCOMMODATIONS

$50–100

Friendship House (728 E. Philadelphia St., York, 717/843-8299, $70), a 1900s-era townhouse, offers visitors a country atmosphere in the city. Two guest rooms (or one room and one two-room suite), all with private bath, include a full breakfast on weekend mornings and continental breakfast the rest of the week. The small garden and patio are open to guests during warm weather. There's also free off-street parking.

The **Cycle Inn** (470 Days Mill Rd., 717/741-6817, $85) is a bed-and-breakfast that often serves hikers or bicyclists on the Heritage Rail Trail. It's about 4.5 miles south of York, near the first intersection of the trail north of Howard Tunnel. The inn offers two rooms, both with private bath, and a hearty breakfast made from fresh produce purchased at the surrounding farms. It's open March–Nov. and is child-friendly.

$100–150
In many cities the downtown hotel is just a memory; in the center of York, the **Yorktowne Hotel** (48 E. Market St., York, 717/848-1111 or 800/233-9324, www.yorktowne.com, $105–122) has been preserved and restored to create a tasteful, modern hotel that retains its 1920s-era charm. All rooms have modern amenities including private baths; the suites also have kitchenettes. A fitness center is available to all guests. A couple of popular restaurants are on the premises.

FOOD
Casual/Inexpensive
The **Blue Moon Café** (361 W. Market St., York, 717/854-6664, www.bluemooncafe.net, Tues.–Sat. 11 A.M.–10 P.M., lunch $7, dinner $15) characterizes its menu as alternative dining and features such local rarities as black bean burritos and Chinese chicken salad. It's a little bit of California in York. The decor is artsy and charming; walls are hung with the work of local painters. The Blue Moon is a pleasant place to contemplate the vicissitudes of life over an espresso.

M Sam & Tony's Pasta House (243 W. Market St., York, 717/852-0059, Mon.–Fri. 11:30 A.M.–9 P.M., Sat. 5–9 P.M., closed Sun.) serves heaping helpings of authentic and delicious Italian-style dishes featuring various pastas, plus eggplant, chicken, and veal. The pasta with clam and garlic sauce (your choice of pasta) is guaranteed to leave fond memories, attract cats, and repel vampires for at least a week. Lunch averages $6, dinner, $12.

Midrange
M Roosevelt Tavern (400 W. Philadelphia St., York, 717/854-7725, www.roosevelttavern.com,

lunch Mon.–Sat. 11:30 A.M.–4 P.M., dinner Mon.–Sat. 4–9 P.M., Sun. 11:30 A.M.–7 P.M.) is a dress-up restaurant (the tavern section is more casual, and includes a full menu) where a lot of local celebrations are held. Prime rib, filet mignon, crab cakes, and chicken Chesapeake are all popular here. Lunch entrées are in the $8 range, dinner around $22.

The **M School of Culinary Arts** (1063 N. George St., North York, 717/846-5000, http://yorkchef.com, Wed.–Fri. seating at 6 P.M. and 8:30 P.M.) is a student-run restaurant that favors adventurous eaters with sophisticated taste on a budget. Menus change regularly (a recent one highlighted world cuisine and featured Vietnamese potstickers, Senegalese soup, and grilled bison rib-eye steak), and diners select three courses from a prix fixe menu averaging $22. The décor is very much like that of a good commercial restaurant—floral arrangements, nice artwork, votive candles, bright and colorful walls—and the food and service are excellent. Check out the menus beforehand on the website and reserve well ahead to get the day you want (Friday is often booked up).

Expensive
The **M Yorktowne Restaurant** (48 E. Market St., York, 717/848-1111, www.yorktowne.com, Mon.–Sat. 5:30–9:30 P.M.) is the in-hotel dining area of the Yorktowne Hotel and has received accolades for its sophisticated menu and wine list. It offers a choice of à la carte or a prix fixe menu, with choices such as an appetizer of warm duck strudel with mâche radicchio and raspberry demi-glace ($12), and entrées such as fricassee of spring rabbit with roast garlic, mashed fingerling potatoes, and seasonal vegetable ragout ($22). This is a good choice for special occasions; reservations required. Dinner entrées average $25.

INFORMATION
To find out more about York and the surrounding area, contact **York County Convention and Visitors Bureau** (149 W. Market St., York 17402, 717/852-9675 or 888/858-9675, www.yorkpa.org).

Lake Erie and the Alleghenies

Imagine life without roads. Imagine walking 20 feet into a forest, turning around, and being unable to see where you came from. The undergrowth and dense forests of northwestern Pennsylvania were virtually impassable to homesteading Europeans until narrow Native American hunting trails were expanded into roads wide enough for horses and wagons. Northwestern Pennsylvania still retains much of this forested character in the vast Allegheny National Forest and Cook State Forest, two of many areas that have been preserved in their wild state.

Waterways—though limited to a few navigable rivers and streams and Lake Erie—provided the most expedient travel routes. When people began to inhabit the northwestern territories of Pennsylvania, it was the water that drew first members of the Erie tribe and, later, European settlers. Rivers connected the trading cabins, hamlets, and villages of the few who were willing to brave the wilderness before the 19th century.

Erie's economy continues to rely on the water, but tourism is providing another sort of boom. The third-largest of Pennsylvania's urban areas

ust-Sees

⊠ **Presque Isle State Park:** An urban park with a surprisingly wild feel and spectacular views of Erie and the lake (page 292).

⊠ **North East Grand Tour:** This auto/cycle trip passes through some green and fertile country, with stops at all the major wineries in the area plus some historic and scenic spots (page 294).

⊠ **Wendell August Forge:** If factory tours are on your schedule, don't miss this classic producer in Grove City; it's a great opportunity to see collectible aluminum ware made (page 300).

⊠ **Brucker Great Blue Heron Preserve:** There are over 250 great blue heron nests in this sanctuary, the largest breeding colony in Pennsylvania. The best time to come is February–May (page 301).

⊠ **Victorian Franklin:** After the discovery of oil, this small town became the center of the business, and the dwelling place for many of the oil millionaires the boom financed (page 303).

⊠ **DeBence Antique Music World:** A charming collection that ranks as one of the top attractions in the state; you'll see and hear lovingly restored nickelodeons, orchestrions, and other mechanical wonders (page 304).

⊠ **Drake Well Museum:** Exhibits here chronicle the petroleum industry from its beginnings to present day (page 304).

⊠ **Straub Brewery:** A phenomenon in itself—a small brewery that chooses quality over quantity—Straub offers great beer, and there's always the "eternal tap" (page 310).

⊠ **Allegheny National Forest:** The forest is a beautiful sight, whether you choose to explore all of its 500,000 acres by foot, boat, or bike, or take the scenic drive, or chug across the fourth-highest railroad trestle in the world on the Knox & Kane Railroad (page 311).

⊠ **Cook State Forest:** Part of "the Black Forest of Pennsylvania," this serene park has stands of virgin forest that began growing in 1644. Some of these over-300-year-old trees stand 200 feet tall (page 314).

view of Erie shoreline from Presque Isle

© JOANNE MILLER

LAKE ERIE
AND THE
ALLEGHENIES

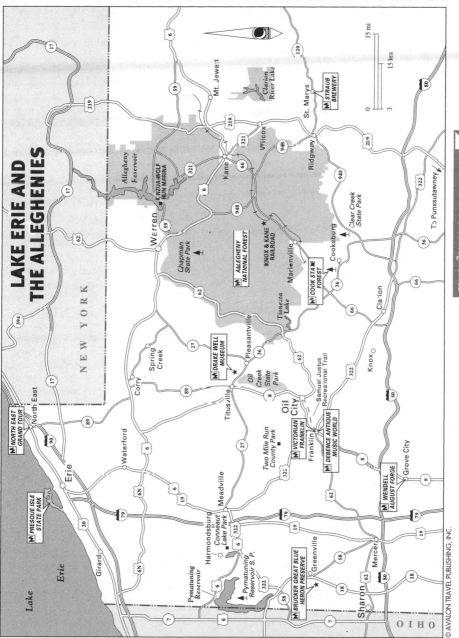

LAKE ERIE AND
THE ALLEGHENIES

NEW YORK

Lake Erie

OHIO

Lake Erie and the Alleghenies

is adapting well to its new popularity as a vacation spot, particularly around Presque Isle. North East has become the "wine country" of Pennsylvania, and Franklin and environs have become a living shrine to the development of one useful and well-known product: oil. A few old industrial towns anchor the landscape; farm towns are surrounded by miles of neat green rows. Farms offer breathing space in the forest. Most of northwestern Pennsylvania remains thick with trees and rivers, as it did 300 years ago. To everyone's benefit, much of this territory has been designated for outdoor recreational use, from the quiet waters of Pymatuning Reservoir to the untamed expanse of Allegheny National Forest.

Two other towns, so unique in character, are worthy of note: Punxsutawney, home of the spring-forecasting groundhog, and St. Marys, a quiet forest town with a wonderful brewery.

PLANNING YOUR TIME

Northwestern Pennsylvania covers a large area, and is best planned in three blocks of at least one week each: one for the Erie/North East Area, another for Crawford/Mercer Counties and Black Gold Country, and the last for the Allegheny Forest region.

Those with a more urban bent will want to spend a week in Erie and North East (based in either location), enjoying the **Flagship *Niagara*/Erie Maritime Museum, Firefighters Historical Museum, Erie Art Museum** and **Erie Zoo** (1–2 hours each) and **Lake Erie,** and **Presque Isle State Park.** This is a great opportunity to combine boating with a variety of other recreation. Plan on adding an extra day if **Waldameer Park and Water World** is on your list.

No trip to the Erie region would be complete without a visit to North East, whether on the **North East Grand Tour** with stops at the major wineries in the area—**Heritage Wine Cellars, Penn Shore Winery and Vineyards, Presque Isle Wine Cellars, The Winery at Mazza** (1 or 2 days). Pick up some mums at the local **farmers' markets.**

The second week would focus on the small towns and attractions of Mercer/Crawford and

Venango Counties, basing in Franklin. Who could pass up the delicious fantasy presented by **Daffin's Chocolate Kingdom and Factory** (30 minutes–2 hours) or the aluminum molding works at **Wendell August Forge** (1–2 hours). Stop by the **Avenue of 144 Flags** for a moving experience. If you're in the area Feb.–May, the **Brucker Great Blue Heron Preserve** (1 hour) is a must-see. The well-preserved homes of **Victorian Franklin** (2 hours) serve as pleasant setting for the incomparable **DeBence Antique Music World,** home of mechanical wonders. The **Drake Well Museum** chronicles the petroleum industry from its beginnings to present day; **Oil Creek State Park** is especially lovely in the autumn.

The **Allegheny National Forest** takes center stage on the third week (or longer). This facility has every type of recreation available—on foot, by boat, auto, bike, horse, and train (and winter sports, too!). When you've had a full dose of nature, mosey over to the **Straub Brewery** (1–2 hours) and sample the "eternal tap." **Cook State Forest**—part of "the Black Forest of Pennsylvania"—has stands of virgin forest that began growing in 1644. Some of these over-300-year-old trees stand 200 feet tall. This is a wondrous and wild place. Both places offer the option of camping in the area, or cabins, or the comfort of some excellent inns and bed-and-breakfasts—now that's roughing it. If you're in the area for a winter visit, make sure to stop down in Punxsutawney and watch Phil do his stuff on a frosty morning in February.

GETTING THERE AND GETTING AROUND
By Air and Bus

Erie has a large airport regularly serviced by USAirways commuter flights from Pittsburgh and Philadelphia. Franklin (Venango County), Jefferson County, and McKean County on the east side of Allegheny National Forest also have airports with connections to Erie and the larger cities.

There is no direct rail service to Erie, but Greyhound Bus Lines (800/231-2222) connects Erie and many of the smaller surrounding towns with

Pittsburgh, Philadelphia, and destinations outside the state. Call for schedule and fare information.

By Auto

As with most of Pennsylvania, the easiest (and often *only*) way to get from point A to point B is by car. From east to west, high-speed I-80 crosses the lower part of northwestern Pennsylvania, and US 6 crosses the upper part. North to south, four-lane I-79 is the main route in the western part, two-lane US 219 meanders up the eastern side. The area is webbed with state roads and a few US routes, all of which are two-lane and mostly in excellent repair.

HISTORY

Early History

Little is known about the indigenous peoples who populated the area around Lake Erie before European colonization other than their name—Eries. Translated, the name means "people of the cat," though the "cat" referred to was more likely a raccoon. The Seneca—one of the five nations who then made up the Iroquois longhouse, or political community—disputed ownership of hunting territory within the boundaries of the Eries. By 1656, the Iroquois Confederacy had dispersed all traces of the Eries, and the Seneca wandered the rich lakeside plain and forests.

Enter the Europeans

French explorers moved down into the Erie area in an attempt to find paths to the Mississippi and the Pacific Ocean, which they thought to be not far west of the Great Lakes. French trappers, unlike the British, were interested in exploration and the fur trade rather than settlement. Beaver pelts were plentiful, and the Iroquois were quick to appreciate the advantages of trade with French representatives. It's believed that the Iroquois thought the French were "just passing through" on their way to other destinations and would disappear once they had found what they came for.

Erie, the only deep-water port in the entire state, became a valuable spoil in the French and

Indian War. The French had already established forts to defend Presque Isle and the surrounding territory when the conflict began. When they were defeated on other fronts, they burned their holdings, and British soldiers rebuilt on the ruins. Forts Presque Isle and LeBoeuf were lost again almost immediately as Pontiac's warriors captured all the northern holdings and held them until the treaty of Fort Stanwix ceded the territory to the British.

Territorial disputes among the colonies—Virginia claimed the Ohio Valley and Pittsburgh, Massachusetts and New York both claimed northwestern Pennsylvania and its access to Lake Erie—were interrupted by the Revolutionary War. After the war, both states gave up their claims by ceding the disputed, sparsely occupied land to the national government. In 1792, Pennsylvania bought the territory for a little more than $150,000. Iroquois knowledge of canoe building and of the intricate maze of waterways feeding the Great Lakes—freely imparted to European traders—enabled pioneers to survive the wilderness, settle, and build a great port on the inland sea.

North East was the first of the lakeshore townships to be settled. Its fertile farmlands drew Vermonter Joseph Shadduck, who bought a tract in 1794. The first road in the territory was built from what is now the town of North East to Freeport, on the lake, in 1797. By the beginning of the 19th century, the township had more than 1,000 settlers, in contrast to the port of Erie, which was little more than a frontier town, with 635 residents. Commercial schooners were already moving between the unprotected ports on Lake Erie, however, and few in the town of Erie failed to recognize the potential value of the protected natural harbor encompassed by Presque Isle. The War of 1812 made that potential manifest.

The Art of War on Water

By the summer of 1812, the British/American duel for control of the Great Lakes was peaking. Britain, with its military base in Canada, held the mouth of the Niagara River on the eastern end of Lake Erie and the Detroit River, which led west to the Michigan territories. There were no supplies for large-scale shipbuilding anywhere on the Pennsylvania side of the lake, and no warship builders. An Erie resident and sailor, Daniel Dobbins, convinced the U.S. Navy that, since the city's harbor was not yet well developed and deep-draft ships could not sail out of the mouth formed by the Presque Isle peninsula, a fleet could be built in secrecy, then floated out of the harbor to join the war effort. He was pressed into service to design and build a fleet of warships for the city's harbor, with help brought in from New York.

In a classic case of politics, Dobbins was not allowed to captain the ships he had built. Master Commandant (Commodore) Oliver Hazard Perry was called in to direct the fleet in action. The core of Perry's new squadron were the brigantines *Lawrence* and *Niagara,* which had to be unloaded and even partially dismantled to clear the undredged harbor mouth to reach open water. Perry, forewarned of fleet size and tactics by an unnamed American spy in the British ranks, sailed out to meet the British ships.

Perry commanded the *Lawrence,* originally in the second position behind the *Niagara,* which was headed by Capt. Jesse Elliott. Commodore Perry's famous flag, "Don't Give up the Ship," flew from the *Lawrence's* head mast. Perry moved the *Lawrence* into the front position to face off with the lead British vessel, the *Detroit.* Together with two small schooners, Perry's ship rapidly closed the distance and came alongside three of the heaviest and best-armed ships in the British fleet. By the time the *Niagara* arrived, roughly two hours later, Perry's ship was in ruins and most of his crew was dead or wounded. In a longboat, he and his remaining men crossed the watery battlefield under fire, and Perry boarded to take command of the *Niagara.*

Perry steered the *Niagara* between the British command ship and the rest of the line and bombarded the *Detroit* until it—and the remainder of the British fleet—hauled down its colors. Through daring and tenacity, Perry had successfully shifted his flag in the midst of a fierce engagement and brought back an entire enemy squadron as a prize of war. British naval power west of the Niagara River was broken.

Questioned later about the amount of time that had elapsed while Perry's first ship was un-

OF SLOOPS AND SCHOONERS, BARKS AND BRIGANTINES

Sailing vessels plied the waters of Lake Erie from the early 1800s into the 20th century. The last known sailing ship in regular service on the lake, the *J. T. Wing,* operated until the mid-1930s. Though it's a simplification, sailing ships can be sorted into four basic categories, distinguished by their rigging (the number of masts) and the shapes of their sails.

Sloops and schooners use fore- and aft-rigged masts with triangular mainsails. Fore and aft rigging means that the sail is attached to a mast from the front (fore) to the back (aft), parallel with the hull of the ship. A sloop has a single mast, fore and aft rigged. This is the design most used for pleasure sailboats. A schooner has two to five masts, fore and aft rigged, usually with a smaller mast forward.

Brigs and barks have square mainsails. Their masts carry yardarms (booms), which are attached to the mast in the middle. The sails are then attached to the yardarms. A brig has two masts and uses square sails. A bark has three or more masts and uses square sails except for the mizzen (rear).

One innovation used commonly on the Great Lakes was the addition of fore- and aft-rigged mizzen masts on barks and brigs instead of square rigging. These hybrid rigs were called barkentines and brigantines. This type of rigging required fewer sailors to operate and gave greater power and control during the notoriously capricious storms on the lakes.

protected, Captain Elliott claimed that the *Niagara* was engaged in battle elsewhere. Though he was never formally accused of dereliction of duty, he requested a Court of Inquiry to dispel rumors that he had mishandled his command. Perry refused to testify, and the matter was never settled.

Commerce on the Wind

Between the War of 1812 and the Civil War, Erie became a major port for builders of commercial ships, notably wind-driven schooners. The forests growing not far from the shore of the lake provided plenty of hard- and softwoods for construction. Sailing ships eventually gave way to steamers, following the popularity of the prototype *Walk in the Water*, built in 1818. By midcentury, 250- to 300-foot Victorian steamers were carrying passengers and freight across the lake on regular schedules. Business was booming in Erie—both in ship manufacture and as a port. In 1844, Erie's shipping community built the Erie Extension Canal, a water route from Erie to Pittsburgh, with an east route (to Conneaut Lake, then to Franklin and the Allegheny River via Meadville) and a west route (to Conneaut Lake, then New Castle and the Beaver River). By 1853, the canal was useless; railroads were built to connect both Buffalo (at the north end of Lake Erie) and Pittsburgh to the east coast. It no longer made financial sense to transport goods over water. When the canal went bankrupt, Erie's source of income changed dramatically. Shipbuilding and shipping both moved to other areas, but commercial fishing expanded, and Erie still provided a transportation center and safe harbor for docking and repair.

The Petroleum Boom and Beyond

For its first 70 years, Franklin, south of Erie, was little more than a rural village. John Chapman (Johnny Appleseed) lived there and cared for a plant nursery in nearby French Creek before wanderlust overtook him. Following Edwin Drake's discovery of oil in nearby Titusville in 1859, however, Franklin soon became a center for worldwide oil production. The discovery of petroleum wells (and, more important, the discovery of profitable new uses for petroleum) turned the sleepy town into a boomtown—literally, since city slickers came to seek their fortunes, their oil wells dotted the forest landscape, and explosions were common. John Wilkes Booth, the assassin of President Lincoln, spent some time here, unsuccessfully seeking wealth in the oil business. Oil did create many millionaires, however, who spent their fortunes on lavish Victorian homes in a variety of architectural styles that still can be seen in Franklin today. The ghost town of Pithole, once the largest oil boomtown in America, is nearby. The boom lasted into the 20th century, until extracting oil from the wells using current methods became unprofitable.

Today, the area remains sparsely settled, though the soil of the Great Lakes Plain supports a lush grape-growing industry and produces fruit for Pennsylvania's finest wines. Frontier towns such as Sharon and Meadville have grown and passed through their industrial periods; like other outposts of 19th- and early 20th-century commerce—small lumbering towns in the Allegheny National Forest and the petroleum boom towns of Franklin and Oil City—they have found new and serene life among the forests and bucolic farmlands of the old frontier.

Erie and Environs

Pennsylvania's third-largest city, Erie, provides the state with an important freshwater port, and a number of excellent cultural and outdoor recreational opportunities.

SCENIC SPOTS

Lake Erie

For someone who has never seen the Great Lakes, the experience is a little disconcerting. Though Lake Erie is among the smallest of these inland seas, the impression is of a vast ocean—until you taste the water.

By 10,000 B.C., the ice sheets of the Wisconsin Glacier had withdrawn north, forming a line from northern Lake Huron to Montreal; the waters that were to become Lake Erie poured over Niagara Falls. Lake Erie took its current form about 2000 B.C., concurrent with habitation by a number of Native American tribes, including the Huron, Wittlesey, Parker, and Petrun on the Ohio, Michigan, New York, and Canadian bor-

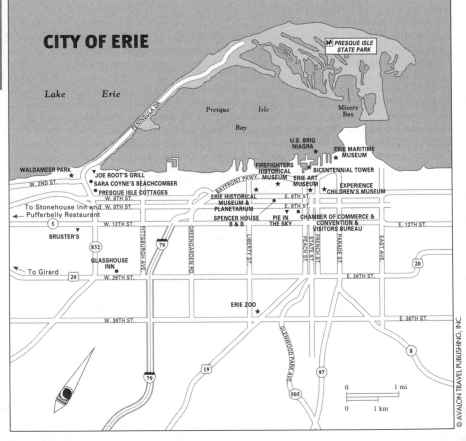

CITY OF ERIE

PRESQUE ISLE STATE PARK

Lake   Erie

PENINSULA DR.

Presque   Isle   Misery Bay

Bay

U.S. BRIG NIAGARA

ERIE MARITIME MUSEUM

FIREFIGHTERS HISTORICAL MUSEUM   BICENTENNIAL TOWER

WALDAMEER PARK

JOE ROOT'S GRILL

SARA COYNE'S BEACHCOMBER   BAYFRONT PKWY.   ERIE ART MUSEUM   EXPERIENCE CHILDREN'S MUSEUM

W. 2ND ST.

PRESQUE ISLE COTTAGES   ERIE HISTORICAL MUSEUM & PLANETARIUM   E. 6TH ST.

W. 6TH ST.   E. 8TH ST.

To Stonehouse Inn and W. 8TH ST.

Pufferbelly Restaurant   SPENCER HOUSE B & B   PIE IN THE SKY   CHAMBER OF COMMERCE & CONVENTION & VISITORS BUREAU

W. 12TH ST.   E. 12TH ST.

BRUSTER'S

PITTSBURGH AVE.   GREENGARDEN RD.   LIBERTY ST.   STATE ST.   PEACH ST.   FRENCH ST.   PARADE ST.   EAST AVE.

GLASSHOUSE INN

To Girard

W. 26TH ST.   E. 26TH ST.

ERIE ZOO

W. 38TH ST.   E. 38TH ST.

GLENWOOD PARK AVE.

0   1 mi

0   1 km

© AVALON TRAVEL PUBLISHING, INC.

ders, and the Eries in Pennsylvania and New York. Arrival of Europeans brought about the eventual use of Lake Erie and the other Great Lakes as commercial waterways, a use that continues today.

To look out over Lake Erie on a stormy day is to see the ghostly shapes of ships, crews, and passengers who were lost during voyages. Between 1797 and today, 429 ships fell victim to Lake Erie's capricious winds and violent storms.

With the advent of advances in vessel technology during the 20th century, traditional shipwrecks became rare. Lake Erie retains its commercial uses, but it's also a source of pleasure. Recreational activities, including boating and swimming, are more popular than ever.

One of the most popular ways to enjoy the lake for a day is a visit to Presque Isle State Park. Hiking, biking, and skating trails crisscross the park, and opportunities abound for picnicking and swimming.

Bicentennial Tower

For a panoramic view of Presque Isle Bay and the bayfront section of Erie, stop by this observation area (7 State St., 814/455-6055). April hours are daily 10 A.M.–6 P.M.; May–Sept. daily 9:30 A.M.–10 P.M. Admission is $2; free on Tues. It was built in 1995 to celebrate Erie's 200th birthday. An elevator is available for those who would prefer not to ascend several flights of stairs.

OTHER POINTS OF INTEREST

Waldameer Park and Water World

Waldameer Park (at the entrance to Presque Isle State Park, Erie, on the west side of Peninsula Dr./SR 832, 814/838-3591, www.waldameer .com) features picnic grounds and a separate area with a Ferris wheel, roller coaster, other thrill rides, and traditional boardwalk games. Water World (inside Waldameer Park) is one of the greatest water parks in the United States, with more than 65 rides and attractions, including a three-story series of water slides. Both Waldameer and Water World are open Memorial Day–Labor Day, with some extra hours during weekends in May. Most of the summer, Waldameer Park is open 1–10 P.M. Water World hours are 11 A.M.–7 P.M.; hours vary at the beginning and end of the season, so call ahead. Admission to Waldameer Park is free, but rides require a fee. Individual

HEROES IN SWIMSUITS

For citizens of the 19th century, professional swimmers, known as surfmen, were the saviors of shipwrecked sailors on the Great Lakes and eastern seaboard. Those who risked stormy waters to rescue others were held in the same regard as today's superheroes. Lifesaving was sport, art, and a romantic form of heroism.

Surfmen were as organized then as contemporary firefighters are now. Lifesaving crews consisted of a coxswain (the captain of the house, much like a fire marshall) and six or more surfmen. The crew trained relentlessly in rowing, Morse code, resuscitation, and firing the Lyle gun, a harpoon-type cannon used to link the rescue boat with a disabled ship. Another important skill was operation of the breeches buoy, a floating device used for moving sailors off a stricken ship. Surfmen had to be certified in all aspects of training to continue their service.

Lifesaving stations used a rapid launch system that propelled a rescue boat from the station house to the water either along steel rails or on wheels. Most of these rowing boats were 25–30 feet long with air compartments which made them virtually unsinkable.

The Erie Lifesaving Station, built in 1876, was three miles west of the Erie Harbor Light. The position soon proved to be impractical because of the distance from disabled ships, and the station was moved to the north pier of Erie's channel entrance. The operations of lifesaving stations formed the foundation for today's Coast Guard activities, and the Erie station, like many others, has since been replaced with a Coast Guard facility.

rides are $1; an unlimited ride pass is $15.50, a pass for those under 42 inches tall is $9.

Water World has a separate admission fee of $12.50, and for those under 42 inches tall, $9. A combined unlimited pass for both Waldameer and Water World is $18 or $12, respectively.

Erie Zoo

The Erie Zoo's main building is home to a variety of animals from Africa and Madagascar, including meerkats and lowland gorillas. The zoo (423 W. 38th St., 814/864-4091) is open year-round 10 A.M.–5 P.M., and in summer on Sun. until 6 P.M. Admission is $6 adults, $5 seniors, and $3 children 3–11.

Pathways through the children's zoo lead visitors past porcupines, potbellied pigs, and arctic foxes. There are also a playground, train, carousel, and picnic area on the 15 acres of grounds. The train ride and carousel require small additional fees.

© JOANNE MILLER

the flagship *Niagara*

MUSEUMS

Flagship Niagara/ Erie Maritime Museum

The re-created ship, which can be viewed from the parking lot, is docked at 164 E. Front St., next to the **Erie Maritime Museum** (150 E. Front St., 814/452-2744). The museum features a reconstruction of the midship section of the *Lawrence,* Perry's first flagship, and exhibits on other seaworthy vessels such as the USS *Wolverine,* plus environmental exhibits on the great lakes. It's open year-round, Mon.–Sat. 9 A.M.–5 P.M., Sun. noon–5 P.M., but the *Niagara* may or may not be in port. When the ship is in port, admission prices are $6 for adults, $5 for seniors, and $3 for youth; when the ship is out of port, admission prices drop to $4 adults, $3.50, and $2, respectively.

On September 10, 1813, under the leadership of Commodore Oliver Hazard Perry, an American fleet of nine ships defeated and captured the British Lake Erie naval squadron consisting of six larger vessels, providing a much-needed victory over the British in the War of 1812. The *Niagara* was Perry's flagship, from which he declared, "We have met the enemy and they are ours."

The original ship was scuttled in Misery Bay off Presque Isle in 1820, as was the custom at the time. In fact, as mechanized vessels took over the tasks of the old wind-driven ships on the Great Lakes, the unwanted hulks were often towed out away from shore and set afire for the amusement of the townspeople.

The remains of the *Niagara* were raised from the bay and rebuilt in 1913 but finally succumbed to old age in the early 1980s. The new *Niagara* was re-created from the original's plans by the International Historical Watercraft Society. The society is made up of a small number of men and women employing shipbuilding, smithing, and rigging skills that have been preserved and passed down since the days of tall ships. Young members of Pennsylvania's Conservation Corps (PCC) assisted the master craftspeople in every aspect of the restoration. The *Niagara* has become the flagship and symbol of the state of Pennsylvania.

Firefighters Historical Museum

Firefighters Historical Museum

The Firefighters Museum (428 Chestnut St., 814/456-5969) captures the romance of firefighting as well as its colorful history. The museum is open May–Aug., Sat. 10 A.M.–5 P.M., Sun. 1–5 P.M.; Sept.–Oct. Sat.–Sun. 1–5 P.M. Special tours are available; call 814/456-5969 or 814/864-2156. Admission is $4. Firefighters, seniors, and children 8–16 receive a discount.

Set within Erie's old Firehouse #4, the museum's walls are lined with embroidered insignia from fire companies all over the world. Inside are all types of firefighting equipment, including an 1889 Remington Howe horse-powered fire engine, antique uniforms, and the stories of those who braved the flames. The guides—all ex-firefighters—speak with great pride about their profession.

Erie Historical Museum and Planetarium

Housed in the Watson/Curtze mansion (356 W. 6th St., 814/871-5790), built in 1891, the museum offers exhibits on regional and maritime history. The museum is open May–Sept. Tues.–Sat. 11 A.M.–5 P.M., Sun. 1–5 P.M.; Oct.–April Wed.–Sat. 11 A.M.–5 P.M., Sun. 1–5 P.M. Admission is $5. Highlights include the period rooms, featuring exceptional woodwork and stained glass.

The planetarium, which offers programs on a variety of stellar topics, is in the carriage house of the mansion. Shows take place Sat. at 1, 2 and 3:30 P.M., Sun at 2 and 3 P.M. During the summer, additional shows are offered. Admission is $4.

Erie Art Museum

The galleries in this 1839 Greek Revival–style building (411 State St., 814/459-5477) display changing exhibits of paintings, drawings, photography, sculpture, and other fine art. The folk art collections are especially interesting. It's open Tues.–Thurs. 11 A.M.–5 P.M., Fri. 11 A.M.–8 P.M., Sat. 11 A.M.–5 P.M., Sun. 1–5 P.M. Admission is $3 adults, $2 seniors and students, $1 children; Wed. free.

ExpERIEnce Children's Museum

This museum (420 French St., 814/453-3743, www.eriechildrensmuseum.org) houses interactive exhibits and educational programming for children ages 2–12. It's open Tues.–Sat. 10 A.M.–4 P.M., Sun. 1–4 P.M.; late autumn–early spring, closed on Tues. Admission is $4, children under 2, free. Though the focus is on science and health issues, there's plenty of fun, too—face painting and dress-up are just a few of the activities. Call for current information about programming and special events.

The museum building has a history of its own: it's the former Boston Department Store livery, built in 1906. The livery sheltered carriages and horses used to transport goods for the store.

Hazel Kibler Museum

This tiny local museum (522 E. Main St., Girard, 814/774-3010 May–Sept. Sun. 2–4 P.M. or by appointment; $2 adults, $1 children) contains memorabilia of circus clown Dan Rice, the model for Uncle Sam. Ephemera from Girard's past, period furnishings, and a large collection of locally manufactured toys from the Marx Company are on display.

OUTDOOR RECREATION

Ⓜ Presque Isle State Park

Presque Isle, a seven-mile-long peninsula that juts in a curve from the city of Erie into the lake, is a rare geological phenomenon. The park office (P.O. Box 8510, Erie, PA 16505-0510, 814/833-7424) has information on activities, nearby accommodations, restaurants, and equipment rentals.

Presque Isle is one of the few places in the world that is continually reforming its glacial sand configuration through the action of winds, currents, and waves. This is no barren sand spit, however; most of the peninsula is covered by a mature forest.

Presque Isle—"almost an island"—encloses both Misery Bay and Presque Isle Bay. It's a popular spot to watch bird migration, especially during May and September. The park has been developed with both ecosystem management and recreation in mind; boat rentals, several picnic areas, and multipurpose trails are available to visitors. A scenic drive circles the peninsula, passing the monument to Oliver Hazard Perry that stands at the mouth of Misery Bay. The west shore of Presque Isle is *the* place to see a sunset on Lake Erie.

Boating: Nonpowered boats and registered powerboats are permitted on the Lake Erie side of Presque Isle, but powerboats are not allowed in the interior lagoons. A watercraft concession on Misery Bay rents canoes, rowboats, motorboats, and electric-powered boats.

Bird-Watching: Presque Isle is a spring and fall stopover for more than 300 different species of migratory birds. Park officials claim that the peninsula is considered one of the 10 best birding locations in the United States. The Gull Point Natural Area is a special management section of the park on the eastern tip, designated as a critical habitat for nesting and migrating shorebirds. The area is open to the public Dec. 1–March 31, closed the rest of the year.

LIGHTHOUSES AND "BLACKBIRDS"

In the early days of Lake Erie shipping, lighthouses were an integral part of movement on the lake. All lighthouses were maintained on a seasonal basis by keepers, who worked for the federal government and received room, board, and a stipend. By the first quarter of the 20th century, most lighthouses were either removed from use or had become automated. The former keepers became yet another statistic of the industrial age. All three of Erie's lighthouses remain standing, and two are still in use.

The first lighthouse on the U.S. side of Lake Erie—the Erie Land Lighthouse—was built in 1818 on the bluffs east of the city, overlooking the channel. This lighthouse was replaced and rebuilt several times; its service was discontinued in 1899. The building still stands at the foot of Lighthouse St. on Erie's east side.

Erie Harbor Light, built in 1830, was originally called the beacon light. It towered above the water, a 50-foot-tall wood-and-concrete structure equipped with powerful lanterns, a foghorn, and a whistle. The light was hit by a schooner in 1857, destroyed, and rebuilt into the metal lighthouse which stands today at the north harbor entrance.

The last lighthouse to be built in Erie was the Presque Isle Light, in 1872. It was originally called the flash light, because of its pulsing signal. It was built and remains on the north shore of Presque Isle.

A profitable form of pirating arose from the presence of lighthouses: blackbirding, the practice of setting up a false beacon during a storm to lure ships aground on shoals. The ship would head for the false harbor, only to ground out. Crews would abandon ship as soon as possible, knowing that they had been lured into a trap. Pirates would then plunder the cargo. Blackbirding accounted for many losses in shipping revenue from the 1840s to the 1860s. The practice was so prevalent at Long Point, directly north across Lake Erie from Presque Isle, that ships began to avoid the area altogether and trust only the Erie lights to guide them safely to their destination.

Hunting and Fishing: Hunting is prohibited in the park except for controlled duck hunting in season.

Fishing is allowed everywhere in the park except the conservation areas. Common species are perch, coho, smelt, walleye, rainbow trout, and bass in Lake Erie, and panfish, perch, bass, muskellunge, walleye, northern pike, crappie, smelt, and coho in Presque Isle Bay.

Multipurpose Trail: A 13-mile trail encircles the park. It's available for use by cyclists, joggers, skaters, and cross-country skiers. The park rents skis Nov.–March 10 A.M.–5 P.M., weather permitting. A commercial bicycle rental place close to the gateway to Presque Isle is **Sara's** (25 Peninsula Dr., 814/833-1957). It's in operation April–Sept.

Swimming: Presque Isle's sandy beaches, washed by the waves of Lake Erie, offer the only surf swimming in the state. Beaches on the Lake Erie side all have lifeguards on duty Memorial Day weekend–Labor Day, 10 A.M.–7 P.M. unless otherwise posted.

Getting There: The main road through Presque Isle is SR 832, which crosses SR 5 south of the town of Erie.

Camping and Cottages

No camping is allowed in Presque Isle State Park, but there are a number of cottages nearby: **Sara Coyne's Beachcomber** (50 Peninsula Dr., 814/833-4560, www.sarasbeachcomber.com) and **Presque Isle Cottages** (320 Peninsula Dr., 814/833-4956) are closest to the Presque Isle entrance and Waldameer Park. Both are closed during the colder months of the year.

ACCOMMODATIONS

$50–100

The **Glass House Inn** (3202 W. 26th St., Erie, 814/833-7751, $49–99) offers more traditional lodging with 30 spotless motel-style rooms. Each has cable TV and air-conditioning, and there are a pool and sauna on the grounds. The Glass House has been maintained by the Merryman family for three generations—as one traveler noted, "Any business that is over 30 years old

with the same phone number must be doing something right."

$100–150

Staying at **The Spencer House Bed and Breakfast** (519 W. 6th St., Erie, PA 16507, 814/454-5984 or 800/890-7263, www.spencerhouse.net, $85–155) is like spending the night at your best friend's house—the friend that comes from a family of 10. Joseph and Laurie Lawrence are the new owners. Four rooms and an apartment (all with private bath) end up feeling like home. The location is excellent, near the scenic part of downtown, but on a street that quiets down in the evenings. West 6th also happens to be a common parade route, and there's no better roost to sip and see than the tearoom on the second floor. Two-night stays are required on holidays and special event weekends (homecoming for the local university, etc.).

FOOD AND DRINK

Pie in the Sky (463 W. 8th, Erie, 814/459-8638, breakfast and lunch Mon.–Sat. 7:30 A.M.–2 P.M., dinner Fri.–Sat. 5:30–9 P.M.) is a charming little café. Coffee and a pastry will run $5 or less, and dinner entrées average $10.

Bruster's (3100 W 12th St., Erie, 814/836-1170, daily 11 A.M.–10 P.M.), .25 mile west of Peninsula Drive, is the place to stop for homemade ice cream, made fresh daily.

Pufferbelly Restaurant (414 French St., Erie, 814/454-1557; Mon.–Thurs. 11 A.M.–9 P.M., Fri.–Sat. 11 A.M.–11 P.M., Sun. brunch 11 A.M.–3 P.M., dinner 3–8 P.M.) has built a reputation on a hearty American menu served in a charming restored firehouse. Locals come for lunch, cocktails (the bar is inviting), and dinner. Broiled seafood, pasta dishes, and grilled meats are favorites. Prices average $11–18.

Joe Root's Grill (35 Peninsula Dr., Erie, 814/836-7668, Mon.–Thurs. 4:30–9 P.M., Fri. 4–10 P.M., Sat. 3–10 P.M., Sun. noon–8:30 P.M.) has the benefit of Presque Isle sunsets in a casual setting. Seafood, ribs, steaks, and pasta make up the menu—Root's is the only full-service bar and restaurant in the immediate area, and

Lake Erie and the Alleghenies

outdoor seating is available during good weather. Prices average $15 for dinner, and there's also an inexpensive ($5) menu for children.

M **The Stonehouse Inn** (4753 W. Lake Rd., Erie, 814/838-9296, www.stonehouse-inn.com, Tues.–Sat. from 5:30 P.M.) is an intimate venue for a celebratory feast. Owner Jim Baldauf insists on absolute freshness of ingredients. Components of the evening meal are chosen daily for no more than 100 patrons. The wine list is sophisticated, international in scope, and moderately pricey. The ambitious menu succeeds, though it occasionally stretches the abilities of the cooking staff. The setting, complete with floating swans in the outdoor pond, is worth contemplating over a cabernet anytime. The Stonehouse is on the western edge of town near the airport; reservations are required. Entrée prices range $18–30.

INFORMATION

Erie's **Chamber of Commerce and Convention and Visitors Bureau** (208 E. Bayfront Pkwy., Suite 103, Erie, PA 16507, 814/454-7191 or 800/524-3743, www.visiteriepa.com, can answer questions and provide additional information on the Erie area.

North East

On the shores of Lake Erie, enterprising growers have created a wine country in Pennsylvania. The vineyards that produce raw material for a variety of vintners surround the small town of North East.

SCENIC TOURS

M North East Grand Tour

This 25-mile loop begins and ends in North East and visits all four major wineries in the area, plus some historic and scenic spots. The terrain is mostly flat, with a few challenging hills—good for reasonably fit bikers. Substantial sections of the route are on main roads, though traffic is light except on the weekends. Since the route passes through North East twice, intrepid walkers might consider a two-day trip. All distances are approximate.

The West Loop: The route starts at the traffic light where US 20 (also known as West Main Road and Buffalo Road) intersects with SR 89 (Lake Street or Station Road). Travel 3.5 miles west on US 20 to Presque Isle Winery at the intersection of Catholic Cemetery Road. Turn right (north) on Catholic Cemetery Road for 1.75 miles until it dead-ends on SR 5 (East Lake Road). Turn right (east) on SR 5. The Penn Shore winery will be on the south side of the road (1.5 miles). Continue east on SR 5 to North Mill Street (2.75 miles). Turn right (south).

This road passes through the area once known as Papermill Hollow, named for the Franklin Papermill; the stone wall across from the blue-timber-and-fieldstone barn is all that remains. Several mills were in operation, powered by the tumbling waters of Sixteen-Mile Creek, on the left. Just before the iron bridge is the Papermill Hollow School, built in 1875, with the original school bell in front of it. North Mill Street intersects with US 20 in 1.75 miles.

The East Loop: Turn left (east) on to US 20 and continue through North East for 2.5 miles. On the left, you'll pass by the oldest brick house in Erie County, the Silliman house, which was competed during the War of 1812.

Make a right turn (south) onto Remington Road. This section of the tour passes by a number of farms that have been owned by the same families for more than a century. Travel south on Remington Road for one mile, then turn left (east) onto Archer Road. Continue for almost 1.5 miles until Archer dead-ends onto Gulf Road. Turn left (north). You'll pass by the farm owned by the Orton family (8515 Gulf Rd.), who own the farm market at the intersection of SR 89 and I-90. When Gulf Road intersects US 20 (one mile), turn left (west) and take a moment to admire Paschke's chrysanthemum farm.

Continue on US 20 less than a mile to Heritage Winery, then make a right (north) on Hirtzel

Road. After a mile, Hirtzel becomes East Middle Road, which, in another mile, intersects with SR 5. The short roads that lead off SR 5 to the shores of the lake contain lakeside estates and cottages built by vacationers from Pittsburgh, Cleveland, and Cincinnati. Turn left (west) on SR 5. Mazza Vineyards is 1.25 miles down the road. Double back from Mazza, and make a right (south) on Dewey Road to East Middle Road (.75 miles). Turn right on East Middle Road (west), and follow it for a little over 1.5 miles to Dill Park Road. Note the octagonal Butts Barn, a local landmark. The barn was built by Alonzo Butt and his son George Will from their grape growing and oil business profits in 1879.

Turn right (north) on Dill Park Road, traveling for a little more than a half mile; make a left (west) turn onto Martin Road. At the intersection, the three-story brick Lake View Summer Resort, which featured its own mineral springs, was a popular summer getaway in the late 19th century. It operated as the Dill Park Hotel in later years. When Martin Road dead-ends on Orchard Beach Road, turn right (north), then left at SR 5. Continue west on SR 5 to Freeport Road (slightly more than one-half mile). Turn right (north) on Freeport Road.

The large brick house on the east side of Freeport Road was built in 1835 as the home of Philetus Glas, the area's first ironmaster. The village of Freeport at the mouth of Sixteen-Mile Creek was a thriving port in 1797. Now it contains a few vacation homes and a small park. Turn and go south down Freeport Road past the SR 5 intersection to Curtis Road, on the left.

Turn left on Curtis Road and drive .4 mile. On the left are the remains of Grimshaw's woollen factory, which was built before the Civil War and manufactured uniforms for the Union Army. The mill burned in 1883 and was rebuilt as a wine cellar. Curtis Road dead-ends into Orchard Beach Road (.5 mile). Turn right (south), and return to North East (1.2 miles).

OTHER POINTS OF INTEREST

The area is known for its mild climate that favors Concord grapes and orchard fruit. Visi-

tors must be at least age 21 to sample wines from the vineyards.

Heritage Wine Cellars

Heritage (12162 E. Main Rd./US 20 at I-90, 814/725-8015 or 800/747-0083, www .heritagewine.biz, mid-May–Oct. daily 10 A.M.– 6 P.M.; mid-Oct.–mid-May noon–6 P.M., closed major holidays) is one of the few wineries in North East that presses fruit from its own vineyards and orchards. The Bostwick family began farming in the region in 1833 and now grows and harvests crops on 200 acres. Niagara, a varietal white, took a gold medal in statewide competitions, and the Bostwicks are proud of their rare Gladwin 113, a varietal dry white available in limited quantities after Thanksgiving each year. Heritage also offers a group of fruit and specialty wines, such as peach wine and a light sherry. Tasting may be done outside the tour. Tours and tastings are free and last approximately 30 minutes. Call for availability.

Penn Shore Winery and Vineyards

Penn Shore (10225 E. Lake Rd./SR 5, 814/725-8688, www.pennshore.com) is in the center of Pennsylvania's grape-growing region along Lake Erie. The winery is open year-round on Sun. 11 A.M.–4:30 P.M.; July–Aug. Mon.–Sat. 9 A.M.– 8 P.M., Sun. 11 A.M.–4:30 P.M.; Sept.–June, Mon.– Sat. 9 A.M.–5:30 P.M., Sun. 11 A.M.–4:30 P.M.

Penn Shore offers a number of varietal wines, such as seyval blanc and vignoles, as well as blended table wines and a number of house specialties, including Kir and Holiday Spice. Penn Shore also produces a sparkling champagne-type wine made from local grapes. Tasting may be done separately from the tour. Tours and tasting are free and are almost always available; tours last approximately one-half hour.

Presque Isle Wine Cellars

Presque Isle Vineyards (9440 W. Main Rd./US 20, 814/725-1314, www.piwine.com) is the favorite of many Erie County wine lovers because of its sophisticated style. The winery produces several varietals, including a botrytized vignoles (a late-harvest grape affected with a natural

GRAPES—THE FRUIT OF AN EMPIRE

Though a number of vineyards on the Great Lakes Plain supply vintners with raw materials, the majority of the grapes grown there are processed into juice and juice products by the Welch's plant in the town of North East. Historically, the agricultural success of northern Pennsylvania's grape-growing region was due to the combined but unrelated work of four men.

In mid-19th-century France, Louis Pasteur developed a heating/purifying process that revolutionized the packaging and longevity of food, and thus its storage and salability. At roughly the same time, a dentist from New Jersey, Dr. Thomas Welch (a staunch prohibitionist), began to bottle grape juice as a substitute for wine in church services. Eventually, Welch's son used the methods of Pasteur to create an international food industry based on grape products. Meanwhile, in Massachusetts, Ephraim Bull, a horticulturist, hybridized a perfect white-fleshed, dark-skinned grape, which he named the Concord. And in North East, farmer Elijah Fay pioneered grape growing in the region with the Catawba and Isabella varieties; however, it was the Concord that thrived in the area's sometimes harsh climate. As news of Fay's bountiful crops spread, vineyards appeared all across the Erie plain. The region was on its way to becoming the largest grower of Concord grapes in the world by 1910 when Welch's opened a major processing facility in North East.

Not all North Easters agreed with Dr. Welch's views on the consumption of liquor; a number of wineries sprang up even before the opening of the Welch's plant. But that plant is today the largest facility of all Welch's plants in America (Welch's itself is now a cooperative owned by more than 1,000 growers nationwide). Though it's not open to the public, the modern plant lends the tiny town of North East a cosmopolitan sheen. But it's the wineries that draw visitors to the scenic area, weaving together the fertile earth and freshwater sea in a wreath of vines.

© JOANNE MILLER

fruit of the vine in North East

sweetening agent) that won a gold medal and a chardonnay and cabernet sauvignon that have won silver medals in state competitions. It's open year-round Mon.–Sat. 8 A.M.–5 P.M., Sun. 12–5 P.M., closed on Easter and Christmas.

Tasting is informal, and the winery also offers supplies and advice for those who wish to try winemaking for themselves. Half-hour tours and tastings are free and usually available on demand.

The Winery at Mazza

Mazza (11815 E. Lake Rd., 814/725-8695, www.mazzawines.com) has won well-deserved silver medals for a number of wines, including a special late-harvest vintage, ice wine of vidal blanc. The winery is open year-round Sun. 11 A.M.–4:30 P.M.; July–Aug., Mon.–Sat. 9 A.M.–8 P.M.; Sept.–June, Mon.–Sat. 9 A.M.–5:30 P.M.

Tours last approximately one-half hour. Tasting is free and may be done outside of the tour. Mazza's table wines are best-sellers, and the winery also features a number of popular fruit wines, such as peach and cherry.

MUSEUMS

The Lakeshore Railway Museum

Railway cars and engines of every type and vintage are parked in the old North East train depot (31 Wall St. at Robinson St.). It's open Memorial

Day weekend–Labor Day weekend, Wed.–Sun. 1–5 P.M.; during Sept.–Oct., weekends only 1–5 P.M. Visitors may wander about exploring the stationary trains; there is no admission fee. The museum hosts special programs on local railway history throughout the summer. When the museum building is open, a small donation is requested. For information and program schedules, call the Lakeshore Railway Historical Society, 814/725-1911.

SHOPPING

Antiques and Handcrafts

Folk art, ephemera, furniture, jewelry—**Interstate Antique Mall** (5446 Station Rd., North East, 814/725-1603) is a collective of antique and collectibles dealers in a warehouse near the intersection of I-90 and SR 89. The place is stuffed with treasures and great pretenders.

The Greenfield Basket Factory (11423 Wilson Rd., North East, 814/725-3419) produces hand-woven wooden veneer baskets in all shapes and sizes. Imaginative lap desks, doll cradles, hampers, purses, and planters are featured, at good prices. The factory will send a product/price list and will take orders over the phone at 800/227-5385 (800/BASKET5).

Farmers' Markets

The area surrounding the village of North East is dotted by farms and farm stores. Three of the most popular include the following.

Arundale Farm and Cider Mill (11727 E. Main Rd., North East, 814/725-1079) was planted in 1877 and is run by the third generation of the Schultz family. They grow eight varieties of apples, in addition to grapes and other produce. Visitors may buy from the farm market or pick their own. Arundale also presses a sweet, natural cider for sale; the farm is open daily Sept.–Nov.

Mums by Paschke (12286 E. Main Rd., North East, 814/725-9860) features a free floral show; visitors are welcome to walk through the chrysanthemum fields behind the farm store between mid-August and mid-November. The market is open daily May–July, offering bedding

plants, and from mid-July–mid-Nov. on also selling seasonal produce.

Apple lovers rejoice! **A. G. Post & Sons** (8893 Gulf Rd., 814/725-3330) excels in apples. It's open July–Feb. daily except Sun.

OUTDOOR RECREATION

Biking

Lake Country Bike (21 E. Main St., North East, 814/725-1338) offers a free cyclist's guide to the area and tour consulting. The shop sometimes rents bikes to the public.

ACCOMMODATIONS AND FOOD

Under $50

An attractive and inexpensive housing alternative with a great view of the lake is the **Colonial Motel** (off SR 5 on Orchard Beach Rd., .5 mile east of the intersection of SR 5 and SR 89,

North East chrysanthemum farm

© JOANNE MILLER

Lake Erie and the Alleghenies

814/725-5513, $35–56). The motel offers rooms with cable TV, a/c, and phone, and efficiencies with a small kitchen. Reservations are appreciated, and the low rates drop even more mid-Oct.–end of May.

$50–100

The Burnhams, innkeepers at the **Vineyard Bed and Breakfast** (10757 Sidehill Rd., North East, PA 16428, 814/725-8998, www.lakeside.net, $65–90) have furnished their turn-of-the-20th-century farmhouse in a comfortable, uncomplicated, modern style. Though close to I-90, the Vineyard is quiet and peaceful. Picture windows in the front of the house overlook the farm, surrounding vineyards, and Lake Erie. All five of the guest rooms have private baths.

$100–150

The Grape Arbor Inn 51-55 E. Main St., North East, PA 16428, 814/725-0048, www .grapearborbandb.com, $80–130) is a first-class bed-and-breakfast in the middle of Pennsylvania's wine country. Innkeepers Gabe and Peggy Houser have thought of everything to make guests comfortable in this carefully restored former stagecoach inn and Underground Railroad stop. The style of the inn is elegant; the details include luxuriously thick towels and terrycloth robes. The Grape Arbor hosts many executives from Welch's Corporation who are used to the best—and they get it here. All rooms have private bath, telephone, and cable color TV—some have fireplaces.

Food

The **Freeport Inn** (11104 E. Lake Rd., North East, 814/725-4607), a homey diner at the intersection of SR 5 and SR 89, is a local favorite that becomes a hot spot at night. It's open Tues.–Thurs. 8 A.M.–9 P.M., to 10 P.M. on weekends; winter hours are Tues.–Thurs. 8 A.M.–8 P.M. and weekends 8 A.M.–9 P.M.; closed on Easter and Christmas. Entrées for dinner hover around $10, and lunch and breakfast prices drop from there. The Freeport makes its own sausage, and breakfasts are big and hearty. It's directly north of the village of North East on SR 89.

INFORMATION

The **North East Chamber of Commerce** (21 S. Lake St., North East, PA 16428, 814/725-4262, www.nechamber.org) has the latest word on the wine country; another resource is the **Erie Chamber of Commerce** (208 E. Bayfront Parkway, Suite 100, Erie, PA 16507, 814/454-7191, www.visiteriepa.com).

Crawford and Mercer Counties

The seat of Crawford County, Meadville, is remarkable for two reasons. First, on Market Street downtown, the 1870 Market House is still the center of community activities and a bustling open-air farmers' market. Second, Hollywood star Sharon Stone was raised within its boundaries. The Stone family home is still there, but the address (sorry, fans) is a closely guarded secret. Crawford County itself is highly recommended for outdoor sports and water recreation, since it contains a large reservoir and a natural lake and is a major stopover for migrating fowl.

Mercer County is an interesting mix of the commercial and rural. The county seat is Mercer, with a population of nearly 3,000. Sharon, a sprawling factory town, has two destinations for chocoholics, complete with factory tours. Grove City is home to a mecca for hand-forged metal collectors, the Wendell August Forge, and the county itself offers real variety in shopping outlets and accommodations.

POINTS OF INTEREST

Conneaut Cellars Winery

This Crawford County winery (on US 322 and US 6, 814/382-3999 or 877/229-9463, www .ccw-wine.com), which uses an old-fashioned vertical press and oak aging barrels, is east of the town of Conneaut Lake and south of Conneaut

Lake itself. It's open for tours and tasting year-round, daily 10 A.M.–6 P.M. The winery produces a variety of wines, including fruit-based "farm wines" and varietals.

Conneaut Lake Amusement Park, Hotel, and Campground

Seasonal schedules vary, but the park (12382 Center St., Conneaut Lake, Crawford County, 814/382-5115) is generally open Memorial Day–Labor Day, Wed.–Thurs. noon–8 P.M., Fri. and Sun. noon–9 P.M., and Sat. noon–10 P.M. Admission to the grounds and parking are free. A day ride pass that includes unlimited use of all park rides and entrance to the water park is $9.95 on weekdays and $11.95 on weekends.

Once a thriving destination on the west side of Conneaut Lake, this park had fallen on hard times. It was revived by an investor and reopened in the spring of 1997, much to the relief of the area's residents, who cherish the turn-of-the-20th-century facility. The Blue Streak, an old-fashioned wooden roller coaster, still offers thrills and has been complemented by a number of modern rides. The horses continue to rear and preen on a well-preserved Muller carousel (see the sidebar "Pennsylvania's Carousels" in the Delaware River Valley chapter), and the water park includes the Otter Creek Adventure River, a 650-foot long, 2.5-foot deep waterway that moves inner tube riders and swimmers around and through waterfalls, fountains, and bubble rapids.

The park was dubbed "Queen of the Inland Resorts" in 1892, and the lake and surrounding woodlands still retain their unspoiled beauty. Conneaut Lake may be explored aboard a sternwheeler, the *Barbara J.*, and the park has its own sandy beach.

The 167-room Hotel Conneaut is next to the park on the lake and features a full-service restaurant (same telephone as the park). Room rates range $35–130. CamperLand (814/382-7750), across the street from the main gate, has 105 campsites (including tent sites and full hookups for RVs) and cabins. Information on all accommodations is available by calling the park information number. Bike rentals and a public boat launch are nearby.

Avenue of 444 Flags

Passing by the Avenue of Flags (Hillcrest Memorial Park, 2634 E. State St., Hermitage, Mercer County, 724/346-3818) off US 62 is a dramatic experience, especially on a windy day. It's reputed to be the largest display of American flags in the world. Each of the 444 American flags represents a day on which 53 Americans were held hostage by Iranian militants between 1979 and 1981. With the help of a group of unemployed steel workers, and using flags donated by the wives of veterans, Tom Flynn, owner of Hillcrest Memorial Park, decided to erect a flag for each day of captivity. On day 100, the parents of hostage Michael Matrinka, of Oliphant (near Scranton), raised the 100th flag and lit a flame, requesting that it be extinguished only upon the return of their son. Three hundred and forty-four days later, Mike Matrinka himself lit the eternal flame, which still burns today in front of the monument.

SHOPPING

Chocolate

Daffin's Chocolate Kingdom and Factory (496 E. State St., Sharon, Mercer County, PA 16146, 724/342-2892 or 877/323-3465, www.daffins .com) is one of the largest candy-makers on the East Coast and is the originator of the hollow chocolate bunny. The retail store and Chocolate Kingdom are open Mon.–Sat. 9 A.M.–9 P.M., Sun. 11 A.M.–5 P.M.

Free tours of the factory (7 Spearman Ave., Farrell), which is three miles from the retail store, can often be arranged on the same day. Reservations are required for tours; call 877/323-3465. The factory is open for tours June–Aug., Tues. and Thurs. 9 A.M.–2:30 P.M.; Sept.–May, Mon., Tues., Thurs., and Fri. 9 A.M.–2:30 P.M.

The retail outlet on East State Street sells every kind of candy imaginable, but the real draw for kids is Chocolate Kingdom in the back. A 15- by 20-foot display space is filled with an ever-changing assortment of giant animals, castles,

Lake Erie and the Alleghenies

© JOANNE MILER

Daffin's Chocolate Kingdom

pumpkins, etc., all made from chocolate. Picture a six-foot milk chocolate squirrel next to a three-foot dark chocolate frog. Free samples are given to visitors, probably to prevent them from munching their way through the exhibit.

Philadelphia Candies (1546 E. State St., Hermitage, 724/981-6341, www.phillyc.com), a family business, has been manufacturing candies in the Sharon area since 1919 (Mercer County). The retail store and factory are open Mon.–Sat. 9 A.M.–9 P.M., Sun. 11 A.M.–5 P.M., but tours must be prescheduled and are sometimes limited to large groups. Founded by Jim and Steve Macris, brothers who had emigrated from Greece, the chocolate factory's name was chosen for its meaning: "brotherly love."

Shoes
Shoe junkies, take note: **Reyers** (69 E. State St., Sharon, PA, Mercer County, 16146, information 877/268-0235, orders 800/245-1550, Mon.–Sat. 10 A.M.–9 P.M., Sun. 11 A.M.–5 P.M.) may indeed be right when it claims itself the World's Largest Shoe Outlet. Approximately 50,000 pairs of shoes, artfully arranged and displayed by color, make up the store's inventory. Both men's and women's styles—from extremely narrow to very wide—are available. Reyers stocks more than 300 popular brands.

Variety Stores and Outlets
Otter Creek Store (S. Courthouse Sq., Mercer, Mercer County, 724/662-2830) is a small shop chock-full of quirky books, games, toys, kites, jewelry, music, and yarn for knitting and weaving. There are even spinning wheels for do-it-yourselfers.

Popular with bargain hunters, **Prime Outlets** (Exit 113 off I-79, Grove City, Mercer County, 724/748-3875 or 888/545-7221) is an outlet mall with Brooks Brothers, Jones New York, OshKosh B'Gosh, and a Coach Factory Store among its retailers.

ⓜ Wendell August Forge
A self-guided tour of Wendell August Forge (620 Madison Ave., Grove City, Mercer County, 724/458-8360 or 800/923-4438, www.wendellaugust .com) is available during open hours; the best time to visit is before 3:30 P.M. The gift shop is open Mon.–Thurs. and Sat. 9 A.M.–6 P.M., Fri. 9 A.M.–8 P.M., Sun. 11 A.M.–5 P.M.; in winter, the shop closes at 5 P.M. Mon.–Fri.

In 1923, Wendell August began a blacksmith forge to produce hand-wrought iron household fixtures. Shortly thereafter, he and his chief designer collaborated with ALCOA in Pittsburgh to develop a method for creating handcrafted aluminum architectural features. As a sideline, August and his designer produced trays and other small items, notably an ashtray to commemorate the inaugural flight of the *Hindenburg* (complete with a glass vial of essodiesel fuel). Their artfully designed and crafted giftware continues to be collected and treasured. The showroom also features outstanding examples of other types of crafts for sale.

OUTDOOR RECREATION

Canoeing and Fishing

Mercer County offers canoeing on Sandy Creek, the Shenango River, Big Neshannock Creek, and Lake Wilhelm.

Maurice K. Goddard State Park, Shenango Reservoir, Shenango River, and Neshannock Creek are popular with anglers.

Pymatuning State Park

Pymatuning Reservoir, near the town of Jamestown (Crawford County), was created in 1931 to control the Shenango and Beaver Rivers and to provide recreational opportunities. Now one of the largest camping areas (657 campsites) in the commonwealth, Pymatuning State Park encompasses state-controlled game areas as well as nearly 4,000 acres of wildlife refuge. The park offers boating, picnicking, hiking, fishing, hunting, sightseeing, and swimming. For more information, contact Department of Environmental Resources, Pymatuning State Park (P.O. Box 425, Jamestown, PA 16134-0425, 724/932-3141 or 888/727-2757). Pymatuning State Park is on the Pennsylvania/Ohio border; its southern boundary is off US 322, and its northern boundary is below US 6.

Conneaut Lake

This body of water, small in comparison to Pymatuning Reservoir (Crawford County), is Pennsylvania's largest natural lake. Fishing and boating are popular pastimes, and the town of Conneaut Lake features a number of restaurants, stores, and sporting goods suppliers.

Ⓜ Brucker Great Blue Heron Preserve

There are more than 250 great blue heron nests in this 45-acre sanctuary (Mercer County), the largest breeding colony in Pennsylvania. Information is available from Brucker Great Blue Heron Sanctuary (75 College Ave., Greenville, PA 16125, 724/589-2117). No entry is permitted beyond the posted signs Feb. 1–Aug. 31; however, the observation shelter is open year-round, daily, from sunrise to sunset (free).

The sanctuary's observation center is a wonderful bird-watching spot. Bring binoculars to see the big birds nesting in the early spring, Feb. May; Sept. 1–Jan. 31, after the herons have left for the year, the entire sanctuary is open to the public and nests may be inspected up close. The site is across SR 18 from Mortensen Road, on the west side of SR 18, three miles south of the town of Greenville. An Agway grain tower is between the road and the sanctuary; a Bristol Consolidator Warehouse is next door.

Shenango Reservoir

This site is administered by the U.S. Army Corps of Engineers (Resource Manager, 2442 Kelly Rd., Hermitage, Mercer County, PA 16150, 724/962-7746) and offers abundant opportunities for swimming, water-skiing, personal watercraft-riding, and other water sports. **RC's Marina** (off Exit 258, SR 18, 724/962-5785) rents fishing and pontoon boats and is the docking area for the *Shenango Queen*, a tour boat that cruises the reservoir.

Camping

Most camping facilities are open early May–mid-Oct. Recommended are **Runamuck Campgrounds** (8896 US 6, Conncaut Lake, 814/382-8185) and **Shadyside Campgrounds** (P.O. Box 345, Harmondsburg, 814/382-2534). Both are in Crawford County.

Rocky Springs Campground (84 Rocky Springs Rd./SR 318, Mercer, Mercer County, 724/662-4415) offers 100 acres of tent and RV sites. It has a swimming pool, playground, and hiking trails.

Junction 19-80 Campground (1266 Old Mercer Rd., Mercer, Mercer County, 724/748-4174) is a campground with a railroad motif. There are full hookups for RVs and tent sites, a swimming pool, and multipurpose trails.

ACCOMMODATIONS AND FOOD

Bed-and-breakfasts reflect the people who run them; Dorothy and Orvil McMillen know how to make comfort a top priority at the ⚑ **Snow Goose Inn** (112 E. Main St., Grove City, Mercer County, 724/458-4644 or 800/317-4644, www.bbonline.com). This pretty turn-of-the-20th-century former boardinghouse was originally built to house college-bound daughters of the gentry. Grove City, home of the Wendell August Forge, is still a small and friendly college town; the Snow Goose welcomes many repeat guests, including cosmopolitan collectors of hand-forged aluminum and other crafts. The breakfast-table conversation is always lively. The inn is open year-round, all rooms have private baths, and rates are $70 per night including breakfast.

⚑ **Quaker Steak & Lube** (101 Chestnut St., Sharon, Mercer County, PA 16146, 724/981-9464, 724/981-7221, or 800/468-9464, is a destination in itself. Steak & Lube is open 365 days a year, Mon.–Wed. 11 A.M.–1 A.M., Thurs.–Sat. 11 A.M.–2 A.M., and Sun. noon–1 A.M. On major holidays, it opens at 7 P.M. Prices range $6–12. A local favorite since 1973, this one-time gas station serves hamburgers, "O-rings" (onion rings), and 18 million buffalo wings (crisp-fried chicken wings served with an assortment of condiments) a year. Vintage and new motorcycles and automobiles hang from the ceiling and sprout from the floor; the restroom stall doors even have steering wheels in case you feel like taking a spin. Anywhere else, it would be a tourist trap—but in Sharon, it's just a local hangout. People come from miles around for the wings.

Both of the following local favorites are owned by the same family. The **Iron Bridge Inn** (724/748-3626), so named for its proximity to the bridge spanning Neshannock Creek, is decorated in a high-rustic style. **Rachel's Roadhouse** (724/748-3193) just down the road is decorated in late Victorian style. Both serve lunch and dinner seven days a week and concentrate on an American-style menu of steaks, chops, pasta, and salads. The Iron Bridge is more formal and serves a lunch buffet Mon.–Fri. and on Sun.; it's known for prime rib. Rachel's is more relaxed and is "the party place"—the bar is hopping nearly every night. Both are five miles south of Mercer on SR 19—Iron Bridge is north of the bridge, on the west side, and Rachel's is south of the bridge on the east side. Food prices range $3–21, and the menu offers a wide assortment, from French fries to lobster salad.

INFORMATION

Crawford County Convention and Visitor Bureau (211 Chestnut St., Meadville, PA 16335, 814/333-1258, www.visitcrawford.org) also maintains a toll-free information number at 800/332-2338.

Mercer County Convention and Visitors Bureau (50 N. Water Ave., Sharon, PA 16146, 800/637-2370, www.mercercountypa.org) will tell you everything you need to know about Mercer and environs.

Black Gold Country

The Pennsylvania oil region, roughly the area between Franklin and Titusville, Venango County, was designated a Heritage Park by the governor in 1994.

SCENIC TOURS
ⓂVictorian Franklin

Before Edwin Drake's discovery of oil, Franklin was a modest village; after discovery, it became the center of the business of oil and land buying and selling, and the dwelling place for many of the oil millionaires that the boom financed. Though many of the buildings within Franklin's city limits are described as Victorian, that description covers more than 20 different styles of architecture. Nowhere is this wealthy individuality more evident than on a walking/biking tour of the city's hill district. The tour is about a mile in length but crosses over some steep hills.

Starting on the 1400 block of Liberty Street, most of the homes were built between 1860 and 1890; they vary from second empire (1416 Liberty St.) to a simple folk style (1433 Liberty). On the corner at 1501 Liberty is the Quo Vadis Bed and Breakfast, a Queen Anne built in 1867. Turn left on 15th Street. The homes again vary in style from Tudor (410 15th St.) to Italian villa (522 15th St.). Turn right up the street at 522 15th St. and you'll enter the Miller Park area of Franklin, so named for its developer, oil millionaire Gen. Charles Miller. Most of Miller Park was built between 1900 and 1920; homes are massive and stylish and were often designed by prominent architects of the day. Up the hill to the right is Twin Gables on Brownsylvania Avenue, originally built as a stable and carriage house for Miller Park residents. It was gutted by fire in 1938 and converted into a residence.

Turn left onto Chestnut Lane, then right onto Adelaide Avenue. The shingle-style house at 612 Adelaide Ave. boasts a set of stained glass windows adorning the round side bay that depict scenes of Miller Park. Turn around and walk back in the direction of Chestnut Lane. Con-

tinue on Adelaide, making a right on Plumer and another right on Sibley Avenue.

General Miller's house, 622 Sibley Ave., is the large brick castlelike structure. The estate included a greenhouse, three tennis courts, and two ponds. The house has been converted into apartments. Continue down Sibley to the bottom of the hill where Adelaide Avenue meets Parkway. Continue on Parkway until it meets 16th Street. Follow 16th to Liberty Street.

Liberty has a number of homes of different styles, including arts and crafts (1525 Liberty St.) and colonial revival (1514 Liberty St.).

Turn left on 15th Street and walk to the end. The Franklin Pioneer Cemetery on the corner of Otter Street contains 243 graves, including that of George Power, the first permanent settler of Franklin. The epitaphs plainly reveal the hardships of pioneer life.

ONE BARREL OF OIL

According to the Drake Well Museum, one 31.5-gallon barrel of crude oil may be processed to produce all of the following items:

280 miles' worth of gasoline for a midsized car
750 pocket combs
540 toothbrushes
170 birthday candles
70 kilowatt hours of electricity
65 plastic dustpans
65 plastic drinking cups
40 miles' worth of diesel fuel for a small truck
39 polyester shirts
27 wax crayons
23 hula hoops
12 small cylinders of liquefied gases such as propane
4 pounds of charcoal
2.9 gallons of jet fuel
1 gallon of tar
1 quart of engine oil
1 quart of solvents

Lake Erie and the Alleghenies

A CURE FOR POVERTY

Early pioneers in Pennsylvania needed a source of food salt and found it by drilling into the ground for reservoirs of salt water. Until the middle of the 19th century, these salt drillers routinely struck petroleum, or black oil. This was not a joyous occasion—salt was considerably more valuable and black oil, which had been known and used as a poor and smoky substitute for other oils in lamps since ancient times, was so common that the Iroquois called it "an-to-no-tons," which means "Ho, how much there is of it!"

Oil had had little practical value; 50 small refineries were in business on the East Coast to transform the crude into kerosene for lamps and lubricants. There was also a small market for petroleum as medicine, touted as "Rock Oil, Celebrated for its Wonderful Curative Powers." Gasoline, a by-product of the refining process, was considered a dangerous substance that contaminated kerosene and made lamps and lanterns explode.

In the early 1850s, New York lawyer and entrepreneur George Bissell sent a sample of petroleum to be analyzed by a chemistry professor at Yale University. Bissell and the professor subsequently developed a variety of petroleum products, suddenly making the unwanted progeny of salt drilling heir to its own throne. As overkill of whales led to depletion of whale oil supplies, black oil came to be seen in a new and more profitable (lamp) light.

The next challenge was getting oil to the surface in quantity. Bissell hired a retired railroad conductor, Col. Edwin Drake, to drill for him on his property in Titusville, attempting to use the old saltwater well system. The drillers were plagued by constant cave-ins until Colonel Drake solved the problem. He had his men drive an iron pipe 39 feet

POINTS OF INTEREST

DeBence Antique Music World

Dairy farmer Jake DeBence and his wife began collecting automated musical instruments in the 1940s, and today their collection ranks as one of the top attractions in the state, with good reason. At DeBence Music World (1261 Liberty St., Franklin, 814/432-8350 or 888/547-2377, www.debencemusicworld.com), nickelodeons, orchestrions, and cylinder- and disk-players from the late 1800s to the 1930s line the sides of the showroom. Music World is open year-round; March 15–Oct. 31 Tues.–Sat. 11 A.M.–4 P.M., Sun. 12:30 P.M.–4 P.M.; Nov. 1–Dec. 23 Fri.–Sat. 11 A.M.–4 P.M., Sun. 12:30–4 P.M., by appointment only the rest of the year. It's closed major holidays. Admission is $8.

Each visitor gets a personal tour, and your guide will flip the switch on the machines that you select—rinky-tink ragtime played on a variety of automated instruments, a carousel, a circus calliope, or perhaps the Wurlitzer Marching Band Orchestrion (guaranteed to draw a crowd or your money back!). Don't miss "the magician," an automated sleight-of-hand puppet that's a real child-pleaser. It's impossible to leave here without a smile on your face.

Drake Well Museum

The Drake Well complex (at the end of Bloss St. in Titusville, 814/827-2797, www.drakewell.org) consists of a reproduction of the first oil well drilled in the United States, several outbuildings that typify life during the late 1850s, and a museum that explores the social and economic significance of the petroleum industry from its beginnings to present day. The museum is open May–Oct., Mon.–Sat. 9 A.M.–5 P.M., Sun. noon–5 P.M.; Nov.–April, Tues.–Sat. 9 A.M.–5 P.M., Sun. noon–5 P.M. It's closed Easter, Thanksgiving, and Christmas. Admission is $5; children ages five and under are free.

Drake Well Museum has one of the largest collections of material about the birth of the oil industry and its development in the world, including documents that trace land ownership from the time Col. Edwin Drake made his lucky strike. Many exhibits in the museum discuss life as it was for settlers who came to cash in on the boom. Drake Well Museum offers another piece of history, an informa-

into the ground, down to solid rock. The well was drilled inside the pipe, and on August 27, 1859, oil bubbled to the surface of the 69.5-foot-deep well.

The first local oil refinery was constructed in 1860, one mile below Titusville. Oil wells sprang up all over the area when others learned of Drake's reliable extraction methods, and the boom was on. Wealth could be measured in barrels per day, and for many, "rock oil" finally made good on its claims as a cure—for poverty.

The next challenge was transportation. There were no railroads in the oil region of western Pennsylvania at the time, so oil had to be hauled by wagon on makeshift roads to Oil Creek, where it could be floated down to Pittsburgh on barges. The weight and number of the wagons churned the roads to quagmires; there were reports of horses who died sinking into the sludge.

Once on Oil Creek, the oil was loaded onto the barges in barrels or was emptied into hollow-hold barges, 50 feet long and 15–20 feet wide. Almost anything that would hold barrels or oil in bulk was used, with little regard for safety. A million barrels of oil and countless lives were lost on the raging waters of Oil Creek and the Allegheny River. By 1874, a 60 mile long oil trunk line was built from the oil region to Pittsburgh, and in 1878, work was begun on a line that crossed the Allegheny Mountains to the Atlantic.

With the growing popularity of gasoline-fueled combustion engines during the first decades of the 20th century, the future of oil was secured. The Franklin oil fields, however, were nearly played out by then, and the industry giants moved west in their search for black gold.

---

tive 27-minute film on oil starring Vincent Price and Alan Hale Jr., the captain from *Gilligan's Island.*

Pithole City was an oil boomtown in 1865, though today its inhabitants are mostly ghosts of the 2,000 hopefuls who rushed in to make their fortunes. The site is being developed and operated by the Drake Well Museum. To get there, take SR 27 east from Titusville to SR 227; follow signs for the turnoff between Pleasantville and Plumer. It's open Memorial Day–Labor Day, Wed. noon–5 P.M. and Thurs.–Sun. 10 A.M.–5 P.M. It continues to be open weekends 10 A.M.–5 P.M. through Oct. Admission is $2.

Oil Creek and Titusville Railroad

This railroad (7 Elm St., Oil City, PA 16301, 814/676-1733, www.octrr.org) travels through "the valley that changed the world." Guides tell colorful stories of the world's first oil "barons," millionaires who built Victorian mansions, and of thousands of other ordinary folks who came to the area during the late 1800s to seek their fortunes. October is the most popular month to ride the train, as the fall foliage in the canyon is spectacular.

The train may be boarded at the following locations: Perry Street Station, 409 South Perry St., Titusville; Drake Well Station, end of Bloss Street at the Drake Well Museum south of Titusville; Petroleum Centre Station (this is a "flag stop" only—the train will pick up bicyclists on the bike trail who flag it down); and Rynd Farm Station, four miles north of Oil City just outside the borough limits of Rouseville on SR 8. The Perry Street round-trip is two hours, 30 minutes in length; Drake Well round-trip is two hours; Rynd Farm round-trip is three hours.

The Oil Creek and Titusville train picks up at each station once per day in the afternoon on this annual schedule: last two weeks in June, Sat.–Sun.; July 1–Aug. 31, Wed., Thurs., Sat., and Sun.; September, Sat.–Sun.; first three weeks in October, Wed.–Sun. (Wed.–Fri. only one round-trip daily, two pickups per day on Sat. and Sun.).

Reservations are recommended, and October tickets should be bought a minimum of two weeks ahead. Credit cards are accepted. Call for the departure schedule and arrive at least one-half hour before boarding. The train will pick up bicycles ($1 plus fare) and canoes ($2 plus fare) from the flag stop. The only working Railway Post Office in the United States is on this line—you can send a postcard from your trip while you ride the rails. A ride runs $12 for adults, $11 for seniors, $8 for kids 3–12. In addition, special excursions are scheduled throughout the year, and fees depend on the trip taken.

OUTDOOR RECREATION

Oil Creek State Park

Oil Creek State Park (visitors' center: Petroleum Centre, intersection of SR 1007, T617, and SR 1004; information: Park Manager, 305 State Park Rd., Oil City, PA 16301, 814/676-5915 or 888/727-2757) is a forested recreational area that illustrates the story of the "black gold rush" that took place after the drilling of the first commercial U.S. oil well in nearby Titusville. One well within the park near the visitors' center is the Coquette well, drilled in 1864 by A. C. Kepler. Kepler, a store clerk in a nearby town, dreamed that he was with a "coquettish young lady" when they were assaulted by an Indian. The lady

autumn in Oil Creek State Park

handed him a rifle and when he shot the Indian, oil gushed from the spot where the Indian had stood. Sometime later, Kepler visited his brother in the village of Petroleum Centre; while walking in the woods, he recognized the spot in his dream. Acting on a hunch, he borrowed money and drilled a well there. It came in at 1,500 barrels a day, making Kepler a millionaire.

Within the park's 7,000 acres are ghostly boomtowns, wells, cemeteries, and other historic sites that can be reached by a network of hiking and biking trails and an excursion train, the Oil Creek and Titusville Railroad. The park adjoins Titusville at its northern end. Oil City is four miles from the southern end. The main entrance to the park is off SR 8, one mile north of the borough of Rouseville.

Biking: One of the park's main attractions is a 9.5-mile paved bicycle trail through Oil Creek Gorge. The path is also a route for hikers and, in the winter, cross-country skiers.

Canoeing: Under normal conditions, Oil Creek is a beginner's stream and offers a gentle and scenic trip through the gorge. The canoeing season runs March–June; launch areas are the bike trail parking area near Drake Well and Fry's Landing near Petroleum Centre. There are no rental facilities in the park.

Hiking: More than 73 miles of hiking and interpretive trails lead visitors through historic and scenic areas within the park. The park's major trail, 36 miles long, runs around the perimeter of it, including a .75-mile interpretive trail at the Blood Farm historic site. Maps are available from the park office.

Hunting and Fishing: All of the park is open to hunting and trapping in season from the day after Labor Day to March 31. All of Oil Creek and its connecting streams are open for bass and trout fishing.

Winter Sports: A 15-mile complex of trails designated for cross-country ski use lie between Petroleum Centre and Plumer. The area includes a large parking area (on SR 1004), warming hut, and restrooms.

Getting There: The most direct route is via SR 8 north of I-80 to Franklin. State Route 8

© JOANNE MILLER

SHOOTING WELLS

Oil wells that didn't produce as expected, or those that were clogged by paraffin (created by natural processes and the friction and heat of drilling) were often "shot" with nitroglycerin, a practice that continues today. During the late 19th century, dangerously unstable nitroglycerine was hauled to well sites in wagons with brightly painted hazard warnings. Not all wagons reached their destinations—wagon-sized craters were a common road hazard in northwestern Pennsylvania at the time.

The well shooter would load his wagon's worth of nitro into slim, torpedo-like containers and then drop them down the clogged well pipes. The underground explosion would usually dislodge the obstacle, break the barriers between one oil pool and the next, or melt the paraffin, as needed.

The Otto Cupler Torpedo Company (in Pleasantville, 814/827-2921) still shoots wells in the oil region and occasionally schedules a demonstration for the public. Call to find out if any shows are scheduled (you may get an answering machine, but the friendly and helpful Cupler folks do return calls). To get to Cupler's, follow SR 8 north to Titusville, then take SR 27 east toward Pleasantville for three miles to Wolfkiels Garage. Turn left; travel one mile to Dotyville, then turn left again (watch for signs).

continues north along the western boundary of the park.

Samuel Justus Recreational Trail

A multipurpose rails-to-trails path, the 5.8-mile Justus Trail connects Oil City and Franklin. Oil City access is 1.6 miles on West 1st Street from the stoplight intersection of Petroleum Street. The gravel road trail turnoff is next to the Penelec building and across from the Venango campus of Clarion University. The parking lot and yellow gate that mark the beginning of the trail are .25 mile down the gravel road. Franklin access is on US 322 south of the city and next to the Allegheny River bridge. There are bike rentals nearby in Franklin.

The river-and-woodland trail passes the mansion of U.S. Senator Joseph C. Sibley, who amassed considerable wealth through his development of a formula to refine crude oil. The trail is open to cyclists, hikers, horseback riders, and cross-country skiers.

Two Mile Run County Park

Less familiar than Oil Creek Park, Two Mile Run, six miles west of Oil City off SR 428, offers nearly 3,000 acres of forest plus a 144-acre lake (for general information, call 814/676-6116).

Swimming, boating, fishing, hiking, and winter sports are available in the park. There's also a family campground open May 14–Nov. 1, with 69 campsites, divided between primitive sites and ones with electrical hookups, plus cabins and cottages. Prices have ranged $75–100 in the past; call for current rates. Reservations for all accommodations may be made 9 A.M.–4 P.M. daily by calling 814/676-6116. Information on boat rentals is also available at that number. There are also organized horseback trail rides (call 814/463-3703 for more information).

The Oil Region Astronomical Society manages an observatory at Lockwood Campground within the park. It's open to the public; call 814/437-2525 or visit www.oras.org to learn more.

ACCOMMODATIONS
$50–100

A carefully restored historic landmark, **Lamberton House** (1331 Otter St., Franklin, PA 16323, 814/432-7908, $65–75) features six bedrooms with either shared or private bath. Three of the meticulously decorated rooms have working fireplaces, and one is set within a romantic turret. The house is on a quiet residential street one block away from French Creek. Innkeeper Sally

Clawson provides a bountiful breakfast and is a walking repository of information on Franklin's colorful history.

Quo Vadis Bed and Breakfast (1501 W. Liberty St., Franklin, PA 16323, 800/360-6598, $65–85), or "Whither goest thou?," is an elegant Queen Anne Victorian among the mansions at the base of Franklin's "Millionaires' Hill," built shortly after Abraham Lincoln became president. The stately house sits at an intersection that is noisy during the day but quiets down at night. The six bedrooms, all with private bath, are furnished with antiques and heirlooms collected over four generations by the present owner's family.

FOOD

Probably the most popular eatery in town, **Leonardo's** (67 Liberty St., Franklin, PA 16323, 814/432-8421, Tues.–Sat. 11 A.M.–9 P.M.) is a favorite with families for its pizzas and Italian dishes—most entrées are under $12 and there's a kids' menu for those under age 10. The place is casual and the food is good; expect a wait if you arrive around 7 P.M.

INFORMATION

Black Gold Country is served by several agencies. **Oil Heritage Region Tourist Promotion Agency** (Franklin, 814/677-3152 or 800/483-6264, ext. 18, www.oilregiontourist.com), has general information on attractions and upcoming events. The **Chambers of Commerce** in Oil City (814/676-8521, www.oilcitychamber.org), Franklin (814/432-5823, www.franklin-pa.org), and Titusville (814/827-2941, www.titusvillechamber.com) have walking tours and tidbits specific to their areas.

Allegheny National Forest and Environs

The forest itself is spread over a huge area where four counties intersect: Warren, McKean, Forest, and Jefferson. Within its boundaries are several small towns and a state park. Clarion, Clearfield, and Cameron Counties are a mix of mountainous forests, farms, and small towns.

Saint Marys is one of those destinations that must be planned. Not that it's hard to find—it's a good-sized town on the eastern edge of the Allegheny National Forest. It's just not on the main routes. Besides being situated in an area of rugged beauty, Saint Marys is home to one of the best commercial breweries in business and a thriving powdered metal industry (think graphite). After a tour of the brewery, you can take advantage of the year-round recreational opportunities the area offers, or just wander down to the airport at sunset and watch the local elk herd drift in to nibble the runways.

Hollywood made much of Punxsutawney's local hero, Phil, the rodent star of Bill Murray's *Groundhog Day*. Phil (and his stand-ins) lead a quiet life most of the year in Punxsutawney (punks-ah-TAH-ney)—the Lenni Lenape called it Ponks-ad-u-te-ny, "town of sandflies" (though I never saw any). Though the movie wasn't filmed in the town, Bill Murray did stop by and pay his respects.

SCENIC TOURS AND SPOTS
Cruising the Elk

If you miss a chance encounter with the elk in Saint Marys, Pennsylvania's largest free-roaming herd can often be seen in early evening on the roads around the village of Benezette, south of Saint Marys. This scenic, approximately 80-mile route travels along the Sinnemahoning River (sin-ma-HO-ning) and through the state park of the same name.

From Saint Marys, travel south on SR 255 to Weedville. Turn left (east) on SR 555. Pass through Benezette on your way to Driftwood—and keep an eye out for those shy, legally protected elk.

At Driftwood (birthplace of the original Hollywood cowboy, Tom Mix), turn left (north) on

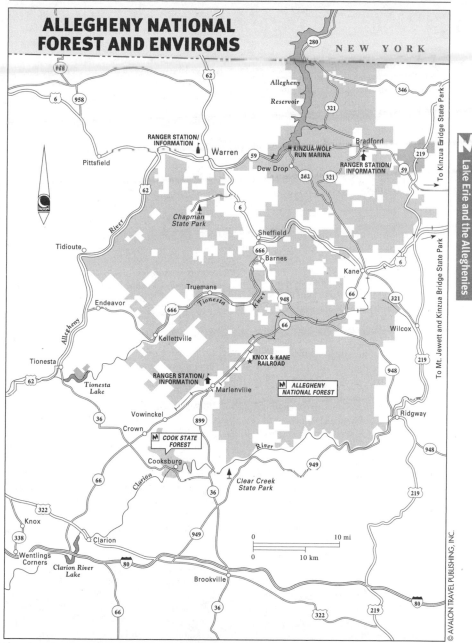

ALLEGHENY NATIONAL FOREST AND ENVIRONS

NEW YORK

Allegheny Reservoir

Lake Erie and the Alleghenies

To Kinzua Bridge State Park

To Mt. Jewett and Kinzua Bridge State Park

RANGER STATION/ INFORMATION
Warren
Pittsfield

KINZUA-WOLF RUN MARINA
Bradford
Dew Drop
RANGER STATION/ INFORMATION

Chapman State Park

Sheffield
Barnes
Kane

Tidioute

Truemans
Endeavor
Kellettville

Wilcox

Tionesta
Tionesta Lake

KNOX & KANE RAILROAD
Marlenville

ALLEGHENY NATIONAL FOREST

Vowinckel
Crown
Ridgway

COOK STATE FOREST
Cooksburg

Clear Creek State Park

Knox
Clarion

Wentlings Corners
Clarion River Lake
Brookville

0   10 mi
0   10 km

© AVALON TRAVEL PUBLISHING, INC.

BIG BOVINE

The Queen of the Herd, Old Kersey Road, Saint Marys, is one of the largest artificial cows in existence and a local landmark. More than half the size of the 30-foot-tall pine trees behind her, "Queenie" looks out over the pastoral fields that make up the Ayershire Dairy Farm, keeping watch over the happy herds. The udderly radiant beauteous bovine is .65 mile west on Old Kersey Rd., off SR 255 south (on the north side of the road), just over two miles from the intersection of SR 255 and SR 120. You can't miss her.

SR 120, winding through Sinnemahoning State Park to Emporium. In Emporium, continue left (west) on SR 120 back to Saint Marys.

OTHER POINTS OF INTEREST

The Winery at Wilcox

The Winery at Wilcox (1867 Mefferts Run Rd., Wilcox, 814/929-5598, www.wineryatwilcox .net), on the east side of Allegheny National Forest, is a dream-come-true for owners Mike and Carol Williams; vintages are often sold out to local buyers before they fully mature. This young winery offers a few varietals (marechal foch and vignoles, among others) and a number of popular blends named in tribute to the surrounding Allegheny woodlands: Bob White, Autumn Leaves, and Clarion River Red. Wilcox must bring in its base juice (the mountain season is too short for growing), so the wines produced are truly a product of the vintner's art. Visitors must be 21 to taste. The winery is 1.9 miles north of the intersection of Mefferts Run Road and US 219. It's open Mon.–Sun. 10 A.M.–6 P.M. Free tours are available depending on season.

Straub Brewery

The name Straub's may not be familiar to those outside Pennsylvania; it's a family-owned business that's been perking along for several generations, and like a lot of businesses here, it's content to produce a high-quality product for a limited but fanatically loyal market. During the tour, you'll have an opportunity to taste great fresh beer, or wait to hang out at the eternal tap—an open keg available to anyone over 21—but you have to wash your glass (as the sign says, your mother probably doesn't work there).

The brewery (303 Sorg St., Saint Marys, 814/834-2875, www.straubbeer.com) began in the 1870s, and out of seven original breweries in the area, survived Prohibition to become the premium producer of quality beer in north-central Pennsylvania. Founded by Peter Straub, a cooper, the business is now in its fourth generation of family ownership.

Straub's uses water from the pristine spring-fed Laurel Run Reservoir and preservative-free barley and corn from the Midwest. The tour is an education in beer-making, from the top floor of the brewery that looks out on the eastern continental divide down to the bottling line where visitors are invited to "grab a greenie" (unlabeled green bottle of Straub's) and taste the freshest prepasteurized beer they've ever had. The eternal tap, something of a legend, is a never-empty keg of beer available to anyone over 21 who would like a beer or two separate from the tour.

Straub continues to be a one-shift-per-day business with only two brews; it stays small out of choice, distributing only in Pennsylvania and eastern Ohio. Straub Light has taken the gold medal in international competition.

All tours must be scheduled by calling the brewery; it's wise to call anyway and make sure the brewery is operating that day. Visitors must be 12 years of age to take the hourlong tour, and 21 years of age to taste. Tours are conducted Mon.–Fri. 9 A.M.–noon and Sat. 10 A.M.—1 P.M. (although the brewery itself doesn't operate on Sat.). The eternal tap is open Mon.–Fri. 9 A.M.–4:30 P.M., Sat. 9 A.M.–1 P.M. The brewery does post a limit: maximum two glasses of beer and 15 minutes at the tap; however, I saw a few of the same people there both before and after the tour. From the photos on the wall, I could see that they were employees, enjoying the fruits of their labor. Tour and tasting are both free.

Knox & Kane Railroad

The K&K Railroad (P.O. Box 422, Marienville, PA 16239, 814/927-6621, www.knoxkanerr.com) makes a steam-powered excursion through the Allegheny National Forest and across the Kinzua Bridge—the fourth-highest railroad trestle bridge in the world, 300 feet above the valley floor. The bridge is also more than 2,000 feet long. Riders can spend the trip spotting wildlife from the windows and enjoying a picnic lunch (inexpensive box lunches may be ordered ahead and paid for at the Marienville Station). Fall is the most popular time of year for this trip, so reservations are recommended. An overnight "caboose camp" trip is also available.

Trains leave from the station on SR 66 in Marienville (long trip) and from the station on US 6 in Kane (shorter trip). The full round-trip from Marienville to the Kinzua Bridge is eight hours. Round-trip from Kane is 3.5 hours. The train picks up passengers once a day from Marienville at 8:30 A.M., and Kane at 10:30 A.M.

The K&K Railroad is seasonal and operates as follows: June, Fri.–Sun.; July and Aug., Tues.–Sun.; Sept., Fri.–Sun.; the first two weeks of Oct., Wed.–Sun., the second two weeks, Sat.–Sun.

Long-trip admission costs $22; the short trip is $16. Children ages three and under are free. For more information and the latest trip schedules, contact Knox & Kane Railroad.

SHOPPING

Punxsutawney Tile and Glass (220 Lane Ave., Punxsutawney, Jefferson County, 814/938-4200) is a small traditional glass manufacturer that produces mouth-blown and stamped glass used almost exclusively by churches—votives, ceremonial containers, and processional holders for candles—plus some art glass pieces and garden globes of great variety and beauty. The company displays some small, collectible glass pieces in its reception area. The work is all produced by traditional methods—several glassblowers are usually at work during the day. Though the company usually arranges tours only for groups, staff members will show fewer visitors around by request. Call ahead and ask for a brief tour. The factory is open Mon.–Fri. 8 A.M.–5 P.M., closed on major holidays. Free.

A holdover from decades past, **The Coolspring General Store** (814/849-2521, Mon.–Sat. 9 A.M.–5 P.M.) sits 10 miles north of Punxsutawney on SR 36 in the village of Coolspring. Wooden benches provide seating around a potbellied stove, and the store stocks penny candy and a jumble of other goods, and there's a deli for sandwiches.

☒ ALLEGHENY NATIONAL FOREST

Covering more than 500,000 acres, Allegheny is the only national forest in Pennsylvania. The park straddles the corners of Forest, Warren, Elk, and McKean Counties. Every kind of recreation is available. There are more than 1,000 miles of roads and trails over ridges, valleys, streams, and meadows for hiking, cross-country skiing, all-terrain vehicles, and snowmobiles. The 90-mile North County National Scenic Trail traverses the park from south to north. The forest is threaded by the Allegheny, Tionesta, and Clarion Rivers and offers deep-water activities via the Kinzua Dam and Allegheny Reservoir in the north and Tionesta Lake in the south.

All parts of the forest are accessible through hiking trails and narrow roads dotted with villages and encampments. The oldest continually operating sawmill in the state is in Endeavor, a bump on SR 666. Truemans, in the village of Fool's Creek, is a general store that's been in operation so long that no one knows when it opened. It's farther on SR 666 between Kellettville and Barnes.

The Civilian Conservation Corps, founded during the Depression, opened its first camp in 1933 near Duhring Road in the Allegheny Forest. Enrollees planted trees, built roads and recreational facilities, and fought forest fires. At the close of the CCC project in 1937, the camp was occupied by conscientious objectors to military service, who performed the same forestry work as the CCC workers. It also became a prisoner-of-war camp during World War II. Many a former prisoner with fond memories of the Allegheny National Forest has returned to the area for a visit.

Information on scenic and historic drives in the Allegheny National Forest is available from Northwest Pennsylvania's Great Outdoor Visitors Bureau (175 Main St., Brookville, PA 15825, tel 814/849-5197 or 800/348-9393, www .pagreatoutdoors.com). Forest County really is away from it all—not only is it Pennsylvania's least populated county, but it has no traffic lights, no radio stations, and no daily newspapers.

For a recreational and land use map of the forest, send a check or money order for $6.36 made out to "ENFIA" to Allegheny National Forest, P.O. 847, Warren, PA 16365, 814/723-5150.

Longhouse National Scenic Byway

This 29-mile route around the Kinzua arm of the Allegheny Reservoir offers spectacular views of forests and the river valley every season of the year. Since the roads are narrow with little visibility, it's recommended for automobiles, not bikes.

The scenic byway circles around, following SR 59 east from Kinzua Point into the forest. Turn south at SR 321 back to the lake, following the road south until it connects with SR 262 to the north.

Biking

Mountain biking is allowed on most trails in the Allegheny National Forest except the Hickory Creek Wilderness, Hearts Content, and Tionesta wild and scenic areas; most trails in the Buzzard Swamp wildlife management area; and Laurel Mill cross-country ski/hike area near Ridgway. Privately owned roads are also off-limits and may be posted. Though the available roads and trails total more than 1,000 miles, the Forest Service recommends specific trails for mountain bike use.

In the western section of the park, suggested routes are Tanbark Hiking Trail, 8.8 miles from US 62 south of Warren to Hearts Content Recreation Area, and Hearts Content Ski Trail,

7.7 miles, in the Hearts Content Recreation Area; Buckaloons Seneca Interpretive Trail, .8 mile, in the Buckaloons Recreation Area; Deerlick Ski Trail, 7.6 miles, near the Sheffield Ranger Station.

In the south-central area, near Marienville (Marienville Ranger District, 814/927-6628) routes include Marienville ATV Trail, 16 miles, on SR 66, south of the Chaffee intersection; Beaver Meadows Trail System, 7.1 miles, around Beaver Meadows Recreation Area; Loleta Trail, three miles, in the Loleta Recreation Area; and Buzzard Swamp Wildlife Management Area hiking trail, 10 miles.

Near the Allegheny Reservoir (Bradford Ranger District, 814/362-4613): Willow Creek ATV Trail, 10.8 miles, off SR 345 east of the reservoir; and Johnny Cake/Tracy Ridge Trail, 5.3 miles, off SR 321 east of the reservoir.

Near Ridgway (Marienville Ranger District, 814/927-6628): Mill Creek Loop Trail, 16.7 miles, accessible from Forest Road 185 off SR 948 north of Ridgway; and Twin Lake Trail, a 12.7-mile trail that starts at the Mill Creek Loop Trail and intersects the North Country Trail at the Tionesta Scenic Area, where bikes are not allowed. Best access points to the Twin Lakes Trail are from Forest Road 148 north of Brookston, SR 66 north of Nansen, or the Mill Creek Loop Trail.

The Allegheny National Forest is continually evaluating and scouting out new bike routes. If you're interested in participating, contact any of the ranger districts listed above.

Canoeing

The Allegheny Reservoir and Tionesta Lake both offer placid waters for canoeing. The Allegheny River, which runs 45 miles from the reservoir to the lake, is studded with islands along its length—seven were designated as wilderness islands by Congress in the 1980s. Camping is permissible on all of the islands within national forest boundaries. Tionesta Creek is another popular waterway. For a guide to access sites, contact the Northern Alleghenies Vacation Region (P.O. Box 804, Warren, PA 16365, 814/726-1222 or 800/624-7802, www.northernalleghenies.com).

There's also a scenic canoe route on the Clarion River, south of the park (see Cook State Forest under Other Outdoor Recreation for more on the Clarion River).

Outback Adventures (across the Tionesta Bridge from Tionesta, 814/755-3638, http://escape.to/outback) is an outfitter that services canoe enthusiasts in the Allegheny National Forest and offers a panoply of choices from cabin rentals to guided tours to two-hour kayak and canoe rentals. Two other rental agencies are **Allegheny Outfitters** (Warren, 814/723-1203) and **Allegheny River Canoe Rental** (Franklin, 800/807-5596).

Hiking

The national forest is threaded with 10 hiking trails totaling 180 miles, varying from six miles to 87 miles in length. The longest of these is part of the North Country National Scenic Trail that runs from the south boundary of the park near Belltown to the New York border. There are also nine shorter interpretive trails from less than a mile to three miles in length. About half of all hiking trails also permit use by bikers and cross-country skiers.

In the western section of the park, suggested routes are Tanbark Hiking Trail, 8.8 miles, from US 62 south of Warren to Hearts Content Recreation Area; Hickory Creek Trail, 11.1 miles, in the Hickory Creek Wilderness; and Minister Creek Trail, 6.6 miles, near Minister Creek.

In the south-central area, near Marienville: Beaver Meadows Trail System, 7.1 miles, around Beaver Meadows Recreation Area; and Buzzard Swamp Wildlife Management Area hiking trail, 10 miles.

Near the Allegheny Reservoir try Johnny Cake/Tracy Ridge Trail, 6.3 miles, off SR 321 east of the reservoir; and Morrison Hiking Trail, 10.8 miles, east of Morrison Run.

Near Ridgway you'll find Mill Creek Loop Trail, 16.7 miles, accessible from Forest Road 185 off SR 948 north of Ridgway; Brush Hollow, 8.5 miles, near Mill Creek Loop; and Twin Lakes Trail, a 12.7-mile trail that starts at the Mill Creek Loop Trail and intersects the North Country Trail at the Tionesta Scenic Area. Best access

points to the Twin Lakes Trail are from Forest Road 148 north of Brookston, SR 66 north of Nansen, or the Mill Creek Loop Trail.

Horseback Riding

Flying W Ranch (SR 666 in Kellettville, 814/463-7663) features trail horses for rent and guided trail rides on paths nearby in the forest.

Hunting and Fishing

The four tourist promotion agencies listed under Information publish a special hunting map designating hunting areas every year. Call any agency to request a map. Streams throughout the park teem with native fish, and most of the waterways within the park boundaries are trout-stocked.

Winter Sports

Several hiking and biking trails become available to cross-country skiers in winter. Among them are Brush Hollow, Deerlick, Hearts Content, Laurel Mill, and Tracy Ridge. In addition: Rimrock Trail, 2.5 miles, east of Allegheny Reservoir; Tidioute Riverside Recreation Trek Trail, 2.5 miles, near Tidioute; and Westline Trail, 9.8 miles, east of the reservoir near Westline.

The park also features 300 miles of designated snowmobile trails and an additional 60 miles of snowmobile/ATV shared-use trails.

Camping

The Forest Service developed seven drive-in campgrounds within the park, a total of 734 sites. Some, such as Buckaloons, Dewdrop, Kiasutha, Red Bridge, Tracy Ridge, Twin Lakes, and Willow Bay are equipped with dump stations for RVs. In addition, five more campgrounds with a total of 88 sites on the Allegheny Reservoir are accessible by boat or hiking trail only. For camping information and reservations, contact the Allegheny National Forest (877/444-6777 or www.reserveusa.com).

Getting There

Allegheny Forest lies between I-80 and US 6. The western boundary of the park is roughly paralleled by US 62 and the eastern boundary by US 219, which intersects both US 6 and I-80.

OTHER OUTDOOR RECREATION

Fishing

East Branch Lake is a haven for trout and warm-water fishing, boating, and water-skiing. The West Branch of the Clarion River offers delayed harvest fly-fishing only, and Big Mill Creek is also restricted to fly fishing. The Clarion River from Ridgway to Clarion permits trout and warm-water fishing; the river is suitable for canoes and floatboats March–mid-May.

Chapman State Park

Chapman, in the western part of Allegheny National Forest, covers 800 acres and offers boating (rentals available), lake swimming, fishing, hunting, and 13 hiking trails, including backpacking trailheads. Campers will find 83 tent/RV sites. The park may be contacted at Chapman State Park (R.R. 2, Box 1610, Clarendon, PA 16313, 814/723-0250).

Tionesta Lake

This lake, which borders the Allegheny National Forest in the southeast, is the result of a dam built and managed by the U.S. Army Corps of Engineers. Tionesta Lake's recreational focus is boating and fishing. It has multiple boat launch sites and tent/RV campgrounds. The launch areas are open year-round, weather permitting, Two primitive campgrounds are open year-round and charge no fee Oct.–mid-April; the third campground, with flush toilets and showers, is restricted to the warm months, May–Oct. For more information on Tionesta Lake facilities, call 814/755-3512. The Pennsylvania Fish Commission State Fish Hatchery maintains a visitors' center and large aquarium nearby in the village of Tionesta.

Clarion River Lake

Another U.S. Army Corps of Engineers property, Clarion River Lake, also emphasizes boating and fishing. The lake is on the southeast side of the national forest. For more information, contact Clarion River Lake's manager (731 East Branch Dam Rd., Wilcox, PA 15870, 814/965-2065).

Boat launch areas, tent/RV sites, and swimming (very popular with "polar bears") are available year-round.

Cook State Forest

Though it's hard to imagine, Pennsylvania's dense forests are mostly secondary growth, particularly in the northern part of the state where the lumber industry of the 1800s clear-cut major sections of the terrain. Cook Forest, south of Allegheny National Forest, is part of the area known in the past as "the Black Forest of Pennsylvania," where some stands of virgin forest still remain. The existing virgin timber in Cook Forest known as the Forest Cathedral began growing afte a severe drought and forest fire in 1644. Some of these over-300-year-old trees stand 200 feet tall and are four feet in diameter. Four of them would be enough to build a six-room house.

The land was originally owned by John Cook, who began his lumber business and sawmill along Tom's Run in 1828. In the 1920s, the state bought the land from the Cook family business to create a preserve and park. In 1994, *National Geographic Traveler* magazine recognized Cook Forest as one of the nation's top 50 state parks because of its ecological and historical significance.

Cook Forest offers camping and all-around recreation, with the exception of biking. On SR 36, which runs through its center, the state park extends from the town of Cooksburg west to Maple Creek Road/Lencer's Drive. For more information, contact Department of Environmental Resources (Cook Forest State Park, P.O. Box 120, Cooksburg, PA 16217, 814/744-8407 or 888/727-2757). Cook Forest is open all year.

Hiking: Cook Forest State Park has 30 miles of trails; the longest is three miles in length. Only two trails are steep and strenuous—Seneca Point and Indian Rocks. Seneca Point is a boulder-laden high point that overlooks the Clarion River Valley; Indian Rocks leads to petroglyphs along the river left by the Senecas, who hunted in the thick forest during the 18th century. One of the most dramatic sights in the park, the Forest Cathedral, is an easy hike along the Longfellow Trail from the Log Cabin Inn Visitors' Center off SR 36. This area contains some of the largest primeval white pine and hemlock trees still standing in the state. The trees were threatened during the summer of 1956; a storm of tremendous force brought down some of the largest. In 1976, a tornado destroyed more trees. In 1997, a hurricane battered the park but fortunately had little effect on the remaining trees. Trail maps are available from the park office.

Horseback Riding: The following stables, among others, offer rentals and guided rides in Cook Forest: **Pine Crest** (SR 36, Cook Forest, 814/752-2200); **Cook Forest Riding Academy** (2613 Forest Rd., 814/927-8391); **Silver Stallion Stables** (Vowinckel-Cooksburg Rd., 814/927-6636); and **Wet & Wild Acres** (SR 36, Cook Forest, 814/752-2600).

Hunting and Fishing: Most of the park is open to hunters during the posted seasons. As with all other parks in the state, any area that sees human traffic forbids hunting. The Clarion River flows along the eastern boundary of the park, and trout, warm water game fish, and panfish are common catches. The park provides a special fishing pond stocked with trout for children under 12 and anglers with disabilities.

Water Sports: The Clarion River is shallow but swift, bottomed by water-smoothed rocks. Supervised wading is possible. The park also has a shallow swimming pool (maximum five feet deep) and wading pool, which is open Memorial Day weekend–Labor Day.

Canoeing is a popular pastime on the river. The Clarion runs by Cook Forest south of Allegheny National Park and on to Ridgway. Canoe rentals are available during the summer from **Cook Forest Canoe Livery** (SR 36, 814/744-8094, weekends only); **Pale Whale Canoe Livery** (River Rd., 814/744-8300); and **Pine Crest Canoe Rentals** (SR 36, Cook Forest, 814/752-2200), among others.

Winter Sports: There are 20 miles of snowmobile trails, a lighted ice-skating pond near River Road, 10 acres of sledding slopes, and three designated cross-country skiing trails in the park.

Other Recreation: The park's property is interspersed with privately owned commercial enterprises along SR 36. There's a golf driving range (near SR 899), and several small amusement/

water parks such as Wet & Wild (SR 36, Cook Forest, 814/752-2600).

Camping: Cook Forest offers 226 tent/trailer campsites and 23 rustic cabins. The campsites are open year-round; however, washhouses with hot and cold running water and showers are not available late Oct.–late May. There is a dump station but no on-site hookups. The cabins are available mid-April–late Dec. Contact Cook Forest State Park (P.O. Box 120, Cooksburg, PA 16217, 814/744-8407 or 888/727-2757) for reservations.

Getting There: Cook Forest is bisected by SR 36; take Exit 78 north off I-80.

Clear Creek State Park

Clear Creek is southeast of Cook Forest State Park. Its 1,700 acres feature 16 hiking trails and river recreation such as canoeing, swimming, and fishing. There are 53 tent/RV campsites; yurts are also available for rent. Contact Clear Creek State Park (R.R. 1, Box 82, Sigel, PA 15860, 814/752-2368).

ACCOMMODATIONS
$50–100

Kane Manor Bed and Breakfast (230 Clay St., Kane, on the east side of the Allegheny National Forest, McKean County, 814/837-6522, www.kanemanor.com, $49–69) is a beautiful stately home built by Civil War veteran Gen. Thomas Kane. The room rate includes breakfast (honeymooners may have breakfast brought up to their room). The manor is next to 10 miles of blazed cross-country ski trails connected to country logging roads for longer outings. There is no fee to use the trails, and cross-county skis are available for rent for $8 a day, $15 for the weekend. The manor offers 10 rooms, seven with private bath.

M Cook Homestead Bed and Breakfast (SR 36 and River Rd., Box 106, Cooksburg, Jefferson County, PA 16217, 814/744-8869, www.cookhomestead.com, $90–105), originally built by lumberman Andrew Cook in 1870, was purchased from his great-granddaughter in 1994 and later converted into a bed-and-breakfast by Denny and Barbara Kocher, with considerable coaching from their dog, Jack. Four bedrooms

GROUNDHOG DAY

Calling a groundhog a public figure may be stretching it, but Punxsutawney Phil makes the national news one day a year—February 2, Groundhog Day. The weather-forecasting rodent is plucked from his man-made stump at 7:30 A.M. to determine the presence or absence of his own shadow and thereby let us humans know when to expect spring. Around 1,500 people bundle up for Phil's frosty prediction, then disperse to more serious pursuits. The big event occurs at Gobbler's Knob, just outside of town, from 4:30 A.M. to 9 A.M. One or two nights before Phil appears, the Pantall Hotel in downtown Punxsutawney hosts an inexpensive preforecast buffet. Phil (there are actually three Phils and one Phyllis) may be visited anytime at the groundhog enclosure across the park from the hotel.

Admission to the event is free, but remember to bundle up—temperatures usually hover around 0°F. Gobbler's Knob is on Woodland Avenue. To get there, follow Mahoning Street/US 119 through town until US 119 turns north and Mahoning continues straight, to the east. Woodland is a right turn off Mahoning (south) about a mile after the separation. Follow the signs to Gobbler's Knob. For more information, contact the Punxsutawney Chamber of Commerce/Groundhog Club (124 W. Mahoning St., Punxsutawney, PA 15767, 814/938-7700 or 814/938-4303, www.groundhog.org).

have private baths; four bedrooms on the second floor share two baths. Perhaps one of the most beautifully situated bed-and-breakfasts in Pennsylvania, the Homestead overlooks the Clarion River at the gateway to Cook Forest; the ranger's station is right next door. Two-night stays are required on weekends during Sept., Oct., and holidays.

Wolf's Den Bed and Breakfast (269 Timberwolf Run, Knox, Clarion County, PA 16232, 814/797-1105, $60–90 depending on room and season) is part of a complex (just off I-80) that includes a restaurant, campground, and nine-hole golf course. The bed-and-breakfast is secluded in a grove of white pine trees and overlooks a small manmade lake. The building features the original (1831) hardwood floors and local fieldstone for the walls. Two bedrooms have private baths, and two share a bath. Wolf's Den is 500 feet north of Exit 53 off I-80, on SR 338 (intersection of SR 338 and I-80).

M The Towne House Inns (138 Center St., Saint Marys, Elk County, 814/781-1556, $58–125) consists of three separate facilities: the Russ building, a 1907 converted manor house; a carriage house; and the Willows, another Victorian building next door (both the Russ building and Willows are Historic Landmarks). The original building has older rooms; the newer facilities in the Willows include some rooms with fireplaces and/or whirlpool baths, and a fitness room, which is available to all guests. The Town House features pleasantly decorated smoking and nonsmoking rooms, some with sophisticated business amenities. All have private bath. In the first floor of the original building, the inn serves breakfast and lunch Mon.–Fri. 6:30 A.M.–1:30 P.M., dinner Mon.–Sat. 5–9 P.M. This is a quality stay for a very low price.

The **Stonehouse Bed and Breakfast** (210 Center St., Punxsutawney, Jefferson County, 814/938-5972, $55–65) is near the local branch of Indiana University. It offers guests two rooms, each with private bath.

The **Pantall Hotel** (135 E. Mahoning St., Punxsutawney, 814/938-6600 or 800/872-6825, www.pantallhotel.com, $45–105) was built in the Victorian era and was renovated in the late 1990s to meet modern standards. Fifty-five clean, functional rooms with full and partial baths and two suites are available. Yes, Bill Murray slept here; his room bears his name. If you're coming for Punxsutawney Phil's February 2 prediction, book at least two months in advance. The hotel is just across the park from Phil's special habitat in the local library. The hotel dining room is the best place in the area for a meal.

$100–150

Scalise's Horton House Bed and Breakfast (504 Market St., Warren, Warren County, 814/723-

7472 or 888/723-7472, $115–145), a lovely old home with a widow's walk and porte cochère, was built during the northwest's oil and timber boom period before 1900. A pleasant alternative to camping, the bed-and-breakfast offers five rooms, all with private baths. It's decorated in the Victorian style, and a full breakfast comes with the room.

FOOD

Kinzua-Wolf Run Marina, a restaurant/lodging/marina combination, is in the Allegheny National Forest on SR 59, 10 miles east of Warren, Warren County. The Docksiders Cafe (814/726-9645, daily 11 A.M.–10 P.M.) offers waterfront dining on the Allegheny Reservoir, complete with spectacular sunsets and live weekend entertainment on the deck. The café offers a full menu—appetizers, sandwiches, burgers, and entrées such as seafood Alfredo, chicken parmesan, and prime rib— until 10 P.M., and the full bar remains open until 11 P.M., with cold beer on tap. Courtesy dockage is available for restaurant patrons. There's also a champagne brunch Sun. 11 A.M.–2 P.M.

In addition to boat dockage, the marina offers Stone Hill Cottage (814/726-3721) as a rental unit. The cottage sleeps four and is close to several hiking, cross-country skiing, and snowmobile trails. Weekend rates are $200 (Fri. 2 P.M.–Mon. 10 A.M.), or $400 for a week.

M The Wolf's Den Restaurant (291 Timberwolf Run, Knox, 814/797-1105, www.wolfsden .com) was originally a working barn during the oil boom era, and the hand-hewn beams, cozy fireplaces, and period antiques ooze rustic charm (the door handles are hatchets). The food is very fresh, well prepared, and priced reasonably—a welcome stop on I-80. The Wolf's Den complex is 500 feet north of Exit 53 (intersection of SR 338 and I-80). The restaurant is open in winter Mon.–Fri. 4 P.M.–8:30 P.M., Sat. 4 P.M.–9 P.M., Sun. 11:30 A.M.–9 P.M.; otherwise, hours are Mon.–Fri. 11:30 A.M.–8:30 P.M. and weekends 11:30 A.M.–9 P.M. Prices range $10–28.

The Pantall Hotel's **M Coach Restaurant** (35 E. Mahoning St., Punxsutawney, 814/938-6600 or 800/872-6825, www.pantallhotel.com, Mon.–Fri. 7 A.M.–8 P.M., Sat. 7 A.M.–9 P.M.,

Sun. 7 A.M.–7 P.M., breakfast and lunch $5, dinner $10) offers tasty homestyle meals—nothing fancy—at down-home prices. The Saturday night and Sunday buffets feature eight hot dishes plus salads, relishes, and the fresh and famous Pantall rolls in a pleasant (though smoky) dining area (all for $8!); you may order from a full menu if you prefer. The **Coachlight Bar** in the Pantall hotel features a restored curly maple Victorian bar, complete with ornate columns and arches. Food may be ordered from the hotel restaurant, and the bar stays open until 2 A.M, daily (open at 11 A.M.). With a little encouragement, the bartender might tell tales from the Pantall's past, such as the diamond deals that took place in the early 1900s, when gems would be spread across the bar and examined for purchase by a local oilman.

INFORMATION

In addition to the information available directly from the Allegheny National Forest, these tourist promotion agencies provide brochures and answer questions upon request: **Northwest Pennsylvania's Great Outdoors Visitors Bureau** (175 Main St., Brookville, PA 15825, 814/849-5197 or 800/348-9393, www.pagreatoutdoors.com—also covering Cameron, Clarion, Clearfield, Elk, and Forest Counties); **Allegheny National Forest Vacation Bureau** (Box 371, Bradford, PA 16701, 814/368-9370 or 800/473-9370, www.alleghenyvacation.com); and **Northern Alleghenies Vacation Region** (315 2nd Ave., P.O. Box 804, Warren, PA 16365, 814/726-1222 or 800/624-7802, www.northernalleghenies.com).

Cook State Park and the other parks mentioned above are spread out over three counties. Cook State Park and Clarion River are in the northernmost part of Armstrong County; contact **Armstrong County Tourist Bureau** (125 Market St., Kittanning, PA 16201, 724/543-4003 or 888/265-9954, www.armstrongcounty.com). Clear Creek is in the northernmost part of Jefferson County and Tionesta Lake is in Forest County; both are handled by Northwest Pennsylvania's Great Outdoors Visitors Bureau, as are St. Marys and Punxsutawney.

Western Amish Country

In colonial times, the "wild west" meant western Pennsylvania—mountainous and rugged, guarded by the impenetrable Allegheny Ridge, and inhabited by hostile natives and teeming wildlife. Industrialization wrested natural riches from the surrounding land, but by the mid-20th century, Western Pennsylvania shed its industrial trappings to return to rural life, agricultural pursuits, and a new role as a scenic recreational area.

Opportunities for outdoor activities abound. Hiking and biking trails can be found in parks and on two-lane byways lined with Amish farms. Boating and fishing locations are a short drive in any direction. Peaceful villages mix with tumbling rivers and mountains densely packed with hardwood forest; for travelers in southwestern Pennsylvania, diverse, uncrowded, pristine scenery is part of the package. It's an unhurried, unadorned place, made for leisurely sightseeing. The peaceful farmlands watered by tributaries of two of Pennsylvania's mightiest rivers are divided into two areas: North of the Ohio (Lawrence, Beaver, and Butler Counties), and East of the Allegheny (Armstrong and Indiana Counties).

PLANNING YOUR TIME

Though the farthest destinations in Western Amish Country are less than four hours apart by auto, it's a good idea to overnight at some point that's central to your area of interest, and plan on 2–7 days, depending on what you'd like to see. This area is excellent for day trips or overnights.

If you expect to stay in Pittsburgh, plan a day trip to Beaver County for a visit to **Old Economy Village** (2 hours) and **Harmony Historic District** (2 hours). **Beaver** and vicinity offer plenty of fun places to eat, shop, and see the sights (especially **Montgomery Locks and Dam** and **Shippingport Nuclear Facility**).

Or spend the day cruising the **North Loop Through the Villages** and keep an eye out for fields plowed by man and horse, and carriages marked with a caution triangle among the surrounding fields and forests (all day). You'll probably want to spend time in **Volant** to do a little shopping and have lunch.

Two hours from Pittsburgh (or worth a stay overnight in the lively college town of Indiana or the villages of Dayton or Smicksburg), the **Jimmy Stewart Museum** (1 hour) can be combined with a slow-paced tour of the surrounding rural area. Get to know **"A Little Town on the Allegheny"** by taking a walking tour of Leechburg (2 hours). Or bike the routes around Indiana for an intimate look at the area in the **Farm Country Cruising** tour (3 hours).

If outdoor activities are your focus, plan to stay in **Raccoon Creek State Park** or **Moraine State Park,** and visit **McConnell's Mill,** or enjoy an extended hike (2 hours–several days) on the **Baker Trail, Armstrong Trail,** or a shorter jaunt on the historic **Ghost Town Trail.**

GETTING THERE AND GETTING AROUND

By Air and Rail
Major access to Western Amish Country is through the Pittsburgh International Airport (see Getting There in the Pittsburgh chapter).

Small craft airports exist throughout the area. Two commuter airlines based in the Pittsburgh Airport are Christman Air (412/225-4000), and Comair (412/566-2100). Call for current destinations and flight schedules.

Rail access to southwestern Pennsylvania is through Pittsburgh (see Getting There in the Pittsburgh chapter).

By Auto
Most (but not all) counties operate their own transportation systems. The best way to see the area is by car.

East-west access is by the multilane, high-speed I-80 in the north, and mostly-two-lane US 422. Major north-south access is by multilane, high-speed I-79 and I-76 in the west. Most of the roads, though narrow, are in excellent condition.

Getting lost on the backroads can be both desirable and hellish. The north and eastern parts of Western Amish Country are farmland and forest, interspersed with small villages. In the warmer months, the countryside looks like a gigantic, well-kept park. There appear to be more riding lawnmowers in use here than anyplace in the world. There is little to orient a visitor as to direction.

If you intend to wander about by auto, it's wise to stop in any gas station and pick up a county map, one that shows county roads (often designated by a letter followed by four numbers, such as T3021 or C4007). These roads frequently go unnamed in real life, but the map will help you approximate your location. A compass isn't a bad idea, either, but step away from the car to use it—a hot engine alters the reading. The beauty of the area becomes secondary when you're tired and hungry and have no idea where you are.

One aspect of rural roads may require psychic preparation: the amount of roadkill in the warmer months. It's due more to the huge animal population than to the usually sparse traffic. Your chances of hitting something increase as the sun goes down, so plan your drive times accordingly.

Must-Sees

M **North Loop Through the Villages:** Keep an eye out for water-driven pumps in the ponds, white cotton curtains swept to one side, and an absence of automobiles in the driveways—you may encounter the Amish in their horse-drawn carriages as you enjoy surrounding fields and forests (page 324).

M **Montgomery Locks and Dam:** Built to control flooding on the Ohio, the dam fronts a 10-mile-long pool. This and the nearby Shippingport Nuclear Facility form an amazing picture of super-sized man-made structures (page 325).

M **Harmony Historic District:** On a much more human scale, these original buildings and a small museum memorialize the first settlement of the 19th-century religious commune known as the Rappites (Harmonists), whose members practiced celibacy and separation of the sexes (page 328).

M **Old Economy Village:** A few miles away from Harmony, this meticulously preserved village was the final dwelling place of the Harmonists. The village contains many of the original buildings and gardens, including the community kitchen and granary (page 328).

M **McConnell's Mill State Park:** The park follows the path of Slippery Rock Creek and contains a

Montgomery Locks and Dam

former water-driven gristmill turned into a museum. A covered bridge marks the northern boundary of Slippery Rock Gorge, a favorite of rock climbers and white-water enthusiasts (page 333).

M **Jimmy Stewart Museum:** Indiana is Jimmy Stewart's hometown, and this museum honors the actor and his career with a multifaceted collection that will appeal to his fans and those who appreciate movie magic (page 341).

M **The Ghost Town Trail:** One of the first rails-to-trails established in America, the path derives its name from once-thriving coal mining communities. The 16-mile-long trail passes by the Eliza Furnace near Vintondale, one of the best-preserved hot blast iron furnaces in existence (page 343).

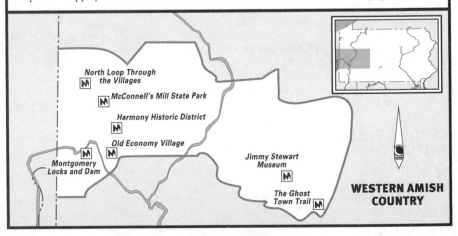

North Loop Through
M the Villages

M McConnell's Mill State Park

Harmony Historic District
M

Old Economy Village
M **M**

Montgomery
Locks and Dam

Jimmy Stewart
Museum
M

The Ghost
Town Trail **M**

**WESTERN AMISH
COUNTRY**

Western Amish Country

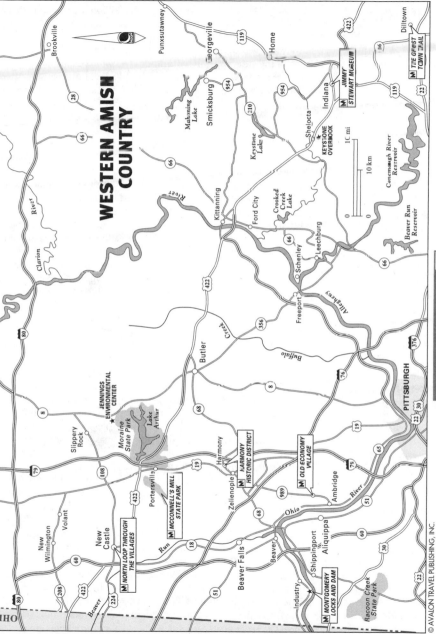

WESTERN AMISH COUNTRY

Western Amish Country

HISTORY

Pre-Colonial Times

Most of southwestern Pennsylvania was uninhabited until around 1750, when the area came under the loose protectorship of the Iroquois to the north. The Iroquois used the area for hunting and permitted their "dependents" (tribes they had conquered in battle or through negotiation, including the Seneca and Lenni Lenape) to do the same.

In 1730, one of the largest Lenni Lenape settlements in the west was established in Kit Han Ne (Kittanning), where an old foot trail crossed a broad river the Lenape called Allegewi (Allegheny). The village was to play a significant role in the French and Indian War as a staging area for raids on white settlements. During Pontiac's War, it was destroyed and its inhabitants were scattered.

Battle for the Frontier

Impenetrable forests prevented settlement of southwestern Pennsylvania until well after 1750. Though the English laid claim to the land, they had made no effort to colonize it. Southwestern Pennsylvania had seen little white exploration at all until territorial disputes with the other European landlord—France—reached an incendiary point in the French and Indian War (so named because each European side claimed native allies).

Not long after the war, numerous Indian tribes in the northeast united to fight under Ottawa chief Pontiac, driving out the few settlers remaining in southwestern Pennsylvania. It remained free of European habitation until a treaty was signed with the Iroquois Confederation in 1768.

Independence

With the 1768 treaty of Fort Stanwix, pioneers once again began to move into western Pennsylvania. Pioneers moved by foot and Conestoga wagon over narrow, rutted roads to a new life. Scots-Irish and German farmers cleared growing room and cities crystallized near the swift-flowing rivers. Farms blossomed, and settlements began to make and ship pig iron and glass south to Pittsburgh in addition to grain and other agricultural products; rivers and rough roads provided the thruways.

Many western colonists who fought in the Revolution did so in expectation of increased access to land and agricultural wealth. After the war was won, however, they found that the governmental powers in Philadelphia didn't necessarily consider the westerners equals.

Growing Pains: Whiskey and Taxes

Ten years after the American government came into being, the issue of balancing the budget was resolved by an old British source of income: taxes. Congress decided to levy a tax on domestic distilled spirits in order to satisfy debts lingering from the Revolutionary War. The burden of this tax fell not on the affluent landed gentry or prosperous businessmen in the east, but on the western farmers who converted their grain crops to easily transportable whiskey, a major source of their income. Spirits were easier to move over the difficult roads of the region and more profitable than the grain that produced it.

The ensuing Whiskey Rebellion of 1794 pitted antifederalists against federalist supporters of the government (then based in Philadelphia) over the issue of unfair taxation. Federalist authorities sent advance troops from a 13,000-man detachment into Pittsburgh in a show of strength. The Whiskey Rebellion ended shortly thereafter without further violence, and the tax was repealed during Thomas Jefferson's presidency.

On the Move

In the 1820s, steamboats and barges routinely transported passengers and freight up and down the rivers. According to the *History of Armstrong County*, written by R. W. Smith in 1883, a large raft holding more than 100 men, women, and children was observed floating down the Allegheny River at Freeport. While some of the men were poling and steering the raft, one man was tending a small herd of horses while a girl milked a cow. Another girl made mush in a shanty and an older woman spun flax on her spinning wheel. All seemed quite content as they floated to new homes in Ohio or Indiana.

If it weren't for the Allegheny River, the towns of Freeport, Ford City, Kittanning, and the other communities along it would not exist. The Allegheny connected the northwestern Pennsylvania settlements of Franklin, Oil City, and Warren with the big city of Pittsburgh. As early as 1807, the river was used to transport lumber to the south; later, it also conveyed petroleum.

Since road travel was frequently impossible because of few thruways and bad conditions, rivers became the arteries and veins of southwestern Pennsylvania. The Allegheny carried tons of freight and passengers down to the Mississippi, while the Monongahela ferried coke (a refined form of coal) to the fledgling steel mills outside Pittsburgh. The coalfields, pig-iron smelters, and coke ovens continued to produce their bounty.

In the first part of the 19th century, improved roads, called turnpikes, were built with private funds. People and goods moved into the western territories on the backs of the rivers and in the rolling hulls of Conestoga wagons.

In the mid-19th century, the iron horse charged across mountains and valleys, giving travelers and transport both speed and a new flexibility. When the War Between the States broke out, southwestern Pennsylvania sent men and weapons to fight under the Union blue. The new railroads transported shot, cannon, food, and other supplies to northern troops.

Farms and Mills

The late 19th century was the golden age of machines. After the Civil War, steel mills appeared in towns along the rivers, churning out rail for the railroads and metal frames and fixtures for buildings. The manufacture of glass for commercial and home use blossomed. Immigrants from the Old World settled all over the southwest. An Italian colony in Avella worked the steel mills; Ukrainians and Germans made glass in Ford City. New machines were being invented daily. James Denny Daugherty, a resident of Kittanning, invented the first typewriter, with the "qwerty" keyboard configuration we still use today, based on manual dexterity and the frequency of appearance of each letter in standard English. The boom seemed endless.

But it wasn't. The need for steel flagged first. The World Wars caused production to soar, but in the lulls men were losing their jobs to plant shutdowns and automation. By the 1950s, many of the steel mills had closed their doors. The boom had ended, and the river country returned to what had sustained it for centuries—agriculture.

North of the Ohio

Beaver County sits above Pittsburgh like a tophat and contains the city's northern suburbs. One resident of Beaver County told me that if I forgot the name of a store or restaurant, I could just call it "Beaver," because everything is named after the Lenni Lenape chief. Though his statement is a bit of an exaggeration, a glance at the map and the phone book does attest to the popularity of the name. Beaver (Tamaqua) of the Lenni Lenape nation was designated "King" by the Iroquois (of whom the Lenni Lenape—or Delaware—were dependents) and sent to negotiate peace with the British after the French and Indian War. He lived briefly in the vicinity of Beaver, moved to New Castle, then settled on the other side of the Ohio border.

The towns that make up Beaver County run into each other with little evidence of seams—appropriate for an area formerly made up of interdependent industries along the Beaver and Ohio Rivers. It would be difficult to guess that a large part of the county is rural, dotted with charming villages, and the home of a large lake and public park a few miles from the Pittsburgh metropolitan area.

The scenic territory north of Beaver County is a hand-stitched quilt of agricultural acreage, rural villages, parks and one town, New Castle. North and east of New Castle, Amish farms prosper as they have for generations. Along the rivers, many mills stand silent—though the small towns around them have flourished as centers of education, commerce, technology, and recreation. In Lawrence County, a large population of Old Order Amish have plowed and planted farms in the Enon Valley and around the villages of New Wilmington and Volant. New Wilmington was established as a borough in 1873 and is the larger of the two villages. It offers a variety of arts and crafts shops (some selling authentic Amish-made pieces), antique shops, bed-and-breakfasts, and restaurants. Volant, a small village nearby, has been turned into an outdoor mall with an Amish-country focus. It's a nice place for a stroll, featuring small shops, cafés, and accommodations.

There's plenty of outdoor recreation in the area: Raccoon Creek, Moraine, McConnell's Mill, and Jennings State Parks.

SCENIC TOURS
M North Loop Through the Villages
Amish farms are distinguished by water-driven pumps in the ponds, white cotton curtains swept to one side, and an absence of automobiles in the driveways. The best time to encounter the Amish in their horse-drawn carriages is on Sunday, in the early afternoon, as they return from

services. The surrounding fields and forests, in shades of gold and green, may be seen by auto or bicycle. Cyclists might consider spending the night in either New Wilmington or Volant, making it a two-day trip.

The center of the city of New Castle is Kennedy Square, with its towering Civil War monument. All roads lead to the square and the traffic circle around it. Since country roads are easy to miss, approximate odometer distances are given for the route; set your odometer at the monument. The entire route is about 40 miles long.

Turn right (north) on SR 18 from the roundabout at the monument and travel to Mitchell Road (five miles). Turn right (east) on Mitchell Road (1.5 miles), then left (north) on Mercer Road (2.5 miles). Make another right turn (southeast) on SR 956, and travel through trees and farms until you see the hand-lettered street sign for Covered Bridge Road on the right side of the road (2.3 miles). Turn left. Over the small hill, the covered Banks bridge is directly in front of you.

There are two ways to go from here. You can pass through the bridge (don't forget to make a

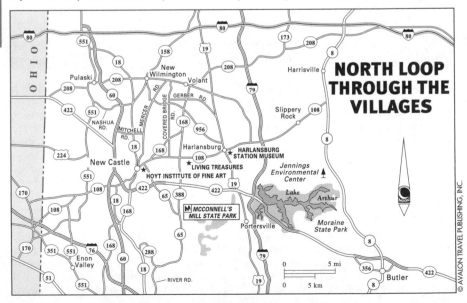

NORTH LOOP THROUGH THE VILLAGES

© AVALON TRAVEL PUBLISHING, INC.

wish and kiss your true love) and follow Covered Bridge Road north into the forest until it dead-ends on SR 208. A right turn at this intersection will lead to Volant (2–3 miles), a left turn to New Wilmington (2–3 miles).

Another option is to turn right directly *before* the bridge onto Gerber Road. Follow it until it ends on SR 168 (2–3 miles). Turn left (north) to SR 208, then left again (west) to pass through Volant on to New Wilmington.

At the traffic light in New Wilmington (there's only one), reset your odometer. Continue west on SR 208 to the intersection of SR 208 and SR 18 (1.5 miles), then turn left (south) on SR 18 (two miles). Turn right on Nashua Road (west, 2.4 miles), right on River Road (north, three miles), then follow SR 208 west to Pulaski, about .5 mile. Turn left (south) at the intersection, and follow the signs for SR 551 south from Pulaski. Continue south on SR 551 (seven miles). Turn left (east) on US 224 and proceed for five miles into the center of New Castle.

© JOANNE MILLER

water power on an Amish farm

SCENIC SPOTS

Riverside Park

This small urban park on Riverside Drive (724/728-5700) parallels the Beaver River in the town of Bridgewater (Beaver County). It's a pleasant place for a picnic or a short walk.

Montgomery Locks and Dam

Visitors can observe operations from the public area of this Ohio River dam (www.lrp.usace .army.mil, free) daily during regular business hours except New Year's Day, Easter, Thanksgiving, and Christmas; during daylight hours, join a tour of the locks (contact the lockmaster, 724/643-8400, Mon.–Fri. 8:30 A.M.–4 P.M.), or see it all from across the river in the village of Ohioview. Entrance to the public area of the dam and locks are off SR 18, about five miles west of the town of Monaca and three miles east of the Shippingport Nuclear Facility. For the best view of the locks and dam, drive west on SR 68 (on the north side of the river), and turn left (south) on any street between Highland and Wilson to reach the road that parallels the river.

The federal government began to construct dams on the Ohio River in the early 1800s. The unpredictable waterway would often flood during the winter and spring, but in summer the water was barely navigable, sometimes averaging one foot in depth between Pittsburgh and Cincinnati, Ohio. The Montgomery locks and dam were built between 1932 and 1936, replacing several smaller wooden dams. The mighty Montgomery is one of a series of 20 massive locks and dams on the Ohio River from Pittsburgh to Cairo, Illinois; the dams work together to control the erratic water level. The Montgomery locks and dam span the wide Ohio, creating a "pool" more than 18 miles long for recreational and commercial use.

Shippingport Nuclear Facility

The sheer size of the stacks and cooling towers of this, the first nuclear facility in the United States, is difficult to comprehend as they appear around the bend in the river from SR 68 (Beaver County). Five cooling towers and two smokestacks fill the

GROWING UP IN BEAVER

Priit Vesilind, senior writer at *National Geographic Magazine*, grew up in the town of Beaver during the 1950s. For this book, he recorded the following reminiscences.

The only things that prevented us from being part of the rural Midwest were the Ohio River and the industrial plants along its shores. In the '50s, the night sky glowed red in the east; light pulsed as the furnaces poured iron more than 10 miles away. It was a home-grown aurora borealis. I still associate certain odors with certain towns: Freedom smells like oil, Ambridge like slag, Beaver like plastics from Koppers Company across the street, where my father worked for 30 years. Beaver moms always complained about soot gathering on window sills, and dirty walls. If you climbed a tree, your pants turned black from a layer of accumulated air pollution.

With some 6,000 people, Beaver was small and familiar. It was built around a square, with a courthouse in the middle, surrounded by parks filled with Norway maple, silver maple, and horse chestnut trees. The square rested on top of the bluff overlooking the Ohio, where many of us fished for catfish and carp, using doughballs and corn. At the time, those scavenger fish were the only survivors in the river, a virtual sewer of industrial effluent. We sometimes sold them to the railroad workers, who didn't seem to care about the sewage. Now the river has been cleaned up, thanks to the Ohio River Commission and the death of heavy industry.

Besides fishing, young boys collected baseball cards, listened to the Pittsburgh Pirates on the radio, sat on cool front porches playing Monopoly or canasta, and traded comic books. The community swimming pool was the focus of the summer. I would roll my bathing suit in my towel, wedge it into my bike frame, cycle up the leafy streets through the old Civil War–era cemetery, and stay at the pool until my lips were blue.

Teenagers hung around Jerry's Cheeseburgers, a drive-in place, Hank's Frozen Custard, and Bert's Bar-B-Cue, which has become a rather sophisticated restaurant now. "Canteen," an informal dance held every Saturday night in the school gym, was the scene of our adolescent blunders and passions. Pegged pants, rolled shirt sleeves, upturned collars, "duck's-ass" haircuts, and cigarettes for "hoods"—the bad guys—were the fashion.

I suppose I remember the time more than the place. We knew each other well in Beaver. We knew the butcher and the baker and the pharmacist. We trusted one another; doors were never locked. We knew who was struggling and who was making it. Our mothers sat in women's clubs together, our dads played golf together. Homes were modest, Sears-Roebuck houses with nice—but not too nice—lawns. Backyards had doghouses, grapevines, flower gardens, old sheds, and clotheslines where moms in housedresses hung out laundry. No one used telephones much. If you wanted your buddy to come and play, you stood in front of his house and yelled, "Hey, Butch!"

In summer, the hollyhocks buzzed with Japanese beetles and honeybees. We would catch them in jars. Summer nights were filled with fireflies, and if you sat in the porch swing eating watermelon you could hear the late-shift mill whistles and the clank of railroad couplings from the line that ran along the river.

When I was a junior in high school, we had an alumnus who came back to talk to us—a man who had gone to a good college and was now a successful diplomat of some sort. His advice to us: "Get out of Beaver!" I did, but much of the way I think and react to the world was formed there, for better or for worse.

© JOANNE MILLER

the old Service United Church

horizon, rising above the low industrial buildings that line the river. Pittsburgh was the first city in America to have electricity supplied by nuclear power. Many reactors went up around the state after the failure of other industries, and nuclear power is still a source of employment for hundreds of Pennsylvanians. Though the facility, operated by Duquesne Light, southwestern Pennsylvania's power company, sometimes schedules tours for schoolchildren, it doesn't normally permit visitors on the plant site. Nuclear power is as controversial in Pennsylvania as in other parts of the United States; the near-disaster at Three Mile Island, near Harrisburg, fueled antinuclear activism across the state, and set the power companies in a self-protective mode that has been even more pronounced since 9/11.

Scenic Churches and Chapels
The tiny **Service United Church and John Andersen Cemetery** have been around since well before the Civil War. The gravestones, set on a hill overlooking the brilliant blue reservoir, read like a primer in U.S. history. The quiet, peace, and beauty of this spot are eternal and otherworldly—perfect for a picnic or a proposal. This is a small and private place, well off the tourist routes (please respect the unique surroundings). The reservoir and church are approximately four miles south of Shippingport on SR 18. Look for the Service Church Road (T482) turnoff on the east side of the road. Follow the road approximately one mile to the church parking lot.

Built by the Greek Catholic Union, a federation of Austro-Hungarian immigrants, the **Saint Nicholas Chapel** (5400 Tuscarawas Rd., Beaver, 724/495-3400 or 800/722-4428, www.gcuusa.com, viewing by reservation, free) is a replica of the wooden structures of the Carpathian Mountain region of central Europe. One hundred and twenty churches in that region were studied to provide a basis for the design of the chapel, dedicated to St. Nicholas. The splendid iconography inside the building, consisting of 20 paintings, may be viewed by request. The public is also welcome to tour one Sunday each month; call for the date. No fee is charged, but donations are appreciated.

HARMONY ON THE MOVE

Within eight years of founding the original Harmony colony in Pennsylvania, the hardworking, wealthy, and hugely successful Rappites had outgrown their own land. They moved to a larger colony (also called Harmony) in Indiana on the banks of the Wabash. At the end of a decade, George Rapp and his followers sold the Indiana property to another charismatic communal leader, atheist Robert Owen, and returned to Pennsylvania, this time to Economy Village, now in the city of Ambridge north of Pittsburgh. One possible reason for the return was restlessness bred by idleness; members of the commune were beginning to ask why they were forbidden to relax and enjoy the fruits of their labor when everything was going so well.

In his lifetime, Rapp faced only one serious threat to the smooth workings of the colony. A traveling salesman from Frankfurt, Germany, posed as a nobleman, integrated himself into the colony, and drew off a number of dissatisfied Harmonists. Rapp offered the "Count" the royal sum of $105,000 to take those who would follow him and leave Economy Village. He accepted Rapp's offer, but his followers dropped away within a decade while the Harmonists continued to thrive.

Rapp died in 1847, at the age of 90. So unshakable was his conviction that he would personally lead his people in the new millennium, he said, "If I did not so fully believe that the Lord has designed me to place our society before his presence in the land of Canaan, I would consider this night to be my last."

Those were his final words.

HISTORIC SIGHTS

Harmony Historic District

This historic district centers around the town diamond in the village of Harmony and includes the Wagner House and Ziegler log house, as well as the Harmonist cemetery, Father Rapp's hillside bench, the Mennonite meetinghouse and cemetery, and the Harmony Museum (218 Mercer St., 724/452-7341 or 888/821-4822, www.harmonymuseum.org, Tues.–Sun. 1–4 P.M., $3.50). The museum encourages reservations for tours on Saturday and for any large groups. A candlelight Christmas open house takes place on the second Sunday in December.

Harmony (alternately spelled Harmonie) was the first settlement of the Rappites, also known as the Harmonists, a 19th-century communal Christian society. The Harmonists produced everything that the group needed and eventually expanded into manufacturing. They occupied this village for eight years before moving to a larger colony in Indiana (the group eventually returned to Pennsylvania).

The graveyard, with its numbered graves, and several of the old buildings are worth exploring. A collection of presettlement Indian artifacts, Harmonist relics, and information about the history of this pious group are on display in the museum. The original one-handed Harmonist church tower clock still stands and still points to the hour.

Old Economy Village

This meticulously preserved village (Church and 14th Sts., Ambridge, Beaver County, 724/266-4500) was the final dwelling place of the Harmonists after their return from Indiana. It's open March–Dec. Tues.–Sat. 9 A.M.–5 P.M., Sun. noon–5 P.M.; closed on holidays except Memorial Day, July 4, and Labor Day. Admission is $5. The village serves as a memorial to the now-defunct sect whose unmarried members practiced celibacy and separation of the sexes. The Harmonists, who shared all aspects of work and leisure, became one of America's most successful economic experiments. The village contains many of the original buildings and gardens, including the community kitchen and granary and George Rapp's home. Old Economy is a fascinating look at an alternative lifestyle that thrived for more than 100 years. The turnoff from SR 65 to the village is marked by a hard-to-see one-foot-square brown sign on the right side of the road (the turn is to the left). The village is within the town of Ambridge, close to SR 65.

OTHER POINTS OF INTEREST

SNPJ Recreation Center

The SNPJ (Slovenska Narodna Podporna Jednota), or Slovene National Benefit Society (270 Martin Rd., Enon Valley, Lawrence County, 724/336-5180 or 877/767-5732, www.snpjrec .com), was organized as a fraternal group in 1904, providing affordable insurance to members. The SNPJ recreation center is a 500-acre resort for members with a trailer court and 60 rustic cabins overlooking a 20-acre lake. The public will enjoy a visit to the Slovenian Heritage Center on the premises and polka dances featuring music by the area's top bands each weekend. Munch on a kielbasa (ka-BAS-a or ke-BAS-ee) sausage and wash it down with a plastic cup of keg beer while listening to Bob "The Turk" Turcola or other polka legends pump out the snappy beat. These dances are major events, attracting people of all ages and backgrounds. I spent the afternoon talking to an Italian polka fan from Ohio as we watched two ponytailed teenage girls spin each other through advanced steps. Dances are scheduled year-round every Sun. 3–9 P.M. Call for information on the bands. Admission varies but is around $5.

POLKA MUSIC IS HAPPINESS

I dare you to try to sit through three polkas in a row and not twitch.

The dictionary defines the polka as a lively round dance originating in Bohemia and performed by couples in duple meter. In fact, polka is music that cures depression, incites movement, and provides a major aerobics workout—all within five minutes.

Polka began as a peasant dance in Bohemia in the 1830s, supposedly started by a Czech servant girl. High society took it over by 1840 and popularized it all over Europe. Courtesy of their wealthy European patrons, several famous composers—Anton Dvořák and "Waltz King" Johann Strauss Jr. among them—incorporated polka rhythms into their work.

Basically a partner dance characterized by a hop-step, the polka has five variations, including a heel-and-toe maneuver that was immortalized in the opera *The Bartered Bride*, by Bedrich Smetana. However, the polka refused to be limited to the rarified realm of classical music. The most popular song in America in the 1930s was the "Beer Barrel Polka," which debuted at a Wurlitzer Jukebox convention in the Midwest. In the 1950s, Lawrence Welk and his Melodymakers (including accordionists and button-box, or concertina, players) popularized the polka on American TV. Welk's famous "An' a one, an' a two . . . " would waft over floating soap bubbles as the band squeezed out a polka-fied rendition of a popular song. Welk's original bubble machine—which provided background for a generation's "champagne music"—now resides in Pittsburgh, at the Westin William Penn Hotel.

Today, polka has hard-core aficionados in Pennsylvania and throughout the Midwest. Variations on the beat—Texas's *conjunto* or *norteña* music, for example (which Joe Cummings, author of *Moon Handbooks Texas*, refers to as Czech-Mex)—are popular all over the United States. Polka weekends—such as the Fourth-of-July Polka Fireworks, hosted by Seven Springs resort—and weeklong polka parties are common events year-round. Hot polka bands have their own sets of groupies, which follow them from one play-date to the next, sometimes forming an RV wagon train.

Polka appeals to all ages, since the main focus of the parties is dancing. Many professional dance groups bring in young people as a way of teaching them their ethnic heritage. Though the emphasis may be on Polish, Czech, German, or Slovenian background, it's always colored with red, white, and blue patriotism.

The eye of the polka hurricane in the Midwest is the International Polka Association (4145 S. Kedzie Ave., Chicago, IL 60632, 800/867-6552). The association boasts a membership of 20,000 and stages its own annual music awards for best band, best vocalist, etc. As the phone message at the International Polka Association says, "Remember . . . polka music is happiness!"

Living Treasures Animal Park

Living Treasures Moraine (four miles west of I-79, New Castle, Lawrence County, 724/724-9571, www.ltanimalpark.com, $6.50 adults, children 3–11 $4.50, under 2 free) is a frequent Pennsylvania phenomenon, a roadside zoo. Living Treasures Moraine is open daily Memorial Day weekend–Labor Day, 10 A.M.–8 P.M., May, Sept.–Oct., Mon.–Fri. 11 A.M.–5 P.M., Sat.–Sun., 10 A.M.–6 P.M.; April Sat.–Sun. 10 A.M.–6 P.M.

Though some of the exotic animals at Living Treasures—antelopes, camels, kangaroos, and zebras—may seem oddly out of place in the Pennsylvania terrain, they appear to be content and well cared for. The more unusual species are often no longer useful to urban zoos or breeding programs and are given an extended life through these exhibition areas. Kids will love the petting/feeding zoo, with its pygmy goats, miniature sheep, llamas, and occasional miniature horse.

Another branch of the organization is Living Treasures Laurel Highlands (SR 711 south of US 31, Donegal, 724/593-8300), open daily Memorial Day weekend–Labor Day, 10 A.M.–8 P.M.; April–May, Sept.–Oct., daily 10 A.M.–6 P.M. Admission prices are the same as above.

MUSEUMS

Merrick Free Art Gallery

This small local gallery (11th St. and 5th Ave., New Brighton, 724/846-1130, http://216.110.178.132/info.html) was established by Edward Dempster Merrick, a local industrialist, in the late 19th century. The gallery is open Tues.–Sat. 10 A.M.–4:30 P.M., Sun. 1–4 P.M.; closed Mon. and major holidays. Summer hours are Wed.–Sat. 10 A.M.–4 P.M., and alternating Sundays 1 P.M.–4 P.M. Admission is free. The Merrick is closed all holiday weekends and Christmas–mid-Jan.

The museum's founder was a descendant of James Merrick, who arrived in Massachusetts in 1636 and made his fortune in the manufacture of horseshoe nails. At the age of 53, he decided to become an artist and collector. The gallery displays a selection of French, German, English, and American paintings of the 18th and 19th centuries and a selection of artifacts from the New Brighton Historical Society.

Air Heritage Museum

A "working museum" at the Beaver County Airport (junction of SR 251 and SR 51, Beaver Falls, 724/843-2820, Mon.–Sat. 10 A.M.–5 P.M., Sun. 11 A.M.–6 P.M., free) invites visitors to help in the restoration of 10 World War II aircraft stored in its hangar. A B-17G "Nine-O-Nine" bomber recovered from a crash during an airshow in 1987 was the first aircraft to be restored and is now on display. All restoration and preservation is done by volunteers during scheduled sessions.

The Harlansburg Station Museum of Transportation

Visitors on the move will appreciate this private collection (intersection of SR 108 and US 19 in the village of Harlansburg, 724/652-9002, www.harlansburgstation.com, $4) in a replica train station complete with four silvery railroad passenger cars. Models and life-sized representations of all forms of transportation, including planes, trains, cars, trucks, trolleys, buses, boats, and bikes are on display. The museum is open March–May and Nov.–Dec. Sat. 10 A.M.–5 P.M., Sun. noon–5 P.M.; June–Oct. Tues.–Sat. 10 A.M.–5 P.M., Sun. noon–5 P.M. Memorabilia, railroad toys, posters, books, magazines, and videos for railroad buffs, plus original art, may be found in the gift shop.

The Hoyt Institute of Fine Arts

This local institution (124 E. Leasure Ave., New Castle, 724/652-2882, www.hoytartcenter.org) was formed by a group of Lawrence County citizens in 1965 to encourage and promote fine art, decorative arts, and performing arts in the New Castle area. In 1968, May Emma Hoyt donated her own mansion, Hoyt East, and Hoyt West (once owned by her brother) to house the activities. Both mansions and the grounds are open Tues. and Thurs. 10 A.M.–8 P.M.; Wed., Fri., and Sat. 10 A.M.–5 P.M. All art exhibitions at

Hoyt East are free. A docent-led tour (call ahead to reserve space) is available for a donation of $3 per person.

Paintings and photography from regional and national artists and an extensive collection of decorative arts are exhibited in Ms. Hoyt's mansion, Hoyt East, which also houses the main office, classrooms, the Shen-ango China collection (crafted locally), and the library.

Hoyt West has been restored to its early 20th-century splendor, and houses a gallery with rotating exhibits and an Oriental room with Asian art; it is the site of performing arts for the institute. The mansions, one Greek Revival and the other Tudor Revival, sit on five acres of landscaped grounds, complete with tiled roofs, carved walnut grand staircases, leaded glass windows, and carriage houses.

SHOPPING
Beaver and Beaver Falls

Beaver and Beaver Falls are old management/industrial towns undergoing transition into tourist areas. Two- and three-story multicolored brick storefronts in varying states of disrepair and polish line the main streets, and there are some bargains to be had. In Beaver Falls, 7th Avenue is the place to shop for antiques. The **Antique Emporium** (818 7th Ave., 724/847-1919, Mon.–Sat. 10 A.M.–5 P.M., Fri. until 8 P.M., Sun. noon–5 P.M.) and **Peggy Smith's Collectibles** (621 7th Ave., 724/843-2622, Mon.–Fri. 11 A.M.–4 P.M., Sat. 10:30 A.M.–5 P.M., Sun. noon–4 P.M. by chance) are a few long-standing outlets. **Riverfront Antique Mall** (2586 Constitution Blvd., Beaver Falls, 724/847-2304 or 800/443-5052, www.riverfrontantiquemalls.com, Mon.–Sat. 9 A.M.–8 P.M., Sun. 9 A.M.–6 P.M.) is the largest antique mall in Western Pennsylvania, with more than 300 dealers.

Zelienople and Harmony

Zelienople (zee-lee-en-O-pul), the town founded by German aristocrat Baron Dettmar Friedrich Basse in 1802 and named for his daughter, Zelie, is a popular spot for antiquing. In the down-

town between 200 and 300 S. Main St., **Main Street Antiques** (204 S. Main St., 724/452-8620, Mon.–Sat. 10 A.M.–5 P.M.) and **VanWhy's Antiques** (300 S. Main St., 724/452-0854, Mon.–Sat. 10 A.M.–5 P.M.) are worth a look; **Olde Country House Antiques** (a few miles north of Zelienople on US 19 north, 724/452-0100, Mon.–Sat. 11 A.M.–5 P.M.) is in a restored stone barn built by the Mennonites in 1814.

Downtown Harmony also offers a host of antiques and crafts shops around Mercer Street such as **In Harmony** (250 Mercer St., 724/452-0203, Mon.–Sat. 10 A.M.–5 P.M.).

SAVING THE STRAND

The heart of many small towns gave way to the convenience of malls in the late 1950s and became little more than boarded-up reminders of a once-thriving community resource. Malls are malls—what makes a community unique are the places that truly belong to it.

In 1914, Gioachino and Rosalia Sapienza converted their grocery store in downtown Zelienople into a movie house christened "The Strand," and ran silent films on an old projector with live piano accompaniment; in the 1920s, they brought in "talkies." Everybody and their kids came to see the latest show.

The Strand (P. O. Box 31, Zelienople, PA 16063, 724/742-0400, www.thestrandtheater.org) thrived as a social center for Zelienople and Harmony for decades, providing a destination for families to meet and be entertained for an evening. With the onset of multiplexes and VCRs, the Strand could no longer compete. One night in the early 1980s, the little theater closed its doors.

Though there's nothing special about the Strand—it's not a historic building or an architectural marvel—it is intimately connected to the lives of generations. A group of local people are working to reopen the Strand as a performing arts center, and with it, to revitalize the interactive community life of downtown—it worked in Pittsburgh; it worked in Baltimore; and it's working in small towns all across America. Let's keep our fingers crossed for the Strand.

New Wilmington

State Route 208 is the main street in New Wilmington; the downtown shopping district lines the streets that cross SR 208. **The Amish Peddler** (405 E. Neshannock Ave./SR 208 east, 724/946-8034, www.800padutch.com, Mon.–Sat. 10 A.M.–5 P.M.) offers Amish-made furniture in several styles, artwork, and accessories. The streets are lined with souvenir and crafts shops, but for the best prices on Amish souvenirs and toys, try **Miller's 5 & 10** (131 S. Market St., 724/946-8322, Mon.–Sat. 10 A.M.–6 P.M.); it's been around since 1961, and will even take in your dry cleaning.

The **Village Gallery** (102 E. Neshannock Ave., 724/946-9181, www.village-gallery.com, Tues.–Wed., Fri. 11 A.M.–5 P.M.; Thurs. 11 A.M.–7 P.M., Sat. 10 A.M.–4 P.M.) features the work of popular local artist J. G. McGill. McGill portrays the daily life of the Amish and other western Pennsylvania subjects in several media. Prints, cards, and originals are available.

Just outside of town, **The Amish Outlet** (intersection of SR 18 and SR 208, 724/946-2318, Mon.–Sat. 10 A.M. to 6 P.M.) is a gift shop featuring furniture, hats, bonnets, and other items handcrafted by local Amish. From spring until late fall, the shop also features baked goods from the kitchens of nearby farms. Though the shop sells numerous items that are not locally made, it provides an opportunity to see local crafts.

Volant

Main Street in the village of Volant, intersection of SR 208 and SR 168, is a shopping area created from a small rural village. Main Street's merchants (www.volantshops.com) make clever use of the existing buildings and railroad cars to house all manner of gift, toy, and clothing shops, jewelers, and restaurants. The shops are divided into several areas: Train Car Shops, Volant Mills, Volant Depot, and Potter Run Landing. Main Street's fancified atmosphere may not be for everyone, but the businesses can provide a lovely day's diversion for those who like to window-shop as well as for serious collectors. The shops are generally open Mon.–Sat. 10 A.M.–5 P.M., Sun. noon–5 P.M. During winter, some shops may limit hours; all are closed on major holidays.

Farmers' Markets and Bulk Stores

The Apple Castle (between New Castle and New Wilmington on New Castle/Sharon Rd./SR 18, Lawrence County, 724/652-3221) is a fifth-generation family farm that sells fresh fruit, corn and other vegetables, cheese, and baked goods. It's open year-round: Jan.–July, Mon.–Sat. 9 A.M.–5:30 P.M.; and Aug.–Dec., Mon.–Sat. 9 A.M.–8 P.M.

Schiestle Country Store (SR 956, 2.5 miles southeast of New Wilmington, Lawrence County, 724/376-3280) offers a rainbow assortment of foods in bulk (more than 25 kinds of flour, a variety of noodles, sugar, spices, etc.), candy- and sausage-making supplies, and specialty dried soups. There's an artesian well on the property—visitors are welcome to fill their containers at no charge. The store is open Mon.–Sat. 10 A.M.–5 P.M.

Helbling Farms (212 Little Beaver Rd., Enon Valley, Lawrence County, 724/336-3276, Mon.–Sat. 9 A.M.–5 P.M., Sun. noon–5 P.M.) is a greenhouse and farm market offering fresh seasonal fruits and vegetables grown on the premises.

OUTDOOR RECREATION

Biking

The 12-mile-long, blacktopped **Stavich Bicycle Trail** (216/536-6221) is suitable for all skill levels and ages. The trail begins in New Castle and ends in Struthers, Ohio. It runs parallel to the Mahoning River and follows the rails of the former Youngstown-New Castle streetcar line. The trail is privately maintained; call for more information.

Canoeing and Rafting

Canoeing enthusiasts recommend the North Fork of the Beaver River, Mahoning River, Shenango River, Slippery Rock Creek (look for white water here in the spring), Neshannock Creek (na-SHAH-nok), and Connoquenessing Creek (ca-nok-a-NESS-in, also nok-a-NESS-in). Contact the Lawrence County Tourist Promotion Agency and Beaver County Tourist Promotion Agency for specifics and recommendations (see Information).

Hunting and Fishing

There are state game lands near Ohioville and Watt's Mills in Beaver County. Lawrence County has five designated state gamelands for hunting in season. Maps and information are available from the Pennsylvania Hunting/Game Commission (814/432-3187).

For fishing information, contact the Pennsylvania Fish and Boat Commission, Southwest Region (P.O. Box 39, Somerset R.D. 2, PA 15501, 814/445-8974, www.fish.state.pa.us). A *Summary of Fishing Regulations and Laws* booklet is available where fishing licenses are sold.

In Lawrence, Beaver, and Butler Counties, the Beaver River, Little Beaver Creek, Neshannock Creek, Slippery Rock Creek, Hickory Creek, Taylor Run, Connoquenessing Creek, Deer Creek, Bessemer Lake, Mahoning River, and Shenango River are popular with anglers.

Raccoon Creek State Park

A large lake and 13 miles of trails distinguish this park (3000 SR 18, Hookstown, 724/899-2200, www.dcnr.state.pa.us, year-round, free), put together from submarginal farmland in southern Beaver County during the 1930s. Workers from the Civilian Conservation Corps and Works Progress Administration began the transformation into what is now a 7,323-acre public recreational space. The park offers a multitude of outdoor opportunities, including boating and bridle paths. The remains of Frankfort Mineral Springs, a nationally known health spa during the 1800s, is within the park's boundaries; the springs may be viewed—there is a short trail near the park office—but are not open for public use.

The park is accessible for people with disabilities. For information and maps, contact Raccoon Creek State Park (R.R. 1, Box 900, Rte. 18, Hookstown, PA 15050-9416, 724/899-2200).

Wildflower Reserve: One highlight of the park is a wildflower reserve with more than 500 species of flowering plants and a variety of habitats such as an oak and hickory forest and floodplain forest. Peak wildflower blooms occur late April–mid-May. The reserve, on the eastern boundary of the park, has five miles of trails.

Water Sports: Swimming is available at Raccoon Lake, on an 800-foot turf beach with a lifeguard on duty. It's open Memorial Day weekend–Labor Day 11 A.M.–7 P.M. The drop from the beach to the lake is gradual enough even for small children. There's a bathhouse and food stand nearby.

Nonpowered and electric-powered boats (with current registration) are permitted. A concession rents canoes and rowboats on the south side of the lake.

For anglers, the lake offers bluegills, sunfish, bullheads, catfish, yellow perch, walleye, muskellunge, crappies, sauger, and bass. Cold-water fish, such as trout, are found both in the lake and in the feeder streams that run through the park.

Winter Sports: Raccoon Creek designates several miles of cross-country and equestrian trails in the uncrowded western section of the park. Snowmobiling is permitted on some of the roads. There's also an area for sledding, ice skating, and ice fishing.

Camping: The park features 10 modern cabins and 172 tent and trailer sites, some up to 35 feet in length. For reservations, call 888/PA-PARKS (888/727-2757) Mon.–Sat. 7 A.M.–5 P.M. Camping is permitted mid-April–mid-Dec.

Getting There: Raccoon Creek State Park is 25 miles northwest of Pittsburgh via US 30.

McConnell's Mill State Park

McConnell's Mill State Park follows the path of Slippery Rock Creek and contains a former water-driven gristmill turned into a museum. Slippery Rock Creek is 49 miles long and is named for one exceptionally slick rock in the vicinity of McConnell's Mill. It is believed that an Indian trail forded the creek at a shelf of sandstone near a natural oil seep, which made the rock slippery and gave its name to the creek, a town, a rock formation, and many local businesses. In the late 1800s, oil wells briefly flourished in the valley, but the oil was swiftly invaded by ground water and the wells were abandoned. The oil wells drained the oil seep, and the Slippery Rock is no longer covered in oil. A Howe truss covered bridge, Kildoo Bridge, marks the northern boundary of Slippery Rock Gorge. The gorge was created

© JOANNE MILLER

McConnell's Mill covered bridge

by glacial movement more than 100,000 years ago, and it still projects an untamed beauty to visitors. While driving on one of the roads that wind through the park, I saw a trio of mature wild turkeys within 10 feet of the road.

No camping is permitted, but two large picnic areas are close to the mill parking area. The river is open to experienced white-water rafters (it varies class II–IV, depending on season). McConnell's Mill Park is open all year, sunrise to sunset. For more information and maps, contact McConnell's Mill State Park (R.R. 2, Box 16, Portersville, PA 16051, 724/368-8091, www.dcnr.state.pa.us).

Climbing and Rappelling: McConnell's Mill State Park is popular with rock climbers and rappellers; two areas have been designated for their use. Rim Road climbing area is across the creek from the mill; the more advanced climbing area is by the unfortunately named Breakneck Bridge, at the intersection of Breakneck Bridge Road and Cheeseman Road. It's fun to watch the many experienced climbers who attend nearby Slip-

pery Rock (a.k.a. Slimy Pebble) University go through their paces.

Hiking: Seven miles of rugged trails follow the path of the gorge. Trails are minimally developed and the creek is aptly named, so be forewarned. The two-mile Kildoo Nature Trail provides the easiest access to the park's greenery.

Hunting and Fishing: Hunting is permitted in season in areas of the park that receive few visitors. Fishing is permitted anywhere along Slippery Rock Creek with the exception of the dam structure. A fly-fishing area is open year-round at the Armstrong Bridge on Harris Road.

Rafting and Swimming: White-water rafting is permitted in rubber rafts, white-water canoes, and kayaks. Rafts must be at least seven feet long and have two air chambers in the gunnels. Life preservers are required. There is no recreational swimming allowed in swift and dangerous Slippery Rock Creek.

Getting There: The park is 38 miles north of Pittsburgh via I-79 to US 19 (Exit 28). The park entrance is about 1,000 feet north of the inter-

THE BRIDGES OF
PENNSYLVANIA COMMONWEALTH

Many people assume that wooden bridges built between 1800 and 1880 were covered to protect either the bridge surface or the carriages and wagons that passed through them. Though both assumptions are correct, many covered bridges were also built by local landowners as toll crossings. Mill owners who built bridges, such as that at McConnell's Mill, would often let customers who brought in loads of grain pass for free. On Sunday, some bridge owners offered a discount for churchgoers and families (and some would even provide a pile of cloths on either end of the bridge so passersby could wipe the dust from their "Sunday best" shoes).

Often referred to as kissing bridges, the covered structures provided private places to romance a sweetheart where prying eyes couldn't see—except when the rafters served as playgrounds for acrobatic children. But theft of privacy paled in comparison to other forms that occurred at the bridges, which were popular places for brigands to lie in wait. Though, since the bridges are also known as wishing bridges, in the belief that reciting a wish while crossing was supposed to guarantee its being granted, one could always wish for a safe passage.

The first wishing bridge built in the United States spanned the Schuylkill River near Philadelphia. In the century that followed, innovation in the design of wooden covered bridges created a knowledge base for the successful engineering of today's massive steel structures. The side walls of covered bridges were constructed in three major forms. the earliest and simplest, the kingpost, had a side wall consisting of a triangle reinforced with upright timbers. The queenpost was a modified version with a truncated triangle with supporting posts. The burr truss combined multiple kingpost-type triangles with an arch for support, permitting spans over wider streams and rivers.

As one bridge builder put it: "Our bridges were covered, my dear Sir, for the same reason that our belles wore hoop skirts and crinolines—to protect the structural beauty that is seldom seen, but nevertheless appreciated."

section of US 19 and US 422 on McConnell's Mill Road.

Moraine State Park

Moraine State Park (on Pleasant Valley Rd. off SR 488, Portersville) is a small paradise reborn from an industrial wasteland. In 1889, oil was discovered in Muddy Creek Valley, the site of the park. Both oil and coal industries flourished there through deep (pit) and strip mining until the 1950s. To transport the spoils, a branch of the Western Allegheny Railroad ran the length of the valley—it was abandoned in 1935. The old railroad grade is still visible in the Upper Muddy Creek finger of the lake and west of the dam.

Two local residents, Edmund Watts Arthur, a Pittsburgh attorney, amateur geologist, naturalist, and writer, and Dr. Frank W. Preston, were instrumental in the process that eventually led to

the reclamation of this area. The Pennsylvania Department of Forests and Waters and the Department of Mines and Mineral Industries combined forces to redevelop the former mine sites.

Before restoration, heavily scarred and pitted earth ran black with polluted acid mine drainage (AMD). Mines were sealed, strip mines were backfilled and graded, and 422 gas and oil wells were plugged; then the 3,225-acre Lake Arthur was constructed and filled, and the swimming beach sited on a former strip mine.

The park was dedicated to public use on May 23, 1970. For all-around recreation, Moraine State Park is a great choice. There are more than 1,200 picnic tables, two beach swimming areas, 11 public boat launching areas, hiking and bicycling trails, environmental education and interpretive programs, a covered shelter designed specifically for waterfowl observation, fishing, hunting, and a host of winter activities. Wheelchair-accessible picnic tables, parking spaces, toilets, fishing piers, and swimming areas are throughout the park. Sailing is especially popular, and races and regattas on Lake Arthur take place throughout the summer—under a clear sky, dozens of colorful sails wheel about on the blue waters. The park is open all year, and admission is free. No camping in the park, but to reserve one of the 11 cabins, contact 888/PA-PARKS (888/727-2757) Mon.–Sat. 7 A.M.–5 P.M. For more information, including park maps, write or call Moraine State Park (222 Pleasant Valley Rd., PA 16051, 724/368-8811, www.dcnr .state.pa.us).

Biking: A seven-mile paved bicycle trail runs along the north shore of Lake Arthur, beginning at the bike rental concession by West Park Drive and ending at the Marina Restaurant. There is also a volunteer-built seven-mile loop trail for mountain bikes that begins near the park's Davis Hollow Marina. The trail is meant for experienced off-road riders in good physical condition; park authorities warn of numerous hazards: steep slopes, rough surfaces, and slippery areas. Ride with caution.

Hiking: The longest and most varied of the hiking trails is the Glacier Ridge Trail, nine miles from the northwest corner of the park (Glacier Ridge trailhead) to the Jennings Environmental Education Center.

Accessible from the Pleasant Valley picnic area, the Sunken Garden and Pleasant Valley Trails are both three-mile loops that interconnect, providing the possibility of nearly six miles for more ambitious hikers. The Sunken Garden Trail also has a shorter (two-mile) return loop. The two-mile-long Hilltop Nature Trail is a self-guiding nature walk on the park's south shore, and the Wyggeston Trail is 4.2 miles long with access points off Old US 422 and SR 528. Maps and information are available from the park office at the Pleasant Valley Road entrance, or from the Forestry and Regional Park office at the Old US 422 entrance.

Hunting and Fishing: Hunting and trapping are permitted throughout Moraine State Park, except for areas subject to heavy recreational use. Off-limit areas are posted, and a map is available at the park office. All hunting is subject to State Park and Pennsylvania Game Commission rules and regulations. The park is closed to hunting and dog training from April 1 to the day after Labor Day. Woodchuck hunting is not permitted.

A number of fish habitat improvement projects have been created by park volunteers throughout Lake Arthur, resulting in a bountiful variety of warm-water species: muskellunge, northern pike, largemouth bass, walleyes, channel catfish, black crappies, bluegills, and hybrids such as tiger muskellunge and stripers. Fishing is permitted everywhere except for posted areas, which include boat docks, launching and mooring areas, the marina, the Game Propagation Area, bridges, or within 100 feet of the beaches. Fishing is subject to the Pennsylvania Fish and Boat Commission rules and regulations for warm-water conservation lakes.

Swimming and Boating: In Moraine State Park, lifeguard-attended swimming is available at two beaches: the turf-and-sand Pleasant Valley Day-Use Area and the sandy Lakeview Day-Use Area, Memorial Day weekend–Labor Day daily 11 A.M.–7 P.M. Boating is permitted everywhere except in the Game Propagation Area; a boat rental facility is at the Pleasant Valley Day-Use Area. Sailing and canoeing are popular activities on Lake Arthur. There is a 10-horsepower limit on boats powered by a motor, and they must display current Pennsylvania boat registration. Nonmotorized boats must display one of the following: 1) a state park launch permit, 2) a state park mooring permit, or 3) a current Pennsylvania boat registration.

Winter Sports: Both the Sunken Garden and Pleasant Valley Trails (accessible from the Pleasant Valley picnic area) have been improved for cross-country skiing. Each is a three-mile loop interconnecting with the other, providing the possibility of a nearly six-mile-long trail. The Sunken Garden Trail also has a shorter (two-mile) return loop. Ice skating and ice fishing are permitted on Lake Arthur.

Camping: There are 11 modern cabins with kitchens and indoor toilets available for rental on a year-round basis within the park. Make reservations through Moraine State Park (R.R. 1, Portersville, PA 16051, 724/368-8811). There are no tent campsites available.

Getting There: Moraine State Park is 40 miles north of Pittsburgh via I-79. It may be reached by taking Exit 28 off I-79 (SR 488) to Pleasant Valley Road, or US 422 or Old US 422 (direct entrance) from SR 528.

Jennings Environmental Center

Jennings, just northeast of Moraine State Park on SR 528, about 1,000 feet south of the intersection of SR 528 and SR 8, encompasses a real rarity in Pennsylvania's dense hardwood forests: a prairie. The Relict Prairie Ecosystem, as it's called, is a remnant of the prairie peninsula that extended out of the Midwest and into western Pennsylvania about 2000 B.C. Indigenous but rare (for Pennsylvania) flora and fauna—notably the blazing star wildflower and Massasauga rattlesnake—live here.

Opportunities to observe a wide variety of animals and more than 134 species of birds are excellent throughout the year; the prairie wildflowers are at their best in early August. Several miles of easy trails interconnect within the 220-acre park. An interpretive center is on the premises, as is a trail accessible to wheelchairs. Cross-country skiing (but not biking) is allowed on all Jennings Environmental Center trails.

The park is open all year, sunrise to sunset. No camping is permitted. Admission is free. For more information, including maps, contact Jennings Environmental Center (2951 Prospect Rd., Slippery Rock, PA 16057, 724/794-6011, www.dcnr.state.pa.us).

Camping

Bear Run Campground (184 Badger Hill Rd., Portersville, Butler County, 724/368-3564 or 888/737-2605, www.bearruncampground.com, April–Oct., $24–45) is a privately owned and operated camping and RV facility 10 minutes from Moraine State Park, Lake Arthur, and McConnell's Mill State Park. The family-style campground offers accommodations and activities reminiscent of the best of childhood summer camps. Available recreation includes a heated pool, children's playground, softball field, horseshoe courts, volleyball, full-sized basketball court in a lighted pavilion, and a recreational arcade with billiards. There are two fishing lakes stocked with trout, one exclusively for kids, plus canoe rentals and access to a boat launch on Lake Arthur.

Accommodations include full-hookup RV sites and pull-throughs (with dump station), water/electric RV and tent sites, group camping areas, wooded primitive sites, a remote walk-in tent area, and improved and primitive cabins. Though it fills the need for a camping area in the vicinity of the state parks, Bear Run's major drawback is its sheer size and the number of people it can accommodate—as in summer camp, it may be difficult to get some private space. In addition, the hot showers are coin-operated.

To get there, take Exit 28 from I-79, then go east 50 yards on SR 488 to the sign. Turn left (north) .5 mile on Badger Hill Road. Daily camping rates are $15, with a discount for week- and monthlong stays. Cabins are about $40 per night.

Rose Point Park (on old US 422 seven miles east of New Castle, Lawrence County, 724/924-2415 or 800/469-1561, www.rosepointpark.com, April–Oct., $18–100) is another family-style privately owned campground that offers tent sites, full hookups for trailers, cabin and trailer rental, and campsites, plus a swimming pool, playground, and other activities. The park is 2.5 miles west of Exit 29 on I-79.

ACCOMMODATIONS
Under $50

In an area with few lodging alternatives, **M The Inn on College Hill** (3233 6th Ave., Beaver, Beaver County, 724/843-6048, $45–65) is a real find. The expansive craftsman-style home of Betty and Howard Mattsson-Boze was built around 1910. It sits in a pleasant residential neighborhood of highly individual homes from the same period. Howard teaches at nearby Geneva College, so the inn attracts collegiate types as well as visitors from the world over. Two of the guest rooms have their own baths, and one has a fireplace and sitting area. It's so quiet at night that the distant rumble of a passing train may cause you to dream of the velvet-lined coaches of coal barons. With luck, Betty will make her special muffins with the "rice" (Swedish pearl sugar) on top.

$50–100

The original four-room house that is the basis of **Felicity Farms** (2075 Dutch Ridge Rd., Beaver, Beaver County, 724/775-0735, www .felicityfarms.com, $85–100) was built in 1786. In 1905, the house was expanded and moved from its original site to its present location on the crest of a hill. Anne Mayerich acquired the property in 1997 and renovated the home to its former splendor. The farmhouse interior is warm, comfortable, and eclectic. Each of the three guest rooms has a private bath. A continental breakfast is offered on weekdays, and a full breakfast is available on Saturday and Sunday.

Rich and Juanita Eppinger make a stay at their warm, comfortable bed-and-breakfast truly special. **M The Inn on Grandview** (310 E. Grandview Ave., Zelienople, Butler County, 724/452-0469, www.fyi.net/~grandinn, $85–140) was known as the Zimmerman Hotel in the early 19th century. It's seen many uses since then, serving as a funeral home, apartment house, and private home. The house was moved from its original location on the corner of Grandview and Oliver to its present site in the early 1900s. After buying the property, the innkeepers gutted and rebuilt the interior and added a cellar. Two years of hard work resulted in a charming and cozy place to stay. The renovation is respectful of the building's original style, updated with modern amenities such as a full bath in each room. One of the rooms features a fireplace and whirlpool bath, another has a claw-foot bathtub and a private second-floor balcony. Juanita, who has a separate decorating business, has put together a mix of antiques (mostly family pieces) and carefully chosen modern furnishings. The spool bed in one of the bedrooms was brought over the mountains from eastern Pennsylvania in a covered wagon. One of the bedroom ceilings has the original hacked post and beams. The Inn on Grandview is a convenient base when exploring western Pennsylvania's Amish country.

FOOD

Inexpensive

In New Brighton, the **Brighton Hot Dog Shoppe** (724/843-4012, Mon.–Thurs. 6 A.M.–11 P.M., Fri.–Sat. 6 A.M.–midnight) is a good place for a quick breakfast or snack. Food prices are mostly under $5.

M Bruster's Ice Cream (1525 Riverside Dr., Bridgewater, 724/774-4155, Sun.–Thurs. 9–10, Fri.–Sat. 9–11) makes its own ice cream on the premises.

Pizza Joe's (209 S. Market St., New Wilmington, 724/946-2515, Sun. noon–10 P.M., Mon.–Thurs. 11 A.M.–10 P.M., Fri.–Sat. 11 A.M.–11 P.M., $10) is the place for Italian specialties. It's part of a chain, and if you want to go to the original, it's not far (1203 Croton Ave., New Castle, 724/652-7355).

Midrange

The **M Willows Inn Family Smorgasbord** (1830 Midland Beaver Rd./SR 68, Industry, near the north side of the Montgomery Locks and Dam, 724/643-4500, www.willowsinnpa.com) serves an inexpensive lunch priced around $12, Tues.–Fri. 11:30 A.M.–3 P.M.; dinner ($15) is served Tues.–Sat. 3 P.M.–8:30 P.M., and Sun. 1–6:30 P.M.; brunch is served Sun. 10:30 A.M.–1 P.M. The big find for big eaters is the Tues.–Sun. dinner smorgasbord with 15 entrées and a big dessert selection. A pub and a decent motel are also on site.

M The Kaufman House (105 S. Main St., Zelienople, 724/452-8900, www.kaufmanhouse .com) has been serving big helpings of delicious, well-priced food since 1859. The structure was renovated in 1888, burned down, rebuilt, and renovated again. It remains a local favorite, with a wide variety of entrées. The Kaufman House is open Mon.–Thurs. 7 A.M.–9 P.M. Fri.–Sat. 7 A.M.–10 P.M. and Sun. 11 A.M.–9 P.M. for breakfast, lunch, and dinner. Lunch prices average $8, dinner $12.

Try **The Shortstop Inn** (124 Neshannock Ave., New Wilmington, 724/946-2424,

Tues.–Sat. 11 A.M.–8 P.M., lunch $6, dinner $10) for tasty home-cooked American food, including fresh bread baked on the premises and the special chicken divan ($10).

A popular place to stop for lunch ($8) and dinner ($13) is the ⛰ **Neshannock Creek Inn** (Main St., Volant, 724/533-2233, Sat.–Thurs. 11 A.M.–5 P.M., Fri. 11 A.M.–8 P.M.); it serves an American menu with lots of fish (hence the late Friday hours), but the local favorite is the gigantic bacon-Swiss-chicken salad ($9).

Expensive

The **Wooden Angel** (308 Leopard Ln., Beaver, 724/774-7880, www.wooden-angel.com, Tues.–Fri. 3 P.M.–9 P.M., Sat. 5–10 P.M., $8–30), is the place to go in town for special occasions. Its all-American wine list has won awards from *Wine Spectator* magazine, and the menu features American food such as eggs benedict thincrust pizza ($9) and the house specialty, rack of lamb ($30).

INFORMATION

The friendly folks at the **Beaver County Tourist Promotion Agency** (526 Brady's Run Rd., Beaver Falls, PA 15010, 724/728-0212 or 800/342-8192, www.co.beaver.pa.us) will send information and answer questions regarding the Beaver area: Ambridge, Beaver, Beaver Falls, Brady's Run Park Recreation Facility, New Brighton, and Industry.

Contact the **Lawrence County Tourist Promotion Agency** (229 S. Jefferson St., Suite 102, New Castle, PA 16101, 724/654-8408 or 888/284-7599, www.lawrencecounty.com) for more information about New Castle, Wilmington, and Volant.

Zelienople, Volant, and Moraine State Park are served by **Butler County Tourism and Convention Bureau** (3008 Unionville Road, Cranberry Township, PA 16066-3408, 724/234-4619 or 866/856-8444, www.visit-butler-county-pennsylvania-pa.com).

East of the Allegheny

The orderly pattern of Amish farms is interrupted only by the larger towns of Kitanning (Armstrong County), Indiana (Indiana County), and an occasional village amid forests laced with rivers.

Since flatboats loaded with grain were poled down to Pittsburgh in the late 18th century, the farms and forests that fan out from the Allegheny River—producers of many of the goods transported via the swift waters—have changed very little. However, the towns that line the banks of the river, which once played a large part in the commerce of western Pennsylvania, have become smaller and more individual since their roles as transport centers have diminished.

The towns hold their history in their names. In 1827, David Leech, a young engineer who built the dam and lock on the new canal beside the nearby Kiskiminetas River, also built Leechburg—four houses, a school, and a gristmill—and became the first mayor. Freeport was so named because it offered the only free boat tie-

ups on the river in 1796. Kittanning (Kit Han Ne), the oldest town in western Pennsylvania, was settled by the Lenni Lenape who migrated from the Delaware Bay before 1700; Kit Han Ne was an important stop on the foot trails that connected native encampments all over the east. Ford City was once the company town of Pittsburgh Plate Glass (PPG). Founded by Captain John Ford, the town was opened to non-PPG residential and commercial development in 1895.

Not all is bucolic, however. Indiana County, Christmas tree capital of the world, has enough power generating stations—many of them nuclear-based—to light 50 million lamps, a combined capacity of five million kilowatts. The tallest nuclear cooling chimney in the United States, at 1,216 feet, is at the Homer City Generating Station. It can be seen along US 119 or SR 556.

In homage to another kind of power, a hardware store proprietor in the town of Indiana once built a window display around a golden Oscar won by his son, Jimmy. Today a sundial marks the former location of J. M. Stewart & Sons Hardware, across the street from the Jimmy Stewart Museum.

The area east of the Allegheny River is a place to pass through leisurely, flowing with the current and swaying down the gentle hills, perhaps enjoying a little outdoor recreation in Crooked Creek National Recreational Area. One of the area's major attractions is its lack of tourist attractions. It really is "away from it all."

SCENIC TOURS

A Little Town on the Allegheny

To take a walking or cycling tour of the village of Leechburg, on SR 56, is to spend time in a typical small river town of today, with a few twists.

Leechburg grew from one family to many since its founding in the early 1800s. The Leechburg Museum (118 1st St., 724/845-6742) was built in the early 1830s as a dwelling place for David Leech himself. It's considered the oldest house in town. The small building behind the house was used as a caretaker's quarters and workshop for the main house. The museum is open Wed. and Sat. 10 A.M.–2 P.M. or by appointment.

The town cemetery with the founder's grave is on Pershing Avenue. The Old Mansion (85 1st St.), now a private home, was built in 1868 by David Leech's son and his wife. The original Hebron Lutheran Church (Main and 2nd Sts.) was built in 1847; the first pastor, Rev. David Earhart, was the grandfather of Amelia Earhart, pioneer aviatrix. The present church, built on the same site in 1888 for $18,000, replaced the small, outmoded original building. The First United Methodist Church (Main and Spring Sts.) was also completed in 1888.

The two-story brick building at 208 3rd St. was once a stagecoach stop on the former native trail from Greensburg to Kittanning. The First National Bank Building (152 Market St.) was built in 1929; this Tennessee marble, Indiana limestone, and cast metal building was the first and finest example of commercial architecture locally.

The First Evangelical Lutheran Church (354–58 Main St.) was built in 1903, and the Clawson Funeral Home (170 Main St.) was originally a Queen Anne–style dwelling for Dr. John Orr and his family. A room on the third floor has been converted into a museum of late-19th-century funeral memorabilia and a library of materials on grief and the grieving process.

Printed walking tours and audio tours detailing the architecture and history of these and other small river towns are available from **Armstrong County Tourist Bureau** (125 Market St., Kittanning, PA 16201, 724/543-4003 or 888/265-9954, www.armstrongcounty.com).

Farm Country Cruising

Take a few minutes to enjoy the prime agricultural area of Indiana County. The approximately 15-mile drive (or bike route) along SR 4015 makes it very clear why the area is called the "Christmas Tree Capital of the World" and also passes by dairy and potato farms. The road begins three miles north of the village of Home on US 119 and winds northwest to Georgeville.

Scenic Spot

For a powerful example of old meeting new, stop at the **Keystone Overlook** on SR 156 between the villages of Shelocta and Idaho, Indiana County. The view takes in miles of farmland and forest as well as the Keystone Electric Generating Station on the South Branch of Crooked Creek. The massive plant is no longer open to the public, but you can find out more at www.pseg.com.

OTHER POINTS OF INTEREST

Kiski Junction Railroad

This working rail line (P.O. Box 48, Schenley, Armstrong County, 724/295-5577, www .kiskijunction.com, May 25–Oct. 31, Sat.–Sun. and Tues. 2 P.M.; Memorial Day–Labor Day Wed. 7 P.M.; $8 adults, less for seniors and children, under 3 free) hauls freight during the week and delighted railroad buffs and children when not on duty. The one-hour trip travels along the Kiski River to Bagdad and returns to Schenley. Fall leaf tours after Labor Day and Halloween tours are available by appointment.

Jimmy Stewart Museum

The Jimmy Stewart Museum is in the Indiana library building next to city hall (845 Philadelphia St., 3rd floor, 724/349-6112 or 800/835-4669, www.jimmy.org, Mon.–Sat. 10 A.M.–5 P.M., Sun. and holidays noon–5 P.M., $5 adults, children five and under and Pookas—large invisible rabbitlike companions—are free). Indiana, a thriving college town, rises like Oz from miles of farm fields. Indiana is Jimmy Stewart's hometown and has honored the actor and his career with a multifaceted museum that will appeal to his fans and to all who appreciate movie magic.

The movie poster collection and family memorabilia (the Stewarts have been in the area since the Civil War) are well displayed. Film clips featuring Stewart run continuously in a restored, 1930s-vintage movie theater. The museum is expanding its offerings to include special events and films reminiscent of the all-American Stewart style.

Windgate Vineyards

Windgate Vineyards (east side of Smicksburg, 814/257-8797, Mon.–Sat. 10 A.M.–5 P.M.; Sun. noon–5 P.M.) is the largest family-owned estate winery in western Pennsylvania. The winery produces varietals that win awards in local, national, and international competitions. To get there, take SR 954 north from Smicksburg three miles. Make a left on Hemlock Acres Road; the winery is two miles farther.

SHOPPING
Farm Markets and Crafts

On Wednesday and Saturday during the warmer months, local farmers sell produce and baked goods at the Franklin Village Mall parking lot (SR 268/West Kittanning exit from US 422, Kittanning, Armstrong County). The market runs 8:30 A.M.–noon.

Also in Armstrong County, Mountain Trails Baskets (seven miles north of Kittanning on SR 66/28, Templeton, 724/545-7666, daily 9 A.M.–5 P.M., tours on request) specializes in handcrafted woven baskets of all shapes and sizes. Each basket comes with an absolute guarantee; if it's ever damaged, it will be rebuilt or replaced at no cost other than shipping. Picnic baskets, baskets with shoulder straps, and hampers are available.

Smicksburg and Environs

The draw in the area surrounding Smicksburg is the countryside, especially along SR 954 and SR 210—miles of rolling hills green with Amish farms. Some of the farms offer handmade goods for sale from the road; others can be found in the village itself. **Handworks** (Clarion St., Smicksburg, 814/257-8891, Fri.–Sat. 10 A.M.–5 P.M., Sun. noon–5 P.M.) offers hand-thrown pottery, hand-carved wooden items, hand-dipped candles, weavings, knit items, and hundreds of hand-woven baskets and unique gift items such as outhouse puzzles, weather sticks, corn-cob potpourri, and horseradish jelly.

© JOANNE MILLER

Jimmy Stewart statue in Indiana

Western Amish Country

OUTDOOR RECREATION

Canoeing, Fishing, and Hunting

In Armstrong County, Mahoning Creek and Redbank Creek are popular canoeing spots in the spring high-water season. Crooked Creek (which feeds Crooked Creek Lake), Buffalo Creek, and the Kiskiminetas River (kiss-key-min-E-tass) are navigable throughout the summer and fall. Contact the Armstrong County Tourist Bureau (125 Market St., Kittanning, PA 16201, 724/543-4003 or 888/265-9954, www.armstrongcounty.com) for more information.

The Allegheny and Kiskiminetas Rivers and Crooked Creek, Keystone, and Mahoning Lakes all provide warm- and cold-water fishing in Armstrong County. For fishing information, contact the Pennsylvania Fish and Boat Commission, Southwest Region (P.O. Box 39, R.D. 2, Somerset, PA 15501, 814/445-8974, www.fish.state.pa.us). A *Summary of Fishing Regulations and Laws* booklet is available where fishing licenses are sold.

Armstrong and Indiana Counties contain five state game lands, totaling more than 5,000 acres. Maps and information are available from the Pennsylvania Hunting/Game Commission (814/432-3187). There is also a Farm/Game Program, with more than 100,000 privately owned acres open to hunters of all types of game. Contact the county tourist promotion agencies (see Information) for specific information.

The Baker Trail

The Baker Trail was established by the Pittsburgh Council of American Youth Hostels (www.hipittsburgh.org) in 1950. It extends from Schenley in Armstrong County north through the Allegheny National Forest—a distance of more than 141 miles—where it connects with the North Country Trail extending all the way to Buffalo, New York. However, shorter segments of the trail make for convenient and scenic day or overnight hikes.

The rugged trail follows forest paths, old jeep trails, and dirt roads through woods and farmlands, along rivers and creeks. Hikers are warned to be equipped for the season—prepared with food, water purification methods, and personal gear, as there are few stores convenient to the trail.

Pittsburgh AYH leads Baker Trail group hikes; hikes are listed in the AYH newsletter, available to members. The *Baker Trail Guide* is a narrative description of the trail and includes topographic maps of the entire trail. Available from Pittsburgh AYH for $7.50 plus $.53 sales tax and $1.50 postage—total $9.53. Mail checks to Pittsburgh AYH (830 E. Warrington Ave., Pittsburgh, PA 15210, 412/431-4910, fax 412/431-2625); call or fax credit card orders.

Trail Camping: There are eight campsites with open-front Adirondack shelters on side trails, and primitive campsites along the trail for tents. There are no signs pointing to the shelters, so you must consult the AYH *Baker Trail Guide.*

Getting There: Because the trail is frequently unmarked, the AYH trail map is a good idea. The trail officially starts in Freeport and crosses the Allegheny River to Schenley. Some hikers prefer to start out in Schenley. The Schenley turnoff (SR 2062) provides access to the Baker Trail about 2.5 miles out of Leechburg on SR 66 east. When driving into Schenley, take the upper road (not toward the post office). Locals say it's all right to use the parking lot on the right next to the water tower, .1 mile from the post office turnoff.

The Armstrong Trail

Originating in Schenley, the 52.5-mile Armstrong Trail (Armstrong Rails-to-Trails Association, 222 Market St., P.O. Box 777, Kittanning, PA 16201, 724/543-4478) follows the east bank of the Allegheny River north to Upper Hillville in Clarion County. In 1992, the Allegheny Valley Land Trust bought and refurbished the old Consolidated Rail Corporation (Conrail) corridor for use as a nonmotorized recreation trail. It passes through a number of historic towns, including rail towns difficult to reach from the main road.

The trail is open to the public for all rail-trail uses, but you'll have to supply your own equipment; there are no businesses that rent sports equipment or horses along the route. For the first 18–20 miles, no food suppliers are available, either, but thereafter, restaurants and grocery and convenience stores can be found in Ford City, Kittanning, and Templeton, all within three blocks of the trail. Parking is available in towns and communities along the way; Pennsylvania Fish Commission parking areas at Rosston, the mouth of Cowanshannock Creek, and Templeton are available to trail users.

Biking and Cross-Country Skiing: This trail is open to bicycles and cross-country skiers along its entire length, but be prepared for some rough patches (narrow passages and/or rocky, broken trail) where trail upgrades are still in the planning stages.

Trail Camping: The Armstrong Trail permits camping in specified areas, by permit. Contact Armstrong Rails-to-Trails. No camping is permitted within any of the borough limits along the trail.

Crooked Creek Lake National Recreational Area

This multiuse area, off SR 66 via CR O3108 on W. T. Heilman Road, 30 miles northeast of Pittsburgh (mailing address Resource Manager, Crooked Creek Lake, R.D. 3, Box 323A, Ford City, PA 16226, 724/763-3161, www.lrp.usace.army.mil) is the largest public recreation area near the Allegheny River. Open year-round, it offers swimming along a sandy beach, a boat launch and rental concession, and fishing for bass, muskie, sunfish, and crappie. Picnicking and hiking along the Baker Trail and other trails are available. The Baker Trail runs along Crooked Creek and the lake for approximately eight miles. Crooked Creek Lake boasts an ice-skating rink, sled riding area, and cross-country skiing on its trails during the winter.

Trailer and tent camping are available. The lake is maintained by the U.S. Army Corps of Engineers. For more information or reservations, contact the resource manager.

The Ghost Town Trail

One of the first rails-to-trails established in America, the Ghost Town Trail (Indiana and Cambria Counties) derives its name from the once-thriving

coal mining communities along its path, Wehrum and Braken. Little remains of these settlements other than one original house and the foundations of several mine buildings. The 16-mile-long Ghost Town Trail extends along the Blacklick Creek Valley from Dilltown in Indiana County to Nanty Glo in Cambria County, passing by the Eliza Furnace near Vintondale. The furnace, a former pig iron foundry operating from 1846 to 1849, is one of the best-preserved hot blast iron furnaces in existence. Pig iron is so named because the molten iron was drained from the blast furnace into a mold dug into the dirt floor. The mold was in the shape of a long, narrow, shallow channel with several ingot-shaped depressions on both sides, giving the impression of piglets feeding from a trough.

The trail is wide and flat, with easy accessibility and gentle grade; it's built on the former railbed of the Black Lick & Yellow Creek Railroad and passes by two cemeteries and a former Indian encampment. Entry points are on SR 403, Dilltown, Indiana County, and Nanty Glo, Cambria County. To get to the Nanty Glo entrance, travel 1.3 miles from U.S. 22 on SR 271 north to the Nanty Glo Fire Department, Station 43. The trail is at the far end of the parking lot. There is also a 1.5-mile-long trail extension west of Dilltown leading to the ghost towns of Scot Glen and Armerford. The packed limestone trail provides an ideal surface for walking, biking, and horseback riding. For more information, call Cambria County Conservation and Recreation (814/472-2110). Trail use is from sunrise to sunset; camping is prohibited.

Camping

In Indiana County, try **Wheel-In** (Plumcreek Rd., Shelocta, 724/354-3693) with tent and trailer sites, recreational activities, and a swimming hole, open April–Sept.

ACCOMMODATIONS
$50–100

The **Dillweed Bed & Breakfast** (Dilltown, Indiana County, 814/446-6465, www.dillweedinc.com, $55–100) is at the Ghost Town trailhead, on SR 403, one mile north of the intersection of US 22. Four rooms decorated in a delightful country Victorian style share two bathrooms, and a little gift shop on the premises sells snacks and jams, gift baskets, and candles.

In Armstrong County, **The Inn on Vine** (241 Vine St., Kittanning, 724/545-7744 or 888/846-3466, $60–90) is a Victorian beauty of a bed-and-breakfast situated on the quiet, tree-lined, residential streets of Kittanning one block from Riverfront Park. Richly furnished with many fine antiques, the inn offers two single rooms that may or may not share a bath, and a master suite with private bath.

The Rebecca House (213 Church St. at Rebecca St., Dayton, 814/257-8323, $55–$70) is a bed-and-breakfast offering comfortable lodging in a Victorian home east of the Allegheny River. One room has a private bath; the other two share a bath. Discounts apply for longer stays.

The town of Indiana offers a number of budget and moderately priced chain hotels. At **Char-bert Farm Bed and Breakfast** (2439 Laurel Rd., Shelocta, 724/726-8264 or 800/475-8264, $70–95), antiques embellish the restored 1850s farmhouse with four large corner bedrooms, each with a unique view and theme and private bath. Ten groomed acres surround the house, shed, and barn in this peaceful rural setting.

INFORMATION

The **Armstrong County Tourist Bureau** (125 Market St., Kittanning, PA 16201, 724/543-4003 or 888/265-9954, www.armstrongcounty .com) has information on all types of recreation in the area (Kittaning, Smicksburg, Dayton), including detailed walking tours of the small towns on the river.

Indiana County Promotion Bureau (2334 Oakland Ave., Suite 7, Indiana, PA 15701, 724/463-7505 or 877/746-3426, www.indiana-co-pa-tourism.org) has the scoop on Indiana, and Smicksburg and environs.

Laurel Highlands

The cities and towns that ring the Laurel Highlands, the southernmost part of the Allegheny Mountains in Pennsylvania, have a variety of entertainment and activities for visitors.

Cambria County is the site of Johnstown, a former industrial center that was devastated during an infamous and tragic flood in 1889; the city now offers an excellent historical museum and several other historic attractions.

Somerset was built on one of the few original roads to traverse the Alleghenies; it's the largest city in Somerset County, and the county seat. It began life as the market village in an area of struggling farms and is still famous for its maple syrup and living history center.

In Westmoreland County, Greensburg—a thriving city with a sophisticated art museum—is the first large urban area southeast of Pittsburgh. The town is building a considerable reputation as a convention center and offers a number of chain hotels among its accommodations. Ligonier is a small mountain town arranged around a diamond in which band concerts still take place in the summer; pleasant shops and restaurants line the streets. Ligonier, originally called Loyalhanna, was the last fortified outpost on the Forbes Road built by the British during the French and

Must-Sees

Look for **M** to find the sights and activities you can't miss and **M** for the best dining and lodging.

M Somerset Loop: The Laurel Highlands are worth a trip any time of year. This route picks out the highlights, including Fallingwater and Ohiopyle State Park (page 352).

M Covered Bridge Hunting in Washington County: Washington County has 25 covered bridges, examples of every shape and style ever built (page 353).

M Fort Necessity National Battlefield: It's loaded with colonial history, but the real reason to visit is the scenic beauty, especially in spring and fall (page 359).

M Idlewild Amusement Park: Idlewild was once designated "Most Beautiful Park in America." Families with young children will enjoy the many activities and peaceful setting (page 362).

M Fallingwater: A spectacular Frank Lloyd Wright design, this home was voted "the best all-time work

of American architecture" by the American Institute of Architects (page 363).

M Kentuck Knob: Seven miles from Fallingwater, this more user-friendly example of Wright's home design also exemplifies his use of setting. Kentuck Knob features an outstanding collection of modern sculpture on the grounds (page 364).

M Johnstown Flood Museum: The haunting displays here chronicle just one event in American history: the devastating torrent that swept through the valley and over the prospering city of Johnstown in 1889 (page 365).

M Westmoreland Museum of Art: An outstanding collection of works by American artists including Mary Cassatt, John Singer Sargent, and Winslow Homer is featured with folk art and decorative pieces (page 366).

M Ohiopyle State Park: The dramatic 1,700-foot-deep Youghiogheny Gorge cuts through the Laurel Ridge Mountains; nearly 19,000 acres of this area, including more than 14 miles of the Youghiogheny River, are set aside for the park (page 370).

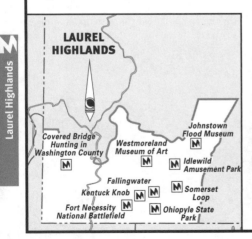

Kentuck Knob

COURTESY OF THE LAUREL HIGHLANDS VISITORS BUREAU

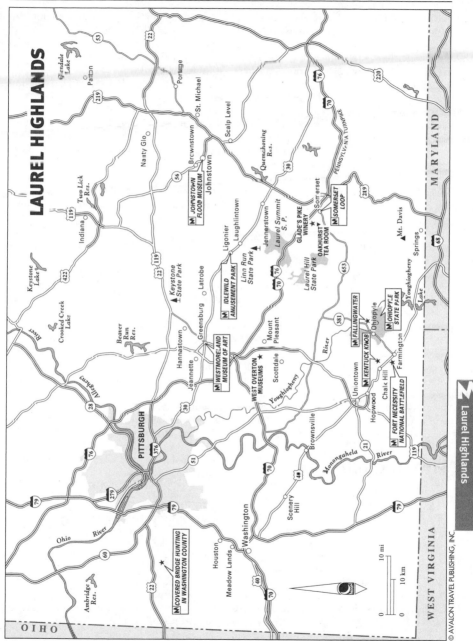

LAUREL HIGHLANDS

OHIO

PITTSBURGH

WEST VIRGINIA

MARYLAND

PENNSYLVANIA TURNPIKE

Gendale Lake

Patton

Portage

St. Michael

Scalp Level

Naaty Glo

Brownstown

Johnstown

Quemohoning Res.

Somerset

M JOHNSTOWN FLOOD MUSEUM

Two Lick Res.

Indiana

Keystone Lake

Ligonier

Laughlintown

Jennerstown

Laurel Summit S.P.

GLADE'S PIKE WINERY

M SOMERSET LOOP

Mt. Davis

Springs

OAKHURST TEA ROOM

Crooked Creek Lake

Beaver Run Res.

Keystone State Park

Latrobe

Greensburg

M IDLEWILD AMUSEMENT PARK

Linn Run State Park

Laurel Hill State Park

Youghiogheny Lake

Hannastown

Jeannette

Mount Pleasant

Scottdale

M WESTMORELAND MUSEUM OF ART

WEST OVERTON MUSEUMS

Youghiogheny

Unontown

M KENTUCK KNOB

M FALLINGWATER

Ohiopyle

Farmington

M OHIOPYLE STATE PARK

Chalk Hill

Hopwood

M FORT NECESSITY NATIONAL BATTLEFIELD

Allegheny River

Brownsville

Monongahela River

Scenery Hill

Washington

Houston

Meadow Lands

Ohio River

Ambridge Res.

M COVERED BRIDGE HUNTING IN WASHINGTON COUNTY

10 mi

10 km

Laurel Highlands

Indian War. The fort itself was rebuilt in the late 1950s, using the original plans from the British War Office, a must-see for visitors with an interest in history. Nearby Idlewild Park has been fulfilling its function as a place of fun and entertainment for almost a century. Through the years, the village of Ligonier has become a popular tourist destination. Hotels and bed-and-breakfasts abound, as do restaurants and cafés. This is country-club country (golf great Arnold Palmer grew up in nearby Latrobe).

After the Civil War, improved transportation and roadways permitted Pittsburgh industrial magnates and their families to come to "the country"—the Laurel Highlands—for recreation and relaxation. Tourism remains an important contributor to the Laurel Highlands economy, second only to agriculture.

Throughout the Laurel Highlands, outdoor activities reign supreme: downhill and cross-country skiers will find paradise among the resorts and parks. Hiking and biking trails traverse the area, and white-water rafting and fishing locations are a short drive in any direction. The Laurel Highlands retain the flavor of exclusivity without the bitterness—spas, resorts, architectural gems, elegant getaways, and peaceful villages mix with tumbling rivers and mountains densely packed with hardwood forest. Everywhere, there is the bursting beauty of a region that continues to renew and replenish itself, and to offer the best in outdoor recreation and luxurious accommodations.

PLANNING YOUR TIME

Though the farthest destinations in the Laurel Highlands are less than three hours apart by auto, it's a good idea to overnight at some point that's central to your area of interest, and plan on 2–7 days, depending on what you'd like to see. This area is excellent for day trips or overnights.

If you plan to stay in Pittsburgh or outside Washington, plan a day trip to the sights of Washington such as the **David Bradford and LeMoyne houses,** the **National Duncan Glass Museum,** or the **Quaker Ridge Winery** (2–4 hours), or spend the day following the **Covered Bridge Hunting in Washington County** tour

(all day), or stop by the **Westmoreland Museum of Art** (2 hours) and **Hanna's Town** (1 hour) in Greensburg, and include a visit to **Bushy Run Battlefield** (1 hour–all day); they're all within an hour's drive.

Another day might be spent making the **Somerset Loop;** the town of Somerset offers good lodging and food choices in addition to the outdoor **Somerset Historical Center** (1–2 hours).

Ligonier is centrally situated, and offers the advantage of **Idlewild Park** for a day's diversion (3 hours–all day), and a visit to the local fort and town (2–3 hours), plus a variety of places to eat.

If outdoor activities are your focus, plan to stay in the vicinity of Ohiopyle or camp in **Ohiopyle State Park** or one of the other state parks—also a great base for Fayette County destinations. From Ohiopyle, it's less than 10 miles to **Fort Necessity** (1 hour–all day), and about the same distance to **Fallingwater** (2–3 hours) and **Kentuck Knob** (2–3 hours). Wherever you stay, it's best to save tours of Fallingwater and Kentuck Knob for a full day.

You may want to spend several days at one of the resorts—all in Fayette County—taking advantage of the activities there, and making day trips. From any of those locations, plan to spend a day in Johnstown, visiting the **Flood Museum** (2 hours) and any of the other historic sights and places of interest in the vicinity—**Johnstown Heritage Discovery Center, Inclined Plane, Johnstown Flood National Memorial, Seldom Seen Coal Mine,** and **Glades Pike Winery,** to name a few (1–4 hours).

GETTING THERE AND GETTING AROUND
By Air and Rail
Major access to southwestern Pennsylvania is through the Pittsburgh International Airport (see Getting There in the Pittsburgh chapter). Small craft airports exist throughout the area. Two commuter airlines based in the Pittsburgh Airport are Christman Air (412/225-4000) and Comair (412/566-2100). Call for current destinations and flight schedules.

Rail access to southwestern Pennsylvania is mainly through Pittsburgh (see Getting There in the Pittsburgh chapter).

By Auto

Most (but not all) Southwestern Pennsylvania counties operate their own transportation systems. The best way to see the area is by car.

East-west access is by the multilane, high-speed toll road I-70/76 south of Pittsburgh, and via scenic US 40 that runs alongside I-79 west of Washington. Major north-south access is by multilane, high-speed I-79 in the west, and two-lane US 119 and US 219 in the east. Most of the roads, though narrow, are in excellent condition.

Getting lost on the backroads can be both desirable and hellish. The south part of southwestern Pennsylvania is mountainous and heavily forested. There is little to orient a visitor as to direction.

If you intend to wander about by auto, it's wise to stop in any gas station and pick up a county map, one that shows county roads (often designated by a letter followed by four numbers, such as T3021 or C4007). These roads frequently go unnamed in real life, but the map will help you approximate your location. A compass isn't a bad idea, either, but step away from the car to use it—a hot engine alters the reading. The beauty of the area becomes secondary when you're tired and hungry and have no idea where you are.

Be prepared for a high roadkill talley in the warmer months. It's due more to the huge animal population than to the usually sparse traffic. Your chances of hitting something increase as the sun goes down, so plan your drive times accordingly.

HISTORY

Early History

The earliest evidence of human habitation in northern America was found just south of Pittsburgh. While wandering the grounds of Meadowcroft Village near Avella, a property owner noticed pieces of flint and a flint knife outside a groundhog's hole. Archaeologists investigated the site and found evidence of human inhabitants dating to the 14th century B.C.—3,000 years earlier than the previous estimate of man's arrival in the area.

About 1600, the Monongahela tribe dominated the area around Pittsburgh for a short time, then mysteriously disappeared. The area remained largely uninhabited, used mainly as a hunting ground by wandering tribal groups. Unfortunately, the game food of choice for Native American (and early European hunters) was an animal found only in the region, the woods buffalo. Smaller than the plains buffalo, it subsisted on spruce and balsam buds but was hunted to extinction in the late 18th century.

The French and Indian War

Impenetrable forests prevented settlement of southwestern Pennsylvania until well after 1750. Though the English laid claim to the land, they had made no effort to colonize it. Southwestern Pennsylvania had seen little white exploration at all until territorial disputes with the other European landlord—France—reached an incendiary point.

When war broke out in Europe between the mother countries, hostilities spread to the New World. The governor of French Canada claimed the forks of the Ohio (Pittsburgh) as a result of La Salle's earlier explorations; he sent a party of 200 French troops and their Huron allies to take possession of the area. Meanwhile, a British charter had granted a half-million acres along the Ohio River to a group of Virginians calling themselves the Ohio Company (Lawrence and Augustine Washington, George's brothers, were members). The colony of Virginia sent 21-year-old George Washington to deliver the news of the charter to the French at Fort LeBoeuf, south of Erie. The French commander fed Washington well but let him know that France planned to take possession of all of southwestern Pennsylvania *tout de suite.*

Upon his return to Virginia, Lieutenant Colonel Washington resolved to drive out the French. He marched in the direction of the French fort on the forks of the Ohio with 300 Virginia frontiersmen. Since no roads existed to the forks, Washington explored the Youghiogheny River by canoe, hoping to float north from the

PONTIAC'S WAR

Near present-day Detroit, Michigan, Pontiac, chief of the Ottawas, initiated and led a Native American campaign to drive the English from western lands after the French and Indian War. Members of the six Iroquois nations east of the Great Lakes tolerated the presence of the French relatively well, since the French appeared to be interested in sharing the abundance of the Americas rather than conquering and settling it. The English, on the other hand, wanted the land free and clear.

Many tribes in the Detroit area, including the Ottawas, Wyandots, Chippewas, and Powatomies, were disturbed by English intentions to openly claim the lands they had recently wrested from French control. European presence had already made major alterations in the lives of the indigenous peoples. When the English perceived resistance from the tribes, they immediately shut down the practice of issuing powder and lead to the Indians. Across the frontier, families of warriors who had become dependent on firearms for hunting began to starve. From the forks of the Ohio north to Erie, Senecas were angry because they had suffered several incidents of European colonists' murdering Indians without penalty, while Indians accused of the murders of Europeans were tried in all-European English courts and hanged. Rumors were spreading that the English planned to exterminate the Indians altogether.

Pontiac laid siege to Fort Detroit in the spring of 1763, and Senecas and Delawares began to attack forts in western Pennsylvania. In June, Indians captured Fort Venango (at Franklin) and Fort Le Boeuf (south of Erie). Several days later, the Senecas joined a party of Ottawas, Chippewas, and Wyandots to capture Fort Presque Isle (at Erie). The Delawares attacked Fort Pitt in late July. The commandant at Pitt, Capt. Simeon Ecuyer, followed a suggestion made by Col. Henry Bouquet and sent the warriors a gift of blankets infected with smallpox.

Colonel Bouquet, a Swiss mercenary in British service, left Carlisle with a company of 460 men for Fort Pitt, leaving some of them in Fort Bed-

ford en route. After provisioning at Fort Ligonier, Bouquet took a shortcut to Fort Pitt through Bushy Run and was immediately ambushed. The well-executed attack was probably led by Mud Eater, a Seneca of great influence within his tribe. An estimated 90 Indians attacked with such force that Bouquet's 400-man party was devastated. "If we have another Action," he wrote, "we Shall hardly be able to Carry our Wounded." Bouquet had his men feign retreat at the center of the line, and when the enemy rushed in, attacked them from both flanks with musket fire and bayonets. The English soldiers inflicted sufficient losses to cause Mud Eater's men to retreat. Bouquet marched on to Fort Pitt, and turned back the Indian attack there.

Soldiers at Detroit managed to overcome Pontiac's forces, but the country outside the immediate influence of Detroit and Fort Pitt fell into Indian hands. For months, Indian war parties attacked settlers and supply trains from Lancaster to the far west.

In 1764, Bouquet marched to Ohio and signed a peace treaty with Pontiac's forces at the forks of the Muskingum River. As part of the treaty, white prisoners in Indian hands were returned to white settlements. Colonel Bouquet's records noted that "there will be many among [the white prisoners] who are very much attached to the Savages by having lived with them . . . [and] may be apt to make their Escape after they are delivered up."

The Shawnees were forced to bind some of the people to be surrendered, and several of the women escaped to return to their Indian families. Author Conrad Richter wrote a fictional account of these events in his novel *A Light in the Forest.*

In spite of the peace agreement, retaliation for the Indian uprising was immediate and brutal. A group of men called Paxton Boys—from the Paxtang (Harrisburg) area—murdered a group of peaceable Christian converts of Native decent, underscoring the government's inability to protect friendly Indians. Other reprisals by Europeans against nonhostile Native Americans ensued, creating an atmosphere of distrust and violence that continues to the present.

Youghiogheny's confluence with the Mononga-hela. The 40-foot Ohiopyle (oh-HI-a-pile) falls stopped him.

Washington managed to push on and bivouac at Great Meadows, near Farmington. He received a message that a small French encampment was in the area. Washington's troops attacked the French in the early morning, firing the first hostile shot of the war. His forces imprisoned the French, even though they insisted they were on a peaceful mission of exploration. Soldiers under Washington's command also killed the French leader, Ensign Coulon de Jumonville— a death that was to be the source of a major setback in Washington's military career.

Necessity

Washington, expecting immediate retaliation, ordered his men to build a field fort—Fort Necessity—in the Great Meadows. But it was two weeks before a French force, led by de Jumonville's half-brother, attacked. Exhausted and low on supplies, Washington and his men surrendered the fort in exchange for the privilege of marching away with their weapons. The French agreed to the terms but demanded that Washington sign a document (in French). Unfortunately for Washington—who was not literate in French—the document twice admitted to his "assassination" of Ensign de Jumonville and to his unprovoked attack on a peaceful mission. French forces burned Fort Necessity to the ground, then publicized Washington's "confession," humiliating both Washington and the British army and forcing Washington to resign his commission.

Braddock's Defeat

Britain then sent Gen. Edward Braddock and two regiments of regular English troops to march from Maryland to western Pennsylvania. Washington volunteered his services as an unpaid aide. The road Braddock's troops cut from Cumberland, Maryland, to Fort Duquesne remained for many years as a principal route to western Pennsylvania (US 40).

General Braddock had no idea how to fight guerrilla style. When warned of an ambush by French-allied Hurons, he replied, "These savages may, indeed, be a formidable enemy to your raw American militia, but upon the King's regular and disciplined troops, sir, it is impossible they should make an impression."

Two-thirds of Braddock's men—including Braddock, who struggled alongside his men in the thick of the fighting—were killed in the ensuing battle.

Washington immediately took command and was able to lead the remnants of the army including the Virginia Regulars, who dived for the bushes at the first assault—back to safety. The French controlled the west for the next three years.

In 1757, William Pitt, a renowned English statesman and orator, took control of British war policy. The plan of his carefully chosen commanders was to capture Fort Duquesne while simultaneously attacking French strongholds on the southern Canadian border. Pitt authorized Gen. John Forbes to build a road from Carlisle to Fort Duquesne, with supply forts at Bedford and Ligonier. A massive British land and naval attack on Fort Louisburg proved successful; meanwhile, British troops found Fort Duquesne deserted and destroyed. They rebuilt it, naming it Fort Pitt. The Battle of Québec ended French domination in northern America.

Growth and Taxes

The Ohio Valley became so sufficiently settled that it could (and did) send soldiers to fight in the War of Independence, but the area's real contribution was iron and weaponry. Industrial production began early on the rivers in the area. Coal and water, necessary ingredients in the production of pig iron, were plentiful.

Less than a decade after the formation of the Union, President George Washington and his cabinet voted to tax the grain alcohol production of western farmers. Those who opposed this tax—called antifederalists—went on to become Republican leaders; Thomas Jefferson and James Madison would, of course, become presidents. Others were not so fortunate; one leader, David Bradford, was forced to flee from his home in the city of Washington (south of Pittsburgh), never to return.

Secret meetings of "the Whiskey Boys" led to an attack on an excise officer (who described his assailants as being dressed in women's clothes) and confrontation with the despised Supervisor of Collection, Gen. John Neville. Rebels were killed in the confrontation, including Revolutionary War hero James McFarlane. Neville's property was burned to the ground. The tax remained in force until 1802.

The Highlands Today

Taxes would remain an issue for a growing nation full of land-hungry immigrants and merchants and industrialists dedicated to making themselves wealthy. As the Industrial Revolution swept over America, the Laurel Highlands produced large quantities of soft coal and coke for steel production while remaining pristine thanks to the hilly terrain. The need for industrial products waned, but agriculture and tourism remained strong. By the end of the 19th century, proximity to Pittsburgh and its millionaires made the area into a scenic and desirable destination away from the grime of the city—this alone remains the central characteristic of the Highlands; a place to get away, relax, and play.

Sights

SCENIC TOURS

Somerset Loop

The Laurel Highlands are worth a trip any time of year, but the first three weeks of October can be absolutely stunning. The tour covers about 60 miles, passes Fallingwater and the village of Ohiopyle (oh-HI-a-pile, or, if you really want to go native, ah-HI-pahl) and begins and ends in the town of Somerset. All distances are approximate.

Travel eight miles on SR 281 (south) to pass through the borough of New Centerville, then an additional 2.7 miles (west) to the village of New Lexington. Bear right (west) onto SR 653 at Stahl's Friendly Market and Best Gas. At the bottom of the hill, 1.2 miles, turn right onto CR 3033 (you'll pass Scottyland, a campground) and make an immediate left onto CR 3014. In less than one mile, you'll cross a "singing" (metal grate) bridge; look for the long Barronvale Covered Bridge, built in 1830, on the right. It's 30 feet from the road and is open to foot traffic only.

Make the next left and travel one mile back to SR 653. To the left of the stop sign is King's Bridge, built in 1802. Bear right on SR 653 up the hill toward the village of Scullton, two miles. Pass through Scullton, and travel another nine miles on SR 653, passing the entrance to Laurel Ridge State Park and the Laurel Highlands Trail, to Normalville and the intersection of SR 653 and SR 381. The small, well-stocked grocery store/gas station at the intersection sells rainbow-hued "Normalville" T-shirts that are hard to resist.

Turn left (south) on SR 381. Drive toward the borough of Mill Run, seven miles down the road (you'll see signs for Fallingwater); after an ad-

sunset over Somerset

© JOANNE MILLER

ditional 3.5 miles, cross the Youghiogheny River into the village of Ohiopyle.

In Ohiopyle, look for the signs that lead to Yough Lake and the village of Confluence, a left turn (east) on Sugar Loaf Road (Local Road 26116). The turnoff (careful— it's easy to miss) is a "Y" just beyond the village. If you see signs for a white-water launch area, you're on the wrong road. The correct road travels up the mountain above the river. The Scenic View sign along the way indicates Baughman's Rock, a lookout that's worth a stop. The turn for SR 281 is about four miles from Ohiopyle on Sugar Loaf Road; turn left (northeast). Pass the entrance to Yough Dam and enter the village of Confluence. Follow the signs to SR 281 north across the iron bridge, turning right at the stop sign. Two miles from Confluence, pass through the borough of Ursina; just beyond the small post office, bear left onto Humbert Road. The Lower Humbert Bridge is one mile up the road on the left. Continue on the main road for six miles and intersect with SR 281 again. Turn left (north) and remain on SR 281 to return to Somerset (15 miles).

Ⓜ Covered Bridge Hunting in Washington County

Washington County, the terminus for the south-westernmost of Pittsburgh's suburbs, has 25 covered bridges, examples of every shape and style ever built. A map of covered-bridge sites is available from **Washington County Tourist Promotion Agency** (273 S. Main St., Washington, PA 15301, 724/228-5520 or 800/531-4114, www.washpatourism.org). The drawings on the map are charming, but the map has one unfortunate drawback: it doesn't indicate all the roads. (While searching for bridges on the Pennsylvania border one afternoon, I found myself on a barely paved road deep in West Virginia.) Still, it's worth the time and effort when the result is a pleasant day's drive combined with a picnic on any of these three backcountry drives.

The first two routes are fairly level and would be suitable for bike trips; the third climbs a mountain and is strictly for autos or two-wheel athletes. All pass through peaceful farmland interspersed with groves of tall trees. There's very little traffic during the week—in the picnic spots, you'll often find yourself alone. You can drive through some of the bridges, others are open to walking traffic only, and some are on private property.

The Northern Loop: Start on US 22, heading west from Pittsburgh International Airport. Turn right on SR 18 (north). From here, the entire route is approximately 12 miles in length.

Go straight (north) on SR 18 through the intersection with a traffic light, where SR 18 crosses County Road 4004 (also known as Pennsylvania Avenue and Old Stubenville Pike). One-tenth of a mile on the left (west) after the light at the intersection is Kings Creek Road. It's a part-paved, part-dirt, seven-mile-long road with a drive-through covered bridge (the Jackson's Mill Bridge). Kings Creek Road returns to County Road 4004 (Pennsylvania Avenue) near the tiny village of Paris. Go left (east) to return to the SR 18 intersection.

Cherry Valley Picnic Loop: From the intersection of US 22 and SR 18, drive south on SR 18, past the American Foods wholesale warehouse on your right (Italian meatballs 69 cents a pound! Ground beef 50 cents a pound!) to Atlasburg (six miles). In Atlasburg, watch for a left turn (east), Atlasburg/Cherry Valley Road (County Road 4017). Set your odometer; from here, the route is roughly 15 miles in length.

At the first "T" intersection (two miles), make a right (south) onto Joffre/Cherry Valley Road (County Road 4015). Zigzag through the tiny community of Cherry Valley (1.5 miles). At the next "T," make a right (west) onto the dirt road, and drive about .1 mile to the Krepps covered bridge. Take a picnic lunch and enjoy this idyllic spot where Cherry Run meets Raccoon Creek. The dirt road on the other side of the bridge continues to SR 18, but it's unpaved and very rough. If you don't have four-wheel drive, return to the paved road.

Go straight (east) through on the paved road to the next "T." Make a right (south), and continue straight (becomes County Road 4015). Turn right at the next "T" (west), then left onto Oak Ridge Road (still County Road 4015) This road will take you south to SR 50 (four miles). A right

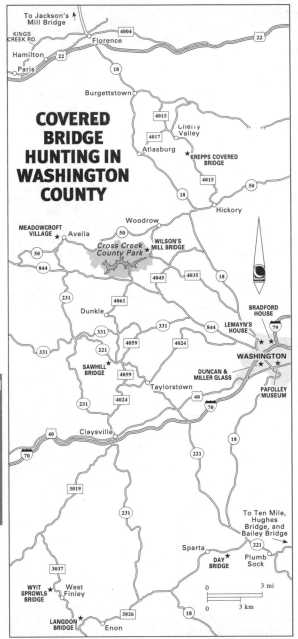

COVERED BRIDGE HUNTING IN WASHINGTON COUNTY

turn (west) will intersect with SR 18 to return back to Atlasburg (north, 4.3 miles), or continue west on SR 50 to reach Avella and Meadowcroft Village (9.5 miles).

Avella to Washington—the Long Way: This route, the longest of the three, takes in the lower half of Washington County and passes through 65 miles of unspoiled pastoral and rural landscapes.

In the town of Avella, follow signs for SR 50 east. Travel toward the village of Woodrow (six miles). You'll pass the turnoff for Cross Creek County Park. Just before Woodrow, look for the right turn (south) on Old Ridge Road (County Road 4035). The road rises into a forest. At the "T" (two miles), turn right (west); within a few hundred yards is the Wilson's Mill bridge and picnic area in a quiet grove of trees. This is the eastern boundary of Cross Creek County Park.

Return to the "T" and go straight through. At the next "T" (1.2 miles), turn right (south) on to County Road 4045. Travel 1.6 miles and turn right again (west) at the next "T" (SR 844, 1.5 miles), then left on Beech Road (south, County Road 4061). Stay on Beech Road (4.5 miles); the road is interrupted at the intersection of SR 331 but continues 100 feet to the right. At the next "T," the intersection of SR 221, the Sawhill Bridge is a few hundred feet to your right. After you've seen the bridge, turn around and head away from it on SR 221 (south). Within one-half mile, you'll reach a "Y"; veer right onto County Road 4059, veer right on County Road 4024, then left on SR 231, always heading

covered bridge in Washington County

south (a total of five miles for the three roads) to Claysville. Turn right (west) at the "T" (US 40).

Continue heading west through the town, following the signs for SR 231. Make a left under the I-70 overpass as if you were going to SR 231 south; within 200 feet of the overpass, turn right (west) on Beham Ridge Road (County Road 3019). Continue, watching for a small sign on the right side of the road that indicates a left turn on County Road 3037 (south, six miles). Ride on the top of the ridge, dropping into a wooded valley. The Wyit Sprowls bridge will be on your right. Stay on County Road 3037; it jogs to the left about a half-mile up the road, just before a "Y" intersection with a stop sign. Veer right (south, still County Road 3037), away from the village of West Finley (Burnsville). Continue until you cross the small concrete Ackley Creek Bridge (two miles). Make an immediate left onto Enon Church Road (east, County Road 3026). Longdon bridge will be on your left, Wheeling Creek on your right. This nine-mile-long road passes the lovely single-steepled Enon Church.

Pass through the village of Sparta; the Day bridge will be on the right one mile west of the village. This route is also marked SR 18. At the "T," turn right (south) on SR 221 (1.5 miles). Pass through the village of Plumbsock; go left (east) at the "Y" to continue on County Road 2020 (2.5 miles). At US 19, follow signs to remain on County Road 2020. One-half mile beyond US 19 on the right is the Bailey bridge. Continue on County Road 2020 until it goes under I-79 (one mile). Make a left on I-79 (north). The Hughes bridge is visible from the interstate on the right. Take I-79 to US 40 (nine miles), and US 40 (west) to Washington (three miles).

SCENIC SPOTS

Eureka Mine-40 and Scalp Level Overlook

The Eureka Mine-40 (Old Scalp Hill off SR 56 east of Richland, two miles north of Windber, 814/467-5646, open late spring–early fall, free), the last mine to be opened by Berwind-White in the area, was established in 1905. The mine was the last mine to be closed by the company and was thus the site at which the company tested and showcased new techniques in mining efficiency. At its peak in 1913, annual production at Mine-40 was just under 800,000 tons. Miners'

Laurel Highlands

housing at the village of Scalp Level includes about 110 two-story, wood-frame duplexes, arranged on a four-street by two-street grid. In addition to the houses, there was a company-owned general store and a school.

Mt. Davis

At 3,213 feet, Mt. Davis is the highest point in Pennsylvania (altitude sickness is usually not a problem). The land surrounding Mt. Davis is a designated natural area containing an unusual set of small concentric stone rings caused by localized frost heaving. Each ring surrounds a spot in the soil that is a little softer than the adjacent ground. When frozen, these soft spots rise as slight humps, and surface rocks on the humps slide off to deposit themselves around the perimeter. The natural area is bounded by SR 2004 on the north, Shelter Rock Road on the east, and Wolf Rock Road via SR 2004 on the south.

The picnic area on SR 2004 is about one mile by foot from the highest point on Mt. Davis. Trails branch out from the picnic area, and the High Point Trail is a fairly easy hike to the viewing area.

Laurel Caverns

Pennsylvania's largest developed limestone cave is an underground maze with more than two miles of passages, including catacomb-like rooms and natural stone sculptures (200 Caverns Park Rd., Farmington, mailing address P.O. Box 62, Hopwood, PA 15445, 724/438-3003 or 800/515-4150, www.laurelcaverns.com, May–Oct. daily 9 A.M.–5 P.M.; March–April and Nov/ Sat.–Sun. 9 A.M.–5 P.M.; closed Dec.–Feb.; adults $9.50, youth Grades 6–12 $7.50, children K–Grade 5 $6.50). Guided tours are one hour long and leave every 20 minutes. Nonslip shoes are necessary. As the cave temperature is a steady 52°F year-round, jackets are advisable. The tour requires extensive walking and may be too strenuous for some. The cave also offers Kavernputt, a 10,000-square-foot underground 18-hole golf course and guided caving experiences to visitors over the age of 12 for an additional fee. Laurel Caverns are between US 40 and SR 857, east of Haydentown. To get there from Farmington, take US 40 west for six miles to the top of Summit Mountain (where you will see the Summit Inn). There you will see a large sign on the left that says, "Laurel Caverns, turn here." Make a left at this sign on to Skyline Drive and follow this road for five miles to Laurel Caverns.

HISTORIC SIGHTS

St. Michael Historic District

During the 1880s, in the town of St. Michael (historic district, 186 Main St., St. Michael, Cambria County, 814/495-5410, free), the South Fork Fishing and Hunting Club counted the elite of Pittsburgh—Andrew Carnegie, Andrew Mellon, Henry Clay Frick, and others—among its members. On the evening of May 30, 1889, the worst storm of the century caused the club's reservoir to overfill, and water flooded over the dam. Fourteen miles down the Little Conemaugh River valley, the city of Johnstown was destroyed. The resort remained abandoned until the 1990s, when a local historical preservation society began to restore the original property. To see where it all started, take US 219 north of Johnstown to the Saint Michael/Sidman exit. Head east on SR 869 for .25 mile. Follow the signs marked National Register, 1889 Historic District. The buildings may be viewed year-round. The area also features the **Miners Memorial Museum** (Lake Rd., Sidman, 814/495-7281), which features coal mining exhibits, artifacts, and interpretation.

Somerset Historical Center

This open-air museum (SR 985 at the junction of SR 601 north of Somerset, 841/445-6077, mid-April to mid-Dec., Tues.–Sat. 9 A.M.–5 P.M., Sun. noon–5 P.M.; closed Memorial Day, July 4, Labor Day; $5) celebrates Pennsylvania's rural heritage. A farmstead, including a log house, smokehouse barn, and maple sugar camp have been reconstructed from the originals or replicated on the property. There is also an exhibit hall of agricultural implements and tools and a general store. An audiovisual program telling the story of the area's pioneers and their self-sufficiency precedes guided tours of the visitors' center and grounds.

Fort Ligonier

Fort Ligonier (S. Market St. at the intersection of US 30 and SR 711, Ligonier, Westmoreland County, 724/238-9701, www.fortligonier.org, May 1–Oct. 31 Mon.–Sat. 10 A.M.–4:30 P.M., Sun. noon–4:30 P.M.; adults $6.75, children 6–14 $3.75) consists of a full-scale re-creation of the fort on its actual site and a spacious, modern museum complete with period rooms and dioramas. Fort Ligonier was built as the last of a chain of supply outposts aimed at recapturing the forks of the Ohio River from the French. In 1758, the fort withstood an attack by French and Indian forces. It was the only fort in western Pennsylvania never taken by an enemy, though British Gen. John Forbes characterized the provincial troops under his command as an "extremely bad collection of broken innkeepers, horse jockeys, and Indian traders." The reconstructed buildings feature accurate lifelike figures of George Washington, General Forbes, and other British soldiers going about their business. Kids will find the history easy to comprehend when viewing these dramatic exhibits.

Hanna's Town

Hanna's Town (Forbes Road, three miles north of Greensburg, Westmoreland County, on CR 1032 between SR 819 and US 119, 724/836-1800, www.starofthewest.org, guided tours $2), on the National Register of Historic Places, is an ongoing archaeological dig that has unearthed nearly one million artifacts. It's open Memorial Day–Labor Day Wed.–Sat. 10 A.M.–4 P.M., Sun. 1–4 P.M.; May 1–Memorial Day and day after Labor Day–Oct. 31, Sat. 10 A.M.–4 P.M., Sun. 1–4 P.M. The reconstructed village consists of the Robert Hanna tavern/courthouse (a handy combination for early juries) and jail, three late-18th-century log houses, a Revolutionary-era fort and blockhouse, and a wagon shed that houses an authentic Conestoga wagon from the late 1700s. Hanna's Town was founded in the early 18th century as the first county seat west of the Allegheny Mountains. The town was destroyed on July 13, 1782, burned to the ground by a troop of Seneca braves during Pontiac's War. The site is administered by the Westmoreland County Historical Society; guided tours

© JOANNE MILLER

Laurel Highlands

gateway to Fort Ligonier

are given by volunteers costumed in 18th century-style garments.

Bushy Run Battlefield

The battlefield (SR 993, Jeannette, Westmoreland County, 724/527-5584 www.bushyrun-battle field.com, adults $3, seniors $2.50, children 6–17 $2) is the site of a decisive battle during Pontiac's War, the attempt by Ottawa Chief Pontiac and a confederation of Ottawa, Seneca, Shawnee, Delaware, and other tribes to regain territory lost to British settlement. The park is open daily Wed.–Sun. 9 A.M.–5 P.M.; visitors' center April–Oct. Wed.–Sat. 9 A.M.–5 P.M., Sun. noon–5 P.M.; Nov.–March Sat. 9 A.M.–5 P.M., Sun. noon–5 P.M. It's 3.1 miles west of the intersection of SR 993 and SR 66, Harrison City.

General Bouquet, on his way to free Fort Pitt from Pontiac's forces, was about to encamp for the night in the vicinity of the park when he was attacked by a group of warriors. Bouquet and his troops narrowly escaped, protected during the siege by sacks of flour brought from Fort Ligonier.

This scenic park, chosen as a top destination by local travel writers, is a peaceful picnic stop and provides an opportunity to learn more about the native inhabitants of western Pennsylvania. The park is out of the way and therefore usually quite empty. Several easy hiking trails weave through the grounds; interpretive brochures are available in the park office.

TRAVELING THE PIKE

In response to the need for better travel routes but impoverished by the Revolution, early individual states chartered private turnpike companies, associations that permitted investors to incorporate and improve sections of road in return for fares received from travelers. These toll-road companies were largely financed by the investment of farmers and businessmen.

In 1806, President Thomas Jefferson authorized the building of a toll road, to be known as the National Pike, from Maryland through Pennsylvania and west to Ohio. The National Pike connected with the Philadelphia Wagon Road near Hagerstown, Maryland. The purpose of the pike was to provide a route for settlement and commerce across the Allegheny Mountains, connecting eastern shipping routes with the western frontier. Many travelers from Philadelphia were on their way west to Pittsburgh to board Ohio riverboats for new lands in the Northwest Territory.

The pike was heavily used from the start. Packhorse trains, of 10–50 horses, traveled over the dirt-and-plank road at the rate of 15 miles a day. New stagecoach lines shortened travel time considerably, averaging a speed of 40 miles a day in summer and 25 in winter. Horses were changed at "stages" along the way—about every 12 miles—providing an average speed of 10 miles per hour.

Gaily painted green, red, black, and yellow U.S. Mail stages (known as the Good Intent Line) would leave Philadelphia at 2 A.M., carrying six passengers, mail, and cargo bound for Pittsburgh.

The iron-wheeled Conestoga wagon, invented in 1750, earned its reputation on the pike as the "ship of inland commerce" and the "prairie schooner." Its chief virtue was a large, well-balanced body, which held up to 10 tons of cargo firmly in place, no matter how rough the road. One observer wrote:

It was a frequent sight to see long lines of Conestoga wagons going towards [Philadelphia], loaded with the products of the West or going in the opposite direction, freighted with the productions of Eastern mills or foreign merchandise.

The considerable amounts of freight and trade goods that moved over the pike gave life to an American legend, the wagoner—a sort of colonial long-distance trucker. Wagoners were a rough lot, notorious for their love of liquor, card games, and fistfights. They moved from one end of the pike to the other under the constant threat of Indian attack, in harsh weather both winter and summer. Wagoners worked for the highest bidder. Some drove liners—freight-hauling wagons that moved from town to town on fixed schedules—while others

Fort Necessity National Battlefield

Fort Necessity (US 40 11 miles southeast of Uniontown, Fayette County, 724/329-5805, www.nps.gov/fone, year-round, daily 9 A.M.– 5 P.M., adults $3, 16 and under free) commem orates the precipitating events of the French and Indian War. In 1754, French troops surrounded George Washington's "fort of necessity" in retaliation for his attack on a peaceful French encampment in Jumonville Glen. They forced his surrender and subsequent resignation from the military. Major Gen. Edward Braddock, a career officer in the British army, took over the command of the British forces (with Washington serving as a volunteer aide-de-camp). Braddock died during a skirmish not far away and was buried along the road in an unmarked grave. His remains were reinterred at Fort Necessity. The reconstructed fort stands in a meadow surrounded by woodlands and is a popular spot during the fall. The grounds also contain the Mt. Washington Tavern, a restored stagecoach stop from the 1820s.

Friendship Hill

Friendship Hill (223 New Geneva Rd., Point Marion, Fayette County, 724/725-9190, www.nps.gov/frhi, mid-Nov.–mid-April Sat.– Mon. 9 A.M.–5 P.M., mid-April–mid-Nov. daily 9 A.M.–5 P.M., free) was Albert Gallatin's family home. Though practically unknown today,

---

sat behind the horses of tramps, which moved at will. Both terms were later applied to ships.

Though wagoners, pioneers, adventurers, and farmers all used the toll road, few liked having to pay for it. Resentment frequently arose against those hired to collect the toll, and toll gates and toll houses were frequently torn down. Under common law, farmers taking grain to mill could use a turnpike free; shrewd travelers sometimes carried grain bags full of bran to defraud toll takers. Rough side roads—shun-pikes—were developed to avoid payment. One notice posted on a toll gate read,

We ast you not to collect no more tole, you must Not collect one cent if you do we are Going to Destroy your House with fire and Denamite . . . We don't want to do this but we want a Free Road and are agoing to have it.

The use of toll roads went into rapid decline after 1832, when the building of canals and extension of the railroads speeded up the job of moving people and freight. A way of life disappeared.

Come all ye wagoners, who have got good wives,
Go home to your farms and there spend your lives.

When the corn is all cribbed and the small grain is good,
You'll have nothing to do but curse the railroad.

From a folksong recorded by Charles Woodmason

With the advent of the automobile, the pikes once again came into heavy use. Many, such as the National Pike, are now free roads. Ninety miles of the National Pike (US 40) pass through southwestern Pennsylvania.

In 1973, Washington County began a Pike Festival, which included simulated wagon trains of the early 19th century. More than 50 wagons, carriages, and horses and riders—most with authentic period dress and equipment—travel the pike in both directions during the months of May and June. One train travels from southern Somerset County west to Brownsville, the other moves from Washington County to Malden. Both trains camp along the route, colonial style. Many of the communities along the way feature flea markets, arts and crafts festivals, and special activities. Fort Necessity National Battlefield, Mt. Washington Tavern, Searight's Toll House, and the towns of Brownsville, Scenery Hill, and Washington all hold special events during the annual trek.

Laurel Highlands

Swiss-born Gallatin was a popular public figure in the early days of the United States. Revolutionary leader Patrick Henry, impressed by Gallatin's learning and diplomacy, proclaimed him "a most astonishing man!" Gallatin lost his political momentum by protesting the whiskey tax that led to the Whiskey Rebellion; however, he never lost his friends in high places. Gallatin later served as Secretary of the Treasury under Presidents Thomas Jefferson and James Madison. At the age of 70, Gallatin became the first president of John Jacob Astor's National Bank of New York.

A self-guiding audio tour is available for the historic sections of the house. To reach Friendship Hill, take US 119 12 miles south to Smithfield, then turn right (west) at the stoplight and continue north toward New Geneva to the park.

Searights Toll House

The Searights Toll House, on US 40 three miles west of Uniontown, Fayette County, was home to the toll collector when US 40 was known as the National Road or Cumberland Road to Pittsburgh. The toll house was erected by the state of Pennsylvania around 1835. A fee was extracted for every vehicle and animal that passed over the road: a horse and rider was charged $.04, driven sheep or hogs $.06 a score. There was a walloping fine of $3 for failure to pay the toll. There is no admission fee. Regular hours are not posted, so seeing the inside of the house is a hit-or-miss proposition.

The LeMoyne House

This historic house (49 E. Maiden St., Washington, Washington County, 724/225-6740, Jan.–Feb. Tues.–Fri. 11 A.M.–4 P.M., March–Dec., Tues.–Fri. 11 A.M.–4 P.M., Sat. noon–4 P.M., $4) was home to the unusual Doctor LeMoyne—a practical visionary. In the mid-1800s, he started colleges for both women and blacks and created a public lending library 30 years before Andrew Carnegie laid the groundwork for his better-known free library system. LeMoyne also ran for public office three times on an antislavery ticket. He never won; his radical ideas—especially his belief in the equality of the sexes and races—made him unpopular in the community. His home, a stop on the Underground Railroad, hid

up to 25 people overnight in the secret reaches of the third floor.

House tours are the best way of getting information on the life of this man of conviction. For more information on this and other historic sites in the Washington area, contact the Washington County Historical Society at the same address and phone.

David Bradford House

A successful attorney and businessman, David Bradford made a fortune shipping flour from his Washington-based mills to New Orleans. In the 1780s, to reflect his wealth and community standing, he built the sophisticated stone manor house that now bears his name (175 S. Main St., Washington, Washington County, 724/222-3604, May 1–mid-Dec. Wed.–Sat. 11 A.M.–4 P.M., $4, $3.50 seniors and AAA members, $2 students 6–18). Bradford fled the house in 1794 to escape arrest for treason for his part in the Whiskey Rebellion, the antitax protest that tested the authority of the newly formed federal government. The home and garden have been refurbished and restored to reflect their colonial origin. During the first two weekends in December, a candlelight tour is given. It is advisable to call ahead because some large tours are scheduled and could make a drop-in visit a little crowded. The house closes for the winter after the last candlelight tour.

OTHER POINTS OF INTEREST

The Johnstown Heritage Discovery Center

The center (Broad St. and 7th Ave., Johnstown, Cambria County, 814/539-1889, www.jaha.org, May–Oct. Sun.–Thurs., 10 A.M.–5 P.M., Fri.–Sat. 10 A.M.–7 P.M.; Nov.–April daily 10 A.M.–5 P.M.; ticket includes admission to Johnstown Flood Museum, adults $6, seniors $5, students $4, children under 6 free) is housed in the 62,000-square-foot former Germania Brewery Building. The center features permanent and temporary exhibition galleries, a museum, classrooms, and community meeting spaces, all focusing on the immigrant experience in America. As visitors cross the century-old footbridge to enter the building, they are immersed in turn-of-the-20th-century Johnstown—the sights, smells, and sounds of a booming industrial town. It's an opportunity to explore the workplaces, home life, and social institutions created by immigrants to turn-of-the-20th-century America. From the cacophony of languages in a steamship agent's office to the heat and sulfur smell of a blast furnace, visitors experience the daily life of the men and women who fueled the Industrial Revolution

Johnstown Inclined Plane

Built in 1891, the Johnstown inclined plane (711 Edgehill Dr., Johnstown, Cambria County, 814/536-1816, www.inclineplane.com) is the steepest in the world, according to the *Guinness Book of World Records*. It's open April–Memorial Day daily

noon–6 P.M.; Memorial Day–Labor Day daily 9 A.M.–10 P.M.; closed Jan.–March; adults $4 round-trip/$2.25 one-way, children 2–12 $2.50 round-trip/$1.50 one-way, children under 2 free, cars $6 one-way, motorcycles $4 one-way, bicycles free. It carries passengers and vehicles 1,693 feet at a 71.9-degree gradient to a visitors' center, observation deck, and restaurant. The parking lot for the incline is off SR 56 east between Walnut and Union Streets in downtown Johnstown.

Grandview Cemetery/ Plot of the Unknown

This cemetery (814/535-2652), at the top of the inclined plane, Johnstown, Cambria County, features the Monument of Tranquillity overlooking the Unknown Plot of 777 graves of victims who perished in the 1889 Johnstown Flood.

UP, UP, AND AWAY: THE INCLINED PLANE

As cable cars are to San Francisco, inclined planes are to southwestern Pennsylvania. In the late 19th century, the mouths of coal mines often opened onto steep hillsides. The mines, and the communities of miners that grew on the hilltops above them, were virtually inaccessible from the towns and transport below. The narrow roads that switchbacked up the rocky mountainsides seldom could accommodate two horses abreast.

Coal was transported by primitive coal hoists, which raised and lowered coal buckets by gravity-and-pulley systems from the mines to the railroads below. These became the forerunners of the era's most popular public transit system—the inclined plane, or incline.

The inclines—pairs of cantilevered cars or elevators mounted on tracks and powered by steam and gravity—were originally built entirely of wood and powered by electricity (they were later rebuilt of iron). Steam or electrical power was necessary to equalize weight in the upper and lower cars via the pulley system, allowing gravity to do its thing.

The new type of transport, comfortable trolleylike cars raising and lowering each other on dual tracks, enjoyed steady patronage. Heavy inclines, such as the one in Johnstown, were designed to carry horses and wagons as well as foot

passengers. All carried light freight. Miners and mill workers rode the inclines to their homes after a long shift. The wives of these men brought groceries up from the shopping areas hundreds of feet below. An early rate card stated, "No charge will be made for one ordinary market basket carried by a passenger."

Most inclined planes were the handiwork of engineer Samuel Diescher, born in Budapest in 1839. He immigrated to Cincinnati and built his first incline there. Diescher moved to Pittsburgh around 1870 and designed and there built the majority of the heavy inclined planes in the United States. He also designed the machinery that operated the Ferris wheel at the 1893 Columbian Exposition in Chicago.

Diescher built several inclined planes in Pittsburgh—at least 17 inclines served the area—and one in Johnstown. As more usable roadways were built into the hillsides, the inclines disappeared. Today, only a few survive. In Pittsburgh, the Monongahela and Duquesne inclines, still open for business, continue to scale 400-foot Mt. Washington. In Johnstown, the inclined plane carries cars and passengers up a steep slope to Grandview Cemetery and the monument to the unknown victims of the Johnstown flood.

Johnstown Flood National Memorial

The visitors' center (733 Lake Rd., South Fork, Cambria County, 814/495-4643, www.nps .gov/jofl, year-round, daily 9 A.M.–5 P.M.; $3, 16 and under free) features exhibits created by the South Fork Fishing and Hunting Club, a film, and programs acted out in period costume; it's on US 219 approximately .5 mile beyond the Saint Michael/Sidman exit.

Seldom Seen Coal Mine

In this former working mine (SR 36, four miles north of the village of Patton, Cambria County, 814/674-8939, www.seldomseenmine.com), visitors have an opportunity to learn about the lives of miners who, since 1900, dug bituminous coal from these veins by hand and loaded it out on mule-pulled cars. Tours begin on the hour at noon (the last tour leaves at 5 P.M.). It's open Memorial Day weekend, July 4th, and Labor Day weekends; June Sat.–Sun.; July–Aug. Thurs.–Sun.; adults/seniors $6, children under 12, $3.50. There are special haunted mine tours in October. The tour guides are former miners who share details of their work experiences; some are descendants of immigrant miners who toiled in these coal banks for as little as $.25 a ton.

Glades Pike Winery

Glades Pike (2208 Glades Pike/SR 31, Somerset County, 814/445-3753, www.gladespikewin ery.com, daily 11 A.M.–6 P.M., free) is a 13,000-square-foot winery with a large deck overlooking its own vineyards. Native American, French hybrid, and other European grapes—all grown in Pennsylvania—are carefully chosen by the wine master and then blended to produce clear, crisp, and exciting wines. Concord, niagara, steuben, diamond, leon millot, seyval blanc, and vidal blanc are among the varieties of grapes used.

Idlewild Amusement Park

Brought to you by the same folks who maintain Sandcastle Water Park and Kennywood in Pittsburgh, Idlewild (US 30, Ligonier, Westmoreland County, 724/238-3666, www.idlewild.com) was once designated "Most Beautiful Park in America" by the *Amusement Park Guidebook*. It's

open the last week in May–June Tues.–Sun., daily July–Labor Day weekend. The gates open at 10 A.M. and close when the crowd thins, sometime between 8 P.M. and midnight. A FunDay Pass to all areas of the park is $21 (seniors $14.50 and under 2, free) and a season pass is $40. If you have young children (or enjoy the freedom of acting like one), this is a must-do.

Idlewild has been around in some form since it was developed as a "pleasure ground" by Pittsburgh's Judge Thomas Mellon. Mellon coincidentally owned the Ligonier Valley Railroad that ran by the grounds on its journey to carry coal from the nearby Fort Palmer mines to Latrobe, then on to Pittsburgh via the Pennsylvania Railroad line. The park was immediately popular and remained so over the years, even after the demise of the railroad that gave it life. The Kennywood Park Corporation took over in 1983 and expanded the park's offerings.

Idlewild is divided into seven sections. The Story Book Forest is a park studded with plaster replicas of scenes from favorite fairy tales such as "Jack and Jill." Jumpin' Jungle is a play zone sized for children *and* adults, with giant rope crawls and bright-colored ball bins. Hootin' Holler is a "wild west" town with shopping, food, and entertainment. The H2Ohhh Zone is a water park with slides, with a separate play area for very small kids. Olde Idlewild features 16 rides from tame to tummy-jolting, including two roller coasters (one an original all-wood model) and an antique merry-go-round. Raccoon Lagoon is eight acres of kiddie rides for the pint-sized set.

The most enchanting section of the park—especially for those of us who grew up (and are growing up) listening to the gentle voice of Mr. Rogers—is Mr. Rogers' Neighborhood, a trolley ride through the land of Make-Believe. King Friday, "X" the Owl, Henrietta Pussycat, and Daniel Tiger are all there. Uncle Fred lives on.

The park has added SoakZone, an assortment of watery amusements for those steamy summer days.

Perhaps the best thing about Idlewild is what it's *not*—slick and Disneyfied. The forest setting enhances the fairy-tale quality for kids; it's a great place to make memories.

Joe's Bar

Joe's Bar (W. Main St., Ligonier, Westmoreland County, 724/238-9980) is a local watering hole with a unique slant. However, a proviso: if sport hunting and collecting are offensive to you, this isn't the place for a quick beer. The bar, corner-pub ordinary in the front, keeps a big-game trophy collection in the back, and what a collection it is! Joe Snyder, the owner, has hunted for big game much of his life. Among the specimens are full-sized bears, any number of African game animals, including an elephant (head and tusks), a crocodile, and a horned oryx. There are also a few "rare" species such as the fur-covered cold fish and the swamp hooger. Among the taxidermic trophies are art objects collected from around the world.

L. E. Smith Glass Company

A center for glass production, this factory (1900 Liberty St. off SR 31, Mount Pleasant, Westmoreland County, 800/537-6484, www.lesmith glass.com, free) was founded in 1907. Store hours are Mon.–Sat. 9 A.M.–5 P.M. and Sun. noon–5 P.M. Factory tours are held Mon.–Fri. 9 A.M.–2 P.M. The factory's gift shop and visitors' center is in an old brick boardinghouse, and the factory itself—one of the few remaining commercial enterprises that still uses individual glass artists—produces a full line of hand-made pressed tableware and collector's glassware.

Fallingwater

Fallingwater (SR 381, halfway between Mill Run and Ohiopyle, Fayette County, 724/329-8051, www.wpconline.org/fallingwater) was voted "the best all-time work of American architecture" by the American Institute of Architects. It's open mid-March–Thanksgiving weekend, Tues.–Sun. 10 A.M.–4 P.M. and the first two weekends in March and Dec., Sat.–Sun. 10 A.M.–3 P.M., weather permitting. Four types of tours are offered: (1) self-guided admission to house and grounds Tues.–Fri. $4, Sat.–Sun. $6; (2) one-hour guided house tours, given throughout the day Tues.–Fri. $10, Sat.–Sun. $15; (3) two-hour in-depth tours starting at 8:30 A.M. Tues.–Fri. $40, Sat.–Sun. $50; (4) three-hour Land of

COURTESY OF THE LAUREL HIGHLANDS VISITORS BUREAU

Laurel Highlands

Fallingwater

Fallingwater tours Sat. at 9 A.M. $50. Children under six are not allowed during regular tour operation; they can be left at the child-care facility for a fee. Special children's tours are available Tues.–Fri. $4, Sat.–Sun. $6. Reservations for all tours are required.

The unique cantilevered design is one of Frank Lloyd Wright's most acclaimed works. Built as a retreat for retailer Edgar J. Kaufmann and his family (Kaufmann's son studied under Wright for a time), the house is built over a waterfall and uses natural materials and lighting throughout to achieve a harmonious blend of nature and comfort. Stones used for the living room floor are waxed to give the appearance of being washed with water. Completed in 1939, this unusual and beautiful dwelling still has a contemporary look. The rhododendron forest that surrounds Fallingwater is in full bloom around the 4th of July.

⋈ Kentuck Knob

Seven miles from Fallingwater, Kentuck Knob (Chalk Hill, Fayette County, 724/329-1901, www.kentuckknob.com, one-hour tours Mon. noon–4 P.M., Tues.–Sun. 10 A.M.–4 P.M.; Tues.–Fri. $10, Sat.–Mon. $15, less for children) is a house of a different color—an example of Usonian residential design from the final decade of Wright's career. It was built for dairy owners I. N. Hagan and his wife in 1954. The Hagans lived in the house until the early 1980s, and then sold it to Lord Peter Palumbo, a London-based businessman, art dealer, and collector of architecturally significant buildings. In 1996, the Palumbos, who use the house for only part of the year, opened the house to the public. The home itself, much smaller and more user-friendly than Fallingwater, is in pristine condition, and views from the windows are spectacular year-round. Make time to enjoy the superb collection of contemporary sculpture and historic artifacts that are placed throughout the grounds.

To get there from Fallingwater: Turn right and go south four miles on SR 381. Turn right onto Kentuck Road at the state park sign at the south end of Ohiopyle. Follow the winding road for 1.5 miles. At the intersection at the top of the hill,

turn left toward Chalk Hill. Go .75 mile to Kentuck Knob. Regular tours are for children six or older. Reservations are recommended.

Linden Hall

Linden Hall mansion (Dawson, Fayette County, 724/529-7543 or 800/944-3238, www.linden hallpa.com) was built and lavishly furnished at the beginning of the 20th century by Sarah Cochran, widow of a local coal magnate. One unusual feature of the mansion is its rare Aeolian pipe organ. The mansion and grounds were purchased by the United Steelworkers of America in 1976 and are now run as a resort. Linden Hall mansion is available for touring (March–Oct. daily 11 A.M.–3 P.M.; tours are on the hour; adults $8, children under 12 $4). The extensive grounds, planted with linden trees imported from Germany, contain an 18-hole, par-72 golf course, swimming pool, tennis courts, lodgings, and restaurant, all available to the public (see Resorts). Linden Hall is between the villages of Dawson and Layton; follow signs from SR 51 at Perryopolis (the grounds are about seven miles from the first sign).

Nemacolin Castle

This Tudor mansion stands at the top of a hill on the north side of the Monongahela River (Brashear and Front Sts., Brownsville, Fayette County, c/o the Brownsville Historical Society, 412/785-6882, www.nemacolincastle.org, mid-March–mid-Oct. Sat.–Sun. 11 A.M.–5 P.M.; June–Aug. Tues.–Thurs. 11 A.M.–5 P.M., Sat.–Sun. 11 A.M.–5 P.M.; adults $6, children under 12 $3). Nemacolin Castle was built on the remnants of old Fort Burd, hastily erected in 1759 during the French and Indian War. In the 1790s, a trading post built by Jacob Bowman came to occupy the spot. As Bowman's business prospered, he added rooms around the original brick-and-wood cabin, which remained in use as the kitchen. Though the outside looks uniform, the rooms were added at different periods; the decor ranges from frontier colonial to Victorian. Most of the interior is restored and contains the belongings and furnishings of the Bowman family, making this an authentic record of the life of a prosperous merchant and his heirs. After Bowman's death, his family continued to add Victorian flourishes to the structure, creating a turreted brick fantasy.

To reach the mansion from US 40 west, turn left at the light on 5th Avenue (the Brownsville hotel is on the north side corner), then right onto Brashear (if you miss it, the next left, 4th Avenue, will get you to the same place).

Meadowcroft Village

This rural town of the 1800s (401 Meadowcroft Rd., Avella, Washington County, 724/587-3412, www.meadowcroftmuseum.org, Memorial Day–Labor Day, Wed.–Sat. noon–5 P.M., Sun. 1–5 P.M., $6.50 for adults, $3.50 for kids 6–16, free under 6) was created by moving authentic dwellings to the property over a period of years.

Meadow Lands harness-racing champion Delvin Miller and his brother turned their family farm into this museum of rural life, complete with blacksmith shop, covered bridge, a one-room school and other log buildings, a country store exhibit, train car, and a museum building filled with horse-drawn vehicles and agricultural equipment. The site is now administered by the Historical Society of Western Pennsylvania in Pittsburgh. The grounds include an archaeological site, the Meadowcroft Rockshelter, containing the remains of North America's earliest inhabitants. The visitor center has a small exhibit on the prehistoric archaeological site, including a short video that explains the significance of this world-renowned site. Kids will enjoy the demonstrations and exhibits (the stuffed racehorse Adios is a favorite) and the opportunity to run off energy on the extensive grounds. Built in 1850, the country store has shelves lined with nostalgic tins and advertisements from a time when snake oil was a cure-all. Meadowcroft sponsors frequent workshops on topics such as blacksmithing, the manufacture of herbal lotions, spinning, and other colonial-era specialties.

Ladbroke at The Meadows

An outstanding harness-racing facility, The Meadows (Race Track Rd., Meadow Lands, Washington County, 724/225-9300, www.latm.com)

opened in the 1960s and is home to many special events during the year. The live racing schedule goes on year-round, Tues.–Sun.; August brings the One Million Dollar Canus Delvin Miller Adios Week, a series of major harness races that culminate in the $500,000 Adios Pace for the Orchids, Pennsylvania's richest stakes race.

Quaker Ridge Winery

The lands of this orchard fruit–based winery (211 S. Wade Ave., Washington, Washington County, 724/222-2914, www.quakerridgewinery.com) were first planted in 1975, on land originally owned by Quaker farmer John England. The tasting room is open Thurs.–Fri. 11 A.M.–6 P.M., Sat.–Sun. 11 A.M.–5 P.M. and by appointment; closed on New Year's Day, Easter, Thanksgiving, and Christmas. Grapes and apples are blended with strawberries, blackberries, cherries, and other fruits to produce a number of award-winning wines varying from sweet to dry. Quaker Ridge also produces personalized labels, and there's a discount on case prices. Tasting is free, and only for visitors 21 and over, of course.

MUSEUMS

▣ Johnstown Flood Museum

This extraordinary museum (304 Washington St., Johnstown, Cambria County, 814/539-1889, www.jaha.org; adults $4, age five and under, free) chronicles just one event in American history: the flood that swept from the neglected dam at the South Fork Fishing and Hunting Club through the valley and over the prospering city of Johnstown in 1889. The museum is open May–Oct., Sun.–Thurs. 10 A.M.–5 P.M., Fri.–Sat. 10 A.M.–7 P.M.; and Nov.–April, daily 10 A.M.–5 P.M. A combination ticket to both the flood museum and the Heritage Discovery Center is $6.

Johnstown shared a similar growth pattern to that of Pittsburgh; during the latter part of the 19th century, thousands of immigrants came from Germany, Ireland, Wales, Slovakia, Croatia, Hungary, Poland, and elsewhere to work in the iron and steel mills, coke ovens, and coal mines in the area. The wall of water that leveled the city was 35–40 feet high; more than 2,000 people died, and hundreds of homes and businesses were destroyed. The flood was the biggest news story and scandal of the time; in the aftermath, aid poured in from all over the United States in support of the victims.

The two lower floors of the museum display information about the flood and feature an Academy Award-winning documentary. Changing exhibits on the third floor tell of the life and times of Johnstown. A recent exhibit featured Johnstown's ethnic heritage clubs (there were more than 100 during the city's industrial boom).

The building, converted from an old Carnegie Free Library, retains a mezzanine-like structure above the third floor. It's a steeply banked running track covered in leather—Carnegie believed in healthy bodies as well as healthy minds. He rebuilt the structure at his own expense after the flood destroyed it.

The Compass Inn Museum

The Compass Inn (US 30, Laughlintown, Westmoreland County, 724/238-4983, www.compassinn .com, May–Oct. Tues.–Sat. 11 A.M.–4 P.M., Sun. noon–4 P.M., adults $6, less for children, under 5 free) is a restored stagecoach stop, built in 1799 and expanded after the 1817 completion of the Pittsburgh-Philadelphia Turnpike. Furnished with period pieces, the working kitchen, blacksmith shop, and barn are reconstructed on their original sites. The Compass Inn is three miles east of Ligonier on US Route 30.

Westmoreland Museum of Art

The Westmoreland (221 N. Main St., Greensburg, Westmoreland County, 724/837-1500, www.wmuseumaa.org, Wed.–Sun. 11 A.M.–5 P.M. and Thurs. 11 A.M.–9 P.M., $3 donation) is an art-lover's open secret. The museum was established in 1950 at the bequest of Mary Marchand Woods. Her will dedicated her entire estate to the founding of a public art museum that would broaden the horizons of the rural communities of southwestern Pennsylvania through cultural acquisitions and education.

Subsequent development has resulted in collections that are varied and visually de-

lightful. The museum curators set about acquiring the work of Pennsylvania artists, such as Rembrandt Peale's *Portrait of George Washington* and Mary Cassatt's *Mother and Two Children*. One gallery is devoted to 19th-century landscapes typical of the Hudson River School; works by Winslow Homer, John Singer Sargent, Thomas Eakins, and J. A. M. Whistler are featured. Another gallery is filled with dramatic scenes of local industries—drawings and paintings of coal, steel, and glass in the making. The second floor holds a collection of fine and decorative arts.

The Westmoreland is one of those rare art museums that children enjoy. The museum has a 2,000-piece toy collection, varying from Civil War–era porcelain dolls to Steiff stuffed animals, cast-iron toys, and more than 250 Barbie dolls. During the Christmas season, the museum exhibits its Barbie and antique toy collections and sets up a large-gauge model train display.

West Overton Museums

In 1838, Mennonite Henry Overholt built a large home, gristmill, and distillery between the towns of Mount Pleasant and Scottdale on what is now SR 819 (West Overton Village, Scottdale, Westmoreland County, 724/887-7910, www.westovertonmuseum.org, May 15–Oct. 15 Tues.–Sat. 10 A.M.–4 P.M., Sun. 1–5 P.M.; Oct. 16–May 14 by appointment; adults $6, seniors and children $4). The distillery produced Old Overholt Whiskey; a workers' community, West Overton Village, grew around the distillery. Most of the village remains intact, and the distillery is now a museum, featuring artifacts, changing exhibits, and a film, *Pillars of Fire,* about the process of turning coal into coke for steel processing. Overholt's great-grandson, Henry Clay Frick, was born in a house on the property and became a millionaire in the coke and steel business.

Pennsylvania Trolley Museum

The Pennsylvania Trolley Museum (1 Museum Rd., Washington, Washington County, 724/228-9256, Memorial Day–Labor Day, daily 10 A.M.–4 P.M., day after Labor Day–Dec. 31 and April

1–day before Memorial Day Sat.–Sun. 11 A.M.–5 P.M., $6) has more than 25 trolleys on display. The oldest dates from 1894, and the collection includes a streetcar named *Desire* from New Orleans. Kids can climb on board many of the vehicles in the car barn, and one even operates on a short length of track. Visitors will enjoy a trip into the past—when public transportation was the sophisticated (and enjoyable) way to travel. The museum also has an extensive collection of trolley memorabilia and trinkets. A picnic grove is nearby. Special programs take place around the Christmas holidays; call for a recorded message.

The National Duncan Glass Museum

This small museum (525 Jefferson Ave., Washington, Washington County, 724/225-9950, www.duncan-glass.com, April 1–Oct. 31 Thurs.–Sun. 11 A.M.–4 P.M., $4) displays pressed crystal and colored-glass pieces produced by the now-defunct Duncan & Miller glassworks. The glassware, designed and crafted for home use during the last century, is prized by collectors for its historical value and beauty. The story of the glassworks, originally established in 1872, and the history of glassmaking in general make this museum a must-see for anyone with an interest in art glass.

Shopping and Recreation

SHOPPING

Johnstown
The Galleria (off U.S. 219 at 570 Galleria Dr., Johnstown, Cambria County, 814/266-6600) has a Boscov's, Bon-Ton, and a Sears.

Somerset County
The **Somerset Antique Mall** 1(13 E. Main St., Somerset, 814/445-9690) is a mix of antiques and collectibles. It's one block south of the Somerset courthouse and is open Tues.–Sat. 10 A.M.–5 P.M., closed Sun.

Factory Shops at Georgian Place (SR 601 north, Somerset, 814/443-3818) is an upscale discount mall featuring Nine West, Izod, and Mikasa stores, among others. Take PA Turnpike Exit 10.

Across from the Factory Shops at Georgian Place, **Pine Haven Village Shoppes** (SR 601) is a cluster of rescued and renovated buildings, including a 200-year-old log home. The buildings house various craft businesses: **The Walker Room** offers early American accessories, furniture, and dried flower arrangements; **Toy Cabin Treasures** features traditional and modern toys; and **Candied Creations** has hand-dipped chocolates.

In the village of Springs, south of Somerset, Saturday is the day for farm-fresh produce at the Springs Festival Grounds, Memorial Day–Sept. 8 A.M.–2 P.M.

Westmoreland County
The village of Ligonier is centered around a diamond with a gazebo—summer evening band concerts are frequent, especially on the weekends. The principal streets, East and West Main and North and South Market, fan out from this central square. Among the sedate dress shops and offices are a number of interesting antique and collectible shops.

On the cross street, an enchanting toy store, **The Toy Box** (108 S. Market St., Ligonier, 724/238-6233, www.toyboxligonier.com, Mon.–Sat. 10 A.M.–5 P.M., Sun. noon–5 P.M.) carries on the theme of the "Land of Make-Believe" from Mister Rogers' Neighborhood in nearby Idlewild Park. Toys, games, and puzzles will keep children and adults busy for hours.

Washington County
Washington Crown Center (1500 W. Chestnut St., at US 40 and I-70, Washington, 724/228-4270) features a Bon-Ton, Sears, Casual Corner, The Limited, and more than 60 other stores.

OUTDOOR RECREATION

Hunting and Fishing
There are hunting areas in Forbes State Forest, Laurel Hill State Park, Linn Run State Park, and Ohiopyle State Park. State game lands are open near Johnstown, Somerset, Uniontown, Vintondale, Wittenberg, Frugality, Confluence, Fairchance, Aleppo, Ashville, and Dunkard. For general hunting information, game season

KEEPING THE WEST WILD

A private organization with nearly 20,000 members, The Western Pennsylvania Conservancy is the state's largest private land conservation organization. Founded in 1932, the conservancy has bought and placed nearly 200,000 acres of prime natural lands throughout western Pennsylvania under its care. Nearly all projects are sold, at cost, to public agencies for parks, forests, and game lands. The money is then recycled into new land acquisition projects.

Much of the land for five of Pennsylvania's state parks—Laurel Ridge, McConnell's Mill, Moraine, Ohiopyle, and Oil Creek—was originally purchased by the conservancy, as were 25,000 acres of pristine state game lands and 19,000 acres of islands and shoreline property along the Allegheny and Clarion Rivers. Possibly the best-known Conservancy project is Fallingwater, Frank Lloyd Wright's architectural landmark, just north of Ohiopyle.

one of the great runs at Seven Springs

dates, and fees, contact the Pennsylvania Game Commission, Southwest Region (339 W. Main St., P.O. Box A, Ligonier, PA 15658, 724/238-9523) or Game Commission Headquarters (2001 Elmerton Ave., Harrisburg PA 17110, 717/787-4250, www.pgc.state.pa.us).

Year-round fishing is available on the Youghiogheny River and at Youghiogheny Lake in Confluence as well as on lakes and streams throughout the area. Laurel Hill Lake is stocked with trout, bass, carp, and bluegills and allows ice fishing.

Tennis

All of the major resorts, Linden Hall, Seven Springs, Nemacolin Woodlands, and Hidden Valley (Fayette County, see Resorts), offer tennis as part of their packages. In addition, Hidden Valley (800/382-2110) offers clinics and tennis camps for all ages and abilities; call for more information.

Water Sports

Laurel Hill Lake, near the village of Trent west of Somerset (Somerset County), features a 65-acre lake with a swimming beach and boat conces-

sion. For more information, contact Laurel Hill State Park (P.O. Box 50, Rector, PA 15677, 724/238-6623).

Winter Sports

Laurel Mountain Ski Resort (201 Summit Ski Rd., Boswell, Somerset County, 724/238-9860, mailing address P.O. Box 657, Ligonier, PA 15658, www.skilaurelmountain), in Laurel Mountain State Park, features a new lodge, state-of-the-art snow-making machinery, quad chair lift, half-pipe snowboarding park, snowtubing run, rental facility, and a ski shop. For a snow report, phone 877/SKI-LAUR(EL) (877/754-5287). Laurel Mountain State Park comprises 493 acres in Westmoreland County. To reach the park go eight miles east of Ligonier or five miles west of Jennerstown on US 30, then turn south on Laurel Summit Road and travel for two miles.

Seven Springs (814/352-7777 or 800/452-2223) in Champion (Fayette County, see Resorts) offers snowmaking capacity and two quad chairlifts, seven triple chairlifts, two double chairlifts, and seven rope tows. There are 14 downhill slopes and 16 cross-country trails. Ski season typically extends Dec. 1–April 1,

Laurel Highlands

Sun.–Thurs. 9 A.M.–10 P.M., Fri.–Sat. 9 A.M.–11 P.M. Call for reservations and general information (including snow conditions and discount packages).

Hidden Valley (general ski information 814/443-2600, snow conditions 800/443-7544; see Resorts) offers 17 slopes with eight lifts, plus 20 miles of groomed cross-country ski trails that link to 20 additional miles of state trails. Packages are available.

Mystic Mountain (in Nemacolin Woodlands; see Resorts) offers eight downhill ski slopes, 15 miles of cross-country trails, and a snowboarding and tubing area.

Kooser State Park

This 250-acre park (SR 31 on Laurel Ridge, between Somerset and Westmoreland Counties, 814/445-8673, www.dcnr.state.pa.us) rents out nine rustic cabins year-round and 45 campsites mid-April–mid-Dec. The cabins have mattresses, refrigerator, stove, and hot water. Renters must bring all cooking and sleeping supplies. To reserve a campsite or cabin, call 888/PA-PARKS (888/727-2757) Mon.–Sat. 7 A.M. to 5 P.M. There is a small lake for fishing and one hiking trail, which is popular during the winter with cross-country skiers. The winter cabins (Dec–mid-March) are handled by a separate concessionaire: to rent a cabin for the winter, call the Winter Cabin Concessionaire (412/720-4074) and ask for Traci Holler.

Linn Run State Park

Linn Run (south of Laughlintown, Westmoreland County, off SR 381/Linn Run Rd., 724/238-6623) is one of the parks in the vast Forbes State Forest, which also includes Laurel Mountain State Park and parts of Laurel Ridge State Park.

Most of the land in Linn Run and surrounding areas was bought by the Commonwealth of Pennsylvania from the Byers and Allen Lumber Company for less than $45,000 in 1909. At the time, critics questioned the wisdom of buying so much "wasteland." Before the acquisition, the entire Linn Run area was clear-cut and scarred by fire. Forester John R. Williams wrote, "fully three-fifths of the reserve has been burned over since lumbering was done."

Little evidence of the "wasteland" remains today. The remarkable ability of the land to heal itself has resulted in heavy second-forest regrowth and lush meadowlands over the entire area. Linn Run offers picnicking, cabins, and five miles of hiking trails.

Hiking: The Grove Run Trail, four miles long, starts on a gentle slope and gets progressively steeper; and the 1.5-mile Wolf Rocks Trail and Vista, which passes examples of frost cracks, frost wedging, and stone exfoliation, are both considered moderately difficult. The Fish Run Trail is the shortest, easiest hike, crossing the path of the now-defunct Pittsburgh, Westmoreland, and Somerset Railroad. Bikes are not permitted on these trails. Trail maps and information are available by calling the park office (724/238-6623) or writing to Linn Run/Laurel Mountain Complex (P.O. Box 50, Rectory, PA 15677-0030).

Camping: Nine rustic cabins and one modern cabin are available for public use year-round, though during the summer season, the cabins are rented out by the week only. The cabins are equipped with fireplaces, electric stoves, and refrigerators. Call 888/PA-PARKS (888/727-2757) Mon.–Sat. 7 A.M.–5 P.M. for reservations.

Keystone State Park

Keystone State Park (north of Latrobe on SR 981, Westmoreland County, 724/668-2939) offers boating, fishing, and swimming on a 78-acre lake, and five miles of hiking, cross-country, and snowmobile trails. Eleven modern cabins and 100 tent and trailer sites are available from the first Friday of April–late Dec. Make reservations by calling 888/PA-PARKS (888/727-2757) Mon.–Sat., 7 A.M.–5 P.M. The park is open mid-April–mid-Dec.

Ohiopyle State Park

The spectacular 1,700-foot-deep Youghiogheny (yock-a-GAY-nee) Gorge cuts through the Laurel Ridge Mountains in southwestern Pennsylvania. Nearly 19,000 acres of this area, including more than 14 miles of the Youghiogheny River, form the basis for Ohiopyle State Park.

The park is open all year, and the visitors' center in the village of Ohiopyle is open May– Oct. For information, maps, or reservations, contact the Department of Environmental Resources, Ohiopyle State Park (PO Box 105, Ohiopyle, PA 15470, 724/329-8591, www.dcnr.state.pa.us).

The beautiful Youghiogheny River, once dead from acid mine drainage (AMD), has made a spectacular comeback in the last few decades. The vast Pittsburgh coal vein runs beneath the area all the way south beyond the Pennsylvania border. For more than 100 years, coal miners worked deep (pit) and strip mines here; many mine sites were left unmarked. When flooded, the mines leached coal waste into the ecosystem. The Youghiogheny now supports a thriving trout population and heavy recreational use, though the danger from unmarked mine AMD remains.

A walk through downtown Ohiopyle will lead you to the local water play area known as "the bump slides" (Cucumber Falls). In high water, it's possible to guide a kayak down the twists and turns of this stream, but most of the year, people prefer to ride several hundred yards downstream on their own rear padding. Ask in the village for directions.

White-Water Rafting: Rafting on the Youghiogheny River, affectionately known as "the Yock," is wildly popular. Depending on the section of the river and the time of year, the river runs up to class IV rapids (class V being the most difficult); by midsummer, the thrills are tamer, though they still provide an enjoyable trip for novices and experts alike. Water level on the river is controlled through a dam upstream.

If you plan to navigate the Yock on your own, call 888/PA-PARKS (888/727-2757) or the Ohiopyle State Park office (724/329-8591) to schedule a launch time. Equipment rentals are available in the town of Ohiopyle. There is a fee to launch boats on weekends on the Lower Yough. During the week, boaters must sign-in at the launch area.

Several rafting companies operate out of Ohiopyle, offering guided trips as well as rentals of everything from wetsuits to kayaks. All are on the one-block-long strip that is downtown Ohiopyle. **Wilderness Voyagers** (724/329-1000 or 800/272-4141, www.wilderness-voyageurs

.com) is the oldest company on the river. It started up in the early 1960s and has a good record of safety and thorough training. A group of boats is sent down the river with two safety men—helmeted kayakers who pick up anyone who takes an unexpected swim—and river guides occupy the lead and last boat. Ages in the groups range from under eight to 60-plus.

Another local company is **White Water Adventurers** (800/992-7238, www.wwaraft.com). Both companies offer equipment rentals, guided trips, and multiple choices for recreation including biking, canoeing, rafting, and a mix of the three.

Hiking and Biking: In addition to the Yough River Trail (see The Youghiogheny River Trail) a separate mountain bike trail and 41 miles of day-hiking trails are available within the park.

Hunting and Fishing: Eighteen thousand acres of the park are open to hunting, trapping, and dog training Labor Day–late May. State Game Lands 51 and 11 are adjacent to the park; all Pennsylvania Game Commission rules and regulations apply.

For fishing information, contact the Pennsylvania Fish and Boat Commission, Southwest Region (P.O. Box 39, Somerset R.D. 2, PA 15501, 814/445-8974, www.fish.state.pa.us). A *Summary of Fishing Regulations and Laws* booklet is available where fishing licenses are sold. The Youghiogheny River is popular for trout, and the Youghiogheny River Lake, at the dam in Confluence, is a favorite for walleye and small-mouth bass.

Winter Sports: Snowmobiling, tobogganing, cross-country skiing, sledding, winter fishing, and hunting are all available. The Kentuck and Sproul Trails were designed with cross-country skiers in mind. These trails connect to a large meadow and are off-limits to snowmobiles.

Camping: The park provides 223 campsites for tents, trailers, backpackers, and RVs. The camping area includes hot showers, flush toilets, and a dumping station. Reservations are necessary; call 888/PA-PARKS (888/727-2757) Mon.–Sat. 7 A.M.–5 P.M.

The Youghiogheny River Trail

This 43-mile trail follows the Youghiogheny River from Confluence in the southern end through Ohiopyle to South Connellsville in the north. The trail will eventually be expanded to Washington, D.C., in the south and Mc-Keesport in the north. It passes through rugged terrain with an abundance of natural hazards, though its completion as a rails-to-trails path has tamed much of the danger. The trail is open to hiking, jogging, biking, and cross-country skiing. Bikes may be rented from several outfitters in Ohiopyle.

Access near Confluence is off SR 281; cross the one-lane bridge over the Yough into Fayette County. Take a sharp right onto Ram Cat Hollow Road, alongside the river. The trail's parking lot and restrooms are two miles up this road. In South Connellsville, access is near the Wheeler Bottom water treatment plant.

Though the trail may be entered at either end in Confluence or South Connellsville, there is an access point in Ohiopyle that breaks the trail into two segments: the south segment, Confluence-Ohiopyle, is 10 miles; the north segment, Ohiopyle-South Connellsville, is 14 miles. The latter segment was named as one of the 18 great walks in the world in a 1994 issue of *Travel and Leisure* magazine. The trail winds through heavily forested areas along the falls and rapids of the river; the trees occasionally thin out to permit a view of the gorge. There are several side trails leading to the river for a quick dip in the four-mile stretch just below South Connellsville. In Ohiopyle, trail access is at the train station/visitors' center downtown (parking may be difficult on weekends). For more information and maps, call 724/329-0986, www.youghrivertrail.org, or contact Ohiopyle State Park (P.O. Box 105, Ohiopyle, PA 15470, 724/329-8591).

Laurel Ridge State Park

Laurel Ridge State Park stretches from the village of Ohiopyle in the west to the Conemaugh River in the east. The park fills in the spaces between several state game lands and other parks (Laurel Mountain, Forbes State Forest, Roaring Run Natural Area, and Ohiopyle State Park). The connecting thread of these wilderness beads is the Laurel Highlands Hiking Trail, which runs

along the Ohiopyle River from the village of Ohiopyle, then veers north across the mountains nearly 70 miles to its end, south of Johnstown. The trail has numerous access points, parking lots, and trail shelters. For more information about the park, contact Laurel Ridge State Park (1117 Jim Mountain Rd., Rockwood, 724/455-3744, www.dcnr.state.pa.us).

The Laurel Highlands Hiking Trail

This 70-mile-long hiking and backpacking trail is the main feature of Laurel Ridge State Park. The trail is open year-round and is marked approximately every 100 feet with two-inch and five-inch yellow blazes; mileage markers appear every mile. Large wooden signs mark trail access points: Ohiopyle trailhead and parking lot, Maple Summit Road, SR 653, SR 51 parking lot, Pennsylvania Turnpike (I-76), US 30 parking lot, SR 271 parking lot, SR 56 (Decker Avenue), and SR 56 trailhead parking lot (in the borough of Seward).

There are eight overnight shelters, placed 8–10 miles apart on the trail. Each area contains five Adirondack-type shelters (with roof and one to four open sides), fireplaces, two nonflush toilets, a water supply, and spaces for 30 tents. Because of heavy use, overnight reservations are mandatory, and one adult, 18 years of age or older, is required to accompany each 10 campers. Reservations may be made up to 30 days in advance; call 888/PA-PARKS (888/727-2757) Mon.–Sat. 7 A.M.–5 P.M.

A hiker's guide to the Laurel Highlands Trail is available from the Pennsylvania Chapter of the Sierra Club (P.O. Box 8241, Pittsburgh, PA 15217). The guide describes the trail, with detailed topographic maps and information of geology, climate, plants, and wildlife.

Commercial Campgrounds

In Farmington (Fayette County), **Benner's Meadow Run** (301 Nelson Rd., 724/329-4097, www.bennersmeadowrun.com) offers a swimming pool, fishing, hiking, a play area, and planned activities for children. It's 12 miles east of Uniontown on US 40, then 2.5 miles north on Nelson Road. Tent sites start at $24.50; rustic cabins are available from $39.50. Full-service cabins and chalets with efficiency kitchens and showers range $85–125.

Additional campsites in Fayette County include: **Tall Oaks** (544 Camp Riamo Rd., Farmington, 724/329-4777) with cabins ($13 per person) and more than 100 tent sites ($9.50 per

adult, less for children), open April–Oct.; and **Yogi Bear Jellystone** (Mill Run, 724/455-2929 or 800/439-9644) offering campsites starting at $28, cabins ($85–152), RV rentals ($90–100), a pool, water slides, and special events (you can party with Yogi in the fur). The park also welcomes day use.

Accommodations

UNDER $50

The 25-bed **Ohiopyle State Park American Youth Hostel** (on Ferncliff Rd., Ohiopyle, Fayette County, 724/329-4476, $15–18) is in an older former single-family dwelling across the tracks from the village of Ohiopyle. It attracts a mixed crowd, including couples with small children and lots of young people who come for the river rafting.

$50–100

The Bayberry Inn (611 N. Center Ave., 814/445-8471, www.bayberry-inn.com, $55–65) is close to the historic Somerset courthouse, on Exit 10 off I-79, Somerset, Somerset County. Each of the five clean and comfortable guest rooms in this urban inn is decorated in a simple turn-of-the-century (1900, not 2000) style and has a private bathroom with shower. A good value.

Ligonier Valley Cottages (75 Lincoln Hwy./US 30, Ligonier, Westmoreland County, 724/238-9696, www.ligoniervalley.com) aren't fancy but are eminently practical and nestled in a beautiful setting. Each cottage sleeps four and comes with most of the comforts of home, including a TV, full kitchen, and bath. Rates range $65–95 per night, $180 for Fri.–Sat., or $375 a week.

In Fayette County, the **Lodge at Chalk Hill** (five miles south of Ohiopyle on US 40 east, 724/438-8880 or 800/833-4283, www.chalkhilllodge.com) has 60 units, some with double or king-sized beds, and efficiencies. The lodge is laid out around a small lake, and children may stay free in their parents' room. Rates range $49–119 for the suite with kitchen.

$100–150

The Inn at Georgian Place (800 Georgian Place Dr., Somerset, Somerset County, 814/443-1043, www9.inetba.com/theinnatgeorgianplace, $95–185) was built in 1915 by local coal and cattle baron D. B. Zimmerman for himself and his family. The original oak paneling, ornate fireplaces, gold-leaf chandeliers, and expansive marble foyer have been kept; private baths, TVs, and telephones have been added to each of the 11 guest rooms. The beautiful interior decor was supervised by innkeeper Jon Knupp with attention to period detail—the rooms, varying from small and cozy to elegant and luxurious, each have a special charm. In spite of the formality of the setting, the inn feels warm and friendly. For die-hard shoppers, the outlet shopping center is next door (see Shopping). Although the inn is a half-mile from a major thoroughfare (Exit 10, I-79), the setting remains untouched by street noise. Breakfast is served to guests in the solarium, an additional treat. Lunch, high tea, cocktails, and dinner are offered to the public during the day in the elegant dining and living rooms (see Food).

Lady of the Lake (next to Idlewild Park on US 30 east, Ligonier, Westmoreland County, 724/238-6955, www.ladyofthelakebandb.com) is a family-oriented bed-and-breakfast where children are welcome. Amenities include swimming in an in-ground heated pool; fishing, canoeing, and paddle boating on a 25-acre pond; tennis; nature trails; and a petting farm. A full six-course country breakfast is included. The main house features rooms with private bath, and an outside cottage is available ($90–125). There is space for camping ($33 per night, includes breakfast).

Laurel Highlands

Entering **The Campbell House** (305 E. Main St., Ligonier, Westmoreland County, 724/238-9812 or 888/238-9812, www.soupkid.com) is like walking into a child's Victorian dollhouse. Innkeeper Patti Campbell, a true romantic and avid collector of both authentic and reproduction memorabilia from the turn-of-the-last-century, has decorated her small bed-and-breakfast (three bedrooms, all with private baths) "for the sentimental of heart." Kewpie dolls, white wicker furniture, and meticulous handmade quilts decorate the rooms. A small kitchen is available for guests to use, and the house itself is three blocks from the center of Ligonier's diamond, a town square complete with gazebo. Main Street, running west and east from the diamond, is lined with shops. Rates range $80–135, less for extended stays.

Yough Plaza (in the center of the village of Ohiopyle, Fayette County, 800/992-7238, $89–164) is a motel-style inn; it offers 10 units with two double beds, and four efficiencies, each with two bedrooms and a kitchen.

M Weatherbury Farm (1061 Sugar Run Rd., Avella, Washington County, 724/587-3763, www.weatherburyfarm.com, $83–175 per night depending on family size and choice of lodging), nestled amid more than 100 acres of rolling farmland in Southwestern Pennsylvania, is a quiet place removed from the cares of the workaday world. The 1870s farmhouse has been restored and redecorated; innkeepers Dale, Marcy, and Nigel Tudor added stenciled walls, fireplaces, paddle fans, family keepsakes, original wide fir floors, and private baths with nostalgic pull-chains. Each room has a sitting area, flowers from the garden, and books. Weatherbury is a working farm with goats, sheep, chickens, ducks, rabbits, and cattle. It's roughly 10 miles west of Washington.

The Century Inn (US 40, Scenery Hill, Washington County, 724/945-6600, www.centuryinn.com, $80–160) was built in 1794 on the old coach road. The 20-room stone inn has been completely restored and can accommodate up to 19 overnight guests; at Zephanie Riggle's House of Entertainment—directly across the street—there's room for another nine guests.

All guest rooms are authentically restored and decorated with antiques, and some have working fireplaces and whirlpool baths.

RESORTS

Resorts are accommodations with restaurants, recreational facilities, and shops. Rates often include all meals or breakfast and dinner, and many recreational activities.

Linden Hall (Dawson, 724/529-7543 or 800/944-3238, www.lindenhallpa.com) offers several recreational activities for the entire family. Swimming, a championship golf course, tennis, and fishing are available on the grounds. There are a restaurant and pub on the premises. Children under 18 may stay for free with their parents in the 74-room lodge. Linden Hall is the most casual and inexpensive of the resorts in this area, with rooms priced $68–82 per night, including use of the swimming pools and tennis courts. Special Getaway and Family Package Plans are available. Linden Hall is between the villages of Dawson and Layton; follow signs from SR 51 at Perryopolis (the grounds are about seven miles from the first sign).

In 1928, Bavarian immigrant Adolph Dupre built his family home on a small parcel of land in the remote Allegheny Mountains. Through the years, he expanded his holdings and designed and built a number of cottages on the property, convinced that the beauty of the area would draw vacationers from Pittsburgh. The Dupres added a primitive auto-engine-powered rope tow for skiers in 1936, offering downhill skiing as an incentive. The tourist trade was a growing business, but the Dupres derived a major part of their income from maple syrup—their grove was the largest in Pennsylvania, producing more than 1,200 gallons a year.

When Adolph Dupre died in 1957, his family continued to expand the resort. **M Seven Springs** (SR 381 two miles south of the intersection with SR 31, Champion, 814/352-7777 or 800/452-2223, www.7springs.com) is now the largest employer in Somerset County, with a major convention center; 10-story hotel, chalets, condominiums, cabins, and other accommodations; an 18-hole golf course; 13 tennis courts; a roller rink; four racquetball courts; a health spa; and a bowling alley. Other recreational pastimes include hiking, swimming, horseback riding, and a variety of supervised activities and programs especially for children. It's become the largest ski area in Pennsylvania, with miles of downhill slopes and cross-country trails including a NASTAR (National Association of Ski Trails and Racecourses) racecourse.

Seven Springs is completely self-contained with several restaurants, bars, and shops. The original Dupre family home has become Helen's, an elegant restaurant with jazz entertainment.

Special events, such as the Wine and Food Festival in August, are scheduled throughout the year. Room rates include use of the swimming pools; exercise room; racquetball, volleyball, and tennis courts; hiking trails; and the family recreation center. Skiing and horseback riding cost extra. All adult rates include breakfast, and though children under age 17 stay free in the same room, they will be charged for breakfast. Rooms in the main lodge range $179–202 winter, $149–490 summer. Condominiums and townhouses range $176–670 winter, $336–730 summer. Chalets and rustic cabins, which can sleep up to 20, start at $330–485 winter (no summer rates). Discount packages are available throughout the year.

Hidden Valley (1 Craighead Dr., about 15 miles west of Somerset on SR 31, 814/443-8000 or 800/458-0175) started off as a small family-run restaurant and inn in the 1950s. In 1993, *Mid-Atlantic* magazine named it as one of the 50 finest regional hotels and resorts. It offers a wide variety of recreational amenities, including an 18-hole golf course, 12 tennis courts, a sports club (with workout equipment), 30 miles of hiking and biking trails, basketball and volleyball courts, a trout- and bass-stocked lake, and four swimming pools. The golf course was selected as one of the best in the mid-Atlantic region by readers of *Tee Time* magazine in 1993. The ski resort offers both downhill and cross-country trails, and ski instruction for all ages (see Winter Sports under

Outdoor Recreation in the Shopping and Recreation section for more information).

Hidden Valley has several restaurants and bars. Room rates include use of the sports club, conference center, pool, tennis courts, and mountain bikes, as well as lake access. Children under 12 stay free in the same room as their parents. Accommodations vary from efficiencies priced $85–195 summer/$85–340 winter to condominiums, townhouses, and large single family homes, $220–350 summer/$400–550 winter depending on size and location. Longer stays are discounted.

At the high-end 2,000-acre resort **Nemacolin Woodlands** (1001 Lafayette Dr., Farmington, Fayette County, 724/329-6387 or 800/422-2736, www.nemacolin.com), perhaps the question is, what *doesn't* it offer? Once a private lodge for a select group of wealthy friends, the original property was bought in 1987 by Joseph Hardy, founder of 84 Lumber, who has devoted himself to rebuilding it into a world-class playground. The property features more than 287 rooms; a drop-dead gorgeous spa (Woodlands Spa); two championship 18-hole golf courses and a golf academy; an equestrian center; a 30-station sporting clays facility and shooting academy; a hummer driving course; an adventure center with ropes course, climbing wall, mountain biking and hiking trails; year-round children's programs and baby-sitting services; 14 specialty shops, Mystic Mountain, a ski facility; several restaurants and lounges; and a multimillion-dollar art collection scattered throughout the property. Oh yes, there's a private airstrip if you'd prefer to arrive by air (like Presidents Clinton and Bush—not together, however).

The main hotel, Chateau LaFayette, is modeled after the classic hotels of Europe—crystal chandeliers, coffered ceilings—nothing understated here ($225–385). The Lodge, an English Tudor with country-style decor, ranges $185–360. Townhouses ($215–365) and luxury homes ($350–3,000) are scattered about the grounds. Falling Rock, on a golf course, is the newest addition to the property ($350–575).

Laurel Highlands

Food and Information

FOOD

Deli and Takeout

The **Falls Market** (69 Main St., 724/329-4973, daily 7 A.M.–5:30 P.M.) in downtown Ohiopyle, has a small food service counter that serves breakfast, sandwiches, and even complete dinners. It also stocks groceries and dry goods and sometimes rents out a room on the second floor. Prices average $6 for a small meal.

Diners and Pubs

The **Summit Diner** (791 N. Center Ave., Somerset, 814/445-7154) is open 24 hours a day, seven days a week, and serves extremely good, inexpensive food (lunch averages $6, dinner $11).

Mel's Restaurant and Bar (127 W. Patriot St., Somerset, 814/445-9841, daily 9 A.M.–2 A.M.) is a third-generation family-owned and operated restaurant and country western bar with live entertainment Fri. and Sat. nights. Pub food—hamburgers, chili, nachos—is under $5, and there are plenty of brews on tap to wash it down.

Ruthie's Diner (south side of US 30, east of the village of Ligonier, 724/238-9930, Mon. and Wed. 6 A.M.–10 P.M., Fri.–Sat. 6 A.M.–11 P.M.; Sun., Tues., Thurs. 6 A.M.–9 P.M., $5–12) serves home-cooked food and tasty pies in a casual, friendly atmosphere. This is where the locals go to eat breakfast, grab a cup of coffee, or meet friends. The phone number listed is actually a pay phone in the restaurant—there is no business phone, but the staff will take "to go" orders over that line.

Sheperd's Farm Restaurant and Ice Cream Shoppe (7553 Kingwood Rd., Confluence, just east of the Somerset County border, 814/395-3448) is another place to grab a quick bite or a more leisurely meal ($2–12).

International

The **Main Moon Restaurant** (113 N. Center St., Somerset, 814/445-3674, daily 10:30 A.M.–9:30 P.M.) features a number of inexpensive combination plates and a buffet for lunch and dinner. Vegetarian specials are on the menu, and everything in this Cantonese/Szechuan restaurant can be ordered as takeout. A block away from the imposing Somerset courthouse, Main Moon is a popular lunch spot for downtowners. Items on the menu average $6 per plate.

Curinga's (1050 Washington Rd., Washington, 724/225-7747) is a local favorite for steaks and seafood as well as pasta dishes. It's open Tues.–Sun. for dinner, and for lunch every day except Sat. Prices range $8–20. The style is Italian with an American twist. Friendly, efficient service and a serene atmosphere make this older eatery a favorite for casual dining as well as for "special events."

Midrange American

Oakhurst Tea Room (2409 Glades Pike, six miles west of Somerset on SR 31, 814/443-2897, www.oakhursttearoom.com) has been serving its famous plate-bending smorgasbords since 1933. It's so well-known that people use the Oakhurst as a geographical point of reference. The luncheon smorgasbord ($8) is available Tues.–Sat. 11 A.M.–4 P.M., dinner smorgy is Tues.–Sat. 4–9 P.M., Sun. 11 A.M.–8 P.M. ($12), and brunch smorgasbord is served Sun. 11 A.M.–2 P.M. During those hours, a regular menu is available; entrée prices average $8–12.

Laurel Mountain Inn (SR 31 between Donegal and Somerset, 814/443-2741, daily 11 A.M.–10 P.M., bar open until 1 A.M.) has plenty of local color and serves huge portions for lunch and dinner. Prices average $12.

The Ligonier Country Inn (Laughlintown, 724/238-3651; winter Fri.–Sun. noon–9 P.M.; summer Thurs.–Sat. 8 A.M.–10:45 P.M., brunch Sun. 11 A.M.–2 P.M., dinner 2–10:45 P.M.) is known for its fine Sunday brunch. It also has a daily lunch and dinner menu, priced around $10 for lunch, $18 for dinner.

The lighthearted **M Ligonier Tavern** (137 W. Main St., Ligonier, 724/238-4831) is a favorite with townspeople and visitors. Situated near the town diamond, the Tavern's lunch and dinner offerings are consistently good, and the menu is varied enough to provide for everyone's taste. Prices are similar to those at the Ligonier Country Inn.

Fine Dining

🞄 The Inn at Georgian Place (800 Georgian Place Dr., Somerset, 814/443-1043, www9.in-etba.com/theinnatgeorgianplace) serves elegant sandwiches and tarts for high tea (noon–2:30 P.M., $10,50), cocktails (daily noon–9 P.M.), and lunch (daily noon–2 P.M., average $12) and dinner (Fri.–Sat. 5:30–9 P.M., Sun. 5:30–8 P.M., average $20) from a continental menu. The setting is elegant, and the food—grilled halibut with caper lemon mornay sauce with mashed potatoes and onion confit, and snow peas $21, for instance—makes dining a special occasion.

🞄 Chez Gérard (1187 US 40 east, Hopwood, 724/437-9001, www.chezgerard.net; Mon., Wed.–Sun. lunch 11:30 A.M.–2 P.M., $13, dinner 5:30 P.M.–9 P.M., entrées average $25, closed Tues.) serves French gourmet cuisine. A prix-fixe six-course dinner runs $42—the cheese course, with about 14 different French cheeses, is a favorite. Guests may also order from an à la carte menu. The restaurant, chosen as one of the top 20 in Pennsylvania by readers of *Gourmet* magazine, is set in the Hopwood House, an inn built in 1790. It's also open for Sun. brunch ($13). Reservations are required.

🞄 The Century Inn (US 40, Scenery Hill, 724/945-6600) is one of the local "destination" restaurants. Lunch and dinner are served daily; entrées average $10 for lunch, $25 for dinner. Reservations are highly recommended. The menu includes many dishes that reflect the historic menus and palates of our pioneer forefathers, including chicken Jacksonian (boneless breast stuffed with scallops and lobster, covered with a delicate vanilla sauce) and seafood treasure chest (shrimp, scallops, and crab in a sherry basil cream in puff pastry).

INFORMATION

The **Johnstown/Cambria County Convention and Visitors Bureau** (416 Main St., Suite 100, Johnstown, PA 15901, 814/536-7993 or 800/237-8590, www.visitjohnstownpa.com) dispenses information on the Johnstown area and Cambria County.

The tourist promotion agency **Laurel Highlands Visitors Bureau** (Town Hall, 120 E. Main St., Ligonier, PA 15658, 724/238-5661 or 800/333-5661, www.laurelhighlands.org) will send information about Somerset, Westmoreland, and Fayette Counties on request. Additional resources are the **Somerset County Chamber of Commerce** (814/445-6431, www.somersetcnty pachamber.org) and **Ligonier Chamber of Commerce** (724/238-4200, www.ligonier.com).

The **Washington County Tourist Promotion Agency** (273 S. Main St., Washington, PA 15301, 724/228-5520 or 800/531-4114, www .washpatourism.org) is the place to go for maps and schedules.

Pittsburgh

Pittsburgh is *the* American success story. A city rebuilt from the ashes of an industrial past, it has become one of the most livable urban areas in America. First-class museums, parks, accommodations, eateries, and amusements sit firmly in a foundation of family-based neighborhoods. The members of these close communities trace their ancestry to hardworking 19th-century immigrants who journeyed to the New World, often perilously, to seek a better life.

Names familiar from America's manufacturing and banking industries and the arts dot its history; Andrew Carnegie, the steel king, and the Mellon family of finance got their starts here. Composer Billy Strayhorn graduated from Westinghouse High School and went on to form a long musical collaboration with Duke Ellington. Both Mary Cassatt, who became a celebrated Impressionist painter in Paris, and Gertrude Stein, the author, were born in Pittsburgh.

Those who haven't been to Pittsburgh recently might associate the city with its sweat-and-grime past of smoking factories, polluted waterways, and a rough-edged sensibility—the rust belt, a postindustrial scrap pile. If the people of Pittsburgh lacked their special character, their desire to fight for and preserve their city, these images might be true. What visitors see are the highly visible and heartening results of the "Pittsburgh Renaissance"—a massive, decades-long collaborative effort by civic and private groups, businesses, and the people who live and work here to

Must-Sees

Look for **M** to find the sights and activities you can't miss and **M** for the best dining and lodging.

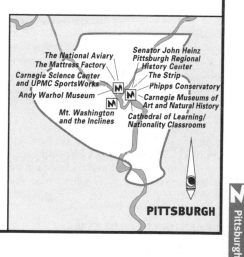 **The Strip:** Join locals for a Saturday tour of this chic warehouse district. Cart vendors and manufacturers vie for your attention in a combination farmer's market/street fair (page 389).

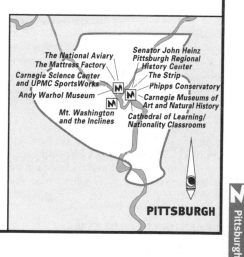 **Senator John Heinz Pittsburgh Regional History Center:** An old icehouse is reborn as a museum, housing a fascinating collection of Pittsburgh memorabilia from the founding of the city to the present (page 394).

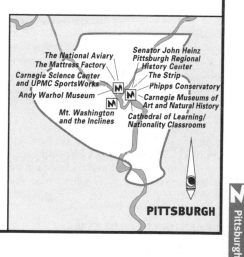 **Cathedral of Learning/Nationality Classrooms:** Each classroom in this University of Pittsburgh building is meticulously decorated to capture a period of time and place in each of the nationalities that make up Pittsburgh's cultural mix, from Chinese to Ukrainian (page 395).

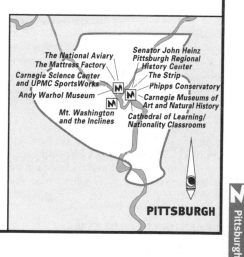 **Carnegie Museums of Art and Natural History:** The Museums of Art, Sculpture and Architecture, and Natural History on the East Side display a mind-boggling array of dinosaurs, gems, animal specimens, fine art, sculpture, architectural models, and more (page 398).

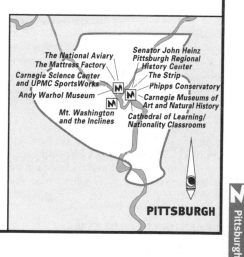 **Phipps Conservatory:** One of the largest Victorian "glass houses" in the country, Phipps features 2.5 acres of evolving gardens and several special shows throughout the year (page 404).

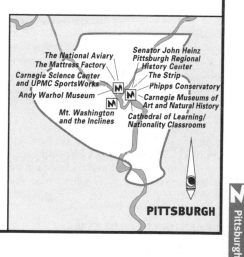 **The National Aviary:** A premier U.S. installation for the study of birds, this zoo for feathered fowl features more than 600 live specimens, and many rare and endangered species. The walk-through habitats are a special treat (page 408).

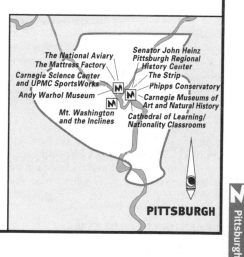 **Carnegie Science Center and UPMC Sports-Works:** It's "an amusement park for the mind," a

many-faceted approach to informal education in science and technology; UPMC SportsWorks offers a combination of play, sports, and learning (page 410).

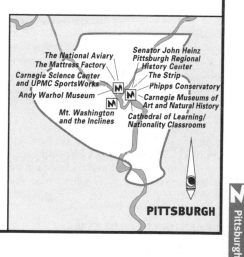 **Andy Warhol Museum:** This ultramodern facility is dedicated to the work of the founder of pop art and his cohorts—a sleek testament to modernism (page 411).

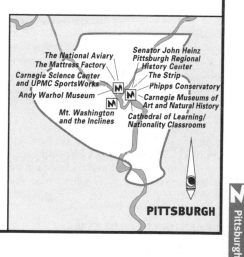 **The Mattress Factory:** The country's premier art collection specializing in large-scale, site-specific installations is fun, sometimes bewildering, and always avant-garde (page 411).

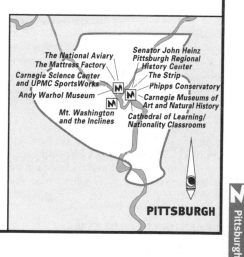 **Mt. Washington and the Inclines:** Take the Duquesne or Monongahela Incline—a rare form of transportation—up Mt. Washington to the Grandview Overlook. *USA Weekend's 2003 Annual Travel Report* named it the No. 2 beauty spot in America (page 413).

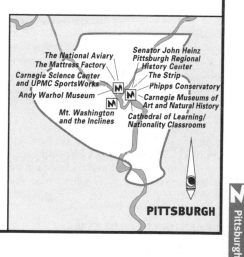

make a once-great city great again. Trees and tumbling fountains now cover the rust-strewn grounds of deserted factories, pleasure craft color the sparkling waters of the rivers, and sophisticated museums and eateries welcome residents and visitors.

In 2003, Pittsburgh was ranked fourth in the United States as an art-related tourist attraction by *American Style* magazine; the Carnegie Science Center was named among the top five museums in the nation by *FamilyFun* magazine, and Pittsburgh was touted as the 17th-cleanest city in the world, according to a survey by the San Francisco–based consultants the William Mercer Company. Pittsburgh's style is never overwhelming or alienating; in fact, *Utne Reader* named it the fifth "Most Underrated Town in America." It's also among the safest urban environments in the United States—the low crime rate is one of the factors that fosters a lively entertainment scene both day and night.

Pittsburgh is home to several richly supported museums, and the world's largest indoor walkthrough aviary. Stunning architecture abounds, as does the love of history and genealogy. Many families who now live in other parts of America can trace their roots to Pittsburgh's ethnic enclaves. Pittsburgh is also home to rabid sports fans; the Penguins (hockey), Pirates (baseball), and Steelers (football) are only the best-known teams quartered here. PNC Park was ranked "Best Stadium in Major League Baseball" by ESPN in 2003.

But most of the people who live here were born here and simply stayed. They often seem surprised that so many people take an interest in Pittsburgh—to them, it's home, a place that feeds the heart.

PLANNING YOUR TIME

Pittsburgh's amusements were built for the people who live there, and they are meant to be enjoyed at a leisurely pace. To see everything would take a week to 10 days. Those with specific pursuits could pare that down, but the best bet is to plan on a week in town and group activities by area—

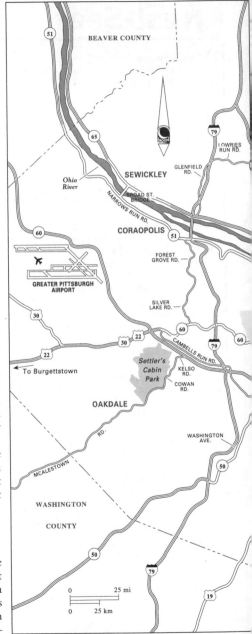

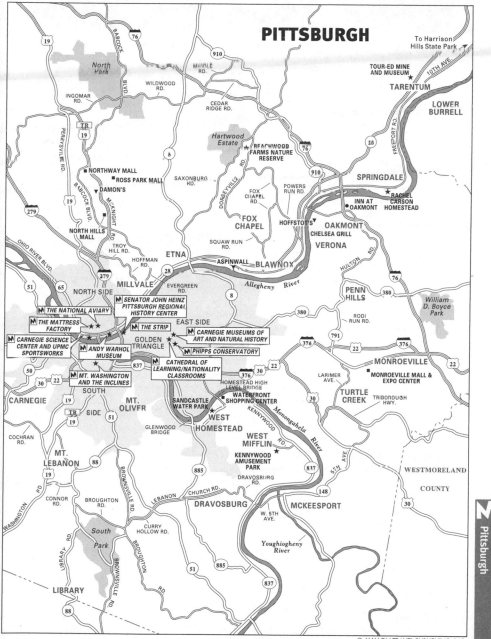

PITTSBURGH

To Harrison
Hills State Park

North
Park

INGOMAR
RD.

WILDWOOD
RD.

MIDDLE
RD.

CEDAR
RIDGE RD.

TOUR-ED MINE
AND MUSEUM

TARENTUM

LOWER
BURRELL

Hartwood
Estate

BEACHWOOD
FARMS NATURE
RESERVE

NORTHWAY MALL

ROSS PARK MALL

DAMON'S

SAXONBURG
RD.

FOX
CHAPEL
RD.

POWERS
RUN RD.

SPRINGDALE

INN AT
OAKMONT

RACHEL
CARSON
HOMESTEAD

NORTH HILLS
MALL

HOFFSTOT'S

OAKMONT

CHELSEA GRILL

VERONA

FOX
CHAPEL

SQUAW RUN
RD.

ETNA

ASPINWALL

BLAWNOX

PENN
HILLS

William
D. Boyce
Park

HOFFMAN
RD.

TROY
HILL RD.

MILLVALE

EVERGREEN
RD.

NORTH SIDE

RODI
RUN RD.

THE NATIONAL AVIARY

SENATOR JOHN HEINZ
PITTSBURGH REGIONAL
HISTORY CENTER

EAST SIDE

THE MATTRESS
FACTORY

THE STRIP

CARNEGIE MUSEUMS OF
ART AND NATURAL HISTORY

MONROEVILLE

CARNEGIE SCIENCE
CENTER AND UPMC
SPORTSWORKS

GOLDEN
TRIANGLE

ANDY WARHOL
MUSEUM

PHIPPS CONSERVATORY

LARIMER
AVE.

MONROEVILLE MALL &
EXPO CENTER

CATHEDRAL OF
LEARNING/NATIONALITY
CLASSROOMS

MT. WASHINGTON
AND THE INCLINES

SOUTH

HOMESTEAD HIGH
LEVEL BRIDGE

WATERFRONT
SHOPPING CENTER

TURTLE
CREEK

TRIBOROUGH
HWY.

CARNEGIE

MT.
OLIVER

SIDE

SANDCASTLE
WATER PARK

WEST
HOMESTEAD

WEST
MIFFLIN

COCHRAN
RD.

GLENWOOD
BRIDGE

WESTMORELAND

MT.
LEBANON

KENNYWOOD
AMUSEMENT
PARK

COUNTY

CONNOR
RD.

BROUGHTON
RD.

DRAVOSBURG
RD.

DRAVOSBURG

MCKEESPORT

W. 5TH
AVE.

South
Park

CURRY
HOLLOW RD.

Youghiogheny
River

LIBRARY

Allegheny River

Monongahela River

CHURCH RD.

© AVALON TRAVEL PUBLISHING, INC.

Pittsburgh

A CITY OF NEIGHBORHOODS

Pittsburgh's planning department recognizes no fewer than 96 neighborhoods in the city. Many of these small, densely settled enclaves began as tiny self-contained villages and were gradually annexed by the growing city. In post-industrial Pittsburgh, strong ethnic neighborhoods serve as repositories of historical and cultural knowledge for the individuals who live in them. Several generations of one family's births and deaths may be recorded at the same local church. One small shoe store shoeing the feet of a toddler today may also have shod the child's great-grandparents. Though increased mobility has diluted the once self-contained neighborhoods, the people of Pittsburgh still tend to identify strongly with "their" part of town.

Even the most distant neighborhoods aren't more than 45 minutes from the downtown area. Many contain sights, food, accommodations, shopping, activities, and entertainment. Some are strictly residential. None of the neighborhoods are ethnically pure, and all of them contribute to the diversity that is Pittsburgh. Some groups, such as those of Asian or Hispanic origins, maintain ethnically oriented organizations but do not claim a single neighborhood as their own.

Pittsburgh's Five Major Areas

Locals divide Pittsburgh into five general areas, each encompassing several neighborhoods: the Golden Triangle and the Strip, the East Side, the North Side, the South Side, and Greater Pittsburgh (which includes the West Side).

The Golden Triangle is the site of Fort Pitt and the original settlement of **Pittsborough.** It has remained the seat of commerce since the city's inception. **The Strip** is a warehouse and industrial district that has become a favorite shopping area for Pittsburghers.

The **East Side** comprises the most numerous (approximately 30) and diverse group of neighborhoods (and also the majority of Pittsburgh's hospitals and universities). In the 1920s, Eastern European Jews began to settle in Squirrel Hill. Irish immigrants who came to western Pennsylvania during the potato famine of the 1840s orig-

---

most are not crowded at any time of day. Try adapting the One Week in Pittsburgh tour in the Discover chapter. You can select additional or substitute activities from Pennsylvania for Art Lovers and History Highlights (also in the Discover chapter) as well as the following family choices.

Family Fun: Families with children won't want to miss the **Pittsburgh Zoo and Aquarium** (2 hours) and the dinosaurs at **Carnegie Museum of Natural Science** (1–2 hours); **Carnegie Science Center and UMPC Sportsworks, Kennywood,** and **Sandcastle** are all-day destinations. Families with younger children will also want to include **Pittsburgh Children's Museum** (1 hour–all day).

HISTORY

Early History

Though evidence indicates much earlier habitation nearby, the first identifiable residents of the Pittsburgh area appear to have been the Monongahela People, who lived briefly in the Ohio Valley around 1600. By the middle of the 17th century, the Iroquois claimed western Pennsylvania and the Ohio Valley to the south, using the area to expand their hunting territory.

For the first half of the 18th century, the Ohio Valley attracted few Europeans other than trappers, traders, and soldiers. The British and French both attempted to maintain peaceable ties with the neutral Iroquois—mostly to keep their profitable fur-trade routes open—and by the mid-1700s, the French recognized the area as a crucial land and water link between their Canadian empire and the tropical riches of Louisiana to the south. The English saw it as an obvious extension of their territory; the fertile valleys linked to navigable rivers provided an opportunity to increase wealth through trade. The French laid claim to the Ohio Valley just as a group of Virginia settlers coincidentally applied to Britain for land grants

inally settled in the Golden Triangle, then moved eastward to the neighborhoods of Oakland and Highland. Point Breeze, the site of one of Andrew Carnegie's homes (since destroyed), is associated with the Scottish. When German and Italian settlers arrived in Bloomfield, in the mid-1800s, the area was indeed a field of blooms. The same influence is evident also in nearby Lawrenceville, in the European-style homes that form small villages within the neighborhoods. Today, Bloomfield and Lawrenceville are enclaves of second- and third-generation Italians. Polish Hill retains the flavor of its original Eastern European inhabitants.

Farther east, the neighborhood now known as The Hill began as a tiny enclave called Haiti, which grew to encompass Quarry Hill, Arthursville, Lacyville, Minersville, and Springfield. The Hill, East Liberty, and Homewood boast the city's largest African-American population, though immigrants from Wales, Germany, Ireland, England, Greece, Italy, Syria, and Russia have also made homes in those areas.

The **North Side** encompasses roughly 20 neighborhoods. It remains a hub of German culture in the area.

Pittsburgh, particularly in the Troy Hill, Spring Hill, and Spring Garden neighborhoods.

The **South Side**, home to Eastern European immigrants who came to work in the mills in the early 20th century, is today alive with many religious, social, and cultural groups of Ukrainian and Slovak heritage. Of the more than 15 neighborhoods, Duquesne Heights, Mt. Washington, and South Side are the most familiar to visitors.

Greater Pittsburgh officially encompasses the largest physical area, including several outlying independent neighborhoods and West End, an M-shaped, 11-neighborhood strip southwest of Point State Park. West End's Banksville, Chartiers City, Crafton Heights, Windgap, Russka Dolina (Russian Valley), and other neighborhoods in the region once were home to heavy industry and a large Russian population. Today, the area is almost entirely residential. Unofficially, Greater Pittsburgh also refers to the surrounding townships and boroughs within Allegheny County, such as Monroeville, which hosts a large concentration of East Indians.

in the area. The hostilities that erupted, known in America as the French and Indian War (referring to the allegiance of the French with the traditional enemies of the Iroquois, the Huron), reflected those taking place in Europe between the two colonial powers.

Colonial Times

George Washington, a 21-year-old soldier under British command, traveled through the valley in 1753 as an emissary of the governor of Virginia, Robert Dinwiddie. His task was to request that the French leave the area. They politely refused. The British hurriedly built a small encampment on the Point but were unceremoniously ousted in 1754 by French troops, who constructed Fort Duquesne (doo-CAIN) there and held the western territory for three years with little opposition.

When British forces captured French-held Fort Louisburg, however, on the southern entrance to the St. Lawrence River near Quebec, the

war turned against France—in both Europe and Canada. Retreating French troops set Fort Duquesne afire, but the English resettled the site in 1758 and built a fort and blockhouse there, naming the encampment after English prime minister William Pitt, the orator and statesman who had assumed responsibility for the colonial war. In 1763, Britain declared victory in both Europe and the New World.

Hardship was the common lot for those who dwelt in the small settlement. A confederation of Delawares and Senecas laid siege to Fort Pitt for nearly two months. To pacify their former enemies, the British outlawed all settlement west of Allegheny Ridge—including the Fort Pitt area. By 1768, Fort Pitt (since renamed Pittsburgh) was again officially open to European settlement—at the price of five pounds (less than $10) per 100 acres, with a 300-acre limit, payment deferred. The province rapidly sold the land to individuals and groups who were willing to make

Pittsburgh

the arduous journey west. The pioneers were chiefly Scots-Irish who had fled British genocide in the Highlands and had paid their way across the Atlantic with years of indentured servitude. Despite several additional British-Iroquois treaties, squatting settlers often encroached upon off-limits Iroquois land, and disputes between Native Americans and settlers continued.

The Pioneer as City Dweller

Pittsburgh's early settlers proved to be stubborn, tough, and of independent spirit. Their disrespect of Indian rights did not extend to the treatment of black slaves, with whom many identified because of their own history as indentured servants. As early as 1750, both French and British sheltered fugitive slaves, and one of the first free black communities was established in Pittsburgh in the aftermath of British victory over the French.

Many settlers openly opposed British rule. In 1775, a group of Pittsburghers met in Semple's Tavern to support "the spirited behavior of their brethren in New England, and . . . approve of their opposing the invaders of American rights and privileges."

Ohio Valley volunteers joined Washington's army outside of Boston; as the war ended in 1783, Pennsylvania set aside 720,000 acres of "depreciation lands" north of Pittsburgh as compensation to Revolutionary War veterans. By 1786, the settlement had only 100 residents but it had already circulated its first newspaper, the precursor of today's *Post-Gazette.*

Early Commerce

Mining and manufacturing began early in and around Pittsburgh; the first British settlers had been mining coal from the hillsides surrounding the town since the early 1760s. In 1800, Pittsburgh increased its mining operations when precious salt was discovered and extracted from the nearby Connemaugh Valley. By that time, the region was producing oceangoing vessels, loading them with produce, and floating them to New Orleans. Beginning in 1787, it served as a staging point for emigrants to the Midwest and Deep South. The emigrants bought flatboats made in Pittsburgh and stocked them with local produce and goods. The city's three rivers were crowded with the bateaux of traders in the 1760s; keelboats and flatboats dominated until 1800, when steamboats, lumber rafts, and oil barges replaced them.

Water Highways

The rivers provided a convenient thoroughfare for the transport of people and goods, at least when they were navigable; during dry spells, depth dropped to less than one foot on the Ohio River. Rivers provided the only means to move goods in bulk before the construction of the canal systems, in the 1830s, and the railroads, in 1850. The first steamboat, the *New Orleans,* was launched from a Pittsburgh boatyard in 1811. Inland water traffic continued to grow from three million tons annually in 1854 to 12 million in 1915. By the dawn of the 20th century, Pittsburgh could boast that the city was the largest inland port in the United States.

Growth of Industry

The War of 1812 turned the economic basis of Pittsburgh from trade to heavy industry. The manufacture of iron, rope, glass, and ships was made possible by the barge traffic on the three rivers. By 1816, Pittsburgh had a population of 10,000—thriving in spite of multiple floods and cholera epidemics. In 1841, the first wire-rope bridge and the first cable suspension bridge were constructed over the rivers, both built by native Pittsburgher John Roebling (who would later design the Brooklyn Bridge in New York). Those bridges were replaced by the "Three Sisters"—the 6th Street, 7th Street, and 9th Street Bridges—around 1925. Meanwhile, on the banks of the rivers, factories and mills had begun to spring up, spurred on by increasingly efficient manufacturing methods, expansion of the railroads, and continuing migration to the west.

Pittsburgh Goes Polyglot

Immigration spurred the growth of the city as many different races and nationalities streamed into Pittsburgh, lured by plentiful work in factories and mills. Settled immigrants from the British

Isles were joined by eastern Europeans and other western Europeans, all of whom formed their own neighborhoods and organizations. African-Americans—both freemen and slaves—arrived to supply the labor-hungry industries. Multiplicity was the norm in Pittsburgh as the fabric of the Union began to tear at the seams.

Allegheny County had given Abraham Lincoln a plurality of 10,000 votes in the 1860 presidential election—the highest tally of any county in the Union. "Where is this state of Allegheny?" Lincoln inquired, and he journeyed to Pittsburgh to present his thanks in person. By the time the Civil War began, the city's population had risen to 50,000. Pittsburgh supplied the Union army with warships, armor plate, shot, shell, and other war materials, including Rodman and Union cannons. After the war, the golden age of industry transformed the world—and Pittsburgh lay at its center.

The Industrial Revolution

In 1869, Judge Thomas Mellon summed up the booming economic climate this way: "Any man who cannot get rich in Pittsburgh is a fool."

Entrepreneurs and innovators such as George Westinghouse (associated with air brakes for railroad cars, alternating electrical current, and the electric locomotive), Col. Alfred Hunt, Charles Martin Hall, and George Clapp (Alcoa Aluminum), Jones and Laughlin (steel), and Henry Clay Frick (coal and steel) made their fortunes both during and after the Civil War, often building from modest means.

Henry J. Heinz planted a small patch of horseradish on his Sharpsburg farm, starting what would become one of the world's largest processed-food companies—by the end of the century, his modest processing plant grew into a mighty complex on the north side of the Allegheny River. Andrew Carnegie worked his way up from bobbin boy in a cloth mill to become the world's undisputed steel tycoon. Cumberland Willis Posey Sr., the son of a slave, left his family's farm to apprentice as a steamboat operator, invested his money and expertise in the manufacture of coal boats, and, in 1890, started the Diamond Coke and Coal Company, the largest

African-American–owned business in the region. He also created the Homestead Grays, one of the first all-black baseball teams.

Factories and Furnaces

With the development of coke—a charcoal substitute made from an easily transportable, purified form of coal—blast furnaces moved alongside the city's rivers. Charles Dickens, reporting on the scene in *American Notes*, first published in 1842, wrote: "Pittsburg is like Birmingham in England . . . It certainly has a great quantity of smoke hanging about it, and is famous for its ironworks . . ."

The furnaces eventually developed into integrated plants that received raw materials and shipped out I-beams, sheet metal, and rail. The first blast furnace in Pittsburgh was built in 1859; in the next 50 years, furnaces rose on all three rivers. Steam, smoke, and the glow of hot metal fashioned its own grandeur in an era that will never be duplicated. In 1901, Pittsburgh ushered in the age of Big Steel (and subsequently the moniker, "Pittsburgh millionaire") when Andrew Carnegie merged his steel empire with eight other leading firms and sold the package for millions of dollars to a banking conglomerate, which then formed the United States Steel Company, now USX.

Strike!

Labor unrest fermented as the pressure to create riches from human toil escalated, pushing workers beyond their limits. As early as 1848, riots erupted when strikebreakers attempted to cross picket lines at the Penn Cotton factory in Allegheny. In 1850, striking iron puddlers and boilers marched to protest the hiring of strikebreakers by Pittsburgh's burgeoning iron mills.

Industrial moguls who opposed organized labor were quick to retaliate. The railroad riots of 1877, in which conductors and trainmen protested wage reductions, culminated in 25 deaths. In 1892, in support of a union protest over management-proposed changes in wages and work hours, more than 3,000 workers from the Homestead Steel Mill staged a walkout. Five days later, under orders from chief executive Henry Frick, a group of hired gunmen known as the "Pinkerton Army" was brought in. After escalating violence, the National Guard ended the strike—destroying the fledgling Amalgamated Association (largest of the unions) in the process.

Mechanical Wonders

Though the innovative thrust in the latter part of the 19th century was toward big industry and big money, some inventions were purely for delight. In 1893, Pittsburgh native George Ferris put his "big wheel from Pittsburgh" on display at the Columbian Exposition at Chicago's World's Fair. Built as a response to France's Eiffel Tower, the first Ferris wheel carried 38 riders within glass-enclosed carriages. In Pittsburgh, Luna Park—one of many new electric amusement parks—attracted crowds of 25,000 people each night. People came to hear band concerts, see daring aerial acts, and brave shoot-the-shoots, a flume ride that careened through splashing "rapids." The park, built at the end of the trolley line in what is now North Oakland, is long demolished but has been re-created (at a cost of $7 million) as Lost Kennywood at the Kennywood Amusement Park south of Pittsburgh.

The New Century

As it entered the 20th century, Pittsburgh settled in, rich and confident in its wealth and capabilities. Industrial production remained high as the city provided for the military needs of World War I. Along with the products of its foundries, Pittsburgh had sent contingents of young men to fight in every war that touched America; in 1918, the first American soldier to die in battle was a Pittsburgher from the North Side, Thomas Enright.

Pittsburgh continued to attract the attention of the nation. The newly published *Pittsburgh Courier* became the largest-circulation African-American newspaper in the country and used its reach and reputation to crusade against racial discrimination. In 1927, Charles Lindbergh took bows for his history-making flight in Pitt Stadium, and Albert Einstein expounded on his theories regarding the use of the atom before a meeting of 400 top scientists here in 1934.

In World War II, Pittsburgh again boasted record steel production in the wake of Pearl Har-

© JOANNE MILLER

the Golden Triangle's "origami building," Fifth Avenue Place—a sign of Pittsburgh's prosperity

bor, with mills working at full capacity. The city represented—in fact and in legend—the best and worst of humankind's early-20th-century push toward economic growth and technological expansion. In 1941, Pittsburgh had the highest rate of pneumonia of any city in the nation. Soot choked the air—on some days, the streetlights came on at noon. Pittsburgh became known as the "Smoky City," to both its pride and shame. The need for mass production of iron and steel that began during the mid-1800s diminished radically during the latter half of the 20th century.

The First Pittsburgh Renaissance

In 1945, the new mayor, David L. Lawrence (who had run on the campaign slogan "Smoke Must Go"), built an alliance with powerful businessmen such as Richard King Mellon. Industry responded to the tough new standards: railroad and shipping interests converted locomotives and tugs from coal-fired to diesel engines; steel and coal industries joined with local universities to develop new coal-burning technologies and methods for recovering smoke and airborne pollutants. Homeowners also adapted, trading coal furnaces for oil, electric, and gas. An urban revitalization effort, copied the world over, rebuilt and renewed the former "hell with the lid off."

PITTSBURGH TODAY

Brownfield Site Development

Pittsburgh's economy continues the process of diversification begun in the late 1940s with the decline of heavy manufacturing; the first renaissance has been followed by several more. Endowed with more urban riverfront (70 miles) than any other inland port city in America, Pittsburgh offers plenty of raw material to work with. The Environmental Protection Agency has picked up the tab for assessing the regeneration of up to 12 "brownfield sites" (abandoned industrial areas), making it easier to develop old mill sites such as those in Duquesne and McKeesport and the Park property in Homestead. The former USX Homestead Works steel mill alone provided 400 acres of developable property along the Monongahela River, the largest section of riverfront in Allegheny County. Redevelopment has proven economically successful—Station Square, a collection of shops, restaurants, offices, and hotel and meeting space that occupies 52 acres along the Monongahela on the South Side site of a former Pittsburgh & Lake Erie Railroad freight yard, attracts millions of visitors annually.

Technology and Business

Pittsburgh's advanced-technology industries involve more than 800 firms and 80,000 employees. All contributed to the city's becoming one of the largest research and development centers in the country at the turn of the 21st century. Major research centers include Carnegie Mellon University's Software Engineering Institute and Robotics Institute; the University of Pittsburgh's Center for Hazardous Materials Research and Center for Biotechnology and Bioengineering; and the universities' jointly owned Supercomputing Center. The city is home to more than 170 academic, industrial, and governmental research laboratories and boasts more doctoral scientists and engineers per capita than Boston or Los Angeles.

More than 220 foreign companies, representing eastern and western Europe, Japan, the Pacific Rim, and other nations, have established operations in the region. Nearly half of these have located their U.S. or world headquarters in the city. One of the nation's leading sites for corporate headquarters, Pittsburgh is home to seven Fortune 500 companies: Alcoa; Westinghouse; H. J. Heinz; PPG Industries; Miles; USX; and Allegheny Ludlum.

Modern Pittsburgh combines the best of its wealthy industrial past with small-town warmth and sophisticated urban pleasures. For good reason, it has repeatedly been named one of the 10 most livable cities in America by Rand McNally's *Places Rated Almanac*.

A PENNSYLVANIA CHILDHOOD

Pulitzer Prize-winning author Annie Dillard grew up in Pittsburgh in the 1950s. She describes the city poetically in her autobiography, *An American Childhood:*

The three wide rivers divide and cool the mountains. Calm old bridges span the banks and link the hills. The Allegheny River flows in brawling from the north, from near the shore of Lake Erie, and from Lake Chautauqua in New York and eastward. The Monongahela River flows in shallow and slow from the south, from West Virginia. The Allegheny and the Monongahela meet and form the westward-wending Ohio. . . . The tall buildings rise lighted to their tips. Their lights illumine other buildings' clean sides, and illumine the narrow city canyons below, where people move, and shine reflected red and white at night from the black waters.

Pittsburgh

The Golden Triangle/The Strip

Stretching from I-579 west to the fountain that billows from the tip of Point State Park, the Golden Triangle is home to a number of American industry's giants. Eight of the world's largest corporations and three of the nation's largest banks have headquarters in this 11- by 11-block area. Architecture downtown is an eclectic mix of styles and periods, varying from narrow preindustrial wooden two- and three-story buildings to gleaming ultramodern designs. Each block has its own character: shabby storefronts displaying Grateful Dead T-shirts open up into multimillion-dollar expanses of glass and steel.

The Strip, a jumble of warehouses and eateries, juts to the north of the Golden Triangle. Manufacturers' outlets, used furniture stores, greengrocers, and shops selling imported products vie with street entertainers and market carts for shoppers' dollars. The Strip is also the site of the sweeping, modern David L. Lawrence Convention Center, across from the 9th Street bridge, chief among several "green-designed" (environmentally low-impact, energy-efficient) buildings in the city.

SIGHTS

Point State Park

The Point—the confluence of the Monongahela and Allegheny Rivers—has been deemed a national historical landmark (888/727-2757, www.dcnr.state.pa.us, daily dusk to dawn, free). The "Mon," as it's referred to locally, is a mudbedded river, while the Allegheny flows over limestone. The two converge at the Point but remain separate ribbons of color as they flow west, creating the Ohio River. The new stadium, the Carnegie Science Center dome, and an old limestone flood wall on the North Side can be seen from the Point and reached by a walkway over the Allegheny River. The Duquesne Incline lies across the river to the south, and a panoramic view of Pittsburgh's skyline rises to the east. The fountain at the end of the Point sends up a dramatic 30-foot-tall plume of water surrounded by 15-foot spray fans; it is active throughout most of the year (closed mid-Dec.–Easter, depending on the weather). Speedboats and water-

Point State Park and its dramatic fountain

Pittsburgh

skiers whiz past in summer, and multicolored leaves carpet the ground in the fall. The Point is a hangout for kids after school as well as for lots of families and older folks. The park is free to the public. However, it's a good idea to take public transportation or walk; parking in the commercial lots in the area is prohibitively expensive—$3 per half hour and up.

Fort Pitt Museum (412/281-9284, Tues.–Sat. 9 A.M.–5 P.M., Sun. noon–5 P.M., closed Mon., $5, free for those under 12) and the **Blockhouse**, within Point State Park at the tip of the Golden Triangle, provide a pleasant afternoon's diversion. The original Fort Pitt was a five-sided structure that measured a half-mile in perimeter, with a bastion at each corner. Two of the walls were built of masonry, the others of rammed earth; the Monongahela bastion has been rebuilt in masonry on its original site to house the Fort Pitt Museum. The Blockhouse, a square brick dwelling, was built by Henry Bouquet in 1764. There is no charge to view the exterior of the Blockhouse—entrance is prohibited.

Market Square

In the downtown area on Market Street between 4th and 5th Avenues, Market Square was literally the center of Pittsburgh in 1784. Today, it's a gathering place for people-watchers and a refreshing place to stop downtown; elders sit holding court like pashas on green park benches, while suited office workers speed by. The square is surrounded by shops and restaurants of varying interest. Chic cafés mix with five-and-dime stores and an occasionally empty storefront.

A few of the Golden Triangle's architectural marvels are close to Market Square. **PPG Place,** home of the largest producer of plate glass in the world, signs the skyline with a part-Camelot, part-ice-crystal fantasy glass tower. The building is glazed with nearly 20,000 pieces of reflective glass that capture the sunset on clear nights, turning the skyscraper into a pillar of fire visible for miles. The **Steelworkers of America Building** is cloaked in a gleaming grid of X's. **Fifth Avenue Place,** a compendium of granite and glass that one wag described as "architectural origami," houses shops and office space. The

Westinghouse Building, center of an empire founded in 1886 by George Westinghouse, sits among its own landscaped gardens near Gateway Center.

◪ The Strip

For a funky and unforgettable shopping experience, join the locals for a Saturday tour of the Strip (open daily except Sunday), just northeast of the Golden Triangle between Penn Avenue and Smallman Street and 12th and 21st Streets. It has become a Pittsburgh tradition to shop one's favorite greengrocer, fishmonger, butcher, and flower wholesaler on Saturday morning. This blocks-long combination of wholesalers and flea marketeers sells everything under the sun; street vendors display clothing from Bali, black-and-white photographs of blues legends, jewelry, and compact discs. Furniture warehouses are jammed chockablock with crafts stores. The aroma of international foods cooked in tiny booths (Thai barbecue on a stick, anyone?) competes with the mouthwatering scent of homemade baked goods. In front of the **Sunseri** bakery and produce store ("If it's Italian, it's at Sunseri's!"), an accordionist holds forth with her version of "Volare." Every ethnic group in Pittsburgh is represented in the shops and on the street. Don't miss this street party/shopping experience.

TRIANGLE HISTORY WALK
Fire and a Flood of Money

Downtown Pittsburgh is a cornucopia for those who are interested in architectural styles of the period 1850–1920. Though all of the Golden Triangle was residential until the late 1800s, post–Civil War urban and industrial growth transformed the area into a central business district. Remnants of the original residential character of the center of downtown can be found in the few small dwellings and churches that remain in the Golden Triangle. When fire destroyed most of the city, in 1845, rebuilding coincided with the growth of the personal fortunes of Andrew Carnegie; his business associates Henry Clay Frick, Henry Oliver, and Henry Phipps; and George Westinghouse, H. J. Heinz, and the Mellons. One of the primary forms of "keeping up with the Joneses" among the new millionaires was to finance bigger and better architecture. The result is a fascinating mishmash of styles produced by the most popular architects and craftsmen of the time.

Frick built four skyscrapers on Grant Street, intending to block the sunlight from Carnegie's headquarters (since replaced). Henry Oliver put some of his riches into a series of buildings in the area bounded by Grant Street, 6th Avenue, and Oliver Avenue. Henry Phipps claimed the area near the Allegheny River and 6th Street and there built five multistory edifices, including the Fulton Building. The Mellons, the banking family that owned more of the Golden Triangle than any of the industrial barons, followed with a half-dozen skyscrapers, including the Gulf Building, at 7th Avenue and Grant, and the Koppers Building. Some of these buildings remain. As industry became dominated by corporations after the 1920s, the newer office buildings became their memorials. A few of the notable buildings, within easy walking distance from each other, are detailed in this section. More information is available from the Pittsburgh Historic Review Commission (see Sightseeing Tours under Services in the Information and Services section of this chapter).

Richardson's Legacy

The Golden Triangle includes the foremost concentration of prominent commercial and institutional buildings from the heyday of Pittsburgh architecture, showcasing the work of some of the best architects in the United States at the time. In 1985, this area was listed in the National Register of Historic Places. The **Allegheny County Courthouse,** at the corner of 5th Avenue and Grant Street, was built by Henry Hobson Richardson in 1888. It was, by his own admission, his masterpiece. The style, with its massive granite blocks, arches, and turrets, has come to be known as "Richardsonian Romanesque." Whether court is in session or not, visitors can view room 321 through the glass windows in the door; it has been restored to its original form. The design, like that of many buildings of this period, relies

THE GOLDEN TRIANGLE/
THE STRIP

To North Side

Allegheny
River

FORT DUQUESNE
BRIDGE

COMMONWEALTH PLACE

Point
State
FORT PITT MUSEUM
AND BLOCKHOUSE ★
Park

HILTON

FORT PITT BLVD.
FORT PITT
BRIDGE
WESTINGHOUSE
BUILDINGS

Monongahela

Pittsburgh

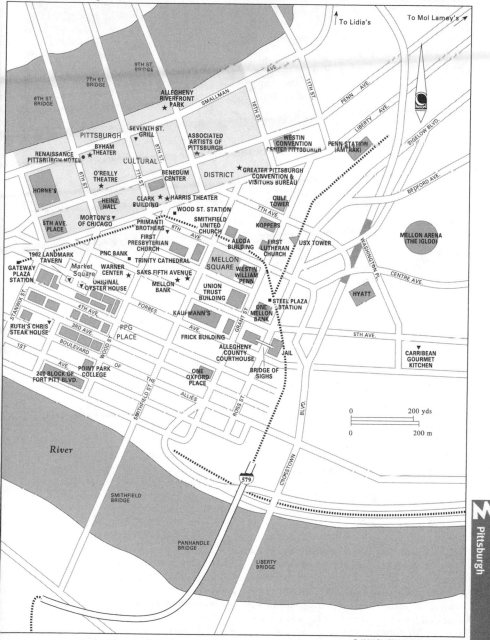

To Lidia's

To Mol Lamey's

9TH ST. BRIDGE

7TH ST. BRIDGE

6TH ST. BRIDGE

SMALLMAN

AVE.

11TH ST.

10TH ST.

PENN AVE.

LIBERTY AVE.

BIGELOW BLVD.

ALLEGHENY RIVERFRONT PARK ★

PITTSBURGH

SEVENTH ST. GRILL ▼

RENAISSANCE PITTSBURGH HOTEL ●

BYHAM ★ THEATER

CULTURAL

O'REILLY THEATRE ★

HORNE'S

HEINZ HALL

5TH AVE. PLACE

MORTON'S ▼ OF CHICAGO

1902 LANDMARK TAVERN

GATEWAY PLAZA STATION

STANWIX ST.

RUTH'S CHRIS STEAK HOUSE

1ST

AVE.

200 BLOCK OF FORT PITT BLVD.

River

6TH ST.

7TH ST.

8TH ST.

ASSOCIATED ARTISTS OF PITTSBURGH

BENEDUM CENTER

DISTRICT

CLARK ★ BUILDING

HARRIS THEATER ★

WOOD ST. STATION

PRIMANTI BROTHERS ▼

FIRST PRESBYTERIAN CHURCH

PNC BANK ■

Market Square

WARNER ★ CENTER

ORIGINAL ▼ OYSTER HOUSE

4TH AVE.

3RD AVE.

BOULEVARD

AVE.

POINT PARK COLLEGE

SMITHFIELD ST.

THE

ALLIES

FORBES

SAKS FIFTH AVENUE ★

MELLON BANK

TRINITY CATHEDRAL ★

SMITHFIELD UNITED CHURCH

KOPPERS

ALCOA BUILDING

MELLON SQUARE

WESTIN WILLIAM PENN

UNION TRUST BUILDING

KAUFMANN'S

PPG PLACE

FRICK BUILDING

ONE OXFORD PLACE

WOOD ST.

GRANT ST.

ROSS ST.

6TH AVE.

7TH AVE.

AVE.

ONE MELLON BANK

STEEL PLAZA STATION

ALLEGHENY COUNTY COURTHOUSE

JAIL

BRIDGE OF SIGHS

WESTIN CONVENTION CENTER PITTSBURGH

GREATER PITTSBURGH CONVENTION & VISITORS BUREAU ★

GULF TOWER

FIRST LUTHERAN CHURCH

USX TOWER

PENN STATION (AMTRAK)

BEDFORD AVE.

WASHINGTON PL.

CENTRE AVE.

MELLON ARENA (THE IGLOO)

HYATT

5TH AVE.

CARRIBEAN GOURMET KITCHEN ▼

CROSSTOWN

BLVD.

579

0   200 yds

0   200 m

SMITHFIELD BRIDGE

PANHANDLE BRIDGE

LIBERTY BRIDGE

Pittsburgh

© JOANNE MILLER

one of Pittsburgh's many lions

heavily on ambient light and is built around a spacious courtyard (this one contains a 10-foot circular fountain). Unfortunately, the building's entrance was moved to the basement some years ago and now gives the visitor the initial impression of being in a series of catacombs rather than a soaring cathedral. Next to the courthouse, connected by the **Bridge of Sighs** (a knockoff of the Venetian original), Richardson's stone jail stands dark and impenetrable.

Grant Street

In contrast, the **Frick Building,** across Grant Street from the courthouse, is a cool and elegant structure in the beaux arts style. The black-and-white marble ceiling and intricate grillwork create a bright and welcoming entrance. The wood-and-glass phone booths in the back lobby add a bit of the glamour of a more refined time. At the rear of the lobby is a bust of Henry Frick, whose fortune powered many Pittsburgh innovations.

The **Union Trust Building** (2 Mellon Bank Center, on Grant Street between Oliver and 5th Avenues) features a rotunda lit by tiers of lights that rise 10 stories to an intricate stained-glass dome. Completed in 1917, this commercial

building was finished with gothic details. The **Westin William Penn Hotel** next door was conceived by Henry Frick to rival the great hotels of New York; it was completed in 1916 (the Grant Street entrance is part of a later addition).

Directly across Grant Street from the Union Trust Building is the new **1 Mellon Bank Center,** designed to echo the stonework of the courthouse, the windows of the Frick Building, and the steeply pitched roofline of the Union Trust Building. Across Grant stands the tallest building between New York and Chicago, the 841-foot-tall **USX Building,** corporate headquarters of US Steel. A corporate and civic symbol, the building is constructed from specially made CORTEN steel to respond favorably to outside temperatures—the 10 triangular exposed support columns are filled with water and antifreeze.

The **First Lutheran Church,** between 6th and 7th Avenues on Grant, is the sole reminder that Grant Street was once residential. On the south corner of 7th Avenue and Grant, the copper-crowned **Koppers Building** is one of the best examples of art deco in Pittsburgh. The north side of the street is anchored by the 44-story former headquarters of the Gulf Oil Company.

WITH AN "H"?

Pittsburghers and their correspondents endured more than a century of confusion over the proper spelling of the city's name. After the French deserted and burned Fort Duquesne, during the French and Indian War, British Brigadier Gen. John Forbes entered the ruins on November 27, 1758, and renamed the area "Pittsborough," in honor of British leader William Pitt. The star-shaped military installation built on the site was dubbed Fort Pitt. No town existed outside the fortification.

As the settlement grew, so did variations on its spelling. The original name on the 1816 city charter was Pittsburg, a spelling that can be found on the rotunda of Pennsylvania Station, at the intersection of Liberty Avenue and Grant Street in the Golden Triangle. Most Pittsburghers continued to add the final "h" anyway. The U.S. Geographic Board of Names complicated matters further when it copied the name from the original charter in its 1894 list of postal addresses. Confusion over the correct spelling of the name reigned until 1911. At that time, U.S. Senator George T. Oliver, publisher of the *Gazette-Times* and *Chronicle-Telegraph* newspapers, intervened at the Board of Names and corrected the problem once and for all. It is officially Pittsburgh with an "h," thank you.

Mellon Square

Behind the Harvard-Yale-Princeton Club on William Penn Place stand a number of small survivors from the Civil War era—the tiny brick, wood, and plaster houses of **Strawberry Way.** The **Alcoa Building,** on 6th and William Penn, is a 30-story skyscraper that was designed as a showpiece for the use of aluminum as a building material. On Smithfield Street, between 6th and 7th Avenues, stands the **Smithfield United Church**—one of three churches that remain on land originally granted by the sons of William Penn in 1781. (The other two churches are both on Oliver Avenue between Smithfield and Wood Streets: **The First Presbyterian Church,** which features a number of Tiffany windows, and **Trinity Cathedral.**)

Mellon Square Park, on William Penn Place between 6th and Oliver Avenues, was donated to the city in 1950 as part of the Pittsburgh Renaissance, intended to provide much-needed open space in the dense downtown. Looking west, one is able to see a 50-foot-high mural honoring Pittsburgh's beloved baseball team, the Pirates. The original entrance to the William Penn Hotel is across from Mellon Park.

Old Water Street

From the beginning, Pittsburgh's ability to move goods and people to points south and west via water made it a strategic destination and launching point. Fort Pitt Boulevard, along the Monongahela River on the southern side of the Golden Triangle, was called Water Street for most of its history. Warehouses and commercial enterprises lined the street, and the (now long-defunct) Monongahela Wharf carried goods from doorway to water. The 200 block of Fort Pitt Boulevard is a well-preserved fragment of the commercial architecture that served river commerce; it remains the best reminder of the role the rivers played in the early history of Pittsburgh. The three- to five-story brick buildings that make up most of the block are typical of the kinds of warehouses built from Market Street to Grant Street after the Great Fire of 1845. To traverse the block from east to west is to step back in time.

The small, three-story structure at 211 Fort Pitt Blvd. is the oldest building on the block, constructed shortly after the fire; the buildings from 213 to 233 were built just after the Civil War and are characterized by the use of Italianate cast-iron storefront and window ornamental elements—a fast, cheap method of construction during that time.

The Queen Anne–style buildings between 235 and 247 reflect prevailing architectural tastes at the turn of the 20th century.

The **Conestoga Building,** the seven-story structure built by financier Jacob Vandergrift, was constructed in the popular Richardsonian

Romanesque style in 1892 by students of Richardson who had worked on the county courthouse. In the original plan for Pittsburgh, laid out by George Woods in 1784, Market Square—a few blocks north via Market Street—was set aside as an open space and public market. It quickly became the commercial center of the city, and Market Street became the principal business street.

The Civil War–era commercial buildings and warehouses between 1st Avenue and Boulevard of the Allies retain the scale and character of that time. One-half block west, the little house at 117 1st Ave., built just after the Great Fire, is one of a handful of early residential structures that have survived as a reminder that, at one time, the Golden Triangle was a village.

GOLDEN TRIANGLE MUSEUMS AND GALLERIES

Ⓜ Senator John Heinz Pittsburgh Regional History Center

This fascinating collection (1212 Smallman St., between 12th and 13th Sts. in the Strip, 412/454-6000, www.pghhistory.org, 10 A.M.–

5 P.M. daily, $6 for adults, $4.50 students and seniors, $3 children 6–18) is housed in the former Chautauqua Lake Ice Company warehouse, originally built in 1899. The center opened in 1996; inside is a 160,000-square-foot museum and research facility devoted to the rich history of the Western Pennsylvania region. The building houses 40,000 square feet of gallery space containing changing exhibits on local history; a world-class research center library and archives; a 300-seat theater; classroom spaces for educational programming; and a Discovery Hall for children. Past exhibits include *Rediscovering Lewis and Clark,* in association with the Smithsonian Institution in Washington, D.C., *Pittsburgh Rhythms,* an interactive exhibit chronicling local musical traditions from Stephen Foster to contemporary jazz, and *George Washington in Western Pennsylvania,* about the first president's wild youth in the Ohio Valley. One favorite is the Heinz exhibit, which chronicles the growth of the famous brand and includes a 1950s kitchen and an array of pickle pins. The vehicles in the Great Hall—a 1949 trolley, Conestoga wagon from pioneer days, and 1967 Westinghouse Markette Electric Car among them—are also fa-

skyline from the green-powered Lawrence Convention Center

vorites. Discounted parking is available at the 11th and Smallman parking garage; it's $3 with museum validation.

Art Galleries
The **Society for Contemporary Craft** is in the heart of the Strip, just north of the Golden Triangle (2100 Smallman St., 412/261-7003, www.contemporarycraft.org; open Tues.–Sat. 9 A.M.–5 P.M., free). The craft displays are innovative and often whimsical; a small café serves snacks. The Society has been here since 1986; it's one of the nation's oldest retailers of handmade contemporary crafts. The original store opened in Verona, northeast of Pittsburgh, in 1971. Paper-and-wire lamps, handbags made from tires, and birdhouses crafted from automobile license plates are a few of the creative wares on offer. The society has added a children's studio and expanded the galleries to include more works in wood, metal, fiber, glass, and found objects.

The Pittsburgh Cultural Trust hosts exhibits from all over the world at the **Wood Street Galleries** (601 Wood St., 412/471-5605, Tues.–Wed. 11 A.M.–6 P.M., Thurs.–Sat. 11 A.M.–7 P.M., free). The gallery is home to 11 small arts organizations and offers art talks to the public. The galleries may be a little hard to find—the address is a "T" station, and one of the two elevators goes up to the galleries (the other goes down to the station). It's well worth it, however, since the exhibits are small but interesting; a recent one featured LED lights as the primary material.

Another gallery of interest in the Strip is **Garfield Artworks** (4931 Penn Ave., 412/361-2262, www.garfieldartworks.com, by appointment), established in 1993. It features contemporary works by local artists.

East Side/Oakland

The neighborhoods east of the Golden Triangle open out like an elegant lady's fan. Many are strictly residential, but a few are of special interest.

Oakland not only packs the internationally flavored amenities of a small college town into a few square blocks, it also offers the attractions of the Carnegie Institutes and Museums and the Phipps Conservatory. Cafés and inexpensive restaurants vie for space with theaters playing black-and-white movies and with shops full of exotic goods. Carnegie and the Pittsburgh Millionaires continued their architectural rivalry here; Carnegie built his institutes, but Frick sold the 14 acres that he owned across the street to the Mellons, who developed the University of Pittsburgh on the site. Frick built his sumptuous Victorian home a few miles away, and Phipps created his glass botanical garden house in Schenley Park.

Shadyside, one of the most popular and well-known neighborhoods in Pittsburgh, is a walkers' and shoppers' paradise, an upscale village with outstanding accommodations and a variety of eateries. True to its name, Shadyside's streets are lined with massive oaks and maples. **Squirrel Hill,** with its kosher markets, Hasidic shoppers,

and unobtrusive delis, could have been plucked out of New York City. And **Bloomfield,** the quiet Italian/Polish/Catholic neighborhood set on a high plateau overlooking the Strip, is home to classic restaurants and food shops.

SIGHTS

◪ Cathedral of Learning/ Nationality Classrooms
The Cathedral of Learning (5th Ave. and Bigelow Blvd., within the University of Pittsburgh campus in Oakland, general information www.pitt.edu) is a 42-story Indiana-limestone gothic tower massed above a city-block-sized Commons Room. In 1925, Chancellor John Bowman envisioned a building that would "[embody] the spiritual, driving and courageous stuff that makes Pittsburgh . . . [a] meeting of the modern skyscraper and medieval cathedral." Seventeen thousand men and women, nearly 100,000 schoolchildren, along with corporations and industries, joined in the campaign to raise $10 million to build Bowman's dream. The Commons Room, 100 feet wide by 200 feet

Pittsburgh

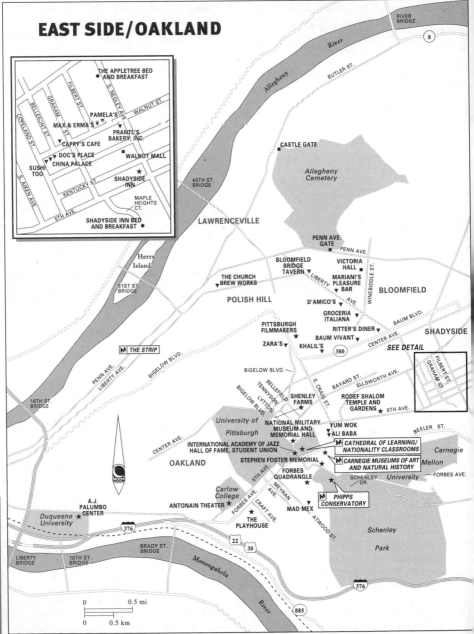

EAST SIDE/OAKLAND

THE APPLETREE BED AND BREAKFAST

PAMELA'S

MAX & ERMA'S

CAPPY'S CAFE

PRANTL'S BAKERY, INC.

DOC'S PLACE

CHINA PALACE

WALNUT MALL

SUSHI TOO

SHADYSIDE INN

MAPLE HEIGHTS CT.

SHADYSIDE INN BED AND BREAKFAST

S. NEGLEY AVE.
WALNUT ST.
FILBERT ST.
GRAHAM ST.
BELLEFONT ST.
COPELAND ST.
S. AIKEN AVE.
KENTUCKY ST.
5TH AVE.

CASTLE GATE

Allegheny Cemetery

RIVER BRIDGE

8

Allegheny River

BUTLER ST.

40TH ST. BRIDGE

LAWRENCEVILLE

PENN AVE. GATE

PENN AVE.

VICTORIA HALL

BLOOMFIELD BRIDGE TAVERN

MARIANI'S PLEASURE BAR

WINEBIDDLE ST.

BLOOMFIELD

Herrs Island

31ST ST. BRIDGE

THE CHURCH BREW WORKS

POLISH HILL

LIBERTY AVE.

D'AMICO'S

GROCERIA ITALIANA

RITTER'S DINER

BAUM BLVD.

SHADYSIDE

PITTSBURGH FILMMAKERS

BAUM VIVANT

ZARA'S

KHALIL'S

380

CENTER AVE.

SEE DETAIL

M THE STRIP

BIGELOW BLVD.

PENN AVE.
LIBERTY AVE.

BIGELOW BLVD.

BELLEFIELD
TENNYSON
LYTTON

S. CRAIG ST.

BAYARD ST.

ELLSWORTH AVE.

FILBERT ST.
GRAHAM ST.

16TH ST. BRIDGE

SHENLEY FARMS

RODEF SHALOM TEMPLE AND GARDENS

5TH AVE.

University of Pittsburgh

NATIONAL MILITARY MUSEUM AND MEMORIAL HALL

YUM WOK

ALI BABA

BEELER ST.

CENTER AVE.

INTERNATIONAL ACADEMY OF JAZZ HALL OF FAME, STUDENT UNION

M CATHEDRAL OF LEARNING/ NATIONALITY CLASSROOMS

Carnegie

OAKLAND

STEPHEN FOSTER MEMORIAL

M CARNEGIE MUSEUMS OF ART AND NATURAL HISTORY

Mellon

FORBES QUADRANGLE

MEYRAN AVE.

SCHENLEY DR.

University

FORBES AVE.

A.J. PALUMBO CENTER

Carlow College

ANTONAIN THEATER

5TH AVE.

FORBES AVE.

CRAFT AVE.

MAD MEX

M PHIPPS CONSERVATORY

Schenley

Duquesne University

376

BRADY ST. BRIDGE

22

30

THE PLAYHOUSE

ATWOOD ST.

Park

LIBERTY BRIDGE

10TH ST. BRIDGE

Monongahela River

376

885

0   0.5 mi

0   0.5 km

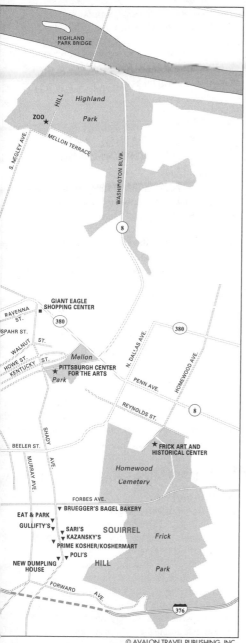

HIGHLAND
PARK BRIDGE

HILL

Highland

ZOO

Park

MELLON TERRACE

S. NEGLEY AVE.

WASHINGTON BLVD.

8

GIANT EAGLE
SHOPPING CENTER

RAVENNA
ST.

380

SPAHR ST.

WALNUT
ST.

380

N. DALLAS AVE.

HOWE ST.

ST.

KENTUCKY

Mellon

PITTSBURGH CENTER
FOR THE ARTS
Park

PENN AVE.

HOMEWOOD AVE.

REYNOLDS ST.

8

SHADY

BEELER ST.

AVE.

FRICK ART AND
HISTORICAL CENTER

MURRAY AVE.

Homewood

Cemetery

FORBES AVE.

BRUEGGER'S BAGEL BAKERY

EAT & PARK
GULLIFTY'S

SARI'S

SQUIRREL

KAZANSKY'S

Frick

PRIME KOSHER/KOSHERMART

NEW DUMPLING
HOUSE

POLI'S

HILL

Park

FORWARD
AVE.

376

long, is floored with one-half acre of green Vermont slate.

Around the perimeter on the first floor and in some spaces of the third floor, 23 of the classrooms have been designed to reflect the many ethnic groups that have contributed to the heritage of Pittsburgh. A visit to these Nationality Classrooms (reservations for tours must be made at least two weeks in advance; call or write Visitor Information, 157 CL, University of Pittsburgh, Pittsburgh, PA 15260, 412/624-6150, www.pitt.edu) is spent in a globally based time warp, ping ponging the viewer from Greece in the 5th century B.C. to 16th century Poland. Most of the rooms may be viewed free without a guide during open hours: Mon.–Fri. 9 A.M.–3 P.M., Sat. 9:30 A.M.–3 P.M., and Sun. and holidays 11 A.M.–3 P.M. Ninety-minute tours led by well-informed students, and self-guided tape-recorded tours, are available every day except Thanksgiving; Dec. 24, 25, and 31; and Jan. 1. The charge for tours: $3. Each room contains original and re-created furnishings and depicts a period within the country's history—the Israeli Room reflects a 1st-century classroom carved from stone, while the Chinese Room is inspired by study rooms in the Forbidden City of the 18th century. Detailing is exquisite; fine woodwork, stonework, stained glass, and ironwork contribute to the accurate re-creation of place and period, right down to the light switches. The rooms often contain artifacts and information about heroes and scholars of the subject country.

The creation of classrooms is ongoing, and each year new ethnic styles and periods are unveiled. Directions and information are available at the Visitor Information Room and Gift Center near the 5th Avenue entrance inside the building.

Other University of Pittsburgh Sights

Next to the Cathedral of Learning at the University of Pittsburgh, the **Heinz Memorial Chapel** (412/624-4157, www.pitt.edu) was built in the French gothic style in 1938 by members of the Heinz family in memory of Henry John Heinz (founder of the Heinz empire) and his mother,

Pittsburgh

Anna Margaretta. The chapel is free and open to the public for viewing Mon.–Fri. 9 A.M.–4 P.M. (minus time for a noon Mass each day). The chapel is also open to visitors Sun. 1–5 P.M. (Catholic and Lutheran services are held during the day, and all are welcome). Guided tours are available; call for information and reservations. The 73-foot-tall transept windows, designed in stained glass by master craftsman Charles Connick, are among the tallest in the world.

Nearby on campus is the **Frick Fine Arts building,** built by Helen Clay Frick in memory of her father. It features a cloistered garden, an art gallery, and a fine arts reference library. Free exhibits are open Tues.–Sat. 10 A.M.–4 P.M. and Sun. 2–5 P.M.

The university also preserves jazz history at the **International Academy of Jazz Hall of Fame** (412/624-4187—jazz department), which displays memorabilia and artifacts in the student union.

National Military Museum and Memorial Hall (4141 5th Ave. and Bigelow Blvd., 412/621-4253, Tues.–Sat. 10 A.M.–4 P.M., closed Labor Day, Thanksgiving, Christmas, and New Year's Day; $4 adults, $3 seniors and veterans, free under 10), built in 1910, was modeled after one of the seven wonders of the ancient world—the Mausoleum of Halicarnassus. The museum displays Civil War relics and memorabilia, including cannons, rifles, photos, and sculpture; there is also a library and auditorium. Scenes from the film *Silence of the Lambs* were filmed inside this classic building.

Sports fans won't want to miss **Wesley Posvar Hall,** largest building on campus and site of former Forbes Field and many historic baseball events. Home plate (site of Babe Ruth's final homer) is preserved under glass on the first floor.

The **Stephen Foster Memorial** (4301 Forbes Ave., 412/624-4100) is also on the university campus, next to the Cathedral of Learning. The auditorium, museum, and research library contain more than 30,000 items pertaining to the Pittsburgh-born composer; the museum commemorates the contribution of music to American life. The collection also reflects a broad cross-section of American popular culture, especially from the 1850s to the 1930s. Foster's grave is in the Allegheny Cemetery (see Parks and Scenic Spots). The library and museum are open Mon.–Fri. 9 A.M.–4 P.M. Entrance to the museum is free; guided tours are available for a fee. Call to make reservations. The museum is closed on university holidays.

CARNEGIE MUSEUMS OF ART AND NATURAL HISTORY

The Carnegie Museums, at three separate locations in Pittsburgh, are composed of the **Museums of Art and Natural History** (4400 Forbes Ave. in the East Side, 412/622-3131, www.cmoa.org), encompassing the Hall of Sculpture, Hall of Architecture, Heinz Architectural Center, the Library of Pittsburgh, and Music Hall for the Performing Arts; the **Science Center** (1 Allegheny Ave., 412/237-3400, www.carnegiesciencecenter.org—see under North Side), encompassing Buhl Planetarium, Rangos Omnimax theater, and SportsWorks; and the **Andy Warhol Museum** (117 Sandusky St., 412/237-8300, www.warhol.org—see under North Side). The Museum of Art, Hall of Sculpture, Hall of Architecture, Museum of Natural History, and Heinz Architectural Center share the same hours: Tues.–Sat. 10 A.M.–5 P.M., Sun. noon–5 P.M.; closed Mon. and holidays. All have separate entrances, but one admission ($8 adults, $5 children 3–18, seniors and students) covers entrance to all. The Music Hall is open for events only; admission varies.

Museum of Art

A brilliantly lit suite of galleries (4400 Forbes Ave., 412/622-3131, www.cmoa.org) is home to a collection varying from ancient Egyptian sculpture and fragments to modern art by Andy Warhol, Roy Lichtenstein, and Alexander Calder. Andrew Carnegie envisioned a museum collection consisting of "the Old Masters of tomorrow" as well as then-popular classical paintings. The rooms are laid out according to the period of artistic style and feature sculpture and furniture as well as paintings and drawings.

Edward Hicks's famous painting *The Peaceable Kingdom* hangs here. One of many versions of the same subject, it was originally painted to address controversies within Quakerism, chiefly the acceptance and equal treatment of heathens by Quakers. Some Quakers believed that freedom of religion referred only to variations within Christianity. In the background, William Penn is shown signing a treaty with representatives from the Delaware tribe. Hicks believed that the peaceful coexistence of the Indians and the Quaker founders of Pennsylvania fulfilled the biblical prophecy of Isaiah: ". . . and the leopard shall lie down with the kid." Works by Frans Hals, Peter Paul Rubens, Maurice Prendergast, and Robert Henri are also part of the permanent collection. The art museum is also home to the biggest contemporary worldwide art exhibition in the United States, The International, which is one of the two oldest in the world—the Venice Biennale began one year earlier, in 1895. A three-story plate-glass-and-granite walkway connects the art museum to other attractions in the complex.

Halls of Sculpture and Architecture

These halls lie off an open three-story gallery adorned with John White Alexander's *The Crowning of Labor,* painted between 1905 and 1908 and restored in 1994. Behind the gallery is the Hall of Sculpture, crafted of Pentelic marble from the Greek quarries that supplied the builders of the Parthenon. Adorned with casts from the classical era, the two-story columned hall replicates the interior of the Temple of Athena on the Acropolis in Athens. Next door, the Hall of Architecture is filled with plaster reproductions of some of the best examples of classical, medieval, and Renaissance architectural details. Today, the museum's collection of plaster casts is unrivaled in the United States, and one of only a few remaining in the world. Of particular interest is the largest cast ever made, the facade of the 12th-century French Abbey Church of St.-Gilles-du-Gard.

Museum of Natural History

This museum opens on a center gallery and relies heavily on filtered natural light for part of its architectural charm. Exhibits change periodically, but the bulk of the museum is made up of dioramas featuring thousands of taxidermy specimens, some of which were collected by Andrew Carnegie himself. Outside the African Hall on the second floor is a stunning diorama, *Arab Courier Attacked by Lions,* re-creating a dramatic and fierce battle between two now-extinct Barbary lions and a man mounted on a camel (final score: courier 1, lions 2). The ornithology wing is a bird lover's dream; the Hillman Hall of Minerals and Gems display offers both scientific and aesthetic appeal; and the perennially popular paleontology section features fossilized skeletal reconstructions of numerous dinosaurs, including *Tyrannosaurus rex* and *Stegosaurus.* Visitors are invited to touch the stony remains of the rulers of the Mesozoic era—all of the skeletons are actual fossil remains except for the skulls and an occasional missing foot bone or vertebra. Standing beneath the looming life-sized figures, it's easy to be transported back to the time when these animals were sentient beings roaming the countryside. In 1898, just three years after establishing the museum, Carnegie spotted a headline in the *New York Journal* proclaiming the discovery of the "Most Colossal Animal Ever on Earth"; he determined to "buy this for Pittsburgh." Carnegie's money went to fund his own research team, which unearthed a number of specimens, including one named *Diplodocus carnegii* in his honor. Another reconstructed animal is the Irish elk, the forerunner of today's timid forest creatures. His rack of horns is broader than a small car— quite a challenge to cavemen on the hunt. The Hall of Dinosaurs is continually expanding with new discoveries, such as dinosaur skin, perfectly preserved dinosaur eggs, and a 25-foot-long slab of rock containing the tracks of two dinosaurs. The collection of reconstructed skeletons is second to none and is a favorite among the short set.

The Museum of Natural History has, since its inception, been involved in scientific research. One of three major curatorial sections (the other two being the Division of Earth Sciences, which includes paleontology, and the Division of Anthropology), the Division of

ANDREW CARNEGIE
AND THE PITTSBURGH MILLIONAIRES

In 1837, Andrew Carnegie was born in Dunfermline, Scotland, and moved with his family to the north side of Pittsburgh as a child. Andrew's formal schooling ended at age 13, and he earned a meager wage as a bobbin oiler and winder. When told of a job opening for a messenger at the newly invented telegraph office, he left the foul-smelling oil vats behind. His unique ability to memorize Morse Code, routes, and names, coupled with an ambitious capacity for hard work, made him popular with both management and customers; his income rose to the princely sum of $25 a month.

During this time, a wealthy local businessman opened his private library to young industrial apprentices in Pittsburgh. Carnegie read Plutarch, Lamb, and a mountain of technical books. When the library refused to lend books to him because he was officially a messenger rather than an apprentice, he launched a successful letter campaign to the local newspaper and gained admittance. Carnegie hoped to become a writer but was turned down by all the local publishers.

His ability to communicate was his greatest asset. He was hired away from the telegraph office by Thomas Scott, the superintendent of the Pennsylvania Railroad, after they shared a long conversation about the future of railroading. When Scott became president of the railroad, Carnegie was made head of the Western Division—at age 24.

Carnegie maintained telegraph and rail connections for Union troops during the Civil War. Sickened by what he witnessed, he became an antiwar activist and later funded an international peace organization. After the war, Carnegie moved to New York.

At this point, he made an interesting resolution. On St. Nicholas Hotel stationery, Carnegie made note of his investments and declared that "the amassing of wealth is one of the worst species of idolatry—no idol more debasing than the worship of money. Whatever I engage in I must push inordinately; therefore I should be careful to choose that life which will be the most elevating in character. . . . I will resign business at thirty-five." He was then 33. Carnegie didn't carry out his plan. Instead, he invested in the future, creating a steel empire for the westward expansion.

Carnegie built his first Bessemer process steel mill in Braddock, 12 miles south of Pittsburgh, during the depression of 1874–1875. The one mill became many, and Carnegie became the undisputed king of steel. Only then did he begin to back away from business, hiring others to oversee his enterprises and buying a vast summer home in Cresson, south of Pittsburgh. At this time, he named Henry Clay Frick executive head of Carnegie Steel. Frick, son of a whiskey distiller, owned and controlled much of the coal-rich land in western Pennsylvania and West Virginia, as well as numerous coke-processing plants, an indispensable factor in steel manufacture.

Carnegie married and began spending six months of the year in Scotland, leaving management of the mills to Frick. When the unionized steel workers of the Homestead plant decided to strike, Frick—carrying out Carnegie's antiunion policies—called on a private army of Pinkerton detectives. Shots were fired, three of the Pinkerton men were critically wounded, and five of the steel workers were killed. News of the strike blazed in newspaper headlines across the country. Carnegie blamed Frick for inappropriate action, and the two men parted ways.

Charles M. Schwab (who once said, "I consider my ability to arouse enthusiasm among people the greatest asset I possess") became president of Carnegie Steel. Schwab, who had risen from the immigrant shacks that surrounded the mills in nearby Johnstown, addressed New York's wealthiest industrialists and bankers one night, telling them of Carnegie's genius—how he had bought and integrated all facets of his industries, from shipping lines to containers. Schwab presented an idea to J. Pierpont Morgan (then the richest man in the world) and Roger Bacon (a friend of Theodore Roosevelt)—to buy all of Carnegie's holdings and integrate them even more efficiently.

Morgan approached Carnegie, who wrote a figure on a slip of paper—more than four hundred million dollars; the United States Steel Corporation was born. Some months later, the two men met on the deck of a Europe-bound steamer. "Pierpont," said Carnegie (he allegedly used the banker's middle name to annoy him), "I should have asked for one hundred million dollars more than I did for that steel business." "If you had," Morgan replied, "I would have paid it."

Approximately 30 associates in various rolling mills, tubing plants, smelters, mining projects, and all the integral factors in Carnegie's empire instantly became rich. Since the bulk of them lived in the Pittsburgh area, the result was an orgy of spending. Mansions with gold-leafed pianos proliferated, and Pittsburgh became a boomtown for those who catered to the newly rich. Lucius Beebe, an author who chronicled the times, reported:

Bohunks from the open hearths . . . whose sartorial tastes had hitherto been limited to a cast-iron Derby that afforded protection from the guided missiles of saloon brawls were confronted with a switch to French champagne for dinner and Scotch-and-soda between meals. The toughened offspring of Mesabi iron miners found themselves distressingly poured into Little Lord Fauntleroy suits and their Buster Brown curls ordered by exquisite barbers.

Meanwhile, Carnegie devoted himself to philanthropy—but with a twist:

Of every thousand dollars spent in so-called charity today, it is probable $900 is unwisely spent: so spent, indeed, as to produce the many evils which it proposes to mitigate or cure.

Carnegie believed that knowledge of the arts and sciences were luxuries that the wealthy should support for the betterment of the people. He acknowledged that scientific expertise was more important than—or at least *as* important as—the ability "to knock down a man now and then," so he built and endowed the Carnegie Institution in Washington, D.C., and the Carnegie Institutes and Museums of Pittsburgh for research and display. Libraries were Carnegie's special projects; he built and stocked nearly 3,000 libraries in the English-speaking world, but also arranged that they would be supported by the communities in which they were built.

Determined to die penniless, he gave away millions to individuals and institutions. When he realized his fortune continued to increase rather than diminish, he arranged for a trust for family and left the rest to the Carnegie Foundation, which continues his philanthropic work today. Carnegie returned to New York as World War I was declared and died at his home in Massachusetts in 1919.

Pittsburgh

Life Sciences maintains a biological field station at Powdermill Nature Reserve south of Pittsburgh, where research focuses on the winter survival mechanisms of small mammals and on bird migration patterns. The museum is also involved in the study of Native American cultures in western Pennsylvania and other sites on both the North and South American continents.

Heinz Architectural Center

Added to the Carnegie Museums in 1994 to further the study of world architecture, this three-story center, built within a former temporary exhibition hall, houses three changing exhibition galleries, a study room, and the curatorial office of the architecture department.

Carnegie Library of Pittsburgh

The jewel of the system of "Free to the People" libraries given to the city by Carnegie is a bibliophile's dream come true (412/622-3114, Mon.–Thurs. 10 A.M.–8 P.M., Fri.–Sat. 10 A.M.–5:30 P.M., Sun. 1–5 P.M.; free). Carnegie said, "A library outranks any other one thing a community can do to benefit its people. It is a never failing spring in the desert."

This branch works hard to stay current with the needs of the public while continuing to renovate and repair the sumptuous architectural details of the original building. Designated a Regional Resource Center for Science and Technology by the federal government, the library also has an extensive music collection and a department dedicated to information on the state of Pennsylvania.

EAST SIDE MUSEUMS AND GALLERIES

The Frick Art and Historical Center

Frick Art Museum and **Clayton,** restored home of industrialist Henry Clay Frick, are within **Frick Park** (7227 Reynolds St., off Homewood Ave., 412/371-0600, www.frickart.org, Tues.–Sat. 10 A.M.–5 P.M., Sun. noon–6 P.M.; café is open for lunch Tues.–Sat. 11 A.M.–5 P.M., tea 3 P.M.–5 P.M., Sun. lunch 11 A.M.–6 P.M., tea 3 P.M.–6 P.M.,

Frick Park

closed Mon.), a superbly maintained six-acre preserve. The Frick Center grounds, Frick art museum, car and carriage museum, and greenhouse are free. Tours of Clayton are $10 adults, $8 seniors and students. Reservations are recommended; the tour is not recommended for those under age 10. The carriage museum, art museum, greenhouse, Clayton, and the gift shop are closed major holidays, though the surrounding park stays open. A small café that attracts well-dressed ladies-who-lunch serves salads, sandwiches, and high tea.

The art museum features works from the pre–20th century European art collection of Helen Clay Frick, Henry's daughter, as well as invited exhibitions from around the country. The quality of the work displayed is consistently superb, and the experience is comparable to being a guest in a very wealthy home—the grounds, carriage museum (featuring elegant horse-drawn and motor carriages owned by the Frick family), art museum, and greenhouse are all worth a look to see how the other half lived. Free docent-led tours of art museum temporary exhibitions are offered Wed., Sat., and Sun. at 2 P.M. The playhouse now serves as the visitors' center and museum shop, which is the starting point for all tours. The crown jewel of the property is Clayton, the perfectly preserved Victorian mansion where Helen Clay Frick spent her childhood.

Pittsburgh Center for the Arts

This neighborhood organization (6300 5th Ave. in Mellon Park, 412/361-0873, www.pittsburgharts.org, Mon.–Sat. 10 A.M.–5:30 P.M., Sun. noon–5 P.M., $6 adults, $3 students) is a renovated mansion that offers regional, national, and international art exhibitions and a sales gallery where more than 500 artists display and sell their work. Exhibitions regularly make the *Pittsburgh Post-Gazette's* top 10 shows-to-see list.

PITTSBURGH ZOO AND AQUARIUM

The 75-acre zoo (1 Wild Pl., in Highland Park, north of Pittsburgh, 412/665-3640 or 800/474-4966, www.pittsburghzoo.com) added an in-

THE PRINCE OF IRONY APPEALS TO THE KING OF STEEL

Mark Twain spent a lot of time in Pittsburgh. In his later years, much of his income was derived from the lecture circuit, and Pittsburgh was a frequent stop. He considered the audiences there to be of a higher caliber than what he referred to as "the rural types," whom he had to work very hard to entertain. One of Pittsburgh's most famous citizens, who was well known for his low opinion of organized religion, was the target of Twain's wry humor in this undated letter from a collection of his works:

To Andrew Carnegie

Dear Sir and Friend:

You seem to be in prosperity. Could you lend an admirer $1.50 to buy a hymn-book with? God will bless you. I feel it; I know it. So will I.

N.B.—If there should be other applications, this one not to count.

Yours, Mark

P.S. Don't send the hymn-book; send the money; I want to make the selection myself.

M

novative and wildly successful 45,000-square-foot aquarium to complement its seven-acre children's area, open-style veldt, and natural habitats. It's open the Sat. before Memorial Day–Labor Day daily 10 A.M.–6 P.M. and the rest of the year 9 A.M.–5 P.M. April–Nov., admission is $8 adults, $6 children 2–13, and $6 adults and $5 children the rest of the year; parking is an additional $3.50.

The zoo was founded in 1898 at the behest of local philanthropist Christopher Lyman Magee and has been expanding and improving ever since. The ambitious recent addition houses more than 40 saltwater or fresh-water exhibits, including a two-story open ocean tank with sharks, an Amazon rainforest, and a stingray tunnel that children can crawl through to view stingrays swimming around them. The ever-popular Kids Kingdom is a combination of play areas, learning environments, and animal-observation areas. Wilderness Walkway winds visitors through trees and wooded terrain, where exhibits explore animal adaptations such as motion, defenses, and domestication; interactive play structures teach children about the animals displayed there. Kids can climb a giant rope spider web or travel with their folks through the treetops on an enclosed Canopy Walk. The Discovery Pavilion's spiral slide whisks visitors through a large hollow "tree" to a 40-foot bat flyway with two simulated cave roosting areas for bat observation. As in the National Aviary in the North Side, thin strands of wire are the only barrier separating the public from the silent flight of night creatures. The meerkat exhibit features a trip into a meerkat burrow, and no one will want to miss the compact naked mole-rat tunnel, which encourages youngsters to discover what it feels like to be in the animals' natural environment (no, you keep *your* clothes *on*).

With the addition of the aquarium, this facility becomes one of the largest zoo-aquarium combinations in the country and Pennsylvania's only public aquarium. Allen Nyhus, zoo critic and author of The Zoo Book, A Guide to America's Best, ranked the Pittsburgh Zoo and Aquarium one of the top three in the United States.

PARKS AND SCENIC SPOTS

Ⓜ Phipps Conservatory

The glittering Lord & Burnham–designed Phipps Conservatory (1 Schenley Park Dr., 412/622-6914, www.phipps.conservatory.org, Tues.–Sun. 9 A.M.–5 P.M., Fri. 9 A.M.–9 P.M.; closed Mon., Christmas Day, and two days before each new seasonal exhibit—call ahead; $6 adults, $5 seniors, $3 children 2–12, special show prices slightly higher) was given to the city in 1893 by Henry Phipps in a friendly gesture of philanthropic competition—his former neighbor and

business partner, Andrew Carnegie, had just given the city several of his famous libraries. The conservatory was originally planted with tropical flora, which Phipps bought from the Horticultural Hall at the World's Columbian Exposition in Chicago and transported to Pittsburgh via railway and horsecart. One of the largest Victorian "glass houses" in the country, the conservatory features 2.5 acres of evolving gardens and several special shows throughout the year; Phipps's desire was "to erect something that will prove to be a source of instruction as well as pleasure to the people." The Discovery Garden is a place where children can learn about the world of plants hands-on. Among the delights in the 13 large display rooms are a number of topiary animals, lush tropical palms and orchids, ferns, and desert plants; several seasonal rooms are changed regularly to present a constantly renewed display. Outdoor gardens include a rose display, aquatic garden, and a Japanese garden ringed with exquisite bonsai.

Allegheny Cemetery

Since 1844, Pittsburghers have enjoyed a peaceful stroll though the romantic landscape of obelisks and mausoleums at the Allegheny Cemetery (look for the "castle" gate, 4734 Butler St. in the Lawrenceville neighborhood, or 4715 Penn Ave., north of Bloomfield, 412/682-1624, www.alleghenycemetery.com, May 7 A.M.–8 P.M., June–Aug. 7 A.M.–7 P.M., Sept.–April 7 A.M.–5:30 P.M., free). Almost as large as Schenley Park and equally carefully tended, it's a well-kept neighborhood secret. The graves of Stephen Foster, Lillian Russell, Gen. Alexander Hays, and Conrad Feger Jackson and Josh Gibson of the Homestead Grays Negro Baseball League team are here. Call to join a guided tour, or wander about on your own.

A Walk Through Schenley Farms

Schenley Farms, a residential area in Oakland, was established about 1905 by the purchase of a teakettle-shaped piece of land from the Schenley estate; the Schenley family had held the land for more than a century. Schenley Farms is essentially a "planned community"—a model of early-

20th-century interest in land-use policies, planning techniques, and urban design. Much of this interest emanated from the City Beautiful movement, which was ushered in by the 1893 World's Columbian Exposition, the same globally themed extravaganza that incited Henry Phipps to go tropical. Schenley Farms is a showcase of eclectic upper-middle-class homes. Plantings—including rows of sycamore trees—streetlights, sidewalks, and retaining walls were designed and constructed to be harmonious even though the home styles differ widely. All utilities were placed underground. The 11 houses on the west side of Lytton Avenue were the first built and appear in a prospectus dated 1907. Several of the houses arc English Tudor style, and all were priced between $20,000 and $30,000. A detailed brochure describing this area is available from the Pittsburgh Historical Review Commission (see Sightseeing Tours under Services in the Information and Services section of this chapter).

Parks and Gardens

Schenley Park (Bigelow Blvd./Schenley Park Dr., Pittsburgh Parks Conservancy, 412/682-7275, www.pittsburghparks.org, free) was Pittsburgh's first public recreational space. Pittsburgh-born expatriate Mary Croghan Schenley—who eloped at age 15 with 43-year-old Capt. Edward Schenley—precipitated a nasty legal battle over her inheritance. She won, and she gave 300 wild acres to the city in 1889 for a public space in perpetuity. Schenley Park is Pittsburgh's flagship; it was designed in the late 19th century by Frederick Law Olmsted, the landscape architect who created New York City's Central Park and Boston's Emerald Necklace. The park's 456 acres offer recreation, cultural amenities—including beautiful Phipp's Conservator—and popular public events, such as the Vintage Grand Prix and the Race for the Cure. Exercise lovers can ice skate, play baseball, soccer, or tennis, or go running at the Schenley Oval, while golfers enjoy the park's 18-hole course. Those seeking a solitary walk in nature can visit Panther Hollow. These grounds are home to the Neill Log House, a cabin dating from 1790 and a typical pioneer home of the time.

Stroll through the splendid beaux-arts campus of **Carnegie Mellon University** (Tech and Frew Sts. on the north side of Schenley Park). The architect, Henry Hornbostel, also designed the Rodef Shalom Temple.

The **Rodef Shalom Botanical Gardens** (4905 5th Ave. at Morewood, 412/621-6566) are landscaped around a Holy Land theme; they provide a quiet oasis in the middle of Pittsburgh's busy East Side. The gardens are open June–Aug., Sun.–Thurs. 10 A.M.–2 P.M. and Sat. noon–1 P.M.; on Wed., the garden is also open 7–9 P.M. Admission is free. The Rodef Shalom Temple, an architectural gem, fronts the gardens.

Highland Park (off SR 8/Washington Blvd., Pittsburgh Parks Conservancy, 412/682-7275, www.pittsburghparks.org, free) is a 380-acre preserve where visitors can swim, jog around a stunning reservoir, or visit the popular Pittsburgh Zoo and Aquarium.

North Side

The area west of I-279 has become one of the finest examples of what people who work together can achieve. Most of North Side was originally set aside as partial compensation for Pittsburgh's Revolutionary War veterans in 1787—3,000 acres north of the City of Pittsburgh was designated a Reserve Tract, commonly referred to as "the depreciation lands."

The area began to undergo increased development in the early 19th century. Several residential neighborhoods flourished in and around the city of Allegheny, chiefly Manchester, Mexican War Streets, and Allegheny West. Manchester, situated on one of Pittsburgh's few level riverside plains, was laid out in a standard grid pattern on the banks of the Ohio River in 1832. Named after the British industrial city by the English immigrants who first settled in the area, Manchester quickly became an important shipping and industrial center. The Pittsburgh Locomotive and Car Works was a notable local industry that produced the first Allegheny-built locomotive. Between 1860 and 1900, a streetcar network linking the area with Pittsburgh changed the character of the neighborhood into a thriving upscale suburb for middle-class merchants and businessmen.

In 1848, Gen. William Robinson Jr. (who later became mayor of the city of Allegheny) returned from service in the Mexican War, subdivided his land, and named the new streets after the battles and generals of that war, giving rise to the community of Mexican War Streets. The modest homes that went up along these avenues gave way to larger and more fashionable residences as the streetcar system made middle-class commuting from Pittsburgh a reality. The neighborhood was well settled by 1872, with the exception of Buena Vista Street, which was occupied by a stockyard (hence the alley named Drovers Way). By 1890, Buena Vista Street became available for construction and was promptly inlaid with Italianate townhouses.

In 1788, Allegheny West was part of the "outlots"—the farming area that lay outside the city of Allegheny. Though initial development was slow (the first structure built was a rope factory), the location of the neighborhood—upwind from the new railroad lines—eventually made Allegheny West the most prestigious section in the city. By 1872, Allegheny West had become an exclusive residential district, with stately homes lining Brighton Road and Ridge Avenue (Pittsburgh's "Millionaires' Row"). The first decade of the 20th century was the high point of the area's prestige and social desirability. The wealthy city of Allegheny and its boroughs were annexed by Pittsburgh in 1908. By 1930, however, the effects of World War I's industrial boom, along with increased population, began to make the area less desirable for its rich residents.

As the streetcar had changed the neighborhoods earlier, the advent of the automobile brought about another shift. Beginning in the 1920s, residents of Manchester, Mexican War Streets, and Allegheny West began to move to outlying suburbs made accessible by the automobile. The Great Depression and World War II discouraged people from maintaining their properties and encouraged higher-density uses, including businesses and apartments. The neighborhoods became increasingly congested and run-down through the 1950s and 1960s. Parts of Manchester were demolished to make way for SR 65, and many of the finest homes in the neighborhoods were destroyed.

In recent years, individuals and neighborhood groups such as the Manchester Citizens Corporation and the Allegheny West Civic Council have worked together to renovate properties and rescue these historic Victorian and Edwardian neighborhoods from the wrecking ball. The neighborhoods still exist, each a unique testimony to the determination of those who cherish them.

The North Side is composed of hills—Mt. Troy, Fineview, Spring Hill, Observatory Hill—each with its own ethnic mix. During the heavy immigration of the late 19th century, Germans, Swiss, and Austrians moved into the area and

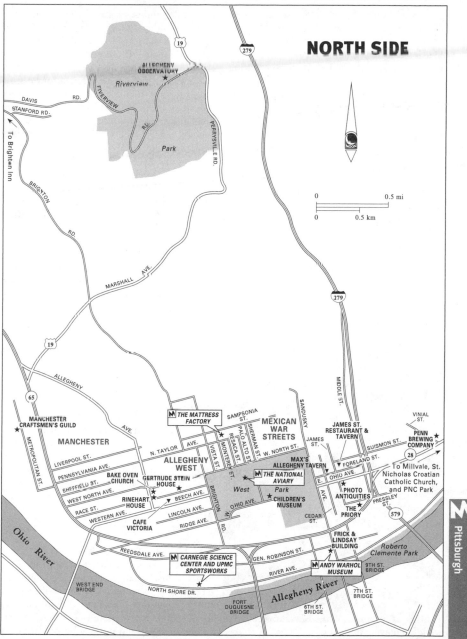

NORTH SIDE

Pittsburgh

gave it a Teutonic flavor. Singing societies were formed, and oompah bands often played in front of the many local breweries. Today, the North Side is rapidly regenerating, a priceless example of how neighborhoods can be rebuilt from within.

THE NORTH SIDE ON FOOT

The quiet residential neighborhoods of Manchester, Mexican War Streets, and Allegheny West are easily accessible by car or on foot. Anyone interested in architectural styles—Italianate, French second empire, Richardsonian Romanesque, Queen Anne, classical revival—can see beautifully restored examples (and some derelicts, as well) within blocks of each other. For detailed maps and information, contact the Pittsburgh Historic Review Commission (see Sightseeing Tours under Services in the Information and Services section of this chapter).

Each neighborhood is unique: Manchester is a mix of small residences and mansions, including the home built in 1830 for Col. James Anderson, Allegheny's first ironmaster (1423 Liverpool

children playing in front of Gertrude Stein's birthplace

St.). Anderson built a foundry and mentored a youthful worker named Andrew Carnegie. The modest row houses of Mexican War Streets provide an intimacy and unity of scale seldom found elsewhere in the city. The Mexican War Streets Society (412/323-9030) offers a tour of preserved historic homes every fall; call for more information. Many of Allegheny West's mansions have been faithfully restored; in addition, fans of literature won't want to miss the birthplace of Gertrude Stein (850 Beech Ave.), just up from the National Aviary. The 1870 Italianate townhouse sits in a neighborhood of homes that formerly housed the families of wealthy merchants and high-level industrial workers. Down the street at 954 Beech, author Mary Roberts Rinehart, an early feminist and promoter of personal freedom for women, wrote one of her many popular mysteries—*The Circular Staircase*—between 1907 and 1911. Across from the Rinehart residence, the stately **Calvary United Methodist Church** sports windows designed by Louis Comfort Tiffany. Allegheny West also contains an unusual example of architect Henry Hobson Richardson's work—one very different from the county courthouse. The **Emmanuel Episcopal Church** (on the corner of Allegheny Ave. and W. North St.) is known as the "bake-oven" church. Richardson originally designed a costly and ornate church for what he assumed was a wealthy parish. When the parishioners were unable to come up with the necessary funds, Richardson completed the church with uncharacteristic simplicity. As a result, Richardson's creation, unlike his Romanesque fantasies, resembles an outdoor bake-oven.

NATURAL HISTORY AND SCIENCE
The National Aviary

The National Aviary (Arch St. between W. North and W. Ohio Sts. in Allegheny Commons Park, 412/323-7235, www.aviary.org, daily 9 A.M.–5 P.M., $5 adults, $4 seniors, $3.50 children 2–12) is one of the premier U.S. installations for the breeding and study of birds. The aviary, much of which is housed in a glass-enclosed for-

© JOANNE MILLER

Pittsburgh

© JOANNE MILLER

sunset at Allegheny Observatory

mer plant conservatory, is built on the original site of the Western Penitentiary (118 officers of the Confederate army were incarcerated there for a year in 1863).

Numerous endangered and exotic species are included in the collection of 600 birds. Habitats are built with an eye for detail, and the entire aviary benefits from plenty of natural light. Viewing areas are evenly divided between natural settings (where birds are separated from people by a series of thin wires nearly invisible to human eyes) and open areas, where the birds fly freely. Visitors are often within close proximity to the birds and can observe unusual species closely before the birds fly to other locations.

The aviary is part of the American Zoological Association's Species Survival Program, essentially computer-dating services for rare and endangered species. Mates are matched from a global bank of species from zoos and aviaries all over the world in an attempt to ensure continuation of small populations. The aviary has expanded its mission and now is collaborating with other conservation organizations to preserve ecosystems for endangered species; for several years, the aviary has supported in-situ research on the rare Mexican thick-billed parrot, and recently reported an upswing in this endangered population.

Visitors can duck (!) for cover under a tropical rainstorm and see open feeding in the walkthrough Wetlands of the Americas and Tropical Forest areas, and meet a friendly African penguin or one of a variety of owls daily.

Allegheny Observatory

Visitors can spend a pleasant Thursday or Friday evening stargazing through the 13-inch Fitz-Clark refractor at the Allegheny Observatory (159 Riverview Ave. in Riverview Park, 412/321-2400; May–Aug. Thurs., April–Oct. Fri. 8 P.M., free, reservations necessary—call Mon.–Fri. 10 A.M.– 4 P.M., not recommended for children under seven). The observatory was founded in 1850 by amateur astronomers to view the comet DeNati and was eventually absorbed by the University of Pittsburgh. Samuel Langley, the first "official" astronomer to supervise the observatory, developed a time service based on an instrument known as the Meridian Telescope. Until the advent of trains, time coordination over long distances was unimportant; as rail traffic increased, however, the necessity of coordinating trains (which were, after all, using the same lengths of track but traveling in opposite directions) became crucial. Langley's service used the telescope and chronograph to check time by star movements, then telegraphed accurate time to railroad way stations, permitting the stationmasters to coordinate the movement of several trains over a wide area and lessening the chance that two or more would attempt to occupy the same space.

Through the years, the observatory has acquired additional equipment, including a 47-foot-long telescope with a 30-inch lens; it's used to photograph and estimate distance to the nearest stars, among other research projects. From 1914 to 1940, the telescope captured more than 10,000 images. The tedious job of tracking and comparing star movements, once done entirely by hand, is now done by computer.

A film and lecture are included in the two-hour tour. The observatory is surrounded by the rolling hills of Riverview Park—many who come bring picnic dinners to enjoy on the hillside before sunset.

Ⓜ Carnegie Science Center and UPMC SportsWorks

The center (1 Allegheny Ave., 412/237-3400, www.carnegiesciencecenter.org) refers to itself as "an amusement park for the mind," and, indeed, one does become entranced exploring this many-faceted approach to informal education in science and technology. It's newest addition, UPMC SportsWorks, is a playground with a purpose—learning about science while playing your favorite sport. Labor Day–mid-June the center and SportsWorks are open Sun.–Thurs. 10 A.M.–5 P.M., Fri.–Sat. 10 A.M.–7 P.M.; mid-June–Sept., the center is open Sun.–Thurs. 10 A.M.–6 P.M., Fri.–Sat. 10 A.M.–9 P.M.; closed Thanksgiving, Christmas, and New Year's Day. General admission to all exhibits is $14 adults, $10 children 3–18; planetarium laser shows and Omnimax shows may be purchased separately.

The original idea behind the center was to make the objects and processes of science accessible through play. More than 40,000 square feet of the 186,000-square-foot center are devoted to interactive exhibits. A joint project of the Buhl

Science Center and the Carnegie Institutes, the complex opened in 1991. Permanent exhibit areas include Kitchen Theater with live cooking demonstrations and a 21-foot-long walk-through digestive system and the interactive SciQuest Gallery that explores forces of nature with "Make Your Own Earthquake" and "Spin Up a Hurricane" displays. There are also a wave tank with six-foot waves and an opportunity to wear foam wings in a wind tunnel. SeaScape is a 2,000-square-foot aquatic environment; its centerpiece is a Pacific coral reef ecosystem with a 150-gallon touch tank. Budding marine biologists can explore artifacts on the sea floor with the help of a yellow submarine and diving suit.

A Pittsburgh tradition since 1954, the 2,300-square-foot Miniature Railroad and Village helps to preserve the past; the railroad displays the rich historical, architectural, and cultural heritage of western Pennsylvania. Many of the sights are recognizable—such as Old Economy Meeting Hall, with its one-armed clock, which still exists north of Pittsburgh in Economy, Pennsylvania, and the 1300 block of Liverpool Street on Pittsburgh's North Side. The Railroad and Village contain 2,000 hand-painted characters and nearly 100 lifelike "animations"—from a lady at a spinning wheel to "Mighty Casey" at bat.

The Henry Buhl Jr. Planetarium is both technologically sophisticated and interactive. Through the use of a digital projection system, the 50-foot domed chamber is capable of simulating realistic three-dimensional flight through space. Beam me up, Scotty.

In the four-story Rangos Omnimax Theater (one of 13 in the country), audience members recline while images are projected onto a 79-foot domed screen tilted to sweep you into the full visual experience of making a dive to the bottom of the sea or watching a rocket launch. The technology uses the largest film frame in motion-picture history and a special 56-speaker sound system. Programs in both the planetarium and theater change regularly.

The center also features the USS *Requin* (French for "sand shark"), a submarine built for World War II duty that made more than 5,000 dives after the end of the war. Decommissioned in

1968, the *Requin* began her final journey in 1990, towed atop four barges on the Mississippi and Ohio Rivers from New Orleans. A mix of science and history, the tours explore the personality of men who volunteer for submarine duty and describe how they lived and worked underwater.

SportsWorks, housed in a separate building near the center, has proven to be enormously popular for good reason. Visitors can participate in a virtual snowboard race, test their running speed and the strength of their karate chop, or fly a jet in an enclosed simulator—all in the name of learning. The varied sports-related exhibits have something for everyone, from trampolines to baseball batting practice.

MUSEUMS AND GALLERIES

Andy Warhol Museum

One of the four Carnegie Museums of Pittsburgh, the Warhol Museum (117 Sandusky St.; 412/237-8300; www.warhol.org; Tues.–Sun. 10 A.M.–5 P.M., Fri. 10 A.M.–10 P.M., closed Mon., $8 adults, $4 students and children) exhibits continually changing works by Warhol from its archives, including video and film clips. The museum also shows special exhibits featuring the work of artists and subjects related to Andy Warhol's unique view of the world. One show featured affecting/scary/peculiar clown paintings scooped up by actress Diane Keaton in flea markets and second-hand shops; another looked at capital punishment in America.

Andrej Warhola, born to Carpatho-Rusyn immigrant parents in a now-dismantled working-class tenement on Orr Street, spent his early years taking Saturday morning art classes at the Carnegie Institute; he later learned graphic design at Carnegie-Mellon and went off to seek his fortune in New York City. Warhola wasn't thrilled about his eastern European, industrial-strength roots—he dropped the "a" ("Maybe they'll think I'm German," he told a friend) and told one interviewer he was actually from Hawaii—but the Andy Warhol Museum revels in the Pittsburghian basis of Warhol's work. His use of assembly-line techniques and commercial images proved you couldn't take the Pittsburgh out of the boy.

The eight-story structure in which the museum is situated is the renovated and redesigned 1911 Frick & Lindsay Building, a terra-cotta, tile-clad warehouse. The exterior now manages to reflect the character of the neighborhood and conceal a brightly illuminated, ultramodern, ultraslick interior. The museum, the largest in the world devoted to the work of a single artist, is a triumph of compatibility between the architecture and the fascinating history of one of Pop Art's founders and chief proponents.

The Pop Art movement began in the late 1950s in Europe and the United States—the style reflected the everyday symbols and values of a changing society by sometimes satirizing the look of ordinary life and the prevalent symbols of materialism. Calling his studios "factories" and making bright art of his familiar Campbell soup cans and repeated images of cultural icons, including Marilyn Monroe, Jackie Kennedy, and Chairman Mao, Warhol seems to have been born to lead the movement in the United States.

Perhaps the most valuable aspect of this collection is the opportunity to view Warhol's less-frequently seen works—particularly the difficult "disaster paintings" and the whimsical graphics for periodicals that launched him into the art scene in New York—as well as his continuing development as an artist. The museum is roughly laid out in decades that reflect Warhol's changing orientations and reveal a serious and dedicated artistic talent beneath the highly stylized work. Warhol's films (The Velvet Underground, Chelsea Girls, etc.) play daily in the museum theater, and every Fri. 5–10 P.M., there's a special event such as a talk, dance party, or film.

The museum sports a cheerful café and a gift shop with some unusual offerings. The Warhol has become a bit of a gathering place for hip art aficionados; it's worth a visit just to see the Silver Cloud room on the fifth floor—dozens of pillow-like silver balloons swirl around, lifting weary spirits. Warhol knew how to play.

The Mattress Factory

Don't miss this, the country's premier art museum specializing in large-scale, site-specific installations (500 Sampsonia Way at Monterey St., 412/231-3169, www.mattress.org, Tues.–Fri.

10 A.M.–5 P.M., Sat. 10 A.M.–7 P.M., Sun. 1–5 P.M., $8 adults, $5 students/seniors, free for children under 12). John Caldwell, San Francisco Museum of Modern Art curator of painting and sculpture, was quoted in the *Wall Street Journal* as saying: "It's one of the great undiscovered cultural resources in America. The art you see there usually can't be seen anywhere else except New York, and often not even there."

Exhibits begin with the selection of 15 international artists a year, who then build their artworks in place. Recent exhibits included roomfuls of household objects bought new and then unevenly worn to a frazzle by artist Curtis Mitchell, Jaroslav Hulboj's narrow yellow spongy foam passageway, *Reconstruction for Lazarus' Situation,* Buzz Spector's *Cold Fashioned Room,* a (literally) frozen room full of Victorian furniture, Rebecca Holland's basement floor made of inch-thick apple green candy (the smell was enough to induce a diabetic coma), and *Infinity Dots Mirrored Room,* a walk-in room projecting colored dots into infinity by Yayoi Kusama. That's just for starters. The art here is so avant that your head will spin, but your mind will be challenged and your heart delighted. Walking through the art in the new expanded quarters next door will make you feel like Alice in Wonderland: something new and strange behind every door.

Pittsburgh Children's Museum

Not just for kids, the Pittsburgh Children's Museum (10 Children's Way in the Old Post Office Building in Allegheny Square, 412/322-5058, www.pittsburghkids.org, Mon.–Sat. 10 A.M.–5 P.M., Sun. noon–5 P.M., $5 adults, $4.50 children and seniors, Thurs. $3.50 for all) offers interactive permanent exhibits such as a two-story climbing sculpture; a studio art area with paint, clay, and computers; a musical swing sculpture; role-playing exhibits that develop and strengthen language skills; and health-related exhibits that focus on respect for the human body and self-esteem. A recent temporary exhibit featured characters from favorite children's books such as *Frog and Toad Are Friends, Arthur's Pet Business,* and *Goldilocks and the Three Bears.*

Art Old, New, and Ethnic

Photo Antiquities (531 E. Ohio St., 412/231-7881, www.photoantiquities.org, Mon.–Sat. 10 A.M.–4 P.M., $6.50 adults, $5 seniors, $3 children 5–12) features an extensive collection of 19th-century photography, daguerreotypes, ambrotypes, tintypes, and vintage prints of Native Americans and Civil War subjects. Victorian-era music plays in the background while visitors peruse the art and history of photography; the museum offers a variety of changing exhibits.

South Side

The South Side of Pittsburgh has historically been a strong community, maintaining much of its eastern European heritage. Once known as Birmingham, the community was annexed by the city of Pittsburgh in 1872. A popular dwelling place for artists and families, the South Side is proudly reacquainting itself with the past—Station Square epitomizes this rebuilt, renewed historical spirit with its museum and multitude of shiny new shops, while East Carson Street remains true to its neighborhood roots. In the fall of 1984, the East Carson Street commercial area was awarded designation as a National Register Historic District and is a National Main Street Center—one of only seven in the country. Restaurants and professional offices join art galleries, antique shops, and neighborhood services to form one of Pittsburgh's most diverse and interesting districts.

M Mt. Washington and the Inclines

The most prominent feature of the South Side is Mt. Washington. To the east and south lie the South Side neighborhoods, and in the opposite direction, downriver, stretches the western edge of the Monongahela River valley. Here, the wide floodplains of this muddy river witnessed the great concentration of the nation's glass-, iron-, and steelmaking centers.

The **Duquesne Incline** (412/381-1665, www.incline.cc, Mon.–Sat. 5:30 A.M.–12:45 A.M. and Sun. and holidays 7 A.M.–12:45 A.M., $1.75 adults, $.85 children 5–11, under 5 and seniors free), with its original cars (built in 1877), was rescued from destruction in 1962 by the residents of nearby Duquesne Heights. They organized bake sales and card parties and sold souvenir tickets and shares of stock during the next year to raise $15,000 to renovate and run

© JOANNE MILLER

South Side hangout

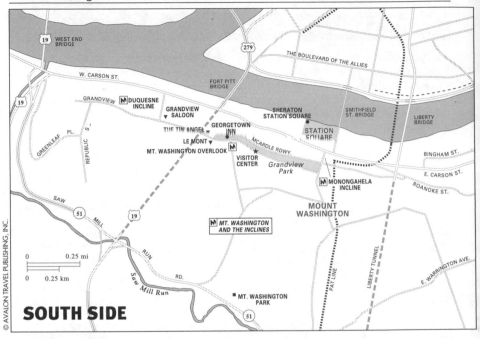

SOUTH SIDE

the incline. The lower station (1197 W. Carson St., just over the Fort Pitt Bridge) is plain and functional. The upper station (1220 Grandview Ave.) features a viewing platform and museum of local history, a storehouse of information on everything that moves on rails in the cities or on cables in the mountains. Hungarian engineer Samuel Diescher designed and built the Duquesne and the Johnstown Inclines, among others, and also engineered the machinery for operating the first Ferris wheel, at the 1893 Columbian Exposition in Chicago. Unusual souvenirs and maps can be had from the gift shop full of Pittsburgh mementos and photos.

Both the Duquesne Incline and the modernized 1870 **Monongahela Incline** (W. Carson St. across from Station Square, 412/237-7309, Mon.–Sat. 5:30 A.M.–12:45 A.M. and Sun. and holidays 8:45 A.M.–midnight, $1.75 adults, $.85 children 5–11, under 5 and seniors free) are run as part of Pittsburgh's transit system.

Station Square

Station Square (W. Carson St. at the Smithfield St. Bridge, 412/261-2811 or 800/859-8959, www.stationsquare.com) is a shopping and entertainment center created from a railyard, the first of several brownfield site redevelopment projects. Once a 40-acre complex of buildings and railroad yards for the Pittsburgh & Lake Erie Railroad, it was the terminus for 76 passenger trains a day and many thousands of tons of freight and mail. Rail use declined after World War II, and almost all rail operations were shifted to other locations, leaving several major buildings standing empty. Pittsburgh History and Landmarks Foundation, which was looking for a large commercial restoration project, assessed the complex and presented its ideas to the Allegheny Foundation, a local family trust, which agreed to support initial reconstruction. The area renewed is equal to 10 percent of the Golden Triangle, making it one of the largest urban-renewal projects in Pennsylvania. Many artifacts rescued

Pittsburgh

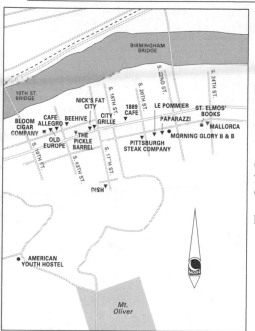

it to steel. Near the Bessemer converter, a 60-foot-long fountain is equipped with mesmerizing dancing waters choreographed to music or a history presentation; each show is extremely well-done, free to the public, and a new program begins about every 20 minutes in the afternoon and evening—this is well worth seeing (May–Nov.). Station Square is also home to the Gateway Clipper Fleet of excursion boats and the Sheraton Hotel.

Grandview Overlook

This small park at the top of Mt. Washington on Grandview Avenue affords a breathtaking view. *USA Weekend's 2003 Annual Travel Report* gave it high praise:

> *In a nation with a wealth of stunning cities full of compelling stories, ranking Pittsburgh as the No. 2 beauty spot is perhaps our most surprising choice. But the Steel City's aesthetic appeal is undeniable, as is its very American capacity for renewal. Standing atop Mount Washington, the steep hill that rises giddily on the city's south side, sightseers enjoy the unforgettable panorama of the Allegheny and Monongahela rivers flowing together to create the mighty Ohio, that waterway so essential in the nation's settlement. The rivers cup downtown's lustrous Golden Triangle, where landmark skyscrapers thrust upward like rockets. At night, lights twinkle on no fewer than 15 bridges.*

Take either of the inclines to reach the overlook.

from demolished Pittsburgh buildings are incorporated into the overall design.

The Grand Concourse—the decorative central hall of the historic Pittsburgh & Lake Erie Railroad Station—was converted into a luxurious 500-seat restaurant (see American under Food and Nightlife). The Freight House was adapted into a "theme" shopping center with shops and restaurants. Several rail cars have been converted into specialty shops. Bessemer Court, an open-air museum, contains the Bessemer converter, the foundation of Pittsburgh's steel wealth and one of two in the United States (the other is in the Smithsonian in Washington, D.C.). This type of converter is a three-story-high, pear-shaped container in which compressed air was blasted through molten iron, burning out excess carbon and other impurities and converting

Museums and Galleries

The **Station Square Gallery** in Station Square features limited-edition prints, photographs, and paintings, often with sports or Pittsburgh themes. A number of small galleries lie along East Carson Street, including **La Fond** (1711 E. Carson, 412/431-3337), which features the work of local and national artists.

Pittsburgh

Greater Pittsburgh

Pittsburgh's urban area sits directly in the middle of Allegheny County. Most of the county is developed, with density decreasing as distance from the Golden Triangle increases. A number of outstanding attractions lie within an hour's drive of downtown Pittsburgh.

Hartwood Acres

Hartwood Acres (200 Hartwood Acres, 412/767-9200, www.county.allegheny.pa.us, grounds open sunrise–sunset daily, free) may seem far to drive just to see another mansion, but it's much more than that. Northeast of Pittsburgh, the countryside is green, peaceful, and very typically Pennsylvanian; neat homes and farms nestle among the trees. This area looks deceptively rural—unspoiled, lush, and beautiful—but in fact, it's mostly upscale residential development. In summer, the air is filled with the smell of new-mown grass.

Hartwood is a stately Tudor mansion that overlooks the rolling countryside; it was designed in 1929 by Alfred Hopkins for John and Mary Lawrence. The property contains a 629-acre park that has several heroic-sized sculptures carefully placed about the grounds; the artwork was added after the estate was taken over in 1969 by the Department of Parks, Recreation, and Conservation. Though the addition of such modern pieces to a classic Tudor estate may seem irreverent, the effect is just the opposite. When viewing the pieces in these settings, one realizes that museums offer only one (limited) display alternative. The wooded hills and meadows seem to be the natural home of these pieces, which were created and donated by well-known artists Lyman Kipp, Jack Youngerman, Betty Gold, Lila Katzen, and others. Sites for the sculptures were carefully selected for harmony and emphasis.

The house, patterned after a 16th-century style, is maintained with its original collection of English and American antiques. Walking around in the gardens close by, a visitor feels almost like an intruder—as if one were invited to a wedding and sneaked away from the festivities to get a look at the setting. The serene grounds are landscaped with towering mock orange, whose

HOLLYWOOD ON THE OHIO

Drawn by the low cost of doing business and an endless variety of architecture, unique neighborhoods, and natural settings, Hollywood film crews have frequently come to Pittsburgh to establish a production base for both feature films and made-for-TV movies. Nick Nolte, Susan Sarandon, Jack Nicholson, Danny DeVito, and Ron Howard have been among the city's more recent guests. There's been a lot of Pittsburgh on the silver and the small screens; shot either wholly or partially in Pittsburgh were *Perils of Pauline*, in 1914; *Angels in the Outfield*, 1951; *Slap Shot*, with Paul Newman, 1977; *The Leatherstocking Tales* (TV), 1980; *Flashdance*, 1982; *All the Right Moves*, with Tom Cruise, 1983; *Dominick and Eugene*, 1988; Oscar-winning *Silence of the Lambs*, 1990; *Lorenzo's Oil*, 1991; *Bob Roberts*, 1991; *Striking Distance*, with Bruce Willis, 1992; *Money for Noth-*ing, 1993; *Finnegan's Wake* (TV), 1993; *Breathing Lessons* (TV), 1993; *Just in Time*, 1993; *Milk Money*, with Melanie Griffith, 1993; *Roommates*, 1993; *Sudden Death*, 1994; *The Piano Lesson* (TV), 1994; *The Oksana Baiul Story* (TV), 1994; *Dog Eat Dog*, 1995; *Kingpin*, with Woody Harrelson and Randy Quaid, 1995; and *Out in the Cold* (TV), 1996; *Diabolique*, with Sharon Stone and Isabelle Adjani, 1996; *Desperate Measures*, with Michael Keaton and Andy Garcia, 1998; *Dogma*, with Ben Affleck and Matt Damon, 1998; and *Inspector Gadget*, with Matthew Broderick, 1999.

Among the films made in the last few years are *Rock Star*, with Mark Wahlberg and Jennifer Aniston, 2001; *The Mothman Prophecies*, with Richard Gere, 2002; *The Guardian* (TV), 2002; and *The Clearing*, with Robert Redford and Helen Mirren, 2004.

gentle orange and honeysuckle scent saturates the air in warm weather. In the summer, theatrical productions are presented under a tent on the lawn behind the mansion. Music and dance performances are held at the Middle Road performance area, approximately a mile from the house (call for a schedule). The grounds are open year-round—for driving, walking, horseback riding, or cross-country skiing—and a mile-long self-guided nature trail winds throughout the park from the mansion parking lot. Guided tours of the mansion, garden, and stable (weather permitting) are available, by reservation (call the number above), Wed.–Sat. 10 A.M.–3 P.M. and Sun. noon–4 P.M. A $5 fee is charged for the guided tours.

Rachel Carson Homestead

The Rachel Carson Homestead (613 Marion Ave., 724/274-5459, www.rachelcarsonhomestead.org, March 11–Nov. 20 Tues.–Thurs. 10 A.M.–2 P.M. and by appointment) lies east of Pittsburgh in the village of Springdale. Carson was born here in 1907, earned a master's degree in zoology, and taught for several years at Johns Hopkins before publishing her National Book Award winner, *The Sea Around Us*, followed by the internationally acclaimed *Silent Spring*, which exposed the dangers of pesticides and herbicides commonly used in American farming. The homestead is open year-round; activities include art exhibits and Rachel Carson Day in late May, featuring live animal exhibits and tours of the Rachel Carson Trail.

Rachel Carson Trail

The Rachel Carson Trail (www.hipittsburgh.org), which passes by the homestead, is a relatively primitive day-hiking trail maintained by Pittsburgh AYH. The full length is approximately 34 miles, extending from North Park, in the north-central area of Allegheny County, to **Harrison Hills County Park**, in the northeast corner of the county. The trail passes near Freeport Road and the Rachel Carson Homestead at its midpoint. Access to the trail near its western terminus in North Park is at the intersection of Pearce Mill Road and Babcock Boulevard—look for the yellow-painted markers. The access to the trail in Harrison Hills Park is at the Watts Memorial Overlook. This trail is a rebuilt section of the original Baker Trail, which was abandoned largely because of development (even today, the trail

---

The city is amazingly versatile, and one's opinion of Pittsburgh may be easily skewed by the particular film viewed. The dreary factories of *The Deer Hunter*, 1978, and the upscale neighborhood of Sewickley in *Houseguest*, 1994, for example, leave quite different impressions. Though parts of both these films take place during the winter, the dull gray overcast that permeates *The Deer Hunter* stands in stark contrast to the festive suburban barbecue and twinkling holiday lights of *Houseguest*.

Pittsburgh has inspired more than its share of ghoulish visions, too, including one of the most famous horror films of all time, *Night of the Living Dead*, which Pittsburgher George Romero made (in black and white) on a shoestring in 1968—one of the very first of the now-towering wave of independent films. Romero also shot *Dawn of the Dead*, 1979; *Day of the Dead*, 1985; and a remake of *Night of the Living Dead*, in 1990. Other bloody-minded shriekers filmed in the city include *Creepshow*, 1982; *Monkey Shines: An Experiment in Fear*, 1988; *Revenge of the Living Zombies*, 1989; and that towering example of the genre, *Blood Sucking Pharaohs in Pittsburgh*, 1988.

The realistic grittiness of Pittsburgh's older neighborhoods also continues to be a draw. It's been used to excellent advantage in *Boys on the Side*, in 1994, and producer-director Danny DeVito's biopic *Hoffa*, with Jack Nicholson in the title role, in 1992. Streets that have been deserted in other urban areas brim with life here, as they have for more than a century. Filmmakers also appreciate the city's looming deserted factories, which have served as backdrops in futuristic destruction pics such as *Robocop*, 1987, and *The Stand*, made for TV in 1993.

changes periodically when new housing is built). The trail is steep in places and covers a varied terrain: traversing several county parks; following power and gas lines; skirting suburban developments and farms; crossing creeks, woods, and fields; and passing along the edge of steep bluffs. Spurs also lead into the mansion area of the Hartwood Estate. The latest edition of the Rachel Carson Trail Guide is available from Pittsburgh AYH (830 E. Warrington Ave., Pittsburgh, PA 15210, 412/431-4910, fax 412/431-2625); call or fax with credit card. The price is $9.53 ($7.50 plus $.53 tax and $1.50 postage).

Tour-Ed Mine and Museum

The Tour-Ed Mine and Museum (748 Bull Creek Rd., Tarentum, 724/224-4720, www .tour-edmine.com, Memorial Day–Labor Day, Wed.–Mon. Sept.–Oct. Fri.–Sun., 1–4 P.M.—last tour is at 3:30, $8) is east of Pittsburgh off Exit 14 from SR 28 north, in Tarentum. Though many associate the life of a coal miner with lung diseases and poverty, the profession also fostered its own mystique and brotherhood, as the Tour-Ed Museum demonstrates. The tour delves into the history of mining, with such esoterica as methane gas detection techniques and the various types of miners' lunch pails, and continues aboard a Mantrip car (a small railway car used to transport miners into work areas of a mine). Inside the mine, a guide discusses the mechanics of mining and displays the machinery used in the local bituminous coalfields from earliest times to today.

Entertainment and Events

SPECTATOR SPORTS

Pittsburgh's sports teams engender rabid support from fans. As a result, last-minute ticket purchases—especially for Steelers and Pirates games—may be difficult. Listed below are the primary sporting teams and their home venues; call for current schedules.

Baseball

The **Pittsburgh Pirates** (information line 412/ 323-5000, www.pittsburghpirates.com) baseball team plays at the newly built PNC Park on Federal Street, North Side; a pedestrian walkway connects the Roberto Clemente (6th Street) Bridge to the park, offering visitors an option of walking from downtown. The major league regular season runs from April to early October, with playoffs in October. Tickets are available through the information line or by calling 800/BUY-BUCS (800/289-2827).

Basketball

A. J. Palumbo Center (1304 Forbes Ave., at Duquesne University, 412/396-6058) stages games for the **Duquesne University** basketball team. The **University of Pittsburgh** basketball team plays at Pitt Stadium (U.P. ticket office 412/648-8300).

The **Robert Morris College** basketball team may be seen at the Mellon Arena, also known as the Igloo (300 Auditorium Pl., 412/642-1800).

Football

Three Rivers Stadium was razed in 2000 to make way for a new 65,000-seat stadium, completed in time for the 2001 season of the **Pittsburgh Steelers** (412/697-7705, www.steelers.com). There is often a waiting list for Steelers season tickets—3,000 tickets for each home game go on sale in May. Call for football information. Tickets are also available from TicketMaster.

The **University of Pittsburgh** hosts home games for its football team at Pitt Stadium (412/648-8300).

Hockey, Soccer, and Wrestling

The Mellon Arena (412/642-1800) hosts the **Pittsburgh Penguins** professional (NHL) ice hockey team and the **Phantoms** (roller hockey).

The **Stingers,** Pittsburgh's indoor soccer team, also play at the Mellon Arena, and you can even find **World Wrestling Federation (WWF)** competition there.

© JOANNE MILLER

PNC Park from across the Allegheny River

PERFORMING ARTS

Pittsburgh has been a mecca for jazz talent (and jazz fans) since the days when musicians were booked from city to city—it's a natural stopover between Chicago and New York. Pianist Art Blakey, song stylist Mary Lou Williams, and balladeer and bandleader Billy Eckstine were born in Pittsburgh. Eckstine lived on Bryant Street and attended Peabody High School; during his long career, he earned 11 gold records. Other notable Pittsburgh performers include musicians Earl Hines, Lena Horne, and George Benson and playwrights George S. Kaufmann, Marc Connelly, and August Wilson.

Many of the city's cultural activities take place at one of the venues of the Pittsburgh Cultural Trust (412/456-6666). The Trust is responsible for the Pittsburgh Cultural District, a renovated 14-block area bounded by Liberty Avenue, the Allegheny River, and 10th and Stanwix Streets in the Golden Triangle. Part of the Cultural Dis-

trict's appeal is its newly landscaped streets in an area of downtown that was once known only for its shabby storefronts. Grants for facade restoration on Liberty and Penn Avenues reclaimed some of the finest turn-of-the-last-century architecture in the city. Other programs have included new utilities and roadways, new brick sidewalks, granite curbs, new lighting, and Bradford pear trees. From the Richard Haas mural on the Byham Theater to the garden maze designed by Pittsburgh area artists, James O. Loney and David A. Ludwig, at the corner of Seventh Street and Penn Avenue, The Trust has a long-standing commitment to developing public arts projects. The additions have positively altered the appearance of the District. The Trust is actively supporting a 25-unit residential project that will house performers from the Pittsburgh Public Theater as well as area residents. The trust owns and operates the Benedum, Byham, Harris, and O'Reilly Theaters. Call for information on events at any PCT facility.

The **Benedum Center for the Performing Arts** (719 Liberty Ave.) was formerly the Stanley Theater. The faithful restoration of this theater reflects the glories of America's theatrical past. The 2,880-seat Benedum is home to the Pittsburgh Ballet Theater, Civic Light Opera, Pittsburgh Opera, and many special performances.

Originally opened as the Gaiety Theater in 1904, the **Byham Theater** (101 6th St.) is Pittsburgh's only remaining vaudeville house. This 1,342-seat theater is enjoying a long-term renovation and is reminiscent of Pittsburgh's theatrical heyday. It now features small- to midsized performing arts productions.

The **Harris Theater** (809 Liberty Ave., 412/682-4111) was renovated in 1995 and is now the new downtown home for Pittsburgh Filmmakers. This 194-seat theater is also used for small live performances. The theater was named in tribute to Pittsburgher John P. Harris, the creator of the Nickelodeon.

The **O'Reilly Theater** (621 Penn Ave.) is the only newly constructed theater in the downtown cultural area, and it is home to Pittsburgh Public Theater. The stage is surrounded on three sides by the 650-member audience.

Pittsburgh

THE SPORTING TRADITION

Pittsburgh is a sports fan's paradise—there's something happening year-round at Heinz Field, the Civic Arena (locally known as the Igloo), PNC Park, or the universities. The city has a long sporting tradition: Pittsburgh staged its first professional football game in 1892 and its first pro hockey game in 1894. The first World Series game took place here in 1903.

During the last decades of the 19th century, Pittsburgh's first professional baseball team, the Alleghenies, became known as the Pirates for wooing and winning infielder Louis Bierbauer away from the rival American Association. They also stole the 1909, 1925, 1971, and 1979 National Championships. Old Forbes Field, the site of many memorable games, is now largely covered by the University of Pittsburgh's Forbes Quadrangle building. However, the home plate over which Babe Ruth smashed his final home run in 1935 continues to be preserved under glass there. Mazeroski's Wall still stands off Roberto Clemente Drive nearby; it's named for Bill Mazeroski, the 1960 World Series batter who hit the winning home run, securing the title for the Pirates against the Yankees.

The early years of baseball were dominated by unrelenting segregation, enforced by Baseball Commissioner Kenesaw Landis, who supported the league's policy barring non-whites. As a result, Pittsburgh was also home to the Pittsburgh Crawfords and the Homestead Grays baseball teams, all-black teams that produced players such as catcher Josh Gibson—considered by many baseball historians to the be greatest player never to play in the major leagues.

Listed below are performing arts, performers, and places to see them. Call for upcoming schedules.

Dance

The **Pittsburgh Ballet Theater** (412/281-4457, www.pbt.org) appears regularly at the Benedum Center for the Performing Arts.

The **Duquesne University Tamburitzans** (412/396-5185), the oldest American folk ensemble dedicated to performing cultural works of Eastern Europe, appear regularly throughout the city. Other dance groups include the **Mary Miller Dance Company** (412/434-1169, www.marymillerdanceco.org), begun in 1984, which presents cross-disciplinary performances.

Music

Performances by the **Pittsburgh Symphony Orchestra,** the **Pittsburgh Symphony Pops,** and the **Pittsburgh Symphony Society** (412/392-2887) are featured at **Heinz Hall** (600 Penn Ave., box office 412/392-4900). An historic building, this Breche opal and Lavanto marble theater was built in 1927 by motion-picture mogul Marcus Loew and saved from destruction in the early 1990s by a 16-month, $11 million renovation.

The Cultural Trust, with the Pittsburgh Symphony and the PACE Theatrical Group, hosts the **Pittsburgh Broadway Series.** This seven-show series features the best the theatrical world has to offer. With performances in the Benedum Center, the Byham Theater, and Heinz Hall, The Broadway Series presents blockbuster hits such as *Phantom of the Opera* and *Miss Saigon.*

An inner-city, minority-directed arts education organization, **Manchester Craftsmen's Guild** (1815 Metropolitan St., 412/322-0800, www.manchesterguild.org) features a variety of jazz performers and various art exhibits. The **Antonian Theater** (3333 5th Ave., Carlow College, 412/578-6685) presents music, theater, opera, and other performances. Call for information.

The **Post-Gazette Pavillion** (SR 18 at SR 22, Burgettstown, Clear Channel Communications, 412/562-9900, www.post-gazettepavilion.com) offers more than 40 concerts per year featuring big names in entertainment from rock, jazz, country, classical, and rhythm-and-blues traditions. The amphitheater also hosts fairs and festivals. **Hartwood Acres** (215 Saxonburg Blvd., 412/767-9200) presents concerts by the River City Brass Band (800/292-7222, www.rcbb.com); the band plays renditions from Bach to Mancini and appears at many different facilities through-

Western Pennsylvania breeds top-rated NFL quarterbacks, too—Johnny Unitas, Joe Namath, Joe Montana, Dan Marino, and Jim Kelly are all local boys made good. One memorable moment in Pittsburgh football: in 1972, with 22 seconds remaining in the fourth quarter of the AFC championship playoff game between the hometown Steelers and the Oakland Raiders, Steelers quarterback Terry Bradshaw threw a desperate pass to running back Frenchy Fuqua. Fuqua collided with safety Jack Tatum, and the ball bounced into the hands of rookie Franco Harris. Harris ran for a game-winning touchdown in what the NFL has come to describe as the "Immaculate Reception." The Steelers have taken the NFL championship four times: Super Bowls IX, X, XIII, and XIV.

In a 1984 miracle on ice, the last-place Pittsburgh Penguins drafted an 18-year-old kid from Montreal named Mario Lemieux. Lemieux scored on his very first shift in his very first game and went on to collect four scoring titles, two season MVP awards, and back-to-back Stanley Cup Championship rings; he who drafts last. . . .

Not all great Pittsburgh sports stories are about winning. Billy Cohn, Pittsburgh native and light heavyweight boxing champion, pitted himself against Joe Louis for the heavyweight title. In their first bout, Cohn outboxed the bigger, stronger Louis and was ahead on points after 12 rounds. Not content to win on points, Cohn wanted to knock Louis out, but he was beaten to the punch by the Brown Bomber himself.

Afterward, Cohn admitted: "I was too stubborn—too Pittsburgh."

out the year. The Pittsburgh Opera, Pittsburgh Symphony Orchestra, and Pittsburgh Ballet Theater also perform at Hartwood.

A variety of musical events take place at the **A. J. Palumbo Center** (1304 Forbes Ave., at Duquesne University, 412/396-6058) and the **Charity Randall Theater** (Stephen Foster Memorial Building, corner of Forbes Ave. and Bigelow Blvd., 412/624-7529, www.pitt.edu). The **Carnegie Music Hall** (4400 Forbes Ave., 412/622-3360) offers concerts, operas, and lectures.

Chevrolet Amphitheater (in Station Square, 412/562-9900, www.ampatstationsquare.com) hosts concerts and festivals.

Poetry

The **Pittsburgh Poetry Exchange** (412/481-7636, pghpoetryexchange.pghfree.net) offers public readings and workshops.

Theater

Hazlett Theater (Allegheny Square, 412/323-7256) is part of City Parks and features live theatre and other performances; call for information. **Pittsburgh Public Theater** (412/316-1600) is one of America's premier regional theater companies. The **Open Stage Theater** (2835 Smallman

St., 412/257-4056) presents the work of modern American playwrights.

City Theater Company (412/431-2489, www.citytheatrecompany.org) has a popular resident theater troupe. **The Playhouse** (222 Craft Ave., 412/621-4445, www.ppc.edu) has a film series and features live children's theater, dance productions, and a professional drama company.

Another theater group about town is the **Kuntu Repertory Theater** (230 S. Bouquet St., 412/624-7298) founded by a professor of African Studies at University of Pittsburgh, has presented plays on the black experience since the mid-1970s.

Vocal Performances

The Benedum Center for the Performing Arts features performances by the **Pittsburgh Opera** (412/281-0912); **Civic Light Opera** (412/281-3973); and the **Broadway Series.**

Other Performance Venues

The **National Military Museum and Memorial Hall** (5th Ave. and Bigelow Blvd., 412/621-4253) offers a wide variety of entertainment: concerts, dance, lectures, circuses, and films. The **Union Ballroom** (Duquesne University Union, 412/396-5810—university events line) features musicals, plays, road shows, dance, rock and jazz

Pittsburgh

concerts, and other events. The **Mellon Arena** (412/642-1800) also hosts various entertainment events.

FILM

Pittsburgh is deeply involved in films—both making them and watching them (see the sidebar "Hollywood on the Ohio") **Pittsburgh Filmmakers** (477 Melwood Ave., on the East Side, 412/681-5449, www.pghfilmmakers.org) is a school that teaches the art of filmmaking and includes classes in video, still, and digital photography. The organization also runs three theaters with special screenings; call for information on films and schedules. Both made-for-TV movies and top box-office hits have been filmed in the city.

Each neighborhood has a minimum of five theaters that show first-run films. **Cinema in the Parks** (www.city.pittsburgh.pa.us) presents free films shown in city parks during the summer.

Shopping

GOLDEN TRIANGLE

The area between Grant and Stanwix Streets and 4th and Penn Avenues contains the majority of Pittsburgh's upscale shops, including showcases for fashions and accessories by top designers such as Armani and Ralph Lauren. **One Oxford Centre** (Grant St. and 4th Ave.), **PPG Place** (200 3 PPG Pl.), and **Fifth Avenue Place** (120 5th Ave.) all contain mixes of shops and eateries. The area is also home to **Saks Fifth Avenue** (513 Smithfield St.), **Lazarus/Horne's** (501 Penn Ave.), and **Kaufmann's Department Store** (400 5th Ave.). Kaufmann's is the descendant of a successful South Side dry-goods venture launched in the 1800s. Edgar Kaufmann, who owned the company through the mid-20th century, was a patron of Frank Lloyd Wright (Kaufmann's son studied with Wright for a time). Kaufmann Sr. commissioned the cantilevered rural retreat Fallingwater (see Other Points of Interest under Sights in The Laurel Highlands chapter).

A former movie palace, the **Warner Centre** (332 5th Ave.), features a retail arcade that preserves many of the building's architectural details. The art deco–style **Clark Building** (717 Liberty Ave.) provides the setting for Pittsburgh's "Diamond District," which features wholesale and retail jewelry, including antique and specialty pieces. For a quick sugar fix while wandering downtown, stop by **Candy-Rama** (212 5th Ave., 412/281-7350, Mon.–Fri. 8:30 A.M.– 5:55 P.M., Sat. 8:30 A.M.–5:30 P.M.); it sells a huge variety of sweets by the piece or pound.

The Strip is the ultimate downtown flea market and giant produce/bakery discount mart. Take the time to stroll down the side streets, which feature numerous specialty shops with merchandise varying from furniture to clothing.

Saturday morning on the Strip

© JOANNE MILLER

True to its meat-packing heart, you'll also find food wholesalers such as **Jo-Mar Provisions** (18th and Smallman Sts., 412/471-1760), the place to pick up Silver Star kielbasa and that side of beef you always wanted.

EAST SIDE

Oakland

Forbes Avenue and 5th Avenue are lined with shops—bookshops, music stores, vintage clothing outlets—and restaurants. The King's Court Theater, on Forbes, looks like a stage mock-up of a medieval castle and plays select recent films.

South Craig Street offers a number of unique shops. East Indian spices and supplies, ethnic clothing and accessories, and Pittsburgh memorabilia and stationery items are a few of the offerings. Insects in amber, discount art supplies, rare and hard-to-find books, and arts and crafts from Haiti and other exotic locales arere also displayed in an ever-changing variety of shops.

Shadyside

The shopping district extends on Walnut Street from South Aiken to South Negley Avenue. A number of chain retailers—Pier 1 Imports, the Gap, the Limited—have moved in in the last few years, causing local wags to start calling this "Mall-nut" Street. However, the quality of the neighborhood is such that the chains have become "Shadysided" rather than the other way around. Small, personal shops still abound, as do a number of excellent restaurants. **Walnut Mall** (5541 Walnut St.) has a number of boutiques purveying women's clothing, home furnishings, pottery, and kitchen crafts. Small shops on Walnut offer crafts from all over the world, shoes for men and women, couture clothing, pets, toys, and leather goods. On the corner of South Craig and Walnut, the Hartwell Building features hard-core couture: Hugo Boss, DKNY, Valentino, and Yohji Yamamoto. Look down the side streets for additional shops, consignment clothing dealers, bookstores, and eateries. In the warmer months, the "Shadyside

stroll" is a popular local Wednesday-evening happening when the shops and restaurants keep their doors open for browsers and the after-dinner crowd.

North of Shadyside, esoteric shops dot Ravenna Street, including a handicrafts shop and a seller of garden statuary, pots, and tiles. At the intersection of Penn Avenue and Ravenna Street is a small shopping center anchored by a Giant Eagle store (dry goods and some groceries).

Squirrel Hill

The three block area on Forbes at the intersection of Forbes Avenue and Murray Avenue offers a number of boutiques and bookstores. A two-block walk down Murray takes you to a shop that focuses on Judaic subjects, as well as a purveyor of esoteric book titles.

NORTH SIDE

This is an audiophile's heaven: **Record-Rama Sound Archives** (1130 Perry Hwy., Pines Plaza Shopping Center off McKnight Rd., 412/367-7330, Mon.–Sat. 10 A.M.–6 P.M.) features more than 200,000 CDs in stock and more than 2.5 million sound recordings, plus cleaning and storage supplies, cassettes, turntables and phonograph equipment, and reference material. The shop will search for obscure recordings of musical artists, and it ships anywhere in the United States.

SOUTH SIDE

Station Square has familiar mall stores such as Casual Corner but also boasts boutiques selling arts, crafts, antiques and collectibles, souvenirs, miniatures, and educational toys. East Carson Street also offers a wide variety of shops.

East Carson Street

A walkable commercial district extends from South 26th to South 10th Streets. Shops come and go, but this commercial district has been a favorite with Pittsburghers of all ages for many years. Restaurants and stores are interspersed with antique and junk shops. The shopping area

Pittsburgh

extends beyond Carson to the side streets with antique stores, art galleries, and cafés. Thanks to low rent in years past, Carson Street was the setting for a gaggle of retro clothing stores, but in recent times, the neighborhood has been edging into a more upscale market, though a few of the old-style shops still exist. Off East Carson on 12th is the **Bloom Cigar Company** (54 S. 12 St., 412/431-4277, Mon.–Wed. 9:30 A.M.–5 P.M., Thurs.–Fri. 9:30 A.M.–6 P.M., Sat. noon–2 P.M., closed Sun.), an old-fashioned tobacconist. On the street, you'll find distinctive American handicrafts, pottery, jewelry, and glass; alternative music; collectible used hardback and selected new books; good deals on furniture and antiques; and beads, findings, and jewelry-making supplies. **The Rex Movie Theater** (1602 E. Carson St., 412/381-6811) shows contemporary films.

GREATER PITTSBURGH

The villages of Verona and Blawnox, on opposite sides of the Allegheny River in the Oakmont area northeast of Pittsburgh, are home to a burgeoning number of collectible and antique shops.

Where the Malls Are

Mall-style shopping and retailers are available in the North Hills area above Riverview Park on the North Side: **Ross Park Mall** (100 Ross Park Mall Dr.); **North Hills Village** (4801 McKnight Rd.); and **Northway Mall** (1550 Northway Mall). To the east, the town of Monroeville contains the **Miracle Mile Shopping Center** (4055 Monroeville Blvd.), and the **Monroeville Mall** (off Business Rte. 22, or "old Rte. 22"—a shopper's paradise with literally acres of major retailers, boutiques of every description, restaurants, and theaters. This suburb is also the site for the **Expo Mart** (105 Mall Blvd., 412/856-8100), which features major shows and exhibits that come to the Pittsburgh area.

Pittsburgh International Airport, west of Pittsburgh, features a number of retail shops. On the South Side, try **Century III Mall** (3075 Clairton Rd., in West Mifflin) and **The Galleria** (1500 Washington Rd., in Mt. Lebanon).

Recreation

PARKS AND TRAILS

Golden Triangle
Point State Park (City Parks, 412/255-2539, www.city.pittsburgh.pa.us), an ideal spot for strolling and people-watching, occupies the tip of the Golden Triangle (see Sights under The Golden Triangle/The Strip).

The Pittsburgh Cultural Trust is responsible for developing the **Allegheny Riverfront Park** (between the Fort Duquesne and 9th St. bridges).

East Side
Frick Woods Nature Reserve in Frick Park has scenic trails, a 1,700-foot paved trail, a nature center, and a lawn-bowling green, while **Schenley Park** (both City Parks, 412/255-2539, www.city.pittsburgh.pa.us) and **Highland Park** (Pittsburgh Parks Conservancy, 412/682-7275) offer walking and jogging trails. (For more infor-

mation on these parks, see East Side Museums and Galleries and Parks and Scenic Spots under East Side/Oakland).

North Side
Roberto Clemente Memorial Park (601 Ridge Ave., City Parks, 412/255-2539, www.city.pittsburgh.pa.us) is the base of Three Rivers Heritage Trail, a recreational greenway and paved hiking/biking path that extends northeast along the Allegheny River for several miles. The large fragment of stone wall that stands near the pathway is all that remains of a former flood barrier.

South Side
Mt. Washington Park (Norton and Ennis Sts.) has a no-frills walking/jogging trail, but the park has been expanded to include playing fields, a swimming pool, and many other amenities.

The E.G. clock, a local landmark, can be seen on the South Side.

Greater Pittsburgh

Beechwood Farms Nature Reserve (614 Dorseyville Rd., Fox Chapel, 412/963-6100, www.aswp.org) is headquarters for the Audubon Society of Western Pennsylvania. This 134-acre park consists of fields, thickets, ponds, and woodlands threaded by five miles of marked trails for hiking, with great bird-watching. It's open dawn to dusk every day. **The Hartwood Estate** (200 Hartwood Acres, 412/767-9200, www.county .allegheny.pa.us) also has hiking/riding trails (see Greater Pittsburgh). **North Park** (Pearce Mill Rd., Allison Park, 724/935-1971) offers more than 3,000 acres of extensive recreational facilities, including a swimming pool, 18-hole golf course, tennis courts, and a full system of trails. **Trillium Trail** (off Squaw Run Rd. in Fox Chapel) is a nature/walking path. **The Arboretum Trail** is a one-mile paved walking trail that replaced abandoned railroad tracks along the river in Oakmont.

The Pittsburgh American Youth Hostel (AYH) maintains a number of trails—from primitive to civilized—in the Greater Pittsburgh area, some

with overnight facilities, others for day use only. The **Rachel Carson Trail** is a 34-mile, relatively primitive day-hiking trail maintained by Pittsburgh AYH north of Pittsburgh (see Greater Pittsburgh). Information on all AYH trails, trail guides, trail patches, and organized hikes is available from the AYH office (830 E. Warrington Ave., Pittsburgh, PA 15210, 412/431-4910, www.hipitts burgh.org). Printed trail guides cost $9.53.

Boyce Park (675 Frankstown Rd., Monroeville, 724/327-8798) has ball fields, an archery range, basketball courts, downhill skiing, and a wave pool in addition to trails. **South Park** (Buffalo Dr., South Park, 412/835-5710) has extensive trails, a wave pool, horseback riding, and summer concerts with performers as varied as the Pittsburgh Opera and Los Lobos.

Settler's Cabin Park (225 Greer Rd., Oakdale, 412/787-2750) has the most heavily used of the county's three wave pools. The location, between the city and the Greater Pittsburgh International Airport, along with an impressive diving platform, adds to the attraction. A log cabin built in 1780 gives the park its name. The region was famous for its high output of shallow coal and was a maze of abandoned open and back-filled mines when the county secured it. Active wells and exposed oil and gas lines were initial problems, but the grading and reforestation of the land has restored it to rolling wooded slopes and meadows. At 1,589 acres, this park was intended to be the largest of the regional parks and still has a wild, rugged, and unexplored quality not found in the other parks.

BIKING

The city maintains several miles of bikeways in Highland and Schenley Parks. Contact City Parks (412/255-2539, www.city.pittsburgh.pa.us) for information. **Three Rivers Heritage Trail**, part of the Steel Heritage Trail project between Sandcastle and Peters Creek in Clairton, is an 11.5-mile paved track running along the north shore of the Allegheny River starting from the site of the new stadium and Roberto Clemente Park. North Park (724/935-1971) has an extensive trail system—a commercial bike rental lies just outside

Pittsburgh

the park on Ingomar Road. South Park (412/835-5710) offers bike rentals noon–dusk at the Outdoor Recreation Center. Any child under age 12 must wear an approved helmet while riding a bicycle.

OTHER RECREATION

Winter Sports
For ice skating, try the **Schenley Park Ice Rink** (412/422-6547). There are also rinks in **North Park** (303 Pearce Mill Rd., 724/935-1971) and **South Park** (Corrigan Drive, 412/835-5710). **Boyce Park** (675 Frankstown Rd., Monroeville, 724/327-8798) has a small downhill ski area. More challenging downhill skiing is available in the Laurel Highlands south of Pittsburgh (see the Laurel Highlands chapter). Cross-country skiing is popular in all the city parks during the winter.

Tennis
For information on public tennis courts, contact City Parks (412/255-2539, www.city.pitts burgh.pa.us). Public courts are open daily 9 A.M.–11 P.M. Court locations include Schenley, Highland, North, and Boyce Parks.

Bird-Watching
The **Audubon Society of Western Pennsylvania** (614 Dorseyville Rd. in Beechwood Farms north of Pittsburgh, 412/963-6100 www.aswp.org) offers monthly programs that include family hikes, lectures, morning nature walks, bird-watching, and animal tracking. The Audubon store is open Tues.–Sat. 9 A.M.–5 P.M., Sun. 1–5 P.M. Visitors who come to the area (open all year, sunrise–sunset) in late December are invited to join the society's Christmas bird count.

AMUSEMENT PARKS

Kennywood Amusement Park
Kennywood (4800 Kennywood Rd., 412/461-0500, www.kennywood.com—a fun website), in the township of West Mifflin (Swissvale exit off I-376; follow signs), has been designated a Na-

Flying Chairs at Old Kennywood

tional Historic Landmark. Kennywood is open mid-May–Labor Day weekend. Gates open at 10:30 A.M. daily; closing time depends on weather and crowd conditions. An all-day, all-rides ticket is $28.95, $13.95 after 6 P.M. Children under three may enter the park for free but must pay for rides. It's possible for adults over the age of 19 and those under 46 inches in height to buy an entry admission for $8 ($7 seniors) and buy individual ride tickets at $.60 each. These tickets are sold only in strips of $3 each for five tickets. Adult rides require one to four tickets; Kiddieland rides require one ticket. Parking in a nearby lot is free. The park reopens in mid-September–late October for Phantom Fright nights, Fri. and Sat. 6 P.M.–midnight (admission is $17.50).

In 1898, the Monongahela Street Railroad Company leased a grove on Anthony Kenny's farm to build an amusement park at the end of its trolley line—mainly to give people somewhere to ride. Luna Park (the common name of amusement parks such as this one, which showcased the new electric bulb) was built on the site by Frederick Ingersoll in 1905. The initial popularity of amusement parks all over the East is largely due to the inventive Ingersoll, who built the world's first roller coaster, The Pittsburgher, in Luna Park/Kennywood. He went on in the next quarter century to build 276 more roller coasters and a number of additional amusement parks. Luna Park/Kennywood survived the world wars and the Depression and is now the only park still in operation out of the nearly 50 similar ones in a 100-mile radius.

Kennywood offers entertainment from a gentler era—the majority of the rides are accessible to most members of the family. The park is well maintained and busy. Small children tug at the hands of their parents while intoning names of favorite rides. The free stunt show, which is performed twice daily, is also from a bygone era. One act featured world champion "skywalker" (highwire artist) Jay Cochran, from Toronto, Canada. He walked across a 1,000-foot-long, .63-inch-thick cable 150 feet above the crowd—without a net. It was both dangerous and thrilling, in a very immediate way.

The current carousel in Kennywood was built in 1926, created by the Dentzel Company of Philadelphia—one of the world's premier handcarvers of carousel animals. The 1916 Wurlitzer band organ that accompanies the bounding horses is the same one that played for the original Kennywood carousel.

Not all of the rides are tame, however. The Sky Coaster hoists riders 180 feet into the air, and then drops them to swing at the end of a long line between two metal towers—somewhere between bungee jumping and suicide. The Pitt Fall soars 251 feet; four riders, on each of four open cars, are pulled to the top with nothing but their shoulder harnesses to hold onto, and then, while they enjoy the miles-long view, the car is dropped to the ground. Whoopee! The park's Steel Phantom roller coaster has made the Guinness Book of Records as having the greatest and fastest drop—225 vertical feet at 80 miles per hour. None of these rides coddle the faint of heart.

In Lost Kennywood—a section built in 1995 that re-creates much of the old Luna Park—deep-fried dough funnel cakes, called "flying saucers," are served with powdered sugar and cinnamon, along with frozen lemonade. The Pittsburg Plunge (no, that's not a typo—when the original was built, the final "h" hadn't been adopted definitely), one of the most popular rides in the park, douses participants and spectators alike.

The grounds are sprinkled with booths selling "fair food" (including Dippin' Dots, the "ice cream of the future," a frozen milk confection consisting of hundreds of small, multicolored spheres). A central restaurant serves entrées such as fish and chips and meat loaf with mashed potatoes—and offers a choice of gravy or melted cheese as a condiment for fries. Pavilions throughout the park offer the usual games of chance—ball tossing, water-gun races—and even the small prizes are cute stuffed toys of decent quality.

Sandcastle Water Park

This water park (1000 Sandcastle Dr., 412/462-6666, on SR 837 between Homestead High Level Bridge and the Glenwood Bridge in West Homestead, www.sandcastlewaterpark.com) is on the site of a former steel mill. The park is open daily June–Aug. and Labor Day weekend, 11 A.M.–6 P.M. The Whitewater pass (general admission, includes all activities) is $21.95 ($16.95 seniors), $15.95 after 3 P.M., and a season pass is $39.95. Children under three are free.

During a hot summer day, it's a family haven with children's and adult pools, 15 water slides, a tube float, and an old-fashioned boardwalk. Blue Tubaluba slides are dual rider, enclosed slides; blue, partly translucent slides let riders experience misters, waterfalls, and total darkness along two 450-foot-long slides before landing in a four-foot-deep pool. The Mon Tsunami features oceanlike roller waves, and little ones will enjoy the 20,000-gallon Wet Willie's pool. A miniature-golf course and Formula 1 Speedway offer additional diversions. The best way to arrive is by water—Sandcastle is on the Mon. There is a charge for parking and boat docking.

Accommodations

Accommodations in Pittsburgh run the gamut from functional to luxurious, from major inner-city "convention hotels" to unique and often luxurious bed-and-breakfasts. Chain hotels cluster around the airport, and nearly all the major chains— Ramada, Sheraton, Hampton Inn, Marriott, Holiday Inn, Howard Johnson, Radisson, Ramada, Red Roof, Econo Lodge, Days Inn, and Best Western—are represented in the neighborhoods; check any phone book for their "800" telephone numbers for address information and reservations. The American Bed and Breakfast Reservation Service (www.abba.com) books reservations for more than 40 listings in the Greater Pittsburgh and Allegheny Valley area. AAA lists smaller, approved lodgings for its members. Low-cost lodgings are scarce; neither the YWCA nor the YMCA offers overnight accommodations.

UNDER $50

South Side

The Pittsburgh branch of **American Youth Hostels** (830 E. Warrington Ave., 412/431-1267, www.hipittsburgh.org) has renovated an old bank building on the South Side and transformed it into a 50-bed dorm-style lodging with some family rooms available. The hostel has a communal kitchen, laundry facilities, and meeting rooms and is wheelchair-accessible. Rates start at $19 per person per night.

$50–100

Accommodations in this price range tend to be available from chain motels and in unadvertised smaller "strip" motels lining the main roads on the outskirts of the city. Contact the reservation numbers listed in Statewide Hotel and Motel Chains (in the Helpful Telephone Numbers section of Resources) for availability. Occasionally, the larger hotels listed below will offer package rates that bring the nightly tariff below the $100 mark.

$100–150

Golden Triangle

Large chain hotels with all amenities in the Golden Triangle include the **Hilton Pittsburgh** (600 Commonwealth Pl., 412/391-4600, $94–149) and the **Westin Convention Center Pittsburgh** (1000 Penn Ave., 412/281-3700, $80–189).

East Side

In Shadyside, the quaint tree-lined neighborhood near the Carnegie, Michael Plesset and his brother Jeffery originally renovated three properties to provide both long- and short-term homes away from home: the **Shadyside Inn** (5405–5415 5th Ave., 5426 5th Ave., and 811 S.

THE WILLIAM PENN HOTEL'S RADIO DAYS

The William Penn Hotel, built in 1916, became not only the social center of Pittsburgh but also a showplace for new technology. The world's first commercially licensed radio station, KDKA, began broadcasting there on November 2, 1920, with news of Harding's defeat of Cox in the presidential election.

The toddling years of radio were fraught with difficulties. Many stations shared the same frequency during the first eight years and voluntarily had silent nights—Pittsburgh would shut down on Tuesday, for example, so broadcasts from other cities could be heard. To complicate matters further, ship-to-shore communications were also on the same frequency. If a ship sent a distress signal, all stations in the vicinity had to shut down so the signal could be pinpointed. Contemporary radio stations owe their use of identity call letters to those very same ship-to-shore wireless transmissions. Ships used letters over the wireless because they were easier to distinguish than numbers.

Negley Ave., 412/441-4444 or 800/767-8483, www.shadysideinn.com, $99–160, dropping for weekly or monthly stays). Two blocks from the Shadyside shopping area on Walnut Street and a few blocks from each other, two of the buildings are in the glass-brick art moderne mode of the 1940s and the other is an arched Richardsonian Romanesque–style delight. All three contain spacious and spotless studio, one-bedroom, and two-bedroom apartment-sized suites with kitchens. Many of Shadyside Inn's customers choose to stay here because the short-term lease is a good value—less expensive and more spacious than a hotel. It's conveniently close to downtown, without the crowds and parking hassles (free off-street parking here). And, it's just plain comfortable—the tubs are big enough to float away your troubles. Movie star Jodie Foster stayed here with a film entourage, as did the family of a former governor of Pennsylvania when he was recovering at a nearby hospital.

North Side

☒ The Priory (614 Pressley St., 412/231-3338, www.thepriory.com, $119–155) is one of the best overall accommodations in Greater Pittsburgh. Hammered-tin ceilings, carefully chosen furnishings, and a flawless restoration of this former residence for Bavarian monks serve to make this bed-and-breakfast inn a favorite among international visitors. German and Swiss settlers banded together in 1852 to build St. Mary's Parish Church and added the priory next door in 1888 to serve as a home for brothers of the Benedictine monastic order. In 1981, the Pennsylvania Department of Transportation closed the church; it was to be razed to make way for I-279. A miraculous change of plans saved the buildings, and restoration work was subsequently begun by the Grafs, who bought the property in 1984. Creature comforts aren't sacrificed for quaintness—the Priory has most of the amenities of a fine hotel. Each of the 24 suites has a private bath, and in warm weather, breakfast is served in a serene courtyard with shade trees sandwiched between the inn and the church. Travelers can also take a free limo to destinations in the Golden

Morning Glory Inn

© JOANNE MILLER

Triangle during the week. The surrounding area has been gentrified into renovated properties similar to the Priory with a few ramshackle dwellings mixed in. An older central shopping district a few blocks away on Ohio Street serves the neighborhood. The Warhol Museum, Children's Museum, and National Aviary are within a quarter-mile radius.

South Side

☒ Morning Glory Inn (2119 Sarah St., 412/431-1707, www.morningglorybedandbreakfast.com, $150–190) is a pleasant alternative to a hotel. The five rooms of this 1862 Italianate Victorian are decorated with both the period and convenience in mind, and the inn is within easy walking distance of the South Side's galleries, jazz bars, and restaurants. Innkeeper Nancy Eshelman and her husband are experts on the area and can tell you about what's new in town; they've made a major effort to make the inn attractive to business travelers. The breakfasts, common

Pittsburgh

rooms, and private courtyard all make this a good choice for those seeking a homier atmosphere.

Greater Pittsburgh

⋈ The Inn at Oakmont (300 Rte. 909, Verona, 412/828-0410, http://theinnatoakmont.com, $100–150) is a newer bed-and-breakfast convenient to either the North or the East Side. The attractive borough of Oakmont, with its blooming dogwood trees and grand old houses, offers fashionable shops and restaurants along its main street, Allegheny Avenue. Up the hill from the town, across from the invitation-only Oakmont Golf and Country Club, the inn provides elegant rooms to weary travelers and golfers alike. The innkeeper, Shelly Smith, along with her parents, Liz and Vance, create a welcoming, intimate atmosphere. Each of the eight guest rooms has a private bath and television, two have whirlpool baths and fireplaces, and two share an adjoining door. Though the rooms are not inexpensive, the value is excellent. Originally, the Smiths searched for a stately older home in Oakmont to create their inn; zoning restrictions forced them to modify their dream. They built the inn from scratch, decorating it with antiques and specially chosen fabrics (often with a subtle golf motif) in 1994. The results are replete with refined old-fashioned charm—including Waterford crystal and silver service—combined with modern conveniences. Shelly serves a gourmet breakfast in beautiful surroundings. These people love to share their home, and the word has gotten around—they book visitors from all over the world. Guests can also reach the inn via the yellow belt (see Getting Around under Transportation). When the belt reaches Hulton Road (the yellow belt continues north), make a right turn to the south instead. The inn is immediately behind the bank.

$150–250

Golden Triangle

The **Omni William Penn** (530 William Penn Pl., 412/281-7100 or 800/843-8664, www.omni hotels.com, $169–199) looks out over Mellon Square Park. Every major city has a grand hotel, an elegant space where debutantes dance illuminated by Baccarat chandeliers and dowagers clink teacups beneath ormolu fixtures. A regal reminder of Pittsburgh's past, the William Penn was built in 1916 by Henry Clay Frick as a showplace for the city; it was created to rival the great hotels of Europe in style, with the added benefit of the budding technological wizardry of the 20th century. And what a marvel it was! Each room featured a telephone (the in-hotel exchange had more operators than the entire city of Johnstown), electrically operated lights and clocks, and a private bathroom—all in an age when most people still used outdoor privies. Considered the most modern hotel of its time, the William Penn was almost entirely a product of Pittsburgh's industries, from the steel girders rolled at Homestead Works to the Louis XVI reproductions that furnished the rooms.

Through the Great Depression and the booms and busts that followed, the William Penn changed hands a number of times; once she narrowly missed destruction, rescued by a group of Pittsburgh investors, who resold her in better times. Now owned and operated by Omni Hotels, the William Penn thrives in a new era that appreciates the fine detailing and service that were the hallmarks of another time. The gilt-and-crystal Grand Ballroom and the art deco–style Urban room (named for Ziegfeld Follies designer Joseph Urban)—with its black glass walls and "Tree of Life" mural—continue to stage many of Pittsburgh's most elegant events. As it has been from the beginning, the hotel is continually booked with meetings and conventions. Afternoon tea is served in the Palm Court Lobby, accompanied by melodies coaxed from a piano once owned by André Previn. The staff serves elegant meals in the Terrace Room, and workers from nearby office buildings gather in the Tap Room for after-work drafts. Lawrence Welk's original bubble machine is given a spin on special occasions. Most important, the pared-down staff still strives to achieve the standard of professional service put forth by former owner Eugene Eppley: "Watch for chances to do special unlooked for, unexpected things which add to the comfort of those within our doors."

The William Penn is an old hotel and suffers occasionally from age-related problems. One significant sign of her origins is the absence of parking—those who arrive by auto must park (and pay) in the locked public lot under Mellon Park across the street. However, this *grande dame* is *the* hotel in the Golden Triangle. Accommodations vary from simple older one-room sleeping quarters and two-room suites to luxury suites with whirlpool baths and apartment-like suite/meeting rooms with three bedrooms that seat 10 and can hold up to 50 people. The Omni William Penn offers visitors a number of fun packages and weekends at bargain prices year-round.

The **ℳ Renaissance Pittsburgh Hotel** (107 6th St., 412/562-1200, www.renaissancehotels .com, $140–250), a Sage Hospitality/Marriott property, is reborn from a historical landmark, the Fulton building. Constructed in 1906 for industrialist Henry Phipps, the building served as a business center, VA hospital administration building, and nightclub (named Heaven) before being carefully renovated in 2001. In the largest project of its kind since the Statue of Liberty restoration in 1986, 40,000 pounds of baking soda went into cleaning the copper cladding in the building's courtyard alone, and the magnificent 30-foot-wide glass rotunda was unshorn of its World War II blackout rubber covering. The wood-and-marble building interior reflects a blend of the best of old Pittsburgh style and the latest technology (including a health club, instant Internet access, and a business center). A restaurant, lounge, and wine bar are also provided for guests (see American under Food and Nightlife). One of the best things about this

lovely four-star hotel is its access to the local performance venues—it's steps away from the Byham Theater, Heinz Hall, the O'Reilly Theater, and the Benedum Center, undoubtedly why many show business people choose to stay here (along with a few private guests of note—Prince Andrew for one). Accommodations vary from large, comfortable rooms to suites, many with a view of the Allegheny River.

The **Pittsburgh Marriott City Center** (112 Washington Pl., 412/471-4000 or 888/456-6600, $149–189) is another good choice in this price range downtown.

East Side

The Appletree Bed and Breakfast (703 S. Negley Ave., 412/661-0631, www.appletreeb-b.com, $150–250) is a beautifully restored Italianate Victorian home in Shadyside. Built in 1884, the home is a grand representation of the era, with intricately designed decorative plasterwork on ceilings and skirtings, original wood floorings, and well-appointed fireplaces. The elegant guestrooms—most are named for varieties of apples—have full baths.

South Side

The 293-room **Sheraton Station Square** (7 Station Square Dr., 412/261-2000 or 800/325-3535, $109–245) is Pittsburgh's premier hotel on the waterfront. It has two restaurants, a fitness facility including indoor pool, and free parking at Station Square for registered guests (the hotel is next to the complex). Special rates are available throughout the year. The Sheraton also offers a Club Level with concierge service and other perks.

Food and Nightlife

Pittsburgh is famous for its ethnic culinary mix. Each of the neighborhood areas has dozens of specialty restaurants, featuring dishes for every taste, from East Indian curry to Guatemala-style enchiladas. For those who prefer the more familiar, chain eateries in the area include the ubiquitous **Eat & Park** (good breakfast specials) and **Bob Evans,** both of which have standard diner menus; **Hoss' Steak House** and **Ponderosa Steakhouse,** meat-and-potatoes lunch and dinner places; and **Chi Chi's,** a Mexican-style food chain with fresh food (very mild unless otherwise requested). **TGI Friday's** is a local favorite for an after-work drink and a light meal. The following are a few Pittsburgh favorites.

BREAKFAST PLACES

Golden Triangle
In the Strip, breakfasts come in the form of eggs any style, buckwheat pancakes, Amish-raised ham, and homemade sausage at **DeLucas** (2015 Penn Ave., 412/566-2195, Mon.–Sat. 6 A.M.–3 P.M., Sun. 7 A.M.–3 P.M.). It's a bargain at less than $6 a plate.

East Side
In Shadyside, a perennial favorite is **Prantl's Bakery** (5542 Walnut St., 412/621-2092, daily 7:30 A.M.–6 P.M.)—reputed to have the best doughnuts in the world.

Forty years ago, Jean Cohen opened the first of a number of small, homey eateries that have become neighborhood institutions. **Pamela's** (5527 Walnut St., 412/683-1003, in Shadyside; 3703 Forbes Ave., 412/683-4066 and 5813 Forbes Ave., 412/422-9457, in Oakland) and **P&G Diner** (232 North Ave., 412/821-4655 in Millvale) are all open Mon.–Sat. 8 A.M.–4 P.M., Sun. 9 A.M.–3 P.M. (Pamela's was named after one of Jean's daughters, who has taken over the business.) The restaurants serve inexpensive hearty breakfasts ($6) and lunches ($7) to locals and visitors alike—the pancakes float off the plate. Get there early on the weekend to avoid the lines.

For breakfast in Squirrel Hill, try **Bruegger's Bagel Bakery** (1719 Murray, 412/422-2814, www.brueggers.com, daily 7 A.M.–2 P.M.), a chain with outlets all over the East Coast. On the next block is an **Eat & Park** (1816 Murray Ave., 412/422-7203, www.eatnpark.com, open 24/7), another chain that offers breakfast, lunch, and dinner at reasonable prices, from under $5 to $15.

South Side
The **Beehive Coffeehouse** (1327 E. Carson St., 412/488-4483, Mon.–Sat. 8:30–1 A.M., Sun. 8:30–midnight) is a neighborhood hangout, papered with local events and artwork and lined with racks of shared reading and free newspapers—a good place to meet the locals and savor the newspaper over a steaming mug and pastry.

DELIS AND QUICK LUNCHES
Golden Triangle
Primanti Brothers (46 18th St., 412/263-2142, www.primantibros.com) is a deli-style operation that's been in business since the 1940s; this stall in the Strip—the original location—is open 24 hours daily. Other locations include a spot under

COURTESY OF THE BEEHIVE COFFEEHOUSE

a morning favorite

Kaufmann's garage on Cherry Way (412/566-8051), and 4th and Forbes Avenues in Oakland (3803 Forbes, 412/621-4444); hours vary at the other locations. Some locals swear that it serves the best (and biggest) sandwiches in Pittsburgh, the classic Primanti consists of a big hunk of grilled meat, cole slaw, hot fried egg, fresh tomato and crisp French fries between two slabs of chewy Italian bread that barely fits into your mouth—all for less than $5.

East Side

Known as "O-Dog," the **Original Hot Dog Shop** (3901 Forbes Ave., 412/621-7388, 10 A.M.–3 P.M., Sat.–Sun. 10 A.M.–5 P.M.), across from the University of Pittsburgh, has been a mainstay of collegiate diets since 1960, the year the Pirates won the World Series. A casino's worth of flashing lights and buzzing neon advertise a fast-food menu that varies from steak hoagies to pizza to pasta—and, of course, the almost-world-famous O-Dog hot dog, served with mustard, relish, onion, pickle, ketchup, chili, sauerkraut, and mayonnaise. Cheese is extra. O-Dog even delivers—and it's cheap, under $5. If you'd prefer an atmosphere with more decorum (and less mustard), the **Carnegie Institutes and Museums** (4400 Forbes Ave.) house a small cafeteria on the ground floor of the Art Museum. It's open for lunch and snacks, with prices averaging $6. Also in the Carnegie is the Fossil Fuels Cafe ("pour on the 40-weight, Mom"), open 11 A.M.–4 P.M., serving coffee and light fare.

Cappy's Cafe (5431 Walnut St., 412/621-1188, Mon.–Sat. 11 A.M.–2 A.M.) offers sandwiches and healthy food choices at around $6. **Max & Erma's** (5533 Walnut St., 412/681-5775, www.maxandermas.com, Mon.–Thurs. 11 A.M.–11 P.M., Fri.–Sat. 11 A.M.–midnight, Sun. 11 A.M.–10 P.M.) is a chain with simple meals in the $6–12 price range.

Sari's (2109 Murray Ave. near Forbes in Squirrel Hill, 412/421-7208, Sun.–Thurs. 10 A.M.–8 P.M., Fri. 10 A.M.–2 P.M., Sat. 6:30 P.M.–11 P.M.) serves fast food from a kosher vegetarian/dairy menu. It's open for takeout during the day, and most items on the menu are under $6.

PIEROGI BY ANY OTHER NAME

Pittsburgh drew wave upon wave of immigrants during the 19th century—first from the British Isles, then later from Europe and Eastern Europe. The result is a fascinating mix of neighborhoods that still retain their identity and restaurants that cater to the unique tastes of a host of ethnic backgrounds.

Two food traditions that are of particular interest are those of Poland and Ukraine: rustic cookery that originated in fertile black-soil valleys that produced grains, fruits, and vegetables (particularly cabbage and potatoes) during the short summer. The long and fierce winters inspired artful use of available ingredients.

Pierogi (peer-O-ghee—boiled, filled dumplings from Poland), piroshki (peer-OSH-kee—small, baked, crescent-shaped pies from Ukraine), and Siberian *pelmeni* (pel-MEN-yeh—a meat-filled dumpling served in broth) are still served in local restaurants.

Both pierogis and piroshkis can have a variety of fillings. The most popular—and traditional—are cheese, potatoes, cabbage, onions, sauerkraut, mushrooms, meat, or combinations of these. A sweet version of pierogi is produced using sour black cherries. *Holubsi* (ho-LOOBS-chee), stuffed cabbage leaves, are also well represented, in both the meat-and-rice version and the vegetarian mushroom-and-rice version. (The Eastern Orthodox church requires abstinence from meat, eggs, and milk products during Lent—the 6.5 weeks that precede Easter—and other religious holidays.) Some of the best kielbasa (kill-BAS-eh—pork and garlic sausage) in America comes from Pittsburgh's local butchers.

The neighborhood of Polish Hill, bordered by SR 380 on the south, lies between the Strip and Bloomfield. The winding streets reveal a number of local delis where visitors may sample Eastern European specialties. Just across the Bloomfield Bridge on the East Side, the Bloomfield Bridge Tavern is reputed to have the best pierogi in Pittsburgh.

Pittsburgh

Expect big helpings of both food and art in Pittsburgh.

South Side

The Pickle Barrel (1301 E. Carson, 412/431-1114, Mon.–Thurs. 6:30 A.M.–6 P.M., Fri. 6:30 A.M.–8 P.M., Sat. 8 A.M.–5 P.M.) has been serving breakfasts, including three-egg omelets, hot dogs, and hamburgers, all under $5, since 1968.

Greater Pittsburgh

Damon's, the Place for Ribs (7221 McKnight Rd., north of Pittsburgh, 412/367-7427, Sun.–Thurs. 11 A.M.–11 P.M., Fri.–Sat. 11 A.M.–12 P.M.) is a favorite quick stop for ribs and sandwiches. Prices range $6–18.

AMERICAN

Golden Triangle

Mortons of Chicago (625 Liberty Ave., 412/261-7141, Mon.–Sat. 5–11 P.M., Sun. 5–10 P.M.) and **Ruth's Chris Steak House** (1 PPG Pl., No. 6, 412/391-4800, Mon.–Thurs. 11:30 A.M.–3 P.M. lunch, 5–10 P.M. dinner; Fri. 11:30 A.M.–3 P.M., 5–11 P.M.; Sat. 5–11 P.M.; Sun. 5–9 P.M.) are dependable upscale steak and prime rib houses, with prices that average $10 for lunch–$20 for dinner.

For a dose of local color, try the **Original Oyster House** (20 Market Sq. in the middle of downtown, 412/566-7925, Mon.–Sat. 9 A.M.–11 P.M.)—a funky but authentic remnant of Pittsburgh's industrial age, with Rolling Rock beer on tap. Snacks are as little as $5; a full meal costs up to $20. The **1902 Landmark Tavern** (24 Market Sq., 412/471-1902, Sun.–Thurs. 11:30 A.M.–9 P.M., Fri.–Sat. 11:30 A.M.–10 P.M.) boasts a faithful period restoration matched in quality by the dishes served. In keeping with the turn-of-the-last-century theme, a raw bar serves clams, mussels, oysters, and shrimp, with prices averaging $10 for lunch, $20 for dinner.

Opus (107 6th St., in the Renaissance Pittsburgh Hotel, 412/992-2005; breakfast Mon.–Fri. 6:30 A.M.–2 P.M., Sat.–Sun. 7 A.M.–2 P.M., $6; lunch daily 11 A.M.–2 P.M., $9; dinner Mon.–Thurs. 5–11 P.M., Fri.–Sat. 5 P.M.–midnight, Sun. 4–10 P.M., $21) serves a standard American menu (steak and grilled onions, pesto-marinated chicken breast, crab cakes, pastas, etc.) in a beautifully renovated room. On the weekends, stop in for the breakfast buffet for $10—it starts at 8:30 and generally runs until noon or 1 P.M. Opus offers a wine bar in the lobby of the hotel, open Tues.–Sat. 5 P.M. until the restaurant closes (sometimes earlier depending on business). The hotel also features the dark wood-and-mirrored Bridge Bar, a full service bar that's open Mon.–Thurs. 2:30–midnight, Fri. 2:30 P.M.–2 A.M., Sat. 11 A.M.–2 A.M., and Sun. 11 A.M.–11 P.M.

East Side

On Baum Boulevard, try **Ritter's Diner** (5221 Baum, 412/682-4852), a classic, if somewhat funky, trip back to the '50s that's open 24 hours every day. Ritter's serves breakfast, lunch, and dinner. Prices are typical diner at $5–15. In Squirrel Hill, **Gullifty's** (1922 Murray Ave., 412/521-8222, Mon.–Fri. 11 A.M.–midnight, Sat. 11 A.M.–1 A.M., Sun. 10 A.M.–1 A.M.), remodeled from an old theater, offers a menu as broad and adventurous (Italian, Mexican, and California cuisine) that it appears to be several eateries in one. Meal prices average $8 for lunch, $15 for dinner.

M The Church Brew Works (3525 Liberty Ave. north of the Strip, 412/688-8200, www .churchbrew.com, Mon.–Thurs. 11:30 A.M.–11:45 P.M., Fri.–Sat. 11:30 A.M.–1 A.M., Sun. noon–10 P.M.) offers a broad range of gourmet entrées such as Asiago crusted pork chops ($17) and vegetarian stir-fry ($15). The pizzas—including a Pittsburgh Pierogie Pizza—are worth exploring (starting at $10). You can get a traditional Pittsburgh salad with chargrilled chicken and mixed greens piled with fries and jack cheese for about $10. Entrées range $10–25. The beers (the award-winning dark Pious Monk Dunkel, and my favorite, Pipe Organ Pale Ale, among them) are what put Church Brew Works on the map; all are made in-house, and the gleaming copper and brass brew tanks stand where the altar once was in this 1902 deconsecrated Baptist Church. Beautiful blue light filters through the stained glass windows into the restaurant, and occasionally, former church attendees will stand before the altar, reviving a memory or two before sitting down to a hearty dinner and a pint.

North Side

The **Brighton Inn** (3889 Brighton Rd., one block north of Benton Rd., 412/766-3110) looks like a rowdy tavern from the street. Inside, faced with a door number one/door number two choice and a tsunami of bar noise, you'll wonder if you should really enter at all. Take the door on the left. It leads to a clean, old-fashioned diner with delicious home cooking and extraordinarily low prices. The bar next door, which is accessible through a doorway in the dining room, is a raucous local hangout. The owner tended bar there for 17 years before he bought the place and became the cook—proof that long engagements work. Takeout is available, and prices average $8.

South Side

Station Square offers a variety of bars and restaurants, fast food, loud food (the Hard Rock Cafe), and elegant sit-down meals, such as the Grand Concourse.

The **M Grand Concourse Restaurant** (1 Station Sq., 412/261-1717, Mon.–Fri. 11 A.M.–10 P.M., Sat. 4–11 P.M., Sun. 10 A.M.–3 P.M. brunch, 4–9 P.M. dinner) is top of the line, and an experience in itself, both for the setting—the elegantly refurbished 1901 Pittsburgh & Lake Erie Railroad terminal—and for the quality of food and service. Dine in the main hall, with its soaring vaulted ceiling, or in the River Room, a former loading platform now enclosed in glass; the setting is reminiscent of a fine rail dining car, and trains rush by, momentarily obscuring a fabulous river and skyline view. The menu is a compendium of American favorites, including crabcakes ($19), steamed mussels, Charlie's seafood chowder ($4 each), surf and turf ($35), and fresh lobster by the pound. Lunch averages $13, dinner $25. Next to the main hall, the Gandydancer Saloon is a popular meeting place and watering hole.

Two local favorites are **City Grille** (2019 E. Carson St., 412/431-1770, Mon.–Wed. 11:30 A.M.–10 P.M.; Thu.–Sat. 11:30 A.M.–11 P.M.)—great rack of lamb with port wine sauce—and the **1889 Cafe** (2017 E. Carson, 412/431-9290, Tues.–Thurs. 10 A.M.–10 P.M., Fri.–Sat. 10 A.M.–11 P.M., Sun. 10 A.M.–9 P.M., $8–13).

For red-meat lovers, the **Pittsburgh Steak Company** (1924 E. Carson, 412/381-5505, Mon.–Thurs. 11 A.M.–11 P.M., Sat. 11 A.M.–midnight, Sun. 4–10 P.M.) serves the Pittsburgh Cheese Steak (steak on a roll with sautéed mushrooms, green peppers, and onions topped with provolone, $9), as well as every cut of beef ever invented, plus chops and seafood. Prices tiptoe from $9–$30. **Blue Lou's** (1510 E. Carson, 412/381-7675, Mon.–Fri. 11 A.M.–midnight, bar until 1:30 A.M., Sat. 11 A.M.–1:30 A.M.) features billiards, darts, and food. Expect to pay around $7 for lunch, $10 for dinner.

For the best view in town, try the **Grandview Saloon** (1212 Grandview Ave., 412/431-1400, Sun.–Thurs. 11 A.M.–10 P.M., Fri.–Sat. 11 A.M.–11 P.M., bar open until 1:30 A.M.). It's close to the top station of the Duquesne Incline and looks out over the city. The menu is American, and lunch is around $8; dinners average $17.

Greater Pittsburgh

Hoffstot's Cafe Monaco (533 Allegheny Ave., in Oakmont, 412/828-8555; Mon.–Thurs. 11:30–10 A.M., Fri.–Sat. 11 A.M.–10 P.M., Sun. 1–9 P.M.; lunch $10, dinner $18) is often packed with happy Oakmonters—and for good reason. The broad menu provides choices for every member of the family, from French-fried chicken to sea scallops Palermo. On the lighter side, inexpensive dinner salads served on generous platters satisfy any appetite (the spinach salad is excellent). Hoffstot's also serves a side of fries for under a dollar anytime and offers weekend specials such as osso bucco. The decor is light and airy—an elegantly comfortable European bistro setting without pretension.

The same people who run Hoffstot's also created the **Chelsea Grille** (515 Allegheny Ave., 412/828-0570, Mon.–Thurs. 11 A.M.–9 P.M., Fri.–Sat. 11 A.M.–10 P.M., Sun. 4–8 P.M.; lunch $7, dinner $20). Where Hoffstot's concentrates on a more European menu, the Grille is all-American, with fresh fish, fajitas, and Cajun-style ostrich medallions.

Near the zoo, try **The Aspinwall Grille** (211 Commercial Ave., Aspinwall, 412/782-6542, Sun.–Thurs. 11 A.M.–10 P.M., Fri.–Sat. 11 A.M.–11 P.M.), a casual pub-style eatery that serves barbecued chicken, steak, and ribs ($11–17), Cajun chicken Alfredo ($14), a variety of seafood, burgers, and sandwiches ($6–18).

Just up the street, the cool, green, slightly more formal **Mulligan's Tavern** (225 Commercial Ave., Aspinwall, 412/781-5190, Mon.–Thurs. 11:30 A.M.–1 P.M., Fri., 11:30 A.M.–11 P.M., Sat. 4:30–11 P.M., closed Sun.) offers a number of specialties such as chicken and dumplings ($3), corned beef ($7 lunch, $12 dinner), and crabcakes ($20). Lunch averages $8.50, dinner $17.

CONTINENTAL

Golden Triangle

Asiago (301 Grant near 4th, in 1 Oxford Centre, 412/392-0225, www.asiagoeurocuisine.com, Mon.–Thurs. 11 A.M.–9 P.M., Fri.–Sat. 11 A.M.–10 P.M., lunch $9, dinner $15) is a very popular chain that serves regional Italian cooking and other dishes with a continental twist.

East Side

On Baum Boulevard east of the Shadyside District, locals swear by the upscale **Baum Vivant** (5102 Baum, 412/682-2620, Mon.–Thurs. 5:30–10 P.M., Fri.–Sat. 5:30–11 P.M., $25–40)—an eclectic menu with a continental slant; reservations are required. The Dover sole is perennially popular.

South Side

Across the street from Bloom Cigar Company on 12th Street off East Carson is **Cafe Allegro** (51 S. 12 St., 412/481-7788, Sun.–Thurs. 5–10 P.M., Fri.–Sat. 5–11 P.M.) voted by *Pittsburgh Magazine* readers Best Overall Restaurant for two years in a row; reservations are recommended. Expect to find dishes such as chef Nolan's bouillabaisse ($23), filet mignon with dark beer and gorgonzola ($28), and goat cheese and watercress ravioli ($19). Prices average $25.

For a formal, upscale dining experience and spectacular views, try **Le Mont** (1114 Grandview Ave., on Mt. Washington, 412/431-3100, www.lemontpittsburgh.com, Mon.–Sat. 5–10 P.M., Sun. 4–10 P.M., $27–48, reservations required);

the **Georgetown Inn** (1230 Grandview Ave., 412/481-4424, lunch Tues.–Sat. 11 A.M.–3 P.M., $8; dinner Mon.–Thurs. 5–11 P.M., Fri.–Sat. 5 P.M.–midnight, Sun. 4–10 P.M. $25, reservations recommended); or **The Tin Angel** (1200 Grandview Ave., 412/381-1919, Mon.–Thurs. 5:30–9 P.M. Fri.–Sat. 5:30–9:30 P.M., reservations required; five-course prix fixe dinners only, $40–60).

Sleek and simple **Dish** (128 S. 17th St., 412/390-2012, 4 P.M.–midnight daily) serves tasty Italian dishes from a brief menu nightly ($15), the friendly bar is a good place to sit and watch the world go by. The South Side used to be filled with little neighborhood bars that were stop-offs for the town's workingmen—Dish is the modern take on tradition—a neighborhood place with a sophisticated feel.

M Old Europe (1209–1211 E. Carson St., www.oldeuroperestaurant.com, Tues.–Sat. 5 P.M.–closing, Sun. 4 P.M.–closing) is a local and regional favorite for its eastern European cuisine and lively old-world bar. Of note are the Bulgarian casserole (layers of feta and kashkaral cheese, onions, mushrooms, tomatoes, and sweet red peppers crowned with egg in a crock pot, $16), Ukrainian beet salad (beets, apples, potatoes, pickles—sounds strange but tastes great, $5) and grilled whole trout ($18).

ETHNIC AND REGIONAL SPECIALTIES

Golden Triangle

Lidia's (1400 Smallman St. in the Strip, 412/552-0150, www.lidiasitaly.com) is a popular branch of the chain. It serves lunch Mon.–Fri. 11:30 A.M.–2 P.M., Sat. 11:30 A.M.–2:30 P.M.; brunch Sun. 11 A.M.–2 P.M.; and dinner Mon. 5–9 P.M., Tues.–Thurs. 5–9:30 P.M., Fri. 5 P.M.–10 P.M., Sat. 4:30–10:30 P.M., Sun. 4–8 P.M. Italian pasta dishes are standard, with the twist of the Pasta Tasting Trio—servers bring three freshly made pastas to your table to taste, and you may have as much of each as you like. Sunday brunch also features the pasta trio, and some Italian specialties such as bacon and egg frico (fried montasio cheese with a savory filling) and potato pancakes

with spinach-poached eggs and prosciutto. Prices average $14 for lunch, $25 for dinner, and $20 for brunch.

In the Strip, **Kaya** (2000 Smallman, 412/261-6565, Mon.–Wed. 11:30 A.M.–10 P.M., Thurs.–Sat. 11:30 A.M.–11 P.M., Sun. noon–9 P.M., lunch $10, dinner $20) is a popular upscale "Karibbean Kuisine" hangout.

East Side

Two-block-long South Craig Street, close to the Carnegie and the Cathedral of Learning, features a variety of restaurants. **Ali Baba** (404 S. Craig, 412/682-2829, Mon.–Fri. lunch 11:30 A.M.–2:30 P.M., dinner 4–9:45 P.M., Sat.–Sun. 4–9:45 P.M., lunch $5, dinner $10) has won awards for its Middle Eastern menu, especially the shish kebab and hummus. Chinese-style **YumWok** (400 S. Craig, 412/687-7777, daily 11 A.M.–10 P.M., $8) completes the international picture.

A wide mix of ethnic restaurants lines Atwood Street (at the intersection of Forbes Avenue) in Oakland. One local favorite is **Mad Mex** (370 Atwood, 412/681-5656, daily 11 A.M.–1 A.M., bar until 1:30 A.M., lunch $7, dinner $10), which repeatedly wins all of Pittsburgh's Best Mex awards in local polls. The combo of Mexican wings and margaritas is unbeatable.

Zara's (3887 Bigelow Blvd., 412/682-8296, Mon.–Sat. 5–11 P.M., $18) serves a southern Italian menu, all homemade; the *raviolis di filamina* (spinach, ricotta, a bit of beef) are a specialty.

Near Shadyside, upscale **Khalil's** (4757 Baum Blvd., 412/683-4757, Sun.–Thurs. 3:30–10 P.M., Fri.–Sat. 4–11:30 P.M., $15) features Middle Eastern specialties. Reservations are required. A touch more expensive than many Chinese restaurants, **China Palace** (5440 Walnut St. in Shadyside, 412/687-7423, Mon.–Thurs. 11:30 A.M.–10 P.M., Fri.–Sat. 11:30 A.M.–11 P.M., Sun. 2–9 P.M., lunch $8, dinner $15) offers a pleasantly serene interior and good service (or delivery), as well as excellent barbecued spareribs. Just down the street, **Sushi Too** (5432 Walnut, 412/687-8744, www.sushitoo.com.123.net, Mon.–Thurs. lunch 11:30 A.M.–3 P.M., dinner 5–10 P.M., Fri.–Sat. 11:30 A.M.–11 P.M., Sun. 1–9 P.M., $13) serves fresh Japanese food. Oddly enough, very

Pittsburgh

little sushi appears on the menu—most dishes are full meals such as chicken teriyaki and tempura. Lunch specials are a good deal at both China Palace and Sushi Too.

Known for its kosher neighborhood, Squirrel Hill's shops and restaurants are interspersed with small greengrocers and purveyors of dry goods. Squirrel Hill's main restaurant area is at the crossroads of Forbes and Murray Avenues, extending down Murray to Forward Street. The neighborhood isn't fancy, but it's safe—both beat cops and beggars patrol the busy street. Inexpensive meal choices are plentiful. Visitors are likely to share aisles with Hasidic men wielding shopping carts at **Prime Kosher/Koshermart,** a grocery store and deli. The deli serves kosher box lunches and prepared meals for around $10. Farther down the road are several pizzerias, Chinese restaurants, and a Middle Eastern deli. Several folks recommended the **New Dumpling House** (2138 Murray, 412/422-4178, Sun.– Wed. 11 A.M.–9:30 P.M., Fri.–Sat. 11 A.M.– 10:30 P.M., $7) for Chinese. **Poli's** (2607 Murray at the corner of Forward, 412/521-6400, Tues.–Thurs. 11:30 A.M.–10 P.M., Fri.–Sat. 11:30 A.M.–11 P.M., Sun. 1–9 P.M., lunch $8, dinner $18) specializes in seafood and Italian dishes such as linguine with sausage.

A real star in the neighborhood is **Kazansky's** (2201 Murray, 412/521-4555, Mon.–Fri. 10 A.M.–11 P.M., Sat.–Sun. 8 A.M.–midnight, $5–15). Once known as the legendary Rhoda's, this is a clean, comfortable, well-decorated restaurant with exceptional food and prices. Homemade chopped liver, delicious cheese blintzes with cherries—the list of big-platter excellent Jewish deli food goes on and on; the corned beef is a local favorite.

Bloomfield, east of the Strip above SR 380, remains true to its village heritage. Liberty Avenue, between Bloomfield Avenue and Edmond Street, has a movie theater, restaurants, grocery stores, foot doctors, clothing stores—everything a family would need. On Cedarville Street, on the corner of Liberty, **Mariani's Pleasure Bar** (4729 Liberty, 412/682-9603, Mon.–Wed. 11 A.M.–10:30 P.M., Thurs.–Sat. 11 A.M.–11:30 P.M., Sun. 4–10 P.M., bar open until 2 A.M., $10) continues to be a fa-

vorite place for roast beef, steaks, and pasta. Some Pittsburghers consider it the quintessential Pittsburgh-Italian restaurant. It offers a terrific lunch buffet Mon.–Fri. 11 A.M.–2:30 P.M. for $6.95. Farther down the block on Cedarville, the **Groceria Italiana** deli sells food to go. **D'Amico's** (on the corner of State Way and Liberty Ave., 412/682-2523, daily 11 A.M.–11 P.M.) serves ample dinners of freshly grilled scampi or more classic Italian dishes, with menu prices hovering around $10. Voted best Polish restaurant and best pierogi in Pittsburgh in local surveys is the **Bloomfield Bridge Tavern** (4412 Liberty Ave., 412/682-8611, daily 11 A.M.–midnight, $9). The tavern features live bands Fri.–Sat.; Tues. is open stage.

North Side

Max's Allegheny Tavern (537 Suismon St., 412/231-1899, www.maxsalleghenytavern.com, Mon.–Thurs. 11 A.M.–11 P.M., Fri.–Sat. 11 A.M.– midnight, Sun. 9:30 A.M.–10 P.M., lunch $5, dinner $11) is an award-winning German restaurant featuring North Side nostalgia. Try the potato pancake reuben ($5.50) here.

South Side

A wide range of moderately priced restaurants lies between South 22nd and South 24th on East Carson Street. **Mallorca** (2228 E. Carson, near 24th, 412/488-1818, Mon.–Thurs. 11:30 A.M.– 10:30 P.M., Fri.–Sat. 11:30 A.M.–11:30 P.M., Sun. noon–10 P.M., lunch $8, dinner $22) specializes in the dishes of Spain and serves alfresco during the summer in a small enclosed courtyard (reservations recommended). *Camerones mallorca* (bacon-wrapped shrimp in a light brandy sauce ($18) and an appetizer, *piquillos* (crabmeat-stuffed red pepper, $9), are local favorites.

Le Pommier (2104 E. Carson, 412/431-1901, Mon.–Thurs. 5:30–9:30 P.M., Fri.–Sat. 5:30–closing, reservations recommended) completes the international picture with French cuisine. Expect dishes such as braised sea bass with savoy cabbage, fingerling potatoes, fennel, roasted tomato, and muscadet cream sauce ($24) and chickpea crepe with boursin cheese, red onion confit, and crisp potatoes and carrots on wild mushroom ragout ($19). Entrées average $27.

Next door is **Paparazzi** (2100 E. Carson St., 412/488-0800, Tues.–Fri. lunch 11 A.M.–3 P.M., dinner 5 P.M.–midnight, Sat.–Sun. dinner 5–1:30 A.M., lunch $9, dinner $15, reservations recommended), an Italian eatery that features live music with dinner.

P. F. Chang's (148 W. Bridge St., in the Waterfront Shopping Center, West Homestead, 412/464-0640, Sun.–Thurs. 11 A.M.–10:30 P.M., Fri.–Sat. 11 A.M.–midnight) is a chain, but the setting is modern and pleasant, and the food is good and reasonably priced. The vegetarian lettuce wraps ($7) and orange peel beef ($11) are especially good. Lunch specials average $7, dinner entrées are $10–20.

BREWPUBS

The area bordered roughly by Madison, Goehring, and Gardner Streets and SR 28 is a worker's town composed primarily of German-American families.

The street spontaneously breaks into cobblestones, and the houses, jammed together rowhouse-style, are an amalgam of various building materials. It's an "unimproved," hardworking, close-knit neighborhood. The look of it so often reflects its origins that Hollywood filmed parts of *Mrs. Soffel* and *Hoffa* on these streets.

The **Penn Brewery** (800 Vinial St. and Troy Hill Rd., across from the Heinz factory, 412/237-9402, www.pennbrew.com, Mon.–Sat. 11 A.M.–midnight, $5–13) features German dishes such as bratwurst and braunschweiger, along with several of its excellent brews to wash them down. Formerly the home of the old Eberhardt & Ober Brewing Company, built in 1848, the brewery complex had been partially demolished and used as a warehouse for 20 years. It was renovated in 1986 by a coalition formed by brewer Tom Pastorius, the North Side Civic Development Council, and a financial group. Four million dollars later, the old E&O complex features a state-of-the-art

BREWERIES IN PITTSBURGH

Home brewing of ale and porter in Pittsburgh coincided with the founding of the settlement. Most of the city's early breweries were content to supply small groups of friends and customers; Pittsburgh's first commercial brewery (its name is lost to history) opened in 1795. Early brewing endeavors in the area relied on plant locations near a hillside, in which caves could be dug for keeping the brew chilled. Hence, the North Side, with its large Teutonic population and the cool recesses of its hills, made the brewing of beer a favored enterprise.

Beer was so popular in the greater industrial environs of Pittsburgh that by 1895, 150 small breweries produced and shipped their product throughout the city. By 1899, business trusts were in vogue and 12 local brewing firms joined nine out-of-town breweries to form the Pittsburgh Brewing Company trust. Among the member breweries were Wainwright Brewing (organized between 1810 and 1820), Eberhardt & Ober, Straub, and Iron City. One of the largest operations, Iron City Brewery had a production capacity of about 50,000 bar-

rels a year, an impressive figure at the time. Continued consolidation of other small producers further reduced the number of independent breweries.

With the passage of the 18th Amendment and the "noble experiment" of Prohibition, few breweries survived. The Pittsburgh Brewing Company, which had become the largest brewing operation in Pennsylvania and the third-largest in the United States, remained in business by producing near-beer and ice cream and providing cold storage.

Today, several breweries operate in Pittsburgh. The largest and most commercial is the Pittsburgh Brewing Company (3340 Liberty Ave., Lawrenceville, 412/682-7400) which was bought by an international corporation in 1986 and returned to local ownership in 1992. A state-of-the-art, large-scale commercial brewery, Pittsburgh Brewing produces that mainstay of mid-Atlantic college parties—Iron City beer and I.C. Light. In 1993, it unveiled J. J. Wainwright Select Lager, a special, limited-edition, all-malt lager, crafted in the tradition of its namesake. The brewery sporadically offers tours; call for information.

Pittsburgh

traditional brewery and two restaurants. Mary Beth Pastorius—who, with her husband, Tom, oversees the operations—says that when people order Penn Dark in the bars, they sometimes ask for "the chick on the horse," a reference to the bottle's Valkyrie-bearing label. The Pastoriuses trace their lineage back nine generations to Daniel Pastorius, founder of Germantown, the first German settlement in America, in 1683.

Penn Brewery has picked up gold medals at the Great American Beer Festival, and its light lager was named best Munich-style beer made in America. Large windows in the Bier Halle restaurant open onto part of the brewing operation: hand-fabricated circular copper kettles 10 feet in diameter mix in the hops, one of the steps toward producing a beer that conforms to *Reinheitsgebot,* the rigid German beer-purity law established in 1516. All of Penn's beers, with the exception of its excellent wheat-based brew, are produced in accordance with this law, which permitted only three ingredients: barley, hops, and water (the original *Reinheitsgebot* didn't specify yeast as a necessary ingredient in brewmaking, as it hadn't been identified in 1516. At the time, yeast wasn't "added" intentionally, but came spontaneously from the atmosphere—and the beer quality varied accordingly. Most modern brewmasters, including those at Penn Brewery, add a controlled quantity of yeast to ensure consistency). On the lower level is the Ratskeller, a party/banquet room. In the courtyard *biergarten,* German-style tuba bands are hired on occasion to coax visitors into rousing polkas.

(See also **The Church Brew Works,** East Side under American in this section.)

NIGHTLIFE

Golden Triangle

The **Tap Room** (in the Omni William Penn, Grant St. entrance, 412/281-7100, daily 11:30–1:30 A.M.) recently completed a decade of renovation and has become a popular place to meet after work. The bar features beers from a variety of microbreweries. The **Pub Bar** (Pittsburgh Hilton and Towers, 412/391-4600, daily 11:30 A.M.–1:30 A.M.) is a quiet meeting place for pregame food and drink during football and baseball season.

In the Strip: **Mullaney's Harp & Fiddle** (2329 Penn Ave., 412/642-6622, Tues.–Thurs. 11:30 A.M.–midnight, Fri.–Sat. 11:30 A.M.–2 A.M., Sun. 4–11 P.M.) features Irish music, an Irish menu, and an irresistible dessert called whiskey cake. The **Boardwalk** (15th and Smallman Sts.) features a number of different nightclubs, a floating stage, and a variety of bands from steel drums to rock. The **Empire** (1630 Smallman St., 412/261-4512, Wed.–Sat. 9 P.M.–2 A.M.) features an 18,000-square-foot dance floor, light show, and a variety of music. Next door, **Rosebud** (1650 Smallman St., 412/261-2232, Thurs.–Sun., varied hours) offers acoustic rock, Latin dance, and world music.

East Side

Club Laga (3609 Forbes Ave., 412/682-2050 and information line 412/687-4636, days and hours vary) is the place for live bands and DJ dancing.

Doc's Place (5442 Walnut St., 412/681-3713, Mon.–Fri. 11 A.M.–2 A.M., Sat. noon–2 A.M.) is a beer-pool-darts hangout both day and night. There's a big-screen TV for sports fans, and Doc's offers pizza, sandwiches, and a full dinner for under $10, Mon.–Sat. The big windows allow maximum viewing for those who just like to watch.

North Side

Stop by **James Street Restaurant and Tavern** (422 Foreland St., 412/323-2222, lunch Mon.–Fri. 11 A.M.–2 P.M., dinner Tues.–Sat. 3 P.M.–2 A.M.) for jazz. Predominantly New Orleans–style in cuisine and music, it also has rock 'n' roll nights.

South Side

In Station Square, **the Hard Rock Cafe** (230 W. Station Sq., 412/481-7625, www.hardrock.com, Sun.–Wed. 11 A.M.–11 P.M., bar until midnight, Thurs.–Sat. 11 A.M.–midnight, bar until 2 A.M.) offers a variety of live performers.

At **Rum Shakers** (1224 E. Carson, 412/431-5910, 5 P.M.–2 A.M.) hip hop DJs spin Wed.–Sat. **Nick's Fat City** (1601–03 E. Carson, 412/481-6880, www.nicksfatcity.com, Wed.–Sat., hours vary) features live entertainment and Pittsburgh's Rock & Roll Hall of Stars—memorabilia spanning more than five decades. Nick's also has a pizza outlet.

Outside the City

At **Moondog's** (378 Freeport Rd., in Blawnox, two miles north of the Highland Park Bridge, 412/828-2040, www.moondogs.us, Mon.–Wed. 7 P.M.–2 A.M., Thurs.–Sat. 2 P.M.–2 A.M.), Monday is jam night, Wednesday is open mic night, and live blues and rock bands perform Thursday–Saturday.

Information and Services

INFORMATION

Tourist Services

The friendly and helpful folks at **Greater Pittsburgh Convention & Visitors Bureau** (412/281-7711 or 800/366-0093, www.visit pittsburgh.com) are the people to contact for local information and guidance. Their business office is in the Alcoa Building (now known as the Regional Enterprise Center) in the Golden Triangle, but it has information kiosks in Station Square and Hines History Center, and two at the Pittsburgh International Airport. Non-U.S. nationals can call the **Pittsburgh Council for International Visitors** (412/624-7800) for referrals and information. **Travelers' Aid** (412/281-5474) is another source.

Information Lines

For a 24-hour events listing free within the Pittsburgh calling area, try the city activities line (800/366-0093). There's also a City Guide phone system (800/462-2489); call, choose your city and state, and type in the appropriate two-number code for attractions, accommodations, transportation, etc. For a list of 12-step meetings, call Al-Anon (412/572-5141 or 800/628-8920).

Personal Safety

Pittsburgh is one of the safest cities of its size in the United States. The crime index is significantly lower than the national average and below that of most other major cities, including Seattle, Buffalo, and St. Louis. In Greater Pittsburgh, crimes involving tourists are rare. The majority of reported personal crimes are "internal"—focusing on personal disputes, gang territory, or drugs—and are largely limited to the neighborhoods of Brushton, East Liberty, and Homewood. The Golden Triangle is patrolled by beat cops on foot or on horseback during the day. All of the neighborhoods are busy with pedestrians during the day and early evening. Even so, the best recommendation for an incident-free visit is self-awareness—know where you are and who is around you. Creeps act on an opportunity—don't give them one. Be strong and smart.

Panhandlers are a fact of urban life nowadays, but there seem to be few in Greater Pittsburgh, even in the summer. Police representatives report that incidents of panhandling are rare and that it isn't considered a problem by either residents or business owners.

SERVICES

Emergencies

For police, fire, and ambulance services, call 911. Travelers' Aid (412/281-5474) is another source of help in an emergency.

Medical Services

Recognized the world over as a center for organ transplants, Pittsburgh has more than 50 medical facilities, which include world-class teaching hospitals. Children's Hospital is home to the largest diabetes clinic in North America. If you need a recommendation, call for medical referral (412/321-5030) or for dental referral (800/917-6453).

Pittsburgh

Services for Visitors with Disabilities

For services or information for people with special needs, contact the Carnegie Library for the Blind and Physically Handicapped (4724 Baum Blvd., 412/687-2440) or Pittsburgh Hearing, Speech, and Deaf Services (1945 5th Ave., voice or TTY 412/281-1375).

Money

Currency exchange is available at Pittsburgh International Airport in the Mutual of Omaha Service Center (412/472-5151); downtown at Citizens Bank (5th Ave. and Grant St., 412/234-4215, open Mon.–Fri. 8:30 A.M.–4 P.M.); and at the PNC Bank (5th Ave. and Wood St., 412/762-2090, open Mon.–Fri. 8:30 A.M.–4:30 P.M.).

Instant teller machines abound; however, not all will accept your bank card or credit card, even if they display the Cirrus or Plus interbank symbol. MAC instant tellers are available at several different banks, and if a Mellon Bank MAC doesn't accept your card, try an Integra Bank machine.

Post Office

Post offices are in nearly every neighborhood in the city. The main post office is known as the General Mail Facility (1001 California Ave., on the North Side, 412/359-7500 or 412/359-7800—customer service). For postal information after 5 P.M. weekdays, and on Sat., Sun., and holidays, call 412/359-7700.

Media

Pittsburgh's general-focus newspapers are the *Pittsburgh Post-Gazette* (in print since the mid-19th century) and the *Pittsburgh Tribune Review.*

Many of the ethnic groups in Pittsburgh have their own newspapers. The African-American community is the focus of the *New Pittsburgh Courier,* and the *Serb National News* has an Eastern European focus. The *Pittsburgh City Paper* (www.pghcitypaper.com) is an excellent free weekly newspaper with arts and entertainment listings.

Sightseeing Tours

The Pittsburgh Historic Review Commission (www.city.pittsburgh.pa.us), a group of seven people appointed by the mayor, meets once a month to review proposals for alteration on all buildings deemed of historic interest by the city, state, or U.S. government. The commission has published an excellent series of guides to detailed architectural walking/driving tours that include a good bit of city history; the guides are available free from the Historic Review Commission on the city's website.

Pittsburgh History & Landmarks Foundation (1 Station Sq., Suite 450, 412/471-5808, www.phlf.org) offers walking tours of neighborhoods all over the city, as well as Tour with Landmarks, tailor-made tour programs that incorporate the interests of the visitor. In the past, PH&LF has organized tours that cover everything from ethnic neighborhoods to the search for lions, gargoyles, eagles, griffins, and dragons in downtown architecture; the organization also offers a three-hour all-city bus tour. Though 10 days' notice is usually required, you may be able to join a preplanned tour. Cost per person averages $10–20.

The **Gateway Clipper Fleet** (9 Station Square Dock, 412/355-7980, www.gatewayclipper.com) has been plying the rivers of Pittsburgh since 1958. A fleet of riverboats is the setting for a pantheon of tours varying from narrated sightseeing cruises to a Riverboat Follies Revue. Prices vary with the event.

Transportation

GETTING THERE

Pittsburgh is within a two-hour flight or a day's drive of more than 70 percent of the U.S. population and 40 percent of the Canadian population.

By Air

Pittsburgh International Airport (412/472-3525, www.pitairport.com) was chosen by readers of *Condé Nast Traveler* magazine as best in the United States and number three in the world in 2002. The airport is served by several airlines providing international and national access to Pittsburgh. British Airways offers direct flights from London; USAirways flies direct from Frankfurt, Germany. Though ticket prices tend to be similar among all American-based carriers, US-Airways has frequent direct flights to Pittsburgh and Philadelphia from most major U.S. airports (Pittsburgh is one of USAirways' hubs). Others (American, Continental, Delta, America West, Northwest, TWA, and United) offer direct flights only through their hub cities, often requiring at least one flight change.

Transportation to town from the airport, which is several miles west of the city, is available by shuttle. Airlines Transportation Company (412/321-8147) charges $16 one-way, $30 round-trip. People's Cab (412/361-3532) and Yellow Cab (412/321-8100) charge about $35 one-way. 401 Limo (412/973-7075) will drive you into town, hassle-free for $46. All major rental car agencies have booths in the airport.

By Auto

Pittsburgh's main access routes are US 22/30, an often congested, mainly two-lane road running east-west; I-76/70, a four-lane toll road running southeast-northwest; and four-lane I-79, which runs north-south. Fifty miles north of Pittsburgh, I-79 intersects I-80, Pennsylvania's main east-west highway.

By Bus

Greyhound/Trailways Bus Lines (800/229-9424, www.greyhound.com) is the main bus service to and from Pittsburgh. Greyhound offers interconnecting service throughout the United States and Canada.

By Rail

Amtrak (800/872-7245, www.amtrak.com) schedules regular runs to and from New York City (the Broadway Limited), Philadelphia, Boston (the Pennsylvanian), Chicago (the Lakeshore Limited), and Washington, D.C. (the Capitol Limited). Passengers arrive at the Pennsylvania Station, across from the Greyhound bus terminal at the intersection of Liberty Avenue and Grant Street in the Golden Triangle.

GETTING AROUND

Finding one's way around Pittsburgh is a challenge. The older part of the city (the Golden Triangle) is patterned in the common numerical street/named street grid, but once out of the downtown area, streets intersect, disappear, and reappear with different names. A detailed recent street map of Greater Pittsburgh is a must. (Rand McNally makes a fairly good one, available at the Duquesne Incline and around the city; it indicates all the neighborhoods and boroughs. AAA's map covers only part of the area.)

By Bus and Rail

Port Authority of Allegheny County (PAT) operates the popular bus and "T" (light-rail) systems around the county. To pick up schedules, go to any "T" station or PAT's downtown office (534 Smithfield St. under Mellon Square, or call 412/442-2000 Mon.–Fri. 7 A.M.–7 P.M. or weekends and holidays 8 A.M.–6 P.M.—TTY, for callers who are deaf or hearing-impaired, is 412/231-7007, www.portauthority.org). Bus routes cover the entire county.

Pittsburgh

The "T" covers a much smaller area; the 2.5-mile route connects the Golden Triangle with the South and North Sides. Service between "T" stops in the Golden Triangle area is free, except for inbound riders during commute hours. Buses and the "T" operate on a zone system—fares increase with distance; exact fare ($.60–3.50) is required. For those who plan to take the bus frequently, a weekly or monthly pass is the most economical choice. PAT operates the Monongahela Incline and also sells tokens for the nonprofit Duquesne Incline. The fare is $1.75 each way.

By Cab

Getting a cab in Pittsburgh usually requires a phone call to Yellow Cab (412/321-8100) or People's Cab (412/441-3200) or walking to the nearest hotel cab stand. Pittsburgh has made a major effort to improve cab availability and service, and it shows. The city even instituted a voluntary service training for drivers. A call will bring a cab within 15 minutes, and the drivers are unfailingly courteous and friendly. Fares start at around $2 for the drop charge (upon entry into the cab) plus $1.60 per mile.

By Auto

Unless you expect to stay within the boundaries of the Golden Triangle-South Side area or plan to use public transportation, renting an automobile is a good idea. Budget, Dollar, Enterprise, Hertz, and Thrifty (check any phone book for their "800" telephone numbers to make reservations) have counters on the basement level of the airport. Car seats for children are also available for rental in the airport near the baggage claim area, lower level. And it's possible to have a car delivered to you in a metropolitan-area location, although a fee is sometimes charged.

Pittsburgh is an old city. The streets—narrow and occasionally poorly marked—were originally built for pedestrians and horses. Charm aside, it's easy to get lost here.

Partly to combat that, the city has been installing a network of 1,500 brightly colored signs that make up the Wayfinder System, which divides the city into five color-coded districts—Downtown (Purple), East Side (Orange), South Side (Green), North Side (Blue), and the northernmost section of North Side, also known as the North Hills (Yellow). Immediately below the Wayfinder symbol each sign announces the area you are heading toward and, below that, the road you are on. The Greater Pittsburgh Convention & Visitors Bureau (412/281-7711) can help with any confusion.

Make sure to carry plenty of quarters—most parking meters take nothing else. Parking lots downtown are painfully expensive (up to $4 per half hour). If possible, park outside the center of town and use the "T" or buses. The Golden Triangle and the different neighborhoods are all very walkable.

The main thoroughfares through the city are I-376, US 22/30, Forbes Avenue, 5th Avenue, SR 380, Bigelow Boulevard, and Penn Avenue (serving the Golden Triangle and the East Side); I-279, US 19, SR 28, and North Avenue (serving the North Side); and, serving the South Side, SR 837 (Carson Street) and US 19 (Saw Mill Run Road). A driver's best friend in Pittsburgh is a good map. West Penn AAA, a branch of the national automobile club, maintains a branch office downtown (near the intersection of Wood St. and 6th Ave., 412/362-3300).

The color belts (Red, Yellow, and Orange), specific routes that bypass the city, were developed to ease traffic in the downtown area. The Yellow Belt is closest to city limits and circles the city. The Orange Belt also circles the city but lies farther out and extends south beyond Allegheny County. The Red Belt rides along the top of the county. Each of the belts is made up of many roads, with the changes occasionally unmarked on the roadway. Visitors may find the 80-mile-long Yellow Belt useful as a sightseeing route.

There are no tolls on any of the city's bridges.

By Bike

Pittsburgh is not a bike-friendly city. The old streets are narrow, often rough, and full of traffic. Bike use, by default, is restricted to parks and trails (see Recreation).

Know
Pennsylvania

The Land

The state covers 45,888 square miles—it's 310 miles wide and 180 miles long. The highest point—Mt. Davis, in Somerset County—has an elevation of 3,213 feet, and the lowest point is at sea level, on the banks of the Delaware outside Philadelphia. There are three major rivers, 50 natural lakes, and 250 man-made lakes—a benefit of decades of flood control.

With only four major urban areas in the state, wilderness is abundant: there are 117 state parks, 20 state forest districts, and 281 game lands. The state forests of Pennsylvania are located in 48 of the state's 67 counties and comprise over two million acres—about one-tenth of the total forest in Pennsylvania.

GEOGRAPHY

On a topographical map of Pennsylvania, the terrain looks as if a giant wildcat's paw swiped across the state in an arc from northeast to southwest. The rock structure that underlies the entire state was formed at the end of the Permian pe-

riod, 200 million years ago. The area was then covered with peaks that rivaled the Swiss Alps. Volcanic action, deposition by streams and lakes, erosion, and glacial movement—especially in the northwest and southeast—reduced the peaks into the varied terrain of today.

There are seven principal topographic regions, though not all are continuous across the state. In the northwest, along the edge of Lake Erie, is the Great Lakes Plain, a 50-mile-wide strip of flat and fertile land that hugs the shore. The fine-grained earth began as the floor of a much larger Lake Erie over 10,000 years ago.

The Great Lakes Plain rises to meet the wall-like edge of the Appalachian Plateau, the largest of the remaining regions, and also the seat of the Pennsylvania portion of the Appalachian Mountain Range that tumbles down the east coast of America. The Appalachian Plateau makes up more than half the total area of the state and is underlain by neatly horizontal layers of rock. On the northeastern edge of the plateau, in the rugged Allegheny Mountains (al-a-GAY-nee),

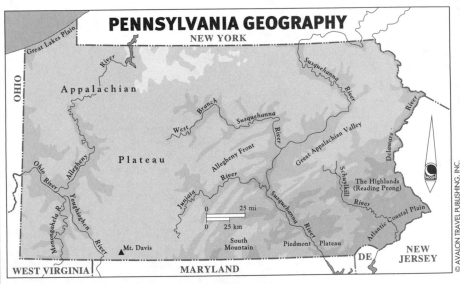

PENNSYLVANIA GEOGRAPHY

PENNSYLVANIA FACTS

State Animal: White-tailed Deer
State Bird: Ruffed Grouse
State Dog: Great Dane
State Flower: Mountain Laurel
State Insect: Firefly
State Motto: Virtue, Liberty, and Independence
Nickname: Keystone State
State Tree: Hemlock

glaciers grew and melted, creating long massive rock structures: Laurel Ridge, Chestnut Ridge, and the Allegheny Front. The softer rock between became narrow lowlands. North of Scranton, the granitic peaks and valleys of the Poconos contrast with the southwestern terrain of smooth, rounded, wooded hills near Pittsburgh, a product of steady erosion rather than ice. South of Pittsburgh, the coal-mining valley that contains the Youghiogheny (yock-a-GAY-nee) and Allegheny Rivers is one of many deep, layered fissures marking the Appalachian Plateau.

The Allegheny Front, variously referred to as Allegheny Mountain and the Allegheny Ridge, on the southeastern edge of the Allegheny Plateau, overlooks a succession of lesser ridges and valleys that make up the Great Appalachian Valley. The ridges—Blue, Tuscarora, Jack, and Bald Eagle—are in turn separated by narrow valleys. In this area, the underlying rock has folded like a paper fan. South of Scranton, and along the Susquehanna River and its tributaries, lie the only anthracite coalfields in America—ancient fields of carbon as smooth and hard as glass.

Between the Great Appalachian Valley and the Piedmont Plateau—the next topographical area to the southeast—are two small regions, South Mountain, on the southern state border near Gettysburg, and the Highlands, reaching almost to Reading from the eastern border. Of all the mountain ranges of Appalachia, South Mountain is the oldest; structurally, it's a continuation of the Blue Ridge Mountains in Virginia. The Highlands is a region of small, rounded summits and is a continuation of the New England Uplands to the north and east.

The Piedmont Plateau, commonly called the Piedmont, is a region of lowlands and gentle hills. The area is extremely fertile; the terrain, covering the hills like velvet in a jewelry box, boasts some of the best farmland in the country. The area has remained productive due, in large part, to the soil conservation methods practiced by the Amish, who have dwelt there in large numbers since colonial days.

Southeast of the Piedmont is Pennsylvania's portion of the Atlantic Coastal Plain, a narrow strip of land along the Delaware River below Trenton, New Jersey. This region extends all along the Atlantic coast. In Pennsylvania, the plain was created by invasion and flooding by the Delaware River and Chesapeake Bay. The Coastal Plain is covered by the city of Philadelphia.

Minerals

Pennsylvania has always had abundant mineral resources. Of these, coal is by far the greatest. The original deposits of bituminous coal in the state have been estimated at more than 75 billion tons, and of anthracite coal at 23 billion tons. Three-quarters of these deposits remain unmined. Next to coal is petroleum, originally estimated at 4.7 billion barrels. Most of this remains underground; as is the case with coal, only a small fraction can be recovered profitably with present extraction methods. Iron ore, magnetite iron ore, clay, limestone, slate, and sandstone are also abundant.

Water

Pennsylvania has three major river systems, which drain more than 90 percent of the state's land. The Delaware is the main river of the eastern part of the state. The Susquehanna (sus-ka-HAN-a) River, with its tributaries West Branch and Juniata (ju-ne-A-ta), flows through the central portion; and the Ohio River, formed at the confluence of the Allegheny and Monongahela (mo-non-ga-HE-la) Rivers, is the main waterway in western Pennsylvania. Of these, only the Delaware and Ohio are navigable. The Delaware is second only to the Mississippi River in the amount of

Know Pennsylvania

© JOANNE MILLER

Susquehanna River near Hyner View

commerce it carries each year; the Ohio is one of the nation's main inland transportation waterways.

The state has approximately 4,400 smaller streams, and 300 lakes, both natural and man-made. Conneaut (con-E-aught) Lake, in the northwestern part of the state, is the largest natural lake within Pennsylvania, though many man-made lakes—including nearby Pymatuning (pee-ma-TOO-ning) Reservoir, are much larger. Flooding has caused major damage throughout Pennsylvania's history, and numerous flood-control projects—especially on the Juniata, Susquehanna, and Allegheny—have reduced but not eliminated the problem.

CLIMATE

Pennsylvania experiences four discrete seasons, though climate varies according to longitude, latitude, and elevation. Winter commonly brings snow (in varying amounts) to most of

the state, and temperatures then range from below zero to the high 30s F. Spring warms up, with temperatures hovering in the 40s and 50s, leading into June's 60s and 70s and eye-dazzling profusion of green leaves and wildflowers. Summer temperatures seldom reach over 100°F, though warm days are often accompanied by high humidity under the lush shade of fully leaved deciduous trees. Evenings during the summer months cool down from daytime highs but usually remain warm. September is generally very warm, but things begin cooling down rapidly through October and November, as the days grow shorter and brilliantly colored trees and shrubs blanket the region. By December, temperatures flirt with the low 20s in preparation for the snows and clean black branches of January.

Rain is common throughout the year, except in the winter months. Hurricanes—most of their wind- and rain-power spent by the time they enter the state—blow through from the south occasionally during the fall and spring. In 1985, a rare but devastating tornado moved through the northern half of the Allegheny Forest, uprooting a number of ancient trees.

The sites of Pennsylvania's three largest cities also have the most moderate temperatures. Southeastern Pennsylvania, including Philadelphia, has the most moderate climate, with a mean annual temperature of 52°F and an average annual snowfall of 30 inches. Southwestern Pennsylvania, near Pittsburgh, and Erie, on the Great Lakes Plain, have similar climates, with slightly lower temperatures and more snowfall. The greatest weather extremes occur in the northeastern and north-central mountains.

FLORA

Trees

Though Pennsylvania was settled as one of the original colonies, 58 percent of it remains unspoiled forest, hosting more than 127 varieties of trees. At the time of European contact, the state, with the exception of the Great Lakes Plain and Atlantic Coastal Plain, was abundant with 300-

to 400-year-old beeches, hemlocks, and sugar maples; it was completely covered with dense forest. The native **chestnut** proved the upcountry's best wood for pioneers' homesteads; it was easily split into logs for cabins and rails for fences. From its split timbers, shingles were rived with mallet and froe to cover houses and barns, From its bark, settlers extracted tannic acid for tanning and dyeing and for medicine. And the pioneers' lean hogs grew fat on the chestnuts the trees produced in fall. The hemlock, growing in the damp glens of the mountains, was almost equally valued.

Though little virgin timber remains (one 4,000-acre exception is the Tionesta Scenic Region in the Allegheny National Forest and Cook Forest), more than 50 percent of the state is wooded, thanks in part to conservation programs begun before the turn of the century. **Black cherry, yellow poplar, white ash, beech, hemlock, red maple,** and **sugar maple** represent the most valuable and widespread tree growth in the Allegheny National Forest today. The trees are maintained and monitored by the U.S. Forest Service and are still used for timber. Over 65 million board-feet of lumber are harvested from the forests every year.

In the northern Appalachian Plateau, native forests of maple, beech, and hemlock thrive. **White pine** and **spruce** dominate the Allegheny Mountains, and southern parts of the state are populated by **ash, aspen, birch, cherry, hickory, locust, red and yellow maple, oak, longleaf pine, poplar, sycamore, wild plum, tulip,** and **black walnut.** Pennsylvanians are justifiably proud of the exquisite color extravaganza produced each autumn, when all of the deciduous trees, in concert with brilliant red **poison sumac,** change the panoply of greens to wind-shifted tones of red, orange, brown, and yellow.

Shrubs and Flowers

Pennsylvania's abundant rainfall and numerous streams and lakes work together to create a bumper crop of hundreds of varieties of native wildflowers and flowering shrubs each year. More than 3,400 species of plants are native to the state. **Azalea, rhododendron, dogwood, redbud,** and **honeysuckle** are common in shady areas. In spring and early summer, the pink,

© JOANNE MILLER

Crown vetch grows wild on the roadsides.

white, and red blossoms of the state flower, the **mountain laurel,** blanket the eponymous Laurel Highlands in the south and the Allegheny Mountains in the northeast. **Blackberry, raspberry,** and **elderberry** are common. Under the forest canopy, spring brings the delicate **wood violet** to bloom alongside **Indian pipe, spring beauty,** jack-in-the-pulpit, **wild grapevine, turkscap lily, trillium, Dutchman's breeches,** and **yellow ladyslipper.** Several types of ferns thrive along streams and rivers, among them **bracken, New York fern, lady fern,** and **Christmas fern.**

Fallow fields and untended meadows are flecked with a sparkling palate of **red wild bergamot, closed gentian** and **fringed gentian, wild valerian, monument plant,** and **black-eyed Susan.** Pink **crown vetch,** introduced to slow erosion on hillsides, greets the traveler along the roadways, mixed with native daisy-like **marguerites.**

FAUNA

Pennsylvania is in a central position biologically—southern animals approach the northern edges of their habitats here, and northern animals approach their southern boundaries. Besides the 63 native species of mammals, 159 fish, 37 reptiles, 36 amphibians, and hundreds of birds, other animals migrate through or visit during severe winters. The diversity of habitat—lakes, forests, bogs, rivers, meadows, ponds, and marshes—allows a wide variety of birds and mammals to exist.

Mammals

White-tailed deer, once severely overhunted and devastated by heavy foresting, are now numerous throughout the state. Though not considered endangered, **black bear** and **wildcat** are rarely seen in their northern mountain habitats. Other animals common to North American forests—**fox, beaver, mink, raccoon, opossum, woodchuck, striped skunk, gray and black squirrel,** and **wild rabbit** have adapted and thrived in all areas. The larger **rusty fox squirrel**

is a familiar sight in western Pennsylvania. Though harder to spot because of their nocturnal habits, both eastern and northern **flying squirrels** are found in Pennsylvania's forests. One of the state's six nonmigratory bat species, the **Indiana bat,** once common in caves in southwestern Pennsylvania, is now on the federal endangered-species list; cave destruction and irresponsible cave exploration are the main threats.

Fish

Pennsylvania is famous worldwide for its game fishing of both warm- and cold-water species. Warm-water lakes and reservoirs abound with **muskellunge, northern pike, largemouth bass, walleye, channel catfish, black crappie, bluegill,** and hybrids such as **tiger muskellunge** and **striper.** Cold limestone streams flow with several species of **trout,** and many streams are stocked to ensure good fishing. All fishing is regulated by the Pennsylvania Fish and Boat Commission. A *Summary of Fishing Regulations and Laws* is available throughout the state where fishing licenses are sold.

Birds

You may often see, at the edges of woodland clearings, two game birds: the **eastern wild turkey,** which stands more than two feet tall; and the state bird, the **ruffed grouse. Bobwhite quail, Hungarian partridge, woodcock,** and **ring-necked pheasant** are common in the woodlands; **mallard ducks** and **Canada geese** gather together on the edges of ponds and lakes during migratory season. **Ospreys, peregrine falcons, eagles,** and other raptors take to the skies along the Allegheny Ridge in the autumn. Nocturnal birds, the **screech, great horned,** and **barred owls** roam the skies in lightly wooded areas and suburbs year-round.

The **siskin, nuthatch, crossbill, pine grosbeak,** and **barn swallow** are common in forest clearings and farmlands and on the edges of urban areas. Another frequently seen bird of brushy woods, the **rufous-sided towhee,** is often mistaken for a robin, though its breast is red only on the sides. The **eastern bluebird,** a perennial favorite, is becoming rare, its habitat threatened by human encroachment.

A shorebird, the **killdeer,** with its long legs and black double necklace, is often spotted far from water, adapting to its environment by finding new hunting grounds in golf courses. The **great blue heron,** a large (three-foot-tall) wading bird, can be found nesting in northwest Pennsylvania.

Reptiles

Pennsylvania is home to numerous beneficial lizards and snakes, which rid farmyards of insects and small rodents. However, more dangerous reptiles also reside here, and hikers and campers should be aware of them.

There are three types of venomous snakes in Pennsylvania. The bite of the **northern copperhead** is highly poisonous, but, because the snake is mostly nocturnal, few bites are reported. A copperhead averages 30 inches in length and possesses a flat, triangular, coppery red head with a pit on each side of the head between the eye and the nose. The snakes have been seen in 54 counties but are rare in the northeast portion of the state.

Timber rattlesnakes, in both their sulfur yellow and black colorations, are found mostly in the sparsely settled northeastern mountain regions. They are the largest of the poisonous snakes, sometimes reaching lengths of five feet, and are found in 46 counties (though they're largely extinct in urban areas). In late summer, the snakes descend into the valleys for water. Rattlesnakes do not always warn (rattle) before they strike. The **Eastern Massasauga rattlesnake,** rare in Pennsylvania, is seen only in a few west-central counties. This yard-long snake is distinguished by a head covered with large plates and squarish spots along the back; it has been placed on the state's endangered list due to wetlands destruction.

With so many streams and rivers, visitors often see one or more of Pennsylvania's wide variety of **turtles** basking in the sun. The three most common are the **stinkpot** (so named for a musky odor excreted by its scent glands), which has a large head and two yellow lines around each eye; the **wood turtle,** which has bright orange-red legs; and the **eastern box turtle,** which can withdraw its legs, head, and tail completely into its shell and seal itself into a "box." Less frequently seen are the **spotted turtle,** with bright yellow spots on its dark shell, and the **map turtle,** its upper shell covered with a network of fine yellow lines.

Amphibians

Frogs, newts, and salamanders inhabit the banks of streams and rivers, and sometimes the damp forest floor all over the state. One dramatic example of the species is the two-foot-long **eastern hellbender,** a flat, giant salamander that lives under rocks near unpolluted streams. In fact, its presence, though disconcerting, is a reliable indicator of the purity of the water; hellbenders are extremely sensitive to pollution. More common (and smaller) amphibians are the **spotted salamander,** purplish-black with yellow or orange spots; the **marbled salamander,** black with white or gray patches; the **eastern tiger salamander,** similar in marking to the marbled but with bright yellow, irregular spots; and the **red-spotted newt,** which spends part of its life strolling forest floors after rainstorms (they're also called efts in this stage and are bright scarlet or orange in color).

ENVIRONMENTAL ISSUES

Pennsylvania took its first significant official action to preserve the environment in the late 19th century, after unregulated lumbering had nearly destroyed the state's forests. The commonwealth established a forestry commission and purchased and replanted thousands of acres. There are now more than two million acres of state forest land.

The state government also established commissions to preserve and protect water resources, soil, and wildlife; soil conservation efforts began in 1937. Recognizing a need for regional cooperation to protect the interactive systems, Pennsylvania joined with surrounding states to develop plans for cleaning and maintaining the Delaware, Susquehanna, and Ohio Rivers. State regulations banned contamination of rivers and streams and authorized reclamation of waterways such as the

REUSING OLD RAILBEDS

By 1916, America had the largest railroad system in the world, with almost 300,000 miles of track. As the century progressed, cars, trucks, buses, and airplanes radically altered the U.S. transportation system and led to the rapid decline of the railroad industry. Today, less than half of that early rail system remains, and 2,000 miles of track are abandoned by rail companies every year.

In 1986, a national, nonprofit membership group, the Rails-to-Trails Conservancy, began a campaign to convert abandoned rail property into a network of multiuse trails. Based in Washington, D.C., the conservancy (1400 16th St. NW, Suite 300, Washington, DC 20036, 202/797-5400) offers technical assistance, advocacy, negotiation skills, and assessments to private groups, public agencies, and individuals who wish to create a site for public enjoyment from a rusty set of old tracks.

The conversion is sometimes an uphill battle. When a rail corridor is abandoned, hundreds of claimants to the corridor may emerge, often with multiple claims to the same piece of land; rail corridors frequently pass through several political jurisdictions, requiring cooperative agreements. Rail companies can choose to turn a quick profit by selling the property to one or two developers rather than waiting for public fundraising, and some fear conversion will lower property values, though the opposite is true.

Pennsylvania boasts 52 Rail-to-Trail conversions—second in the nation only to Michigan, which has 55. Rail-to-Trails of varying lengths are found in nearly every county in Pennsylvania. Though surface treatments differ, the paths are usually covered with hard-packed crushed limestone. They're open to walkers, joggers, cyclists, cross-country skiers, horseback riders, and wheelchairs. The trails are for day use only and are free to the public.

Schuylkill River (SKOO-kul), long clogged and polluted by coal runoff.

Wildlife is protected and monitored by the State Game Commission, which regulates hunting and has acquired nearly a million acres as refuge for animals and birds in addition to state game lands, which are opened to hunting on a wildlife-population basis.

Most of the state has been organized into conservation districts. In 1972, Pennsylvania ratified a constitutional amendment guaranteeing a pure and aesthetically pleasing environment. However, pollution continues to exist, especially in the state's waterways. PCBs, chlordane, and mercury—all long-lived chemical residues—continue to turn up in Lake Erie, all the major river basins, and some tributaries. The Fish and Boat Commission issues an annual advisory on which fish and areas to avoid.

The greatest threat to wildlife today in Pennsylvania isn't hunting but rather destruction of habitat. Since 1682, the vast forests that covered the state have been tamed and conquered by the advancing human population. The last bison

was shot around 1801, the last moose in 1790, and the last native elk in 1867. The eastern timber wolf, the wolverine, and possibly the mountain lion are now extinct in Pennsylvania. In all, 12 species of mammals, six species of birds, two species of reptiles, 27 species of fish, and one species of amphibian have been officially declared extinct in the state.

As with the forests, conservation efforts by state and private organizations have turned back time. A subspecies of **elk,** brought in from Yellowstone National Park, was let loose in the Allegheny Forest around 1900; their progeny may be seen, drifting in casual herds, near the town of St. Marys. **River otters,** killed as vermin and depleted by water pollution, are now making a comeback. **Fishers,** sleek relatives of the weasel, were recently reintroduced into the northern part of the state. Several birds of prey are starting to replenish; the osprey and the peregrine falcon, both victims of DDT poisoning, had been rarely seen since the mid-1940s. The **bald eagle,** now seen nesting around the Pymatuning Reservoir, is a national success story.

History

Early History

Pennsylvania was largely uninhabited prior to European settlement. An ancient, dense hardwood forest spread over the hills and valleys west of the Delaware River, broken only by rivers and streams that fed the land. Native hunters roamed over footpaths established for generations. They and their families settled on the edges of the forest; tribes of Lenni Lenape planted maize on the banks of the Delaware River (and subsequently became known as Delawares); Susquehannocks lived in the Susquehanna Valley, near Harrisburg; Eries built villages on the shore of Lake Erie; and a few Shawnee migrated from the southern sections of the continent. The entire territory was under the undisputed protection of the vast Iroquois Confederacy, which controlled most of the eastern seaboard.

Penn is Mightier Than the Swedes (and the Dutch)

Pennsylvania's first nonnative inhabitants were Scandinavian; in 1638, New Sweden Colony was established on the site of what is now Philadelphia. Less than 20 years later, in 1655, the Dutch, at the behest of New Amsterdam director general Peter Stuyvesant, overran the colony and took possession of it. But the Dutch proved unsuccessful in fully settling the area, and in 1673, King Charles II of England declared the Pennsylvania portion of the colonies (along with New Amsterdam) to be British soil.

Meanwhile, back in England, radical preacher George Fox was gaining both adherents and opponents with his religious teachings, insisting that God valued each individual equally—a notion that shook the foundations of the British class system. Fox was decried as a heretic, and his followers were widely persecuted and imprisoned until a charismatic young aristocrat appeared on the scene and embraced Fox's teachings.

By becoming a Quaker, young William Penn—set to inherit both wealth and station from his loyalist father, Admiral William Penn—carried off the 17th-century social equivalent of Patty Hearst's joining the Symbionese Liberation Army. The younger Penn's religious inclinations created problems for the elder Penn's great friend, King Charles II. Quakerism challenged the status of the established churches and the hierarchy of the king and upper classes—who ruled, after all, by divine right. William Penn was high-profile and very vocal, a fiery speaker who published numerous tracts declaring the rights of the individual. Quakers, along with other Protestants, were being sent to the stake all over Europe. Charles was troubled by young Penn's outspoken Quakerism, but what was a king to do? If Penn had been an ordinary troublemaker, he would have simply been hauled off to jail (or worse). But because the admiral had lent the king about $40,000—a debt that was now a considerable burden—the crown came up with a unique solution. In 1681, the king gave Penn some pretty but useless land in the colonies and shipped him off on the next packet out of Liverpool—getting rid of both annoyances at one stroke. Everybody was happy.

The name of the territory honored Penn's father in a poetic concatenation of "Penn" and "sylvan," meaning, roughly, "Penn's Woods." The territory began at the Delaware River and had no western boundaries. For more than a century after Penn won the charter, Pennsylvania's boundaries were disputed by other colonies, including Connecticut, Maryland, and Virginia. The dispute with the first resulted in internal conflicts known as the Pennamite Wars; those with the latter two were largely settled through the efforts of three astronomers: Britons Charles Mason and Jeremiah Dixon and Philadelphian David Rittenhouse (for whom Rittenhouse Square is named). Mason and Dixon surveyed the eastern portion of the boundary, working until 1767, and Rittenhouse completed the western extension in 1784. The boundary, which came to be known as the Mason-Dixon line, played a significant part in the Civil War, dividing free states from slave-holding states, North from South.

William Penn the younger saw the territorial award as a great opportunity to offer a place of refuge to persecuted religious minorities such as his Quaker brethren. He sailed to the New World and immediately negotiated with the Lenni Lenape for leased property rights. Many of the Lenni Lenape migrated west and north, along with other displaced tribes like the Tuscaroras and Nanticokes. Thousands of Quakers and other sectarians bought property—and with it the dream of freedom—from Penn's land company. They sailed to America and began settling in Philadelphia, then moved westward to farms and small towns in the fertile Piedmont.

Penn's dealings were so well respected that his treaties with the natives were honored for almost a century after his death. Though Penn's ideals formed the basis of the legal and representational systems of Pennsylvania, he actually spent very little time in the New World. He visited exactly twice, each time for less than three years. He left all of his extensive landholdings to his children and second wife, who proved to be a sharp and effective businesswoman.

Philadelphia Becomes a City

Due to its central position in the colonies, its Chesapeake Bay shipping access, and the enormous amount of wealth generated by the surrounding area, Philadelphia became the largest and most important city in the colonies by the time of the American Revolution. Meanwhile, pioneers arrived by the shipload, often paying for passage by indenturing themselves as servants

VOLKSKUNST: PENNSYLVANIA FOLK ART

The highly stylized arts and crafts produced in the early days of Pennsylvania were a result of two major forces. First, the "plain" artistic mode was a uniquely American creation, a conscious attempt by Pennsylvania's German immigrants to distinguish their work from the effete rococo style popular in Europe at the time. Household items and pottery were stripped to reflect their basic function—two of the most common chair designs were the ladder-back with a cane bottom and the curved, slat-backed Pennsylvania Windsor. To reflect the Quaker disdain for upholstered luxury, neither was padded. Second, during the early stages of colonization, most craftsmen were farmers, and household goods were created out of necessity. The strict lines of utilitarian furniture such as chests and chairs often bore stylized natural elements; flowers and animals were common, as were symbols of religious faith, which permeated every aspect of life. The most functional objects—iron trivets and hinges, pottery plates, storage chests, and quilts—took on a new life as local craftspeople innovated in design according to their needs.

The guild system for craftsmen in Europe required a lengthy apprenticeship; the journeyman phase through master credentialing was simply not necessary in the New World. Anyone, regardless of birth or training, could try his or her hand at pottery, glassmaking, silversmithing, or a mix of any number of crafts once relegated to a rigidly qualified segment of the population. As a result, the bright colors and stylized patterns of "primitive" manufacturers developed into the decorative styles we associate with Pennsylvania Dutch crafts today.

This combination of high functionality and folksy decoration is reflected in dower chests, pottery, painted and punched tin, glassware, and quilts, which are all popularly collected. Dower chests were commonly given to girls between the ages of eight and 12 and contained linens to be used when the girl married; she often embroidered her own and added to the collection provided by other female members of the family. These brightly painted hope chests often displayed the name of the owner and have been passed down through generations. Tin, which was commercially produced, was saved, burned, or scrapped and repainted in the style known as tole.

Glassware was frequently produced and enameled or etched in fanciful designs. One manufacturer, Heinrich Stiegel, the son of middle-class German parents, sometimes called himself Baron

for varying periods. Many stayed in the city, but those who wanted to work their own farmland—as was common of many of the Germanic peoples—moved north and west.

Colonial Movement

That northern and western progress from Philadelphia continued steadily until pioneers reached the Allegheny Ridge. The only trails through the densely forested mountains were native trails too narrow for horses and wagons. Compounding the difficulty of surmounting the terrain was the fact that the native dwellers in the western lands were hostile to European incursion. The Shawnee, an Algonquian-language group unlike the Iroquois, came north from the Virginias, then moved west to the Ohio River. They frequently warred against other tribes, and

Shawnee living in the Ohio Valley offered the greatest resistance to colonization; many of the bloodiest massacres in colonial history were Shawnee reprisals against the westward movement of the pioneers. As a result of the difficulty of movement and dangerous conditions, the Atlantic Coastal Plain, the Piedmont, and the Allegheny Valley were settled well before lands north and west of the Allegheny Plateau, which remained sparsely populated until the canal system made travel more feasible.

The Colonial Wars

In 1753, the French sent troops south from their Canadian territory to occupy and claim the Ohio Valley. This aggression mirrored the conflict then taking place in Europe between the French and British. Most of the Native American tribes in the

and signed his name "von Stiegel." He became owner and producer of several glassworks in the mid-18th century. His work is prized today for its quality and beauty. Ceramic plates and other forms of pottery were decorated with biblical sayings, humorous quips, or folksy sentiments accompanied by highly stylized natural elements. Quilts, perhaps the most popular of today's collectibles, had their origins based upon need and community social interaction; quilting bees produced innumerable works of art in fabric.

Other homely arts flourished: every young girl practiced and became proficient in needlework and embroidery. Samplers and tablecloths often told the history of births and deaths within the families that created them. Even carved wooden toys reflected the freedom of the New World—birds and animals of the forests joined farm animals to become animated by the playful imaginations of children.

The documents known as *fraktur*, a distinctive early Pennsylvania art, were often decorated with natural forms. *Fraktur* is a style of manuscript writing and illumination that uses a broken or fractured style of lettering to create designs. This style, in which capitals and many of the small letters were formed with breaks between the strokes, de-

veloped from medieval forms. Significant events were memorialized in *fraktur*—awards, religious documents, house blessings *(Haussegen);* since the work was usually done on paper, authentic pieces are rare today.

Other types of art endure. The most celebrated folk painter in early 19th-century Pennsylvania was the mystical Quaker traveling minister, Edward Hicks, who painted his favorite subject, the *Peaceable Kingdom,* in many versions.

Portrait painting and fine arts had a significant place in the New World. Quaker Benjamin West was one of the earliest "plain" painters in Pennsylvania during the 18th century. His American work brought a new realism to popular art, though he later painted in a more fashionable allegorical style. He became president of the prestigious Royal Academy in London and served as teacher and mentor to a number of Pennsylvania painters, including Robert Fulton (who would find fame not as the wielder of a paintbrush but rather as inventor of the steamboat). Chief among West's students was Charles Willson Peale, who founded the Peale artistic dynasty. Peale and his brothers, sons, and grandsons painted many portraits of Revolutionary War figures, including 35 versions of George Washington.

region allied themselves with one or the other of the European forces—hence, the French and Indian War. The Iroquois remained neutral, hoping to play one side against the other and therefore continue a lucrative fur trade. The French hoped to make use of the Ohio River as a direct route to the Mississippi and French-held New Orleans. British forces based in eastern Pennsylvania made several unsuccessful attempts to drive them out and finally took possession of western Pennsylvania only after English troops defeated the French back on home soil in Europe.

British military movements into the area yielded one significant benefit—a series of forts and a primitive road were built to supply and support the troops, making access to the interior easier than it had ever been before for land-hungry pioneers. However, the French and Indian War was followed immediately by a native uprising, Pontiac's Rebellion, which kept the settlers out of the area for several more years.

The Revolutionary War

By 1773, the wild western portions of Pennsylvania, like the central and northern areas, had seen an influx of settlers. The Ohio Valley and the town of Pittsburgh had already become an in-

dustrial and shipping center, and Pennsylvania's narrow valleys were yielding grain, tobacco, and other desirable agricultural products. After many years of a hands-off approach, Britain began to clamp down on the wealthy colonies, imposing new taxes and making successful commerce increasingly difficult. In 1774, delegates from each of the colonies except Georgia met to protest the restrictions and formed the First Continental Congress, in Philadelphia. Matters escalated, and finally the British sent troops against the colonials in 1775; in Concord, Massachusetts, Paul Revere rode to warn colonists that British redcoats were on the march, and the revolution began in earnest. Though British General George Cornwallis surrendered to French and American forces at Yorktown, Virginia in 1781, the Revolutionary War lasted until 1783, when both sides signed the treaty of Paris, freeing the colonies to form their own nation.

Industrial Expansion and the Civil War

The rise of mining and manufacturing, along with the building of state-financed turnpikes, canals, and railroads, changed the face of Pennsylvania. By 1840, the hundreds of acres of

THE PRICE OF PACIFISM

Following the promise of religious freedom, Quakers owned much of the choicest land and most profitable businesses in Pennsylvania by 1776. Though many Friends did fight in the Revolution, others—adhering to their religious beliefs—refused to take up arms. As revolutionary fervor was heating up, a petition encouraging wavering Friends to back the pacifist position was circulated bearing the names of several wealthy and prominent Philadelphia Quakers. Delegates to the Second Continental Congress meeting in Philadelphia recommended that the local government apprehend those who had signed the petition on the grounds that they were "notoriously disaffected" against the Revolution and possibly even British supporters and spies.

The suspects demanded a hearing by Congress,

which was refused. Six guards were assigned to gather the signatories of the paper, who were forced into wagons and driven west, toward Lancaster.

Much of Philadelphia's citizenry, sympathetic to the wrongful imprisonment, lined the streets as the wagons passed, but the same wagons were stoned in Reading by patriots who believed that Quakers were traitors. Eventually, the prisoners were moved to Winchester in Virginia, where they remained for nearly six months, harassed by the locals for their "traitorous" beliefs. After repeated petitions to the Pennsylvania Council for a hearing, they were allowed to journey back to Lancaster and granted a hearing of their petition. They were finally allowed to return home and spent the remainder of the war unmolested.

wilderness that lay beyond the Allegheny Ridge were dotted with villages and encampments. In the north-central area, towns grew around lumber camps in the forests; in Erie, a ship transport and shipbuilding industry was thriving. Though the Piedmont remained the agricultural center of the state, Pittsburgh and Philadelphia were expanding exponentially as the demand for their coal, iron, and other industrial products brought millions of immigrants into new jobs. Many members of the Society of Friends (Quakers) worked together to secretly transport runaway slaves via the Underground Railroad to Canada—an activity that was both illegal and socially unpopular. By the time of the Civil War, in 1861, Pennsylvania pledged full support to the Union, and the state's booming industries produced ships, guns, and supplies in abundance. The decisive battle of Gettysburg, near South Mountain in south central Pennsylvania, was the "high-water mark" of the war—the northernmost point reached by the Confederate army during battle.

The Industrial Revolution

The Civil War was followed by an unprecedented period of industrial growth for Pennsylvania, as railroads crossed the nation and westward expansion, which once stopped at the Mississippi River, now moved across the prairies to the west coast of the continent. Rail, iron, and steel made multimillionaires out of poor boys such as Andrew Carnegie and the Scranton brothers and created a new class of Americans—self-made men. By the beginning of the 20th century, however, once-abundant natural resources—coal, iron ore, petroleum, and timber—were running out. The immigrants and African-Americans who had come to the state because of job opportunities were being laid off and were unable to find work in the communities where they had settled their families and made their lives.

World Wars

American history supports the idea that nothing revives a slumping economy quite as well as a war. World War I revitalized Pennsylvania's economy by

paper mill in Tyrone—modern industry in action

creating new markets for the state's industrial base; a demand for ships and tanks with which to fight World War II ameliorated the Great Depression and put millions of people back to work.

When the wars ended, demand for steel and iron fell. That, combined with a growing emphasis on different building materials, caused yet another crisis in Pennsylvania's major industries. In addition, Pennsylvanians were beginning to suffer from and rebel against the outrageous levels of pollution in the cities.

Contemporary Pennsylvania

Through a series of government and citizen initiatives, Pennsylvania has experienced a rebirth. Agriculture, once the economic cornerstone of the state, is again the chief source of wealth. The rivers and towns, once horribly polluted with foundry chemicals, coal-mine runoff, and filthy air, have become showplaces—models for the rest of the industrialized world. The state also relies on tourism now; Pennsylvania, inexpensive by East Coast standards, with no tax on clothing or foodstuffs, has become a regular shopping and recreation destination for the surrounding states and for foreign visitors including Canadians, Europeans, and Asians. Many come to be immersed in U.S. history—and no state offers more of that. Others enjoy the sparsely inhabited forests and mountains, the superbly endowed museums, or the best restaurants in America. The state maps available from the tourist board bear the legend "America Starts Here." And so it does.

Government and Economy

Government

The Commonwealth of Pennsylvania functions under an amended constitution first adopted in 1873. Executive authority is vested in a governor (who serves a term of four years and may serve two terms in succession), a lieutenant governor, an attorney general, an auditor general, and a treasurer—all also elected for four years. The governor has considerable power, appointing—subject to the approval of the state legislature—all department heads except those popularly elected, and members of independent boards and commissions. Gubernatorial power includes filling vacancies in offices when the legislature is not in session. The governor's veto may be overridden by a two-thirds vote in both the senate and house. The senate's 50 members are elected for four years, and the 203 members of the house of representatives are elected for two years. The lieutenant governor presides over the senate but has no vote on legislation.

Pennsylvania's supreme court dates from 1722. Its justices are elected for 10 years and form the court of last resort within the state system. The superior court, whose judges are also elected for 10-year terms, hears appeals from the courts of common pleas. The commonwealth court, created in 1968, has jurisdiction over civil actions involving the state.

Pennsylvania has 67 counties. Each county, like the state's townships, cities, boroughs, and other civil subdivisions, is self-governing. Almost all county officers are elected to their posts.

FIRST IN AMERICA

Pennsylvania is first in the nation in the following areas:

Mushroom production
Number of covered bridges
Number of licensed bakeries
Number of licensed hunters
Number of meat-packing plants
Potato chip production
Pretzel production
Rural population
Sausage production
Scrapple (pork bits in cornmeal cake) production
State game land area

The state was overwhelmingly Democratic between 1800 and 1860 but emerged from the Civil War strongly Republican, in support of Abraham Lincoln and his abolitionist platform. Business and financial interests also supported Republican positions on high tariffs and sound currency. In the latter part of the 19th and the early years of the 20th century, Pennsylvania was dominated by a dynasty of political bosses. Between the Civil War and 1934, Democrats won the governor's seat only twice, although they have increased their strength in recent decades. Labor, African-Americans, and Roman Catholics, concentrated in the cities, have boosted membership in the state's Democratic Party. Democratic governors have been elected from time to time since 1934; today the balance between the two major parties in Pennsylvania is very close.

Economy

Agriculture is the leading source of income in the state. There are estimated to be at least 56,000 farms within Pennsylvania's boundaries. Farmland occupies roughly 8.3 million acres, and 120,000 people work on farms. More than two-thirds of these are farm owners and their families. Dairying is the primary farm occupation in the northeast and northwest, where the soil is less fertile than in the southern part of the state. There, dairying is often combined with general farming. Milk is Pennsylvania's most important farm product, followed by eggs, chickens, and fresh produce.

Tourism is Pennsylvania's second-largest industry after agriculture. In terms of dollars spent by visitors, the state ranks eighth in the nation. Pennsylvania's cities draw large numbers of business travelers as well as casual tourists, but the rest of the state is increasing in popularity as word of its recreational attractions spreads.

Ever since colonial times, mining, manufacturing, and commerce have played important parts in the economy. Inland waterways, abundant natural resources, fertile farmlands, and a strategic position on the Atlantic seaboard have shaped the state's economic history. Pennsylvania is still one of America's industrial leaders and ranks seventh among the states in terms of manufacturing output. Pennsylvania's iron-and-steel industry led the nation in production and output for more than a century, but in the 1970s, national economic recession and foreign competition closed many mills. However, the state produces *all* of the nation's anthracite coal and is third in production of bituminous coal.

The People

Demography

Pennsylvania's current population is around 12,009,000. Population distribution between urban and rural areas has remained relatively stable in the last century, with approximately 66 percent of the populace inhabiting the cities and the remainder in rural areas. Since 1970, rural areas in western Pennsylvania and the Allegheny Forest region to the north, and the urban Scranton/Wilkes-Barre area, have lost population while southeastern Pennsylvania, Harrisburg, the Poconos, and the west—around Beaver County—have gained 25 percent to 50 percent or more in population. The remainder of the state, mostly rural, shows slow gains, up to 25 percent.

Pennsylvania has an unusually diverse ethnic mix, due, in part, to its central role as a major port of entry for immigration since the 17th century. Pennsylvanians generally place great emphasis on religion and ethnic background. Every village, town, and city has an abundance of churches, and the state is home to more than 100 different religious groups. Many of the groups reflect their founders' ethnic heritage. For example, the Amish and Mennonites speak English, High German (primarily for religious services), and a variation of German known as Pennsylvania Dutch.

About 15,000 Native Americans inhabited the Pennsylvania area when Europeans arrived, and approximately the same number live in the state today. Early Dutch, Swedish, Finnish, and Welsh colonists who initially settled the Delaware Valley left few traceable descendants. English, Scotch-Irish, and Germans, who mostly arrived in the 18th century, reinforced by 19th-century immigration, continue to account for large population sectors in the state. Today, Americans of English heritage are prominent in the southeast around Philadelphia; German-Americans are a major group in the Piedmont; and descendants of Scotch-Irish pioneers are prevalent in the south-central region, from Harrisburg to Pittsburgh.

After the 1870s, Slavs, Poles, Ukrainians, Italians, Jews, Russians, and Greeks joined the mix. Pennsylvania's African-American population increased greatly after the Civil War and in the early 20th century. During the 1960s and 1970s, Hispanics arrived in large numbers. The latest immigration surge has been from Asia.

Since the state's beginning, each new wave of immigrants has created a backlash from those already settled in the area. Though agents of William Penn encouraged Germans from the Rhineland region to immigrate to Pennsylvania, not everyone felt the same way. Benjamin Franklin was disturbed by the newcomers, and, in 1751, wrote, "Why should the Palatine boors [farmers] be suffered to swarm into our settlement, and by herding together, establish their language, and manners, to the exclusion of ours? Why should Pennsylvania, founded by the English, become a colony of aliens, who will shortly be so numerous as to Germanize us, instead of our Anglicifying them, and will never adopt our language or customs any more than they can acquire our complexion?" Ben's whining made little impact; after all, every newcomer was "Pennsylvaniacized."

Ethnography
Though the term Quakers refers more to members of a religious group—the Society of Friends—bonded by belief rather than to racial heritage, the majority of Quakers who immigrated to Pennsylvania after 1682 were, like William Penn, **British.** By 1720, two years after

Penn's death in England, 10,000 Quakers in Philadelphia and the Piedmont retained most of the land and all of the political power in the colony. By 1776, although their numbers had reached 100,000, the Quakers' political power had been eroded by their refusal to fund against Indian raids on the frontiers, combined with an uneasy pacifism during the French and Indian War (they finally supported Britain) and during the Revolutionary War (when those who eschewed pacifism threw in their lot with the colonies). Small enclaves of Friends continue to exist in every part of the state, having been completely assimilated into the mix.

One of the major purposes of William Penn's land grant was to provide a place of refuge for his Quaker brethren, some of whom were **German.** Other early German immigrants to Pennsylvania consisted of persecuted followers of various other Protestant sects, among them Moravians, Mennonites, Schwenkfelders, Dunkards, and the Ephrata Brethren. In general, the Germans were farmers and skilled craftsmen who avoided the city and moved into the surrounding areas. One of their significant contributions was in the field of agriculture; they introduced the three-field rotation system of planting, natural fertilizers, and multicrop planting. The extreme fertility of the soil today in the Piedmont, after 200 years of use, is a testament to their skill.

The first German settlement, Germantown (northwest of Philadelphia) was founded by educator and poet Francis Daniel Pastorius. By 1750, 70,000 German-speaking people dwelt in the counties surrounding Philadelphia. Their numbers were significant enough to demand money for frontier defense from the Quaker-run Pennsylvania Assembly in Philadelphia. During this time, the assembly tried on several occasions to force Germans to learn English, an act that succeeded in alienating them all the more. The result was to create a subculture in Pennsylvania that retains its own customs and cultural mores, as well as a distinctive language. Heavy immigration from German-speaking countries continued until about 1820; their numbers grew to 100,000 by the end of the 18th

SAMPLING THE MIX

In the cities and the surrounding countryside, visitors are continually aware of Pennsylvania's rich ethnic mix. As they immigrated, various ethnic groups often formed enclaves with their own churches, shops, and foods. Pittsburgh remains largely a city of neighborhoods, all at one time tiny ethnic villages. Today, African-Americans and people of Nordic, German, and Eastern European descent continue to maintain their own benevolent societies and churches, food shops, and special events. In Philadelphia, the cultural heritage of Italy, England, Africa, Ireland, and China are equally well preserved.

Because of this marked ethnic pride, Pennsylvania offers an unprecedented opportunity to enjoy America's mix. One of the best ways to take advantage of the opportunity is to search through local papers for announcements of church bazaars and other activities; these often feature food, crafts, and performances. In Pittsburgh, look for performances by the Tambouritzens, a group that performs folk dances and other entertainment from Eastern Europe. Ethnic festivals occur regularly in both the cities and the outlying areas. Philadelphia offers many opportunities to celebrate African-American heritage; the city publishes its own city guide (see the Philadelphia chapter).

Know Pennsylvania

century. Today, German-Americans form a significant part of Pennsylvania's rural population.

Though **Scotch-Irish** immigrants (people of Scottish descent who had been living in Ireland) appeared in Philadelphia as early as 1685, it wasn't until 1717 that great numbers of them began arriving. Most of this initial large group settled in Lancaster and Chester Counties. In 1740, a third wave, possibly 12,000 more, came to America, and another nearly 30,000 immigrated to Pennsylvania between 1771 and 1773. Most came because of religious and political differences with the British government, and also for economic opportunity. The majority were farmers, craftspeople, small businessmen, and traders. Like the Germans before them, they moved to the frontiers of Pennsylvania, and they joined with the Germans in protesting the lack of protection from Indian attacks. The combined German/Scotch-Irish efforts resulted in construction of a system of frontier forts, many of which still exist in some form today. The land-hungry Scotch-Irish, who often made passage by indenturing themselves, were more daring in their land acquisition than the Germans and, by 1790, 63,000 of them had settled in the counties west of the Allegheny Ridge—the most dangerous and difficult territory in the state. Their enthu-

siastic support of colonial forces during the Revolution ensured their representation in the new America.

Welsh immigrants, many of them Quakers, formed the largest ethnic group in Pennsylvania for the first two decades of the colony's existence; by 1700, some 6,000 Welsh resided in the state. These early inhabitants initially settled into a 40,000-acre tract west of the Schuylkill River, in present-day Merion and Haverford (which explains the local presence of names such as Bala-Cynwyd and Bryn Mawr, named in memory of the home of Welsh pioneer Rowland Ellis). Provincial authorities divided the tract in 1685 and allowed settlers of other ethnic and national groups to buy land there, scattering the Welsh settlers to other parts of Philadelphia.

By 1776, the Welsh population had doubled to 12,000. During the next century, Welsh families settled in Scranton, Carbondale, and the north counties, mainly to work in the anthracite fields; by 1880 almost 30 percent of the mine workers were Welsh. The *Eisteddfod*, an annual Welsh traditional gathering of musicians, poets, and writers, has continued to this day in some areas of northeastern Pennsylvania.

Irish immigrants, also often traveling as indentured servants, began settling in Philadelphia around 1700. Their numbers increased dramatically in 1800, when a failed uprising against England brought well-educated, political Irish dissidents and their families to the new state. During the early part of the 19th century, agricultural disasters and a potato famine in Ireland brought 5,000 additional Irish to the anthracite coal regions. Competition for the same labor jobs led to riots in Luzerne County among the Irish, British, and Welsh and in Philadelphia between Irish and African-Americans. "Old-stock" Irish (those who had arrived in or before 1800) considered the newer immigrants lazy and stupid. The great migration of the 1840s brought 72,000 more Irish to Philadelphia.

Many of these immigrants participated bravely in the Civil War, but the collective reputation of the Irish was sullied by the activities of the Molly Maguires, a secret society that ruthlessly avenged maltreatment of coal miners and their families in acts of sabotage and murder against the powerful mine owners (see the sidebar "The Molly Maguires," in the Poconos and Black Diamond Country chapter). After Black Friday, when several Molly Maguire leaders were hanged, the Irish began to move into the building trades, small business, and politics. Today, Pennsylvania's Irish-Americans tend to dwell in the state's cities and make up one of the largest and most politically active groups in the state.

The first **Italians** to immigrate to Pennsylvania, in the 1860s, were a group of professional musicians, painters, physicians, and educators from northern Italy. They settled in south Philadelphia and, within 20 years, were joined by another 7,000 people from southern Italy. Many who came to America from Italy's southern provinces were farmers, but the industrialization of Philadelphia and other cities offered steady, well-paying work in factories and mills. In 1882, the United States passed the first laws limiting immigration, but by the first decade of the 20th century Italians and Italian-Americans numbered 77,000 in Philadelphia alone. The prosperous 1920s saw unprecedented emigration from Italy; more than three million workers and their families arrived in the U.S. hungry for jobs and an op-

portunity to build their own communities. By 1920, peoples of Italian descent, along with those of Irish descent, formed the largest ethnic groups in Philadelphia. Further restrictive immigration laws cut the flow to a trickle by 1952, but Italian-Americans continue to have a highly visible and politically active presence in Philadelphia.

Another ethnic group defined by religious ties, **Jewish** settlers had homesteaded in Lancaster, Easton, and Philadelphia by the early 18th century. Like all other colonials, Jews took various sides during the Revolution, though Haym Solomon, a Philadelphia businessman and broker, was responsible in large part for raising most of the money needed to finance the Continental army—and, later, to keep the new nation from ruin. In the 1790s, a census counted 3,000 Jews in Pennsylvania. The population grew to 250,000 by 1870, and Eastern Europe's pogroms and repressive laws over the following two decades brought a further increase in Jewish immigration to Pennsylvania. By 1810, two million Jews had entered the United States. Many stayed in the cities, establishing religious and secular schools and temples. Currently, 500,000 American Jews live within greater Philadelphia alone.

In the mid- to late-19th century, thousands of **Poles, Russians, Lithuanians, Hungarians, Slavs, Croatians,** and **Ukrainians** arrived in Pennsylvania, often fleeing strife in their home countries. Most had been peasants with rustic backgrounds, who found industrialized urban Pennsylvania a rough fit. Adapting skills learned in fields and farms, they began to provide the labor that built America's coal and steel fortunes.

They used their strong backs to carry coal out of the anthracite mines of the northeast and their hardened hands to wield picks and shovels in the bituminous mines in the Ohio Valley, and they built their close-knit communities around the coal breakers. The first Ukrainian Catholic Church was established in Shenandoah in 1865, and the Ruthenians built a Byzantine rite church, St. Michael the Archangel, in the same town; in 1867, a Croatian bank was begun in Pittsburgh. Today, the Pittsburgh area is home to the highest concentration of Eastern Europeans in the state, and more people of Eastern European descent dwell in Pennsylvania than in any other state in the nation.

Steel mills all over Pennsylvania absorbed thousands of workers and their families. Though most Eastern Europeans stayed in the industrial trades (a local folklore legend, Joe Magarac, a Polish Paul Bunyan who could lift a 50-ton ladle of molten steel, typified the manly ideal), some went on to other professions. Leopold Stokowski became the conductor of the Philadelphia Symphony in 1915; in 1936, Hungarian-born Eugene Ormandy took over the baton. Not all musical interest leaned toward the classics; in the 1950s, a young Polish singer named Bobby Vinton hit number one on the pop charts with "My Melody of Love," and entered a pantheon of '50s pop heroes during the birth of rock 'n' roll

Originally brought from Africa to the New World as early as 1639, most of the 10,000 **Africans** in Pennsylvania during colonial and revolutionary times were slaves. Freedom was a hotly contested issue prior to the Civil War, with Mennonites and Quakers leading the abolitionist contingent. Many Pennsylvanians agreed with the freedom issue but not with the idea of equality. After the Civil War, segregation was the rule not only on streetcars but also in mines, mills, and shipyards. In 1867, a widely signed petition ended segregation on streetcars, but the battle for equality and representation in political, economic, and cultural venues goes on. Pennsylvania's cities—particularly Harrisburg, Philadelphia, and Pittsburgh—continue to provide opportunities for work and cultural enrichment; there are more than one million African-Americans living in Pennsylvania, and about 900,000 of them in Philadelphia.

Hispanic immigrants, consisting largely of Puerto Rican tenant farmers (already U S. citizens), began coming to the state in the 1920s, seeking greater opportunities than existed in their homeland. More than 120,000 live in Pennsylvania today, including 90,000 in Philadelphia. Puerto Rican immigrants have formed close-knit communities of extended families, creating their own grocery stores *(bodegas)* and churches.

Chinese have been in Pennsylvania for hundreds of years, mostly settling in large cities. Philadelphia has a thriving Chinatown, once the exclusive province of Chinese immigrants. Most recent newcomers have been **Vietnamese, Thai,** and **Cambodians** driven out of their own countries by brutal wars. Asians have tended to stay in the state's urban areas; even so, they form less than 10 percent of the total population of Philadelphia and constitute lower percentages in other areas of the state.

Culture

RELIGION

Every religious doctrine is currently represented in Pennsylvania—Baha'i to Judaism, Wicca to Baptists. Religion led to the founding of the colony, played crucial roles in the state's history, and continues to exert an absolutely inextricable influence in the lives of the people who live in, pass through, and visit Pennsylvania. The following spiritual belief systems initially influenced and often continue to be identified with Pennsylvania.

Society of Friends (Quakers)

In 17th-century England, traveling preacher George Fox's intimation that God valued each individual was a revolutionary idea that challenged the legitimacy of both the class system and established religions. The British court joined with Catholic and Episcopal hierarchies in labeling Fox's teachings heresy. His followers, who called themselves Friends and met by gathering in silence, were derisively referred to as "Quakers" because they were thought to "tremble at the word of the Lord." Members of the sect were continually being imprisoned for not showing proper respect to the upper classes; they refused to bow or remove their hats in the presence of anyone but God.

Famous for their dedicated pacifism, many Quakers have continued to choose noncombatant service over active military duty throughout the history of the United States. Some, such as David Harris during the Vietnam War, have endured jail rather than condone violence against their fellow humans. Though the Society of Friends forgoes active proselytizing, the group remains strong throughout the world today. Nearly every county in America has a weekly meeting at a private home or meetinghouse.

Mennonites and Old Order Amish

All Amish and Mennonites trace their roots to the Swiss Anabaptist ("new birth") movement of

1525, an offshoot of the Protestant Reformation. Anabaptists disdained the formality of both Protestant and Catholic worship, believing instead in each individual's direct relationship to God. They also promoted adult baptism—a criminal offense at the time. "Anabaptist hunters" were paid to track down, torture, and kill believers (a number of whom were burned at the stake).

Toward the end of the 17th century, the Anabaptist movement split over several issues, chief among them the practice of "shunning," social ostracism of community members for disobedience. A conservative sect dwelling primarily in the Alsace region of France was determined to continue the practice, so the Anabaptists separated into two main camps—the pro-shunning Old Order Amish and the more liberal Mennonites. Since the original schism, each of the main branches has split many times.

Mennonites and Amish alike immigrated to Pennsylvania during the 18th century, seeking freedom from religious persecution. The oldest Amish community is thought to be Shartlesville (then called Northkill), near Reading, dating from 1738. In 1900, fewer than 500 Amish lived in Lancaster County; some 16,000 now live in that area alone, with Amish and Mennonite communities thriving side by side in all parts of Pennsylvania. Large colonies farm the Piedmont, which includes Lancaster County, the Big Valley (Kishacoquillas Valley) area south of State College, and the area north and east of New Castle in western Pennsylvania.

Mennonites are active international missionaries, and most sects under the broad Mennonite umbrella interact with the world in every way. Though they share a deeply religious lifestyle with the Amish, they're indistinct as a group. Dress ranges widely from fashionable clothing to near-Amish plainness, and their use of cars and other modern conveniences characterizes them as a fundamentalist group with strong Pennsylvanian-American roots.

Though completely obliterated in their European homeland, Old Order Amish have flourished in the New World. The Anabaptist persecution instilled a deep mistrust of the outside world into Amish culture. With their quaint clothing, horse-drawn buggies, and bucolic lifestyle, the Amish appear to have rejected—and perhaps transcended—the modern world. Though all Amish practice both symbolic and social separation from the worldly communities that surround them, they maintain a carefully thought-out balance between their strict religious traditions and the seductive sway of progress.

Shunning is still practiced today, a result of rigid enforcement of boundaries for behavior among the Old Order. The price for rebellion by baptized members is a period of attempted persuasion by friends and elders followed, finally, by excommunication. The entire community "shuns" the excommunicated individual, refusing to interact with him or her. Those who do not wish to repent often join one of the more worldly Amish sects or Mennonite groups.

Among the Amish, the price of contentment is the surrender of personal aspirations to community goals. In exchange for the novelty offered by an urbanized, commercialized, rapidly changing world, members receive a durable identity, a solid sense of belonging, direction, and purpose.

Religious Communes

Led by charismatic figures, three unique sectarian groups also migrated to Pennsylvania to escape persecution and to pursue the utopian ideal of communal life. Two of these religious communes exist only in memory; the other has adapted to the demands of a changing society. The belief systems of Pennsylvania's three major communal groups—the Ephratans (EFF-ra-tenz), the Harmonists, and the Moravians—were rooted in the religious reformation of the 16th century. Adherence to strict biblical interpretation characterized these groups—sex was often seen as the original sin, so the Harmonists insisted on total celibacy and the Ephratans and Moravians imposed strict limitations on marriage and con-

jugal life. The welfare of the marital unit was always secondary to that of the group.

The **Ephratans** followed the teachings of German mystic Conrad Beissel and came with him to America in 1732 to establish the Ephrata (an ancient name for Bethlehem) cloister. The log, stone, and half-timbered buildings—which still stand today—are based on the architecture of the Rhenish homeland of the group.

The Ephratans recognized three orders of citizens: married couples and their young children, who lived outside the cloister; celibate men ("Brethren"); and celibate women ("Spiritual Virgins"). The celibate orders lived on the property in separate houses and engaged in communal farming and fruit growing, basketmaking, papermaking, book production, printing, carpentry, and milling.

Acts of charity were highly valued by Ephratans; travelers and visitors were routinely lodged and fed free of charge. During the Revolution, several hundred wounded soldiers, fresh from the battle at Brandywine, were nursed by members. (The buildings used as hospitals were later burned to prevent spread of infection.)

After Conrad Beissel's death, in 1768, and the end of British rule in the colonies, membership declined, reflecting both the loss of leadership and a growing lack of interest in a life of self-denial. In 1814, the remaining householders incorporated into the Seventh Day German Baptist Church.

Today, the buildings and grounds of the cloister, a few miles north of Lancaster in southeastern Pennsylvania, are open to visitors and are maintained and administered by a nonprofit membership organization.

The Christian-based communal sect known as the **Harmonists**, or Rappites, organized in Germany at the end of the 18th century. The group was formed around a part-time preacher and vintner, George Rapp, who believed in the intrinsic rewards of hard work as well as the imminent second coming of Christ. In 1804, Rapp led his flock from bitter religious intolerance in Europe to Harmony, Pennsylvania, where they farmed, practiced animal husbandry, built a textile mill and a distillery, and provided for themselves in every way.

A waning population of believers tolled the death knell for the Harmonist colony. Since commune members were celibate, the community relied for survival on the adoption of children and the conversion of adults. As the years went on, fewer Harmonist immigrants arrived from Germany. The decrease of commune membership combined with an aging population forced the hiring of non-Harmonists—mainly Japanese and Chinese laborers—to run the Harmonists' factories. However, the success of the colony seemed to rely directly on the hands-on dedication of its fading membership. By 1876, only 100 elderly men and women walked the cobblestone streets of Economy, and the factories were idle. In 1915, there were only two living Rappites, and by 1921 the last member had died. The state maintains both Economy Village and the Great House at Harmony as museums, monuments to the most commercially successful commune in American history.

One of the German groups that immigrated to Pennsylvania in the 1700s was the Fratres Unitas, followers of the religious martyr John Huss. The sect, which came into existence after Huss's death, in 1457, originated in Bohemia and Moravia. By 1754, its members founded three colonies in Pennsylvania—Emmaus, Nazareth, and the largest, Bethlehem. The Fratres Unitas are known today as **Moravians,** and they maintain active churches and missions all over the world.

A love for education, art, and music permeated the lives of the Moravians. They created some of the earliest and most complete school systems in the area, including a school for both boys and girls in 1742. Each congregation was grouped according to age, sex, and marital status and arranged into choirs. On Easter on the hill behind the meeting house, the Bethlehem congregation gathered to sing in celebration in the Moravian cemetery (God's Acre), where their dead lay buried in choirs, rather than family groups, to symbolize their membership in the larger world of the church.

The Moravian Church today retains many of its original qualities, such as love for education

and the arts. Missionary work has proven very successful over the years; so many converts have been made in Tanzania that the Moravian Church's black members now outnumber every other ethnic group in the world congregation.

LANGUAGE

English is the prevalent language in Pennsylvania. However, you will find small pockets of traditional communities whose members speak High German or Pennsylvania Dutch—a patois full of German colloquialisms, something like Yiddish.

FESTIVALS AND EVENTS

Pennsylvania offers a host of events from tiny village festivals to celebrations of the state's primary business: agricultural fairs take place throughout the state during July, August, and September, featuring champion livestock, homemade goods, amusement rides, parades, and other entertainment. For a copy of the Pennsylvania fair schedule, contact the Pennsylvania Department of Agriculture (Attn: Agricultural Fair Program, 2301 N. Cameron St., Harrisburg, PA 17110-9408, 717/787-4737, www.pda.state.pa.us).

An annotated list of festivals and special events by month and book chapter follows; contact the tourism boards in each chapter for more information:

January
Mummers Parade, Philadelphia (Philadelphia chapter): Practice your struts for New Year's Day; a frosty version of Mardi Gras, with costumed banjo-playing bands and dancers.

Transportation Celebration, Pittsburgh (Pittsburgh chapter): The Recreational Vehicle Show, Boat Show, Custom Car Show, and Automobile Show all take place in January or February.

February
National Ice Carving Championships, Scranton (The Poconos and Black Diamond Country chapter): Contestants create fine art from the union of fire and water, sculpting huge ice blocks

with blowtorches, chainsaws, and specially adapted carving tools.

Pennsylvania Horticultural Society's Flower Show Philadelphia (Philadelphia chapter): This show is one of the most prestigious garden events in the United States.

Groundhog Day, Punxsutawney (Lake Erie and the Alleghenies chapter): Calling a groundhog a public figure may be stretching it, but Punxsutawney Phil is *the* eponymous groundhog, and he makes the national news every February.

March

St. Patrick's Day Parades, Philadelphia and Pittsburgh (Philadelphia and Pittsburgh chapters): Parades celebrate the strong Irish communities in both cities.

Annual Trout Stocking, Volant (Western Amish Country chapter): This is a call for anglers to fluff up their lures. Millions of fingerlings are released into specified rivers and streams in the area.

April

Spring Flower Show at Phipps Conservatory, Pittsburgh (Pittsburgh chapter): This flower show is spectacular, with each of the conservatory's glass-enclosed rooms decorated in a special theme.

Penn Relays, Philadelphia (Philadelphia chapter): America's oldest track meet (begun in 1885) takes place at the University of Pennsylvania.

Old Pike Days, SR 40 (Laurel Highlands chapter): This event celebrates America's first federally built thoroughfare, the National Road. Costumed participants in the wagon train camp at Addison, Great Meadows, Uniontown, and Brownsville, and each of the encampment areas has food and entertainment; Fort Necessity hosts a crafts fair.

May

Dad Vail Regatta, Philadelphia (Philadelphia chapter): The regatta brings together more than 3,000 rowers from 60 colleges and universities to participate in the largest rowing competition in America.

Devon Horse Show and Country Fair, Chester County (Delaware River Valley chap-

ter): This is the nation's largest outdoor equestrian event.

June

Bark Peeler's Convention, Coudersport (Endless Mountains chapter): Here's an opportunity to warm up your chaw—the event features a state-championship tobacco-spitting contest and demonstrations of woodsmanship, blacksmithing, fiddling, and greased-pole climbing.

Elfreth's Alley Fete Days, Philadelphia (Philadelphia chapter): The oldest residential street in the nation opens its homes to the public. The event includes a colonial crafts show, bagpipers, and other entertainment.

Gettysburg Civil War Heritage Days, Gettysburg (Railroad and Civil War Country chapter): The Civil War battle is commemorated with living-history encampments, band concerts, a 4th of July program, lectures, and a battle reenactment.

Sentimental Journey Fly-In, Lock Haven (Endless Mountains chapter): The Fly-In takes place each summer, usually at the end of June. Pilots from all over the country participate as an average of 200 makes and models of aircraft, including antique and classic planes, fly by and perform stunts.

July

4th of July Parade, Philadelphia (Philadelphia chapter): The annual parade begins on 20th Street and JFK Boulevard and winds through town. It's a great time and place to celebrate the birth of a nation.

Three Rivers Regatta, Pittsburgh (Pittsburgh chapter): An opportunity to enjoy hundreds of beautiful boats on the spectacular confluence of the Monongahela, Allegheny, and Ohio Rivers.

Harborfest, Erie (Lake Erie and the Alleghenies chapter): Hot-air balloons, musicians, the U.S. Navy SEALs skydiving team, and an amusement arcade make for four days of family fun.

August

Old Thresherman's Reunion, Kinzer (Pennsylvania Dutch Country chapter): This event has

...n held at the Rough & Tumble Museum since 948. Expect to see an odd assortment of old arm machines, accompanied by an army of tinkerers and mechanics.

Grange Encampment and Fair, Centre County (Endless Mountains chapter): This ultimate weeklong country fair has taken place in Centre County since 1874; livestock parade around the show rings between tractor pulls and marching bands.

September

Penn's Colony Festival and Marketplace, Pittsburgh (Pittsburgh chapter): Features battle reenactments, colonial food, an arts and crafts market, and entertainment.

Wine Country Festival, North East (Lake Erie and the Alleghenies chapter): The festival honors northwestern Pennsylvania's own wine country and the fruit of the vine with hay rides, a farmers' market, winetasting, music, and arts and crafts exhibits.

October

Polish American Heritage Month, Philadelphia (Philadelphia chapter): In October Philadelphia celebrates Polish American Heritage Month with exhibitions, lectures, music, and performances across the city.

Pennsylvania State Flaming Foliage Festival, Renovo (Endless Mountains chapter): For two days each year, the small town of Renovo celebrates with an annual old-fashioned parade and crafts festival.

November

Holidays at the Nationality Classrooms, Pittsburgh (Pittsburgh chapter): During the holidays, the ethnic-decor concept goes one step further and adds Christmas decorations.

Enchanted Colonial Village, Philadelphia (Philadelphia chapter): This is a traditional Philadelphia favorite; it's an animated reproduction of an 18th-century village on display at the Atwater-Kent Museum.

December

Historic Houses in Fairmount Park, Philadelphia (Philadelphia chapter): The historic houses are especially pretty during the holiday season, when each is decorated by local garden clubs.

Washington Crossing the Delaware, Washington Crossing Historic Park (Delaware River Valley chapter): A reenactment of Washington's victorious march to Trenton, with a parade of colonial officers and soldiers; General Washington himself addresses the troops.

Bethlehem Christmas, Bethlehem (Delaware River Valley chapter): A walking tour, candlelight concerts, horse-drawn carriage rides, and a colonial handicrafts market, among many other events.

Victorian Christmas, Bellefonte (Endless Mountains chapter): Businesses, schools, churches, and government agencies work together to decorate the town, creating a 19th-century atmosphere. Sleigh rides and other special events are scheduled each year.

Entertainment and Recreation

ART AND CULTURE

Pittsburgh and Philadelphia are repositories of fabulous art, professional symphonies, opera companies, ballet companies, and theater. Resorts in the Laurel Highlands and Poconos and large-scale venues near the big cities often feature big-name rock bands, singers, comedians, and other entertainers, and almost every county has a local theater troupe that performs musicals and plays.

AMUSEMENT PARKS

Amusement parks, large and small, are one of the state's unique attractions. They are as varied as Sesame Place, near Philadelphia, which focuses more on children's active participation than on passive entertainment; the wooded fairyland of Knoebels, in Elysburg (Poconos and Black Diamond Country); the intricate water slides of Waldameer Amusement Park, in Erie; and Pittsburgh's Kennywood, which has reconstructed part of the original Luna Park.

Of historical and artistic interest are the classic carousels in many of the parks. Artisans from two of America's most famous and fabulous carousel companies—both situated in Philadelphia—carved many of the leaping horses, roaring tigers, and bounding ostriches that populate the carefully restored and original merry-go-rounds throughout the state.

SHOPPING AND CRAFTS

Two features make Pennsylvania a mecca for shoppers. First, the state is the birthplace of discount outlets—the originals, in Reading, are still going strong, as are dozens of discount outlets all

LUNA PARK

On a warm, humid summer night, imagine holding your mother's hand, damp where your palms touch. You're barely able to suppress your excitement as the trolley you ride rattles and clanks through a series of stops, until houses and shops fall away, leaving only an occasional small house dimly lit, glimpsed from the road. The air, now perfumed with mock orange and the damp smell of the forest floor, closes around you; the trolley rocks, but you will not be lulled. You stick your head out the window of the car, bringing admonitions from both your mother and older brother, but there! You caught a glimpse of it! Through the black trees on this moonless night, a fairyland blazes, not far! The lights twinkle through the openings in tree branches until the trolley finally reaches the turnaround, the end of the line, and the families disgorge to approach the gated entry, the archway lit with a hundred shining white lights. At last! Luna Park.

Throughout the state, Pennsylvania has kept alive an old-fashioned, family-oriented form of entertainment—the amusement park. Most of the parks were built during the birth of the 20th century and celebrated the advent of electricity. Many were built at the end-of-the-line stops of the newly built trolley systems that provided public transportation for each municipality. The parks, commonly called Luna Parks, were built to encourage whole families to travel on the trolley and were festooned with thousands of light bulbs, which allowed them to be seen from miles away in the dark evening hours. In the beginning, the parks were little more than picnic grounds, places where adults could socialize and let the kids run wild. Through the years, the parks that survived have changed with their patrons. Rides were added, perhaps a merry-go-round, and, later, a Ferris wheel. Though some parks offer intense thrill rides, most are family oriented, and perfect for a warm evening's entertainment.

:r the state. Second, there's no tax on clothing, hich makes purchases a double bargain.

Crafts, particularly handmade quilts and Amish-built wooden furniture and toys, are sold throughout the state. Country crafts, such as handmade baskets and candles, are also popular and reasonably priced.

OUTDOOR RECREATION

Cycling

The rails-to-trails movement, which converts unused railroad corridors to multiuse trails, has added 190 miles of multiuse trails all over the state. The Loyalsock Trail, a demanding wilderness passage through Lycoming and Sullivan Counties, crosses mountain peaks with elevations averaging over 1,700 feet. The state website (www.dcnr.state.pa.us) has rail-trails maps and information. Mountain bikers and hikers can take advantage of hundreds of miles of multiuse and specialty trails in the state parks.

Fishing

Fishing is a consummate preoccupation in Pennsylvania. Twenty-five species of game fish, their numbers often supplemented by state breeding programs, inhabit Lake Erie and thousands of the state's smaller lakes, rivers, ponds, and streams. The Laurel Highlands alone are home to 120 freshwater lakes and streams, and the Allegheny National Forest offers three reservoirs loaded with warm-water game fish. Many of the state parks offer ice fishing to those who can't wait for warm weather.

Fishing is strictly controlled by the Pennsylvania Fish and Boat Commission. Licenses are required for anyone over the age of 16 and are available from more than 1,700 licensed issuing agents across the state (usually sporting goods and department stores) as well as county treasurers and Fish and Boat Commission regional offices. Fishing license fees are $17 for residents ages 16–64, $4 for resident seniors (65 and up), $16 for a resident senior lifetime license, $35 for nonresidents 16 and up, or $15 for a three-day tourist license. A trout-permit stamp is an additional $5 (prices include an issuing agents charge of $.75 for each license.

Licensing, season, and location information is available from the **Pennsylvania Fish and Boat Commission Main Office** (P.O. Box

LONG-DISTANCE TRAILS

Erie

Tanbark Trail

Baker Trail

North Country Trail

North Country Trail

Twin Lakes Trail

Bucktail Path

Quehanna Trail

Donut Hole Trail

Susquehannock Trail System

Loyalsock Trail

Scranton

Pinchot Trail System

Thunder Swamp Trail System

Mid-state Trail System

0   25 mi
0   25 km

Rachel Carson Trail

State College

Baker Trail

Forbes Trail

PITTSBURGH

Harrisburg

Appalachian Trail

Allentown

Horse-shoe Trail

Warrior Trail

Catawba Trail

Laurel Highland Trail

Link Trail

Tuscarora Trail

Conestoga Trail

Forbes Road Historic Trail

Appalachian Trail

Gettysburg

Mason Dixon Trail

Mason Dixon Trail

PHILADELPHIA

67000, Harrisburg, PA 17106-7000, 717/705-7800, www.fish.state.pa.us; the fishing license division is 717/705-7933). Both numbers are on the Verizon phone system, which may require dialing the number twice (a voice prompt will ask for your "10-digit number"—just redial). Season dates for sportfishing vary, but American shad, herring, striped bass, carp, sunfish, yellow perch, catfish, rock bass, and sunfish are open year-round.

Hang-Gliding and Small Aircraft

Hyner View State Park, in Clinton County in north-central Pennsylvania, is recognized among hang-glider pilots as one of the best spots in the nation. The thermals that waft along the mountain gorges here have also helped set records for gliders, and several airports offer rides and instruction. Pennsylvania is the home of the original Piper Cub (in Lock Haven); small airports and aircraft are everywhere. Hot-air-balloon rides are also offered at many of the airports during summer festivals.

Hiking

For general information on *all* Pennsylvania state parks, call Pennsylvania Parks (888/727-2757, www.dcnr.state.pa.us). Most state parks offer some type of camping facilities.

Allegheny State Forest and the northern half of the state offer the wildest parks with long stretches of forested land. With few exceptions, state game lands are open year-round to hikers and backpackers and are used by hunters only during the appropriate season, mid-Oct–mid-Jan. There are 24 designated National Recreation Trails for hikers, bikers, and backpackers.

The Appalachian Trail, stretching 229 miles from Franklin County to the Delaware Water Gap, is open to hikers and backpackers—and is only one of 34 long-distance trails in the state.

Hunting

Hunting remains one of the state's most popular outdoor activities; the Game Commission issues roughly 1.1 million licenses each year. Funds collected by the commission for licensing and fees have gone to acquire more than 1.3 million acres of private property, which have been turned into public game lands. Of the state's 67 counties, all but two— Allegheny (Pittsburgh) and Philadelphia—contain state game lands. These lands are open year-round to hikers, backpackers, and to hunters in season.

GUARDING THE WEALTH

Pennsylvania's wealth as a young colony was based on the fur trade, and hunting and trapping were the main sources of table fare for the majority of its population. By the mid-1800s, unrestricted hunting had brought about the extinction of several prized fur species—beaver, otter, and fisher—and the near-eradication of several game species that were once common everywhere in the state, among them white-tailed deer, black bear, and wild turkey. Toward the end of the 19th century, hunters and wildlife enthusiasts alike lobbied the state government for protective measures. Up until that time—with the sole exception of songbirds—no animals, including severely endangered species such as the passenger pigeon, were monitored or protected. In 1895, the governor created the Pennsylvania Board of Game Commissioners (now the Pennsylvania Game Commission) to enact and enforce season and bag limits on selected species. The commissioners were not universally welcomed.

During the first 25 years of the commission's existence, game wardens were occasionally bushwhacked, attacked, and even killed by hunters who refused to obey the laws. Eventually, opposition faded away, and the commission was able—through monitoring, limitation, and reintroduction—to restore many of the most popular and endangered species. Black bear, beaver, and elk were reintroduced some years ago and are making a comeback. White-tailed deer, wood ducks, and wild turkeys are now plentiful again. With some exceptions, Pennsylvania's wildlife is now more abundant than it was at the turn of the last century.

PENNSYLVANIA STATE PARK FEES

Note: Nonresidents pay higher fees.

Park-Operated Swimming Pools

day use $1.75–6
seniors $1.50–4
children under 38 inches tall ....free
book of 20 tickets $25–50
park camper or cabin occupant $1–4
nonswimmer ....free

Campsites Per Night

backpack camping: $3–4
Class A site (near toilets/showers): $11–13
Class B site (no running water): $9–11
campsite w/ electricity (30 amp or less): $11–15
campsite w/ electricity (more than 30 amp): $14–16

Cabins

Rustic cabins that sleep up to nine or up to 11 people are available.
Higher fees reflect weekend stays and nonresidency (Sun.–Thurs. stays are less expensive).

rustic cabin sleeping 2–3: $19–$38 per night; $127–152 per week
rustic cabin sleeping 4–5: $26–51 per night; $172–204 per week
rustic cabin sleeping 6–7: $32–64 per night; $213–254 per week
modern cabin sleeping up to 6: $47–95 per night; $316–381 per week
modern cabin sleeping up to 8: $59–118 per night; $394–472 per week
modern cabin sleeping 10–12: $62–123 per night; $414–492 per week

During the summer season—from the Friday after Memorial Day to the Friday before Labor Day—all cabins must be rented for a one-week period, beginning on a Friday. The rest of the year is considered off-season, and cabins may be rented by the week, half-week, or nightly, up to a maximum of 14 consecutive days. Cabin reservations are accepted beginning of the first Saturday in February for a one-year period from April 1 of the current year to March 31 of the following year. Reservations must be made at the appropriate park office; call Pennsylvania State Parks at 888/PA-PARKS (888/727-2757) for a list of parks, facilities, and phone numbers. During the first week reservations are available, they will be accepted by telephone only. After that, reservations may be made by telephone or in person. Full payment for a tentative reservation must be received within four weeks after being scheduled.

The **Pennsylvania Game Commission** (2001 Elmerton Ave., Harrisburg, PA 17110, 717/787-4250, www.pgc.state.pa.us) has general licenses and current information on hunting areas, seasons, and bag limits. Licenses and information are also available from issuing agents across the state (usually the same folks who sell fishing licenses), county treasurers, and all six of the commission's regional facilities. Licenses may be purchased by mail from the main office or the offices for the Northwest Region (814/432-3187); the Southwest Region (724/238-9523); the North-Central Region (570/398-4744); the South-Central Region (814/643-1831); the Northeast Region (570/675-1143); or the Southeast Region (610/926-3136).

A general hunting license, good for almost all game July 1–June 30 of the following year, costs $20 for an adult resident, $6 for a junior (under 16) resident, $101 for an adult nonresident, $41 for a junior nonresident, and $13 for resident seniors (over 65). Additional fees are required for archery deer season, use of muzzle-loaders (flintlock season), and bear hunting.

Rafting, Kayaking, and Canoeing

The Lehigh River, in the Endless Mountains, with Class I to Class III rapids, is ideal for those just starting out on white water. So is the Pine River, in Pennsylvania's Grand Canyon, near Wellsboro. Both areas feature scenery spectacular enough to keep even experienced rafters and kayakers entertained.

The Youghiogheny River, in the Laurel Highlands of southwestern Pennsylvania, is one of the best white-water rivers in the eastern United States. Three sections of the river deliver mild to wild (Class IV) thrills. The most challenging section features a drop of more than 115 feet per mile. Each river is serviced by outfitters who rent equipment and guide trips.

The Susquehanna (the eastern border of Dutch Country), Allegheny, Clarion, Tionesta (all in the Lake Erie and Alleghenies area), and Delaware Rivers (eastern border of the state), along with hundreds of smaller streams throughout the state, provide milder settings for canoeing enthusiasts. Canoes may be rented from many riverside liveries.

Sailing, Boating, and Swimming

Sailing is both a participatory and a spectator sport on Lake Arthur, in Western Amish Country, where several regattas are held each year. Lake Erie offers a freshwater sea for sailors who crave the open water.

Hundreds of Pennsylvania's marinas, state parks, and reservoirs rent oar boats; most also permit electrically powered boats, but any boat must have current Pennsylvania registration. Contact the **Pennsylvania Fish and Boat Commission State Headquarters** (P.O. Box 67000, Harrisburg, PA 17106-7000, 866/262-8734, www.fish.state.pa.us) for information about boat registration.

Many state parks offer public Olympic-sized swimming pools, as do most larger municipalities. Streams and lakes abound and often have roped-off swim areas staffed by lifeguards.

Spelunking

Thanks to its limestone karst underpinning, Pennsylvania offers unusual opportunities to explore several different types of caves. The state welcomes visitors in eight commercial caverns, varying from water-based Penn's Cave, in Centre County, to the unique catacombs of Laurel Caverns, in southwestern Pennsylvania—one of only two such caves in the United States. "Wild" caves are not open to the public and are off-limits because of the risks of habitat destruction and personal injury. The **Pennsylvania Cave Conservancy** (www.caves.org) lists most state caves, including restricted areas, and "grottos," member groups all over the state. Another good source of information is the **National Speleological Society** (2813 Cave Ave., Huntsville, AL 35810, www.caves.org).

Winter Sports

If you're looking for miles of thrilling downhill ski runs, you can get them in Pennsylvania (even if it may turn out to be the same mile over and over).

Know Pennsylvania

Given that the highest point in the state, Mt. Davis, is slightly over 3,000 feet tall, it stands to reason that the major runs may be challenging but will not be long. Steep thrills *are* available, however; Potter County's Denton Hill State Park, in north-central Pennsylvania, boasts the East's Avalanche run, a slope with a 6 percent incline that provides the sensation of hurtling toward the ground with your face parallel with the bottom of the mountain. The state has 33 ski areas, and nearly all offer something for all levels of ability. Blue Knob, in Railroad and Civil War Country, is one of the most popular. Many, such as Seven Springs in southwestern Pennsylvania, have the added advantage of being resorts offering many other activities. The Poconos have been a destination for downhill skiers for half a century.

Cross-country skiing is a major sport here and is practiced everywhere from city parks to groomed trails in the state parks and Allegheny National Forest. Snowshoeing is also becoming popular. The Laurel Highlands offers 70 miles of trails with overnight areas and shelters for both cross-country skiers and snowshoe enthusiasts.

Getting There

By Air

There are 16 major airports sprinkled through Pennsylvania: Pittsburgh, Westmoreland County, Franklin, Erie, Johnstown, Roaring Spring (Blair County), McKean County, Jefferson County, State College, Williamsport, Harrisburg, Scranton, Allentown, Reading, Lancaster, and Philadelphia. Of these, Pittsburgh and Philadelphia receive international traffic from 31 foreign and domestic carriers. USAirways has bases in both cities and operates flights daily to and from all major U.S. cities and also commuter flights to many Pennsylvania destinations. Dozens of smaller airports connect the traveler with every region.

By Rail

The state has more than 60 railroad companies, six of which are Class One (passenger) rail lines. Cross-state Amtrak passenger service (800/872-7245, www.amtrak.com) is available, and Philadelphia is the hub of the Northeast corridor between Boston and Washington, D.C.

By Bus

Greyhound (800/822-2662, www.greyhound .com) offers dozens of connecting routes from all over the United States and within the state. Call for specific departure times and destinations; staff will give schedules and prices over the phone.

By Water

Pennsylvania has three major ports. Philadelphia is the largest freshwater port in the world and services ocean liners. Erie is one of the major Great Lakes ports, and Pittsburgh is the nation's largest inland port, providing access to an extensive, 9,000-mile inland waterway system all the way to New Orleans.

By Auto

The major route through the state from east to west is I-80, which begins at the Delaware River in New Jersey and ends above Youngstown, Ohio. The route neatly bisects the state into northern and southern halves and provides access to all counties via smaller U.S. and State Routes (SR). State Route 6, a mostly two-lane road of unusual scenic beauty, crosses the state in the north. Most roadways in Pennsylvania are paid for by gas taxes and are free to travelers. The Pennsylvania Turnpike, US 76, from Philadelphia through Pittsburgh to the Ohio border, south of Youngstown, is a toll road. Tolls vary depending on distance traveled, and exits occur only every 10 miles or so. The turnpike has 22 "service plazas," with restaurants, service stations, restrooms, telephones, and picnic areas, along its length.

From New York, I-81 out of Binghamton is the north/south route to Scranton; it continues as I-476, from Scranton to Philadelphia. I-84 enters

Pennsylvania at the New York/New Jersey border; it, too, ends in Scranton. From Phillipsburg, New Jersey, I-78 travels through Allentown and Harrisburg to Carlisle. In the south, I-79 travels from West Virginia north through the western section of the state, and a branch of I-70 als enters the state from Wheeling, West Virginia, in the southwest. Access north/south from Maryland is via I-70 (Hancock), I 81 (Hagerstown), and I-83 (Maryland Line).

Getting Around

Intercity Mass Transit

All 15 of Pennsylvania's larger urban areas are served by mass transit, and most of the smaller cities have some form of public transit. Pittsburgh and Philadelphia are justifiably proud of their intercity systems, and travel within those urban areas makes an automobile a burden, especially considering the high cost of parking.

By Auto

Car travel is the best way to appreciate Pennsylvania's rural beauty and also to visit some of its less accessible attractions. Of Pennsylvania's 115,000 miles of streets and highways, 41,000 are maintained by the state. The larger roads are designated as interstates; there are also US roads, which cross more than one state, and state roads. (The road signage varies—only the numbers appear on some signs, while others also bear the designation "PA" or a silhouette of the state. In this book, state roads are denoted by "SR," as in SR 202.) The 470-mile Pennsylvania Turnpike opened in 1940 as the first high-speed (70 mph average), multilane highway in the United States. The highway speed limit in Pennsylvania is 55 mph unless posted otherwise. Children under four must ride in approved safety seats, and drivers and front-seat passengers must wear seat belts.

The Pennsylvania Department of Highways does an excellent job with signage on the major routes, but the counties take a more casual approach on the smaller roads—sometimes the signs are very good, but you may often find yourself missing your turn the first time and having to find your way back. Driving at night is twice as adventurous; the rural nature of much of the state makes the night roadways a hit-or-miss proposition for both you and the resident wildlife. If you're planning to sightsee by auto, by all means stop at a gas station or convenience store for a local map that shows the county roads (CR), also designated as local roads (LR) and township roads (T); these roads are often unmarked and can lead you on hours-long wild turkey chases.

Visas and Officialdom

Overseas visitors need a passport and a visa to enter the United States. This means (except for diplomats, students, or refugees) a nonimmigrant visitor's visa. You must obtain this in advance at a U.S. consulate or embassy abroad. Residents of Western European and Commonwealth countries usually receive these readily; residents of other countries may have to provide the consulate with proof of "sufficient personal funds" before the visa is issued.

Upon your arrival in the United States, an immigration inspector will decide on the time validity of your visa—the maximum duration of a temporary visitor's visa (B-1 or B-2) is six months. If your U.S. visa has expired, you can still enter the country (for a stay of 29 days or shorter) with a transit visa, but you may be required to show proof of onward travel, such as an airplane ticket or ship travel voucher.

Conduct and Customs

Carriages

Amish families traveling by horse-drawn carriage don't drive on the interstates or highways, but they do use Pennsylvania's many two-lane roads—so you're liable to encounter them anywhere in the state.

Carriages are impossible to miss; all carry red reflector triangles. In general, etiquette calls for automobile drivers to slow as they approach until a clear path for passing is available; then pass slowly—just fast enough to get around—and accelerate away, also slowly. You don't want to spook the horses; even though they're accustomed to cars, it's entirely possible to startle them. I made that egregious mistake only once, and the driver hurled a few choice (and well-deserved) German epithets at me while he struggled to control his frightened team.

Religious Observance

While its best-known religious sects may represent a minority of the state's populace, Pennsylvania is fairly devout and takes its religion seriously. It's worthwhile to remember this, and not only on Sunday, when the state virtually shuts down. Many Pennsylvanians—who are among the nicest people you will ever meet—are very conservative. Taking the Lord's name in vain—even in as relatively mild a statement as "My God"—may create noticeable discomfort

among those within earshot, particularly in Mennonite and Amish communities.

Worship Meetings

If you have an interest in attending services in an unfamiliar religious tradition, use the following guidelines. Quakers welcome anyone to their worship meetings and are quite tolerant in general—Quakerism is close in attitude to Unitarianism elsewhere. Mennonites and Moravians are a measure *more* welcoming—missionary work plays a significant part in their beliefs. Old Order Amish meetings are closed to all but members (unless you know someone in the community).

Photography

Show the Amish the courtesy you would show anyone else: don't trespass on their property and don't photograph them without permission. Many, though not all, consider a photograph in which they may be identified as a "graven image" or a sign of vanity—and therefore a violation of biblical precepts.

Liquor Laws

Pennsylvania restricts the sale and consumption of booze, and penalties for driving under the influence are astronomical; the situation is amusing when considering that many of the colony's

Quaker settlers established distilleries, and that taverns and roadhouses in colonial days did a whopping business. Wine, liquor, and beer are served in bars, taverns, and most restaurants but are not available to take out. Neither are they sold in grocery stores. The state operates 675 Wine and Spirits Shoppes, which offer a variety of wines and stronger stuff; as expected, the selection is often limited. Beer may be purchased in package outlets and taverns but not in grocery stores. Residents are accustomed to driving across state lines (Pennsylvania shares borders with six other states) for better selections of wine and hard liquor.

Police

The interstates are regularly patrolled, and main highways also get a fair share of police pass-throughs. Pittsburgh, Allentown, Scranton, Erie, and Philadelphia are major American cities whose police forces and meter maids are on par with those of comparable municipalities. In Pennsylvania's smaller towns, law enforcement is often represented by part-time police or volunteers, who are occasionally overeager to nab out-of-staters, speeders, and other scofflaws. When nearing a town of any size, slow down and be careful. Police officials of any type are scarce on less-traveled thoroughfares and backroads.

TIPS FOR TRAVELERS

Though the cities pose the usual urban threats to women traveling alone, they and seniors, students, and gay and lesbian travelers all will find few difficulties along the road in Pennsylvania. Because of the settled, small-town nature of much of the state, newcomers are occasionally met with suspicion, though such attitudes are decreasing as tourism grows. A friendly, polite attitude will win over the most conservative Pennsylvanians, and you'll find helpful and kind people everywhere in the state.

Pennsylvania's city dwellers are ethnically mixed, but the rural population tends to be of white European origin. Visitors of different ethnic origin traveling alone in the more isolated parts of the state are as exotic as parrots; some visitors may experience the acute discomfort of some locals. This is either an opportunity to educate the populace or move on; trust your instincts. Families, in any form, are met with open arms.

Both Philadelphia and Pittsburgh offer advantages and facilities for travelers with disabilities, including wheelchair access, and services for hearing- and vision-impaired visitors. Outside the cities' boundaries, however, access and services are limited. The Pennsylvania Office of Travel Marketing offers specially formatted information for hearing- and vision-impaired visitors.

Health and Safety

Falling ill in a strange place can happen to anyone, but fear shouldn't prevent visitors from enjoying the varied charms of Pennsylvania. Travelers who take regular medication should bring enough to cover their expected stay, though most prescriptions are available everywhere.

Larger cities, such as Philadelphia, Pittsburgh, Erie, Williamsport, State College, York, Allentown, and Scranton all have excellent hospitals, pharmacies, and emergency medical services; extensive police services; and fire stations. Firefighters are frequently trained in emergency medical procedures. Any of these services are only minutes away by phone (dial 911 in case of emergency), and the appropriate agency will respond, whether it's an ambulance for transport to a hospital or a police officer). Hospitals often require some form of assurance of payment upon admittance, usually medical insurance billable in the United States, cash, or credit cards.

Police and fire services are free to everyone. Though street crime is more common in the big cities—pickpocket theft, car break-ins, and muggings are the crimes most reported by visitors—Philadelphia and Pittsburgh have police who patrol the streets downtown on foot, making crime less likely. Both large cities make major efforts to educate and protect travelers. The usual rules apply—don't wear flashy jewelry, fan yourself with a wad of cash, or stroll aimlessly in questionable neighborhoods—leave that to the police decoys. Crime against visitors in the smaller cities is virtually unknown, and the villages and rural areas are quite safe.

As the town size decreases, so do the number of health and safety services. Cities with populations of more than 1,000 are minimally equipped with a clinic that will handle emergency health problems, and small police and firefighting forces. In villages and rural areas with fewer than 1,000 residents, these services are provided by visiting

SNAKES AND TICKS, OH MY

Though rare, snakebites do happen, and a wound from any of Pennsylvania's venomous snakes is considered dangerous. Immobilize the bitten part and transport the victim immediately to a physician for serum treatment. Antivenin should be administered at the earliest possible opportunity. The Hollywood rescue—tourniquet applied between the wound and the heart, incision between the fang marks with a sharp, clean instrument, and suction by mouth to attempt to remove the venom—should be used only if no other treatment will be available for several hours.

Lyme disease, a group of bacterial infections transmitted by deer ticks, the tiny dark cousins of common field ticks, has been a concern in the past few years. Unusually mild winters have caused an explosion in the deer tick population, and cases of Lyme disease have burgeoned. Lyme disease is no joke, causing fever, depression, fa-

tigue, arthritis, and a host of other unpleasant symptoms, made worse if the infection goes undetected. Deer ticks like to hang out on long grasses, waiting for unsuspecting victims, so wear light-colored shirts and long pants when hiking, and tuck the bottoms into your socks or close the pants legs off in some fashion. Check for ticks on your clothing and skin when your hike is done. Deer ticks are quite small—about the size of the head of a pin—and drop off the body after feeding within a few days. Some victims develop a bullseye-shaped rash somewhere on the body after being infected, but many do not. Within three days of infection, a victim develops flulike symptoms, which clear up, followed three weeks later by much more severe aches and pains. When in doubt, see your doctor. Early treatment (usually a 30-day course of antibiotics) shortens the severity of the disease.

medical personnel and volunteer police and fire-fighters. The dangers of snakebite, bear or wild-cat maulings, tick bites, and other wildlife-encounter indignities are negligible outside the more isolated hiking trails. Use the emergency procedures outlined below to get help.

Highway Patrol cars are frequently seen on the interstates and highways of more than two lanes, but they are seldom seen on the miles of two-lane roads that net the state—a boon to those who trifle with speed limits, but a problem for those who are lost or have suffered an auto breakdown. Fortunately, there's usually some kind of dwelling within walking distance if an emergency occurs. People are remarkably helpful, but respect their privacy. Knock on the door, then step away so they can get a good look at you. Be prepared to ask your questions through the door, and request that they call the emergency service for you. Sometimes, you'll be invited in for coffee and cake.

Emergency Services

In any of the larger cities and towns, police and medical emergency services can be reached by dialing 911 (there is no charge for the call if you make it from a public phone). Since so much of the state is rural and the towns and villages may be few and far between, however, a 911 call may not get a response. In that case, call the operator (dial "0") for the number of the local clinic and park or police authorities. State parks are usually staffed full-time during the day, and an office on the premises will dispatch necessary help.

Information and Services

MONEY AND BANKING

Currency

U.S. paper currency is all the same size and color. If you're not acquainted with it, you would be well advised to familiarize yourself with the common denominations to avoid making expensive mistakes. Coins in circulation come in denominations of $.01 (penny), $.05 (nickel), $.10 (dime), $.25 (quarter), $.50 (half-dollar), and $1. Paper currency (bills) comes in denominations of $1, $2 (uncommon), $5, $10, $20, $50, and $100 (there are two different editions of $20 and $100 bills in circulation). Bills larger than $100 are not in common usage.

ATMs, Traveler's Checks, and Credit Cards

Pennsylvania generally participates in all the benefits and conveniences of modern life, including automated teller machines (ATMs) and instant credit-card approval. However, a vast majority of Pennsylvania is extremely rural, and you will find that many of the state's smaller settlements and villages don't have banks or ATMs and won't accept payment by personal check, traveler's check, or credit card. For this reason, you should carry a reasonable amount of cash when you're heading to the hinterlands. (You're generally safe to do this—and certainly safer in Pennsylvania than in a lot of other places.) A rule of thumb: if a town has a stoplight, it probably has a bank branch, and possibly an ATM. Almost all are equipped to handle Cirrus and other bank cash-transfer requests.

COMMUNICATIONS AND MEDIA

Newspapers

Some small towns print and distribute their own newspapers, full of local merchants' ads and the latest high-school basketball victories. However, most readers rely on the state's major papers for news. The two largest are published, not surprisingly, in Pennsylvania's two biggest cities. The *Philadelphia Inquirer* has won Pulitzer prizes and is available daily across the state. The *Pittsburgh Post-Gazette* has been in print since the mid-19th century. Both cities also boast wide selections of specialized, alternative, and free papers. (Pittsburgh is even home to the *Serb National News,* among others.)

Magazines

Pennsylvania (800/537-2624 in Pennsylvania, 717/761-6620 outside the state, www.regional magazines.org) is a bimonthly magazine featuring articles of contemporary and historical interest. Call or visit the website for subscription information

Pennsylvania Heritage (P.O. Box 1026, Harrisburg, PA 17108-1026, www.paheritage.org) is a slick, well-written magazine with articles and stories chronicling the history up to the present of many of the state's features. It's published quarterly by the Pennsylvania Historical and Museum Commission; send subscription inquiries to Pennsylvania Heritage at the address given.

TOURIST INFORMATION AND MAPS

Tourist Information

Pennsylvania has an excellent **Office of Travel Marketing** (800/847-4872) in Harrisburg. Call for a copy of its free and comprehensive *Visitors Guide,* which also lists contact numbers for the state's localized (usually by county) tourist bureaus and agencies; all are listed by area in the text of this book. All of the county tourism websites are also listed at www.pacvb.org, with links to those that offer websites of their own. Visitors with hearing impairments may request a copy of the guide by calling the office's TDD number, 800/332-8338. The Office of Travel Marketing also has an edited version of the guide in tape format for vision-impaired visitors, available by calling 800/237-4363 Mon.–Fri. 8:30 A.M.–5 P.M.

The **Bureau of State Parks** (888/727-2757, www.dcnr.state.pa.us) publishes a free *Pennsylvania State Parks Recreational Guide,* which includes general information on all state park facilities. The bureau also publishes exceptional "blue books" on individual parks—small pamphlets that detail trails, layout, and a little background on each park. The bureau will either send you the pamphlet or will give you the phone number of any park you're interested in so that you may contact the park directly.

The **Bureau of Forestry** (main office 717/783-7941, www.dcnr.state.pa.us) handles the state forests, natural areas, and wild areas, which comprise more than two million acres. Not all state parks are in state forests, and vice versa. The bureau publishes public-use maps of the state forests; these show roads, towns, streams, trails, topography, natural and wild areas, and vistas. Also available are separate maps showing major hiking trails, snowmobile trails, cross-country ski trails, campsites, and ranger stations and points of interest within each park's boundaries.

The **Heritage Affairs Commission** (Room 309, Forum Building, Harrisburg, PA 17120, 717/783-8625) provides contacts for ethnic and folklife organizations throughout the state. For information, write to the Heritage Affairs Commission, or call during business hours.

Maps and Directions

In Pennsylvania, you *will* need maps to get around. The Office of Travel Marketing (800/847-4872) will include a copy of the basic Pennsylvania Highway Department state map when you request a visitor information packet. For smaller, more localized areas, your best bet is to buy the local maps wherever you are. Gas stations and convenience stores often carry them.

Also, if you're going to be spending any time driving Pennsylvania's back roads, it really is a good idea to carry a compass with you. The roads are often poorly marked or unmarked, and a compass can reduce the time you spend driving around (even Admiral Perry could have gotten lost in Pennsylvania, with or without a snowstorm).

Time and Tax

Pennsylvania is in the Eastern Standard Time zone.

In the larger cities, merchants keep longer hours and days, but elsewhere, food, clothing, and general-goods stores are normally open Mon.–Sat. 10 A.M.–5 P.M. Many shops close on Sunday, and those that cater primarily to tourists often shorten their hours during the winter. Hotels, inns, and bed-and-breakfasts are generally open daily year-round. Some restaurants are open daily, but most close one day a week—Sunday, Monday, or Tuesday. Many restaurants open early, around 6 A.M., and stop serving at 10 P.M.

Sales tax varies from county to county, averaging 8 percent. There is no tax on food or clothing, but restaurants and hotels usually charge a premium tax over the county tax, totaling an average of 11 percent.

WEIGHTS AND MEASURES

The United States does not use the metric system; instead, it measures distance in inches, feet, yards, and miles (see the conversion table at the back of this book). In the United States, dry weights are measured in ounces and pounds, liquid weights in ounces, pints, quarts, and gallons. Temperature is measured using the Fahrenheit, not the Celsius, scale.

Suggested Reading

ARTS AND CRAFTS

Stoudt, John. *Early Pennsylvania Arts and Crafts*. New York: A.S. Barnes and Company, 1964. This definitive work explores the origins and interconnections among a wide variety of arts and crafts. The book is amply illustrated.

CAROUSELS

Dinger, Charlotte. *Art of the Carousel*. New York: Mann Publishers, 1983. Stories and photo-illustrations of the collectors' pieces and carousels in general.

Fraley, Tobin. *The Carousel Animal*. Berkeley, CA: Zephyr Press, 1983. Text by animal restoration expert Fraley combined with beautiful photos of individual pieces by Gary Sinick make this book a visual treat.

Manns, William, with Peggy Shank. *Painted Ponies*. Millwood, NY: ZON International Publishing, 1986. A very readable and cleverly illustrated book that offers complete bios on all the major carousel manufacturers and master carvers, plus a list of locations of operating carousels in the United States.

DESCRIPTION AND TRAVEL

Avery, Ron. *Philadelphia: Beyond the Liberty Bell*. Philadelphia: Broad Street Books, 1991. The author explores a number of oddities and sites that don't make the guidebooks and adds some interesting commentary.

Patrick, James, ed. *Longwood Gardens*. Rhode Island: Fort Church Publishers, 1995. The photographs in this book are so sumptuous you might believe that they've been enhanced; not so—Longwood Gardens *really* looks like that.

Chase, Henry, ed. *In Their Footsteps*. New York: Henry Holt and Co., 1992. Chase, the editor of *American Visions* magazine, has compiled this book of African-American heritage sites all over the United States.

Stone, D., and D. Frew. *Waters of Repose*. Erie, PA: Erie County Historical Society, 1993. A well-researched and interesting book on the maritime history of Lake Erie, with suggested activities.

FICTION

Shaara, Michael. *The Killer Angels*. New York: Ballantine Books/Random House, 1975. Shaara's poetic rendition of the Civil War, and especially of the Battle of Gettysburg, won him a Pulitzer Prize and became the basis for the film *Gettysburg*.

Cooper, James Fenimore. *Leatherstocking Tales*. New York: Viking Press, 1985. A series that covers almost a century of U.S. history.

...chter, Conrad. *A Light in the Forest.* New York: Bantam/Knopf, 1984. Native-European relations during the westward expansion.

FOOD

Miller, Mark. *Amish Cooking.* New York: Crown Publishers, 1989. This beautiful book of photographs and recipes is adapted from the original 1980 version printed in Scottsdale, Pennsylvania. The recipes are authentic, gathered from Amish households—the shoo-fly pie is to die for.

von Bremzen, Anya, and John Welchman. *Please to the Table.* New York: Workman Publishing, 1990. For those who long for a decent pierogi, this is the definitive guide to food recipes from the Baltics to Uzbekistan.

HISTORY

Wallace, Paul. *Indians in Pennsylvania.* Harrisburg, PA: The Pennsylvania Historical and Museum Commission, 1993. This book, one of a series of anthropological studies, is a respectful and informative look at the state's first people.

Rouse, Parke. *The Great Wagon Road: From Philadelphia to the South.* New York: McGraw-Hill, 1973. A kaleidoscopic picture of colonial times, when it was, as Rouse quotes, "a great life for dogs and men, but . . . hell on women and steers."

Nofi, Albert. *The Gettysburg Campaign.* New York: Gallery Books, 1988. A detailed history of the incident.

Dowdey, Clifford. *Death of a Nation: The Story of Lee and His Men at Gettysburg.* New York: Knopf, 1988. The author explores the personalities in the great conflict.

DeVoto, Bernard, ed. *The Portable Mark Twain.* New York: Viking, 1975. A collection of Mark Twain's works, including his letter to Carnegie.

Stevenson, Robert Louis. *The Travels and Essays of Robert Louis Stevenson.* New York: Charles Scribner's Sons, 1895. This book contains many of Stevenson's travel essays, including a brief bit about Pennsylvania in "Across the Plains."

Serrin, William. *Homestead: The Glory and Tragedy of an American Steel Town.* New York: Times Books/Random House, 1992. A fascinating and well-written book that takes an intimate look at the people, culture, and history of one of America's greatest steel towns. Homestead is across the Monongahela River, south of Pittsburgh.

Dickens, Charles. *American Notes.* New York: St. Martins Press, 1985. Dickens's record of his travels across the United Stares 1840–1842.

Kraus, Michael. *The United States to 1865.* Ann Arbor, MI: The University of Michigan Press, 1959. Straightforward history.

Smedley, R. C. *History of the Underground Railroad.* New York: Arno Press and The New York Times, 1969. The original of this publication is in the Harvard College Library Collection. Dr. Smedley wrote the manuscript of this very readable study (published as part of *The American Negro, His History and Literature* series) of the Underground Railroad in Chester and neighboring counties for the *Lancaster Journal* newspaper in 1883.

Del Tredici, Robert. *The People of Three Mile Island.* San Francisco: Sierra Club Books, 1980. The author focuses on the residents in the areas surrounding Three Mile Island and their reactions to the nuclear incident of 1978.

PENNSYLVANIA PERSONAGES

Shippen, Katherine. *Andrew Carnegie and the Age of Steel.* New York: Random House, 1958. Carnegie's story, simplified for younger readers.

Carnegie, Andrew. *The Autobiography of Andrew Carnegie.* Boston: Northeastern University Press, 1986. From the horse's pen.

Beebe, Lucius. *The Big Spenders.* Garden City, NY: Doubleday & Company, 1966. Chapter 11, titled "The Plutocrats of Pittsburgh," tells some entertaining, gossip stories about Andrew Carnegie and the Pittsburgh millionaires. Beebe was a master of the snide aside

Oates, Stephen. *To Purge This Land with Blood: A Biography of John Brown.* New York: Harper & Row, 1984. History and times of the radical abolitionist.

Paterno, Joe, with Bernard Asbell. *Paterno by the Book.* New York: Random House, 1989. Joe tells all—his philosophy of winning, his background, and his mistakes. Plenty of info on former players and teams, and great insights into the politics and payoffs of college football.

Dillard, Annie. *An American Childhood.* New York, Harper & Row, 1987. Dillard's poetic and beautiful autobiography about growing up in 1950s Pittsburgh.

RAILROADS

D'Aulaire, Emily and Per Ola. "Freight Trains are Back and They're on a Roll." *Smithsonian.* (June 1995): 36–49. An entertaining exploration of railroading, including history, modern organization, and a look at Choo Choo U.

Moedinger, William. *The Road to Paradise.* Lancaster, PA: Strasburg Rail Road Shop, 1983. The story of the rebirth of the Strasburg Railroad.

RELIGIOUS COMMUNES

Nordhoff, Charles. *The Communistic Societies of the United States.* New York: Hillary House Publishers, 1961. First published in 1875, this book looks at communal life—both religious and secular—at the time of its greatest flowering.

Horwitz, Elinor. *Communes in America: The Place Just Right.* Philadelphia and New York: J.B. Lippincott Company, 1972. An entertaining and fast-paced look at communal life from a modern perspective.

Know Pennsylvania

Helpful Phone Numbers

AIRLINES

The following major airlines fly into both Pittsburgh and Philadelphia:

Airline	Domestic Flights	International Flights
American Airlines	800/433-7300	800/624-6262
Continental Airlines	800/523-3273	800/231-0856
Delta Airlines	800/221-1212	800/241-4141
Northwest Airlines	800/225-2525	800/447-4747
Trans World Airlines	800/221-2000	
USAirways	800/943-5436	
United Airlines	800/241-6522	

STATEWIDE HOTEL AND MOTEL CHAINS

The following chains have facilities throughout the state, usually in the larger towns. McIntosh Inns specialize in southeastern Pennsylvania. For specific locations or to book rooms, call the 800 number listed for each chain directly. (Rooms may also be booked through a travel agent.)

Hotel/Motel	Telephone Number
Best Western	800/528-1234
Days Inn	800/DAYS-INN (800/329-7466)
Hilton	800/HILTONS (800/445-8667)
Holiday Inn	800/HOLIDAY (800/465-4329)
Howard Johnson	800/466-4656
Knights Court	800/THE KNIGHTS (800/843-5644)
Knights Inn	800/843-5644
Knights Lodging	800/843-5644
McIntosh Inns	800/444-2775
Wyndham	800/WYNDHAM (800/996-3426)

Internet Resources

PHILADELPHIA

Philadelphia Tourism Marketing Corporation
www.gophila.com

Philadelphia Convention & Visitors Bureau
www.pcvb.org

AOL's cityguide
www.digitalcity.com/Philadelphia

DELAWARE RIVER VALLEY

Brandywine Conference and Visitors Bureau
www.brandywinecountry.com

Chester County Visitors Center
www.brandywinevalley.com

Valley Forge Convention and Visitors Bureau
www.valleyforge.org

New Hope
www.newhopepa.com

Bucks County B&B Association of Pennsylvania
www.visitbucks.com.

Bucks County Conference and Visitors Bureau
www.experiencebuckscounty.com

Lehigh Valley Convention and Visitors Bureau
www.lehighvalleypa.org

Bethlehem Visitors' Center
www.bethlehempa.org

Easton
www.easton-pa.com

PENNSYLVANIA DUTCH COUNTRY

Pennsylvania Dutch Convention and Visitors Bureau
www.padutchcountry.com

Hershey
www.hersheypa.com

Hershey Capital Region Visitors Bureau
www.hersheycapitalregion.com

Berks County Chamber of Commerce
www.berkschamber.org

THE POCONOS AND BLACK DIAMOND COUNTRY

Northeast Territory Visitors Bureau
www.visitnepa.org

Scranton-Lackawanna home page
www.pocono.org/scrantonpocono

Wilkes-Barre Convention and Visitors Bureau
www.tournepa.com

Pocono Mountains Vacation Bureau
www.800poconos.com

Jim Thorpe Network
www.jimthorpe.net

Schuylkill County Visitors Bureau
www.schuylkill.org

Pottsville Commission on Tourism
www.easternpa.com

Columbia-Montour Tourist Promotion Agency
www.itourcolumbiamontour.com

Susquehanna Valley Visitors Bureau
www.visitcentralpa.org

ENDLESS MOUNTAINS

Endless Mountains Tourism Bureau
www.endlessmountains.org

Tioga County Visitors Bureau
www.visittiogapa.com

Potter County Visitors Association
www.pottercountypa.org

Northern Alleghenies Vacation Region
www.northernalleghenies.com

City of Lock Haven
www.lockhavencity.org

North Central Pennsylvania Portal
www.mywol.net

Lycoming County Tourist Promotion Agency
http://williamsport-pa.com

Valleys of the Susquehanna
www.pavalleys.com

Clinton County Economic Partnership
www.clintoncountyinfo.com/Tourism

Penn State
www.psu.edu

Boalsburg, Bellefonte, and State College
www.visitpennstate.org

Central Pennsylvania Visitors and Convention Bureau
www.centralpacvb.org

RAILROAD AND CIVIL WAR COUNTRY

Allegheny Mountains Convention and Visitors Bureau
www.alleghenymountains.org

Bedford County Conference and Visitors Bureau
www.bedfordcounty.net

Huntingdon County Visitors Bureau
www.raystown.org

Juniata River Valley Visitors Bureau
www.juniatarivervalley.org

Gettysburg National Military Park
www.nps.gov/gett

York County Convention and Visitors Bureau
www.yorkpa.org

York County Parks
www.york-county.org/gov/Parks

LAKE ERIE AND THE ALLEGHENIES

Erie Chamber of Commerce and Convention and Visitors Bureau
www.visiteriepa.com

North East Chamber of Commerce
www.northeastchamber

Crawford County Convention and Visitor Bureau
www.visitcrawford.org

Mercer County Convention and Visitors Bureau
www.mercercountypa.org

Oil Heritage Region Tourist Promotion Agency
www.oilregiontourist.com

Oil City Chamber of Commerce
www.oilcitychamber.org

Franklin Chamber of Commerce
www.franklin-pa.org

Titusville Chamber of Commerce
www.titusvillechamber.com

Northwest Pennsylvania's Great Outdoor Visitors Bureau
www.pagreatoutdoors.com

Northern Alleghenies Vacation Region
www.northernalleghenies.com

Allegheny National Forest Vacation Bureau
www.allegheny-vacation.com

Armstrong County Tourist Bureau
www.armstrongcounty.com

WESTERN AMISH COUNTRY

Beaver County Tourist Promotion Agency
www.co.beaver.pa.us

Lawrence County Tourist Promotion Agency
www.lawrencecounty.com/tourism

Butler County Tourism and Convention Bureau
www.visit-butler-county-pennsylvania-pa.com

Armstrong County Tourist Bureau
www.armstrongcounty.com

Indiana County Promotion Bureau
www.indiana-co-pa-tourism.org

LAUREL HIGHLANDS

Johnstown/Cambria County Convention and Visitors Bureau
www.visitjohnstownpa.com

Laurel Highlands Visitors Bureau
www.laurelhighlands.org

Somerset County Chamber of Commerce
www.somersetcntypachamber.org

Ligonier Chamber of Commerce
www.ligonier.com

Washington County Tourist Promotion Agency
www.washpatourism.org

PITTSBURGH

Greater Pittsburgh Convention & Visitors Bureau
www.visitpittsburgh.com

University of Pittsburgh
www.pitt.edu

Allegheny County Parks
www.county.allegheny.pa.us/parks

Pittsburgh City Paper
www.pghcitypaper.com

STATEWIDE OUTDOOR RECREATION

National Parks and National Historic Sites
www.nps.gov

Pennsylvania rail trails
www.dcnr.state.pa.us/rails

Pennsylvania Fish and Boat Commission
www.fish.state.pa.us
www.dcnr.state.pa.us/stateparks

Pennsylvania Game Commission
www.pgc.state.pa.us

Pennsylvania Cave Conservancy
www.caves.org/conservancy/pcc

AMERICAN HISTORY

Independence National Historical Park
www.nps.gov/inde

Atwater-Kent Museum, Philadelphia
www.philadelphiahistory.org

State Museum of Pennsylvania, Harrisburg
www.statemuseumpa.org

Steamtown, Scranton
www.nps.gov/stea

Path of Progress National Heritage Route, Hollidaysburg
www.sphpc.org

Horseshoe Curve National Historic Landmark
www.railroadcity.com/curve

Gettysburg National Military Park
www.nps.gov/gett

MAJOR AIRPORTS

Philadelphia International Airport
www.phl.org

Pittsburgh International Airport
www.pitairport.com

INTERCITY TRANSPORTATION

Philadelphia—SEPTA
www.septa.org/inside/travel.html

Pittsburgh—Port Authority of Allegheny County (PAT)
www.portauthority.org

Index

Amusement Parks and Water Parks

Carousels

Museums

State Parks

general discussion: 472, 480
Archbald Pothole State Park: 168–170
Black Moshannon State Park: 228–229
Blue Knob State Park: 234, 248, 249–250
Buchanan's Birthplace State Park: 261
Canoe Creek State Park: 249
Chapman State Park: 314
Cherry Springs State Park: 198, 213
Clear Creek State Park: 315
Colton Point State Park: 209
Cowans Gap State Park: 259–261
Frances Slocum State Park: 170–171
French Creek State Park: 154
Hickory Run State Park: 178
Hyner Run State Park: 220
Hyner View State Park: 220
Keystone State Park: 370
Kooser State Park: 370

Laurel Ridge State Park: 372
Leonard Harrison State Park: 209
Linn Run State Park: 370
Locust Lake State Park: 190
McConnell's Mill State Park: 320, 333–335
Moraine State Park: 335–337
Nockamixon State Park: 112–113
Ohiopyle State Park: 346, 370–371
Oil Creek State Park: 306–307
Ole Bull State Park: 213–214
Pine Grove Furnace State Park: 272–274
Point State Park: 388–389, 424
Presque Isle State Park: 282, 292–293
Promised Land State Park: 177–178
Pymatuning State Park: 301
Raccoon Creek State Park: 333
Ricketts Glen State Park: 160, 193–195
World's End State Park: 205–206

Steelworkers of America Building: 389
Stein, Gertrude: 408
Stephen Foster Memorial: 398
Stewart, Jimmy: 339–340, 341
Stiegel, Heinrich: 454–455
Stingers: 418
St. Michael Historic District: 356
Stony Valley Railroad Grade: 144–145
Stone Valley Recreation Area: 227, 255
Stoy Museum: 144
St. Patrick's Day Parade: 467
Strand, The: 331
Strasburg: 129–130, 133, 134–136
Strasburg Railroad: 129–130
Straub Brewery: 310
Strawberry Mansion: 57
Strawberry Way: 393
Strip, The: 382, 389, 423–424
Stuart, J. E. B.: 258
Sturgis Pretzel House: 136
Sugar Valley Loop: 215–216
surfmen: 289
Susquehanna River: 447–448
Susquehannock people: 236–237
Susquehannock State Forest: 212–213
Swatara Creek: 145
Swedish immigrants: American Swedish Historical Museum 50

Sweetbriar: 57
swimming: 472, 473; Blue Knob State Park 250; Canoe Creek State Park 249; Cowans Gap State Park 260; Crooked Creek Lake National Recreational Area 343; Frances Slocum State Park 170; French Creek State Park 154; Hyner Run State Park 220; Laurel Hill Lake 369; Locust Lake State Park 190; McConnell's Mill State Park 334; Moraine State Park 336; Nockamixon State Park 112; Ole Bull State Park 214; Pine Grove Furnace State Park 273; Poconos 175; Presque Isle State Park 293; Promised Land State Park 177; Pymatuning State Park 301; Raccoon Creek State Park 333; Ricketts Glen State Park 195; Settler's Cabin Park 425; Shenango Reservoir 301; Two Mile Run County Park 307; World's End State Park 206
Switchback Trail: 183–184

T

taxes: 481
taxis: 88, 444
technology industries: 387
temperature: 448
Temple University Shoe Museum: 55
tennis: 227, 369, 426
Tennis Club: 227

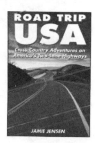

U.S.~Metric Conversion

1 inch = 2.54 centimeters (cm)
1 foot = .304 meters (m)
1 yard = 0.914 meters
1 mile = 1.6093 kilometers (km)
1 km = .6214 miles
1 fathom = 1.8288 m
1 chain = 20.1168 m
1 furlong = 201.168 m
1 acre = .4047 hectares
1 sq km = 100 hectares
1 sq mile = 2.59 square km
1 ounce = 28.35 grams
1 pound = .4536 kilograms
1 short ton = .90718 metric ton
1 short ton = 2000 pounds
1 long ton = 1.016 metric tons
1 long ton = 2240 pounds
1 metric ton = 1000 kilograms
1 quart = .9463 liters
1 US gallon = 3.7854 liters
1 Imperial gallon = 4.5459 liters
1 nautical mile = 1.852 km

To compute Celsius temperatures, subtract 32 from Fahrenheit and divide by 1.8. To go the other way, multiply Celsius by 1.8 and add 32.

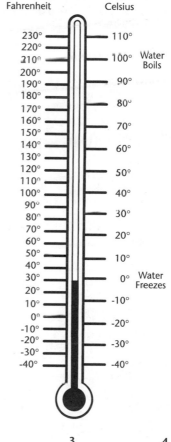

Fahrenheit	Celsius	
230°	110°	
220°		
210°	100°	Water Boils
200°		
190°	90°	
180°		
170°	80°	
160°		
150°	70°	
140°		
130°	60°	
120°	50°	
110°		
100°	40°	
90°		
80°	30°	
70°		
60°	20°	
50°		
40°	10°	
30°		
20°	0°	Water Freezes
10°	-10°	
0°		
-10°	-20°	
-20°		
-30°	-30°	
-40°	-40°	

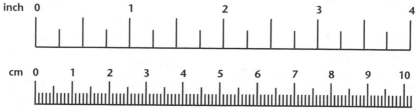

inch	0	1	2	3	4

cm	0	1	2	3	4	5	6	7	8	9	10

Keeping Current

Although we strive to produce the most up-to-date guidebook humanly possible, change is unavoidable. Between the time this book goes to print and the moment you read it, a handful of the businesses noted in these pages will undoubtedly change prices, move, or even close their doors forever. Other worthy attractions will open for the first time. If you have a favorite gem you'd like to see included in the next edition, or see anything that needs updating, clarification, or correction, please drop us a line. Send your comments via email to atpfeedback@avalonpub.com, or use the address below.

Moon Handbooks Pennsylvania
Avalon Travel Publishing
1400 65th Street, Suite 250
Emeryville, CA 94608, USA
www.moon.com

Editor: Kathryn Ettinger
Series Manager: Kevin McLain
Acquisitions Editor: Rebecca K. Browning
Copy Editor: Karen Gaynor Bleske
Graphics Coordinator: Deb Dutcher
Production Coordinators: Jacob Goolkasian, Karen Heithecker
Cover Designer: Kari Gim
Interior Designers: Amber Pirker
Map Editors: Olivia Solís, Kevin Anglin
Cartographers: Mike Morgenfeld, Suzanne Service
Proofreader: Michael Gardner
Indexer: Deana Shields

ISBN: 1-56691-585-6
ISSN: 1096-9543

Printing History
1st Edition—1998
3rd Edition—February 2005
5 4 3 2 1

Avalon Travel Publishing
An imprint of
Avalon Publishing Group, Inc.

AVALON
publishing group incorporated

Some photos and illustrations are used by permission and are the property of the original copyright owners.

Front cover photo © Garry Black/Masterfile

Printed in Canada by Transcontinental